India—A Travel

It is a comprehensive guidebook on India—an authentic answer to the needs of international and domestic travellers who want to know everything about the country. The author has tried to respond to all the questions that were asked by the travellers while he worked overseas. He has rendered all the information in a frank and forthright manner, neither concealing anything, nor exaggerating the charms of his country. It has been written by a person who has seen most of the major tourist attractions of this vast country. And the places which he has not visited, his source of information has been the tourist officers of the Government of India—many of them trained by him.

Pran Seth was a senior official in the Department of Tourism, Government of India, for almost three decades. For 16 long years, he headed the Government of India Tourist Offices in the diverse markets of the Americas, Europe and Asia, providing tourist information to thousands of travel agents, tour operators, airlines staff and independent travellers about the destination he knew best—India. Since the early eighties, he has been penning columns for consumer and travel press and authored several books on travel, tourism and tourism management. Pacific Asia Travel Association (PATA) honoured him with the best travel writer's award in 1983, at its Mexico conference.

Seth's involvement with the travel industry has manifested itself in several other ways. He was a consultant to Travel Agents Association of India; undertook specialised assignments for World Tourism Organisation; coordinated and taught tourism management to post-graduate students of Delhi University for several years; trained the tourist officers of Government of India and state governments through the Indian Institute of Travel and Tourism Management (IITTM).

> To
> *My grandchildren*
> *the four tourists of tomorrow*
> **ABHIMANYU & SAURABH**
> *(Sons of Meena & Dr. Anil Seth)*
> **ARJUN & RISHAV**
> *(Sons of Sushma & Ravi Bhat)*

Published by
Sterling Publishers Private Limited

INDIA
A Traveller's Companion

PRAN NATH SETH

Assistance in Research
MANMOHAN SADANA
(Director, Department of Tourism Govt. of India)

KING STREET PRESS

published in Europe by
KING STREET PRESS
a division of ABC Ltd.
38 King Street,
London, WC2E 8JT

India: A Traveller's Companion
©1998, Pran Nath Seth
ISBN 0-9516055-1-8

All rights are reserved. No part of this publication may be reproduced, stored in a retrieval system or transmitted, in any form or by any means, mechanical, photocopying, recording or otherwise, without prior written permission of the Sterling Publishers (P) Ltd., L-10, Green Park Extension, New Delhi-110016 INDIA.

Published by King Street Press.
Lasertypeset by Glory Graphics (P) Ltd., New Delhi.
Printed at Gopsons Papers Ltd., Noida, (India).
Cover design by Narendra Vashishta
Illustrations: Arjun Rathore

FOREWORD

It is with a sense of great pleasure and pride that I recommend Pran Nath Seth's latest effort in writing yet another book on Tourism. Pran happens to be one of those dedicated souls who never give up their passion for a cause which they hold so dear to them. Having been associated with dissemination of information and planning and marketing of Indian Tourism for over three decades, he is admirably qualified to write a guidebook on Indian Tourism aptly titled *India—A Traveller's Companion*.

Till a few years ago, most travellers to India saw our great and diverse country with the help of material compiled by foreign travel writers or through the eyes of foreigners. Many of them did an excellent job. It is only recently that our own travel writers have taken to preparing such informative books. These are bound to prove useful for visitors to India.

Tourism in India, both domestic and international, has yet to find its rightful place in the Indian Economy. The fastest growing industry in the world, tourism promises to contribute one out of every nine jobs in the world, generate approximately 11 per cent of the world revenue and grow at a rate faster than the world trade. But it has yet to find acceptability at different levels in our country. Today, about 11 million Indians travel in our country every day by train and another 40 million travel inter-city by surface transportation. But our share of international arrivals is only 2 million, all of whom are not necessarily tourists.

The founding fathers of our country, soon after independence, rightly dedicated the first four decades to developing infrastructure for essential activities such as agriculture, irrigation, education, public health, housing and industry. With our limited resources, we could think of tourism only in the last decade and, that too, with limited financial and human resources. While one can understand and even appreciate that tourism planning must remain under the charge of the Ministry of Tourism, tourism marketing ought to be undertaken by marketing professionals, be they from the services or from the private sector.

I have known Pran Nath Seth for forty years even since he joined the Department of Tourism as Director of Publicity. He has dealt with almost all aspects of tourism and headed Government of India Tourist Offices in North America, Europe and Japan. He knows what the visitors to India want to know about his country. This book by him will certainly fill the existing void in tourism literature and serve as a guidebook for not only foreign visitors but also for our domestic *Paryataks*.

Inder Sharma
President
Sita World Travel Ltd.
New Delhi
(Former President Pacific
Asia Travel Association (PATA)
San Francisco)

CONTENTS

Foreword v

Part I
INTRODUCING INDIA

1. **Land, People and Geography** 3
   - India: The Land and its Geography 5
   - Ancient Land, Young Nation 8
   - What to read and see before coming to India 19
   - India, Today and Tomorrow 22
   - Facts for Visitors 28
2. **Getting Ready for India** 35
   - Let Us Plan a Trip 36
   - How Visitors Travel to India 40
   - Journey Time 42
   - Air India 42
   - Other International Carriers 42
   - Domestic Air Travel and Indian Airlines 44
   - Planning an Itinerary 52
3. **At Home with the Indians** 67
   - Meeting the Indian People 68
   - Travel in India 69
   - Where to Get Travel Information 71
   - Government of India Tourist Offices in India 71
   - Leading Travel Agents and Tour Operators 72
   - Languages 75
   - Media 76
   - Health 78
   - Mail and Telecommunication Services 81
   - Interesting Facts 82
   - Hindi Vocabulary for Tourists 84
4. **India's Cultural and Artistic Heritage** 91
   - Religion and Philosophy 92
   - Indian Dance and Music 98

	Indian Architecture and Sculpture	105
	Paintings	113
	Festivals and Fairs	116
5.	**Dining Choices in India**	**125**
	Spicy Pleasures	126
	Range of Curries and Bread	127
	Regional Choices	129
	Refreshments	134
6.	**Shopping in India**	**135**
	Shopping Bargains	136
	Range of Shopping	136
	Selling in India	142
7.	**Special Interests**	**143**
	From the Window of an Indian Train	144
	The World of Adventure	153
	Call of the Wild	163
8.	**Hotel Accommodation**	**173**
	Indian Hotel Chains	174
	Tariffs and Prices	174
	Major Hotel Chains of India	175

Part II
EXPLORING INDIA

9.	**Jammu and Kashmir: Himalayan Paradise**	**187**
	Srinagar	191
	Gulmarg	198
	Sonamarg	199
	Amarnath	199
	Pahalgam	199
	Anantnag	200
	Ladakh	200
	Leh	202
	Jammu	204
10.	**Himachal Pradesh: The Himalayan Retreat**	**213**
	Shimla	215
	Kulu and Manali	217
	Lahaul and Spiti	218
11.	**Punjab and Haryana: The Fertile Land**	**225**
	Chandigarh	228
	Amritsar	229

12.	**Delhi: A Tale of Seven Cities**	**235**
	An Ancient City	237
	The New City	238
13.	**Rajasthan: The Land of Palaces, Forts and Camels**	**253**
	Jaipur	257
	Alwar	260
	Ajmer	262
	Chittorgarh	263
	Udaipur	263
	Mount Abu	264
	Jodhpur	265
	Jaisalmer	265
	Bikaner	266
14.	**Uttar Pradesh: The Heart of Hindustan**	**279**
	Nainital, Almora, Ranikhet, Corbett Park	283
	Agra	286
	Fatehpur Sikri	289
	Lucknow	
	Allahabad	294
	Gorakhpur and Lumbini	295
	Varanasi	295
	Sarnath	297
15.	**Madhya Pradesh: India's Tribal Province**	**311**
	Khajuraho	313
	Mandu	323
	Kanha National Park	328
	Jabalpur	329
16.	**Gujarat: The Land of Gandhi and Merchant Princes**	**341**
	Surat	347
	Vadodara	347
	Ahmedabad	348
	Lothal	350
	Modhera	351
	Unjha	351
	Patan	352
	Saurashtra	352
	Rajkot	352
	Jamnagar	352
	Palitana	352
	Junagarh and Girnar	354
	Gir Forest	354
	Somnath	356
	Ahmedpur Mandvi	357

	Daman and Diu	357
	Dadra and Nagar Haveli	358
17.	**Maharashtra: The Land of Caves, Forts and Temples**	**365**
	Mumbai	367
	Pune	377
	Ajanta - Ellora	379
	Aurangabad	380
	Daulatabad	380
	Matheran	381
	Khandala and Lonavala	382
	Panchgani and Mahabaleshwar	383
	Nasik	384
	Nanded	384
	Shirdi	384
18.	**Goa: India's Tourist Haven**	**395**
	Hindu temples with Portuguese names	400
	The Taverna Spirit of Goa	401
	Old Goa	403
	Other Important Towns	404
	Beaches of Goa	404
19.	**Karnataka: The Land of Great Monuments and National Parks**	**411**
	Bangalore	415
	Mysore	416
	Bandipur Wildlife Sanctuary	421
	Hampi	422
	Aihole	424
	Pattadakal	424
	Badami	425
	Bijapur	426
20.	**Kerala: India's Tropical Paradise**	**435**
	Thiruvananthapuram	441
	Kovalam Beach	442
	Quilon	443
	Alleppey	443
	Cochin	444
	Kottayam	445
	Periyar Wildlife Sanctuary	445
21.	**Tamil Nadu and Pondicherry: Land of Sculptural and Architectural Beauty**	**455**
	Madras	459

	Chingleput and Covelong	462
	Tirukalikundram	463
	Mahabalipuram	463
	Kanchipuram	466
	Vellore	466
	Vedanthangal Bird Sanctuary	467
	Tiruvannamalai	467
	Chidambaram	467
	Tanjore	467
	Tiruchirapalli	469
	Madurai	470
	Rameshwaram	472
	Kanniyakumari	473
	Courtalam	474
	Kodaikanal	474
	Ootacamund	475
	Pondicherry	476
22.	**Andhra Pradesh: Land of Silks, Spices and Temples**	**487**
	Hyderabad	489
	Warrangal	496
	Tirupati	497
	Vijayawada	498
	Vishakhapatnam	500
23.	**Orissa: Past Splendours and Contemporary Expressions**	**505**
	Bhubaneswar	508
	Puri	510
	Konark	511
	Cuttack	512
24.	**West Bengal: The Land of 24 Parganas**	**521**
	Calcutta	523
	Chandarnagore	532
	Darjeeling	533
	Kurseong	535
	Cooch Behar	535
	Jaldapara Wildlife Sanctuary	535
	Vishnupur	536
	Durgapur	536
	Santiniketan	536
	Sriniketan	536
	Nabadwip	537
	Digha	537

	Malda	537
	Murshidabad	537
25.	**Bihar: The Land of the Buddha and Ashoka the Great**	**543**
	Patna	545
	Bodh Gaya	546
	Lumbini	547
	Rajgir	547
	Vaishali	548
	Kushinagar	548
	Sarnath	548
	Sravasti	548
	Gaya	550
	Nalanda	551
	Pawapuri	552
	Parshnath Hill	552
	Maner	552
	Bihar-Sharif	552
	Sasaram	552
	Ranchi and Hazaribagh	553
	Jamshedpur	554
	Bhagalpur	554
	Rajarappa	554
26.	**Assam and its Six Sisters**	**559**
	ASSAM	562
	Guwahati	563
	Kaziranga Wildlife Sanctuary	564
	Manas Wildlife Sanctuary	565
	MEGHALAYA	566
	Shillong	566
	ARUNACHAL PRADESH	567
	NAGALAND	568
	MANIPUR	570
	MIZORAM	571
	TRIPURA	572
27.	**Sikkim: India's Fairy-Tale State**	**581**
	Gangtok	585
28.	**Island Resorts of India :**	**591**
	ANDAMAN and NICOBAR	593
	Port Blair	594
	LAKSHADWEEP	596

Part III
INDIA'S NEIGHBOURING COUNTRIES

29.	Nepal: A Destination for All Seasons	603
	Kathmandu	610
	Kirtipur	613
	Bhaktapur	617
	Rapti Valley	619
	Pokhra	622
30.	Bhutan: The Land of the Dragon	631
	Paro Valley	636
	Thimphu	638
	Punakha	639
	Wangdiphodrang	640
	Tongsa	640
	Tashigang	641
	Mongar	641
	Index	643

INTRODUCING INDIA

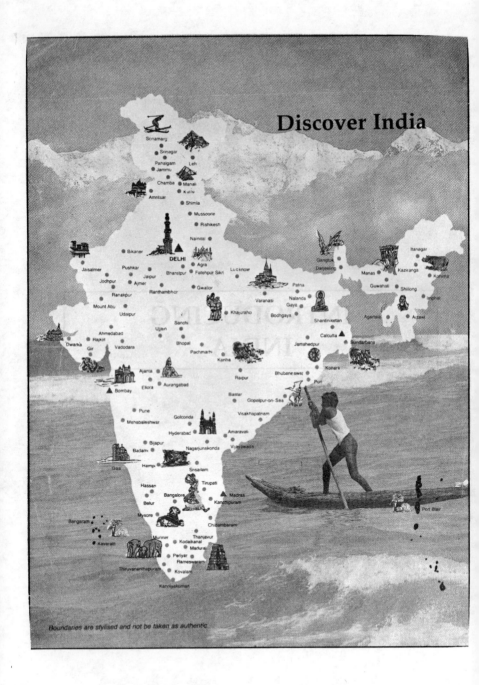

Chapter 1

LAND, PEOPLE AND GEOGRAPHY

1. India: The Land and its Geography
2. Ancient Land, Young Nation
3. What to read and see before coming to India
4. India : Today and Tomorrow
5. Facts for Visitors

INDIA

Capital	:	New Delhi
Area	:	3,287,263 sq km (1991 census)
Population (1996 UN est.)	:	953 million
Male	:	
Female	:	
Absolute Increase (1981-91)	:	160,601,764
Decadal Growth (1981-91)	:	23.5%
Density	:	267 per sq km
Literacy	:	52.11%
Male	:	63.86%
Female	:	39.14%
Female-Male Ratio	:	959 : 1000
National Income (1991-92)	:	Rs. 47,325 million (at current prices)
Per Capita GNP (1993-94)	:	$ 335
Per Capita Real GDP (1993)	:	$ 1,240
(Figure by World Bank)	:	Rs. 6,150.00
Inflation Rate	:	8%, Sep., 1995
States	:	25
Union Territories	:	6
Current US $ 1	:	Rs. 36.50

INDIA - THE LAND AND ITS GEOGRAPHY

GEOGRAPHICAL FEATURES

India, it is often said, is not a country but a continent. The real character of the country is masked by its continental dimensions. Not many have the time, opportunity and patience to see the whole country.

Consider the vastness of the country and you will appreciate its diversity. From the icy heights of the Himalayas in the north to the tip of Kanyakumari perpetually washed by the waters of the Indian Ocean in the south, it covers a distance of 3,500 km. It extends the same distance from the Rann of Kutch in the west to the forests of Assam in the east. The country has 7,000 km. of coastline, and an area of 3,287,263 sq. km. It encompasses geographical conditions, climate, scenery and people as diverse as those in Europe or the USA. Here lie some of the highest peaks, the longest plains and the wettest, the hottest and the coldest regions in the world. In the forests of the country are various species of rare animals such as the Asian lion, the rhino, the sinewy tiger, the sambhar, and a vast variety of deer, elephants and other mammals.

India has a distinct geographical entity. Separated from Asia by the Himalayas in the north and bounded by the sea on three other sides, it has a unity of its own which has been preserved and nurtured in the Indian way of life.

The land mass of India falls into three natural regions: the Himalayas in the north, the Deccan Plateau in the south and the Indo-Gangetic Plain in the middle. The north of the country is bordered by the long sweep of the Himalayas, the highest mountain range in the world. They run in a south-east to south-west direction right across the north of India and separate India from China and Bhutan in the east and Nepal in the centre. Bhutan, Nepal and Darjeeling lie along the Himalayas. So do the Indian Himalayan States of Jammu and Kashmir, Himachal Pradesh and northern Uttar Pradesh, the Garhwal Himalayas. The Himalayas are not a single mountain range but a series of ranges with beautiful valleys as in Himachal Pradesh and Kashmir.

Highest Peak	Largest River
Godwin-Austin also known as K² (Himalayas)— 8611 metres	Ganga or the Ganges

The highest peak in India is Godwin-Austin, also known as K^2 (8611 m). Mount Everest, the highest Himalayan peak (8848 m) is in Nepal. It is visible on a clear day from Darjeeling city in India.

South of the Himalayas is the vast 2,500 km. long Indo-Gangetic Plain watered by the Sutlej, the Ganga, the Yamuna and the Brahmaputra

rivers. It provides a great contrast to the soaring mountain peaks. The northern plain is oppressively flat and slopes so gradually that all the way from Delhi to Calcutta there is a drop only of 200 metres. The mighty Ganga is the greatest river of India. It has its source in the Himalayas. The Brahmaputra, flowing down the north-east of the country, is another major river. In the north-west, the mighty Indus flows through Ladakh in India but changes its course to Pakistan through India's State of Jammu & Kashmir.

The fertile Indo-Gangetic Plain has been the cradle of the Aryan civilisation which is known for its remarkable achievements in science and literature. In the north on the banks of Yamuna, lies Delhi, a city which has been built at least eight times. On the Ganga is situated the picturesque city of Varanasi, a seat of Hindu learning. Here in the Deer Park at Sarnath, Lord Buddha gave his first message of compassion to the suffering humanity. Further in the east lies another great city - Patna - ancient Pataliputra and the famous capital of Emperor Ashoka, the Great. Between Patna and Calcutta lies India's Ruhr, the modern centre of Jamshedpur, and an area rich in coal, iron and many other minerals.

Highest Rainfall	Biggest Cave Temple
Cherrapunji in Meghalaya	Ellora in Maharashtra

South of the northern plains, the land rises up to the high plateau known as the Deccan. The triangular peninsula in the south has the Vindhya Ranges for its base and the craggy ghats lapped by the waves of the sea on its either side. The Western Ghats are higher and have a wider coastal strip than the Eastern Ghats. The two ranges meet in the Nilgiri Hills. In these Ghats nestle the southern hill resorts of Matheran and Mahabaleshwar. In the extreme south are the Nilgiris wherein lie the famous resorts of Ooty and Kodaikanal.

Two major rivers, Krishna and Cauveri, rising in the Western Ghats, flow into the Bay of Bengal. The two other important rivers, Tapti and Narmada, flow westwards into the Arabian Sea.

In the north-west of the peninsula lies Bombay, India's principal centre for trade with the West. About 400 km. to the north-east of Bombay are the ancient cave paintings of Ajanta and sculptures of Ellora temples, not far from Aurangabad city.

Further down south along the narrow stretch of the west coast with the Arabian Sea to its west, are the luxuriant tropical forests of Kerala with their peaceful lagoons.

The peninsula is a great seat of Indian culture which finds its expression in beautiful temples, dance, drama and music that have been preserved in their unspoiled form.

LAND OF ALL SEASONS

India has been called the Land of All Seasons. The country experiences five seasons—summer, the monsoons or rainy season, autumn, winter and spring.

For purposes of convenience, we divide the Indian seasons into three: Hot, Wet and Cool.

The summer months (April-June) are hot in most parts of India. In some parts, temperatures at noon can soar as high as 47°C. The weather is dry and dusty. This is the time to move to hill resorts as most affluent Indians do. Among the hill resorts are Shimla, Kulu-Manali, Mussoorie, Nainital, Kashmir, Darjeeling, Ootacamund (new name Udhagamandalam), Kodaikanal, Panchmari, Mount Abu, etc. The choice is yours.

During the wet season, the monsoon brings relief to the plains of India. Between June and September, the country is suddenly transformed into a vast expanse of verdure. The monsoon is experienced all over India except in south-eastern areas which receive most rainfall between mid-October and December.

Largest Lake
Chilka Lake in Orissa

Largest City
Bombay

However, the monsoon is not to be dreaded. It is the time for merry-making for farmers. It does not rain all day. Intermittent showers are followed by a cool breeze, and then the weather becomes dry again, enabling the visitors to move around.

This is also the trekking season in Kashmir. In Himachal Pradesh, trekking starts with the beginning of the monsoon showers and goes on till heavy rains arrive. In Nepal, trekking is done during winter, the monsoons being too treacherous.

Finally, around October, the monsoon ends and the real holiday season starts. The weather is not too hot or too cold. The air is cool in the Himalayas as well as in the northern plains. It can be quite cold at nights. At times, the Dal Lake in Kashmir freezes in winter.

Snow once again attracts Indians to ski resorts. Although the Himalayan regions and the northern plains are cold, the southern peninsula has a crisp, spring-like climate. One seldom needs woollens here.

ANCIENT LAND, YOUNG NATION

India has a continuous civilisation of over 5000 years. The country derives its name from the river Indus which flows through north-west India—now north-west Pakistan. The first Aryan settlers in India called this great river Sindhu, meaning a large sheet of water like the sea.

More than five thousand years ago, civilised communities lived in India in planned cities with adequate arrangements for sanitation. They built houses of brick, wore cotton clothes, made beautiful gold and silver jewellery, pottery and toys. Their fine steatite seals bore a pictographic script which is still to be deciphered.

Largest Museum	Largest State
The Indian Museum in Calcutta	Madhya Pradesh

THE INDUS VALLEY CIVILISATION

This period of Indian history has been called by historians as the Indus Valley Civilisation. Its remains are found in Mohenjodaro and Harappa in Pakistan and Kalibangan, Lothal, and Sukortada and other cities in India. Lothal was a prosperous seaport in Gujarat. One can see in these cities a process of continuous development—cereal cultivation, animal husbandry, crafts, architecture and even ideology. The solidity of construction in cities like Mohenjodaro is testified by the fact that it has withstood the ravages of time for 5,000 years.

The Indus Civilisation was firmly based on a prosperous agricultural economy. Apparently, the Indus region had a fertile soil and lots of rain. The weather has since changed. Today, it barely gets 10 cms of rain in one year.

Apart from the Indus, the Ravi and the Saraswati rivers, referred to in the *Vedas*, the Sutlej and the Beas flowed through the fertile region of the Indus Valley. Saraswati has since vanished.

The Aryans

How and when these highly urbanised people of the Indus Valley disappeared from the scene are questions which cannot be answered yet. They were perhaps submerged by the successive waves of Aryan migrants who began pouring into India about 1500 B.C. through the mountain passes of the north-west. The newcomers had learnt the use of iron and had tamed horses. This gave them a superiority in warfare over

Tallest Tower	Largest Zoo
TV Tower in Delhi (235 m high)	The Zoological Gardens in Calcutta

the pre-Aryans, who were defeated. In time, a new pattern of life emerged from the fusion of the two people.

The sports-loving pastoral Aryans evolved a type of rural life which has remained basically unchanged to this day. To their functional organisation of society is to be traced the origin of the caste system. They worshipped the sun, the moon and the rivers and composed songs in praise of them. The poems addressed by them to *usha* (dawn) are considered some of the best in the world's literature. Their spiritual efforts are enshrined in the *Vedas*, the *Upanishads* and the two famous epics, the *Ramayana* and the *Mahabharata*, which have exercised a powerful influence on the people of India through the ages. Their contribution to science included the decimal system of notation and the concept of zero. They developed a system of medicine and surgery. The tales and fables with which they entertained their children found their way to the Western world. The Aryans were pioneers in the sciences of Mathematics, Astronomy and Medicine which reached the west through Arabs.

GAUTAMA BUDDHA

With the passage of time, many undesirable tendencies made their appearance among the Aryan (Hindu) society. The name "Hindu" for the people of India came from *Sindhu* and was perhaps given by the Greeks and others who followed them. Excessive ritualism robbed it of its former simplicity. Gautama Buddha, who founded Buddhism in the 6th century B.C., and Mahavira, the first Jain apostle, led the revolt against ritualism and urged the people to lead an ethical life and follow the principles of the Golden Mean. The latter laid emphasis on *ahimsa* or non-violence—the source of the pacific strain in Indian thought and philosophy. They had no place for worship of idols in their original philosophy but later their followers installed them in their temples.

GREEKS COME TO INDIA

In 326 B.C., Alexander the Great invaded India at the head of a large Greek army. That was the West's first contact with India. The Greek invasion left a permanent impact on Indian art and mythology. The Greeks borrowed a lot from Indian science, mathematics and philosophy, which reached the rest of Europe through them.

An historian accompanying Alexander wrote, "Indians grow wool on trees." He was referring to cotton. Till then, the Greeks had not known

Tallest Statue	Largest Railway Platform
Statue of Lord Gomateshwara (Karnataka)	Kharagpur (S.E. Railway Zone)

about cotton. They wore animal skins to cover their bodies or cloth made from wool of the animals.

There is an account left by Aristoxenus, a disciple of Aristotle, about a talk between an Indian traveller to Athens and Aristotle.

"What is the scope of your philosophy?" he asked the celebrated Greek philosopher.

"An inquiry into the phenomenon that is man," replied Aristotle.

The Indian burst into laughter. To the perplexed philosopher, he then said, "How can you make an inquiry into the phenomenon that is man without knowing God?"

The laughing traveller's attitude had been moulded by Indian philosophical treatises like the *Upanishads*. The enigma of life cannot be understood until the seeker goes to the source—Brahma, the Creator. Only on realisation of God can one understand the mystery of all other creations of God.

The first Indian empire took shape soon after Alexander's withdrawal. Its founder was Chandragupta Maurya, grandfather of Ashoka the Great. Assisted by Chanakya, who wrote *Arthashastra*, a famous treatise on politics and administration, he defeated the Greek General, Seleucus Nikator and welded India into a single and mighty political entity.

ASHOKA THE GREAT

When Ashoka came to the throne in 273 B.C., his empire included almost the whole of India and Afghanistan. The conquest of Kalinga (modern Orissa), accompanied as it was by a tremendous loss of life, produced in the emperor's mind a deep revulsion against war and violence. He embraced Buddhism and decided to conquer men's minds with love rather than by sword. He caused monolithic stone pillars to be erected throughout his far-flung empire. To propagate the *dharma*, he had them inscribed with a code of morals based on the teachings of the Buddha. He forbade the killing of animals on certain days of the week. This humane emperor sent out missionaries to Central Asia, Burma and Sri Lanka to spread the gospel of the Buddha.

INDIANS GO EAST : THE MAKING OF GREATER INDIA

With the dawn of the Christian era began yet another fascinating era of Indian history. Merchants and adventurers left the shores of their home country to set up colonies in Java, Sumatra, Bali, Cambodia, Thailand and Malaya. They were followed by princes, missionaries, architects and artists. The Indian colonies in time grew into kingdoms and empires. The

Most Thickly Populated State
Kerala

Ellora temple, Maharashtra

inhabitants of these lands adopted the Indian way of life. Indian philosophy, religion, art and architecture became part of their daily existence. From the first to the middle of the 15th century, the whole of South-East Asia was under Indian cultural and political influence.

The Golden Age of Indian History

The confusion that followed the decline of the Mauryan empire and the invasion of the north-west by tribes from Central Asia was cleared up by the Guptas. The rule of the Guptas (A.D. 320 to 495), known as the Golden Age of Indian history, was a period of remarkable achievements in the arts, literature and material prosperity. The finest paintings and sculptures in the caves of Ajanta and Ellora are ascribed to this period. Kalidasa's *Shakuntala* and *Meghadoot* belong to this period and so were many other poets and scholars. Aryabhatta, the astronomer, argued that the planet earth circled around the sun. He was ignored but not killed. An iron pillar erected at Delhi during the Gupta period still stands erect in the open to this day without a trace of rust, evidence of the Indians' advanced knowledge of metallurgy. A Chinese traveller, Fa-Hien, who visited India during this period, gives a graphic account of the peace and prosperity that prevailed then.

ADVENT OF ISLAM

The next important phase of Indian history began with the impact of Islam in the 8th century. First came the Arab traders and invaders, then the Turks and the Afghans and, finally, the Mughals. The Mughals, who made India their home, were great builders and their monuments include the Taj Mahal at Agra, the Red Fort and the Jama Masjid at Delhi and the majestic palaces of Akbar at Fatehpur Sikri. Excellence was achieved in paintings, particularly in miniatures, music, dance and poetry. The advent of Islam did not disrupt the continuity of Indian life. The rulers came, plundered cities and went away. Some, like the Mughals, stayed on and made India their home. They married Hindu princesses and the Hindu princes fought for the Mughal empire. In fact, the great emperor Akbar encouraged the movement for fusion of Hindu and Muslim ways of life into a single national culture. His efforts came to an end as his successors thought differently.

Keen on setting up an 'Islamic' state in India, much against the policy of his predecessors like Akbar and Shahjahan, Aurangzeb had no time for the finer things of life. In a desperate bid to make an appeal to the emperor about their plight, the musicians and artists of Delhi took out a funeral

Longest Tunnel	Largest Dome
Jawahar Tunnel (J&K)	Gol Gumbaz (Karnataka)

procession, wailing and crying about the death of music. The Emperor heard their loud wails and wanted to know why they were crying.

He looked out and the mourners said, "Your Majesty, we are musicians going out to bury music because there is no royal patronage."

"Bury it deep so that it never surfaces again," responded the angry emperor.

For the sake of sitting on the throne of Delhi, the emperor, Aurangzeb, killed all his brothers and imprisoned his father Shahjahan in Agra Fort which he had built. Shahjahan lived for several years in imprisonment, lonely and distraught.

The Mughal empire ceased to exist by the time Aurangzeb ended his rule in 1707 after a reign of 50 years. It had been crumbling under pressure from the Marathas in the West, the Sikhs in the North, and the British throughout India.

EAST MEETS WEST

Till Vasco da Gama discovered the sea route to India in 1498 via the Cape of Good Hope, India had no direct contact with Europe. Trade with India was channelled through the Arabs. Later, the Portuguese, through their mastery of sea routes, controlled the trade with India throughout the 16th century. But apart from acquiring some trading posts on the west coast of India, the Portuguese could not seize any political power in the country. Their monopoly was broken in the 17th century, first by the Dutch, and later by the British and the French. The British originally started trading from the west coast at Surat. Later, they acquired Bombay, the tiny seaport at that time given to King Charles II of England as dowry to Catherine of Braganza, who married the British King. On the east coast, they set up trading posts at Madras and Calcutta.

The foreign trading communities remained under check so long as the Imperial Government at Delhi was able to inflict punishment on them for infringement of trading norms imposed on them. But as soon as the Imperial power in Delhi weakened, they started meddling in the political affairs of local chieftains by taking sides, one against the other. The British and the French were already well-entrenched in India as it was easy for them to fight their political battles through the contending princes.

In their struggle for power, the British were able to sideline the French, first on the Carnatic coast and later in Bengal. In Bengal, their leader, Robert Clive, with the help of Indian malcontents defeated the forces of the Mughal Viceroy at Plassey in 1857. The British forced the

Largest Mosque	Highest Minaret
Jama Masjid in Delhi	Qutub Minar in Delhi

Imperial power to delegate to them the revenue administration of the three States of Bihar, Bengal and Orissa.

Having taken over the vast and fertile plains of the Indo-Gangetic region, the British took on other viceroyalties of the Mughals. In 1803, the Marathas were decisively defeated by the British and the whole of India was now open to British penetration. Only the Sikh empire in the North remained to challenge them. The Sikhs, under the wise leadership of their King, Maharaja Ranjit Singh, avoided any major confrontation with the British. After the death of Maharaja Ranjit Singh, the Sikhs, too, were humbled and the whole of Punjab fell into the hands of the British. The State of Jammu and Kashmir, which was part of the Sikh empire, was acquired by a Dogra General, Dhyan Singh of the Sikh Army, for a paltry sum of 7.5 million rupees.

By the beginning of the 19th century, the British East India Company, which was set up in the 17th century to trade with India, was ruling over the entire Indian subcontinent.

British rule in India lasted for 130 years (1818-1947).

Up to the Sepoy Mutiny in 1857, the forces of the British East India Company were on an expansion spree. They acquired more territories of Indian princes on one pretext or the other. The Indian princes were shaky and resentful. In 1857, they joined hands under the leadership of the Mughal emperor Bahadurshah Zafar, whose empire was localised to the four walls of Delhi, and started a revolt. They were joined by the Indian sepoys of the British Army. Luckily for the British in India, not all the Indian soldiers joined the rebellion. The armies of some of the Indian princes, including the Sikh Army, remained faithful to the British. The mutiny was quelled and the British Crown took direct control of the Indian administration, eliminating the role of the British East India Company. The Queen assured the Indian princes that their territorial integrity would be respected. Of course, they were in turn expected to behave and remain loyal to the British.

From the time of failure of the War of Indian Independence in 1857 till World War I was an era of consolidation of the British Empire in India and subsequent introduction of reforms. Among the major administrative reforms taken up during this period were the formulation of a new education policy and introduction of English as the official language in the country. A modern judicial system with uniform legal and penal codes was launched. Another important development was the establishment of a regular civil service on an All India basis. Railways appeared on the scene, so did a Posts and Telegraph system. A common currency and a customs service brought a new sense of unity to India.

Longest Road	**Highest Gateway**
Grand Trunk Road	Buland Darwaza in Fatehpur Sikri (U.P.)

Post-World War I period was one of mass awakening among the Indian people who began to realise their plight as a slave nation. They were determined to win freedom. A humble beginning was made in 1885 when an Englishman, Mr. A. Hume, founded the Indian National Congress to fight for the legitimate civil rights of Indians. In course of time, the Indian National Congress was taken over by staunch nationalist leaders like Mahatma Gandhi and Lokmanya Tilak who articulated the Indian demand for self-rule. The British resorted to delaying tactics, forcing the Indian National Congress under the leadership of Mahatma Gandhi and Jawaharlal Nehru to give up their modest demand for Dominion Status and to seek total Independence in 1932. They called it *Swaraj* — self-rule. In order to divide the people, the British encouraged the Muslims to organise themselves in a separate organisation. The All India Muslim League was their answer to the Indian National Congress. The Muslim League opposed the demand of the Indian National Congress for Independence, saying it did not want to be dominated by 'Brahmins', moneylenders and shopkeepers — that is how its leader, Mohammad Ali Jinnah, described the majority of Hindus.

Simultaneously, the British were trying to win over the Indians by offering them some minor reforms and a kind of representative government. Mahatma Gandhi did not accept the offer and started a non-violent civil disobedience movement. Millions of Indians, irrespective of their religious beliefs, courted arrest. He also started a Non-cooperation Movement asking Government servants to leave their jobs, teachers and students to quit schools and people in general not to buy British-made textiles and other goods. The movement paralysed the British administration. Following a minor case of violence, however, Mahatma Gandhi suspended his movement which was then at its height. He wanted a moral victory through non-violence. The people were dismayed but they followed Gandhi's orders. India became calm once again, but only to start another struggle.

During World War II, the Viceroy, Lord Wavell, announced India's participation in the war in 1939 without consulting the Indian leadership. Infuriated by this action, they announced a movement asking the British to "Quit India". The movement overtook the whole country by storm and millions of Indians once again courted arrest.

It now became clear to the British Government that there was no option for it but to concede the demand for the independence of India. But the Muslim League leader, Mohammad Ali Jinnah, wanted the British to "Divide and Quit". It also became clear to the Congress leaders that the only alternative to Jinnah's demand for separation was a Civil War.

Longest Cantilever Span Bridge
Howrah Bridge in Calcutta

The new British Government headed by the Labour Party decided to grant independence to India, and gave the responsibility for the transfer of power to a new Viceroy, Lord Mountbatten. Both Jawaharlal Nehru, the leader of the Congress, and Mohammad Ali Jinnah, the Muslim League leader, refused to have a loose Federation as proposed by the British Government. Jinnah declared, "I will have India divided or India destroyed." Mahatma Gandhi declared that he would have India divided over "his dead body". But, nobody listened to his pleadings in the prevailing surcharged atmosphere. India was divided into two parts on the basis of Hindu and Muslim majority areas. Pakistan comprised two wings — West Pakistan extending from the North West Frontier to Lahore in Punjab, and East Pakistan (now Bangladesh) comprising half of Bengal and a small part of Assam. The two wings were separated by 2500 kilometres of Indian territory. The remaining part of India was called India or *Bharat*.

The princely states were released by the British from their obligations and were required to join one country or the other. There were some 560 princely states in the subcontinent.

In the euphoria of independence — August 15, 1947 — evacuation of over 200,000 British was a smooth and an uneventful affair. Indians had forgotten their humiliation and bitterness. India accepted Lord Mountbatten as the first Governor General of the country.

INDEPENDENCE AND AFTER

As the subcontinent of India was divided into two nations, Pakistan became a Muslim state and pushed non-Muslims out of it. India decided to remain secular providing equal opportunities and justice for all religious and ethnic minorities. But the frenzy in Pakistan caused by the new zeal of Islam and Islamisation led to violence and the exodus of Hindu and Sikhs from their homes in Pakistan. Train-loads of non-Muslim refugees moved out of Pakistan, so did the Muslims from India. In one turbulent year, some ten million people moved in opposite directions to find safety. Never in the history of the world had such a massive migration taken place. Thousands of people lost their lives and properties in the holocaust that took place in the wake of partition.

It was a colossal task for the Indian Army to control the situation. At this critical juncture, Mahatma Gandhi came to Delhi and started his fast unto death calling for peace and sanity. People listened to him and order was restored. Gandhi urged the Hindus to make sure that their Muslims brethren did not leave their hearths and homes in India. The strife-torn

---

Largest Delta
Sunderbans in West Bengal

---

subcontinent started breathing peace. Later, a bigoted Hindu youngman, Nathu Ram Godse, shot Gandhi dead on January 30, 1948. His grouse was that Gandhi had favoured the Indian Muslims who should have been allowed to go to Pakistan. The nation was stunned. Blood-letting came to an end. Nehru announced in a voice choked with grief, "The light has gone out of our lives." The assassination of Gandhi shocked the country, restored sanity, giving Nehru time to build a new India.

Sardar Patel, India's Home Minister and a leader of great vision, was able to merge 362 princely states of India into the Indian nation. The only exception was Kashmir. The Maharaja of Jammu and Kashmir, a common border with India and Pakistan, vacillated for some time as he was a Hindu and the majority of his subjects were Muslims. The leadership in Pakistan, who wanted to grab Kashmir in a hurry, launched an attack on Kashmir by sending tribal hordes into the state. The Muslims of Kashmir, under the leadership of Sheikh Abdullah, however, had been urging the Maharaja to accede to secular India. The savage attack on the State left no option for the Maharaja but to sign the instrument of accession, asking for the help of the Indian Army to defend his State. The Indian Army acted promptly, saved Srinagar airport and pushed back the hordes. This led to the outbreak of war between the Indian and Pakistani armies. The United Nations intervened ordering a ceasefire. One-third of Jammu and Kashmir territory had come under Pakistani occupation. The ceasefire line became the de-facto international frontier.

Islam could not preserve the unity of Pakistan. East Pakistan fought a battle of independence against the Punjabi-dominated Pakistan leadership and became free in 1971. Pakistan fought three wars with India over Kashmir. Presently, Pakistan has launched a low-intensity proxy war in Kashmir in yet another attempt to forcibly grab Kashmir.

While India gained its independence on August 15, 1947, it retained the Dominion Status till January 26, 1950, with Lord Mountbatten as Governor General. When it became a Republic, Dr. Rajendra Prasad was elected as its first President. Both August 15 and January 26 are celebrated in India as national holidays. On January 26, every year, there is a massive

---

THE NATIONAL FLAG

India's National Flag is a horizontal tri-colour of deep saffron at the top, white in the middle and dark green at the bottom in equal proportions. The ratio of the width of the flag to its length is two to three. In the centre of the white band is a wheel, in navy blue, which represents the *chakra*, Wheel of Dharma.
Its design is also that of the wheel *(chakra)* which appears on the abacus of the Sarnath Lion Capital of King Ashoka.

parade of the Indian Armed Forces in Delhi. Folk dances from all over the country come to Delhi to join the Parade.

India continues to be a member of the British Commonwealth of Nations — the first republic to have joined it. Since then, several other countries freed from British Raj have followed India's example.

The New India

Forty-nine years are but a short period in the life of a nation. In India, however, this has been a period of remarkable achievements. The numerous princely states and provinces which the nation inherited have been welded into a single political entity and the political map of India has been redrawn on a rational basis. A Constitution, which enshrines the aspirations of the Indian people and the best traditions of democratic liberties, was framed and came into force on January 26, 1950.

WHAT TO READ AND SEE BEFORE COMING TO INDIA

BOOKS

If you want to really enjoy your visit to India, try to read some good books on it. There are many outstanding Indian writers of English whose works are worth reading. Among these are Gandhi, Nehru, Dr. S.Radhakrishnan, R.K.Narayan, Ved Mehta, S.Rushdie, A.R.Jhabvala and Khushwant Singh.

THE STATE'S EMBLEM

The State Emblem of India is an adaptation from the Sarnath Lion Capital of King Ashoka as preserved in the Sarnath Museum. The Government adopted it on January 26, 1950, the day India became a Republic.

In the original of the Sarnath Capital, there are four lions, standing back to back, mounted on an abacus, with a frieze carrying a sculpture in high relief on an elephant, a galloping horse, a bull and a lion separated by intervening wheels *(chakras)* over a bell-shaped lotus. Carved out of a single block of polished sandstone, the Capital is crowned by the Wheel of the Law *(Dharma Chakra)*.

In the State Emblem adopted by the Government, only three lions are visible, the fourth being hidden from view. The words, 'Satyameva Jayate' from the *Mundaka Upanishad*, meaning "Truth alone Triumphs", are inscribed.

Trinidad Indian, V.S.Naipaul, who visited India to rediscover the country, initially saw an "area of darkness" in it, which he has described in one of his books by the same title. He, however, changed his views in his later book, *India - A Million Mutinies Now*.

Some of the books which you may read with advantage are:
1. Basham, A.L., *The Wonder That Was India* (London. Reprint 1985 - *An History of Ancient India*).
2. Gandhi, M.K., *The Story of My Experiments with Truth* (London, 1982).
3. Mehta, Ved, *Mahatma Gandhi and His Apostles* (London, 1982).
4. Fisher Trevor, *India File* (London, 1983).
5. Forster, E.M., *A Passage to India* (London, 1922).
6. Collins, L. and Lapiere Dominique, *Freedom at Midnight* (India, 1976).
7. Lapiere Dominique, *The City of Joy* (Century, 1986). (The book is about Calcutta).
8. Naipaul, V.S., *A Wounded Civilisation* (London, 1977).
9. Naipaul, V.S., *India - A Million Mutinies* (London, 1990).
10. Rushdie, S., *Midnight's Children* (London, 1984).
11. Mehta, Geeta, *Karma Cola* (This is an amusing book on India, looking to the West and the West discovering the wisdom of the East).
12. Thereux, Paul, *The Great Railway Bazar* (London, 1980).
13. Kaye, M.M., *The Far Pavilions* (London, 1978).
14. Chaudhri, N.C., *The Autobiography of An Unknown Indian* (London, 1991).
15. Galbraith, J.K., *John Kenneth Galbraith Introduces India* (London, 1979).
16. Nehru, J., *An Autobiography* (London 1989).
17. Nehru, J., *Discovery of India* (London, 1990).
18. Jagannathan, Shakuntala, *Hinduism - An Introduction* (Vakils, Jeffer and Simons, Bombay, 1985).
19. Khushwant Singh : *Train to Pakistan* (London). (A novel about the trauma of partition).
20. O.P. Ghai, *The Bhagavad Gita* (Sterling Publishers, New Delhi, 1991).
21. Rajagopalachari, C., *Mahabharata* (Bharatiya Vidya Bhawan, Bombay 1989).
22. Mark Tully, and Z. Masani, *From Raj to Rajiv* (BBC Books, UK. 1986).
23. Akbar, M.J., *Nehru, The Making of India* (London, 1989).
24. B. Seshadri, *Call of the Wild* (Sterling Publishers, New Delhi, 1995)
25. D. Bolland, A Guide to Kathakali (Sterling Publishers, New Delhi, 1996)

Higest Waterfall
Jog Falls in Karnataka

FILMS

India's tourist offices overseas have excellent libraries of films and videos on India. These include films on arts, dance, music, crafts, and other fields of Indian culture. The films are loaned free of charge, specially to clubs, schools, colleges and universities.

Among the popular films on India produced overseas is 'Gandhi', produced by Sir Richard Attenborough. The film is about India's struggle for independence.

The well-known novel *Far Pavilions* has been made into an excellent film. *A Passage to India* and *Heat and Dust* have also been made into interesting films.

A young Indian producer, Ms Meera Nair, has produced a film, 'Salaam Bombay', on the street children of Bombay. The film has won much acclaim.

India's Film World

India tops the world in the number of films produced every year. It made 836 films in 1992 and 812 in 1993. The major film centres of India are Bombay, Madras, Hyderabad and Calcutta.

NATIONAL ANTHEM

Rabindranath Tagore's song 'Jana-gana-mana' was adopted by the Constituent Assembly as the National Anthem of India on January 24, 1950. The first stanza out of the five stanzas of the song forms the National Anthem:

Jana-gana-mana-adhinayaka jaya he
Bharat-bhagya-vidhata
Punjab-Sindhu-Gujarata-Maratha
Dravida-Utkala-Banga
Vindhya-Himachal-Yamuna-Ganga
Uchhala-jaladhi-taranga
Tava shubh name jage, Tava shubh asisa mange
Gahe tava jaya-gatha
Jana-gana-mangala-dayaka, jaya he
Bharat-bhagya-vidhata
Jaya he, Jaya he, Jaya he
Jaya jaya jaya, jaya he.

Largest Freshwater Lake
Wular Lake in Kashmir

INDIA, TODAY AND TOMORROW

VARIETY AND DIVERSITY OF INDIA

India does not lend itself to easy generalities. It is too vast a country with too long a history. Men of exceptional merit and intelligence have been wrong in the past. Macaulay who shaped the education policy of the British rulers in India, did not find any tasty fruits in the country though India has all varieties of tropical and non-tropical fruits. Abbe Dubois, who lived in South India for forty years, did not find any fragrant flowers! And, most British writers could not find anything more interesting in India than the "heat and dust" and the *Shikar*. They never wrote about the snowy mountains of the Himalayas or the rolling hills of the Nilgiris. The rules about India are riddled with exceptions. Evidence could be made available to prove any theory about India — but it could be misleading and erroneous.

What are, therefore, the most apparent realities of India which may strike a visitor on arrival? Undoubtedly, it is its bewildering variety as he drives through the streets of Bombay or Delhi after checking out of the airport. Variety is evident everywhere — in landscape, colour, in costumes, in facial features of the people, in languages and in flora and fauna. A visitor may find people talking in a babel of languages which he cannot understand. But, if he stops someone to ask for directions, more often than not, he will get the reply in English. Indians in cities know more than two languages and can easily understand each other despite the 17 official languages and hundreds of dialects. You will see people with blue eyes and European complexions. You will meet Indians who look like the Chinese and others with negroid features. India is a melting pot of races who found sanctuary in the country during different periods of history in the last 5000 years.

The variety of India may be bewildering to a visitor from overseas, but not to an Indian. For us, it is unity in diversity, the basic cultural and political unity which permeates the nation. Hindu places of pilgrimage are there in every nook and corner of the country. A thousand years ago, Shankaracharya, a saint from Kerala in the south, visited the major pilgrim centres in the north, south, east and west of India. He declared those places as the most holy ones which Hindus must visit at least once in their lifetime. Hindus still go there in millions every year. There is a ceaseless flow of pilgrims from one part of India to another. Television has its reach to all parts of India conveying the message of one nation.

Largest Desert
Thar (Rajasthan)

Politically, India has grown from strength to strength after each general election.

A visitor is often bewildered by several of our activities as he judges us by his country's standards. It should not be forgotten that India lives simultaneously in the 17th and the 21st century. One can see both the centuries co-existing. Le Corbusier, the renowned French architect, built Chandigarh, one of the most modern cities in the world, but the workers engaged for it carried cement and sand in iron trays over their heads as their forefathers did 400 years ago. A swank Mercedes develops an engine trouble on a highway and is pulled by a bullock-cart to the nearest service station! A speeding bus running at 100 kilometres an hour is made to halt on a highway as a herd of cows and buffaloes blocks its way! A modern warship, manufactured in an Indian shipyard is launched with a prayer to the Sea God written some 2000 years ago followed by the ceremonial breaking of coconuts. A research laboratory is opened on a date fixed by the astrologers on the basis of calculations regarding the position of the sun, the moon and stars — the way it was done when Indians first evolved the decimal system. These are facts of real life in India.

SCIENCE AND TECHNOLOGY

While the ancient is everywhere, the modern is preferred. People are keen to use science and technology to better their lot. The Government launched its Community Development Programme in villages some thirty-five years ago to transform rural India. The link in this self-improvement programme of rural India is the Village Level Worker who oversees development work in groups of 5 to 10 villages. The countryside is changing. Mud houses are being replaced by more permanent structures. Tractors are replacing bullock carts. But bullock power is also there to let the farmers take their produce to the market or to till the soil. Old silverware is being beaten to make new vessels. Village crafts which were on the verge of extinction during British rule have been revived and the Government has stepped in to protect and encourage them. The change overcoming the country is interesting. While villagers are acquiring plastic dolls for their children, their handmade dolls now adorn the mantelpiece of the sophisticated household in urban areas. Visitors from the West are patronising Indian handicrafts. Handicrafts are now one of the country's major export items. A visitor has just to go round the rows of handicrafts emporia in the Indian capital to discover that every State of India has its own exclusive crafts.

As India became free, Jawaharlal Nehru, the first Prime Minister of India, wanted Indians to imbibe "scientific temper". To achieve this

---

Largest Artificial Lake
Gobindsagar Lake on Bhakra Dam, Punjab

objective, the Government opened numerous research laboratories, technical colleges, schools and institutions all over the country. There are some 190 universities in India. By now, India is credited with having the third largest technical manpower in the world after the USA and the erstwhile USSR. Many Indians migrate to other countries for better opportunities as doctors, engineers, architects, teachers and lawyers. India cannot absorb them all. Indians are everywhere—in developed as well as in developing countries—to make a living. It may be a brain-drain but they do send their remittances back home revitalising the Indian economy.

ACHIEVEMENTS

In their own country, Indians have a lot to be proud of. They were the sixth nation to detonate a nuclear device in 1965, though only for peaceful purposes. In their space programme, they are among the top seven nations. They build their own ships, certain categories of planes, railway engines and coaches, satellites and motor cars. India is the only developing country which can undertake turnkey projects in other developing and developed countries. The country now ranks among the ten largest industrial nations of the world. In traditional terms, India is the fourth largest military power. When India became free, the late Prime Minister of England, Churchill, said that power was going into the hands of "men of straw". These men of straw suddenly became men of steel and reshaped the country into one nation despite the fact that the British had left some 500 independent and autonomous states ruled by Maharajas and Nawabs.

On the economic front, change has been brought about through a system of planned development. After a slow start, the Indian economy began improving. It was only in the 1980s that it recorded an average yearly increase in GDP of 5.4 per cent. During the same decade, the economy was liberalised and opened to foreign investments. Joint ventures in India and abroad and technical collaborations with foreign companies were encouraged. The growth performance was not equal to the economy of some newly industrialised countries like Korea, Taiwan, Singapore or Hong Kong. But that is the price a country pays for development through democratic processes.

The most significant achievement of India in the area of economy was the attainment of self-sufficiency in foodgrains and several other agricultural commodities like sugarcane and cotton. There was a noteworthy expansion in the production of fruits, vegetables, milk and eggs. In India, 75 per cent of area under cultivation is watered by rains. Therefore, the monsoon plays a major role in this.

State with Largest Forested Area
Assam

The physical infrastructure has shown an even greater growth. Electricity generation and crude production were up. There has also been a rapid expansion in rail, road and air transportation. Power generation is still behind in the country's requirements, limiting industrial growth.

India is a potential industrial giant since it possesses all the essential minerals. The iron ore is of high quality. India has huge reserves of oil, which have yet to be exploited. And, above all, it has skilled manpower in plenty.

Social indicators of development in India have been impressive. Life expectancy has gone up from 32 years in 1950 to 60 in 1992. Death rate has declined from 27 per thousand to 10. Birth-rate, though curtailed from 39 per thousand to 30 at present, is still above the danger mark. The need for family planning is evident to every individual and the 1991 Census birth-rate indicates a slight decline. Literacy has gone up to 52 per cent from 16 per cent at the dawn of independence. The current Eighth Five Year Plan which started in 1991 aims at raising the literacy percentage to 70 per cent and by the end of the twentieth century totally wiping out illiteracy. Already, some of the progressive states of India like Kerala and Pondicherry have been declared fully literate while some pockets in other parts of the country have achieved cent per cent literacy.

The public sector has played an important role in the economic development of India. At one stage, it achieved commanding heights in the economy. More than 50 per cent of economic growth in India can be attributed to the public sector. But, no restrictions were imposed on the private sector. It may be interesting to know that five of India's large public sector units are listed among the 500 largest industrial corporations of the world listed by *Fortune* magazine. Indian Oil stands at the 106th position while the Oil and Natural Gas Commission ranks 278th.

During the period of controls and licensing, the public sector was favoured but the private sector was encouraged. There were no restrictions. Nor was there discrimination. The private sector grew at a faster rate and created new wealth. It is, today, in a position to replace or take over public sector units which are not doing well

The opening of the economy to outside influences in the 1980s by Prime Minister Indira Gandhi led to massive imports of goods, some of which were not very important for India. This led to a crisis in the balance of payments. The problem was accentuated during Rajiv Gandhi's government which introduced more doses of liberalisation leading to a spurt in imports. This worked very well in accelerating industrial growth. In order to meet new demands, the country had to approach IMF and World Bank for loans. All industries are now open to foreign investments

Highest Bridge	Largest Railway Bridge
Chamba Bridge	Sone Bridge in Bihar

and collaboration except those related to defence and nuclear power. A clear signal has been given that foreign technology and investment are welcome.

The new innovative financial instruments have lent sophistication to the financial market. Financial and money markets now offer more choices to savers, investors and borrowers. It may be interesting to know that India's saving rate is one of the highest in the world—21 per cent, next only to Japan's.

Although the achievements of India since independence both in political and in economic terms, are impressive, the country still has about 250 million people who are living below the poverty line. The challenge is about the future.

INDIAN WOMEN TODAY

Traditionally, women in India have been respected and admired through the ages. In ancient Vedic literature, woman has been described as *Aradhangini* or half part of man's body.

In Hindu mythology, disastrous consequences have followed whenever women were ill-treated. For example, Rama took to arms against the mighty Ravana in the epic story of *Ramayana* because Ravana tried to insult his wife Sita. Similarly, the great war of Mahabharata took place because Draupadi was insulted by the Kauravas, the rival cousins of the Pandavas.

And, much later in historic times, wars were fought to protect the honour of women according to the rules of chivalry whenever disrespect was shown to them.

Respect for women is an intrinsic part of India's culture. In India, a woman can travel long distances more safely all by herself or in a group than in most western countries.

However, marital and family relationship have been heavily weighed in favour of the male. Manu, the ancient Hindu law-maker, lent his support to the vulnerability of women. "A woman may obey her father as a child, her husband when she is married, and sons when she grows old," he ordained.

Dress codes have changed too. Indian women seldom wore tight jeans and blouses - now these are in fashion. The *dopatta*, which covered the chest, has virtually disappeared.

Education and Awakening

The new industrial revolution led to movement of people to areas where there were jobs. This has resulted in the slow disintegration of the joint

---
Longest Corridor in the World
Rameshwaram Temple Corridor (4,000 ft. long)
---

family. It has also led to young educated wives taking up jobs. Young and eligible bachelors now seek brides holding jobs. Matrimonial columns in daily newspapers are full of such advertisements. In the 1960s, women sought jobs as teachers, nurses, secretaries, clerks and telephone operators. In the 1990s, they are attacking all male citadels including the Army, Air Force, Police and Engineering.

Social changes have encouraged many people to educate their daughters and make them employable before marriage. What still prevents Indian women, particularly Muslim women, from taking their rightful place in modern society is the old prejudices against educating the girl child. Often, the excuse is that the girl has only to look after the family. She is not to seek a job and she must be good in household work. In the countryside, most women have always worked in the fields, though some upper class women were not allowed to dirty their hands in the fields because of their high 'status'. Here again, the pattern is undergoing a change.

Mahatma Gandhi brought about tremendous change in the attitude of Indians towards women. He involved women in the independence struggle and millions of them came out in the streets to court arrest.

Jawaharlal Nehru followed his mentor's dedication to the rights of women. He brought the Hindu Code Bill on the Statute Book giving Hindu women the right to divorce, as in Western societies, and equal share in property. A Hindu could not remarry till he had divorced his first wife. Earlier, he could marry as many women as he liked. Another law has been enacted making dowry a penal offence. Dowry has been, and still is, a major problem in Indian society. Good bridegrooms fetch huge dowries in the marriage market. Although the dowry system has been declared illegal, dowry is now given and taken discreetly.

A new awakening is evident among educated Indian women. They have organised their own clubs and societies which have been successfully challenging the traditional inequality in the society.

Job Opportunities

Why this metamorphosis in the Indian woman? The entry of women into the work-force in large numbers over the decades is a major reason. The Indian woman, in fact, had a head-start over women in Europe with the freedom movement catapulting her beyond the domestic walls and into the streets. Independence brought both men and women the vote. Voting age has been reduced to 18 years. Now women have 30 per cent reservation in village Panchayats-elected local bodies.

Highest Straight Gravity Dam in the World
Bhakra Dam

Also it brought them jobs. Traditionally, teaching, medicine, and later law, were considered 'suitable professions' for urban women. India had a woman Prime Minister, Indira Gandhi. The US never elected a woman president. In the 1980s, women became deans of municipal hospitals and department heads in areas other than gynaecology and obstetrics.

The new Indian woman is also learning to live without men. Single women are adopting children.

The daughter in the family is taking up new roles and responsibilities. She is gradually becoming her parents' keeper. The changing power structure of the nuclear family pushes parents to the fringe in their son's home. Parents tap daughters for emotional and monetary needs and they respond willingly. In a land where the birth of a son was essential for salvation, older people are openly expressing preference for daughters.

In another fifty years, Indian women will leave their European sisters behind. On the road to equality, Indian women have an advantage. Their men love the family and they are likely to continue doing so. Men are not seeking life out of the family.

FACTS FOR VISITORS

VISAS

Foreign nationals wishing to visit India must be in possession of a valid passport and a visa granted by an Indian Mission abroad. Indian Missions are located in 140 countries of the world.

The Government of India does not allow any visa-free entry.

Nationals of Nepal and Bhutan are exempted from obtaining a visa. They can enter India without a passport and visa provided they have their identity papers.

Visas are of different kinds. The period of their validity is subject to certain restrictions. The visa must be checked before entering India. All visas specify the number of times a visitor may enter a country. A multi-entry visa must be obtained if one is visiting some of the neighbouring countries like Nepal and Sri Lanka and re-entering India.

On arrival, passengers are expected to fill in a Disembarkation Card. Often, it is given to them while on flight. For those having language problems, airline hostesses help them do the needful.

Tourist Visas

Foreigners coming to India for a holiday should ask for a tourist visa — a multiple-entry tourist visa, if they intend to visit one of the neighbouring countries. A tourist visa is granted for up to 120 days.

A transit visa for three days is also available from Indian Missions. But it is advisable to apply for a tourist visa, as it costs the same fee. The visa fee is normally US $ 5 for all countries of the world except UK, where it is £ 23.

Among other categories of Indian visas are: (a) Student visa for those joining Indian universities, (b) Business visa for those coming for business, and (c) Conference visa for those coming to attend a conference.

If the primary purpose of your visit to India is a holiday, ask for a tourist visa. It is the easiest to obtain; other visas may take longer.

BUSINESS VISAS

Foreigners wishing to come to India for business purposes can obtain multi-entry business visas valid for a period of five years from the date of issue.

STUDENT VISAS

Foreign students who have been admitted for academic studies in Indian universities or other recognised institutions can obtain student visas valid for a period of five years or for the duration of the course, whichever is earlier, subject to the production of evidence of admission and the means of sustenance while in India.

CONFERENCE VISAS

Foreign delegates coming to India to attend international conferences are granted conference visas. Foreign delegates are advised to apply for conference visas to the Indian Mission well in advance.

VISAS FOR FOREIGN TECHNICIANS

Foreign technicians/experts coming to India in pursuance of bilateral agreements between the Government of India and a foreign Government or in pursuance of a collaboration agreement between foreign and Indian firms can obtain multiple-entry visas for a period of five years or for the duration of the agreement, whichever is less.

VISAS FOR MOUNTAINEERING EXPEDITIONS

Foreigners wishing to undertake trekking, botanical expeditions, mountaineering expeditions, canoeing, rafting, etc., in a team are granted visas for the required duration on the presentation of full details of the touring members, nature of the event, area to be visited and any other information that may be asked for by the Indian Missions.

Visas for Sports Teams/Individual Sports
Sports teams or individual sportsmen visiting to participate in international sports events held in India may apply to an Indian Embassy/Mission for the grant of visas for the required duration.

Visas for Foreign Journalists (Media Persons)
Documentary/features film-makers desirous of coming to India for coverage and shooting of films can obtain short-term visas from Indian Mission abroad by completion of the formalities advised by the Missions.

Group Landing Permits
There are no short-term landing permit facilities for individuals arriving in India without visas. Every foreigner must have a valid visa for India. A limited facility exists for group tours consisting of sponsored groups by a travel agency recognised by the Government of India. Tourist groups arriving by air, ship or by chartered or scheduled flights are granted collective landing permits for a period of up to 30 days by the immigration authorities on landing, provided the groups are sponsored by a recognised travel agency and a pre-drawn itinerary is presented along with details of passports, etc., of the members. The travel agency must give an undertaking to conduct the groups together.

Registration
Foreigners coming to India on a long-term visa of more than 180 days should obtain a registration certificate and residential permit from the nearest Foreigners' Registration Office within two weeks of their arrival. No registration is required for foreigners arriving on a visa valid for up to 180 days. Addresses of the Registration Offices are given in the local telephone directory.

If a foreigner who has arrived on a visa valid for up to 180 days decides to stay in India for more than the specified period, he should immediately make an application to the nearest Foreigners' Registration Office.

Restricted and Protected Areas
Foreigners are not permitted to visit restricted/protected areas, normally in remote border areas. Information about these areas is available from Indian Missions/Tourist Offices overseas. Most of these areas are away from the normal tourist circuits.

Foreigners Arriving via Nepal
Foreign tourists coming to India via Nepal can enter India through any of the six land checkposts, namely, Raniganj, in West Bengal, Sonauli,

Banbasa, Nepalganj Road (Rupaidiha), Gauriphants in Uttar Pradesh, Rexual in Bihar or by air through Delhi/Varanasi/Patna/Calcutta.

Visits to Bhutan

Visitors desirous of travelling to Bhutan are required to obtain a visa from the Royal Bhutan Government or its Missions in New Delhi or New York. A transit permit from the Ministry of External Affairs will be required if the foreigner wants to enter Bhutan through Assam. Foreigners entering Bhutan through West Bengal do not require a permit.

EXTENSION OF VISAS

For extension of a visa, an application must be made to the Foreigner's Registration Office nearest to his place of residence. Extension is normally not given for more than six months except in exceptional circumstances.

HEALTH REGULATIONS

Foreign tourists should be in possession of a yellow fever vaccination certificate in accordance with the International Health Regulations if their travel is originating or transiting through yellow fever endemic countries. India does not insist on any other health formality.

Aids Test

Foreigners coming to India with the intention of staying for one year or more have to undergo an AIDS test in any one of the nearest surveillance centres. In case a foreigner is found to be infected with the AIDS virus, he will be deported.

Foreigners having HIV-free certificates issued within one month before their arrival from any of the WHO collaborating laboratories are exempted from the AIDS test.

CUSTOMS FORMALITIES

You can bring with you one bottle of whisky, 200 cigarettes and any amount of money, small items like bottles of perfume and other gifts, personal clothing and jewellery. These need not be declared. Larger items like video cameras, computers or TV sets, must be declared in the Tourist Baggage Re-export Form to ensure that the passenger takes them out of India when he leaves the country.

If you have nothing to declare, you can walk through the Green Channel in the customs enclosure. If you have something dutiable, go through the Red Channel.

MONEY MATTERS

Indian currency is based on the decimal system—100 paise to the rupee. Coins are in the denominations of 5, 10, 20, 25, and 50 paise, though 5, 10 and 20 paise coins have virtually vanished, thanks to inflation.

Bank notes are in the denominations of 1, 2, 5, 10, 20, 50, 100 and 500 rupees.

FOREIGN CURRENCY REGULATIONS

You may bring in any amount of foreign currency or travellers' cheques to India. It is desirable to declare it in the Currency Declaration Form handed out to you at the time of arrival. If you have only $1,000 you need not declare it.

When you change your money in Indian currency, do it at the branch of a bank or go to an authorised money-changer. Get an encashment receipt from the money-changer. It helps you to reconvert the leftover Indian currency.

In metropolitan or other major cities, it is possible to change currency at airports, hotels and banks. In small towns there may be a little problem. So change your money before you go to a small town. It may be advisable to bring some US dollars and British pounds which can be exchanged more easily in smaller tourist centres.

If you do business of changing money with a street tout in the hope of getting a better rate, the likely chance is that either you get cheated in conversion or you may get counterfeit currency. The difference is so little that it is not worth doing it. It is also illegal. Soon the Indian rupee may become freely convertible.

BANKING SYSTEM

The central banking institution is the Reserve Bank of India (RBI) which is authorised to issue bank notes. There are many other banks, several of them Government-owned. There are dozens of foreign banks in India representing practically all major countries of the world.

CREDIT CARDS

Most major international credit cards—Visa/American Express, Diners—are accepted in international hotels, shops and restaurants.

EXCHANGE RATE

The Indian rupee floats against a basket of currencies. The rate is subject to change. Check the latest exchange rate of the Indian rupee in any of the business magazines or at your point of entry from the airport bank. Exchange a part of your money at the bank at the airport. It always gives you a better rate than your hotel.

OTHER FORMALITIES

Departure from India
Foreigners leaving by road, air or sea have to fill up an embarkation card at the time of departure. Registration certificates, if any, are to be surrendered.

Foreign Travel Tax
There is a tax of Rs 300 (US $ 10) for all persons leaving India for foreign countries. This is applicable both to foreigners and Indians. The tax on travel to neighbouring countries is only Rs 150 ($ 5). The tax is also applicable to children and infants.

Export of Antiquities
Antiquities — sculptures, paintings and other works of art and craftsmanship illustrative of ancient art, crafts, religion of bygone ages and of historical interest which have been in existence for more than 100 years—cannot be exported without a valid permit from the Department of Archaeology. Items less than 100 years old can be exported without a permit.

Export of Articles made from Animals, etc.
The Government of India is concerned about the conservation of its endangered and rare fauna. With this view, export of all wild animals indigenous to the country and articles made from the skins of such animals, furs and ivory are also not allowed.

Weights and Measures
The metric system is used in India. Precious metals — especially gold— are sold by the traditional *tola*, which is equal to 11.5 grams.

Gems are weighed in carats (0.2 grams).

Financial outlays and population are usually expressed in terms of lakhs (100,000) and crores (100 lakhs or 10 million).

Electricity
India has the 220 V, 50 Cycle system of electricity. Most hotels can provide step-down transformers to enable you use your electrical appliances.

Business Hours
Government of India offices work five days a week, from 9 a.m. to 6 p.m. every day, post offices and banks observe a 6-day week. Major Telegraph/Post Offices work 24-hours a day throughout the week. Some State

Governments also observe a 6-day week. Sundays are official holidays. Shops are generally open from 10 a.m. to 7 p.m. The weekly closed day varies from locality to locality.

Hotel - Restaurants are usually open till 1 o'clock at night. Hotel coffee shops are open 24 hours.

Chapter 2

GETTING READY FOR INDIA

1. Let Us Plan a Trip
2. Indian Tourist Offices Abroad
3. How Visitors Travel to India
4. Getting There by Air
5. Journey Time
6. Air India and Other International Carriers
7. Domestic Air Travel
8. Planning an Itinerary
9. Popular Tours—Long and Short

LET US PLAN A TRIP

India is one major tourist destination where you must plan ahead unless you are on a package tour, where you travel like a well-cared-for baby. First-time visitors may as well buy a packaged tour - it is hassle-free, economical and the service provided by travel agents in India is excellent. A business traveller flying to India for a short visit does not need any advance planning. The hotel where he stays will bring the whole world at his doorstep.

INDIAN TOURIST OFFICES ABROAD

If you plan to do India on your own, do read something about the country and get the requisite information. Everything becomes so simple. The best source of information for you is the Government of India Tourist Office nearest to your home. There are some 17 Government of India Tourist Offices located in countries from where most tourists come to India. If there is no Government of India Tourist Office in your country, write to or call the Indian Embassy, Consulate or the Air India Office in your country. They stock tourist literature produced by the Government of India. Your travel agent, too, will have information on India.

LIST OF GOVERNMENT OF INDIA TOURIST OFFICES OVERSEAS

Cable addresses of Tourist Offices Overseas is TOUR INDIA.

AUSTRALIA
Castlereagh Street,
Sydney NSW 2000
Tel.: (02) 232 - 1600
Fax: (02) 223 - 3003

CANADA
60, Bloor Street,
West Suite No. 1003,
Toronto, Ontario M4W 3B8
Tel.: (416) 962 - 3787/88
Fax: (416) 962 - 6279

FRANCE
9 8 Boulevard de la Madeleine,
75009
Paris 9
Tel.: 4265-83-86
Fax: 4265 - 0016

ITALY
Via Albricci 9,
20122 Milan
Tel.: 804952
Fax: 7202168

JAPAN
Pearl Building,
9-18 Ginza,
7 Chome Chuo Ku,
Tokyo 104
Tel.: (03) 571 - 5062/63
Fax: 571-5235

BAHRAIN /UAE
PO Box 26106, Manama
Bahrain
Tel.: 973 - 715793
Fax: 973 - 715527

MALAYSIA
Kuala Lumpur Wisma HLA,
2nd Floor, Plot No. 203,
Jalan Raja Chulan-50200
Tel.: 2425285
Fax: 2425301

SINGAPORE
20, Karamat Lane,
01-United House,
Singapore-0920
Tel: 235-3800
Fax: 235-8677

SPAIN
Avenida PIO XII 30-32,
Madrid-28016
Tel: 3457339
Fax: 4577996

SWEDEN
Sweavagen 9-11, S-III-57
Stockholm-11157
Tel.: 215081
Fax: 210186

SWITZERLAND
1-3 Rue de Chantepoulet,
1201 Geneva
Tel.: 732 - 1813
Fax: 73 - 15660

THAILAND
3rd Floor, 62/5 Thaniya Road,
Bangkok-10500
Tel.: 2352585,
Fax: 2368411

U.A.E./DUBAI
P.O. Box 12856,
NASA Building,
Al Makhdum Dubai
Tel.: - 274848
Fax: 971 - 274013

UNITED KINGDOM
7 Cork Street,
London WIX 2AB
Tel.: 437 - 3677/78
Fax: 494 - 1048

U.S.A.
30 Rockefeller Plaza,
Room 15,
North Mezzanine, New York
Tel.: 586 - 4901/2
Fax: 582 - 3270

LOS ANGELES
3550 Wilshire Blvd,
Suite 204,
CA 90010
Tel.: 380 - 8855
Fax: 380 - 6111

GERMANY
Basler Street-48,
60329, Frankfurt Main-1
Tel.: 235423/24
Fax: 23-4724

A few leading Travel Agencies of India maintain their promotional offices abroad. Some of these are:

TRAVEL CORPORATION INDIA OFFICES

OVERSEAS

BARCELONA
Aribau 276 602A
08006 Barcelona
SPAIN
Tel: (343) 2001415
Telex: 81032 TCIN E
Fax: (343) 2017201
Attn: Mr. P. Kumar

FRANKFURT
Joachim Becher Strasse 8,
6000 Frankfurt Main I,
GERMANY.
Tel: (4969) 565353/565335
Telex: 4189131 TCIF D
Fax: (4069) 5604165.

LONDON
Suite 235, High Holborn House,
52-54 High Holborn.
London WCIV 6RL
U.K.
Tel: (4471) 831-0417/242-9930
Telex: 265637 TCI G
Fax: (4471) 404 5023

LOS ANGELES
26710 Fond Du Lac Road,
Rancho Palos Verdes,
CA 90274, Los Angeles,
U.S.A.
Tel: (310) 791 3130
Fax: (310) 791 3132

MILAN
Via Ronchi 39,
20134 Milan,
ITALY.
Tel: (02) 214 0824
Fax: (02) 2152581

NEW YORK
408, 8th Avenue, Suite 205,
New York,
NY 10001,
U.S.A.
Tel: (212) 659-3920/1025
Fax: (212) 695-4123

PARIS
22-24 Avenue Foch,
92250 La Garenne,
Colombes
FRANCE.
Tel: (331) 4785-2533
Telex: 250 303 PUBLIC PARIS
Fax: (331) 47862765.

SEOUL
1310-HO, 337-Dong, Hanshin Apt.
Seo-Cho Ku, Cham-Won Dong.
Seoul,
KOREA.
Tel: (822) 595 6560
Telex: TELENET K25548
Fax: (822) 595 5170

SYDNEY
7, Bridge Street, Balmain,
NSW 2041,
AUSTRALIA,
Tel: (612) 555-1079
Fax: (612) 555-1279

TOKYO
901, Royal Plaza,
3-4-12 Azabudai, Minato-Ru,
Tokyo 106,
JAPAN.
Tel: (03) 3585-6262
Telex: TCITYO-J-27942
Fax: (03)-3585-6128.

SITA OFFICES ABROAD

COLOMBO
Sri Lanka (Ceylon)
SITA World Travel
(India) Pvt. Ltd.
130, Glennie Street,
Colombo-2
Phones: 421370, 421101
Telex: 22241, 21389 KEELLS-CE
Cable: "SITATRAVEL"
Fax: 449659

FRANCE
SITA World Travel
1, Rue Edouard Colonne
75001-Paris
Phones: 42335531, 42335532
Telex: 215 782 F SITATUR
Fax: 331-4233 4175

NEPAL
SITA World Travel
(Nepal) Pvt. Ltd.
Tridevi Marg
Thamel-Kaiser Mahal
P.O. Box 394
Kathmandu,
NEPAL
Phones: (977-1) 418363, 418738
Telex: 2446 SITA-NP
Fax: (977-1) 227557

FRANKFURT
SITA World Travel
Leerbach Str. 118
6000 Frankfurt Main 1
Phones: (069) 5978535, 550647
Telex: 417938, 417949 Str d
Fax: (069) 598933

MILAN
SITA World Travel (India) Pvt. Ltd.
viale Romagna N 17
Milan-20133
ITALY
Phones: (02) 76110163,
76110184
Telex: 333840-LUCEXP I
Fax: (02) 76110184

MERCURY TRAVEL OFFICES

FRANKFURT
6 Kurhessenstrasse
6000 Frankfurt Main 50
Tel: (069) 512620
Tlx: 414352MERCE D
Fax: (69) 521849

NEW YORK
820, 2nd Avenue,
New York - 10 017
Tlx: 225069MERCUR
Cable:MERCINDIA
Fax : (212) 9835692

TOKYO
204, Villa Hirose
2-302 Yayagi
Shibuya-Ku-Tokte
JAPAN - Zip code 151
Tel: 03 375 7908
Fax: 03 375 7916

PARIS
72, Rue de la Glaciers
Tel: 43-36-74-99
75013 - PARIS
Fax: 43-37-60-78

These offices are in a position to recommend a tour or tell you about a reliable agent in your country who markets their tours. The offices are in constant touch with travel agents in the host country providing them with the latest information on new developments and new travel products.

Although you can make all arrangements for your travel on arrival in India, these can be time-consuming. For instance, air bookings on domestic routes could be difficult in the busy tourist season - October to March. But if you want to rough it out on buses and trains, welcome aboard, join the Indian crowds.

HOW VISITORS TRAVEL TO INDIA

Most tourists - 97 per cent - come to India by air though they can reach it by sea or road also. Till the mid-seventies, some 10 per cent of visitors to India came through the Asian Highway via Turkey, Iran, Afghanistan and Pakistan. But, now, this is becoming increasingly difficult because of disturbances in some countries en route.

INDIA BY AIR

India has direct air links with all the five continents, except South America. The introduction of new long-range aircraft has made it easy to fly to India. There are flights from New York to India, with a short stopover in Europe, which takes only 16 hours.

AIR INDIA AND OTHER INTERNATIONAL CARRIERS

Over 50 international carriers fly to and through India.

Air India - India's national carrier - is one of them and has a share of some 30 per cent of inbound and outbound traffic.

Although the flag carrier of second most highly populated country in the world, Air India is not a large airline by international rating. It ranks 23rd among the IATA airlines in the world.

Founded in 1932 as a private pioneering venture by Mr. J.R.D. Tata to improve communications within India, Air India had begun

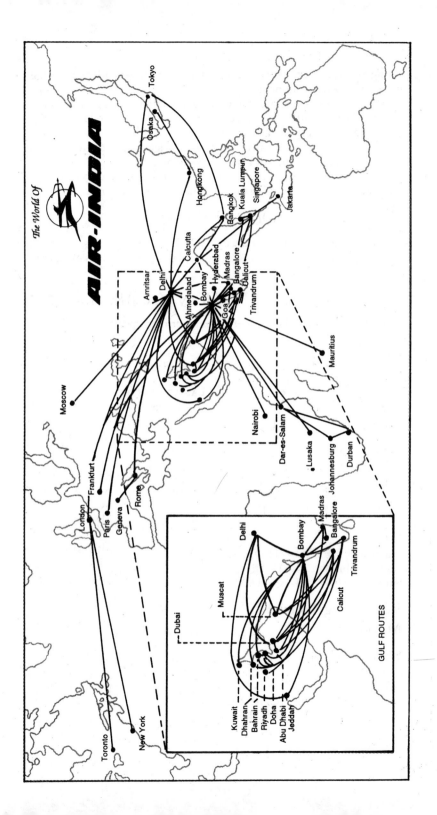

taking its present shape by the time India became independent in 1947. It flies to all the five continents.

Over the years, Air India has built its reputation as a superior airlines in term of service, efficiency and cuisine — both Western and Indian. It is known for its well trained, charming Indian and Western hostesses and for its warm hospitality. The interiors of the planes have distinct Indian motifs, providing an introduction to an Indian holiday.

In recent years, Air India has made its services most convenient for international travellers flying non-stop to Europe and Japan.

JOURNEY TIME

USA is 16 hours away from India by Air India while Europe is only eight hours. Japan too is eight hours away. No place in the world is more than 24 hours away from India.

OTHER INTERNATIONAL CARRIERS

The following is the list of international airlines operating from major tourist markets:

U.K.	AI, BA, PA, TG	Switzerland	AI, SR
U.S.A.	AI, DL, BA, KL, LH, SR, AZ, AF	**EASTERN EUROPE**	
Sri Lanka	IC, UL	Czechoslovakia	OK
Germany	AI, LH, PA, DL	Poland	LO
France	AI, AF,	Russia	AI, SU, HY
Japan	AI, SR, AZ, CA, TG	**AFRICA**	
Canada	AI, BA, KL, LH, SR, AZ, AF	Ethiopia	ET
		Kenya	AI, KQ
Australia	CX, SQ, TG, NH, AI	Libya	BG
		Mauritius	MK/AI
Italy	AI, AZ	Nigeria	AI
Malaysia	AI, MH, OK, SU	Seychelles	MK/AI
Saudi Arabia	AI, SV, AF	Tanzania	AI
Singapore	AI, SQ, SU, MH	Egypt	MS, TW
		Zambia	QZ/AI
Remaining Tourist Markets		South Africa	
		WEST ASIA	
		Israel	
WESTERN EUROPE		Bahrain	AI, GF
Belgium	KL	UAE	AI, RB, KU, GF, EK, BG, CX, BA, DY
Greece	BG		
Netherlands	BG, TG, AI, KL		
Spain	SR, AF, LH, KL	Iraq	AI, IR

Kuwait	AI, KU		HY	- Uzbekistan Airway
Oman	AI, GF		BA	- British Airways
Qatar	AI, GF		IA	- Iraqi Airways
Syria	RB		BG	- Bangladesh Biman
Yemen	DY		IB	- Iberia Airlines
			CX	- Cathay Pacific
SOUTH ASIA			IC	- Indian Airlines
Afghanistan	IC, FG		DY	- Alyemda
Bangladesh	IC, BG		IR	- Iran Air
Iran	IR		DL	- Delta
Nepal	IC, RA		IY	- Yemen Air
Pakistan	IC, PK, UL, IR		EK	- Emirate Airlines
			JL	- JAL
SOUTH-EAST ASIA			ET	- Ethiopian Airlines
Indonesia	SQ, MH, TG		KL	- KLM
Philippines	SR, AF, NH, SG, TG		KQ	- Kenya Airways
			QZ	- Zambia Airways
Thailand	AI, IC, TG, CX, AF, SR		KU	- Kuwait Airways
			RA	- Royal Nepal Airlines
EAST ASIA			LH	- Lufthansa
China	SR, ET, AF, TG		RB	- Syrian Arab Airlines
Hong Kong	AI, BA, CX, AF, SR, AZ		LO	- LOT Polish Airlines
			SQ	- Singapore Airlines
Korea	SR		MH	- Malaysian Airlines
			SR	- Swissair
AUSTRALASIA			MK	- Air Mauritius
New Zealand	CX, SQ		SU	- Aeroflot
			MS	- Egypt Air
Airline Codes used above			SV	- Saudia
AF	- Air France		OK	- Czechoslovenske Aeroline
FG	- Bakhtar Afghan Airlines		TG	- Thai Airways
AI	- Air India		PK	- PIA
GF	- Gulf Air		UL	- Air Lanka
AZ	- Alitalia			

INTERNATIONAL AIR CONNECTIONS TO SMALLER AIRPORTS

Airports	Flights operating to/from
Goa	Dubai, Kuwait, Europe
Hyderabad	Jeddah
Patna	Kathmandu
Trichy (Tiruchirapalli)	Colombo
Trivandrum	Abu Dhabi, Colombo Dhahran, Dubai, Kuwait, Male, Ras-a-Khaima, Sharjah.
Varanasi	Kathmandu

AIR FARES TO INDIA

Deregulation of airlines has left international airfares in a state of flux. You should check with a reliable travel agent who is in touch with the changing fares to know exactly what your trip will cost. Fares also depend on the class you wish to travel.

There are excursion fares from many countries to India including USA, Canada, UK, France, Germany, Japan and Australia. For New York, Air India's economy return fare with stopovers en route is US $ 3944. The excursion fare is US $ 1,774 during low season and US $ 2,182 in high season. From UK the economy fare is £ 1,466 while the excursion fare is £ 770 throughout the year.

Excursion fares impose some restrictions on minimum and maximum periods of stay. These fares are most economical for tourists.

It is interesting to note that all-inclusive package tours from USA and UK can be bought for the price of economy fares to India. Packaged tours, therefore, have a definite advantage for people going on a holiday.

Charter services are also available mainly from the European Continent. The Government of India encourages charter flights and some 1000 charter flights operate every year.

If you buy a ticket to India from the United States, it is possible to make one stopover each way in Europe and possibly two. Try to check with Air India, Delta or United Airlines as these airlines fly directly to India from the United States.

A recent addition is Tower Airlines from Bombay.

DOMESTIC AIR TRAVEL AND INDIAN AIRLINES

Air India and Indian Airlines—these are two different airlines under two different managements. While Air India normally flies on international routes, Indian Airlines connects points within India and in the neighbouring countries. India's domestic carrier - Indian Airlines - is a much bigger carrier, flying some 7.7 million passengers every year, while Air India carries only 2 million international passengers annually.

With the introduction of private airlines, Indian Airlines' share in traffic has declined.

Before 1953, India had a number of small privately run airlines. Since these were not working efficiently, the Government nationalised aviation by merging them. Thus a viable Indian Airlines was born. It has the most modern fleets of Airbuses A-320, Boeing 737, etc. Every two minutes, one of its flights takes off or lands in some part of India. The airline has an excellent safety record.

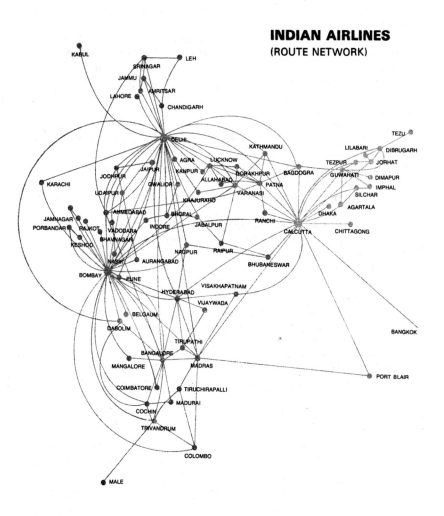

Indian Airlines connects some 53 towns in India and 14 destinations in the neighbouring countries - Pakistan, Bangladesh, Nepal, Sri Lanka, Maldives, Singapore, Thailand, UAE, Oman, Malaysia and Kuwait.

Indian Airlines has computerised reservations. Its reservations overseas can be done through major mega Central Reservation Systems (CRS) in a matter of minutes. Travel agents and airlines have direct access to these CRSs.

It is desirable to book on Indian Airlines in advance during the tourist seasons - September to March - as there is heavy demand during this period. Foreign passengers are given preference in Indian Airlines reservations. 25 per cent of seats on tourist routes are reserved for foreign travellers until three days before the departure of the flights when these seats are released to wait-listed Indian passengers.

Passengers with confirmed reservations are generally expected to reach the airport one hour before the departure of a domestic flight. Security checks take a little more time than necessary. At some airports, the passenger is asked to identify his checked-in baggage before it is loaded in the plane.

An airport tax of Rs 150 is levied for flights to neighbouring countries. Rs 300 is charged for flights to other countries.

The inflight service of Indian Airlines is quite good. Snacks and soft drinks are served on short flights and dinner or luncheon on long-distance flights - if it is luncheon or dinner time. Alcohol, including beer, is not served on domestic flights. There are no cancellation charges.

Indian Airlines is a member of IATA and has interline agreements with most of the airlines. Travellers can make Indian Airlines reservations through the originating international carrier in their country. Employees of IATA airlines are entitled to a 50 per cent discount. Tickets are valid for travel for one year from the date of travel.

CONCESSIONAL FARES

The following are concessional air-fares on Indian Airlines applicable to foreign visitors:

DISCOVER INDIA FARE: US $ 500 FOR 21 DAYS

This fare is available to foreign visitors and non-resident Indians against dollar payment for unlimited travel for 21 days. No city is allowed to be touched more than once except for transfer connections.

> Coach services from city to airport are low-priced and dependable. Metered taxis too are not expensive. Hotel taxis often cost twice the amount charged by the yellow-top taxis because they include the return fare and their quality is much better.

INDIA WONDER FARES: US $ 200 EACH

These consist of four fares each of $ 200, allowing unlimited travel to passengers for one week within North, East, West or the South Zones. Port Blair, the capital of Andaman Islands can be added to the South or East Zone by payment of additional US $ 100.

YOUTH FARE: 25% OFF

Those between the ages of 12 and 30 are entitled to 25% discount of the US dollar tariff within India and the Indo-Nepal sector, any time of the year.

COMMON INTEREST GROUPS: 10% OFF

Groups of 10 or more adults travelling together for common purpose are allowed 10% discount on Indian Airlines international sectors and connecting domestic flights.

SAARC GROUP EXCURSION FARE: 30% OFF

A discount of 30% is offered to groups of 10 or more persons travelling within the SAARC region touching at least three countries and staying at least two days each. Maximum stay is 21 days.

SOUTH INDIA: 30% OFF

This special fare is available to foreign visitors against dollar tariff on specified south India sectors of Madras, Tiruchirapalli, Coimbatore, Tiruvananthapuram, Bangalore and Madurai when combined with travel from either Sri Lanka or the Maldives.

All these concessions are available throughout the year.

APPROXIMATE JOURNEY TIME ON DOMESTIC ROUTES

From Delhi to	Time Taken Hrs.	Mins.	Stops en route
Agra	0	40	
Ahmedabad	1	25	
Amritsar	0	50	
Aurangabad	3	30	2
Bagdogra (for Darjeeling)	1	55	
Bangalore	2	30	
Bhopal	2	05	1
Bhubaneswar	3	20	1
Bombay	1	55	
Calcutta	1	55	
Cochin	4	05	1
Guwahati	3	35	1

Goa	2	25	
Hyderabad	2	10	
Indore	3	50	2
Jaipur	0	40	
Jodhpur	1	55	1
Khajuraho	1	55	1
Leh (Ladakh)	1	15	1
Lucknow	0	55	
Madras	2	30	1
Patna	1	25	
Pune	2	00	
Srinagar	1	15	
Tiruvananthapuram	5	05	2
Udaipur	1	55	2
Varanasi	1	15	

From Bombay to

Ahmedabad	1	00	
Aurangabad	0	45	
Bangalore	1	30	
Bhopal	2	15	1
Calcutta	2	20	
Cochin	1	45	
Coimbatore (for Ooty)	1	50	
Delhi	1	55	
Goa	1	00	
Hyderabad	1	15	
Indore	1	05	
Jaipur	1	30	
Jodhpur	2	25	2
Lucknow	3	25	1
Madras	1	45	
Srinagar via Delhi	3	15	2
Tiruvananthapuram	1	55	
Udaipur	2	20	1
Varanasi	2	10	

From Madras to

Ahmedabad	3	35	1
Bangalore	0	45	
Bombay	1	45	

Calcutta	2	05	
Cochin	1	50	1
Coimbatore (for Ooty)	0	45	
Delhi	2	30	
Hyderabad	1	0	
Madurai	0	50	
Port Blair	2	05	
Trichy (Tiruchirapalli)	0	45	
Tiruvananthapuram	2	35	1
Visakhapatnam	1	10	

From Calcutta to

Bagdogra (for Darjeeling)	0	55	
Bangalore	2	25	
Bhubaneswar	0	55	
Bombay	2	40	
Delhi	2	05	
Guwahati	1	10	
Hyderabad	2	05	
Lucknow	2	20	1
Madras	2	05	
Patna	0	55	
Port Blair	2	0	
Shillong (by Vayudoot)	1	35	
Visakhapatnam	1	20	

DISTANCES FROM THE AIRPORT

	km.		km.
Agra	7	Jaipur	15
Ahmedabad	10	Jodhpur	5
Amritsar	11	Jorhat	6
Aurangabad	10	Keshod	3
Bagdogra	14	Khajuraho	5
Bangalore	13	Leh	8
Belgaum	14	Lucknow	15
Bhavnagar	5	Madurai	12
Bhopal	11	Madras	16
Bhubaneswar	4	Nagpur	10
Bombay	26	Patna	7
Calcutta	16	Porbandar	4
Chandigarh	11	Port Blair	4

Cochin	6	Pune	8
Coimbatore	23	Srinagar	14
Dabolim (Goa)	30	Trichy	8
Delhi	13	(Tiruchirapalli)	
Gorakhpur	7	Tiruvananthapuram	7
Guwahati	22	Udaipur	24
Gwalior	12	Varanasi	22
Indore	9	(Benaras)	
Jabalpur	15	Visakhapatnam	14

AIR INDIA'S DOMESTIC FLIGHTS

Besides Indian Airlines, which had virtual monopoly of domestic routes till recently, Air India is allowed to carry domestic passengers on its linking flights between Bombay, Delhi, Calcutta, Madras, Bangalore and Tiruvananthapuram. These flights leave from international terminals. Indian Airlines tickets are also valid on these sectors.

VAYUDOOT

A decade ago, a third government-run carrier Vayudoot, had appeared on the aviation scene. It is now a Division of Indian Airlines and its principal objective is to provide 'feeder' or third level airlines services in regions where these are most needed, i.e., Eastern India.

Started in 1982, the airline had a meteoric rise and in five years it connected as many as 100 cities. But this expansion was short-lived and the airline ran into massive losses. The number of cities it now connects does not exceed 25 — many of them in eastern India. The new airline could not be a commercial success as it flew some second-hand Avros of Indian Airlines or a small fleet of new 18-seater Dornier aircraft. Under Vayudoot Rent-a-Plane scheme, the 18-seater Dornier or the 48-seater Avro can be chartered for the movement of groups.

PRIVATE SECTOR DOMESTIC AIRLINES

In recent years, the Government has deregulated aviation and allowed private sector airlines to compete with Indian Airlines.

A few private sector airlines have come up. Among them are East West Airlines, Damania, Jet Airways, Modi Luft and Sahara Airlines. These airlines are giving tough competition to the Indian Airlines and have snatched about 25% of Indian Airlines traffic.

The Government of India has decided to disinvest part of its equity of Air India and Indian Airlines to private sector. The level of disinvestment

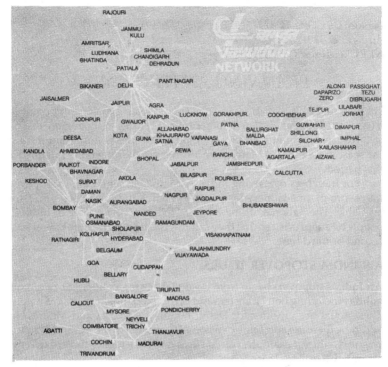

is not yet known though there is a case for Government disinvesting 51 per cent of the equity and relinquishing control of the two airlines.

PRIVATE AIRLINES
NEW DELHI

Jet Airways - *City* ☎ 3724728/29 *Airport* ☎ 3295402.
Fax : 011-3714867

East West: *City* ☎ 3721510, 3716138/29.
Airport ☎ 3295126/5498. *Fax :* 011-3755166

Sahara India Airlines
City Off.: ☎ 3326851/52
Fax: 3326858/56 *Airport:* ☎ 3295715

Modi Luft: *City Off.:* ☎ 3712222. *Fax:* 6430929. *Airport:* 5481351

Damania: *City Off.:* ☎ 6881739. *Fax:* 011-6886286.
Airport: 3295482/84
Archana: *City Off.:* ☎ 68411690/1985. *Fax:* 011-6847762.
Airport: ☎ 3295768, 3295126 *ext.* 2354.

Jagson: *City Off.:* ☎ 3711069. *Fax: 011-3324693.*
Airport: ☎ *329126 extn. 2200*
NEPC Airlines: *City: 3322525*

PLANNING AN ITINERARY

For planning an Indian itinerary, you should select a major entry point as a base. The tour can radiate to other tourist centres in the region.

Advance planning and reservation of Airlines is important during the season - October to March. The airlines are running quite full during this period.

For travellers overflying India, Air India has a number of stopover tours - pre-planned itineraries at very attractive and subsidised prices are available. The national airline is interested in giving a taste of India to people on a short visit so that they can re-visit the country for a longer stay second or third time.

AIR INDIA STOPOVER TOURS

Air India's stopovers begin from US dollars 29 for a one-night-two-days holiday including hotel transfers and accommodation in standard hotels. These tours are on offer for Delhi, Bombay, Calcutta and Madras. In addition, there are add-one extensions. If you want to see Agra and Jaipur, besides Delhi, for example, you can do it on a two- nights-three-days tour for only US dollars 185.

Extensions from Delhi include Agra, Jaipur, Srinagar, Goa and Kathmandu. Extensions from Bombay are to Aurangabad and Goa. From Calcutta, you can opt for Bhubaneswar/Puri and Konark. From Madras, there is a week-long southern safari. So take advantage of these stopover tours, you may call the nearest Air India office.

For most India tours, you need an Indian Airlines timetable for detailed planning because travel by road takes more time. Indian Airlines has frequent and convenient flights to some 60 major cities of India. It is now in a position to provide seats at short notice. Its capacity has been augmented. Indian Airlines is on line with major CRS's of the world and your travel agent can get you instant reservations. Private Airlines bookings are also available on major CRSs.

POPULAR ITINERARIES

The following are some of the standard and popular tour itineraries of India:
5-Day Tour of Delhi-Jaipur-Agra-Delhi
TOUR NO.1
Day 1 : DELHI
Arrive Delhi. Afternoon half day sightseeing tour of Old and New Delhi.

DAY 2 : DELHI - JAIPUR
Depart for Jaipur - the Pink City - by car. En route visit the early 17th century Amber Fort. Afternoon, city sightseeing.

DAY 3 : JAIPUR - AGRA
Depart for Agra by car. En route visit the 15th century deserted city of Fatehpur-Sikri. Afternoon, free.

DAY 4 : AGRA - DELHI
Morning, visit the world famous Taj Mahal built in the 16th century, the Fort and the Tomb of Itmad-ud-Daula. Afternoon, depart for Delhi by car. En route visit Emperor Akbar's Tomb at Sikandra.

DAY 5 : DELHI
Depart for Delhi.

TOUR NO 2
7-day North India
DAY I: DELHI
Arrive Delhi. Afternoon half-day sightseeing tour of Old and New Delhi.

DAY 2: DELHI - JAIPUR
Depart for Jaipur - the Pink City - by car. En route visit early 17th century Amber Fort. Afternoon, city sightseeing tour.

DAY 3: JAIPUR - AGRA
Depart for Agra by car. En route visit the 15th century deserted city of Fatehpur Sikri. Afternoon, free.

DAY 4: AGRA
Morning, visit the world famous Taj Mahal built in the 16th century, the Fort and the Tomb of Itimad-ud-Daula. Afternoon free.

DAY 5: AGRA - JHANSI - KHAJURAHO
Depart for Jhansi by train. Proceed to Khajuraho by car (172 kms.). En route visit the medieval Orchha. Afternoon, free.

DAY 6: KHAJURAHO - VARANASI
Morning visit the world famous 9th to 12th centuries Khajuraho Temples. Afternoon, depart for Varanasi by air.

DAY 7: VARANASI - DELHI
Early morning, boat excursion on the holy Ganga river. Later visit Sarnath where Lord Buddha gave his first sermon. Depart for Delhi by Air on Varanasi-Delhi sector.

TOUR NO 3
India - Nepal
(10-day tour of Delhi-Jaipur-Agra-Khajuraho-Varanasi-Kathmandu)
DAY 1: DELHI
Arrive Delhi. Afternoon, city sightseeing tour of Old and New Delhi.

DAY 2: DELHI - JAIPUR
Depart for Jaipur - the Pink City - by car. En route visit the early 17th century Amber Fort. Afternoon, city sightseeing tour.
DAY 3: JAIPUR - AGRA
Depart for Agra by car. En route visit the 15th century deserted city of Fatehpur - Sikri. Afternoon, free.
DAY 4: AGRA
Morning, visit the world famous Taj Mahal built in the 16th century, the Fort and the Tomb of Itimad-ud-Daula. Afternoon free.
DAY 5: AGRA - JHANSI - KHAJURAHO
Morning, depart for Jhansi by train. Proceed to Khajuraho by car (172 kms.). En route visit the medieval Orchha. Afternoon free.
DAY 6: KHAJURAHO - VARANASI
Morning, visit the world famous 9th to 12th century Khajuraho temples. Afternoon, depart for Varanasi by air.
DAY 7: VARANASI - KATHMANDU
Early morning boat excursion on the holy river Ganga. Later, city sightseeing tour and Sarnath excursion where Lord Buddha gave his first sermon. Afternoon, depart for Kathmandu by air.
DAY 8: KATHMANDU
Morning, city sightseeing tour. Afternoon, excursion to Patan.
DAY 9: KATHMANDU
Morning, excursion to Bhodnath, Pashupathinath and Bhadgaon. Afternoon free.
DAY 10 : KATHMANDU
Depart for Delhi, Bombay, Calcutta or Delhi or Europe/Far East. Air travel on sectors Khajuraho-Varanasi-Kathmandu.

TOUR NO.4
North India and West
11-Day tour of Delhi-Agra-Jaipur-Jodhpur-Udaipur-Aurangabad-Bombay (also available in reverse direction from Bombay)
DAY 1: DELHI
Arrive Delhi. Afternoon, sightseeing tour of Old and New Delhi.
DAY 2: DELHI - AGRA
Depart for Agra by car. En route visit 16th century Akbar's tomb at Sikandra. Afternoon, visit the world famous Taj Mahal built in the 16th century; the Fort and the Tomb of Itimad-ud-Daula.
DAY 3: AGRA - JAIPUR
Depart for Jaipur by car. En route visit the 15th century deserted city of Fatehpur-Sikri. Afternoon free.

DAY 4: JAIPUR
Morning, excursion to early 17th century Amber Fort. Afternoon, city sightseeing tour.
DAY 5: JAIPUR - JODHPUR
Depart for Jodhpur by air. Afternoon, visit the Jaswant Thada Cenotaph, the Mehramgarh Fort and the market.
DAY 6: JODHPUR - UDAIPUR
Depart for Udaipur by air. Afternoon free.
DAY 7: UDAIPUR
Morning, visit City Palace and Museum, Jagdish Temple, Saheliyon ki Bari and Fatehsagar Lake.
Afternoon free.
DAY 8: UDAIPUR - AURANGABAD
Depart for Aurangabad by air. Afternoon, excursion to the eighth century Ellora Caves.
DAY 9: AURANGABAD
Full day excursion to the sixth century Ajanta Caves.
DAY 10: AURANGABAD - BOMBAY
Depart for Bombay by air. Afternoon, city sightseeing tour.
DAY 11: BOMBAY
Depart for Bombay by air.
Notes: The Elephanta Caves excursion operates only mid-September to mid-May. This tour can be prolonged by taking extensions of air travel on sectors Jaipur-Jodhpur-Aurangabad-Bombay.

TOUR NO. 5
15-day tour of Delhi-Agra-Jaipur-Jodhpur-Jaisalmer-Jodhpur. Ranakpur-Mt. Abu-Udaipur-Aurangabad-Bombay
DAY 1: DELHI
Arrive Delhi. Afternoon, sightseeing tour of Old and New Delhi.
DAY 2: DELHI-AGRA
Depart for Agra by car. En route visit Emperor Akbar's Tomb at Sikandra. Afternoon, visit the world famous Taj Mahal built in the 16th century; the Fort and the Tomb of Itimad-ud-Daula.
DAY 3: AGRA - JAIPUR
Depart for Jaipur by car. En route visit the 15th century deserted city of Fatehpur Sikri. Afternoon free.
DAY 4: JAIPUR
Morning, excursion to the early 17th century Amber Fort. Afternoon, city sightseeing tour.
DAY 5: JAIPUR - JODHPUR
Depart for Jodhpur by car. Afternoon, visit the Jaswant Thada Cenotaph; the Mehramgarh Fort and the Market.

DAY 6: JODHPUR - JAISALMER
Morning city sightseeing tour. Afternoon free.
DAY 8: Morning city sightseeing.
Afternoon free.
DAY 9: JODHPUR - MT. ABU
Depart for Mt. Abu by car. Afternoon, city sightseeing tour.
DAY 10: MT. ABU - UDAIPUR
Depart for Udaipur by car. En route visit the Jain Temples at Ranakpur.
Afternoon free.
DAY 11: UDAIPUR
Morning, city sightseeing tour.
Evening boat cruise on Lake Pichola.
DAY 12: UDAIPUR - AURANGABAD
Depart for Aurangabad by air. Afternoon, excursion to Ellora Caves.
DAY 13: AURANGABAD
Full-day excursion to Ajanta Caves.
DAY 14: AURANGABAD - BOMBAY
Depart for Bombay by air.
Afternoon, city sightseeing tour.
DAY 15: BOMBAY
Depart Bombay.
Air travel on sectors Udaipur-Aurangabad-Bombay.

TOUR NO. 6
12-Day tour of Madras-Trichy-Thanjavur-Madurai-Periyar-Cochin-Bangalore - Mysore-Madras
DAY 1: MADRAS
Arrive Madras. Afternoon, city sightseeing.
DAY 2: MADRAS
Full-day excursion by car to Mahabalipuram and Kanchipuram temples built between 5th and 8th centuries.
DAY 3: MADRAS - TRICHY
Depart for Trichy by air. Afternoon, city sightseeing tour.
DAY 4: TRICHY - THANJAVUR-MADURAI
Depart for Madurai by car. En route visit the famous 9th century Chola temple of Brihadeeswara at Thanjavur.
DAY 5: MADURAI - THEKKADY
Depart for Thekkady by car. Afternoon, boat cruise on Lake Periyar to view wildlife.
DAY 6: THEKKADY - COCHIN
Depart for Cochin. Afternoon, city sightseeing tour.
DAY 7: COCHIN
Morning, motor boat cruise on the backwaters (lagoons). Afternoon free.

DAY 8: COCHIN - BANGALORE
Depart for Bangalore by air. Afternoon, city sightseeing tour.
DAY 9: BANGALORE - MYSORE
Depart for Mysore by car. En route visit Srirangapatnam, the summer Palace of Tipu Sultan built in the 18th century. Afternoon, city sightseeing tour of Mysore including the Palace of Maharaja of Mysore.
DAY 10: MYSORE - BELUR - HALEBID - MYSORE
Full-day excursion to the 11th century temples of Belur and Halebid.
DAY 11: MYSORE - BANGALORE - MADRAS
Depart for Bangalore by car and later for Madras by air.
DAY 12: MADRAS
Depart for Madras by air.
Note: Air travel sectors: Madras-Trichy and Cochin-Bangalore-Madras

TOUR NO 7
12-Day tour of Bombay-Aurangabad-Udaipur-Jodhpur-Jaipur - Agra-Delhi (also available in reverse direction)
DAY 1: BOMBAY
Arrive Bombay. Afternoon, city sightseeing.
DAY 2: BOMBAY - AURANGABAD
Depart for Aurangabad by air. Afternoon, excursion to eighth century Ellora Caves.
DAY 3: AURANGABAD
Full-day excursion to sixth century Ajanta Caves.
DAY 4: AURANGABAD - UDAIPUR
Depart for Udaipur by air. Afternoon, motor boat cruise on Lake Pichola.
DAY 5: UDAIPUR
Morning, city sightseeing tour. Afternoon free.
DAY 6: UDAIPUR - JODHPUR
Depart for Jodhpur by air. Afternoon, city sightseeing tour.
DAY 7: JODHPUR - JAIPUR
Depart for Jaipur by air. Afternoon, city sightseeing tour.
DAY 8: JAIPUR
Morning, excursion to early 17th century Amber Fort. Afternoon free.
DAY 9: JAIPUR - AGRA
Depart for Agra by car. En route visit the 15th century deserted city of Fatehpur Sikri.
DAY 10: AGRA - DELHI
Morning, visit the world famous Taj Mahal built in the 16th century, the Fort and the Tomb of Itimad-ud-Daula. Afternoon depart for Delhi by car en route visiting Emperor Akbar's Tomb at Sikandra.
DAY 11: DELHI
Morning, city sightseeing tour of Old and New Delhi. Afternoon free.

DAY 12: DELHI
Depart from Delhi by air.
Notes: Elephanta caves excursion operates only mid-September to mid-May. Air travel on sectors Bombay-Aurangabad-Udaipur-Jodhpur-Jaipur.

TOUR NO. 8
14-Day tour of Bombay-Hyderabad-Bangalore-Mysore-Madras-Trichy-Thanjavur-Cochin-Bombay

DAY 1: BOMBAY
Arrive Bombay. Afternoon, city sightseeing tour.

DAY 2: BOMBAY - HYDERABAD
Morning excursion of Elephanta Caves. Depart for Hyderabad by air.

DAY 3: HYDERABAD
Morning, city sightseeing tour including Salar Jung Museum. Afternoon, visit Golconda Fort, built in the 15th century.

DAY 4: HYDERABAD - BANGALORE
Depart for Bangalore by air. Afternoon, city sightseeing tour.

DAY 5: BANGALORE - MYSORE
Depart for Mysore by car. En route visit Srirangapatnam, the Summer Palace of Tipu Sultan built in the 18th century. Afternoon, city sightseeing tour including the Palace of the Maharaja of Mysore.

DAY 6: MYSORE - BELUR - HALEBID - MYSORE
Full day excursion by car to the 11th century temples at Belur and Halebid.

DAY 7: MYSORE - BANGALORE - MADRAS
Depart for Bangalore by car and then for Madras by air.

DAY 8: MADRAS
Full-day excursion by car to Mahabalipuram and Kanchipuram temples built between 5th and 8th centuries.

DAY 9: MADRAS - TRICHY
Morning, city sightseeing tour of Madras. Afternoon, depart for Trichy by air.

DAY 10: TRICHY - THANJAVUR - MADURAI
Morning, city sightseeing tour of Trichy. Afternoon depart for Madurai by car. En route visit the famous 9th century Chola temple of Brihadeesvara at Thanjavur.

DAY 11: MADURAI - THEKKADY
Morning, city sightseeing tour of Madurai. Afternoon, depart for Thekkady by car.

DAY 12: THEKKADY - COCHIN
Morning boat cruise on Lake Periyar to view wildlife. Afternoon, depart for Cochin by car.

DAY 13: COCHIN
Morning motor boat cruise on the Backwaters (lagoons). Afternoon, city sightseeing tour.

DAY 14: COCHIN - BOMBAY
Depart for Bombay by air and the same day for onward destination. Air Travel on sectors: Bombay-Hyderabad-Bangalore-Madras-Trichy and Cochin-Bombay.

TOUR NO. 9
7-Day tour of Calcutta-Bagdogra-Darjeeling-Pemayangste - Gangtok-Calcutta

DAY 1: CALCUTTA
Arrive Calcutta. Afternoon, city sightseeing tour.
DAY 2: CALCUTTA - BAGDOGRA - DARJEELING
Depart for Bagdogra by air and then proceed by car to Darjeeling.
DAY 3: DARJEELING
Early morning excursion to Tiger Hill to view the sunrise. Later, city sightseeing tour. Afternoon free.
DAY 4 : DARJEELING - PEMAYANGSTE
Depart for Pemayangste by car. Afternoon visit the monastery.
DAY 5: PEMAYANGTSE - GANGTOK
Depart for Gangtok by car. Afternoon, city sightseeing tour.
DAY 6: GANGTOK
Morning visit Rumtok Monastery.
Afternoon, free.
DAY 7: GANGTOK - BAGDOGRA - CALCUTTA
Depart for Bagdogra by car (127 kms.). Then for Calcutta or Delhi by air.

SHORT OR STOPOVER TOURS

To enable visitors in a hurry to see a little bit of India, we give below short tours which can be undertaken from major entry points in India. We have listed them as stopover tours.

FROM DELHI

Stopover 1 - DELHI - 1 to 2 days.
Ist Day: Morning, tour of Old Delhi. Afternoon, tour of New Delhi.
2nd Day: Free for shopping; visit to museums, etc.

Stopover 2 - AGRA - JAIPUR-3 days.
Ist Day: Morning, drive to Agra visiting Sikandra en route. Afternoon, tour of monuments of Agra.
2nd Day: Morning, visit Fatehpur Sikri en route to Jaipur. Afternoon, sightseeing of Jaipur.
3rd Day: Morning, drive to Delhi, visiting Amber Fort en route.

Stopover 3 - AGRA - KHAJURAHO - 3 days
DAY 1: Morning, fly to Agra. Drive to Fatehpur Sikri. Afternoon, Tour of Agra.
DAY 2: Morning, fly to Khajuraho.
Afternoon, visit temples.
DAY 3: Fly to Delhi.

Stopover 4 - KASHMIR - 3 days
DAY 1: Morning, fly to Srinagar. Afternoon, visit Mughal Gardens.
DAY 2: Full day excursion to Gulmarg.
DAY 3: Morning, free.
Afternoon, fly to Delhi.

Stopover 5 - AGRA - VARANASI - 3 days
DAY 1: Morning, fly to Agra. Drive to Fatehpur Sikri. Afternoon, tour of Agra.
DAY 2: Fly to Varanasi. Afternoon sightseeing tour of city and Sarnath.
DAY 3: Early morning boat ride on the Ganga. Early afternoon, fly to Delhi.

Stopover 6 - JAIPUR - UDAIPUR - 3 days
DAY 1: Morning fly to Jaipur. Tour of Jaipur city. Afternoon, elephant ride to Amber Fort.
DAY 2: Morning, fly to Udaipur. Tour of city. Afternoon, cruise on Pichola Lake.
DAY 3: Morning, fly to Delhi.

FROM BOMBAY

Stopover 7 - BOMBAY - 1 to 2 days
DAY 1: Morning, visit to the Elephanta Caves. Afternoon, tour of city.
DAY 2: Morning, tour of suburbs. Afternoon, free for shopping

Stopover 8 - AJANTA - ELLORA-3 days
DAY 1: Morning, fly to Aurangabad. Visit Daulatabad Fort and Ellora Caves. Afternoon, tour of Aurangabad.
DAY 2: Full day visit to the Ajanta Caves.
DAY 3: Morning, fly to Bombay.

Stopover 9 - GOA - 3 days
DAY 1: Early afternoon fly to Goa. Evening, free to swim.
DAY 2: Morning, tour of Old Goa and Ponda. Afternoon, free to swim and sun-bathe.
DAY 3: Morning, free to visit other beaches. Afternoon, fly to Bombay.

Stopover 10 - GIR FOREST - 3 days
DAY 1: Afternoon, fly to Keshod. Drive to Gir.

DAY 2: Morning, visit Somnath Temple and Museum. Lunch at Chorwad Beach Resort. Afternoon, proceed to forest to see lions.
DAY 3: Morning, drive through forest. Afternoon, fly to Bombay.

Stopover 11 - INDORE - MANDU - 3 days
DAY 1: Morning, fly to Indore. Visit Kanch Mandir and drive to Mandu.
Day 2: Full day sightseeing of Mandu monuments. Evening, drive to Indore.
DAY 3: Morning, fly to Bombay.

FROM MADRAS

Stopover 12 - MADRAS - 1 to 2 days
DAY 1: Morning, tour of City. Afternoon free for shopping.
DAY 2: Full day excursion to Mahabalipuram.

Stopover 13 - MAHABALIPURAM - KANCHIPURAM - 2 days
DAY 1: Morning, drive to Mahabalipuram. Tour of monuments. Afternoon, free for swimming.
DAY 2: Morning, visit Sculpture School. Afternoon, visit Kanchipuram. Evening, return to Madras

Stopover 14 - BANGALORE - MYSORE - SOMNATHPUR 3 days
DAY 1: Morning, fly to Bangalore. Afternoon, tour of city.
DAY 2: Morning, drive to Mysore. Full day tour to Mysore and Srirangapatnam.
DAY 3: Visit Somnathpur and Sravanabelagola. Drive to Bangalore. Fly to Madras.

Stopover 15 - MADURAI - TRICHY - 2 days
DAY 1: Morning, fly to Madurai. Tour of City. Evening, visit to Temple and Son-et-lumiere show.
DAY 2: Morning, drive to Trichy. Tour of Srirangam temple town and Rock Fort, Trichy. Evening, fly to Madras.

Stopover 16 - BANGALORE - HYDERABAD
DAY 1: Afternoon, fly to Bangalore.
DAY 2: Morning, tour of city. Evening, fly to Hyderabad
DAY 3: Morning, sightseeing tour.
Evening, fly to Madras.

Stopover 17 - COCHIN - TIRUVANANTHAPURAM (Kovalam) - 3 days
DAY 1: Morning, fly to Cochin. Afternoon, boat ride on the backwaters.
DAY 2: Morning, tour of city. Afternoon, drive to Kovalam Beach.
DAY 3: Morning, on the Beach. Afternoon, drive around Tiruvananthapuram. Evening, fly to Madras.

From Calcutta

Stopover 18 - CALCUTTA - 1 to 2 days
DAY 1: Full day tour of city, Botanical Gardens and Belur Math.
DAY 2: Free to visit cultural institutions, theatres, shops, etc.

Stopover 19 - DARJEELING - 3 days
DAY 1: Afternoon, fly to Bagdogra. Drive to Darjeeling.
DAY 2: Early Morning, drive to Tiger Hill to see Mount Everest and visit Ghoom Monastery. Afternoon, tour of Darjeeling.
DAY 3: Fly to Calcutta from Bagdogra.

Stopover 20 - BHUBANESWAR - PURI - KONARK - 3 days
DAY 1: Morning, fly to Bhubaneswar. Afternoon, tour of Temples.
DAY 2: Full day excursion to Konark and Puri. Overnight at Puri.
DAY 3: Morning, free to swim at Puri. Afternoon, drive to Bhubaneswar. Evening, fly to Calcutta.

Stopover 21 - VARANASI - 2 days
DAY 1: Morning, fly to Varanasi. Afternoon, tour of city and Sarnath.
DAY 2: Early morning, boat ride on the Ganga. Morning, visit University Campus. Evening, fly to Calcutta.

Stopover 22 - BODH GAYA - RAJGIR - NALANDA - 3 days
DAY 1: Morning, fly to Patna. Drive to Rajgir. Afternoon, sightseeing of Rajgir.
DAY 2: Full day excursion to Bodh Gaya and Nalanda. Evening, drive to Patna.
DAY 3: Fly to Calcutta.

Note: Most of the above itineraries are by air and road. However, all of these itineraries can be undertaken by rail and road, if necessary.

INDIA'S INTERNATIONAL AIRPORTS

About 97 per cent of foreign visitors to India come by air. Bombay and Delhi are the major entry points. Together they receive about 75 per cent of the visitors to India.

Others enter through Madras and Calcutta. There are a few small international airports as well where flights from foreign countries land but not so frequently. Among these are Varanasi and Patna (from Nepal), Hyderabad and Thiruvananthapuram (from the Gulf and Maldives), Dabolim (Goa) charters from Europe.

Many long-haul flights often land in India at midnight or after to suit the regulations on landings and take-offs in Europe and the Far East. India has no night curfew for landings and airlines take advantage to reach India at an unearthly hour.

The four international airports are well served by 50 international airlines. The facilities at these airports are adequate and are being constantly improved.

All airports have left luggage facilities. Porters and licensed metered taxis are available. In Delhi and Bombay the authorities have arranged what is called the "prepaid" taxi system. You pay the fare in advance to the authorised agents outside the airports and taxi drivers collect it from the agent after delivering the passenger at his hotel or house. They are paid the fare only after they produce to the authorities a signed voucher from the passengers. There are no hassles about the fare and no complaints of overcharging.

There are duty-free shops at all the international airports. A visitor to India can buy duty-free goods also at the arrival lounge before going through the customs. Prices are comparable and even cheaper than Singapore and Hong Kong.

INDIA BY SEA

Passenger liners are no longer operating to India. However, some parts in India like Bombay, Margoa, Cochin and Madras are 'stops for luxury liners' round-the-world cruises. They normally touch India between October and March. Among these the most well-known is Q.E.II.

Some freighters too offer passage to India. Excellent accommodation is always available on these ships.

Among the shipping lines having regular freighter are the Shipping Corporation of India, the American President Line, the British India Steam Navigation Company and Lloyd Triestine.

INDIA BY ROAD

India has a wide network of roads - well over 2 million km. in length. Nearly half of these are good, metalled roads. A number of roads connecting various states have been classified as National Highways and are generally in very good condition but are not comparable to the 4 or 6 lane highways in USA or Germany. In the second category are the State Highways or the roads maintained by local bodies. These are also generally in good condition.

Travel by road can be an exciting and rewarding experience. A traveller gets to see the countryside and know how people in villages live and work. While driving on a highway you find different kinds of vehicles sharing the road with you. Among the road-users will be bullock carts, tractors with large families as passengers, three-or two-wheeler vehicles, bicycles and, of course, cars, buses, trucks, etc. But they crowd roads

leading into big cities. On rural roads, you can drive for miles without many vehicles coming in your way. Caution is the cardinal principle of driving in India. Driving at a speed of 60 to 70 km an hour on a national highway and 40 to 50 km during city drives can be perfectly safe.

In India, the rule is to drive on the left side of the road but in practice Indians drive on every side of the road. Referring to the chaos on Indian roads in the cities, William K. Stevens of the *New York Times* wrote, "India has more than half the number of traffic deaths in the United States which has nearly forty times more vehicles." He had other interesting observations to make, "Cars and heavy vehicles routinely breeze through the centre of a village at high speed relying on people and animals to scatter and save themselves." About scooter drivers, he said, "They are particularly vulnerable, and the danger is often compounded when a whole family - father, mother and perhaps three children - zips through on a single two-wheeler." On Indian highways, you will be better off to give the right of way to truck drivers or bus drivers. They seem to feel and act like kings of the roads.

Using the horn to warn other drivers is an accepted practice in India and many vehicle drivers often seem to blow it all the time. Perhaps they enjoy it and want everybody on the road to know it. Traffic on the Indian roads can be noisy especially if you are coming from a European city where the noise level is very low.

RENTING A CAR

Renting a car with chauffeur is inexpensive in India, in fact cheaper than what you pay for self-driven cars elsewhere. Till recently, Indian law did not allow self-driven rental cars. But now it has been amended and it is possible to rent a self-driven car. Moreover, facilities of renting a car at one place and leaving it at another are not yet available. Hertz, Budget and Europa cars are operating in India through their associates. Chauffeur-driven cars from these companies may work out cheaper and the driver can also act as your friend, philosopher and guide. Most of the chauffeurs in rental car companies can communicate in English. And, if you agree to do some shopping in their company, they will be excited and go all out to help you for they get a cut from the shops. For an additional charge, chauffeurs will accompany you for an out-of-town trip. The Government has fixed rates of hiring tourist cars and also additional charges for out-of-town journeys. Check before you rent a car and you may add a little tip to make the driver happy. You do not have to make arrangements for the accommodation and food of the driver. It is included in the cost paid by you and if you are a generous traveller, give him a few rupees to eat. Basically, a chauffeur-driven car is a long-distance taxi and you may be able to hire it for an all-inclusive rate — Rs 400 a day depending on the distance covered and the length of hire.

For city sightseeing, you can rent either an imported or an Indian car. Several of these vehicles are air-conditioned, but you do not need air conditioning during winter months. For each type of car, charges are different. City bus tours, which are very inexpensive, are also available. You can make a booking at the tourist office itself.

Cars can be rented from the transport counters of hotels or by calling a rental company. Central reservation offices of the three multinational companies are:

1. BUDGET
   G 3, Arunachal, Barakhamba Road,
   New Delhi-110001
   Tel 371 - 5657.

2. Europa
   Travel House, Basant Lok,
   Vasant Vihar, New Delhi
   Tel: 331-8695

3. Hertz
   18, Barakhamba Road
   Connaught Place,
   New Delhi-100001
   Tel. : 331-8695.

Not many foreign visitors bring their own cars to India as the overland journey has become difficult due to disturbances in Afghanistan, Iran and Pakistan. But, you cannot go wrong if you buy a car or motor cycle in India and sell it after 4 to 6 months. There is very high resale value of used cars in India.

INTER-CITY BUS SERVICES

Inter-city or inter-state bus services are frequent and inexpensive. For a little more than US$3, you can travel from Delhi to Chandigarh, a distance of 250 kilometres in a very good bus - they call it 'deluxe' in India. Add another 5 dollars and you can travel the same distance in an air-conditioned deluxe train (Shatabdi) with snacks thrown in.

The latest additions are video-coaches where Indian movies are shown on long-distance routes - a very noisy way of travelling!

CITY TRANSPORT

Within cities, there are many bus services. But most buses are crowded and a visitor may find it difficult to locate the bus which will take him to his destination unless he is an everyday traveller. In the Indian capital, the authorities have introduced Green and White Line buses which are not very crowded because the fare is slighty higher.

The cheapest, but not the most convenient, way of negotiating short distances would be to ride in an autorickshaw. It is an experience by itself and costs half the fare of a normal taxi. Two or three people can sit in it. Autorickshaws have fare metres. Avoid the autorickshaw driver who says his metre is not working. He wants to overcharge you. Also avoid long distance drives on autorickshaws if you are not young. It may be tiring.

There are plenty of yellow top ordinary taxis in major cities. There is never a shortage . Taxi drivers welcome a foreign visitor as he is more likely to be a compulsive tipper. You need not disappoint him.

Drivers take good care of their vehicles and some of them have been driving them for as long as thirty years. If the vehicle ever breaks down, you can be sure the driver will fix it in a matter of minutes. Most taxi drivers are good mechanics too.

A taxi driver will be happy if you retain him for the whole day. Retention charge is only Rs 15 per hour. There is a 25 per cent addition as night charge between 10 p.m. and 6 a.m.

Chapter 3

AT HOME WITH THE INDIANS

1. Meeting the Indian People
2. Travel in India
3. Where to get Travel Information
4. Government Tourist Offices in India
5. Leading Travel Agents and Tour Operators
6. Languages
7. Media
8. Health
9. Mail and Telecommunication Services
10. Interesting Facts
11. Hindi Vocabulary for Tourists

MEETING THE INDIAN PEOPLE

India has undergone tremendous changes since its independence in 1947. It is a modern country with ancient beliefs and traditions. In major cities, educated people can communicate well in English which continues to be one of India's official languages. Indians can be as extrovert as the Americans. A *New York Times* correspondent based in New Delhi wrote, "Indians can out-talk the Americans..." They can also be very shy and conservative. It depends upon how the foreign visitor looks at the people in the host country and how he wants to communicate with them. There are not many Indians who will take the first step to talk to a foreigner except the street-smart salesman (there are plenty of them in Delhi) who want to sell you something. Once the ice is broken, there are no barriers. Your friend may invite you to his home. Most Indians are proud of the achievements of their progeny. They would like to introduce them to you. You may be invited to dinner and, if things go well, for luncheon the next day, provided you are willing. Although they are very hospitable and warm, you must be able to say 'no' if you have other interesting things to do. They will understand. Even the poorer Indians will do the same provided you show some interest.

India is a democratic country and a visitor is free to move about anywhere he likes. A few tips, however, may be useful for the-first time visitors.

While the universal language of smile and gracious nod may result in an instant warmth in India, women should generally be greeted with folded hands. Shaking hands, except in westernised circles, should be avoided. On meeting you, people will bow their head slightly, fold their hands and say 'Namaskar', which means "I honour you". However, when men meet and greet each other, they usually shake hands. Greeting with folded hands may be more appropriate though the Indian himself will offer his hand for you to shake.

HOLY PLACES

Most Indians are religious-minded. A majority of them regularly visit temples, mosques, gurudwaras or churches. To respect their sentiments, take off your leather shoes while entering Hindu or Sikh temples. In Sikh gurudwaras, we also cover our heads on entry. You may tie your handkerchief on your head and that will suffice. There are no such restrictions on entering ancient monuments where no worship is offered.

The famous Velanganni Church, Tamil Nadu

WOMEN TRAVELLERS

Foreign women tourists in their traditional and graceful attire are not an object of curiosity in India. They mix well with Indian women, especially the educated ones. But foreign women wearing revealing clothes may attract attention and perhaps cat calls too from Indian Romeos! Just walk past, ignoring them. Any little indication of friendliness can be misunderstood. Women travelling alone in Indian cities during the day and early evenings are perfectly safe. But it can be risky for women travelling alone late at night, as in any other metropolitan cities of the world crime against foreign women is virtually unknown in India.

Few golden rules for women travelling alone:
(a) Avoid men too eager to help.
(b) Avoid accepting lifts which you have not asked for.
(c) Avoid asking a man for a lift. No harm when he is accompanied by a female.
(d) Avoid free and frank talk with strangers.

WEDDINGS

If you happen to be in India during the marriage season - all months are not auspicious for Hindu marriages - do try to attend one. Tourist offices may help you get an invitation to a wedding.

A Hindu marriage is a loud, festive and happy occasion, full of fun for relatives and friends. It is preceded by a lavish dinner. Families love to have foreigners as guests.

There is nothing very private in a Hindu wedding. The couple is surrounded by a large number of friends and relatives while they go through the ceremonies seated around the sacred fire. After these are over, the couple are made to go round the fire seven times to take a vow to love and respect each other. The elders bless the newly-weds and shower flowers on them.

FUNERALS

Hindu funerals, however, are very personal and solemn occasions. Families would not like to have strangers around. The mourning colour in India is white and not black as in the West.

TRAVEL IN INDIA

Affluent foreign travellers with a tight time schedule, are very well looked after if they entrust their travel arrangements to an Indian travel agent who is recognised by the Government of India. A list of leading travel agents is given at the end of this chapter. Such visitors are met on arrival, escorted to their hotels, taken on conducted sightseeing and then moved on their next halt in the itinerary where they receive similar services. They are not likely to encounter any difficulty during their entire journey except in the event of nature disrupting traffic or an airlines flight being delayed or cancelled.

Travel agents in India are highly professional and give excellent value for money.

Free and Independent Travellers (FITS) who want to travel on their own may face different kinds of problems. They should seek services of travel agents for making their air and rail bookings and other arrangements. The cost will be nominal.

In India, there is no dearth of helpful 'volunteers' offering their services as escorts or as friends without any cost to you. But, beware of such 'friends' at the airports or in the streets. They must be avoided.

WHERE TO GET TRAVEL INFORMATION

If you are an FIT, you can never go wrong if your first contact is with the Government of India Tourist Office in the city. It will correctly guide you on how to see the city at a very reasonable price. You can take a city bus tour alongwith other Indian tourists. You can eat at a clean and air-conditioned restaurant, sampling fine Indian or western food at fair prices. The Tourist Office will tell you where to eat and where to stay.

GOVERNMENT OF INDIA TOURIST OFFICES IN INDIA

Cable address of Tourist Offices in India is INDTOUR

Place	Address	Phone
New Delhi	88, Janpath, New Delhi 110 001	332-0005/ 332-0008
Bombay	123, M. Karve Road, Bombay 400 020	2032932/ 2033144
Calcutta	'Embassy', 4, Shakespeare Sarani, Calcutta 700 071	2421402/ 2421475
Madras	154, Anna Salai, Madras 600 002	8269685/ 869695
Agra	191, The Mall, Agra 282 001 (U.P.)	363377
Aurangabad	Krishna Vilas, Station Road, Aurangabad 431 001	31217
Bangalore	KFC Building, 48, Church Street, Bangalore 560 001	5585417
Bhubaneswar	B-20, Kalpana Area, Bhubaneswar 751 014	54203
Guwahati	B.K. Kakati Road, Ulubari, Guwahati 781 007	547407
Hyderabad	Sandozi Building, 26, Himayat Nagar, Hyderabad 500 029	660037
Imphal	Old Lambulane, Jail Road, Imphal 795 001	21131
Itanagar	P.O. Naharlagun, Itanagar 791 110	328
Jaipur	State Hotel, Jaipur 302 001	372200
Khajuraho	Near Western Group of Temples, Khajuraho 471 606	2047/2048
Kochi	Willingdon Island, Kochi 682 009	6683521

Panaji	Communidade Building, Church Square, Panaji, Goa 403 001	43412
Patna	Sudama Palace, Kakarbagh Road, Patna 80020	226721
Port Blair	V.I.P. Road, Junglighat, Port Blair 744103	21006
Shillong	G.S. Road, Police Bazar, Shillong 793 001	225632
Thiruvananthapuram	Airport, Thiruvananthpuram	451498
Varanasi	15 B, The Mall, Varanasi 221 002	43744

At places where there are no Government of India Tourist Offices, the State Governments have their own Tourist Bureaus. There will be no language problem—the staff speak English and are helpful to foreigners. Some of the tourist officers can speak foreign languages other than English too. Tourist literature is not sold in these offices. It is given free of charge.

In a country like India where travel is very safe, it is a great experience to travel independently. But you need plenty of time and flexibility in your travel plans. Remember, the average period of stay of foreign tourists in India is one month. Surely, some tourists stay for two to three months to make that average.

GUIDE SERVICES

All major tourist cities have trained English and other foreign language speaking guides. Their charges are fixed, and do not exceed $ 10 to $ 15 for a whole day. Guides can be hired from Government of India Tourist Offices. They can also accompany you for outstation assignments for an additianal charge.

LEADING TRAVEL AGENTS AND TOUR OPERATORS

There are some 100 travel agents and tour operators approved by the Government of India. Listed below, are a few of the better known and reliable agents who handle inbound business. Some of them have offices all over India and also overseas promotional offices in major markets:

BOMBAY

1. Travel Corporation of India (TCI), Chander Mukhi, Nariman Point Bombay

   Tel.: 2021881
   Telex: 011 82366
   Cable: TURING
   Fax: 29424

2. Indtravels,
   Nicol Road,
   Ballard Estate,
   Bombay-400 038.

   Phone: 2615
   Telex: 011 - 73534 AFTION
   Cable: INDTRAVELS
   Fax: 91 - 22-26105%

3. Trade Wings,
   30, K. Dubash Marg,
   Bombay - 400 050.

   Phone: 244 - 334
   Telex: 011 - 2494/5470 TWBB IN
   Cable: TRAVEL
   Fax: 91 - 22 - 2044223

4. Cox and Kings (India),
   270/272, Dr.D.N.Road,
   Bombay - 400 001.

   Phone: 2043065
   Telex: 011 - 2865
   Cable: COXSHIP
   Fax:

5. Thomas Cook (India),
   Dr.D.N.Road,
   Bombay - 400 001.

   Phone: 2048556
   Telex: 011 = 2096
   Cable: THOMASCOOK BOMBAY
   Fax: 91 - 22 - 2871069

6. American Express,
   274, Dr. D.N.Road,
   Bombay

   Phone: 204694
   Telex: 011 - 3134
   Cable: AIRAGE
   Fax:

7. Diners World Travels,
   Raheja Chambers,
   213, Nariman Point,
   Bombay - 400021.

   Phone: 244949
   Telex: 011 - 6897
   Cable: DINCLUB

NEW DELHI

8. Sita World Travels,
   Malcha Marg,
   Shopping Complex,
   Diplomatic Enclave,
   New Delhi - 110021.

   Phone: 301 - 1122
   Telex: 31-65141 SITAIN
   Cable: SITATUR
   Fax: 011-301-0123

9. Mercury Travels,
   Jeevan Tara Building,
   Parliament Street.

   Phone: 321-403
   Telex: 011-351413
   Cable: MERETRAVEL

10. Orient Express,
    70, Janpath,
    New Delhi - 110001.

    Phone: 322-2142
    Telex: 031-3533
    Cable: OREXPRESSEO
    Fax: 11 - 332-519

11. Travel House,
    Basant Lok,
    Vasant Vihar,
    New Delhi-110057.

    Phone: 603400
    Telex: 031-66644
    Cable: SIMPTRAVEL
    Fax: 091-11-679107

12. Everest Travel
    11C, Prem House,
    Connaught Place,
    New Delhi-110001.

    Phone: 332-1117
    Telex: 031 - 63039
    Cable: EVERETT
    Fax: 91-11-332-6778

13. Holiday Maker,
    USO House,
    6, Special Institutional Area,
    Near Qutab Hotel,
    New Delhi-110067

    Phone: 6868630
    Telex: 031-72219
    Fax: 11-6853425

14. Paradise Tour Company,
    20B, Community Centre,
    Basant Lok, Vasant Vihar.

    Phone: 606712
    Telex: 031-72458
    Fax: 011-687511

15. Wild Life Adventure Tours,
    606, Akashdeep, 6th Floor,
    Barakhamba Raod,
    New Delhi - 110001.

    Phone: 331-2773
    Telex: 031-65617
    Fax: 011-331-2984

16. Creative Travels,
    Creative Plaza,
    Nanakpura, Moti Bagh,
    New Delhi-110021.

    Phone: 679192
    Telex: 031-82047
    Fax: 011-675353

17. Kai Travels,
    A 312-314, Kai Suite
    Ansal Chambers, No. I,
    3, Bhikhaji Cama Place
    New Delhi - 110066.

    Phone: 878444
    Telex: 031-72081
    Fax: 011 - 6883155

18. Ashok Travels and Tours,
    Kanishka Plaza,
    19, Ashok Road,
    New Delhi-110001.

    Phone: 332-4205
    Telex: 031-61858
    Cable: TOURIST
    Fax: 011-360233

CALCUTTA

19. Balmer Lawrie,
    21, Netaji Subash Road,
    Calcutta - 700 001.

20. Trade Wings (Calcutta),
    32, Chowranghee Road,
    Calcutta - 700 071.

21. Speedways International,
    3, Chowranghee Square,
    Calcutta - 700 072.

22. Ganges Tour & Travels,   *Phone*: 2490619
    Jawaharlal Nehru Road,   *Fax*: 0091 (33) 4732030
    Calcutta-700087

MADRAS

23. Ashok Travels,   *Phone*: 8251583
    34, Pantheon Road,   *Telex*: 0410450 EDC In
    Madras - 600 008.

24. Bharat Travels,
    159, Lingha Chetty Road,
    Madras - 600 001.

LANGUAGES

India has 18 officially recognised languages. This is an evolution in a land of myriad dialects. The 1991 census had listed 1652 languages as mother tongues spoken in India.

With independence, the question of a common language came up. The Constituent Assembly could not arrive at a consensus in the matter. The question was put to vote and Hindi won by a single vote — the casting vote of the President. Hindi, however, was only one of the many regional languages of India. The Indian National Congress had advocated the formation of linguistic provinces. The acceptance of this policy involved the statutory recognition of all the major regional languages.

The Constitution, therefore, recognised Hindi in the Devanagari script as the official language of the Union and the regional languages as the official languages of the States. English was recognised as the authoritative legislative and judicial language. A schedule - the 8th Schedule - was added to the Constitution to indicate all regional languages statutorily recognised. The Schedule contains the following 18 languages:

1)	Assamese	2)	Bengali	3)	Gujarati
4)	Hindi	5)	Kannada	6)	Kashmiri
7)	Malayalam	8)	Marathi	9)	Oriya
10)	Punjabi	11)	Sanskrit	12)	Tamil
13)	Telugu	14)	Urdu	15)	Sindhi
16)	Nepali	17)	Manipuri	18)	Konkani

Of the 18 languages listed in the Schedule, all except three - Sanskrit, Kashmiri and Sindhi - are official languages of one or the other state.

MEDIA

PUBLICATIONS

Of the 2,856 daily newspapers in India, some 209 are in English and 1182 in Hindi. The rest are in different Indian languages. The best known daily newspapers in English are *The Indian Express, The Times of India, The Hindu, The Hindustan Times* and *The Statesman*. India does not have tabloid daily newspapers. *The Indian Express*, published from 15 cities, enjoys the highest circulation among English dailies followed by *The Times of India* which is published from six cities. The Lucknow-based *Pioneer*, the 130- year-old newspaper with which Sir Winston Churchill was once associated as a reporter, has started publication from Delhi in addition to Lucknow. It is a good newspaper for foreign visitors as it carries more foreign news. *Sunday Times, Times of India*, Sunday publication has the longest circulation of a week.

Among news magazines, the fortnightly *India Today*, patterned on *Time Magazine* and published from Delhi, and the *Frontline*, published from Madras, are very popular. *India Today* has the highest circulation among news magazines published in English. It has several language editions too. *Sunday*, published every Sunday from Calcutta, is another popular weekly news magazine in English. *Gentleman* and *Debonair* (monthlies) magazines try to cater to the tastes of men!

Indian magazines appear to be inward-looking. They publish detailed stories on politics and politicians. Politics appears to be the Indian passion as well as a hobby. There are a few popular magazines dealing with business, i.e., *Business India, Business Today* and *Business Standard*. *Economic Times* and *Financial Express* are the two well known financial dailies published from major cities.

Indian editions of *Time, Newsweek* and *Readers' Digest* are readily available. Compared to the prices of Indian magazines, prices of *Time* and *Newsweek* are quite high. Foreign magazines do not have very large circulations in India, perhaps due to their high prices. *Readers' Digest* is doing well and is also published in Hindi.

There are several well produced English magazines for women: *Femina* and *Savvy* are more popular. There is a proliferation of magazines dealing with the film world. They contain scandals about film-stars, often deliberately planted to generate publicity for them. Among those published in English are *Stardust, Filmfare, Star and Style, Movie*.

Sports magazines are in plenty in keeping with the Indian passion for sports. But, apart from cricket and tennis, there is not much about other international sports. Cricket, hockey, tennis and football are popular sports of India.

TELEVISION

Although television started as a pilot project in India in 1959, it was only in the early 1980s that it acquired the role of a major mass medium. That was the time when the Asian Games were held in India. Colour television was introduced much later. Manufacture of television sets was also encouraged. Now-India not only meets its own requirements of colour and black and white television sets but also exports its surplus production. The Government-run television system in India is called *Doordarshan*. A second channel has been introduced with the participation of private sector. Doordarshan has also started a few satellite channels broadcasting in regional languages.

Television has great influence on the life of the people of India. By 1995, Doordarshan had reached 90 per cent of the population of India and 80 per cent of its area. The reach of television is being extended and during the next two years it will cover the whole of India.

India has been using its own space satellites to beam television programmes to viewers in Asia.

Indian television is presently Government controlled. It enables the Government to telecast educational and informational programmes. Most entertainment programmes on TV consist of popular Indian films, music items and serials from the life of the people. News in English and Hindi are broadcast at regular intervals.

Major cities have 2 channels - one primary channel for All India coverage and the second one for entertainment. There are several other channels to cater in different languages of the country. Most hotels are now linked by cable to international networks like Star TV, BBC, CNN, etc.

About 70 million sets are available with Indian families. But the impact of TV is much greater as many villages have community television sets.

The Government uses TV to promote family planning, thrift, environmental protection, cleanliness and national integration, which are important issues facing the nation.

Doordarshan accepts advertising with popular films and serials. Advertisements are shown briefly at the start of a programme and are not interspersed.

ALL INDIA RADIO

Radio broadcasting in India started in 1927. Initially called All India Radio, its name was changed to *Akashvani*. Radio has greater reach than television. You can see people listening to Akashvani while mending shoes, cooking food or selling goods in shops. At present, it is Government-controlled. The programmes are an interesting mix of entertainment and information. There are special programmes catering to all segments of the population. Emphasis is on farming, family planning, good housekeeping. Film music keeps the people tuned in to *Akashvani*. A special All-India Channel called Vividh Bharati broadcasts film music day. It is a commercial channel and accepts advertising. Ten per cent of broadcasting time is allotted to advertisements.

A national radio channel has commenced broadcasting since 1988. The transmission originating from Delhi, is beamed all over the country through a 1000 kw transmitter located at Nagpur. The News Services Division of Akashvani broadcasts every day 273 news bulletins for a duration of 37 hours in its home, regional and external services. In its home service from Delhi, 78 bulletins are put out in different Indian languages for over 11 hours every day. The external services broadcast daily programmes for nine hours in 23 languages. Akashvani's external programmes reach many countries of Europe, USA and Canada.

There is a strong public demand to make both Doordarshan and Akashvani autonomous organisations on the lines of BBC in the United Kingdom.

To be fair to Indian television and radio, it can be said that the bias in favour of the ruling party is marginal. The opposition party immediately go in for *dharna* (sit-in strikes) outside Broadcasting Houses as and when they find that their case is being unfairly projected and corrective measures are taken immediately.

HEALTH

Foreign visitors should not come with the impression that India is infection prone. It is not. The country has been declared free of smallpox and cholera by the World Health Organisation (WHO) and no vaccinations are required for entry into the country. India uses the same methods to treat its water as is done in the West. But by all means come along with your favourite medicines.

Change of weather and water may affect any sensitive stomach. There is no dearth of bottled mineral water in India. It is brought from the Himalayan springs - perfectly safe - from a height of 1500 metres. It is inexpensive, too, and is available in big cities of the country. You always have the alternative to drink bottled soft drinks.

There is no better health care than precaution. Eat less than what your stomach demands, especially the tasty Indian curries. After a couple of days, your stomach will adjust itself to the changes and you can increase your intake of food.

First class air-conditioned hotels have no mosquitoes. However. If you are travelling in the countryside, take necessary precautions.

And, if in spite of every precaution, you get a toothache in Agra, do not panic. Indian dentists are well qualified and well trained to take care of you. Some of them may have had their degrees from American or British medical colleges. For any health problem, hotels have doctors on call. They will take care of you in a matter of minutes.

Health Care: Indian Style

Caring for the body is a part of the Indian tradition. Natural therapies, herbal medicines and beauty aids are a part of it. Indians through the ages have learnt to depend on nature for most of their requirements. Nature provides plants, herbs, barks of tree, fruits, flowers, milk and honey to take care of the health of men and women. Indians are also of the view that a healthy mind rests in a healthy body.

Yoga institutions all over the country teach fitness, mental calm and emotional relaxation. Yoga is often used medicinally in conjunction with massage to preserve energy, improve sleep and relieve stress. It may be interesting to take a few Yoga lessons. And, if you feel the difference, you may learn a few more simple postures and exercises for breathing. As you repeat these exercises daily, the relaxation increases.

Yoga clinics around the country give advice on how to continue your exercises and meditation.

Along with Yoga, Ayurvedic massage is popular in India. Massage oil varies according to what is available in different parts of the country. In the south, it is coconut oil, in the north mustard oil. These are absorbed better than the thicker almond oil which is used for the feet only. The aim of the massage is to open the skin pores, so that the oil enters and lubricates the skin tissues, veins and muscles. Massage promotes blood circulation and removes congestion.

PRECAUTIONS

India is not a theft-prone country. But a lot of people are poor and they can be tempted to steal - if you leave your things unattended. Cash and other expensive items must be put in the hotel locker or kept in locked suit cases. These should not be left scattered in the room.

In crowded areas, take extra precautions with your wallet. Bus-stops, railway stations and busy bazars are such areas. Pickpockets may find you an easy victim if you are wandering alone.

In case of loss, contact the local police. It can be contacted on telephone number 100 in most cities. Make a written complaint and take a copy duly receipted by the police post. The copy is called First Information Report (FIR). It helps!

SOME MORE PRECAUTIONS

Make a photo copy of your passport and keep it in your luggage. In the unlikely event of its loss, it always helps make a new passport. Note down the number of your credit cards or travellers' cheques separately in your notebook.

TOURIST POLICE

To help tourists, Delhi has a special tourist police willing to assist the visitors. Its services extend to international and national airports, Connaught Place, the Inter-State Bus Terminal and important monuments.

INSURANCE

It may be advisable to have adequate insurance cover against theft and ill health.

ALCOHOLIC DRINKS

Although many Indians shun alcohol, specially the women, the upper crust of society do enjoy alcoholic drinks which are a luxury for most Indians.

Imported liquors like Scotch Whisky are very much prized. But Indian-made whiskies, rums, and brandy are not far behind their western counterparts. These are also popular with foreign residents.

There are some 30 varieties of Indian beer available. Popular brands are *Kingfisher, Heyward* and *Rosy Pelican*. Indian beer is good.

Alcoholic drinks and beer must be bought from licensed shops. India does not produce very good wines. Try them for their taste.

Drinking in public is prohibited and is not desirable. You are welcome to drink in your hotel room or in the hotel bar if you want company. Some Indian states enforce prohibition - especially Gujarat, Tamil Nadu and Andhra Pradesh. But foreigners in hotels can get permits for drinking.

TIME

Indian Standard Time is 5½ hours ahead of Greenwich Mean Time and 10½ hours ahead of US East. Thus noon in India is 1.30 a.m. in New York. Nepal sticks to its ancient sundial time which is ten minutes ahead of Indian Standard Time. Indian Standard Time has no variation in summer or winter.

MAIL AND TELECOMMUNICATION SERVICES

Mail in India is very reliable and is frequently sent by air. The basic rate of inland letters is 75 paise for an aerogram. A one rupee stamp is required to be fixed on the cover of an envelope to be mailed within India, Nepal and Bhutan.

An air-letter costs Rs 6.50 and is valid for all the countries of the world. An envelope (20 grams) mailed to any foreign country needs stamps worth Rs 11 only. Picture postcards for foreign destinations need Rs 6 worth of stamps. Book-post by (120 gms) cost only Rs. 6.

Have your letter weighed at a post office to avoid under-stamping. Try to get the stamps defaced by the postal clerk in your presence.

SPEED POST

Speed Post delivers time-bound mail in 24 to 72 hours from the time of booking. The system money-back guarantees in case of late deliveries. Booking can be done at major post office of the cities. It is one of the world's largest courier systems run by government-owned Postal Department.

There are several private courier services, too. Among them are Blue Dart, Express and Skypack etc.

India has one of the world's largest postal systems comprising 150,000 post offices. In terms of handling mail, India ranks among the top after UK, Japan, and France. It employs about 600,000 people all over India for postal services alone.

PARCELS

Parcels should normally be mailed from major post offices. Avoid asking small shops to ship your purchases. Government emporia or large departmental stores will readily ship your goods and can be trusted.

Try to carry your small souvenirs with you as unaccompanied luggage.

OVERSEAS TELEPHONE AND TELEX SERVICES

Besides hotels, international telephone facilities exist in major post offices and markets. There are telephone booths for local and international calls in busy market areas all over the country. Telephoning from these places works out cheaper than from your hotel room.

India has a direct dialling system linking over 190 countries of the world, including China. Within India, Subscribers Trunk Dialling (STD) is available for 900 cities!

During your travels you will see big signs ISD/STD. You can call anywhere in the world from these booths. These are not automatic, there is always an attendant to assist you. International calls made between 11 p.m. and 6 a.m. earn a discount of 30%. If you are a visitor you can call the world through AT&T. From India dial 001-117 using your AT&T card or call collect.

City calls can be made from any telephone booth by inserting a one-rupee coin.

INTERESTING FACTS

NIGHT LIFE

Night life is virtually non-existent in the villages of India. In the metropolitan cities of Bombay, Delhi, Calcutta, Madras and Bangalore, however, there are plenty of discos, floor shows and an array of cultural events which can keep you occupied in the evening. The cultural scene in Indian cities becomes more alive in winter months with dance performances, plays, musical evenings and sometimes English plays. Rich and educated Indians lead a hectic social life and love to wear formal and fashionable clothes. If a visitor is drawn into a well-connected party circuit, he may see an India of the elite with lavish parties at home, in exclusive clubs or in 5-star hotels. The time-honoured tradition is that guests are offered drinks as long as the party lasts.

Most 5-star hotels have discos, but these are expensive. Hotel guests however pay a nominal entry fee. Only sons and daughters of the very rich can afford this luxury.

WHAT TO CARRY

Remember that India, despite its poverty, is one of the ten largest industrial countries of the world. Therefore, you do not have to bring in much of toiletries, cosmetics or medicines. Most international brand names like Old Spice, Ponds, Forhans, Colgate are generally available in general stores alongwith many exquisite Indian brands.

You can also avoid bringing a large wardrobe. First, the climate in the country is mild and, secondly, you can add to your wardrobe designers' clothes stitched by experienced tailors at short notice. Devaluation of the Indian rupee has made India the world's bargain centre. Prices of cottons, silks, leather shoes are cheaper than in Hong Kong, Thailand and Singapore. And, what a variety! Jewellery comes in many shapes and designs. Indian gold and diamond jewellery is known all over the world. In fact, it is India's largest export item. Handicrafts and utility goods of all varieties are available in different parts of India. You cannot resist shopping in this country.

PHOTOGRAPHY

Films are easily available in India. Imported film rolls may be a little more expensive. It would, therefore, be useful to bring enough supply of films for your personal use. If you are left with some rolls, you can always gift them to your Indian friends who will appreciate such a gesture.

Camera repair services are available in major cities. Photographic equipment should be checked before departure. If the equipment is new, make sure to test it by shooting a roll.

Film- processing facilities are available even in small towns and often this can be done within 24 hours.

The best time for shooting in India is two hours after dawn and two hours before sunset. The weather may be dry or hazy during dry months demanding special care.

Most Indian people love to be photographed and will be willing to pose for you.

Photography is prohibited at airports, defence installations, railway stations, etc., for security reasons. Photography is also not allowed in some tribal areas. Special permission is needed for using artificial lights at ancient monuments.

DAIRY PRODUCTS AND ICE-CREAMS

India manufactures good quality dairy products and chocolates. They are not very different from Swiss or Dutch products. Amul, Nestle and Cadbury's are the popular brands.

Ice-cream is a speciality in India. You will find excellent ice-cream sold at street corners through vendors or corner shops. Famous names are Milkfood, Dollops (Cadbury's), Kwality and Gaylords. These are safe and are made the same way as in the West.

INDIAN TEA

India is the largest producer of tea in the world. Indian tea is known for its taste and flavour. There are many brands. Do not forget to take some home - like the famous Darjeeling and Assam tea. It comes in attractive packs and can make very good and inexpensive gifts for friends and relatives.

SOFT DRINKS

Being a tropical country, India offers several varieties of exotic soft drinks including some foreign brands like Pepsi and Coca Cola. India's

Thums-up, Limca, Citra, Gold Spot and Maaza - a mango drink—
maintain the same standards as foreign brands. Maaza is also marketed
in the USA and the Middle East. Thums-up is sold in some countries of
the Middle East.

FAST FOOD

Indigenous chains of fast food outlets have come up everywhere - not
very different from their American counterparts. You may soon see a
MacDonalds, Yankee Doodle or a Pizza Hut, and there are the Wimpy's,
a British fast food giant, and the Nirulas, an Indian chain which
specialises in fast foods.

WESTERN FOOD

Indian food is not curry alone as you will read in the chapter on Indian
cuisine. It need not be hot and spicy, either. Order food in a good
restaurant and you will not be disappointed. Western and Chinese food
are available almost everywhere. There are speciality restaurants for
French, Italian, Chinese or Japanese food in every major town. Recently,
some Thai restaurants have also come up in Bombay and Delhi. You can
surely have your choice and do not have to depend on curry for your
sustenance.

HINDI VOCABULARY FOR TOURISTS

English is spoken and understood in most parts of India, specially by
people who have been to high school. English is a compulsory subject in
high schools and often students start learning it from the fifth class. In
many colleges and universities, science subjects are taught through the
medium of English. It continues to be an administrative and official
language of the central Government, besides Hindi. Although you may
not be stuck up anywhere in the country if you are familiar with English,
it is always desirable and enjoyable to know a few words of the local
language - in this case Hindi - to communicate with the common people
of India.

English too has absorbed many words of Indian languages and not
many people can now trace their origin to India. For example, "I live in a
bungalow which is situated on the edge of a *jungle*", "We sit in the
verandah on chairs made of *teak* wood", "We change into *pyjamas* and
wear *sandals*", "We *shampoo* our hair", etc. The English language is full of
many such words, a legacy of close association of Britain with India.

The glossary that follows lists some important Hindi words with their English translations - words you may hear again and again during your travels.

Acha:	OK.
Acharya:	A revered teacher.
Ahimsa:	non-violence.
Arrack:	An alcoholic drink made from coconut sap or rice wine.
Ashram:	A spiritual retreat.
Ayah:	A maidservant.
Ayurvedic:	Indian herbal medicine.
Baba:	A religious Guru, father; a term of respect for older people.
Babu:	A lower grade office worker.
Bahhut Accha:	Very Good.
Bagh:	Garden.
Bahadur:	Brave.
Baksheesh:	Tip.
Bandar:	Monkey.
Bandh:	General strike.
Baaen:	Left.
Bada:	Big.
Bearer:	Waiter.
Begum:	A Muslim woman of high rank; a form of address.
Betel:	Nut of the betel tree.
Bhagavad Gita:	A holy Hindu scripture; Lord Krishna's teaching to Arjuna before the epic battle of Kurukshetra.
Beedis:	Small hand-rolled cigarettes.
Black Money:	An Indian term for untaxed money.
Brahmin:	The highest Hindu caste; often a member of the priestly class.
Bustee:	A slum area.
Cantonment:	A military area. The British kept the military in separate areas. The system continues.
Chalo, Chalo:	Let us go.
Chappal:	Sandal.
Chappati:	Unleavened Indian bread.
Chhota:	Small, younger.
Chhela:	Disciple.
Cheeni:	Sugar.
Choli:	Saree blouse.
Chowkidar:	Watchman.
Crore:	10 million.
Daaen:	Right.

Dacait:	Robber.
Darshan:	Audience or meeting with a guru ; having a glimpse of a temple deity.
Darwaza:	Gateway, door.
Dhaba:	A cheap Indian restaurant.
Dhal:	Lentil curry; what most Indians take with bread or rice.
Dharamsala:	A religious guest house which provides free accommodation.
Dharma:	Hindu ethical code.
Dhobi:	Washerman.
Dhoti:	Worn like the *lunghi;* the cloth is pulled up between the legs and tucked.
Diwan-i-Aam:	The Hall of Public Audience in a ruler's palace.
Diwan-i-Khas:	The Hall of Private Audience.
Durbar:	Royal Court.
Durga:	Name of a Hindu goddess, symbol of power.
Doodh:	Milk.
Faqir:	A Muslim ascetic, a beggar.
Feni:	A spirit—drink made from cashews.
Gaddi:	Throne.
Ganesh:	The Elephant-headed god; the God of Wisdom.
Ganga:	River Ganges.
Ghee:	Clarified butter.
Gherao:	A kind of Indian protest by workers who lock up senior managers, peacefully, of course.
Goondas :	Toughs or ruffians.
Gurudwara:	A Sikh religious temple.
Guru:	Teacher; a holy person.
Haaji:	A Muslim who has made a pilgrimage to Mecca.
Hanuman:	Hindu god with the face of a monkey.
Harijan:	The so-called untouchables. Now, untouchability is not practised and they get preference in jobs, etc.
Hartal:	Strike of any kind—that of workers or students.
Hookah:	Water-pipe for smoking tobacco.
Imam:	Muslim religious leaders
Indra:	Another Hindu god, god of rain.
IMFL:	Indian made foreign liquor; a better quality Indian made whisky.
Jatakas:	Stories from the past lives of Lord Buddha.
Kali:	Hindu goddess; manifestation of power.
Karma :	Fate.
Khadi :	Handspun cloth. Mahatma Gandhi had ordained its use to make India self-sufficient.
Kothi :	Residence, usually a large mansion.

Kotwali :	A police station.
Krishna:	Hindu God who delivered the sermon in the Gita.
Kurta :	Indian style loose shirt.
Lakh:	One hundred thousand. (10,0000)
Lassi :	A refreshing, popular sweet yoghurt drink.
Lathi :	Baton.
Mahabharata :	A Hindu epic.
Mahal :	Palace.
Maharajah :	A Hindu ruler.
Maidan :	A large open ground.
Mali :	A gardener.
Mandir :	A Hindu temple.
Mantra :	A Hindu prayer.
Masjid :	A mosque.
Mela :	A fair.
Memsahib :	A form of address for wealthy women, often used for white foreign women.
Mughals :	A dynasty of Muslim rulers who ruled Northern India for 200 years.
Moksha :	Salvation from cycle of births and deaths.
Monsoons :	Rainy season in India from June to October.
Narayana :	A name for Vishnu, the Protector.
Nawab :	A Muslim ruling prince.
Naxalites:	An ultra-left political movement.
Namada :	A term used for a rug.
Namaste :	An expression with which a person may be greeted at any time of the day.
Padayatra :	A journey by foot often used by Indian politicians to carry their message to rural people.
Pandit :	Hindu priest.
Puja :	Prayer.
Puranas :	Ancient Hindu scriptures.
Purdah :	Isolation in home practised by Muslim women.
Raga :	Melody or rhythm.
Raj :	Rule or government.
Rajput :	A warrior class from Rajasthan.
Ramayana :	One of the two major Hindu epic stories. It is known all over South-East Asia.
Rani :	Wife of a princely ruler.
Rasta Roko :	A form of protest by stopping all traffic.
Rath :	Often used as a temple chariot.
Rikshaw :	Two-wheeled vehicle pulled by a man using a cycle.
Rishis :	Sages.
Sadhu :	An ascetic.

Salwar :	Trousers worn by Punjabi women; now by most Indian young girls.
Satsang :	A gathering for a holy discourse.
Satyagraha :	Non-violent protest popularised by Mahatma Gandhi.
Shakti :	Spiritual energy or Life Force.
Shikar :	A hunting expedition.
Sardar :	A term used for leader; Sikhs are also addressed as Sardars.
Sitar :	An Indian stringed instrument.
Swami :	Title often used for a Hindu holy man.
Shri/Shrimati :	Mr/Mrs.
Shukriya :	Thank you.
Tabla :	A pair of kettledrums played with fingers.
Thali :	Traditional Indian metal plate for serving food.
Tonga :	Two-wheeled horse or pony carriage.
Thug :	A cheat.
Upanishads :	Ancient Hindu philosophical scriptures.
Varuna:	A Hindu God - the Lord of Oceans.
Vedas :	The four scriptures which the Hindus believe were revealed by the Gods through ancient sears.
Vihar :	Buddhist monastery.
Yajna :	Pious Hindu ceremony; chanting of ancient prayers around the sacred fire.
Yatra :	Pilgrimage.
Yoni :	Female fertility symbol.
Zamindar :	Landowner.
Zenana :	Female apartment in a Muslim household.

Numbers

Ek :	One
Do :	Two
Teen :	Three.
Chaar :	Four.
Paanch :	Five.
Chhe :	Six.
Saat :	Seven.
Aath :	Eight.
Nau :	Nine.
Dus :	Ten.
Bees :	Twenty
Tees :	Thirty
Chalis :	Forty
Pachas :	Fifty.
Saath :	Sixty.

१ २ ३ ४ ५

६ ७ ८ ९ १०

२० ३० ४० ५० ६०

७० ८० ९० १००

Sattar :   Seventy.
Assi :   Eighty.
Nabbe :   Ninety.
Sau :   One hundred.

COMMON INDIAN DISHES

Daal Makhni :   Lentil curry, richly spiced and fried in butter.
Shahi Paneer :   A dish made of fresh cheese, cream and tomatoes.
Baingan Bhartha :   A dish made of egg plant, mildly spiced.
Rogan Josh :   Curried lamb, often mutton.
Biriyani :   A popular rice dish mixed with mutton or chicken pieces - spiced and saffron coloured.
Tandoori Dishes :   Baked in clay oven - often chicken, mutton or fish.
Idili :   Steamed rice cakes eaten with fresh coconut chutney.
Malai Paneer :   A curried dish of creamy cheese.
Mattar Paneer :   A curried dish of fresh cheese mixed with fresh peas.
Chapatti :   Crisp thin bread made over a plate on slow fire.

Rumali Roti :   Paper-thin large bread baked in clay oven.
Naan :   Fluffy, yoghurt-leavened bread baked in clay oven.
Paratha :   A soft and tasty wheat bread thinly fried in butter.
Kulcha-Bhatura :   A soft doughy bread eaten with spicy chick-peas.

Dosa : Freshly made form of crepes from lightly fermented rice flour often stuffed with spiced potatoes. Almost a full meal eaten with Sambhar - lentil and vegetable soup and coconut chutney.

DESSERTS

Kulfi : Indian version of ice-cream flavoured with cardamom, pistachio, nuts and saffron.
Rasgullas : Cream cheese balls dipped in syrup.
Burfi : Cakes of sweets made from pure milk.
Gulab Jamun : Spongy ground fried balls dipped in hot syrup.
Kheer : Rich, thickened milk with rice, raisins and nuts.
Firni : A popular rice pudding.

Chapter 4

INDIA'S CULTURAL AND ARTISTIC HERITAGE

1. Religions and Philosophy
2. Indian Music and Dance
3. Architecture and Sculpture
4. Paintings
5. Festivals and Fairs

RELIGION AND PHILOSOPHY

The earliest Indian were not city-dwellers. They lived in forests and enjoyed the kind of life the dense forests offered. They lived in harmony with nature. So, most of their earlier myths revolved around trees, *Yaksha* and *Yakshinis,* snake spirits, *Nagas, Nagins,* etc.

HINDUISM

The earth itself is Aditi, the Mother Goddess. Strong and violent phenomena of nature are all symbolised by God who resembles Shiva. We also come across images of Mother Goddess and Shiva in the remains of Mohenjodaro and Harappa.

The Aryan tribes who began to cross the Hindukush mountains about fifteen centuries before Christ were mainly pastoral people, driving their herds of cattle to better pastures, racing in chariots, and intent on conquering new territories. The challenge of the high ranges of the Himalayas and the dense jungles was formidable. In the hymns and poems sung by them during their progress towards the Indus and Gangetic plains, several deities appear, who seem to be the personification of the nature gods to be worshipped and appeased. Among them are Agni, the fire; Varuna, the all-encompassing spirit of heaven; Rudra, the force of storms; Usha, the dawn; Surya, the sun.

The nomadic Aryans had brought few women with them on their arduous journeys and they began to inter-marry with the indigenous Dravidians. And, through intermingling, some of the native poetry of the conquerors absorbed the primitive but potent magical beliefs and practices of the conquered.

Thus most of the beliefs which are known to be part of Vedic culture are probably a fusion of the genius of the two strains of peoples in early India's history. The gods of both the races began to be worshipped together. According to the practice of henotheism, God is exalted to the supreme place at one time or another, the rest being considered merely incarnations of the Supreme Spirit. Also, the doctrine of birth and rebirth, according to good or bad deeds, emanates from a popular belief.

To begin with, the fair-skinned Aryans did not favour the dark-skinned Dravidian whom they subdued. This divided the population into a caste order, based originally on *varna* (colour) but subsequently on nature of men's occupations. The division, which was flexible at first, became rigid in time and led to social discrimination in later centuries. Originally, the movement from lower to higher castes was common.

In the process of assimilation, tension arose in this mixed society. And some of the men of the second highest caste, the Kshatriyas, and many more of the first caste, the Brahmins, began to retire into the forests, to meditate on the problems of Life and Death and of the relationship between man and God. The sayings of these thinkers later took the form of forest books called the *Upanishads*. There are many points of view expressed in the aphorisms, fables and proverbs in them. Some of them are even contradictory. One main doctrine emerges from the philosophy propounded by the *Upanishads*. There was a Supreme God, Brahman, the One. From the sheer compulsion of desire, this One split Himself into Many. And thus the universe arose, with a corresponding desire in the hearts of the many to seek Union with the Supreme One, to become one with *Brahman*. The way enjoined for this Union is meditation and prayer.

The exalted doctrine of the *Upanishads* was, however, mixed up by the priests with superstition and intricate rituals. The dominance of the upper castes became oppressive. The people revolted when it became intolerable.

BUDDHISM AND JAINISM

Prince Gautama, scion of a small principality on the borders of Nepal and India, was roused to profound inquiry into the existing beliefs and practices of the Hindu faith. A sensitive young man, he felt the cruelty of life, of sickness, old age and death assailing the people.

He sought to fathom the depths of human experience. In his despair at not finding a plausible solution, he settled down to meditate under a *peepal* tree in Bodh Gaya, and attained enlightenment. He became the Buddha, the Enlightened One or the one with knowledge. Pain is at the core of life, he said. And there is no escape from suffering in the birth and rebirth to which all beings are committed. Only the moral path of right thought and right deed could relieve human sorrows, he propounded.

The Buddha did not speculate about God, but considered salvation from the rigours of this world to lie in the attainment of *Nirvana* or freedom from the cycle of birth and death. Many feudal princes, as well as millions of humble people, listened to the message of the Buddha and found solace in his teachings.

Another prophet with a similar attitude of tenderness towards all beings was *Mahavira* the *Jina*, who founded Jainism around 500 BC. He rejected the Hindu gospel that the Supreme Creator had engineered this universe. He believed that it was infinite and eternal. Mahavir preached complete renunciation of desire and the material world for spiritual salvation.

Jain monks became embodiments of total renunciation - wearing few clothes. A begging bowl and a stove were their only possessions. They covered their mouths to avoid any living insect accidently entering their mouth. That is how they preached non-violence. In course of time, non-violence also became an essential element of Hinduism.

It is very difficult to separate Hinduism from Buddhism and Jainism. Hindu philosophy adjusted itself to the needs of time. You were not called to question if you differed with the prevalent belief. Respect for others' beliefs was a cardinal principle with the Hindu thinkers. So, Buddhism and Jainism became indistinguishable from Hinduism.

RELIGIOUS TREATISES

While the religious and philosophical beliefs of the early Hindus are summed up in the *Vedas* and the *Upanishads*, the actual history of the Aryan penetration into the plains of India seems to have been recorded in the two great epic poems, the *Ramayana* and the *Mahabharata*. All the kings and queens, who figure as heroes and heroines in these stories were later deified. And, one of the gods, who played an important part in the great war, was exalted to the position of Supreme God. This was Krishna, who was later to become one of the most favoured symbols of the human aspiration for union with the divine. His discourse to Arjuna, who was confused while facing his own kith and kin in the battle, has been enshrined in a long poem called the *Bhagavad Gita*. It is, today, the principal code for action for the Hindu masses. It sums up the philosophy of Hinduism and all Hindus swear by the *Bhagavad Gita*.

Between the fourth and ninth centuries, the various ancient gods of the Vedic period, *Brahma, Agni, Surya, Indra* and *Siva* had been added to by the names of Vishnu, Shakti and a host of *apsaras* (flying angels), demons and spirits, making a vast pantheon. They also found their way on the walls of Hindu temples.

The enormous body of Hindu religious doctrines, practices and beliefs was codified, during the medieval period, in books called the *Puranas*. These constitute a kind of encyclopaedia of the Hindu faith. The beliefs were supported by Puranic stories which were very effective with illiterate masses.

During this time, the original pure doctrine of Gautama was similarly also corrupted. It led to the decay of Buddhism.

VARIOUS CULTS

Subsequently, many Hindu reformers dedicated their energy to the revival of a more synthetic doctrine based on the original faith. Most of the original faiths had been transformed into dogma. Some of these reformers emphasised the realisation of the Supreme God through personal devotion. The movement was called *Bhakti*. Hinduism assumed the form of Brahmanical Theism.

There were three main forms of Brahmanical theism current among the Hindus since the medieval period. These were associated with the worship of three different gods. *Vaishnavism* exalts God Vishnu, the

Blessed one. Apart from Vishnu and His consort Lakshmi, God King Rama, and the heroic God, Krishna, are honoured as incarnations of the Supreme in the Vaishnava cult.

Shaivism insists on the supreme position of the beneficent and terrible God, Shiva - the Creator, preserver and destroyer of the universe.

Shaktism emphasises the role of Shakti, the consort of Shiva, as Durga, Mother Kali (destroyer) and Parvati (preserver of the universe). Many esoteric doctrines and practices are associated with this cult.

The variegated beliefs of Hinduism were influenced by Islam, Sikhism and Christianity during its long career. A significant result of these contacts was the strengthening of faith in one God - the Supreme Being. The country gave birth to many philosophers who emphasised the essential unity of all religions. God, they said, was the same by whatever name one may describe Him.

The fundamental postulates have survived the test of time and still command the adherence of the bulk of the population. They worshipped both Rama and Rahim.

The reform movements of the Arya Samaj, with its emphasis on the "pure" Vedic doctrine, and the Brahmo Samaj, with its insistence on synthesis between Hindu and Christian teachings, introduced more rational concepts and practices into Hinduism.

A great advantage of Hinduism is that it is a thinking man's way of life and like Christianity and Islam it does not enforce infallible concepts and beliefs. Hinduism offers a philosophy for a good and happy way to lead life without invoking the wrath of God.

ISLAM

Muslims are the largest minority of India. Their population is almost the same as in Pakistan. Only in the Kashmir Valley do they constitute a majority, elsewhere they are evenly spread with strong pockets in Uttar Pradesh and Bihar.

Arab traders sowed the first seeds of Islam in India when they beached their sailing vessels along the southern coast during the 7th century AD, bringing news of the recently founded faith of Prophet Mohammed. Mohammed was born in AD 570. They also brought the Muslim canon, the *Quran,* a collection of messages from Allah (God) spoken to Mohammed. The overwhelming feature of Islam was its forceful zeal to spread the word — by persuasion and, if it did not work, by the sword. Beginning from Arabia, Islam spread east over the centuries and eventually took firm roots in three continents: Asia, Europe and Africa. Unlike the Hindu religion which required its adherents to be born Hindus, conversion was their mission. Conversion in Islam is easy. To become a Muslim, it merely requires uttering of the words "There is no God but Allah and Mohammed is His prophet."

Early in its history, Islam experienced a schism that remains to this day. The majority of Muslims are *Sunnis*, whose allegiance is to the descendants of Mohammed's direct successor, the Caliph, while other Muslims are Shiaites who follow the descendants of the Prophet's son-in-law, Ali. Both aspire to make a pilgrimage to Mecca, prophet Mohammed's birthplace, and wish to become *Hajji*. But the two sects are often at loggerheads over their faith. In Indian and Pakistani cities, there are frequent skirmishes between the followers of the two sects.

SIKHISM

Sikhs constitute about two per cent of the Indian population. Sikhism is a fairly new religion, having broken away from Hinduism in the 16th century. Sikhism grew in response to friction between Hindus and Muslims in Punjab provoked by the terrible repression by the Muslim rulers, who tried to forcibly convert the Hindus. Aurangzeb was so hostile to Sikh religion that he offered as reward a gold coin to any citizen who brought the severed head of a Sikh. Provoked by this, the tenth Guru, Gobind Singh, enjoined upon all Sikhs to take the surname 'Singh' (Lion) and turned them into a volunteer army always ready to fight the Muslim rulers.

Founded by Guru Nanak (1444-1538), Sikhism originated as a Bhakti movement, rejected the caste system, treating everyone on an equal footing. The Sikhs believe in one God and worship Him in their temples called *gurudwaras*. Their holy book is the *Granth Sahib*, a collection of the teachings of their Ten Gurus and other contemporary saints, both Hindus and Muslims. The tenth Guru, Gobind Singh, ordered that there would be no more Gurus after him and that their sacred book, the *Granth Sahib*, alone should be read for guidance.

Their holiest city is Amritsar with its Golden Temple called *Harmander Sahib*.

Sikhs are known for their pragmatism, humour and common sense. They are also known for their bravery and valour.

CHRISTIANITY

Christianity too is a major religion of India. Most people are surprised to hear that Christianity took root in India within half a century of Christ's lifetime.

Saint Thomas arrived in Kerala in AD 54 and spread the Christian faith. It is amazing how Indians showed tolerance to foreigners who took shelter in India. Jews had arrived in India before the Christians. Christians and Jews were at loggerheads elsewhere in the world. But, as Apostle Saint Thomas, a disciple of Jesus Christ, landed on the Indian soil, he was received by a Jewish girl. Since Apostle St. George had come from Syria, the Christians in Kerala came to be known as Syrian Christians. Christianity, therefore, was not unknown when the Portuguese, Dutch and the English came to India to spread Christianity of their respective brands. Christianity was accepted mostly by low-caste Hindus. There are some 18 million Christians in India. Most of them are concentrated in the State of Goa, which was a Portuguese territory till 1960 and in the north-eastern States of Mizoram and Meghalaya, where Christian missionaries converted the tribals, often by offering some allurement.

JEWS

Jews in India have lived in Cochin for almost 3000 years. Their immigration dates back to AD 973 when King Soloman's merchant fleet started trading with Kerala for spices and silver. They originally settled on the Malabar coast. The Dravidian King of Cochin treated them well and granted a piece of land to one Josepin Rabban, a Jewish leader. They prospered and have lived peacefully over the centuries in Kerala. Now, only a handful of white Jews have been left as most have migrated to Israel. It is possible to see some old Jews in the Cochin synagogue, one of the oldest in the world.

According to records left by Mores Fereya de Perva of Amsterdam, who visited Cochin in 1686, tens of thousands of Jews had arrived in Cochin in the 4th century AD. Some of them seemed to have arrived in the 1st century AD.

ZOROASTRIANISM

A good example of India's hospitality towards the persecuted people of the world can be seen in the treatment of Zoroastrians who came to Gujarat (India) from Iran around AD 766. Called Parsis in India, there are some 100,000 of them living in Bombay and other places of India. Over the centuries, they have tried to preserve the purity of their blood by inter-marrying among themselves, creating some problems for their race. This system is breaking down as many Parsi boys and girls do not feel the necessity to marry among themselves.

Zoroastrianism was founded by Prophet Zoroaster around 800 BC. The advent of Islam in Iran led to their persecution and they found safety in India. They were a peace-loving people.

The Zoroastrian holy book is the *Zend-Avesta*, which describes the ongoing battle between good and evil. Their God is Ahura Mazda, who is symbolised by fire. Parsis worship nature's elements and are fire-worshippers, keeping the symbol of their belief burning in their temples.

INDIAN MUSIC AND DANCE

Of all aspects of Indian life, music is the most intriguing and elusive. The reaction of most visitors to India who are not born to Indian music ranges from mild bewilderment to confusion.

For instance, it is quite possible for an Indian audience of one thousand to listen enrapt for hours to a veteran singer of eighty-five with a cracked voice — amazing to Western ears which habitually demand tonal quality from music. Nor does a physical break, such as might be occasioned by a fit of coughing, or a hubbub in the back rows, become a calamity as it would be in a European concert. The reason for these strange phenomena is that in Indian classical music what is said is valued much more than the manner in which it is said. There is no denying that a melodious voice is an asset even in Indian music, but at the same time the lack of it does not disqualify an otherwise gifted musician from saying his piece. Before understanding what it is that the singer or the player has to say, let us get acquainted with the concepts of *raga* and *rasa*.

RAGAS

Raga literally means that which tinges the mind with a particular feeling, passion or emotion. The structure of each *raga* and the melodic movement within its framework are governed by definite and extensive rules laid down in ancient treatise on music written much before the Christian era. Indian music recognises twenty-two notes and microtones in the octave. The technique of a *raga*, put in the simplest form, consists in the use of certain fixed notes and microtones to the deliberate exclusion of others. Within this fixed framework, however, there is unlimited scope for improvisation. Each artiste can have his own individual interpretation and vision of a particular *raga*. No two renderings of the same *raga* by the same singer or player may be exactly the same. There is no written composition in the Western sense of the term.

Emotion is the raw material with which the Indian musician works. There is no narration or image-making. Each note in the octave has a definite expression and emotional value which is determined by its relation with the tonic. A constant drone always accompanies a singer or player so that the tonic might remain fixed in the mind of the listener. Particular groups of notes also combine to produce phrases with definite emotional expressions, such as the pathetic, the noble, the grave, etc. A musician mixes his notes and phrases much as a painter may mix his colours. The difference is that the final picture does not tell a story, but is the portrait of an emotional state. It is this that a singer tries to convey through subtle but acute suggestion, to develop and exalt until the listener is suffused with its distinctive flavour. The enjoyment of a particular emotional flavour is called *Rasa*.

Indian *ragas*, which form the main body of classical music in the country, deal with four *Rasas:* The erotic, the pathetic, the beatific and the heroic.

There are numerous *ragas*, each falling within one of these four categories. Theoretically speaking, if every permissible permutation and combination of notes was exploited, it would yield 38,000 *ragas*. As it is, only about 200 are prevalent. Many *ragas* are common to the two main systems of music in India, the HINDUSTANI and the CARNATIC prevalent in the North and the South, respectively.

The basic framework of Indian music is melodic. The voice never isolates individual notes from the melodic line, but glides over the intervals that separate them.

The constant accompanying rhythm, explicitly and prominently beaten out on a percussion instrument, is a feature of Indian music which every Indian takes for granted but which strikes others as extraordinary. Slow, medium and fast tempos are used in accordance with the mood of the musical passage. There is a very large number of rhythmic patterns, most of them of great intricacy, within which the performer moves with perfect ease.

Classical music in India owes much to folk music which has been brought on the stage in cities. In many spheres of public entertainment, folk music has become more popular but it seldom loses touch with the classical.

EAST MEETS WEST

During the past 40 years, there has been growing interest among the young people in America and Europe in Indian music. Musicians — both of the classical and the pop variety — have seriously experimented with modes of music outside the usual Western tradition. Pop groups — following the lead given by the Beatles — use instruments like the *sitar* and *shehnai* for exploration of eastern themes. Renowned musicians like YEHUDI MENUHIN and classic guitarists like JULIOUS BREAM have worked out new ways of collaborating with well-known Indian musicians. Modern composers like ALAN HOVHANESS have incorporated elements of Indian music in their work. JOHN MEHANGHLIN and ZAKIR HUSSAIN created Indo-Jazz fusion music. Indian musicians like PANDIT RAVI SHANKAR and VILAYAT KHAN have toured the concert halls in the West with thousands of young people listening to them with rapt attention. Ravi Shankar creates his own discipline for attention. He tells his audience not to smoke while he plays and the audience listens — a discipline no Western musician can enforce.

CLASSICAL DANCES

In recent years Indian dance has travelled all over the world. Some young people in the west have started learning the techniques of Indian dance. Its statisque quality and rhythm have caught the imagination of the people. Performance by Indian dancers in major capitals of the world attract large audiences.

Indian classical dancing, like the music, subscribes to a rigorous code and depends for the conveyance of its total import on a large body of previously understood conditions. But its statisque quality has a direct appeal to the eye. In recent years, Indian classical dancers have travelled to all parts of the world.

The origin of Indian dance is lost in time. There is a myth that when Lord Shiva shook his hand drum, the world heard its first rhythm. As he moved his body in tune with its beat, the universe came into being. All dancers conceive of classical dance as the highest form of worship. They dedicate themselves to Shiva — the dancing Nataraja and the supreme symbol of cosmic energy.

Dance forms an intrinsic part of worship in the temples where Hindus offer flowers to the God for worship. So do they offer him dance and music, being the most beautiful expression of the human spirit. Indians alone have the concept of a god who dances — Shiva, Nataraja, the king of dancers, one who creates the rhythm of the Universe.

In Indian dance, the concept of *rasa* or the aesthetic mood holds the central place. Nine *rasas* are recognised - *Shringara* or love in all its variations, devotion, humour, pathos, heroism, fury, terror, disgust, wonderment and peace.

The dance of India has an unbroken tradition of over 3,000 years. Its themes come from the vast treasure-house of myth, legend and ancient literature with which it has been associated through its long history.

Bharata's canonical treatise on dramaturgy, written in the 3rd century B.C., the *Natya Sastra*, is generally recognised as the most authoritative work on the subject. According to Bharata's exposition of the art of histrionics, dancing is a part of drama, and the classical dancer is, therefore, essentially, a storyteller, with the descriptive power of a poet. For this purpose, traditional Indian dancing employs a highly developed, symbolical gesture language which is almost as eloquent as poetry. A *hastamudra* (hand gesture), for instance, can be used to convey such a wide range of meanings as pearl, fragrance, a drop of water, silence, salvation, generosity, testing medicine, and calling the beloved. There are numerous *mudras* and the possibilities of expression through their combinations are infinite. There is always a set pattern for the musical accompaniment. The literary content of the song is interpreted in *abhinaya* or mime, of which hand gestures are an important part.

A characteristic feature of classical dancing is the use of intricate patterns of rhythm which are evident in the footwork and are generally emphasised by the jingling ankle-bells. The patterns of rhythm are cyclic and have their counterpart in the drums of the accompanying music.

Bharatanatyam

Four distinct schools of classical dance are generally recognised today. What is commonly referred to as *Bharatanatyam* is a dance technique of the South which was used by *devadasis* or temple dancers for centuries. It is by far the oldest of the classical styles and follows the ancient treatises more closely. A typical performance involves a single dancer, who represents various characters in the story or the theme portrayed. The themes of *Bharatanatyam* are usually lyrical, but there is also great scope for the dramatic. The rhythmic patterns of this dance style are particularly beautiful and are accompanied by corresponding beats on the *mridangam,* a long drum which tapers at both ends. Dancers dance to the music. The principal singer is also the director of the dancers.

Kathakali

Kathakali (originally called Ramkatham—the story of Rama, the hero of the *Ramayana*) is a dance-drama of Kerala. Its themes are taken from the ancient epics and an elaborate language of hand gestures and minute facial expressions is used to portray situations and emotions. The performance opens with tempestuous drumming in order to transport the spectator to another world peopled with gods and goddesses, and a host of Hindu myths and legends. The towering

headdresses, the elaborate facial make-up, the dim light and the precise and smooth gestures create this illusion with effortless ease. The art of the *Kathakali* performer and his pantomime lies in the fact that without any stage sets or scenery whatsoever he can conjure up convincing visions of forests, oceans, palaces and the infernal regions. The Kathakali performance lends itself best to the dramatic. The music and orchestra which form an integral part of *Kathakali* are of a very high order and excellence. *Kathakali* plays are written in Malayalam verse and set to music in appropriate *Ragas*.

The singer, who actually directs the dance, sings the lines to the accompaniment of the drums timed to the beating of the gong and cymbals.

Manipuri

Manipuri dancing is lyrical in character and its movements are supple and delicate. The Manipuri style is reminiscent of the medieval sculpture of India, with its emphasis on curves and circles rather than on lines and angles. In recent times, many choreographers have adapted the techniques of Manipuri and Kathakali to modern ballets based on contemporary themes. The costumes of Manipuri dancers are very pretty and colourful. The costumes and dances add a very cheerful note to India's heritage of dance.

Kathak

The *Kathak*, developed as a result of Mughal patronage in the 16th to

17th centuries, has also grown directly out of the ancient tradition of Indian dancing. This style of dancing belongs to North India and has an elegance and sophistication indicative of the urban society in which it flourished. The dancer's feet take up the challenge of the drums. Lightning footwork and ankle bells echo each subtle nuance of the accompanying tabla (drum) and the dancer stamps out the most intricate patterns in complicated time measures and contrapuntal rhythms.

Each of the four generally recognised classical styles is rooted in folk dances. The tribal and rural people of India literally dance their way through life. It is to them the most natural medium of self-expression. Nature, silently and unobstrusively, fashions their performance. As dancers from the Himalayan regions sway and bend, they recreate the vast, undulating ranges of the Himalayas. The agitated movements and abrupt changes of posture in the otherwise gentle rhythms in the folk dances of Assam signify violent storms and the uprooting of trees.

The tense and watchful attitudes in the dancing of the Nagas and the Gonds denote the perils of the jungle. The dances of the fishermen of Bombay suggest the roaring, mounting waves of the sea. The folk dances of the plains people, by contrast, impart a sense of peace and harmony.

The folk dances of India are ageless, but the prestige associated with them is new. They now form the most colourful part of India's Republic Day pageantry. Folk dances have now travelled from rural to urban areas.

Dimsa Dance (Araku)

Dance Today

There has been a major revival of the classical dances of India. They are now performed in the capital cities of India far from their places of origin. They are also performed in major capitals of the Western world. There have been experiments with Indian dance forms to adapt them to modern ballets by great artists like UDAY SHANKAR. But, in general, they have remained close to their traditional classical form and do not generally attempt to portray contemporary themes.

MUSICAL INSTRUMENTS OF INDIA

The flute, *nadaswaram, veena, gottuvadhyam, thavil, mridangam,* and the plain drum are some of the ancient instruments of music in India. The *sitar* and the *tabla* were latecomers. The *sitar* appears to have infiltrated from Persia and has assumed great popularity. Except for the *veena,* which is neatly fretted, all instruments are negotiated by the method of trial and error. Their handling depends on the ingenuity and dexterity of the player. The flute and the *nadaswaram,* as also the *shehnai,* are wind instruments. The *veena, gottuvadhyam* and the *sitar,* and now the *sarod* from Afghanistan, are stringed instruments. The drum varieties are percussion instruments.

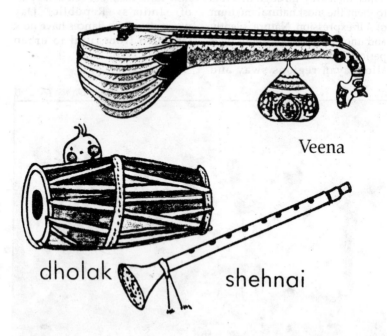

INDIAN ARCHITECTURE AND SCULPTURE

Indian architecture is as old as the history of civilisation. The earliest remains of recognisable building activity in the Indian subcontinent dates back to the third millennium in the Indus Valley cities. These cities are among man's earliest attempts to organise urban environment. The Great Baths of Mohenjodaro are some of the good examples of building.

The Vedic period that followed was marked by the anonymous pastoral settlements of mud, thatch, bamboo and timber in the valleys of the Ganga and the Saraswati. Although we do not have any extant example of perishable timber structures of that period, our knowledge is based on evidence left by subsequent Buddhist sculptures of the 2nd and 3rd century BC, which often depicted episodes from the life of Buddha, in the architectural setting of the Vedic period.

THE HINDU TEMPLES

Among India's ancient monuments, the most characteristic are the Hindu temples. Large or small, they are easily recognised by the typical pyramidal spire. They dominate the countryside with their presence, particularly in the South. The temples of KANCHIPURAM, MADURAI, SRIRANGAM, RAMESWARAM and other centres of pilgrimage in the South are busy places of worship. These are rivalled in the North only by the ancient city of VARANASI. Hindu temples were destroyed in the North. Floods too added to the devastation of architectural monuments.

Shivpuri Temple

The magnitude of the destruction wrought by time and invasions in the North can be had from the fact that Varanasi, the holiest city of the Hindus, has hardly a monument that can lay claim to antiquity. The great temples that have survived are in out-of-the-way places like KHAJURAHO in Madhya Pradesh, and BHUBANESWAR and KONARK in Orissa, where they could escape the fury of the invader's religious zeal to destroy.

Indian temples were built at centres of pilgrimage, near a river, a lake or a man-made tank because water was needed by the worshippers for ablutions and, at the same time, it was invested with an inner meaning. The symbolic meaning runs through the architecture of the temple itself with its three parts, namely, the base, the walls and the spire, corresponding to Earth, the intervening space and Heaven. In other words, the Feet, the Body and the Head of the Cosmic Man. The temple is regarded as the Universe in microcosm, a house of God, an altar at which the devotee makes his offering to the Presence enshrined within. This is the fundamental meaning of the temple building. Even the humblest shrine carries this significance.

THE STUPA

It was around the 3rd to 2nd century BC that Buddhism became the dominant religion of India, and stone was introduced for the first time in Indian art and architecture.

More ancient than the temples are the Buddhist stupas. Mound-shaped, they enshrine the relics either of the Buddha or of a great figure of the Buddhist church. Fundamentally, they too are invested with some symbolic meaning. Being identified analogically with the subtle body of the Buddha, the stupa is, like the temple, a place of worship.

From simple beginnings, the *stupa* evolved into an elaborate structure with beautiful sculpture adorning the encircling balustrades and the gateways. The finest example of the sculpture is the stupa at Sanchi, dating from the 3rd century before Christ. Episodes from the life of the Buddha are depicted here together with the various deities of the folk religion, which the Buddhist religion had absorbed.

ROCK-CUT ARCHITECTURE

It was in the field of rock-cut architecture, however, that remarkable Buddhist monuments were produced in areas such as Bihar in the east and Maharashtra in the west. Buddhist monks enlarged and transformed the natural grottos and caves in the hillside, excavating great and glorious prayer halls and monasteries out of huge cliffs. Despite the use of the rock-cut mode, the plan and elevation of these caves closely resemble the earlier brick and wood buildings. The monk-architects who carved the caves introduced windows, balconies and huge arch-shaped openings. In carving these "wondrous, caverns of light" out of rocky hillsides, these monk architects added a unique distinction to the Indian architectural tradition. Although rock-cut caves exist elsewhere in the world, there is no parallel to the aesthetic achievements of India in this field.

Rock-cut temple at Mammallapuram

MAURYAN SCULPTURE

Considerable architectural and sculptural activity must have preceded the execution of the fine carvings at S<small>ANCHI</small> but few specimens of it have survived. In fact, the earliest remains outside the proto-historic finds of the Indus Valley culture of which rich remains have been discovered in India at R<small>OPAR</small> and L<small>OTHAL</small> near Ahmedabad, are those of the Mauryan period (322-185 BC). Mauryan stone sculpture, the best specimen of which are to be seen in the country's many museums, had a rare feeling for monumental form and majestic power. Exquisitely finished, it was characterised by a brilliant polish that has not lost its lustre even today. Among Mauryan sculptures is the Lion Capital in the S<small>ARNATH</small> M<small>USEUM</small> which has been adopted as the State seal of this country.

Numerous Buddhist as well as Jain stupas were built at Mathura during the rule of the Kushans (1st-2nd century). Though none of them now remains, many of their splendid sculptures are to be found in the local museum. The female form is now treated with fresh vivacity, and innumerable decorative motifs.

As Buddhism spread from the north to the south, the deep impact of the new faith on the latter is evident from the remnants of the great stupas of AMARAVATI and NAGARJUNAKONDA. Here, the sculptor's art is executed on marble in bas-relief and possesses great animation and nervous energy. The crowded scenes depict the social life of the times and often relate the elevating tales of life of the Buddha.

CAVE ARCHITECTURE — BUDDHIST AND HINDU

Cave architecture received great elaboration during the Buddhist period (3rd century BC). Its best specimens are to be found in the hills of the western coast where the quality of the rock made them suitable for excavation. The caves, mostly in groups, were self-contained monastic establishments with rooms for monks to live in and temples where the Buddha was worshipped.

The great cave at KARLA is probably the finest of the cave temples. Imposing in size, its interior illuminated by soft light from a great window, the Karla cave induces in the visitor the feeling of benevolence and peace. The sculpture, comprising human couples, is characterised by free rhythm, grace and elegance.

Cave architecture was developed by the Hindus in a later period and the great cave temples at BADAMI, ELEPHANTA and ELLORA are remarkable monuments. The Mahesmurti of Elephanta (near Bombay), representing Shiva in his three aspects of Creator, Preserver and Destroyer, has been singled out by many as possibly the finest single piece of Indian sculpture. The great Buddhist, Hindu and Jain rock temples of Ellora vie with one another in splendour and size, the most staggering achievement being the KAILASA TEMPLE (8th century). Entirely hewn out of a rock, it has the appearance of a small man-made mountain, duplicating the heavenly mountain-abode of Lord Shiva.

THE GOLDEN AGE OF INDIAN ART - THE GUPTA PERIOD

Temple sculpture reached near perfection in the Gupta period (AD 320-495), the Golden Age of Indian Art, although the temple architecture was yet to be developed. The figures of gods and goddesses carved during this period have vitality and grace and are suffused with spiritual feeling. In the DASAVATARA TEMPLE at DEOGARH, Hindu iconography was given a form which it possesses even to this day. Fine images of Hindu deities as well as Buddhist and Jain pantheons are found in the country's museums.

TEMPLE ARCHITECTURE (MEDIEVAL)

The characteristic North Indian temple with a pyramidal spire was developed in the post-Gupta period. A wave of architectural activity swept the country during the 10th and 11th centuries. Great temples were built at Khajuraho in Madhya Pradesh (c.10th-11th centuries) and Bhubaneswar in Orissa (c.8th-11th centuries). The marble Jain temples at DILWARA (c.11th-13th centuries) represent a late phase of this style.

Most of the temples of this period are lavishly decorated with sculptures that are to be viewed not as individual pieces but as forming a part of the elaborate texture of the walls. The sculptures represent images of deities in numerous delicate poses and attitudes, and amorous couples. Mythical animals, in various combinations of elephant, lion and bird, are popular motifs. Also, there are long friezes depicting scenes of hunt and court as well as processions of soldiers.

The erotic element in medieval Indian sculpture may need a word of explanation. Though no single explanation of its significance is possible, it is important to consider that the bliss of ultimate spiritual union is, in Hindu thought, comparable to physical union. As a man embraced by his beloved knows not of 'I' and 'Thou', so is the union of man and God, full of joy and bliss. It has also been suggested that some of the erotic sculptures represented the ritual aspect of forgotten cults.

TEMPLE ARCHITECTURE OF THE SOUTH

From the 7th century there was an upsurge of building activity in South India. The BRIHADEESVARA TEMPLE at THANJAVUR, probably the largest Indian temple surviving from antiquity, was constructed by the Chola king, Rajaraja I, towards the end of the 10th century.

The foundations of a vital movement of sacred architecture were laid during the Pallava period with the construction of rock-cut temples at MAHABALIPURAM (c.7th-8th centuries). Here, the excellent sculpture has a gentle movement and quiet dignity. The later Pallava temples at Kanchipuram represented the same style.

Chola architecture is conceived in much more grandiose proportions. Besides the Thanjavur temple, another colossal

Temple at Somnathpur

Modhera temple, Gujarat

temple was built at GANGAIKONDACHOLAPURAM by Rajaraja's son, Rajendra (11th century).

The creative impulse in the South lasted much longer than in the North where the last masterpiece was probably the KONARK TEMPLE (13th century). Conceived in the form of the chariot of the Sun God, it is a remarkable example of Hindu architecture and sculpture. This achievement was made possible by the comparative safety from foreign invasions which was achieved during rule of the valiant rulers of VIJAYANAGAR (c. 1350-1600). Their deserted capital at HAMPI is a monument to their lavish patronage of art and architecture.

A word may also be said about the ornate medieval temples in HALEBID, BELUR and SOMNATHPUR in the modern state of Karnataka. They are remarkable for their exceptionally rich carvings made possible by the quality of the stone, which is soft and easily carved when freshly quarried but hardens with exposure.

MUSLIM ARCHITECTURE

Muslim architecture traces its history to the first Turkish invasions and gradually acquires a distinct national character that distinguishes it from the architecture of Islam. Many fine early monuments are to be found in DELHI, the most famous being the JAMA MASJID, built by Qutb-ud-din Aibak, near the famous QUTUB MINAR in early 13th century. The rise of the Sultanates of Gujarat, Malwa and Jaunpur, during the 15th century, marked the emergence of provincial styles of great beauty assimilating Hindu architecture and its decorative motifs. The most splendid phase of Muslim architecture in India, however, was the one initiated by the Mughals under Emperor Akbar. The AGRA FORT and the deserted capital city of FATEHPUR SIKRI near Agra (16th century) bear testimony to the greatness of his vision and the catholicity of his taste. Also, near Agra is the splendid mausoleum of Akbar, known as SIKANDRA, conceived by the Emperor in his lifetime but completed in the reign of his son Jahangir. The principal attraction of Agra, however, is the TAJ MAHAL, a tribute of Emperor Shahjahan (1627-1658) to his beloved queen, Mumtaz Mahal. Of chaste proportions, and built entirely of marble, it never fails to please in the charming setting of fountains in a beautiful garden. Shahjahan, whose passion was architecture, also built the magnificent RED FORT and the famous JAMA MASJID near the Red Fort. Before he could complete the Red Fort, he was dethroned by his ambitious son, Aurangzeb, and moved to the Fort at Agra where he lived for another decade gazing vacantly at the monument of love he had built — the Taj Mahal.

Aurangzeb had no time or aptitude for architecture — he was so busy with wars and rebellions during this period. He built a poor

Qutb Shahi Tombs

imitation of the Taj Mahal, BIBI KA MAQBARA, in AURANGABAD to commemorate the death of his wife.

Fine buildings were, however, erected in the Deccan, where the Islamic architectural tradition had grown up during the time of the Bahamani Sultans. Rulers of the Adil Shahi Sultanate of BIJAPUR built several excellent buildings in the capital city, of which IBRAHIM RAUZA, the tomb of Ibrahim Adil Shah II (1580), GOL GUMBAZ, and the tomb of his successor Muhammad, are easily the most outstanding. Hindu rulers continued to build side by side with the Muslims, the PALACE OF RAJA MANN SINGH TOMAR at GWALIOR being an outstanding achievement of civil architecture. The FORT and the PALACE AT AMBER, near Jaipur, as well as other Rajput citadels of this period are imposing works of art. The River GHATS OF VARANASI, built mainly during the 18th and 19th centuries by many Hindu princes of India, represent indigenous architecture in a state of decline. Viewed as a whole, they do not fail to move the visitor by their complexity and size.

MUSEUMS AND ART GALLERIES

India offers superb museums for the visitors, especially for those interested in history, archaeology and art.

In addition to large museums in major metropolitan cities, you find smaller ones close to the archaeological sites. These museums provide you a lot of information in understanding ancient monuments and ruins.

The Indian Government encourages people to visit museums. Therefore, entry fees are either nil or nominal. There are some additional charges for taking photographs. Most museums are open from 10 a.m. to 5 p.m. on all days except Mondays.

Admission to temples is free though you are welcome to leave something for charity.

There is a nominal fee for admission to major archaeological monuments like the Taj Mahal in Agra or the Red Fort in Delhi.

Of about 250 museums in India, we list below a few prominent ones. If the city happens to be on your itinerary, try not to miss them:

Bombay
1. Prince of Wales Museum.
2. Victoria and Albert Museum.
3. Jahangir Nicholson Museum of Modern Art.
4. Nehru Science Museum.

Calcutta
1. Indian Museum.
2. Victoria Memorial Hall Museum.
3. Rabinder Bharti Museum.

Delhi
1. National Museum.
2. National Museum of Natural History.
3. Crafts Museum.
4. Red Fort Museum.
5. Rail Transport Museum.
6. International Dolls Museum.

Madras
1. Government Museum Natural History.
2. Fort Saint George Museum.

PAINTINGS

Despite the great gap in our knowledge of continuous history, the story of Indian paintings can begin with the art of the primitive man in rock shelters and caves. It has survived at many places — to name only a few, HOSHANGABAD, MIRZAPUR and BUMBETKA.

Subsequently, we found the remains of a well-developed urban civilisation in India — Indus Valley Civilisation (2000 BC - 1500 BC). Most of its remains lay buried for some thousand years under the earth till these were discovered less than a hundred years ago. Among the remains, there are beautiful samples of colourfully painted pottery. From those samples, we conclude that the Indus Valley people must have had a rich tradition of painting too, but the super structure had totally vanished.

AJANTA MURALS

The earliest examples of a fine Indian painting tradition is found in Ajanta Caves in the modern Maharashtra — from first century BC to the eighth century AD. The spirit of the compassionate Buddha is their inspiration. *Jataka* tales pertaining to Buddhist mythology form the themes of these paintings. Anonymous artists painted them collectively in sinuous line and sensitive colours.

The world of Ajanta is peopled with sensitive characters from the various former lives of the Enlightened One, the Buddha. Tropical vegetation, insects, birds, animals, human and angelic forms, textiles, jewellery and architecture are shown in varied colours. The themes are presented on the walls as a continuous narrative or story. The stream of shapes, as if encompassing the manifest world, frequently congeals into groups held together with the tension of the inner relationship of being to being. An elaborate language of gestures intensifies the expression.

When the ancient Buddhist missionaries went to foreign lands to spread the message of peace, the brush and the chisel accompanied them. Ajanta became the fountainhead of all Buddhist murals in Asian countries. We notice the impact of Ajanta on the paintings in Sirgirya Caves in Sri Lanka, Bamyan in Afghanistan and at many places on the old silk route to China, Korea and Horiyuji in Japan. The sweep of Indian artists was wide indeed!

In India, the mural tradition continued with a little less momentum in Chalukyan Badami Caves (6th century), Pallava Panamalai (7th century), Chola Tanjore (12th century). The tradition continued in Kerala at many places till the middle of the 18th century.

MANUSCRIPT PAINTINGS

By the 11th century, the murals had been scaled down from the extended mural surface to the size of a palm leaf strip — again in the tradition of Ajanta. Later, there was a decline in the quality of paintings and the line became brittle and angular. These manuscript paintings came from Bengal and Nepal, again telling the Buddhist stories. The style soon spread to western India and we can see many illuminated manuscripts dealing with Jain texts during the period 12th - 15th century. Manuscript paintings diversified their theme by illustrating the lyricism of the well-known romantic poems.

Before the Mughals appeared on the Indian scene, Indian paintings had established and stabilised a fine tradition of pictorial style. It was subsequently influenced by the tradition of Persian miniature art.

The arrival of temple-bulldozing Muslims wiped out great chunks of the Hindu artistic tradition. In their zeal to build empires and to convert Hindus to Islam, they had little time for art or culture. It was only Akbar the Great — when the Mughals were firmly established in

India — who emerged as a patron of arts. He encouraged miniature paintings from a blend of Persian and Islamic styles. He recruited a large number of Indian artists. Each painting was often a cooperative effort of Indian and Persian artists, one doing the drawing, the other colouring and the third filling the details. The indigenisation received further momentum when Akbar commissioned the translation and illustration of Hindu Epics like the *Ramayana* and the *Mahabharata*. The artists in Akbar's court primarily painted portraits, courtly life, battle scenes, exquisite wildlife, the nature. The tradition received more encouragement under Jahangir, Akbar's son, who was also a great patron of arts and architecture. An artist's palette often included malachite, lapis lazuli, gold, silver and an ingenious substance called Peori, a yellow dye extracted from the urine of cows, on mango leaves.

The artists trained in the court of Akbar and his son Jahangir went away to the courts of Rajput princes. They improved upon their techniques and skills. Thus emerged several new schools of miniature paintings, each having its own distinctive style. Among these are Rajasthan or the Mewar School of Paintings, Jammu or the Pahari School and Basohli or the Kangra School. In the hill states, the artists could work undisturbed by the political upheavals of the plains of northern India.

CONTEMPORARY PAINTINGS

During the British Raj, the East India Company commissioned Indian artists to paint picturesque landscapes in oil and water colours. These painters were often referred to as the Company school. The ingredients of the new painting of the end of the 19th and early 20th centuries, however, are not merely anachronistic delvings into myth and history in quest of vanished glory. The combination of aristocratic and popular elements from the past with contemporary events, and the feeling of discovery of a national identity created works which reflected the mood of the times. Apart from the already assimilated European influences, Mughal, Rajput and Persian miniatures and the contemporary traditionalistic work from Japan were among the stylistic and technical determinatives.

ABANINDRANATH TAGORE, GAGANENDRANATH TAGORE and NANDALAL BOSE are among the most important painters of this movement, often called the Bengal School. Abanindranath developed a highly sophisticated style with a leaning towards portraiture. Gaganendranath was a brilliant cartoonist-critic of social and political wrongs. Nandalal, more of a technical revitalist than the two Tagore brothers, became known for his epic themes. Subsequently, he developed into a bold explorer of vast fields of Asian art.

While developing within the tenets of nationalism, a few among the more conscious painters discovered the indigenous and elementary vitality of folk forms. The deliberate orientation that followed continues to the present day. JAMINI ROY, AMRITA SHER-GILL, BENODE MUKERJEE and RAM KINKAR were among the more significant artists of the time. And among the new painters we can add the names of M.F. HUSSAIN and KRISHAN KHANNA.

FESTIVALS AND FAIRS

There is not a single day in the Indian calendar when you may not be able to locate a festival in some part of the country. There are festivals for all occasions. All major Indian religions have their share of colourful festivals to celebrate. Then, there are festivals to celebrate change of seasons. Next are the festivals connected with the harvesting or sowing of crops. Every happy occasion calls for a celebration with dance and music. Not all the festivals are celebrated all over the country but some are. Besides, there are festivals connected with pilgrimages. Hindu, Buddhist, Jain and Sikh pilgrimage centres are located in each corner of India attracting millions of devouts who move from one part of the country to another. For instance, the KUMBH MELA at HARIDWAR or PRAYAG (Allahabad) attracts a few million people each time. Kumbh is celebrated every twelve years.

In no other country of the world are people so frequently motivated by a religious urge to travel as in India. One can take off for a holiday with an easy conscience when it comes to a religious pilgrimage. Fortunately for the Hindus, most of their places of pilgrimage are at scenic places in the Himalayas or near the sea.

There are some national festivals which are celebrated all over India. On January 26 each year, Republic Day in India is celebrated with a massive parade of the Army, Navy and the Air Force displaying latest military hardware. On this day in New Delhi one can see the whole of India capsuled. It reflects the pride, glory and joy of independent India.

While the dates of the national festivals are known, other festivals follow the lunar calendar and the dates can vary from year to year. However, they do not vary too much. Broadly, they fall within the same month as in the previous year.

If you plan to include a festival in your itinerary, please check the date with the nearest Government of India Tourist Office. They know the dates at least one year in advance. The following are some of the important festivals of India. We will describe them in greater detail while dealing with areas where they are celebrated.

PONGAL (January)

A harvest festival celebrated mainly in Tamil Nadu, it is a three-day festival. The first day, known as BHOGI PONGAL, is confined to domestic festivals. On the second day, SURYA PONGAL, cooked rice is offered to the sun. On the third day, MATTU PONGAL, cattle are washed, their horns painted and decorated, and they are fed the rice offered to the sun. Festivities involve bull fights and the snatching of money bags tied between the horns of ferocious bulls.

BHOGALI BIHU (January)

This is a harvest festival celebrated in Assam. Thatched pavilions are put up and feasts held in them at night. In the morning the pavilions are set on fire followed by a lot of feasting, dancing and singing.

REPUBLIC DAY (January)

January 26 is of great historical importance to the country. India became a republic on this day in 1950. Republic Day is celebrated all over the country — traditionally with hoisting of the national flag, a parade of Army and Police and official festivities. The main attraction is at New Delhi where a spectacular parade consisting of the Armed Forces, school children and youth, folk dancers followed by elaborate floats from all the states of India move down from the magnificent RASHTRAPATI BHAWAN (President's House), past INDIA GATE and on to the historic RED FORT. On January 29, a breathtaking Beating the Retreat ceremony takes place. Set

against the Rashtrapati Bhawan, the Armed Forces bands play martial music and march forming intricate patterns. This is followed by a colourful display of flares and illumination of Rashtrapati Bhawan and other buildings around it.

KITE FESTIVAL (January)

Coinciding with MAKARA SANKRANTI, the kite festival of AHMEDABAD is held at a time when the azure skies are festooned with multi-coloured kites of all patterns and dimensions. There is a general air of festivity with the entire city populace on roof tops flying kites attached to brightly coloured strings. Kitefliers take on bids to cut each other's strings. Besides kite flying, displays of Gujarati cuisine, handicrafts and folk arts are other attractions. The festival marks the end of the winter season.

ELEPHANT MARATHON (January)

TRICHUR (Kerala), the venue of the Elephant Marathon, has over 100 elephants participating in it. Events like a cruise on the backwaters, boat races and tugs-of-war between elephants and the participants in the Marathon are the other major attractions.

YOGA WEEK (January)

The Yoga festival is celebrated at RISHIKESH, a picturesque town at the foothills of the Himalayas. To popularise Yoga, a week-long programme of lectures and demonstrations of *asanas* (postures) by prominent exponents is held. Water sports on the Ganga is another attraction.

VASANT PANCHAMI (January-February)

This festival of spring has people wearing clothes in bright shades of yellow and participating in music, dance and merriment. It is also the day when in some parts of the country, especially in Bengal, the goddess of learning, Saraswati, is worshipped.

DESERT FESTIVAL (January-February)

The exquisite medieval Fort of JAISALMER in Rajasthan forms the backdrop to a spectacular DESERT FESTIVAL. Puppeteers, folk artistes and dancers regale the audiences. There is also a unique sound and light show on the desert sands on the full-moon night.

SURAJKUND CRAFTS MELA (February)

A spectacular handloom and handicrafts fair is organised in the rural setting of SURAJKUND (Haryana State) in the vicinity of New Delhi. At this annual week-long *mela*, crafts people from all over the country meet and bring alive the age-old living crafts tradition. Visitors can see them at work and buy some of their exquisite handicrafts. This is the best occasion to see rural craftsmen at work.

SHIVARATRI (February-March)

As the name indicates, SHIVARATRI is celebrated by the devotees of Lord Shiva who, it is believed, danced the *Tandav* — his celestial dance—on this night. Preceding the feast is a night of strict discipline. Orthodox devotees remain awake all night listening to sacred texts and hymns. Devotees throng the various Shiva temples all over the country and most temples become venues of fun-filled fairs.

KHAJURAHO FESTIVAL (February-March)

Set against the ancient erotic temples of KHAJURAHO in Madhya Pradesh, a week-long festival of classical dance is held every year featuring the best artists of the country. It is an occasion to see various Indian dance forms in a setting one can never forget.

HOLI (March)

Popularly known as the COLOUR FESTIVAL, Holi is a spring festival celebrated normally over two days in North India. On the evening of the first day bonfires are lit to symbolise the destruction of evil but also seen as the end of winter in the north. On the second day, cold coloured water is thrown on people, even on strangers and passersby. The festival is great fun and later people visit each other and distribute sweets, affectionately hugging each other.

GANGAUR (March)

This is popular festival of Rajasthan when Lord Shiva and his consort Parvati are worshipped. One of the most colourful festivals held anywhere in India, it is the occasion for Rajasthani women to don their traditional costume of *lehnga, choli* and *odhni*. They congregate around the idols of Shiva and Parvati, sing, dance and offer prayers.

RAMA NAVAMI (March-April)

This is celebrated as the birthday of Lord Rama and is most popular, especially in Uttar Pradesh. Given the importance of Lord Rama to the Hindus, RAMA NAVAMI is observed all over the country. During the eight days preceding Lord Rama's birthday, it is considered auspicious to read or listen to the epic *Ramayana*. Celebrations include reading and staging of the *Ramayana* in various folk forms.

THE GOA CARNIVAL (March-April)

A boisterous, colourful carnival spread over a week, is held every year in Goa just before Lent. The festivities include an extravagant parade consisting of theme-floats. It is generally a time of great fun and frolic for Goa's Christian population.

MAHAVIR JAYANTI (March-April)

The birth anniversary of Mahavira, the founder of Jainism, is observed by the Jains, an important religious sect. It is celebrated in a comparatively quiet manner with visits to sacred places and with the offering of prayers.

UGADI (March-April)

The New Year in Andhra Pradesh and Karnataka is called UGADI and is celebrated with a rich feast. The day is considered auspicious for beginning new ventures. It is believed that the behaviour of people on this day will set the pattern for the rest of the year. So everyone tries to be pleasant and avoids ill will.

MEENAKSHI TEMPLE FEAST (April)

The temple of Meenakshi, the wife of Lord Shiva, in MADURAI, is known for its magnitude and architectural excellence. It is also the venue of an annual feast to celebrate the marriage of the goddess. Car processions of the goddess and the god are some of the colourful features of this festival.

RAMZAN ID/ID-UL-FITR (April)

This is one of the joyful festivals of Muslims. It marks the end of RAMZAN, a month of fasting by day and eating only at night. It is the Christmas of the Muslims.

URS SHARIF (April-May)

A large fair is held in AJMER during the Urs of Khwaja Mohiuddin Chishti, a Sufi saint. The Urs commemorates the symbolic union of the saint with God. Millions of Muslim pilgrims pour into the city during the Urs and the fair.

INTERNATIONAL FLOWER FESTIVAL (April-May)

This spectacular International Flower Festival held every year has beautiful flowers and unique plants along with 500 odd varieties of orchids displayed at GANGTOK in Sikkim. River-rafting and yak-safari are some of the other events during this blooming extravaganza. Lovers of flowers cannot miss Gangtok at this time of the year.

BAISAKHI (April-May)

This is an important day for the Punjabis. It was on this day that Guru Gobind Singh founded the *Khalsa* — the pure among the Sikhs. In all gurudwaras of the country, the *Granth* is read from beginning to end and taken out in a procession. After this, there is a lot of feasting and in most villages folk dances, especially the vigorous *Bhangra*, are performed.

It is good to be in AMRITSAR on Baisakhi day and be able to visit the GOLDEN TEMPLE. Basically, it is a harvest festival, when farmers symbolically start harvesting the wheat crop.

ID-UL-ZUHA/BAKR-ID (June)

This Muslim festival commemorates Ibrahim's sacrifice of his son in obedience to a command of God. An animal sacrifice is an integral part of the festivities. Mutton and vermicelli delicacies are served on this day.

RATH YATRA (June-July)

This fascinating temple festival is held at the JAGANNATH TEMPLE in PURI, Orissa. Wooden images of Lord Jagannath, his sister and brother, are taken out in a procession in large chariots or *raths*. The main chariot is nearly 14 metres high, 10 metres square and has 16 wheels. The other two are comparatively smaller. The chariots are drawn by millions of devotees over a distance of nearly two kilometres.

TEEJ (June-July)

This is an important festival of Rajasthan that heralds the advent of the monsoons. The presiding deity of the festival is the goddess Parvati. Idols of the goddess are taken out in colourful processions accompanied by song and dance. Decorated swings are put up and women in exotic dresses swing on them singing devotional or romantic songs.

HEMIS FESTIVAL (June-July)

This fair is held at HEMIS GOMPA, about 50 kilometres from LEH (J & K State), to celebrate the birthday of Padmasambhava, the founder of Lamaism. The ritual dances by masked dancers are its main attraction. There are displays of local handicrafts too.

MANGO FESTIVAL (June-July)

SAHARANPUR, in Uttar Pradesh, is the venue of this unique mango festival held every mango season where innumerable varieties of the fruit are displayed. It is a 'mango-ful' affair—full of juicy mangoes from different parts of India. If you are a mango lover, do not miss this festival.

RAKSHA BANDHAN/NARIAL PURNIMA (July-August)

RAKSHA BANDHAN is celebrated mainly in North India when brothers and sisters reaffirm their bonds of affection. The sisters tie colourful threads or amulets on the wrists of their brothers who in turn give them gifts and symbolically promise to protect them. The sea god, Varuna, a Vedic deity, is also worshipped by many on this day by throwing coconuts into the sea, which is why the day is also called NARIAL PURNIMA or 'Coconut Full Moon'.

NAAG PANCHMI (July-August)

This is a festival of serpents. Live cobras or their images are worshipped by feeding them with milk. It is fairly common in Bengal and South India.

MUHARRAM (July-August)

This is a day of mourning as it commemorates the martyrdom of Prophet Mohammed's grandson, Hussain. Gorgeous replicas of the martyr's tomb are carried in procession through the streets while men beat their chests and wail as an expression of grief on the death of Hussain. The *tazias* (processions) of LUCKNOW and HYDERABAD are famous.

JANMASHTAMI (August-September)

This is Lord Krishna's birthday celebrated at midnight all over the country. The main celebrations are held at MATHURA, his birthplace, where at the Krishna temple his birth is symbolically re-enacted. At BRINDABAN, adjoining Mathura, colourful *Raslilas,* song and dance dramas depicting the life of Lord Krishna, are performed all day and night. In Maharashtra and Gujarat, the celebrations include the breaking of earthen pots containing yoghurt or butter hung high up between poles and houses by men forming human pyramids. This is an act in imitation of the Lord who, as a child, often stole butter and yoghurt kept in earthen pots out of his reach.

SAIR-E-GUL FAROSHAN (August-September)

This is a flower festival jointly celebrated by Hindus and Muslims as a symbol of communal harmony in the town of MEHRAULI, close to New Delhi. It is also called the Pankha festival because of the large palm-leaf fans decorated with flowers that are taken out in a procession led by fire-dancers.

GANESH CHATURTHI (August-September)

This is the birthday of the elephant-headed god, Lord Ganesh. He is worshipped on this day to remove obstacles and ensure smooth progress in all ventures during the year. In Maharashtra, especially in BOMBAY, small, big and gigantic images of Lord Ganesh are worshipped for days, after which they are taken out in mammoth processions to the waterfront for immersion. Thousands of idols carried by devotees in trucks or specially constructed chariots are brought to the waterfront. Each locality vies with the other in displaying its idols.

TARNETAR MELA (August-September)

This is a rather unique fair in that it acts as a sort of marriage market for the tribals of TARNETAR in Saurashtra. The fair concludes with a festival at the TRINETESHWAR TEMPLE to celebrate the wedding of the legendary MAHABHARATA hero, Arjuna, with Draupadi. The tribals dressed in their colourful best sing and dance.

ONAM (August-September)

This is a unique festival of Kerala. It is celebrated in honour of an *asura* or demon. Puranic legend has it that Vamana, an incarnation of Lord Vishnu, obtained the Kingdom of Mahabali. Mahabali was exiled by Vamana. As Mahabali was very fond of his land and his subjects, he was allowed to visit the land once a year - on the day of Onam. The folklore of Kerala considers the reign of Mahabali as Kerala's golden age. The festival marks the end of the monsoon and the beginning of the harvest season. People decorate their homes with colourful flower carpets, wear new clothes and prepare a sumptuous lunch for Mahabali. A major attraction of the Onam celebrations in Kerala is the famed snake boat races held in its picturesque backwaters.

DUSSEHRA (September-October)

This is a festival that finds many manifestations all over the country but always celebrates the triumph of good over evil. Normally, it is a ten-day festival during which nine days are spent in worship and the tenth day in celebration of Lord Rama and his victory over the demon Ravana, or in paying respect to the goddess Durga, as in Bengal.

In North India, the RAMLEELA, a folk play depicting the life and times of Lord Rama, is staged in various localities. On the tenth day effigies of the demon Ravana, his brother and nephew, are burnt. These effigies are often a couple of hundred feet high.

In West Bengal exquisitely decorated idols of Goddess Durga are installed and worshipped. On the tenth day the idols are taken out in huge processions and immersed in tanks, rivers or the sea.

In South India, during Dussehra or NAVRATRI, as it is known there, houses are decorated with displays of dolls, toys and idols. MYSORE witnesses a magnificent procession with caparisoned elephants and horses, as the erstwhile Maharaja goes from his palace to the temple.

In KULU it is famed for its colourful processions. As an idyllic holiday resort, Kulu provides trekking and water sports during the festival.

DIWALI (October-November)

Diwali, a contraction of the Sanskrit word DEEPAWALI, means a row or cluster of lights. It is one of the most celebrated festivals of India. The origin of the festival has many versions but the most popular one traces it to the *Ramayana* and Lord Rama's coronation after his 14-year exile in the forest. It is said that the people illuminated their houses and streets with earthen oil lamps to welcome the Lord. The process has been repeated every year since then. Besides earthen lamps, people now illuminate their houses with electric bulbs and candles.

To the business community, especially in Western India, Diwali marks the New Year involving the worship of Lakshmi, the goddess of wealth. They open new books of account on this day. At night, along with illuminations, fire crackers are lit in almost every house, sweets are distributed, new clothes are worn and games of chance are played.

Diwali is easily the brightest and noisiest Indian festival.

PUSHKAR MELA (October-November)

This fair is held annually on the banks of LAKE PUSHKAR in Rajasthan. During the mela, major attractions are the camel and cattle fair and camel races. It has become a major tourist draw for people from all over the world, particularly Europe.

GURU PURAB (October-November)

The Sikhs observe the birthdays of all their Gurus as holy days. But the birthdays of Guru Nanak (October-November) and Guru Gobind Singh (December-January) are celebrated as festivals. The *Akhand Path* or the continuous reading of the holy book, and the *Granth* (holy book) being taken out in a procession are the two main events.

CHRISTMAS (December)

The birth of Lord Jesus Christ is celebrated by the Christians in India as elsewhere in the world. The Christmas spirit pervades in all markets which offer attractive bargains.

SHEKHAWATI FESTIVAL (December)

The SHEKHAWATI region of Rajasthan, known for its painted *havelis* (palaces), celebrates the Shekhawati festival. One can see Rajasthani folk dancers along with the cuisine and crafts which are on display.

ELLORA FESTIVAL

As in Khajuraho, a festival of classical dance and music is held every year at ELLORA against the backdrop of the ancient caves, which are justifiably famous all over the world.

NEW YEAR

January is celebrated as the New Year with a lot of revelry by most people. Each community has its own traditional New Year, like Diwali for some, Vishu for the Malayalese of Kerala, Gudi Padva for the Maharashtrians, Ugadi in Andhra Pradesh and Karnataka, Jamashed Navroz or Pateti for the Parsis, Baba Barsha in Bengal, Laser in Ladakh, Goru in Assam. But the first of January is everybody's New Year.

Chapter 5

DINING CHOICES IN INDIA

1. Spicy Pleasures
2. Range of Curries and Bread
3. Regional Choices
4. Refreshments

SPICY PLEASURES

Thanks to hundreds of Indian restaurants which have mushroomed in the capitals of the world, Indian cuisine is no longer a mystery. The myth that surrounded Indian food that it was all curry and nothing else is gradually vanishing. In UK, Indian curry is the third most popular dish among the Britons. Among the Japanese, curry rice has pride of place, the second most popular dish according to a recent survey.

The number of Indian restaurants in UK exceeds 1,000; the number in USA, Canada and Japan is over 100 each. Other major capitals in Europe too have a sprinkling of Indian restaurants. Paris has quite a few. That makes it easier for India's tourism promoters to sell India for a holiday. India attracts over 2 million foreign visitors in a year for an average stay of one month — the longest average stay for any country in the world!

So great is the variety of food in India that a visitor who has grown on the notion that it is the land of curry and rice is in for a surprise. Curry, to the Indian, is not the name of a dish. It encompasses a whole class of dishes. There are any number of curries, made with meat, fish, chicken, vegetables and, on occasions, fruits. The only common factor is that they all contain freshly ground spices, including turmeric, and have a 'gravy'. The combination of spices, often passed from mother to

daughter or from one chef to his son, makes one curry totally different from other curries. There is no standard curry powder mixture. Every housewife has her special mix of spices. And the proportions vary from recipe to recipe.

It may be interesting to note that most of these spices have a medicinal value which Westerners, often with their antibiotic obsessions, tend to disregard. But an Indian cook knows which spice will have what effect on the digestive system and uses it accordingly to help it.

The most commonly used spices and herbs in Indian cooking are asafoetida, cardamom, clove, cinnamon, coriander, garlic, ginger, turmeric and aniseed. Let us examine their uses.

Turmeric is used almost in every dish. It helps to preserve food and gives the dish a pleasant yellow natural colour. It has also digestive properties. Ginger is considered good for digestion and many people like it not only in their food but also eat it as a salad. Coriander seeds or beans are used in most Indian dishes. They are supposed to have a cooling effect on the body of a person who eats the food. Cardamoms are strong and sweet. They have a nice flavour. They are used in all dishes and in some curries too. They help in digestion. Saffron, the most expensive spice, can create a lot of effect and fragrance with a little quantity. To produce one pound of saffron, several thousand flowers are needed. It is grown in the valley of Kashmir and is used for its flavour. Mustard, cinnamon, nutmeg, pepper, cloves, poppy and caraway seeds are also used in Indian dishes.

Masala is the name for a blend of many spices. It may be dry or in liquid paste. The chef decides what will go in the spice blend. Garam Masala is a blend of fragrant spices only. It can be prepared in advance and stored. Now, various blends of packed *Garam Masalas* are available in stores. The packet tells you for what kind of dish it could be used. The *Garam Masalas* are generally cinnamom, cloves, cuminseeds, mace, coriander seeds, nutmeg, and black pepper.

RANGE OF CURRIES AND BREAD

There is a whole range of curry dishes from different parts of India, each having its own distinct flavour. For the purpose of convenience, we can broadly divide Indian food into four different regions — corresponding to Delhi for the North, Bombay for the West, Madras for the South and Calcutta for the East. As will be seen, food habits have been formed over the years depending on the type of raw materials available in a region. In North India, there is abundance of meat, vegetables, almonds, dairy

products, chillies and wheat. Therefore, we find people have a preference for wheat bread in the shape of *nan, roti, puri* or *parathas*. Contrary to the belief that North Indians are meat-eaters, a meat dish is only an additional dish while a vegetable curry and *dal* (lentil curry) are generally a must in a total meal served in an Indian home.

Cooking media in the north is pure *ghee* (clarified butter) though it is now used sparingly due to its high price. Other vegetable fats are now more commonly used as cooking media.

In the west and east rice is the staple diet. Fish is plentiful. So most dishes revolve round these raw materials. The south is predominantly vegetarian except places on the coast. A whole lot of vegetarian cuisine has been developed over the centuries. There is so much of variety that a visitor is dazzled by the choice offered to him.

If the preparation of food is important to Indians, its presentation is no less significant. Traditionally, Indian food is served either on a well-washed large banana leaf or in a *thali* (a large plate made of brass, steel or silver). On it, several *katoris* (little bowls) are placed to hold small helpings of each dish. A typical meal may consist of a meat or fish dish, two vegetable dishes, *dal,* yoghurt and a sweet dish of *kheer* or *halwa*. Other accompaniments would be pickles, *chutneys, papads,* etc. A small piece of lime may be placed in the *thali* to be used by the guest, if he so wishes.

Porcelain plates are a Western innovation introduced in affluent Indian homes in recent years.

REGIONAL CHOICES

NORTH INDIAN FOOD

North Indian cooking is the most succulent in India. It owes a lot to the Mughals who came to India, and the *Mughlai* food, associated with northern India, derives its name from the influence of Muslims.

Bread is more commonly eaten than rice. The omnipresent *chappati* is the common man's fare. *Nan* is kind of a luxury and goes well with *tandoori* food. Another variety of bread is *paratha*, a rich bread of wheat flour made with clarified butter. It is tasty and soft.

The West is more familiar with India's *tandoori* food as most Indian restaurants overseas serve it. *Tandoori* chicken or mutton is a barbecued food which is spiced and marinated in yoghurt for a few hours before it is cooked. *Tandoori* chicken with *nan*, green salad and a dessert is really the food for a maharajah. Foreign visitors to India cannot resist its temptation. It is not overly spiced and is nearest to Western cooking.

Delhi is also the *kabab* country. Meat *kababs* come in many varieties. Some of these are: *Boti Kabab, Reshmi Kabab, Pasinda Kabab, Seekh Kabab,* and *Shammi Kabab*. The last one is made with a spiced paste of ground meat mixed with spices and fried over a low fire.

The other delicacies of the Northern Indian cuisine are *biryani* which is a dish of rice, saffron and marinated lamb or chicken. At VIP receptions, this dish is often served. *Pulao* is a slightly less complicated version of *biryani*. There is another exciting version — sweet pulao — made with rice, coconut, almonds, mangoes and papayas.

If you are not eating *tandoori* dishes of mutton, fish or chicken, your other choices are *Rogan Josh,* lamb curry, *Kofta, Korma* or *Do-Piaza*. *Do-Piaza* is made with lots of onions, *Korma* is particularly rich and *Koftas* are meat-ball curry. *Koftas* come in many forms, small and large. The large ones are stuffed with boiled eggs. Accompanying the North Indian meal will be a small helping of *dal* (lentil soup). For people who do not eat meat, there are several options - *Paneer* (peas with cheese), *Sag Paneer* (cheese with spinach), *Bharta,* a delicious vegetable made from egg plant and several other curry dishes combining cauliflower, potatoes and other vegetables. Now they cook cauliflower and cheese dishes also in a *tandoor*. The dessert often made is *kheer, firni* (pudding) or *halwa*.

Kashmiri food has also been influenced by *Mughlai* food. It has more varieties of meat dishes. There is plenty of lamb in Kashmir. Kashmiri food is a little more spicy than the typical North Indian dishes.

If you are not watchful, tea time in North India may make you forget about dinner. With tea comes stuffed pastry, *samosas,* fritter-like *pakoras* and any number of sweets made from milk paste, i.e., *Rasgulla,*

Gulab Jamun or *Barfi*. As is the Indian tradition, the host always insists you eat more, telling you that you have eaten very little — but it is your stomach!

BENGALI SPECIALS

In Bengal, food is plainer and depends on rice as the mainstay of the meal. Catering is perhaps the most serious business in the life of a Bengali. The first thing he does in the morning is to shop for food and vegetables and travels several miles to buy his fish, vegetables and sweets from his favourite shops.

For most Bengalis, seafish is infra-dig. Their preference is for fresh water fish. Fortunately there is an abundance of it in many homes in rural Bengal having their own fish ponds. Mustard seeds and mustard oil are generally used in cooking their fish dishes. *Bekdi*, a special fish of Bengal, specially lends itself to Western style of cooking and is recommended while you are in Calcutta.

If Bengali's first love is fish, then without doubt the second is sweets. Special and typical sweets that come from Bengal are *Sandesh* and *Rasgullas*, made in different ways from cottage cheese. One notable exception is *misti doi* (sweetened yoghurt). Bengali cuisine is unique in India where plain yoghurt is missing in its bill of fare.

Traditionally, no sweets are made at home. They are always bought at a confectioner's and this goes for *misti-doi* also. And just as well. The recipe seems to be a closely held secret which no housewife has yet successfully been able to penetrate.

SOUTH INDIAN FIESTA

South Indians eat a lot of rice. It is also in the south that curry should be regarded with respect. Their curry may be rich as in North India but it certainly is hot.

For vegetarians, South India is a heaven. Their vegetarian food provides a lot of variety, especially the Brahmin cuisine which is different from the non-Brahmin food. The orthodox South Indian Brahmin is a strict vegetarian steering away from even garlic and onion for smell and from tomatoes because of their colour (of the blood!). His diet in all the four states is based on the bounty of the countryside. Tamarind grows here and so do chillies. Coconut is freely available. And the lentil that grows here is *arhar*, a yellow lentil. It is a combination of this with tamarind, spices and vegetables which makes *Sambhar* their staple dish and is eaten twice a day. *Rasam* (Mulligatawny) a thin, peppery, lentil-based soup, is taken at both lunch and dinner. And if old wives' tales are to be believed, it is this that is responsible for the Brahmin brain power. *Rasam* is also the forebear of the now famous mulligatawny soup, the name itself being a corruption of the Tamil *milagu tannir*, or pepper water. A typical meal in the South consists of *sambhar, rasam*, two or three vegetable preparations, often cooked with grated coconut and yughurt and eaten with boiled rice.

However, the most popular dishes that have come out of the South are *dosas* and *idlis*. Their popularity has spread throughout the country to an extent that the *idli* and *dosa* eating joints can be found as far in the Himalayas as Leh in Ladakh or in Sikkim, Bhutan and Kathmandu. Both are made with a mixture of ground fermented rice and *dal*. They are served with *sambhar* and coconut *chutney*. *Dosas* are griddle-fried pancakes; *idlis* are more like steamed dumplings. Though there is a measure of similarity between the foods of the four states of South India, there is one pocket where the cuisine is different. This is Hyderabad which was once ruled by the Muslim Nizams. Typical Hyderabadi food has Muslim overtones and includes several dishes that are unique to this area, such as *baghara baigan*, a distinctive dish of mutton. The *biryani* in Hyderabad also tastes different.

DELIGHTS FROM WEST INDIA

Food in Bombay is different from food in the rest of the country. This is perhaps due to the presence of small but influential communities of Parsis, who came from Iran a thousand years ago, and other minorities like the Sindhis, Punjabis, Goans and Khoja Muslims.

Dhansak, a contribution of the Parsis, is a dish made with chicken or lamb and cooked with generously spiced puree of a mixture of lentils and vegetables. *Dhansak* is served in many restaurants of Bombay, specially on Sundays.

Till a few years ago, Goa was occupied by the Portuguese (it was liberated in December 1961). The Portuguese influence is evident in its cuisine. One of Goa's best known dishes is *Vindaloo*, chicken pork or fish cooked with spices and vinegar, which took the name from the Portuguese *vinadalhos*. Unlike other Indians, Goans eat a lot of pork and *vindaloo* is often cooked with pork. Their fresh sausages have also a special taste. They also eat a lot of fresh seafood.

Belonging to Bombay are also two Muslim communities, the Boras and the Khojas. Each has its own style of cooking.

The Sindhis, who migrated from Sindh in Pakistan, have brought their own cuisine. It is very popular and is more often meat-based.

Bombay Duck is the nick-name of a seafish, very tasty when curried or fried.

The Maharashtrians and the Gujaratis, the original natives of this region, have their quota of meat-eaters. But the majority of them are vegetarians. Like their counterparts among South Indian Brahmins, they have mastered the art of vegetarian cooking. Their cuisine involves subtle spicing and light cooking using sprouted lentils — to produce palatable and nutritious meals. They favour sweet and sour dishes.

People in the western region eat, both wheat and rice, though more rice than wheat.

Food in India has now become an All-India affair. One can eat any kind of regional food in major cities of India. Therefore, if you want to eat North Indian food in Bombay, just ask your hotel for information. They will direct you to a restaurant in the hotel itself or, if you prefer, in the city.

BREADS

India offers a vast variety of breads. Unlike in the West, these breads are the mainstay of Indian meals.

Chappatis and *nans* are cooked in an oven or *tandoor*. Thin and small *chappatis* are painstakingly made on an iron griddle placed on gas or fire. Some breads like *puris* are fried in deep fat and *parathas* are panfried with a little fat, preferably pure clarified butter (ghee).

The commonest bread is the chappati which you can see Indians making in any odd corner over *angithis* or *chulhas* using wood or charcoal. Basically, the *chappati* is just flour and water dough rolled very thin and cooked like a pancake on slow heat. These are hot and fresh and you can eat several of them with your vegetable or meat curry.

A richer version of the *roti* is the *paratha*, which is cooked with butter. It comes out soft and delicious. Indians also make *parathas* stuffed with potatoes or other vegetables. Stuffed *parathas* are complete meals and are eaten with plain yoghurt and pickles.

Puris are made from the same basic dough rolled out thin and round with a wooden roller and deep-fried in clarified butter or vegetable fat. Similarly, a hot bread made of slightly different dough is called a *loochi* in Calcutta. It tastes very different from *puris*.

In the south, *dosa* and *idli* substitute for bread. *Dosa* is made from rice and cooked like crepe. *Idli* is steamed rice cake. *Dosa* is often stuffed with vegetables to make a complete meal. Both are eaten with a vegetable soup called *sambhar*.

Papad, spiced with pepper and aniseed, go with every meal. They taste very good when served hot from the oven. They go better with drinks.

DESSERTS

India is a country of sweets, and Indians, if they can afford, want to eat sweets with almost every meal. Each region has its own specialities.

Basically, various regional recipes are different forms of rice puddings, milk puddings, vegetable fruits dipped in sweet syrup. Besides, there are varieties of milk-based *Barfies* and pastries. Combinations of all these offer hundreds of varieties. These are decorated with raisins, almonds, pistachio and the like.

Most Indian sweets are made by boiling down milk to remove the moisture. It is called *khoa*. Adding butter, sugar and many other flavours, these are turned into *barfi, malai, kheer, rasgulla* and *sandesh*.

Indian sweets may taste too sweet to Western visitors.

PAAN

As the meal comes to an end, there is this item *Paan* which is a betel leaf wrapped around a variety of ingredients. Every *paan*-seller has his special recipe to make. There are as many styles of *paan* as the states of India. The *paan* made of betel leaf is the most popular. It is considered to be digestive. You may try one if you do not mind your lips showing the colours of the lipstick!

RECOMMENDED RESTAURANTS FOR INDIAN FOOD

The following are some of the well-known Indian restaurants serving Indian food in different parts of India. You cannot go wrong if you eat in any one or more of them to familiarise yourself with good Indian food:

Bombay
1. Tanjore, Taj Mahal Hotel
2. Dum Pukht, Sea Rock
3. Sheraton Hotel
4. Kandhar, Oberoi Towers
5. Mewar, Oberoi Towers

New Delhi
1. Kandhar, Oberoi Towers
2. Chaupal, Ashok
3. Aangan, Hyatt Regency
4. Pakwan, Le Meredien
5. Frontier, Ashok
6. Haveli, Taj Mahal
7. Darbar, Ashok
8. Bukhara, Maurya Sheraton
9. Tandoor, President
10. Balauchi, New Delhi Hilton

Madras
1. Peshawari, Chola Sheraton
2. Thanjavur, Trident
3. Dakshin, Park Sheraton

Calcutta
1. Mughal Room, Oberoi Grand

Bangalore
1. Afghan, Windsor Manor Sheraton
2. Karnavati, Taj Residency

Hyderabad
1. Firdaus, Krishna Oberoi

Bhubaneshw
1. Chandni, The Oberoi

REFRESHMENTS

A word about refreshments. Since India is a semi-tropical country, there is a lot of choice of soft drinks.

In North India, *lassi* is the most popular drink. Sweet or salty buttermilk is freshly prepared in your presence. The South and the West offer fresh coconuts as their most refreshing drink. Coffee - cold or hot - is available in all restaurants of the South with your meal.

Tea is popular all over India. Indians take tea at any time of the day, often at 11 a.m. and 4 p.m. If you enter a friend's office, he will probably offer you a hot cup of tea or coffee.

Juices — mango, sweet lime, pineapple and orange — are available fresh and also in bottles or packs. Aerated drinks are many. Foreign brands like Pepsi and Coke can also be had.

Ice-creams are many and safe. Well-known brands are Kwality, Dollops and Gaylord. Some international brands have also joined the race.

Liquor stores abound in major cities. Imported whisky and other alcoholic drinks are expensive. Bring your own bottle or two of whisky. You are allowed to do so.

Indian liquors are very reasonably priced and are popular among foreign residents in India. Indian beer is of excellent quality and inexpensive. Its cost goes up quite a lot when you drink it in a restaurant of any five-star hotel.

Chapter 6

SHOPPING IN INDIA

1. Shopping Bargains
2. Range of Shopping
3. Selling in India

SHOPPING BARGAINS

As you plan a trip to India, leave plenty of space in your baggage for shopping that you are bound to do in India. The assortment of wares is staggering and so are low prices, which may often be one-fourth of what you may pay in New York or London. The recent devaluation of the Indian rupee has made India a bargain country, more attractive than Thailand, Singapore and Hong Kong. Except for electronic goods, India has a price edge over all goods — carpets, textiles, jewellery, leatherware, readymade garments and a vast array of handicrafts. Its handicrafts reflect centuries of tradition and the art has come down to the artisans from generation to generation. Indian handicrafts are not an organised or commercialised industry but represent an unhampered expression of craftsmen to meet the daily needs of people as well as the inner aesthetic urges of the community. Recent economic liberalisation has brought international brands—available in India at modest prices.

The country is full of bargains. It is a storehouse, at once, of art treasures and contemporary high-tech consumer goods. You can pick up in a shop delicate pastel patterned dinner and tea-sets which you can be sure will not be departmental store copies. There is an immense variety in designs and colours. If you are adventurous, you can order a whole range of furnishings from this country to do up your home to make it distinctive— and at a price unbeliveably low ! Many come to India regularly to replenish their supplies of clothes, children's garments, linen, home furnishings and other goods of daily use. This may need planning. But even if you are rushed and do not have much time for shopping, there are stores brimming with stuff waiting to be picked up.

RANGE OF SHOPPING

CARPETS AND RUGS

Perhaps an appropriate place to begin would be with carpets. It may be interesting to know that India produces and exports more handcrafted carpets than any other country in the world. In KASHMIR, where India's best carpets are produced, the carpets are

crafted in the Persian tradition. Silk carpets are Kashmir's speciality. These are not found anywhere else in the world. The art flourished under the Mughal kings and today carpet-weaving is a popular cottage industry in Kashmir, thanks to the worldwide demand. During winter snow, when people keep indoors, the carpets are woven by families of craftsmen. And when the weather opens up, a large supply is available for customers. Besides Kashmir, carpets are produced in India at the carpet centres of MIRZAPUR in Uttar Pradesh and in Rajasthan. Tibetan refugees who left their country for India in the early fifties have settled down in India and now provide a large supply of original Tibetan carpets.

Cotton rugs, called *durries,* come in many varieties and designs. There is a plethora of colours. *Durries* can adorn any drawing room. They are washable too and have several uses, including decoration as wall-hangings.

LINEN

It is possible to get linen to match your rugs. In fact, some of the fabulous hand block-printed linens on cotton resemble closely the provincial prints of French linen. From dining-sets to bedcovers, from table mats to runners, the choice is vast. An exquisite example of linen is worked with *zardozi* or gold embroidery specially on silk.

SILKS

Silk has been manufactured in India since Vedic times. There is a reference in *Arthashastra,* a second century manuscript, to the silks of Bengal and Assam. Although wild silks have also been spun in the remote areas of Assam for thousands of years, knowledge about the mulberry tree and silks was imported from China. And now silk weaving is a major industry of India.

Silk has a special significance in India. It was considered a pure fabric to be worn on all auspicious occasions, marriages and other religious ceremonies. Among the major production centres of silk are VARANASI, AHMEDABAD, KANCHIPURAM, SURAT and THANJAVUR.

Working with overseas designers, India is one of the important suppliers of fashion silk garments for the Western world. Often samples of the latest fashions can be picked up for a song in India. Western dresses can be fashioned from silk by experienced Indian tailors at a notice of one or two days. Readymade garments are one of India's largest exports.

SAREES

Widely used by much of India's female population, sarees are the best known objects of daily use. This graceful attire is simply one length of material, usually five and a half metres in length and a bit over one metre in width. It is worn without pins, buttons or fastenings. A petticoat worn on a lady's waist holds it well and a fitting blouse called a *choli* adds to the charm of the lady.

Sarees range from gossamer thin *Chanderis* woven in silk to the thick *Kanjeevaram* silks of Tamil Nadu. Both types are distinguished by the restrained use of motifs. But *Ikats* from Orissa, in handspun cottons of earthy colours, are woven with traditional motifs obtained by precise dyeing and weaving techniques. Indian sarees take as their themes parrots or elephants, seashells or stylised flowers, and sometimes an architectural-geometrical pattern of Muslim architectural details.

Silk sarees are manufactured in many parts of India. Each has a distinctive mark of the region where it is made. A saree length can be fashioned into any kind of Western dress in a tailor's shop. Often the blouse piece comes with a good saree to match its colour.

HANDICRAFTS

Handicrafts can be classified by the medium

on which they are worked. Objects of wood that range from fragrant sandalwood to ebony are carved, sculptured or inlaid with brass wire, ivory or mother-of-pearl. Stonework includes marble mosaics inlaid with semi-precious stones and soapstone carvings. Metalwork ranges from enamelled brassware and bronze religious statuettes to folk art figures. Pottery encompasses terracotta toys ranging from rural India to ornamental objects distinguished by bright blue motifs and a high glaze. Ivory carvings of incredible intricacy and miniature paintings on ivory represent crafts of the classical tradition. Cane and bamboo crafts highlight the everyday art of India.

Sumptuous silk brocades woven with gold thread and pure silk carpets of Persian designs are collector's items. These are bought equally for their beauty as for their investment value.

While *shatoosh* shawls from Kashmir are a once-in-a-life-time purchase, lambswool stoles can be had for a modest price. For every piece of real jewellery, there is costume jewellery which looks equally elegant.

Handicrafts have evolved from three principal sources: royal courts, religious use and folk art. The kings of the erstwhile princely states were patrons of some of the country's greatest art traditions, of which miniature paintings are one example. In the absence of royal patronage, some of the country's master-craftsmen would have been forced into other occupations. But tourists took their places and they are again in business. Brass lamps of Tamil Nadu were, and still are, used in Hindu temples. Paintings of religious themes are often part of temple decoration. Folk art and objects of daily use, which range from clay pottery to embroidered leather, personify India's  ongoing traditions of crafts from one generation to another.

Many crafts are still made by craftsmen in the traditional way. But they cater to the ever-expanding international market. Thus, brassware exotics are made alongside flower vases of contemporary design; and *bidri* work *hooqa* bases in Hyderabad coexist with elegant jewellery cases in the same work.

Traditional handicrafts are not the only buys from India. High fashion, quality leather jackets, shoes and handbags are available in sheep's leather and cow-hides. Designs for silver and costume jewellery change with international fashions. Lambswool winter wear are widely exported. Household linen is prized for its durability and attractive designs. Durries, woven cotton rugs mentioned earlier, once only available in ethnic designs, have now found their way into exclusive stores of USA and Europe.

For the shopper in a hurry, the government-run Central Cottage Industries Emporium has branches in each major city. These are well-appointed multi-storeyed complexes containing a selection of handicrafts from every corner of the country. Cottage Emporia, in common with many fine stores, accept all major international credit cards. Each branch has an air-freighting section where bulky purchases are delivered right at your doorstep back home. These are very reliable organisations. While Government emporia and hotel shops can be trusted with shipment, it will be desirable to take your shopping with you if you buy something from a small businessman. Likewise, many other higher stores in India will pack and air-freight your bulky purchases. In NEW DELHI, a whole street full of State Government emporia on BABA KHARAK SINGH ROAD provides the shopper with virtually everything that is available in the country. Each state of India specialises in one thing or another.

Above all, shopping in India is fun. From the myriad shops that cater to the tourist where bargaining is almost obligatory to local bazars, where you rub shoulders with village women trailing colourful veils, from picking up a trinket for a fistful of small change to investing in an enamelled gold wine cup that may become priceless after a few years! The bazaar around CHARMINAR in HYDERABAD is crowded with shops where ladies bargain for real pearls or glass bangles. Pearls were bought and sold in Hyderabad much before the Japanese came up with their own artificial version. Such experiences are interesting for sightseers, photographers and shoppers.

To cater to budgets that range from the generous to the modest, crafts have developed accordingly, tailored to the discerning collector as well as to the modest buyer. The difference in price may be enormous, and the difference in quality barely discernible to the uninitiated. However, skill, labour and material vary vastly, catering to both ends of the market. The souvenir seeker is happy to acquire a handcrafted object for very little money. The discerning shopper is also satisfied with his purchase.

Each state in the country has something different to offer, for crafts are essentially the interrelationship between available materials and local tradition. The theme shopper, if he wishes, can collect only

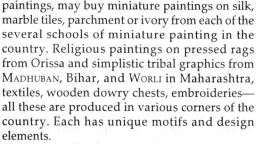

paintings, may buy miniature paintings on silk, marble tiles, parchment or ivory from each of the several schools of miniature painting in the country. Religious paintings on pressed rags from Orissa and simplistic tribal graphics from MADHUBAN, Bihar, and WORLI in Maharashtra, textiles, wooden dowry chests, embroideries—all these are produced in various corners of the country. Each has unique motifs and design elements.

Stores in most cities are open from Monday till Saturday from 10 a.m. to 7 p.m. Some areas are open even on Sundays. All State capitals have government-run emporia where you can be sure of price and quality.

JEWELLERY

Jewellery is never an inexpensive commodity anywhere in the world. However, craftsmanship being cheaper in India, it is possible to buy exquisitely wrought gold jewellery (22 carat) at very attractive prices. India's largest export in terms of value are gems and jewellery. Precious and semi-precious gemstones can be bought loose or set. Indian jewel craftsmen are highly skilled and can set loose stones into any pattern, just by looking at a picture.

However, the whole point of shopping in India is that you may spend as much — or as little — as you wish. For the souvenir hunter there is an astonishing variety of attractive buys that make inexpensive mementoes. Frequently, every item is available in a staggering variety of price ranges.

SELLING IN INDIA

Budget tourists have often wondered what they could sell in India on profit to augment their monetary resources. A few years ago, affluent Indians were willing to grab anything *FORIN* as foreign goods had a 'status' value. No longer, India now produces quality goods and these are available at half the price of goods bought in developed countries. Even watches and pocket calculators which fetched high price in the past are cheaper in India than in Japan or Hong Kong. Dutiable goods like VCRs or expensive cameras which may fetch good prices are recorded on a visitor's passport and will have to be re-exported.

Of course, your bottle of Scotch whisky may get you two or three times the price you paid at the duty-free shop. Smugglers do thriving business in imported whisky — even passing on fake bottles as genuine! But liberalisation has brought Scotch whisky to Indian shops to be bottled and sold here. The profit in your imported whisky today is also declining.

Recent liberalisation has allowed the marketing of foreign brands of liquor in India in collaboration with Indian manufacturers.

Chapter 7

SPECIAL INTERESTS

1. From the Window of an Indian Train
2. The World of Adventure
3. The Call of the Wild

FROM THE WINDOW OF AN INDIAN TRAIN

A trip by train from one end of India to another can be a memorable experience. Whether in the train or at stations en route, it is microcosmic of an Indian way of life, so different from the rest of the world. It is society in motion. Everyone is willing to talk to every other person, keen to share details of their families and the problems they face. Food is shared too. Nothing is secret and sacrosanct. Sometimes friendship made in the train endures for life.

You may not be a train enthusiast, but you cannot forget the initial surge of excitement mingled with awe as a great, long train drawn by giant locomotives pulls into a station. The ubiquitous *coolie* (porter) clad in red and carrying mountains of luggage of all shapes and sizes jostles the passengers that pour through the railway stations everyday. On the platform is the *chaiwalla*, serving tea in small cups of clay that are thrown away after use, and the fruit-seller selling seasonal fruits. The other vendors offer cold drinks, snacks and sweets. Newspaper hawkers loaded with newspapers, journals, thrillers and romances rush up and down the platform. Food, beverages, literature — all are available without your leaving the train, just put your head out of a window and yell to the nearest vendor!

RAILWAY NETWORK

Indian Railways are Asia's largest and the world's second largest rail system in the world. Over ten million passengers travel on the trains every day. Approximately 11,000 trains run everyday connecting over 7,000 stations and covering a route length of 60,000 km.

When you arrive in India at any of the international airports of Delhi, Bombay, Calcutta or Madras, there is an instant Booking-cum-Reservation counter at each of these airports. They facilitate your onward journey by train.

INDRAIL PASSES

Indrail Passes are extremely popular and provide unlimited travel on trains for the period of their validity. The rates vary according to the number of days of travel and the class you wish to travel by. Indrail Passes can be bought through General Sales Agents of Indian Railway overseas or at the major railway offices and at reservation counters in New Delhi, Bombay, Calcutta or Madras. They are also available at railway reservation offices in Hyderabad, Rameswaram, Bangalore, Trivandrum and Jaipur and are valid for a year from the day you start your journey. Indrail Passes can be purchased 360 days in advance. Payment must be made in US dollars or pounds sterling, in cash or traveller's cheques. The fares cover reservation charges on berths at night. However, the purchase of an Indrail Pass does not ensure a reserved seat on the train. Reservations have to be made separately, but if the train is full you can avail of the tourist quota or even the emergency VIP quota. Though visitors get preference and they have their quota for the purpose, yet in case of any difficulty the Chief Reservation Officer or Station Superintendent will assist you.

What does it cost?

The cost of an Indrail Pass is dependent on the "class" and "period" of travel. The table below indicates the position.
FROM 01 MAY 1992

Period of Validity (Days)	A.C. Class	(in U.S. Dollars) 1st Class	2nd Class
7	270	135	70
15	330	165	80
21	400	200	90
30	500	250	110
60	720	360	165
90	960	480	210

Note: Children below the age of 5 travel free when accompanied by parents travelling on an IRP: those between 5 and 12 pay half (approx).

Advantages of an Indrail Pass

* No sleeper surcharge for night journeys for any class of accommodation (Indirect saving of Hotel cost).
* No extra charge for travelling by superfast trains.
* No reservation fee for berths or seats; reservations can be arranged from your country if IRP is purchased well in advance.
* Free meals in Rajdhani Expresses.

* Railway retiring rooms at nominal charges (subject to availability).
* Free luggage allowance:
  A.C. class - 70 kg, 1st Class - 50 kg, 2nd Class - 35 kg.
  (Children between the ages of 5 and 12 are eligible for half of this.)

To assist tourists plan their itineraries, there is a brochure available suggesting 32 model itineraries covering major cities, monuments, forts, palaces, wildlife sanctuaries, hill and beach resorts and other tourist attractions. You can request the nearest Government of India Tourist Office for a copy.

RAILWAY CLASSES

There are three main class gradations on the Indian Railways — second class, first class and air-conditioned first class. There are sub-divisions within these classes. The second class has both 'two-tier' and 'three-tier' sleepers. The two-tier sleeper is padded and more comfortable. There is also the second class air-conditioned sleeper which, unfortunately, is not available on all trains. When available, it is an excellent value for money. Ordinary first class is comfortable when the weather is good but may not be so when temperature soars into the 44^0C.

On some of the superfast trains to the main cities of India you can travel by chair-car, which is air-conditioned. The chair-car has reclining seats like those in a plane. Fares are very reasonable. If you are on a low budget, and want to keep cool, the chair-car is your best buy.

First class air-conditioned is the most comfortable and luxurious. You will love the experience. There are attendants attached to each coach who take care of all your requirements. The cost is the same as on an air journey.

The Indian Railway system is one of the most extensive in the world and is the legacy of the British Raj. On August 16, 1853, India entered into the era of railways. The first train pulled out of Bori Bunder station in Bombay and puffed its way down 35 kms to Thane.

After the Indian Mutiny in 1857, India was brought under the direct rule of the Crown. The British found it prudent to develop a unified network of trains to maintain law and order. Journeys which took months were completed in days.

THE HILL TRAINS

There are some very beautiful little railway trains in India which haul up passengers from the steaming plains during summer to cool mountains up to five to six thousand feet or more. Four fascinating little mountain railways were built during the heyday of the Raj so that people could escape from the intense summer heat of the Indian plains. Engineers spanned the vast rivers of this country with great rail bridges, laid tracks through dense jungles and desert sands and conquered the steep

gradients of mountainous terrain. By the turn of the 20th century, SHIMLA, the summer capital of British India, OOTACAMUND in the Nilgiris, MATHERAN, a hill resort near Bombay, and DARJEELING, the heart of the tea-growing area of the Eastern Himalayas, were all connected to the plains by their own unique train system. To each of these hill stations the people of Delhi, Bombay, Calcutta and Madras — the four major cities of India — travelled up the mountainside in a leisurely fashion. Today, these little trains are still plying. But how long they remain is anyone's guess. Until very recently, all the four train systems used steam locomotives. Today we are down to two. The Matheran and Shimla trains have moved on to diesel engines, undoubtedly fast but not so romantic.

The Darjeeling train, built along the old Hill Cart Road that was used by horse-drawn traffic and bullock-carts, uses the same alignment most of the way. Where the gradient is too steep, ingeniously built loops and spirals, zigzags and reverses are used to continue the train's journey up the mountain slopes. Surprisingly, there are no tunnels on this line and passengers have an uninterrupted view of the breathtaking scenery.

In contrast, the Kalka-Shimla line weaves in and out of tunnels and over multi-level arched bridges that look like Roman aqueducts. The mountains were conquered head-on with heavy engineering and you go through 103 tunnels on a 94-km journey.

The Matheran train takes incredibly sharp curves and the Ooty train system has a central toothed rail in the centre of the track. This mechanism assists the engine in steep climbs and prevents it from rolling backwards. The engine, which is probably the last of its kind in the world, is placed at the rear of the train. So, in fact, the train is pushed up the mountainside. For the comfort of nervous passengers, the engine has four sets of brakes.

The Nilgiri train starts in METTUPALAYAM, off the foot of the Nilgiris and winds its way up to Ooty, or OOTACAMUND (now called Udhagamandalam). The scenery en route is spectacular for all the 46 km of its route. The landscape changes from vistas of plains and arecanut plantations to lush green rain forests. The train chugs through terraced fields, eucalyptus and cypress groves and Toda tribal villages, and finally into its terminus.

INDIA'S PALACE ON WHEELS

Ever had a holiday in a moving train which is also your home for one week? Perhaps not. Try India's new Palace On Wheels, put together by pooling luxurious railway saloons used by the Maharajas and Viceroys of India a century ago. Since the Maharajas are no longer recognised in democratic India, the train, which had its inaugural run in October 1991 after major refurbishment, is now patronised by the new "Maharajas" — rich and affluent foreign tourists. But one does not have to be very rich to buy a seven-day package on this train. It costs US $ 300 (double occupancy) per day inclusive of travel, meals, sightseeing and all other services in the train. The price is no more than the tariff quoted by major international hotels for a night's stay.

The original Palace On Wheels was started in 1982 by the Indian Railways. A British travel agent suggested to the then Chairman of Indian Railways, M.S. Gujral, that a special train be started for British visitors to experience the nostalgia of the British Raj. Gujral immediately thought of starting a train by locating old, historic saloons used in the past by Maharajas and Viceroys and running it through some of the most exotic and popular tourist spots of the country in comfort and style.

Within a year, the train was readied for a journey starting from DELHI and passing through the 'pink city' of JAIPUR, the historic CHITTORGARH FORT, the lake city of UDAIPUR, and the ancient fort towns of JAISALMER and JODHPUR in the Thar desert. The train also passes through the famous bird sanctuary of BHARATPUR, followed by trips to FATEHPUR SIKRI, the abandoned capital of Emperor Akbar, and the 'poem in marble' in AGRA — the Taj Mahal. The itinerary ends in Delhi, but a visitor can get off earlier. The maximum the train can accommodate is 104 passengers in 13 luxurious saloons. Two saloons have been manufactured and designed to serve as royal dining-rooms for guests and yet another is a 24-hour well-stocked bar and a quiet library.

The train is operated on a metre gauge track as in olden days. Convenient stops have been arranged to enable travellers to move to and from dining rooms or to the bar of their respective saloons. The train is not really subject to the normal railway schedules, and stops can be made, if necessary, for the convenience of passengers. The journey covers 2,230 km and is completed in eight nights and seven days. Recently the track has been widened.

Every saloon has four cabins for passengers, accommodating two each. Each saloon has two attendants attached to it — a "captain" and his assistant, a "Man-Friday". They are only a call-bell away. The saloons have their own pantries which are also homes for the two attendants to sleep. Breakfasts, drinks and snacks can be ordered from the pantry while one lies comfortably in bed. Another special feature of each saloon is its lounge where passengers can relax, read or watch a movie on the television. There is a telephone, too, for inter-saloon communications. James Sherwood, the billionaire owner of the Orient Express, travelled on this train and was so impressed that he offered to buy it to operate it in Europe. But, Indian Railways declined the offer.

Several modern features, such as airconditioning, have been added to the new Palace on Wheels. The old coaches — some of them about 100 years old—were becoming unsafe for operation. Indian Railways, therefore, built a new train at their coach factory in Madras — a replica of the old one — to make use of its tourist potential for India. Although the old train had become a legend with 95 per cent average occupancy, visitors were bothered by the heat in the absence of air-conditioning and

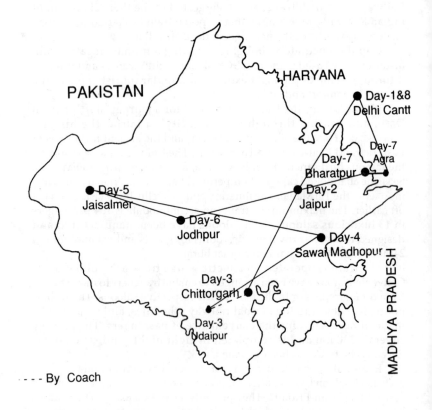

Route of 'Palace on Wheels'

the bath-rooms were so small that it was not possible to install geysers. The present train is more comfortable, complete with modern facilities and the ambience of the old train.

Dining can be a gourmet experience reminiscent of feudal times when service and attention were key words in hospitality. The Rajasthan Tourism Development Corporation, which is a partner with Indian Railways in the Palace on Wheels project, provides all the services including meals. Each luncheon and dinner runs into 8 to 10 courses of Indian, Western and Chinese dishes. Food is served by uniformed waiters, dressed like the Maharajas' servants, as in the past with traditional turbans.

A few lunches are arranged at hotels. For instance, Rambagh Palace Hotel hosts lunch in Jaipur, Lake Palace in Udaipur, Umaid Bhawan

Palace Hotel in Jodhpur and the Taj View Hotel in Agra. Some dinners are organised in exotic settings. The dinner in Jaipur is arranged against the background of the NAARGARH FORT, followed by entertainment by folk dancers and music. Another dinner is in the exotic setting of Moomal Hotel in Jaisalmer where entertainment lasts till the wee hours of the night with guests learning to dance the Rajasthani way.

A trip on the Palace on Wheels is a trip through the history of a thousand turbulent years — in an environment of hospitality which brings you memories of days when indulgence without qualms was a way of life. The train leaves Delhi every Wednesday between August and March. Reservations can be booked through travel agents anywhere in the world or General Sales Agents of Indian Railways in key cities of the world.

The tariff includes cost of travel, full catering on board, (i.e., morning tea, breakfast, lunch, evening tea and dinner), conducted sightseeing tours in deluxe coaches, entrance fees, elephant ride at Jaipur, camel ride at Jaisalmer and boat ride to and fro the Lake Palace Hotel at Udaipur and Bharatpur, a bird sanctuary. The guests have to pay for their liquor.

Information: Manager, Palace on Wheels, Tourist Reception Centre, Bikaner House, New Delhi-110001; *Tel: 3381884/33389525; Fax: 011-3382823.*

Another 'Palace on Wheels' from New Delhi through Gujarat state called 'Royal Orient' was launched in 1995 and is proving very popular. A few more similar trams are in the offering providing new options to visitors to India.

OTHER TRAINS

If a visitor has not enough time to undertake a long train journey, there are other options to experience a train trip. For example, the TAJ EXPRESS leaves from New Delhi Railway Station every morning for Agra and returns the same evening. It is the most convenient way to witness the splendours of the ancient Mughal capital of Agra. The Taj Express also goes on to Gwalior. The GWALIOR FORT is spectacular, the town itself charming and, all in all, it is a very pleasant trip.

The SHATABDI is yet another train which connects Delhi, Agra and Gwalior.

The PINK CITY EXPRESS runs from Delhi to Jaipur, a good weekend excursion.

New Shatabdi trains now connect Delhi-Jaipur and Delhi-Chandigarh.

There is the fabled DECCAN QUEEN that commutes between Bombay and Pune. Due to the phenomenal increase in rail traffic on this sector, double-decker carriages have been introduced, all produced locally.

The Shatabdi Express runs on two routes: from New Delhi to Kanpur and from New Delhi to Bhopal. The name Shatabdi commemorates the birth centenary of India's first Prime Minister, Pandit Jawaharlal Nehru.

The Shatabdi Express is today the fastest train in India. It maintains an average speed of 130 km/h.

THE RAIL MUSEUM

For the rail enthusiasts, India offers an excellent rail transport museum. It is located in the Chanakyapuri area of New Delhi. As one wanders through the open yard, the history of railways in India unfolds itself through the specimens of locomotives and coaches set on rail tracks complete with signals and tunnels. Twenty-six vintage steam locomotives, seventeen luxury coaches and saloon-cars that once transported viceroys and maharajahs and their entourages across the country, give us an insight into a time and way of life that has vanished. A few diesel and electric counterparts of the steam locomotive on display bring us back to the hurly-burly of present times. The museum's most prized exhibit is the FAIRY QUEEN, the oldest surviving locomotive in the world today. It was built in Leeds in England in 1855 and used during the Mutiny of 1857. Later, it was used for hauling light mail trains between Howrah and Ranchi. Skilled craftsmanship is evident in its brass tubes, wooden brakes, copper and brass ornamentation and rich green and gold livery.

Other vintage locomotives are the black and grey engine of the OUDH and ROHILKHAND RAILWAY built in Manchester in 1870 and fitted with two whistles, each one emitting a different sound; another steam engine built

for the RAJPUTANA RAILWAY in 1878, has its boilers placed on either side of the engine. An old veteran on display, manufactured in 1891, was used in the NIZAM OF HYDERABAD'S STATE RAILWAY. This was the most extensive rail network amongst the princely states and covered about 2,000 km. Also on display is the first indigenously built locomotive. It was built at Ajmer in Rajasthan for the RAJPUTANA MALWA RAILWAY in 1895. Other interesting pieces at the museum are two enormous green engines built for the haulage of heavy minerals. One can also view two electric engines built in 1930 for shuttle between Bombay and Pune that are named after two governors of Bombay — SIR ROGER LUMLEY and SIR LESLIE WILSON.

A special feature of the museum is the MAHARAJAH OF PATIALA'S MONORAIL. A pale blue-coloured train, it covered about 75 km of the state. The Maharajah was known for his whims and eccentricities and his train had its very own peculiarity — it ran on a single track along one side of the road ! On this rail were the load-bearing wheels of the train and on the other side larger, flat wheels ran along the road and provided the necessary balance ! Four German locomotives were specially designed for this mono-rail system which was in use for almost 20 years until finally abandoned in 1927. The train was used for joy-rides.

THE WORLD OF ADVENTURE

A major attraction of India for the young as well as for the not-so-young are the lofty Himalayas. Geologically, the Himalayas are still young and growing. Only 60 million years ago the Himalayas were formed when a travelling crust of earth from the South Pole collided with Eurasia, folding up the Himalayas. Today, this great mountain system has an invaluable role in determining life in the Indian subcontinent. The mountain ranges control the climate of India by holding the monsoons till the appropriate time, on the one hand, and protecting the land from the Siberian cold winds, on the other. The snows from the Himalayas feed the perennial northern rivers assuring water for drinking and for farmlands.

The climate and geological diversity of the Himalayas have led to the creation of a unique ecosystem which holds rich natural resources, both living and non-living. The sharp zoning in vegetational types and the resultant habitats are the home of a large variety of birds and animals. Himalayan flora is unique. It encompasses forests of all types — tropical swampy forests, deciduous forests, coniferous forests, rhododendron forests, alpine meadows and even hot and cold forests.

The Himalayas are, however, not just a refuge for primitive forms of life. Human civilisations and cultures flourish here. The mountains are a melting-pot of plants, animals and human groups. The Himalayas are more than the world's youngest and highest mountains. They are a treasure-house of knowledge that is waiting to be explored.

MOUNTAIN CLIMBING AS A SPORT

The Himalayas are like a magnet, all those who have the will to challenge its slopes and glaciers. For centuries, sages have crossed their high and hazardous passes to discover places of pilgrimage like KAILASH, KEDARNATH, GANGOTRI, YAMNOTRI and AMARNATH — some of the most beautiful places on the earth. Traders, hunters and porters have crossed Himalayan passes thousands of feet high to discover the natural wealth of the mountains. They established trade routes and connected many regions of the Himalayas, unifying people. These traders did not have the luxury of modern mountaineering equipment. They evolved crude but functional mountaineering aids, like an all wool mountain boot, walking sticks with ferrule to maintain balance on slopes, yak-hair ropes and jackets of lambskin.

Mountaineering as a sport in the Himalayas began in 1883 when W.W. Graham, a European, came to the Himalayas for the sole purpose of climbing. Graham was not the first foreigner to explore the Himalayas. Some preachers and surveyors had been there earlier. As interest in Himalayan mountaineering grew, Indians helped as porters and agents. In 1951, Gurdial Singh led the first full-fledged Indian mountaineering expedition to Trishul and successfully climbed the peak.

Traditionally, Indians were reluctant to climb these peaks as they believed that gods lived there. Today, as many as 100 mountaineering expeditions venture into the Himalayas every year. And 20,000 foreign trekkers and 10,000 Indian trekkers walk across its fascinating slopes and valleys. The Himalayas are no longer inaccessible. Improved road communications, reliable weather forecasting and well-organised search and rescue facilities have made mountaineering and trekking a safe sport.

REGULATIONS FOR MOUNTAINEERING EXPEDITIONS

Foreign mountaineering expeditions desirous of climbing in the Indian Himalayas have to get clearances from the Government of India through the Indian Mountaineering Foundation (IMF) Headquarters, Benito Juarez Road, Anand Niketan, New Delhi - 110021.

All foreign expeditions have to be accompanied by an Indian Liaison Officer who is a mountaineer and will assist the expedition with local arrangements. Permission also has to be sought to import and use wireless and communication equipment and to take photographs in restricted areas.

LET US EXPLORE THE HIMALAYAS

GARHWAL HIMALAYAS

It is in these mountains that the holy Ganga finds its source. The Garhwal Himalayas stretch just over 290 km and are separated from the Punjab Himalayas by the river Sutlej. Garhwal was the first part of the Himalayas to be explored and surveyed, and the highest peak in these mountains is less than 8000 metres. Garhwal is flanked by Tibet in the north, Kumaon in the east, Bijnor in the south and Tehri and Dehradun in the west.

NANDA DEVI, called the 'Pearl of the Himalayas', is the highest peak of the Garhwal mountains. It has twin peaks, the main peak and the east peak. It is revered since ancient times and worshipped as the Goddess Nanda. T. G. Longstaff, one of the earliest explorers of the Garhwal region, has said, "No mountain in the world is more beautiful than Nanda Devi."

Another popular peak in the Garhwal region is KAMET. Ten expeditions were attempted on this peak before it was finally scaled in 1931.

At the traditional source of the Ganga, the GANGOTRI, one finds the most fascinating mountaineering area in the world. A few kilometres above the icy cave from which the river takes off are the meadows of TAPOVAN and NANDANVAN. The peaks are mainly over the 20,000 feet mark and still have some unclimbed faces. All along the 30 km length of the Gangotri glacier are side glaciers, some not yet fully explored. One can also traverse to the southern face of the crest which provides steeper ice faces.

Further eastwards, Kumaon provides fairly easy access to the SUNDER-DHUNGA glacier and other fascinating mountain ranges.

Skiing in Garhwal

JOSHIMATH, traditionally a pilgrim town, is now being developed as a skiing resort for Garhwal. A ropeway takes visitors from the town at 6,000 ft. to the slopes of AULI and GORSAIN near the KUARI PASS at 12,000 ft. The panorama of Himalayan snow peaks from Kuari is spellbinding.

The bonus for winter visitors to Joshimath is the weather. For three months (January through March) of the skiing season, there are no clouds at most times of the year. The clear blue sky and the surrounding snow make this an ultimate ski-resort.

KASHMIR AND LADAKH HIMALAYAS

The arid ZANSKAR RANGE parallels the Himalayan watershed in the north. LADAKH, a part of the State of Jammu and Kashmir, often referred to as "Moonland" or "Little Tibet", is a high altitude desert and snow-covered peaks rise over barren and treeless landscapes. The Zanskar and the parallel Ladakh range contain few large peaks, but some like Sasir Kangri (7672 metres) are only 50 km north of Leh, the capital of Ladakh. The Zanskar range also contains the famous peaks of Nun (7135 metres) and Kun (7085 metres), popular with mountaineers because of their rocky structure, altitude and glacial face. Around these are White Needle (6500 metres), Pinnacle (6930 metres) and z-1 (6400 metres). These peaks are located at the head of the Shafat glacier. The 'Z' series also cluster around the Durung Drung glacier.

The Ladakh chain is ideal for rock climbing as its mountains are bare and eroded. The valley of Zanskar is separated from that of the Indus by the Stok chain which has popular peaks like Meru (5,700 metres), Kanjitu (5,800 metres), Mashro West (5,950 metres) and Stok Kangri (6,120 metres).

Kishtwar, a popular mountaineering area in Ladakh, has been explored by climbers only in recent years and is a jagged profusion of peaks, sharp fluted and icy. These are only a few days march from the road. There are also many summits of alpine character between 4,800 and 5,800 metres.

Skiing in Kashmir

Kashmir is the best known and most developed region for skiing in India. The valley's premier upland resort, Gulmarg, is situated at 2,730 metres and is the country's largest and best equipped winter sports resort. There are good snow conditions from December to April. Modern facilities such as T-bars, ski lifts, chair cars and ropeways have been built. Ski equipment is available for hire and is of international standards. Instructors trained at European ski resorts are available for training.

Gulmarg has an Indian Institute of Skiing and Mountaineering. It can organise training programmes for beginners. For those who enjoy ski-mountaineering or Nordic skiing, there are other possibilities. A popular ski mountaineering route is to go from Gulmarg to Khilanmarg (3,045 metres), 5 km away. This place affords some magnificent views of the valley and the surrounding ranges.

THE HIMACHAL HIMALAYAS

The State of Himachal Pradesh is made up of ten districts with a total area of 56,019 sq. km. The northern border of Himachal Pradesh is bounded by Tibet. In the north-west it borders Kashmir, in the south lie the plains of Punjab and the eastern border meets the hills of Uttar Pradesh. The State is rugged and mountainous. The valleys of Lahaul and Spiti are the dreams of mountaineers.

The Lahaul and Spiti valley is a desolate region compared to the lush Beas valley of Kulu, also a popular mountain area of the state. Spiti, which overlooks Tibet across the Sutlej river, is Tibetan in landscape with its sparse population characteristically Tibetan. Kulu and Lahaul are good areas for mountaineering practice, both alpine style ascents and ski-mountaineering. The jagged ice peaks of Kulu offer good routes for the ambitious mountaineers. A popular peak in this area is DEO TIBBA (6,001 metres) which is visible from SHIMLA, the capital of Himachal Pradesh.

The MENTHOSA snowpeak in CHAMBA at 6,445 metres has never been conquered, nor has DHARMASURA (6,446 metres) in the BARA SHIGRI glacier region. The MILANG RIVER BASIN has more than a dozen peaks over 6,000 metres high. Himachal may well hold the record for peaks that have defied ascent till today.

Skiing in Himachal

Himachal too has skiing facilities. NARKANDA lies 60 km. north of Shimla on Kipling's famous Hindustan-Tibet road at a height of nearly 3000 metres. The nearby peak, HATHU, dominates the great watershed of India. From here one can see both the Sutlej and the Giri rivers which flow into the Indus and the Ganga system, respectively.

The skiing season in Narkanda starts in January and lasts into the first week of April. While there is six to ten feet of snow, the motor road to Shimla usually remains open making Narkanda conveniently accessible. The government-run ski classes provide their own equipment for skiing. A major advantage of Narkanda is that after an overnight journey from Delhi, one can fit in a skiing weekend at rates that are easily the lowest in the world.

While Narkanda is quite developed, skiing at KUFRI is still taking off. Kufri has the advantage of proximity to the plains.

Important Peaks of
INDIAN HIMALAYAS

Name of Peak	Height (m)	State
Abi Gamine	7,355	Uttar Pradesh
Badrinath	7,138	Uttar Pradesh
Brammahi	6,416	Jammu and Kashmir
Changabang	6,864	Uttar Pradesh
Deo Tibba	6,221	Himachal Pradesh
Dunagiri	7,066	Uttar Pradesh
Indrasan	6,221	Himachal Pradesh
Kamet	7,756	Uttar Pradesh
Kokthang	20,167 ft	Sikkim
Kullu Pumori	6,553	Himachal Pradesh
Kun	7,087	Jammu and Kashmir
Leo Pargial	6,770	Himachal Pradesh
Mana Peak	7,273	Uttar Pradesh
Menthosa	6,443	Himachal Pradesh
Mulkila	6,517	Himachal Pradesh
Nanda Devi	7,817	Uttar Pradesh
Niligiri Parvat	6,474	Uttar Pradesh
Nilkanta	6,904	Uttar Pradesh
Nun	7,135	Jammu and Kashmir
Papsura	6,451	Himachal Pradesh
Panchchuli	6,904	Uttar Pradesh
Rathong	22,000 ft	Sikkim
Shivling	6,543	Uttar Pradesh
Sickle Moon	6,575	Jammu and Kashmir
Tarangiri	6,415	Jammu and Kashmir
Trishul	7,120	Uttar Pradesh
White Sail	6,446	Himachal Pradesh

The MANALI region offers scope for both winter and summer skiing. When the snows herald in winter, the area around SOLONG NALA attracts skiers to its extensive natural slopes. In the summer months, possibilities of skiing on the slopes of the ROHTANG PASS are there.

SIKKIM HIMALAYAS

The Sikkim Himalayas are characterised very strongly by the culture of the region. Prayer flags line several routes to upper Himalayan monasteries.

Only two peaks in Sikkim are open to mountaineering expeditions — those of RATHONG (22,000 ft.) and KOKTHANG (20,167 ft.). There are, however, many other challenging peaks.

ADVENTURE SPORTS

In recent years, India has been changing its image from purely a cultural destination to a composite destination for varied outdoor activities. Adventure sports are on top of India's new face. India with its diverse terrain sustains practically every conceivable adventure sport. The canvas of unusual adventure sports is large-running the dangerous rapids in northern rivers or rock-climbing close to metro cities. Then there are hang- gliding or ballooning, motor-rafting or crossing the desert on camel back. The choice is unlimited.

River-Running

The snowfed mountain rivers that trace their origins to the Himalayas descend from their icy heights across high cliff-suspended gorges and tortuous, boulder-strewn beds before they change into a smooth flow across the great Indo- Gangetic plains. As they cut against rocky banks, crashing into rocks, and falling down caverns and breaking into white water rapids, the waters foam and swirl. The awesome might of the rivers in these parts and their apparent navigational invincibility has given impetus to river running. Leading river-running experts have opined that India has the potential to become the river-running capital of the world.

River-running is a fairly young sport in India. But the challenge of the rivers in the upper Himalayas makes it among the best regions in the world. Amateurs and first-timers have their choice of quieter waters, with promise of a passage through some of the most picturesque riversides. Professionals can run better known and more difficult routes on rapids listed as Grade IV to VI on the international scale.

The ZANSKAR RIVER, in the Zanskar valley, can offer a professional and exciting six days on the river, starting from PADAM. The rapids are frequent, and as they can be dangerous, the best season to raft them is when the waters, in the months of August and September, are low.

The GANGA, the most sacred of Indian rivers, attributes a holy legend to its origin. It is sacred to the Hindus all over the world, its water is purifying. Legend apart, its mountainous terrain affords some of the most spectacular river-running in the country — ideal for both paddle-rafting and car-rafting. A more popular programme is a run that begins 10 km above RISHIKESH — a fascinating experience.

A new run has been mapped out on the SUTLEJ from RAMPUR BHUSHAIR to TATTAPANI and on to SALAPAR BRIDGE, a 92-km run on a stretch graded IV-V on the international scale.

River-running expeditions in India are organised and managed by professional Indian teams who have been trained abroad in some of the most difficult water stretches of the world. Recently, Indians won the prestigious Engadine Trophy at the international river rafting competition on the Inn river of Switzerland.

Motor Rally

The topographical distribution of India makes it ideal for running rallies from desert roads to beach, hill, mountain and forest tracks. A rally can take many turns, and the picturesque vintage car rally is a periodic and recurring event in many Indian metros. Participants come dressed in cheerful, period costumes and some with very rare, collectors' cars. The rallies may include a '35 Jaguar Convertible or a '54 Austin Saloon Deluxe or even an 1898 Humberette.

But vintage rallies aside, major competing events in India have become regular. The Federation of Indian Rally Drivers Championship (FIRDC) organises championship rallies of national and international status. There are the SCISSORS ACTION RALLY (national) sponsored by the Coimbatore-based Automative Sports Club, the HIMALAYAN CAR RALLY (international) sponsored by the Himalayan Rally Association, Bombay, the KARNATAKA 1,000 RALLY (national) organised by the Karnataka Motor Sports Club, the RALLY D' ENDURANCE (national) organised by the Indian Automative Sports Club, Bangalore, and the Charminar Sports Club. Apart from these, there are rallies organised by associations from August through December. But the one rally that is a cut above all others, and attracts international attention, is the Himalayan Car Rally, now vying for championship status. Rallyists from around the world gather for this premier event, and spirits run high as the rally is flagged off from New Delhi, which is its beginning and concluding points.

A rally is not a race, it is a test of the skills, endurance of a car and its driver. Discarding heavy traffic roads, a rally takes to lesser known and traversed routes. The Himalayan Car Rally goes a step further with detailed charting of its route, using dirt roads, forest roads, dry river beds and mountain roads.

The Himalayan Car Rally is open to anyone who possesses a valid driving licence. The rally routes, or legs, may permit regrouping halts of

2 to 5 hours duration en route. The event is run in compliance with the international sporting code of the Federation Internationale de l' Automobile, the regulations of the Federational Internationale du Sport Automobile, and the national competition rules of the Federation of Motor Sports Clubs of India.

Usually, the Himalayan Car Rally is divided into four legs totalling over 3,200 km concentrating on the mountain terrain of Himachal Pradesh and Uttar Pradesh. The normal Himalayan run, though it changes every year, may pass through some major towns en route, like DELHI, MUSSOORIE, DEHRADUN, HARIDWAR, DHARAMSALA, SHIMLA, NARKANDA, MANDI, NAINITAL, RANIKHET, CORBETT NATIONAL PARK and GARHMUKTESWAR. New tracks are marked into the rally every year, as more undiscovered routes are discovered, or because a dirt road may possibly have been washed away. This helps in retaining the surprise element.

Ballooning

Ballooning, too, has become a popular sport in India. Giant balloons billow out their folds and rise in the sky in a colourful parade. The balloonists look like those precariously hung on baskets. Standing in the basket is a delightful sensation. It feels reassuringly solid, just like standing in a floating balcony. The average basket carries two or three persons, but ten can travel depending on the size of the balloon. When alone, a balloonist can rise to the height of 800 feet. Groups may be restricted to heights of 200 to 500 feet.

The Balloon Club of India is located at New Delhi's Safdarjung Airport and has three balloons and 50 members. Begun in 1970, the club has organised international balloon fairs with great success.

Camel Safari

An exciting sport of the Thar desert is the camel safari for those who can spare time and want to sample a unique experience. It is a holiday with a difference — an adventure sport that calls for little exertion. Its mounting popularity reflects a new rapport between man, the desert, and the beast. Camel safaris can trace their origin to the age of overland trade between India and China, when

camel caravans would journey along established trade routes laden with spices, herbs and jewels.

The Thar has a world of its own, an endless ocean of sand, dotted with dunes and patchily covered with xerophytic shrubs. It has its distinctive wildlife. Route navigation in the desert is an acquired art. Caravans must be led by riders who know how to study the stars but also recognise the shifting sands of the terrain. Aided by the warmth of the hospitable villagers en route, the camel safari becomes a once-in-a-lifetime experience. The swinging giant of the desert — camel—is neither very comfortable nor easy to get used to! It is a real-life adventure.

For those interested in camel safaris, variations from 4-day to 15-day safaris can be organised. Safari organisers attempt to recreate the atmosphere of old caravan journeys. Musicians accompany the caravans, and halts are called outside villages where the local people are invited to enjoy campfire hospitality. Cooking equipment, twin-bedded tents form a regular part of the safari. Staff is available for all assistance, including the pitching of tents, and providing services. For those who may not have enough time, one-day or two-day trips can also be organised on request.

Hang-Gliding

Hang-gliding has been introduced only recently in India. Several sites have been identified by hang gliders and those that merit note are the SRINAGAR VALLEY in Jammu and Kashmir, BILLING, KANGRA, DHARAMSALA, SHIMLA and KASAULI in Himachal Pradesh, PUNE, KAMSHET on the Bombay-Pune Highway, TALEGAON, SATARA, SINHGARH as also MURUD JANJIRA in Maharashtra, the NILGIRI HILLS in Tamil Nadu, MHOW, INDORE in Madhya Pradesh, the CHAMUNDI HILL and areas around BANGALORE-MYSORE in Karnataka and SHILLONG in Meghalaya.

Hang-gliding clubs in India are centred at Pune, New Delhi, Bombay, Chandigarh, Shimla, Devlali, Bangalore and Kalahati. Most of the clubs have their own hang-gliders which are indigenously manufactured.

Most Indian hang-gliding sites have been highly rated, and those in the lower reaches of the Himalayas are among the best in the world. Kangra and Kasauli are being developed as major hang-gliding centres. An international championship has brought the former into focus. A Kasauli take-off can prove exhilirating for the glider who may find himself floating into Chandigarh with the utmost ease. The Himachal Gliding Rally at Kangra is held during the second week of May as good thermal currents prevail during this season.

Reputed travel agents can arrange exciting ski-gliding experiences at SOLANG NALA in Manali, Himachal Pradesh and KHILANMARG above Gulmarg in Kashmir.

Heli-Skiing

India also offers attractive winter sports options. In January 1988, in collaboration with the famous Swiss born ski-mountaineer, Sylvan Saudan, heli-skiing was introduced in Kashmir. India is the first Asian country to offer heli-skiing facilities. A heli-skier is dropped on the top of a mountain or ridge by a helicopter, saving the skier the arduous task of climbing up. The skier may then negotiate the virgin, uncharted terrain and experience the thrill and the danger of skiing on powdery snow.

A necessary prerequisite of this dangerous though thrilling sport is skiing experience and careful prior study of physical features, cornices, crevasses, wind direction and potential avalanche hazards in the area.

Kashmir has an edge over Canada, a favourite destination of most heli- skiers. In Canada, heli-skiers have to set off from small resorts and are often marooned by bad weather miles away from civilisation. In Kashmir, the beautiful Himalayan range is always in front of the heli-skier. Besides, there are more than 5,000 first skill descent locations available. Trained Indian instructors are there to help newcomers.

CALL OF THE WILD

India has a long tradition of protecting and preserving wildlife. Indian literature is full of concern for earth as well as for forests and those who live in them.

Although British rulers and the Indian Maharajas played havoc with India's wildlife, the Government of independent India has shown a remarkable concern to protect it. In India, wildlife has been protected both by the Central and the State Governments through legislation since 1970. Prime Minister Jawaharlal Nehru and later his daughter Indira Gandhi took a keen interest in the protection of wildlife. Thanks to their efforts, the species which were going to be extinct have survived once again, i.e., the tiger, the rhinoceros, the lion, etc.

INDIA'S WILDLIFE PARKS

The total area of India's protected wilderness is approximately 90,000 sq km and constitutes 3 per cent of the country's land area. The emphasis has been not only on protecting wildlife in reserved forests, but also in areas where man and animal continue to live in harmony. The country's protected wilderness consists of 53 national parks and 247 sanctuaries, many of which fall under the purview of the Project Tiger. The climatic and geographic diversity makes India the home of over 350 mammal and 1,200 bird species — some of which are unique to this subcontinent.

India's faunal assemblage varies from habitat to habitat. Whereas some sanctuaries aim at protecting individual species, most aim at providing total harmony for their wildlife population. The subcontinent is the home of many species that are not found elsewhere, like the white tiger, the royal Bengal tiger, the snow leopard, the Asiatic lion, the lion-tailed macaque, the Himalayan tahr, the Andaman teal, the great Indian bustard and the monal pheasant.

Wildlife tourism in India is designed to give the visitor opportunities of exploring the country's rich natural heritage without disturbance to its fragile ecosystem. Several of India's national parks and sanctuaries are conveniently accessible and have designated tourism zones with good accommodation and transport.

India's wildlife sanctuaries have not received much publicity overseas mainly because most of them are located in far-flung regions. And that is perhaps good for the sanctuaries. Indian sanctuaries are not inundated with hordes of visitors!

Since a visitor to Indian wildlife sanctuaries may have already been to Africa, it may be relevant to explain the difference between the two regions. Africa's wide open plains have led to the evolution of large herds of animals which can be easily seen from a safe distance. In Indian sanctuaries, however, animals are found in small herds in dense forests or in isolated places where one can only shoot them with camera. The animals are hidden in dense forests or keep themselves screened in tall grass. They venture forth to watering holes avoiding man. The tiger, particularly, can be very elusive. You always have a chance to see it on the first day, but you can miss it too —despite extending your stay from one to three days. In India, the authorities do not bring the tiger for viewing by offering him a bait. A visitor goes into the jungle on elephant back. Everything which moves can be noticed from the high seat and if you are lucky, you can see a rare animal. Herds of deer are, however, seen in plenty. It is real fun tracking the animals on elephant back. Wild elephant herds, too, can be seen if one has patience, specially in the PERIYAR WILDLIFE SANCTUARY in the South. They all come to the lake to quench their thirst. Sighting of animals in India has a thrill of its own — not known in Africa. It is believed that while India has a greater variety of wildlife to offer than Africa, the latter has a greater number of animals.

Project Tiger

India launched a major conservation project called Project Tiger in 1973 with a grant of US $ one million from the World Wildlife Fund matched by a similar amount from the Government of India. Initially, there were nine areas designed as Project Tiger; now there are 15 covering a total area of 24,712 sq. km. As a result of this special attention, the tiger population in each sanctuary is on the increase.

The most accessible and popular sanctuary to see wild tigers is the KANHA NATIONAL PARK in the heart of Central India — five hours drive from Jabalpur or six hours from Nagpur. The other place for sighting the tiger is nearer Delhi in the CORBETT NATIONAL PARK in Uttar Pradesh, in the foothills of the Himalayas. Named after the well-known English writer of jungle books, Jim Corbett, it is only six hours drive from the Indian capital, New Delhi. It supports a wide variety of mammals including tigers and over 585 species of birds.

For bird watching, the most easily accessible sanctuary is at BHARATPUR, only three hours from Delhi and one hour from Agra city by car. During winter months, migratory birds come here all the way from Siberia, including the rare Siberian Crane. A very quiet and serene place to watch rare Indian and foreign birds.

Another three hours from Bharatpur is one more Project Tiger sanctuary, RANTHAMBOR. An Indian success story in saving wildlife is the protection given to the one-horned rhinoceros which is exclusive to India. In Assam, wedged between the Brahmaputra river and the Miki Hills of eastern India, the population of rhinoceros in the KAZIRANGA SANCTUARY has reached saturation point. In 1960, only 80 rhinoceros were left; today they number 900. Some rhinoceros are being moved to other sanctuaries.

The following is a comprehensive chart of wildlife sanctuaries and parks in India. We have listed only those which are easily accessible to foreign visitors:

Do's and Don'ts for Visitors to Sanctuaries

To enjoy a visit to a wildlife sanctuary, the following guidelines may be kept in mind:

1. Be as quiet as possible. Avoid radios, transistors and music in the jungle. It disturbs the animals.

2. Dress in khaki, or brown or olive green to merge with the surroundings.
3. Avoid pollution of air, soil or water.
4. Look for and enjoy all kinds of wildlife — not necessarily the big game.
5. Use the services of a local guide to take you around and to explain.
6. Do not forget your camera and binoculars at home. There are great moments to record for your grandchildren.

IMPORTANT NATIONAL PARKS & SANCTUARIES IN INDIA

(Courtesy: World Wildlife Fund, India)

Name of National Park/Sanctuary	Best time for visiting	Species found
Andhra Pradesh		
1. Kolleru Pelicanry	December-March	Pelicans, flamingo, heron, painted stork, avocent, teal and tern
2. Nagarjunasagar Srisailam Sanctuary	October-June	Tiger, panther, sloth bear, wild boar, chital, sambar, nilgai, blackbuck, jackal, fox, wolf and crocodile.
Assam		
1. Kaziranga National Park	February to May	Great Indian one-horned rhinoceros, wild buffalo, elephant, gaur, leopard cat, wild boar, civet cat, swamp deer, hog deer, sambar, tiger, python, pelican, partridge and florican.
2. Manas Wildlife Sanctuary	February	Elephant, tiger, panther, gaur, wild buffalo, great Indian one-horned rhino, golden langur, civet cat, otter, swamp deer, hog deer, sambar, pygmy hog, water monitor, wild boar, great pied hornbill, florican.

Bihar

1.	Hazaribagh Wildlife Sanctuary	October to June — Tiger, leopard, sambar, chital, nilgai, wild boar, wild cat, peafowl, etc.
2.	Dalma Wildlife Sanctuary	October-June — Elephant, leopard, wild boar, wild cat, peafowl, etc.
3.	Palamau Wildlife Sanctuary	All the year around elephant, panther, wild boar, barking deer, gaur, chital, sambar, peafowl, etc.

Goa, Daman and Diu

1. Mollem Wildlife Sanctuary — November-May — Gaur, sambar, mouse deer, barking deer, panther, flying squirrel, porcupine, civet cat, ant-eater, slender loris, grey junglefowl.

Gujarat

1. Gir National Park — December-mid June — Asiatic lion, panther, striped hyena, sambar, nilgai, chital, four horned antelope, chinkara, wild boar, crocodile.
2. Wild Ass Sanctuary (little Rann of Kutch) — January-mid June — Wild ass, nilgai, wolf, chinkara.
3. Pirotan Marine Sanctuary — November-February — Corals, octopus, pufferfish, stork, heron, ibis, flamingo, pelican, wader.

Jammu and Kashmir

1. Dachigam Wildlife Sanctuary — April-November — Leopard, black bear, brown bear, serow, musk deer, hangul (barasingha).

Himachal Pradesh

1. Manali Sanctuary — April-June, Sept. to October — Tahr, serow, goral, black bear, kalij, chir, koklas, chakor, partridge, civet, marten, flying fox.

Karnataka

1. Bandipur National Park — March-August — Indian elephant, tiger, gaur, sambar, chital,

	(Tiger Reserve)		barking deer, wild dog, wild boar, jackal, sloth bear, panther, four-horned antelope, Malabar squirrel, green pigeon, junglefowl, partridge, bush quail, etc.
2.	Bennarghatta National Park		Throughout the year elephant, sloth bear, chital, barking deer, grey partridge, bush quail, junglefowl, etc.
3.	Nagerhole National Park	October to March	Elephant, tiger, panther, chital, sambar, sloth bear, junglefowl, partridge, etc.
4.	Ranganathittoo Bird Sanctuary	July-August	Open-billed stork, white ibis, little egret, cattle egret, darter, cormorant, pond heron, river tern, spoonbill, crocodile, etc.

Kerala

1.	Periyar Wildlife Sanctuary (Tiger Reserve)	October-April	Elephant, tiger, panther, wild dog, gaur, sloth bear, nilgai, wild boar, sambar and barking deer.
2.	Parambikulam Wildlife Sanctuary	October-April	Elephant, gaur, leopard, tiger, sloth bear, nilgai, chital, sambar, crocodile.

Madhya Pradesh

1.	Kanha National Park	March-June	Tiger, panther, gaur, barasingha, chital, sambar, blackbuck, four-horned antelope, barking deer, mouse deer, nilgai, wild dog, boar.
2.	Bandhavgarh National Park	November-June	Tiger, panther, gaur, chital, sambar, nilgai, chinkara, barking deer, bear, wild boar and a variety of upland birds.

3. Satpura National Park — March-June — Tiger, panther, gaur, chital, sambar, barking deer, sloth bear, wild bear, etc.

Maharashtra

1. Tadoba National Park — May-June — Tiger, panther, sloth bear, gaur, sambar, nilgai, chital, chinkara, crocodile.

2. Dhakna-Kolkaz Sanctuary (Tiger Reserve) — April-May — Tiger, panther, gaur, sloth bear, sambar, barking deer, four-horned antelope, wild boar, chital. Bird life is plentiful.

3. Karnala Bird Sanctuary — January-April — Ashy minivet, paradise fly-catcher, sharma, Malabar whistling thrush, racket-tailed drongo, woodpecker, etc. Other wildlife seen are the panther, four-horned antelope and common langur.

Manipur

1. Keibul Lamjao National Park — February-April — Brown-antlered deer, wild goat and water birds.

2. Dampa Wildlife Sanctuary — November-February — Elephant, tiger, leopard, sambar, barking deer, Himalayan bear, wild boar, wild dog, wild cat, gaur, leopard cat, king cobra, python, hornbill, pheasant, etc.

Nagaland

1. Intangki Wildlife Sanctuary — November-March — Gaur, boar, elephant, barking deer, bear, clouded leopard, panther, tiger, pangolin and various kinds of reptiles.

Orissa

1. Satkosia Gorge Sanctuary — Summer and winter — Gharial and mugger, tiger, leopard, jungle cat, civet, gaur, ratel, four-

2.	Bhitar Kanika Sanctuary	Winter	horned antelope, hornbill, junglefowl and other birds. Salt-water crocodile, leopard cat, hyena, jungle cat, leopard, wild boar, chital, sambar, giant squirrel, water monitor, sea-turtle, king cobra, python, painted stork, adjutant stork, openbilled stork, white ibis, black ibis, etc.
3.	Chilika Sanctuary	Winter	Blackbuck, chital, ibis, crane, cormorant, egret, flamingo, and pelican.
4.	Simlipal Wildlife Sanctuary (Tiger Reserve)	Winter	Tiger, elephant, gaur, chital, leopard, mouse deer, flying squirrel and mugger.

Punjab

1.	Harike Headworks Sanctuary	October-March	Duck, pochard, teal, coot, waterhen, geese, nilgai and wild boar.

Rajasthan

1.	Tiger Project Ranthambore (Tiger Reserve)	All year round except July, August & September	Tiger, panther, hyena, jungle cat, civet, sambar, chital, nilgai, bear, wild boar, partridge, green pigeon, red spur fowl, etc.
2.	Sariska Project (Tiger Reserve)	All year round except July, August & September	Tiger, panther, hyena, jungle cat, civet, sambar, chinkara, nilgai, four-horned antelope, partridge, green-pigeon, red spur fowl.
3.	Ghana Bird Sanctuary, Bharatpur	October to February	Siberian crane, cormorant, stork, spoonbill, quail, coot, heron, teal, tern, sambar, chital, black-buck, wild boar, civet, etc.

4. Desert Sanctuary	All year round	Great Indian bustard, blackbuck, chinkara.

Sikkim

1. Khangchendzonga National Park	February to April October & Nov.	Snow-leopard, clouded leopard, marbled cat, civet, binturong, Himalayan black bear, red panda, Tibetan wild ass, blue sheep, serow, goral, takin, musk deer, pheasant, partridge, green pigeon, etc.

Tamil Nadu

1. Mudumalai Wildlife Sanctuary	February-June	Elephant, gaur, chital, sambar, tiger, panther, sloth bear, wild dog, etc.
2. Anamalai Wildlife Sanctuary	February-June	Lion-tailed macaque, elephant, gaur, chital, sambar, tiger, panther, sloth bear, wild dog, etc.
3. Mundanthurai Tiger Sanctuary	September-Nov.	Tiger, chital, sambar, wild boar, lion-tailed macaque.
4. Point Calimere Sanctuary	January-September	Black-buck, chital, wild boar, flamingoes.
5. Vedanthagai Water Birds Sanctuary	November-February	Different water birds.
6. Kalakad Sanctuary	Whole year	Lion-tailed macaque.

Uttar Pradesh

1. Corbett National Park (Tiger Reserve)	November-May	Elephant, tiger, panther, sloth bear, nilgai, sambar, chital, wild boar, porcupine, peafowl, red junglefowl, partridge, both species of Indian inland crocodiles, goral and four-horned antelope.
2. Dudhwa National Park	November-May	Tiger, panther, sloth bear, sambar, swamp deer, chital, hog deer, barking deer, nilgai,

3. Kedarnath Sanctuary	September-October May-June	peafowl, junglefowl, partridge, etc. Himalayan brown and black bear, snow-leopard, bharal, musk deer, tahir, serow, goral.

West Bengal

1. Jaldapara Wildlife Sanctuary	December to May	Rhino, elephant, tiger, leopard, wild boar, gaur, barking deer, hog deer, sambar and a variety of birds.
2. Tiger Reserve, Sunderbans	September to May	Tiger, different species of deer, wild boar, estuarine crocodile, Gangetic dolphin.

Chapter 8

HOTEL ACCOMMODATION

1. Indian Hotel Chains
2. Tariffs and Prices
3. Major Hotel Chains

INDIAN HOTEL CHAINS

India has some superb hotels. At least a dozen of them are listed among three hundred best hotels of the world. There are four major chains of Indian hotels. Three of these — Oberoi, Taj and Welcomgroup — are chains of deluxe hotels. If you book with any of their hotels in India, you can never go wrong. They comparefavourably with international deluxe hotels. Price-wise, too, they offer value for money. Their charges are lower than similar properties in Europe, North America and Asia. The service is outstanding and so is warmth and hospitality.

The fourth chain — Ashok — is a composite chain of deluxe, standard and budget hotels. It offers good value for money.

The Taj and Oberoi chains are also managing and operating deluxe properties in different parts of the world including USA, UK, Middle East, Australia, Indonesia, Sri Lanka and Egypt. India also has its quota of Holiday Inns, Le Meredien, Hyatt Regency, Kempinsky, Hilton International Ramada and Quality Inns, etc. Besides, some of their properties have marketing tie-ups with foreign chains. Taj's Bombay property is affiliated to the Inter-continental Hotels Chain. Six Welcomgroup hotels in India are part of the Sheraton International chain.

TARIFFS AND PRICES

Major hotel chains quote prices in US dollars. Chains like Ashok and Centaur quote in rupees, though payment has to be made in dollars. We quote approximate prices according to the class of the hotel (they are subject to change). Prices include taxes.

Hotel Prices in US Dollars

	Metropolitan Town	Major Resorts	State Capitals	Small Resorts
Deluxe Single/Double	150-200	100-150	50-75	20-50
First Class Single/Double	70-100	50-100	30-50	15-30
Second Class Single/Double	20-40	15-30	10-25	10-15
Budget Hotels Single/Double	15-25	10-20	10-15	8-12

INDIA GIVES BEST VALUE

India is beckoning if your credit card is overwhelmed and your stomach is cast-iron. The world's most populous nation is also the cheapest holiday destination, according to an international survey conducted by travel agency giant Thomas Cook.

The land of the Taj Mahal, saris and teeming millions ranks number one in eight of the 14 bargain categories in the survey - and in the top two or three of the remainder.

Looking for a three-course meal in a quality restaurant for $16 - or a rental car for around $25 a day? Go no further than India. There you'll also find the world's cheapest suntan lotion and taxis that, while hair-raising, offer tremendous value.

Egypt, Malaysia, Florida and California are next in line in the value-for-money list.

The Caribbean Islands can be horrifying - and Barbados, Jamaica, Bermuda and St Lucia will stretch the budgets of even the wealthy. Fancy an 'ordinary' three-course meal for $ 96 at St Lucia - or hire a car (bottom of the range) for $ 960 a week in Jamaica!

Seychelles is another place to steer clear of if your means are modest. There, a three-course meal and a bottle of modest wine in a reasonable restaurant will relieve you of $ 125, and petrol for that $ 800-a-week rental car will set you back $ 2.30 a litre.

Restaurant Prices (For Dinner) — Per Person - Drinks not included

	Major Cities	Major Resorts	Small Resorts
DE LUXE	Rs.400-500	Rs.300-400	Rs.100-150
FIRST CLASS	Rs.200-300	Rs.150-250	Rs.100-150
MODERATE	Rs.100-150	Rs.100-125	Rs.50-100
INEXPENSIVE	Rs.75-100	Rs.50-75	Rs.50-100

MAJOR HOTEL CHAINS OF INDIA

The following is a list of hotels operated by the four chains in India.

ASHOK HOTELS

It is a hotel chain operated by a government-owned organisation called India Tourism Development Corporation (ITDC). Operation of hotels is one of its important functions. Others are operation of transport units all over India, running duty-free shops at airports and providing travel-related services.

A. HOTELS

Name of Hotel	No of Rooms	Name of Hotel	No of Rooms
New Delhi		**Aurangabad**	
Ashok	576	Aurangabad Ashok	65
Ashok Yatri Niwas	558	**Bangalore**	
Janpath	212	Hotel Ashok	181
Kanishka	318	**Bhubaneswar**	
Lodhi	207	Kalinga Ashok	28
Qutab	62	**Calcutta**	
Ranjit	186	Airport Ashok	148
Samrat	268	**Hassan**	
Agra		Hassan Ashok	46
Agra Ashok	58		

B. BEACH RESORTS

Name of Hotel	No of Rooms	Name of Hotel	No of Rooms
Kovalam		**Madurai**	
Ashok Kovalam Beach Resort	122	Madurai Ashok	43
Ashok Kovalam Grove	56	**Mysore**	
Mamallapuram		Lalith Mahal Palace	54
Ashok Temple Bay	23	**Patna**	
Imphal		Pataliputra Ashok	56
Imphal Ashok	45	**Pondicherry**	
Jaipur		Pondicherry Ashok	20
Jaipur Ashok	63	**Shillong**	
Jammu		Pinewood Ashok	40
Jammu Ashok	48	**Udaipur**	
Khajuraho		Laxmi Vilas Palace	34
Khajuraho Ashok	40	**Varanasi**	
		Varanasi Ashok	84

C. ASHOK TRAVELLERS LODGES

Name of Hotel	No. of Rooms	Name of Hotel	No. of Rooms
Bodh Gaya	12	**Forest Lodge**	
Kulu	6	Bharatpur	18
Manali	10		

RESERVATIONS

A. **In India**
>Ashok Reservation
>Service,
>ITDC.
>New Delhi.
>*Phone: 600121*
>*Telex: 031-65207*
>*Cable: TOURISM*

B. **Overseas**
1. Air India Offices overseas.
2. ITDC has international linkages for overseas marketing and reservations.
   (a) Odner Hotel Representatives (OHR), Hong Kong. OHR has 15 offices in South-East Asia.
   (b) Golden Tulip Worldwide Hotels Sales and Reservation Offices or KLM Booking Offices.
   (c) Trusthouse Forte Hotels Sales Offices worldwide.

TAJ GROUP OF HOTELS

Founded in 1903, the Taj Group of hotels started as the dream of a pioneering visionary Sir Jamshedji Tata, who wished to build a hotel in India which could excel hotels in Europe. From the late 1960s the company expanded into a hotel chain, first in India and then overseas. The group now operates 25 hotels in India. Four of the Taj Hotels are included in the Leading Hotels of the World International listing.

Name of Hotel	No. of Rooms	Name of Hotel	No. of Rooms
Bombay		*Bangalore*	
The Taj Mahal Intercontinental	650	Taj Residency	180
Hotel President	300	West End Hotel	138
New Delhi		*Calcutta*	
The Taj Mahal Hotel	350	Taj Bengal	200
Taj Palace Hotel	504	*Goa*	
Agra		The Aguada Hermitage	40
Taj-View Hotel	130	The Fort Aguada Beach Resort	120
		The Taj Holiday Village	100

Taj Garden Retreat, Coonoor.

Name of Hotel	No. of Rooms	Name of Hotel	No. of Rooms
Jaipur		*Ootacamund (Ooty)*	
The Rambagh Palace	110	Savoy Hotel	60
The Jai Mahal Palace Hotel	102	*Udaipur*	
		The Lake Palace	85
Raj Mahal Palace	11	Shivniwas Palace	30
Ramgarh Lodge	16	*Varanasi*	
Madras		Hotel Taj Ganges	120
Taj Coromandal	240	*Cochin*	
Connemara Hotel	138	Malabar Hotel	37
The Fisherman's Cove	100		

RESERVATIONS

A. **In India**
 1. Central Reservation Service
    Taj Group of Hotels, Bombay.
    Phone: 2023366
    Telex: 011-2442 TAJBIN
    Cable: PALACE
 2. Regional Sales Offices

B. **Overseas**
 1. New York - c/o. Intercontinental Hotels
    Phone: (212) 812-7939

2. Representation Worldwide of THE LEADING HOTELS OF THE WORLD.
3. UTELL INTERNATIONAL Sales & Reservation Offices (Worldwide) for all Taj group of hotels.

OBEROI GROUP

The story of this chain of hotels is the story of Mr. M.S. Oberoi who rose from the post of an accounts clerk in Cecil Hotel, Shimla, to one of the leading hoteliers of the world. After expanding his network in India, he was the first Indian to manage luxury hotels overseas. He has been aptly described as Conard Hilton of India.

At present, the Oberoi chain operates 12 hotels in India and 13 abroad. The Calcutta, New Delhi and Bombay hotels are included in the Leading Hotels of the World International listing. Their Indian hotels are listed below.

Name of Hotel	No. of Rooms	Name of Hotel	No. of Rooms
Bombay		*Darjeeling*	
Oberoi Towers	700	Oberoi Mount Everest	70
The Oberoi	375	*Gopalpur-On-Sea*	
Calcutta		Oberoi Palm Beach	20
Oberoi Grand	300	*Hyderabad*	
New Delhi		Krishna Oberoi	300
The Oberoi	300	*Khajuraho*	
Oberoi Maidens	75	Jess Oberoi	54
Bhubaneswar		*Shimla*	
Oberoi Bhubaneswar	70	Oberoi Clarkes	35
Srinagar			
Oberoi Palace	100		

RESERVATIONS

A. In India
1. All Oberoi hotels can be booked through the Oberoi Corporate Sales & Marketing Office, Delhi.
   Phone: 2525464
   Telex: 031-56461
   OMDL IN
   Cable: AHI
2. Bookings can also be made through any of the Oberoi Hotels in India.

B. Overseas
1. Through Oberoi Hotels Overseas in Melbourne, Aswan, Fayoum, Cairo, El Arish, Bali, Baghdad, Kathmandu, Dammam, Singapore, Colombo and Kandy.

2. ReservationWorldwide THE LEADING HOTELS of the world.
3. LOEWS Representation International (LRI) Offices.

WELCOMGROUP HOTEL CHAIN

It is the youngest but the fastest growing hotel chain in India. A subsidiary of the India Tobacco Company, one of the country's largest corporate house, all its properties are deluxe. Six of them form part of the Sheraton chain.

WELCOMGROUP SHERATON HOTELS

Name of Hotel	No.of Rooms	Name of Hotel	No.of Rooms
Agra		*Madras*	
Mughal Sheraton	500	Chola Sheraton	100
Bangalore		Park Sheraton	160
Windsor Manor Sheraton	140	*New Delhi*	
		Maurya Sheraton Hotel and Tower	500
Bombay			
SeaRock Sheraton	400		

OTHER WELCOMGROUP HOTELS

Name of Hotel	No.of Rooms	Name of Hotel	No.of Rooms
Andamans		*Jodhpur*	
Bay Island	48	Umaid Bhawan Palace	94
Aurangabad		*Khimsar*	
Rama International	100	Royal Castle	14
Baroda		*Mangalore*	
Welcomegroup Vadodara	102	Manjarun	100
Bhavnagar		*Patna*	
Nilambag Palace	14 Suites	Maurya Patna	80
Gwalior		*Srinagar*	
Usha Kiran Palace	27	Gurkha Houseboats	
Jaipur		Nedous	
Rajputana Palace	224		

RESERVATIONS

For any Welcomgroup Sheraton Hotel call IIT Sheraton Hotels Worldwide or ITC International Ltd, 110 Hillside Avenue, Suite 203, Springfield, New Jersey, 0781 USA. *Tel. (201) 379-773/8990. Fax- 201-379-1473.* Any Welcomgroup hotel in India or General Manager, Marketing, Welcomgroup Maurya Sheraton, Diplomatic Enclave, New Delhi-11021. *Tel.301-0101. Fax- 301-2892.*

HOLIDAY INNS

Name of Hotel	No. of Rooms	Name of Hotel	No. of Rooms
Hyderabad		*Bangalore*	
Holiday Inn Krishna	150	Holiday Inn Bangalore	200
Bombay			
Holiday Inn Bombay	210		

QUALITY INNS

A recent entrant on the Indian hotel scene, the following is a list of their franchised hotels. These hotels offer excellent value for money — and are moderately priced.

Name of Hotel	No. of Rooms	Name of Hotel	No. of Rooms
Ahmedabad		*Goa*	
Quality Suites Shalin	72	Comfort Inn Whispering Palms	54
Bangalore		*Mysore*	
Comfort Inn Ramanashree	67	Quality Inn Southern Star	72
Bombay		*Ootacamund*	
Quality Inn Rangsharda	70	Quality Inn Southern Star	67
Corbett National Park		*Madras*	
Quality Inn Corbett Cottages Jungle Resort	18	Quality Inn Aruna	
Hyderabad			
Quality Inn Green Park	160		

HILTON

Name of Hotel	No. of Rooms
New Delhi Hilton	500

Comfort Inn Jothi Park Ooty

RESERVATIONS

Outside India call Choice Hotels International - toll - free. In India - *11-675-347*.

OTHER HOTEL CHAINS

Name of Place	No. of Rooms
Meridien, New Delhi.	375
Hyatt Regency, New Delhi.	535
Leela Kimpensky, Bombay.	435

MAJOR BEACH RESORTS

Leela Beach, Goa
Majorda Beach Resort, Goa.
120 and 12 Cottages

PALACE HOTELS IN INDIA

There are palaces in India where you can still live like a prince. You can dine under crystal chandeliers, recline on chairs inlaid with ivory, walk on ancient Persian rugs and sleep between silken sheets.

Yes, you can live like a Maharaja in the royal retreats - the palaces of erstwhile Maharajas who have been retired in the Republican India. Their residences were built with lavish opulence that only royalty could have possessed. With all modern conveniences, these palaces now turned hotels offer luxury that no modern imitation can match.

The following is a list of some select Palace Hotels which can be recommended to anyone who wants a new experience.

Jodhpur

Umaid Bhawan Palace: Maharaja Umaid Singh's Palace of Jodhpur is one of the largest and grandest residences in the world.

Jaipur

Rambagh Palace: Built in 1835, it was a suburban palace where royal house parties and fairy-tale weddings took place.

Jai Mahal Palace: It was the creation of a lineage of rulers who took Rajput architecture to its acme. It is here that one sees the refined tastes that guided their prodigious efforts.

Udaipur

Laxmi Vilas Palace: A former royal guest house of Maharaja Bhupal Singh, Laxmi Vilas Palace overlooks the serene Fatehsagar lake.

Lake Palace: In a classic princely style, Prince Jagat Singh built his palace in Lake Pichola - a marble isle in the tranquil waters. It is an airy complex with graceful granite columns built only for royal pleasure and relaxation. Now it is all yours!

Welcomgroup Sheraton Towers

The Ashok Group

Quality Suites Shalin
Ahmedabad

The Oberoi Grand
CALCUTTA, INDIA

Bhavnagar
Nilambag Palace: Built at the turn of the century, this royal residence of the rulers of Bhavnagar reflects the ruler's love for modern and his passion for the past.

Khimsar Castle: Mentioned in the diaries of Emperor Aurangzeb. Romantic in its isolation, one can experience royal hospitality within its formidable walls. It is reached after driving over a moat.

Kolhapur
Shalini Palace: Built in the nineteenth century, the residence of Kolhapur rulers nestles in thick greenery by the side of the serene Renhala Lake.

Gwalior
Usha Kiran Palace: Built shortly after the turn of the century, it was the retreat of royal ladies of The Scindia Court. The palace reflects the romantic past of a bygone era.

Srinagar
The Oberoi Palace: There are few who have not succumbed to the charm of this palace — summer residence of the Maharaja of Kashmir on the picturesque Dal Lake.

Mysore
Lalith Mahal: Globe lights, patterned marble floors and a bushed ambience — Lalith Mahal Palace makes history come alive in its resplendent best.

If you are on a long trip to India and would like to know details about every hotel in India and its tariff, including budget hotels, the best reference book is: *Hotel and Restaurant Guide, India - 1996,* published by the Federation of Hotels and Restaurant Associations of India, M-75 (Market), Greater Kailash-II, New Delhi - 110048.
Telephone: 6411779

EXPLORING INDIA

Chapter 9

JAMMU & KASHMIR
Himalayan Paradise

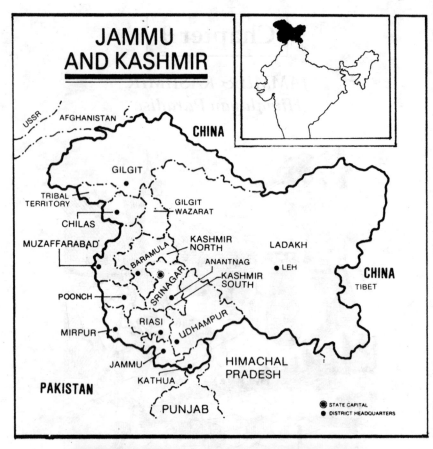

The snowclad Himalayas

Scenic beauty, Gulmarg.

The Himalayan Valley of Kashmir is known all over the world for its beauty and charm. But, few outside the Indian subcontinent know that the State of Jammu and Kashmir is not merely the Vale of Kashmir. It is a very large State, only slightly smaller than the British islands. It has three distinct entities with different climates, flora and fauna and cultures. Not only do the people in three different regions of the State — Jammu, Kashmir and Ladakh — live differently but also speak different languages, worship different gods and have different ethical and moral codes.

This northernmost State of India has an area of 222,236 sq. km. and a population of over 6 million. The State capital is SRINAGAR, a city of beautiful lakes, Mughal gardens and wonderful shopping opportunities. But, winter is so cold in Srinagar that the Government moves down to Jammu during the colder months. The Jammu region in the south, on the periphery of the plains of Punjab, has the legendary JAMMU CITY, home of Hindu Dogras. It is also the winter capital of the State.

To the north lies the Kashmir valley, some 300 km. from Jammu city across forested ravines and steep mountain passes. It is an oval plateau over 5000 feet high and is framed by three Himalayan ranges—the KARAKORAM, ZANSKAR and PIR PANJAL. The capital, Srinagar, nestles amidst the valley's huge lakes, meadows and unique floating gardens.

The third important region of the State is LADAKH — in the north-eastern corner of the state and bordering China. Few realise that it is further north than Tibet. For thousands of years, caravans loaded with goods made their way into the plains of India through Kashmir. The international flavour continues till today. One sees many races, national costumes and traditions. Among the Kashmiris, Kashmiri Pandits who are Hindus (men of letters), are a progressive community, scattered all over India. Pandit Jawaharlal Nehru and Indira Gandhi were part of the Kashmiri Pandit fraternity. Most Kashmiri Pandits have recently been forced to leave Kashmir due to a communal frenzy by Muslim fundamentalists. Ladakh is also popularly called the 'Little Tibet' as its topography, culture and religion are very much similar to Tibet's. In Ladakh, you can see the 7000 metres high peaks of the Zanskar range. It still looks and feels like a medieval Buddhist kingdom, with scores of monasteries on the mountain crags and hundreds of monks wearing red robes and prayer flags fluttering everywhere.

Although Kashmir valley is predominantly Muslim, Jammu and Ladakh are predominantly Hindu and Buddhist, respectively.

Most travellers prefer to fly directly into Srinagar which is less than two hours from the Indian capital, Delhi. LEH, the capital of Ladakh, is also accessible by air from Srinagar but is also reached directly by Indian Airlines flights from Chandigarh. The Srinagar- Leh flight which operates twice a week is one of the most scenic and exciting short flights in the world. It glides through the most beautiful snowclad ranges of mountains in the world. Some young travellers prefer the overland routes to Ladakh via Himachal Pradesh or from Srinagar itself but these routes are arduous.

There are regular bus services to the Jammu and Kashmir State from Delhi and from Pathankot in Punjab to Srinagar via Jammu. The bus journey from Pathankot to Jammu and then to Srinagar can be gruelling but if you take an overnight stop en-route, it can be exciting as you pass through some of the very beautiful areas of the Himalayas.

Another interesting mode of travel to Srinagar is by overnight train from Delhi to Jammu, the rail-head, and then take a taxi to Srinagar. It works out less expensive than the airfare if you have a family to travel with you. The advantage of a taxi ride is that you can stop at any of the numerous scenic spots on the way. There are wayside Indian style restaurants en-route where you can certainly enjoy a hot cup of tea and snacks, and a full meal.

THE VALE OF KASHMIR

Kashmir formed part of the far-flung empire of Emperor Ashoka three centuries before Christ. He spread Buddhism in Kashmir and beyond to Tibet, China and Central Asian Republics. In the 7th and 8th centuries, there was a succession of Hindu kings who gave Kashmir its first impressive monuments. Then followed a dark epoch of feudalistic disarray in which power passed from one ruthless commander to another till a Tibetan Muslim prince took over. He died in 1338 and Commander Shah Mir usurped the kingdom and started a Sultan dynasty. The eighth and the most celebrated Sultan of this dynasty was a popular and wise king, Zainul-Abdin known as Badshah or the Great

King. He patronised art, music and encouraged studies in Hindu and Buddhist scriptures. The king was very popular with the local population as they considered him their patron saint who introduced such arts as shawl making, embroidery, carpet-weaving, papier-mache, silver and wood carvings. He invited guilds of craftsmen from Persia and Samarkand to settle down in the Kashmir valley.

When Mughal Emperor Akbar conquered Kashmir in 1587, he lost his heart to the Valley. Declaring Kashmir as "his private gardens", he indulged himself in boating, water fowling and amused himself through eccentricities like trying to fit in as many of his valets in a hollow Chenar tree as possible — 34 was his best accomplishment. Four generations of Mughal kings made Kashmir their home to avoid the heat and dust of summer. On his way to Kashmir, Akbar's son Jahangir fell ill and when he was asked to express his last wish, he said, "Kashmir... and nothing else." The Mughal kings created elaborate pleasure gardens, marble pavilions and intricate irrigation systems in the valley. By concentrating their attention on Kashmir, they also succeeded in converting the majority of local Hindus into Islam.

As the Mughal power waned, Afghan warlords captured the valley till they were ousted by the Sikh Maharaja Ranjit Singh. Kashmir became part of the Sikh empire. When the Sikhs lost their war against the British in 1846, the latter demanded an indemnity of 500,000 pounds. Since they could not meet this demand, the Sikhs offered Kashmir to the British. The Dogra Maharaja of Jammu offered the British twice the amount asked for as indemnity and thus became the Maharaja of the combined State of Jammu and Kashmir. His descendants ruled over the State till 1947 — when the State acceded to India and became part of the Indian Republic. Pakistan did not like the accession, claiming it should have formed part of Pakistan as it had a majority Muslim population. The strategically important State became the battleground between India and Pakistan during 1948, 1965 and in 1971 wars when Pakistan lost also its other eastern wing which is now the independent Bangladesh. Pakistan is still trying to grab Kashmir by aiding and abetting terrorism in Kashmir. As a result, the Kashmir valley is no longer the bliss it was. Although there are no travel restrictions to Kashmir Valley, not many foreign visitors have been frequenting it due to law and order problems. Trips to Ladakh have increased as there are no terrorist activities there. Jammu is attracting more domestic Indian visitors.

SRINAGAR

Srinagar, the City Beautiful, was established by Emperor Ashoka some 2300 years ago when his daughter Charumati took a fancy to the DAL LAKE during her visit to the region. The present city was founded in the sixth century by King Pravarsen. The king created many of the serpentine waterways that still wriggle through the city like backdoor

entrances to the sprawling Dal Lake, and to the smaller and more secluded NAGIN LAKE. Srinagar's old houses on the Jhelum river with labyrinthine alleys appear not to have changed since the times of the Mughals.

The beauty of the Kashmir valley is such that it transforms itself into a different world every season. It is snowbound and harsh in cold winter when even the Dal Lake is frozen and sometimes you can play cricket on it. But, winter is also the season for sportsmen who throng to nearby GULMARG for skiing and other winter sports. During spring, it is most beautiful with flowers blooming all over the valley, snow melting and trees taking a new shape.

Summers in Kashmir are idyllic and autumns ablaze with burnished copper, scarlet and golden brown leaves. Kashmir is also at its best in April and May when the melting snows cleanse the lakes. The flower-bedecked meadows are drenched in colour. The apple, almond, walnut, cherry, pear and apricot orchards burst into fragrant blossoms. June and July are the two good months for trekking, trout-fishing and water sports. By October, there is scarf-and-sweater weather and in December the first snows are on the horizon.

Houseboats of Srinagar

A unique charm of Srinagar is its 1300 or more houseboats — the floating little hotels on the edge of the Dal Lake or in the secluded areas of the Nagin Lake. How these houseboats originated is an interesting story. The British had taken a fancy to Kashmir and wanted to come here for a holiday during summer. But the wily Maharaja had different ideas. He did not

want the British to come in large numbers and indulge in conspiracies to dethrone him. Therefore, he forbade the non-state subjects to own landed property in Kashmir. But, the ingenious British had a clever idea. They built houseboats which were moored on the waters of the Lake. From these newly-built houseboats, they issued 'at home' invitations to their friends dodging the Maharaja's orders. They trained their Kashmiri cooks into the British gastronomic legacy — they still cook the best English meals this side of the Suez Canal. The British visitors enjoyed their cruises on water in tiny hand-pedalled "Shikaras" — the little boats with giant mattresses, cushioned seats and curtains. Although most of the old British houseboats are no more, there are better and roomier imitations today, some of which could surpass the comforts of a 5-star hotel. The owners compete to woo the tourists with interesting names, like White House, Washington, Love-in-the-Mist and Noorjehan. The owner and his family live in an adjoining separate houseboat where the members of the family join hands to provide service to the guests. A mooring in the idyllic surroundings of the smaller Nagin Lake could in itself be a memorable holiday, as you are totally cut off from the outside world — no telephones, etc. Your only contact with the world is the tiny "Shikara" which is at your beck and call and you can hail it in case you want to go to the shore. For the rest of your needs, you do not have to leave the boat as even the Post Office comes to your boat to sell you postage stamps and deliver letters; so does the flower and fruit sellers. You can also buy film rolls and toothpaste from the vendors who come on boats. And for shopping, you may be sick of people who want to sell you shawls, carpets, silk garments and famous handicrafts of Kashmir. Kashmiris are great salesmen and they can sell you anything — bargaining depends on your skill to haggle. Do not be surprised if a salesman sells you something for Rs. 200 for which he had originally quoted Rs. 1,000. To avoid aggressive salesmanship, do not let any salesman enter your boat. If you allow one, others will not be far behind.

There are some 1,300 houseboats moored on the waters of the lakes and about 1,000 are on the official approved list of the Tourist Department of the State Government. Government has fixed tariff for each houseboat depending on the facilities it offers — the best one is the deluxe category. The Kashmiri boatmen are quite pushy. It is better to book your houseboat through a travel agent in Delhi or check with the TOURIST RECEPTION CENTRE on arrival at Srinagar about the type of boat you need. It is suggested that no houseboat should be hired unseen.

The daily tariff that you pay to the houseboat includes three meals including the breakfast. The cook and his family may present the drab Western food which they think is the right English food. If you have no intention to savour the British menus, tell the cook to make you some of the fine Indian dishes like *Biryani,* excellent *Seekh Kabab* in yoghurt or the *Tandoori* delicacies. These items will whet your appetite. There are some particularly tasty Kashmiri dishes that we recommend — one is *Gushtaba*. Trained Kashmiri cooks pound meat for hours into sausage-like pulp to make meatballs, which are served in creamy sauce and pepper red curry. There are other interesting Kashmiri curries and you can read about them in the chapter on Indian cuisine in the first part of the book.

If eating at the houseboat is no longer attractive, visit the OBEROI PALACE or CENTAUR LAKE VIEW HOTEL where luncheon or dinner for two may cost less than Rs. 500. These hotels can be trusted for good Indian, Kashmiri and Western cuisine. There are other reasonably good cafes and restaurants in the city.

Living in a houseboat may be an exotic way of spending a holiday in Srinagar, but if you value comfort above everything, then go for the Oberoi Palace Hotel, the Royal Palace where Maharaja Hari Singh stayed till 1947. It is built on a 20-acre area on the edge of the sprawling Dal Lake and is now operated by India's major international hotel chain, the Oberois. From its vast, green lawns, you can view the rising and the setting sun on the lake.

An interesting story is told of Lord Mountbatten's visit to this Palace where he stayed when he came in 1947 to persuade Maharaja Hari Singh to accede to India. He shocked the servants of the Palace by sunbathing in the nude.

The Maharaja, it is believed, had agreed to accede to India but the Pathan tribesmen led by officers of Pakistan Army were already approaching Srinagar airport. The Maharaja decided to go for siesta ordering his servants to shoot him in case the Indian army did not reach Srinagar before the tribesmen did. The Indian Army flew down from Delhi in the nick of time to save the airport and also the Maharaja. He, however, abdicated soon after in favour of his only son, Karan Singh, who is now a political leader.

Getting around in Srinagar

The most delightful way of getting around Srinagar is to go by *shikara* — the little "Gondola" of Asia's Venice, i.e., Srinagar. You can hire a shikara to go round the Mughal gardens, gliding on the placid waters of the lake. If you do not want the boatman to accompany you, you may as well borrow his paddle and canoe and move independently. But, do it for a short trip. A long trip can be tiring.

Another way of going round Srinagar is to hire a bicycle and go round the MUGHAL GARDENS through Srinagar's wide boulevards. Srinagar is too spread-out to visit all the places on foot. It is great fun to cycle around the lakeside avenues lined with tall chenar trees or along the narrow causeway from beneath the HARI PARBAT FORT which cuts across the Dal Lake to the NISHAT GARDENS. It is also an inexpensive way of seeing the city. Avoid the crowded streets of the central city with heavy traffic and the smoke emitted by vehicles.

There are plenty of taxis and autorickshaws in town but they are unmetered. You may need some bargaining skill to pay the right fare. If you are not in a bargaining mood, buy a sightseeing bus tour of the city organised by the Department of Tourism, or take a bus trip to Gulmarg and Pahalgam. The cost of an organised tour is only a fraction of what it costs by hired taxis

What to see in Srinagar

Srinagar has been described by some Western visitors as the *Venice of the East* and Kashmir as the *Switzerland of Asia*. Srinagar has many characteristics which are neither Venetian nor Swiss. Its flowering housetops, for instance, are uniquely its own. For a few weeks of April and May before the summer sunburns them up, the roof-tops of Srinagar turn into top-storey flower gardens. The houses of Kashmiris are traditionally made of earth. Watered by the rains and snows of winter, they change into fields of grass in early spring. Soon the flowers start blooming. Many such houses on the Jhelum still blossom into flower gardens, pleasing the onlookers.

The traffic on the Jhelum river is another thing that will fascinate visitors. Families huddled in large vessels move up and down the river to transport timber. Between the large vessels, you can see scores of shikaras go by with their beautiful names and cushioned interiors. From Jhelum, these shikaras glide gently into the Dal and Nagin Lakes. It is here that they serve the residents of the houseboats to take them around.

The scene in the bazars of Srinagar is right from the pages of the book of *Arabian Nights*. You will see men dressed in robes which are uniquely Kashmiri — a long, loose robe *(Choga)* which hangs down to their knees. In winter, they carry under this robe a burning *Kangri* (wicker basket) to keep them warm. The women of Kashmir are strikingly beautiful with almond-shaped eyes and Tartar cheek-bones.

The horse-drawn "tongas" ply on the roads of Srinagar offering an alternative mode of transport to visitors. Old men wearing turbans — mostly white — and younger people wearing fur caps are seen on the roads. Smoking the *hookah* is a habit shared by most Kashmiris. The shops are full of handmade goods — embroidered fabrics or leather, carved woodwork, shawls made of Pashmina wool, papier-mache, silverware, jewellery and carpets in various colours.

Apart from its bazars, the city has a unique landmark — the SHANKARACHARYA TEMPLE. It is located on a sharp hill, 1,000 feet high overlooking the city. Stone steps take you right on top where a small temple dedicated to Lord Shiva stands. It was built in memory of the great Shankaracharya who came to Kashmir from Kerala some 1200 years ago to revive Hinduism which had been eclipsed by Buddhism.

From the top of the Shankaracharya Hills, you can see down a panoramic view of the Valley not only of the city but also of the confluence of the Jhelum and the Dal Lake. There are other temples in Srinagar and in the Kashmir valley. There is the eighth century stone temple built by King Lalitaditya at Martand, near the present-day village of Matton on the road to Pahalgam. The temple lies in ruins. There are more ruins of Lalitaditya's capital city called PARIHASPUR, 5 km. off the road to BARAMULLA. Ruins of another ancient Buddhist settlement are found above the village Harwan near SHALIMAR GARDENS.

The capital, Srinagar, is predominantly Muslim and the town has many mosques. The JAMI-MASJID (built in 1402) is the largest in Kashmir. The PATHAR MASJID was built by Jahangir's wife Noorjahan. The pagoda-like SHAH HAMDAN mosque on the NASEEM LAKE claims to have a relic — the sacred hair of the Prophet Mohammad. Made entirely of wood, the mosque is named after the saint who is credited with the peaceful conversion of millions of Hindus into Islam. Non-Muslims are not allowed into the Mosque but you can peep through the door to see the intricately painted papier-mache ceiling and doors. Unlike the muddy colour of the snow-fed waters of Jhelum, the waters of the two lakes — Dal and Nagin—are transparent. But, due to overuse of the Dal Lake over the years for tourism and other purposes, its size has been reduced to almost half. Besides, the Kashmiris have been growing vegetables and food on its floating gardens, thereby reducing the lake even further. Government is now trying to clean up the lake but its attempts have so far been not very successful.

From your houseboat on the Dal or Nagin Lake, you can see the vegetable market. It is only a short shikara ride away. The farmers emerge early morning from a maze of floating gardens and canals bringing boat-loads of their produce. They gather in an open waterway to buy, sell or barter their produce. The first rays of the dawn tinge the wild gardens of lotus flowers with a delicate pink. The kingfishers are seen darting about, flashing their wings. As the day breaks, the lakes are alive with other activities. It is a unique world of its own not seen anywhere else.

The famous MUGHAL GARDENS of Srinagar are around the Dal Lake. The boulevard road skirts the lake and you can either take the road to see the gardens or hire a leisurely shikara, to see them. The first one to be seen is the CHASHMA SHAHI, which is set into the slopes of its circling hills. Chashma Shahi is attributed to Shahjahan. It means the Royal Spring, named after a natural spring that flows here. The spring waters are believed to have curative properties. You can see many visitors filling up their flasks to take water home or to their hotels. Nearby is the PARI MAHAL which was the Sufi Garden College. Both are small, but offer you beautiful views over the lake.

NISHAT and SHALIMAR are two larger Mughal Gardens, located much further down the boulevard. Nishat is the larger of the two and has an impressive plantation of chenar trees on its highest terrace. The trees were planted during the Mughal period perhaps by the kings themselves. Shalimar is the more famous of the two, due to its romantic association with Emperor Jahangir and his lovely queen Noorjahan. An interesting Sound and Light Show on the love story of the two has been mounted here. Both the gardens are built on a symmetrical plan of central waterways with fountains dividing a series of gardened terraces.

The central piece on the upper terrace of Shalimar is the Baradari. It was here that Jahangir relaxed with his beautiful bride surrounded by a million roses and the heady smell of all of them.

Nagin Lake

A circular drive through apple orchards and rice fields take you from Shalimar to Nagin Lake. Visitors take this drive to see HAZRATBAL, the Muslim shrine which is believed to have the sacred hair of the prophet. A short distance from the mosque is the tomb of Sheikh Mohammad Abdullah, who at one time was called the "Lion of Kashmir" and was the undisputed leader of the Kashmiris, belonging to all religions. But, during recent revival of fundamentalist Islam, the memorial has been threatened by terrorists. Nagin Lake is cleaner and provides quiet solitude to tourists seeking it in houseboats moored on its waters. Beyond Nagin Lake, is the famous HARI PARBAT built three hundred years ago by Emperor Akbar. It is a relatively small fortress atop a hill. Across the lakes from Hari Parbat is the famous Hindu TEMPLE OF SHANKARACHARYA. The view from the fortress is superb — the lakes and their houseboats, waterways and gardens — and the seven original bridges spanning the serpentine flow of Jhelum river.

CRAFTSMEN OF KASHMIR

Kashmir is known for its exquisite craftsmanship which has flourished over the centuries. During the long and dreary winter months in the valley, craftsmen work in the warm comfort of their homes to make handicrafts and sell them to tourists coming there during summer months. If you drive through the countryside, you will see hundreds of carpet looms hidden in crumbling village homes. The hand-knotted Persian rugs are washed in open courtyards. Delicate wool embroidery is often done by men stitching away under the apple boughs. Fine quality shawls made from small goats found in Ladakh are expensive. The royal *Shahtoosh* shawls are so soft that they can be passed through a finger ring.

Then there are more traditional rugs of Kashmir called *Namdas*. These are decorated with simple designs and are popular with the visitors as they are inexpensive.

Among other crafts of Kashmir are the papier-mache work. It includes beautifully painted boxes, ashtrays and other utility goods. The art has been passed from one generation to another.

Wood carving is another special Kashmiri art which has a certain uniqueness about it. The walnut furniture made in Kashmir is exquisite and work done on the furniture speaks of Kashmiri patience and workmanship.

Kashmiris love dance and music, and marriages and other festive occasions provide them with opportunities to enjoy themselves. Influenced by their Hindu forefathers, Kashmiris are seen worshipping wayside shrines dedicated to holymen throughout the Valley.

On festive occasions, Kashmiris serve a feast called Wazwan. It consists of 36 meat dishes prepared specially by highly trained chefs and eaten together — all dipping their fingers in the same pot, perhaps an expression of Islamic fraternity.

GULMARG

Beyond Srinagar, the Kashmir valley has many other beautiful places to visit and see. Two most easily accessible and popular spots are GULMARG and PAHALGAM. Gulmarg, the Meadow of Flowers (height 8500 feet), is only 52 km. from Srinagar to the southwest. Here you will find in rather Europeanised surroundings with an 18-hole Golf Course, a club and several nice hotels. During the British Raj, Gulmarg hosted the British Resident and his fellow Europeans. They created a European hill resort which is very much still there in spirit as well as in environments. Walking along Gulmarg's circular path you only have to look down to have a complete view of the valley including the capital, Srinagar. A fine view can also be had of NANGA PARBAT — the naked mountain — which is over 26,000 feet and dominates the entire region. A few kilometres before returning to Srinagar, take a turn to the left on Baramula Road at SANGRAMA — the track leads to WULAR — the largest fresh-water lake in

Kashmir and the second largest in India. It is something like the Lake Geneva of Switzerland. It has a beautiful setting, with HARAMUK MOUNTAIN at its head. The sunset at the lake is breathtaking. Leaving Wular and only a few kilometres away is another lake — MANASBAL. It is known for its lotus blossoms. From here, you may take the road that branches to the left at GANDARBAL into the SINDH VALLEY. As you pass through the Valley, the mountains seem to come down precipitously on both sides. The hills around are covered with a special kind of Kashmiri pine trees. The average height of this great conifer is over one hundred feet.

SONAMARG

At the head of the Sindh Valley is SONAMARG, a small but uniquely beautiful hill resort. It is located on the road to Ladakh and has in recent times accommodated travellers on the way to ZOJI LA PASS. At an altitude of 8,860 feet, Sonamarg is 84 km. from Srinagar. Literally translated, it means "The Golden Meadow", deriving its name from the golden colour of its massed spring flowers.

AMARNATH

As you ascend the LIDDER VALLEY, the scene is more majestic. Coming down again, you pass the sacred cave of AMARNATH where Hindu pilgrims come in thousands from all parts of India to have a glimpse of Shivalingam formed from iced snow. The cave is situated amidst iced snow at a height of 13,000 feet — and is totally cut off from the rest of the world during winter. The most auspicious occasion to visit Amarnath for a pilgrimage is on the night of the full moon in the month of *Shravan* (July-August) every year.

PAHALGAM

Down the Lidder Valley is another very popular hill resort of the Kashmir valley — PAHALGAM. While Gulmarg was the favourite of the British during the Raj, rich Indians patronised Pahalgam. Climatic conditions favour tent life and visitors prefer to spend their holidays under specially pitched tents on its vast camping grounds along the Lidder river. At a height of 7,200 feet the tourists do not feel fatigue as they do at higher altitudes. The flora and fauna is good and the scenery captivating.

It is from Pahalgam that the pilgrim groups often take off for the Cave of Amarnath — a 4-day trip. Dotted around the town are clusters of government-owned tourist huts, tented camps and private lodges. Foreign visitors like Pahalgam because they can relax in a surrounding that compares favourably with the Swiss Alps or they can undertake adventure treks into the high altitude meadows beyond.

Tents and pack ponies can be hired at Pahalgam for a trek to the 11,800 feet high KOLAHOI GLACIER. The trek is done in three days. Ladakh from Pahalgam is an arduous ten-day journey on foot.

On the way to Kolahoi in summer, you may find it interesting to share your camping grounds with nomadic Bakarwals — shepherds who move into higher grounds to let their sheep, goats and buffaloes graze. The men are tall, sturdy and handsome. Their women plait their hair into hundreds of tiny braids. They move with families, children tied on the backs of pack ponies with pots and pans.

Continuing the journey up the bridle path on the way to the glacier, you see a beautiful resting spot, LIDDERWAT. Although the sun shines brightly here, yet the tall encircling pines keep the shades very dark. Moving from Lidderwat, you arrive at the great frozen river that stands motionless. This is Kolahoi Glacier. And, if you drink a little bit of the melted water, you feel great relief — like having a chilled glass of champagne.

Trekking in the high altitude area of Himalayas is not without hazards and must be done in the company of trained guides. Up to May and June, the snow bridges can be relied upon. Later, they can be treacherous and undertaking a trek after October is undoubtedly risky.

ANANTNAG

Down the Lidder Valley is ANANTNAG, a little town, where we rejoin the Vale of Kashmir. Again, it is the land of spreading chenars and the poplar avenues which have welcomed and charmed visitors for centuries.

EXPLORING LADAKH

Ladakh, as we mentioned earlier, is a separate province of the State of Jammu and Kashmir and distinct in its culture and topography. It is a region which was opened to tourists only a few years ago. Since then, foreign tourists, particularly young visitors have thronged to Ladakh to see its unspoiled beauty.

The Ladakh region is part mountain, part flat terrain and is quite arid. It is a high altitude desert and its capital LEH, is located at an altitude of 3,330 metres — 11,500 feet above sea level. The landscape is glorious but stark — the surrounding mountains are painted in colours that only Nature could choose.

The region is predominantly Buddhist and several important Buddhist monasteries dominate the region. Some of them are located within visiting distance from LEH. The spectacular ZANSKAR mountains are where the venturesome go for river-rafting and for exhilirating treks. The clean, dry air, magnificent scenery and the warm hospitality of the people makes Ladakh truly memorable.

The territory of Ladakh represents some 70 per cent of area of the State of Jammu and Kashmir with a population of 1,20,000 only. It has one of the lowest density of population in the world — less than one or two per square kilometre. The effect of elevation and isolation amid snowy mountains has made the countryside forbiddingly arid and produced one of the most unusual climates in the world. Burning heat during the day is followed by extreme cold at night, and everything is pierced by dryness in the air. The average annual rainfall is less than four inches. As you drive up and down this arid, barren, sun-beaten and wind-swept countryside, you get a peculiar feeling that you are somewhere on the lunar surface.

Despite this forbidding description of the climate, Ladakh has its charm and great tourist attraction. The blue sky, brisk sunshine and green valleys dot the region like oasis and make up for its starkness. The cultural life of the people inhabiting different valleys is very interesting.

Ladakh can be divided into a number of valleys — the principal one among them being the Indus which runs through the entire region from southeast to northwest.

Ladakh is connected with the Kashmir valley by a black-topped road which remains open from May to November. Besides, there are air services to Leh. Another route has now been charted through the Kulu-Manali valleys of Himachal Pradesh.

The road from Srinagar passes through picturesque villages on the banks of the Sindh river. Leaving the green Sindh Valley at Sonmarg, the first pass to be crossed is Zoji La — at a height of 11,578 feet. On the other side of Sindh Valley is Dras Valley which is arid. Below Tashgram starts the granite country. Mountains rise on both sides to serrated ridges of 17,000 to 18,000 feet.

After a tortuous drive, you reach the second largest town of Ladakh—Kargil. The population is less than 3,000 people. Kargil is situated in Suru Valley where the Suru river flows and meets the Indus at a place called Marul. There are a few villages in this valley at a height of 9000 feet. The valley has less snow in winter and the ultra-violet rays are stronger. That explains why it has an abundance of fruit trees, mainly mulberry and apricot. Willows and poplars grow along the water courses.

After crossing the Suru, the road goes through a sandy plateau followed by another narrow valley. You then reach Mulbekh village, which has an important monastery, perched on a high rock. A large statue of Maitriya — future Buddha — is carved on the roadside. You cross another pass, 12,000 feet. Namika-La. Later, the road winds up to the highest pass on the Srinagar-Leh Road — Fatula, 13,497 feet above sea level.

Another half hour's drive, takes you to the mysterious Lamayuru — Ladakh's oldest monastery — looming like a Hollywood movie backdrop of Shangri-La. Lamayuru is venerated. It is believed that one of the great Tibetan teachers, Norapa, meditated here for several years. Like all Ladakh monasteries, it is also a complex of buildings with shrines dedicated to different gods and incarnations of Lord Buddha.

In Ladakh, monasteries are traditional centres of culture and religious activities. Monasteries are also the biggest landowners. Always depending on donations, they have now switched to charging visitors admission fees ranging from Rs. 10 to 20, a small amount.

The road crosses the Indus near KHALSE with ruins of ZORAWAR FORT adjacent to the bridge. From Khalse, the road follows the Indus and is more or less level. You are nearing Leh, the capital of Ladakh, passing through a number of terraced plains.

LEH

Leh is a compact town of 12,000 people. Its most striking building is the abandoned palace of the former rulers. Houses cover the lower slopes that rise up to the spur on which the Palace stands, rising boldly for ten storeys from the rock. Higher up on the same ridge is the monastery and the towers of an old fortification. On the plain below is the new part of the town which is rapidly spreading in all directions. While Leh has come a long way from the time when Polo was played on its main street, it retains its pleasant traditional quality. There are lovely vegetable sellers dressed in coral necklaces and turquoise-encrusted headgear, sitting comfortably behind the baskets of vegetables. Thanks to tourism, the city now has some 80 registered hotels and guest-houses — some even 2-room family apartments for hire during the tourist season. But tourism has also changed the place.

On arrival, the visitors should take a day of rest due to exertion caused by Leh's high altitude. It is not advisable to start exploring Leh immediately after leaving the plains. It is necessary to get used to the high altitude.

Monasteries

Leh is the town of Buddhist monasteries. A look at the monasteries gives you also a peep into the life of the people of Ladakh. The most visited monasteries are SHEY, THIKSEY and HEMIS, all spread along the river Indus. It does not take very long to visit them. The best time to visit the monasteries is early morning or late evenings when the priests are saying their prayers and doing their mystical chanting. The ringing of bells and blowing of long brass horns lend a magical touch.

Shey is the oldest of the three monasteries. But, it is not in regular use. It is, therefore, open only till nine in the morning. The monastery has a 2-storey high statue of Lord Buddha seated in meditation. Above and below are the crumbling walls of the old summer capital of Ladakh.

Chortens above Tso-Moriri

Thiksey is situated on a hill-top in picturesque surroundings. From here, you can enjoy the view of the Sindh Valley below. The monastery has rooms full of statues, stupas and Tankhas — religious paintings of all kinds. It is 17 km. from Leh and is one of the largest monasteries.

HEMIS GOMPA is the biggest and very richly endowed monastery of Ladakh. It is about 40 km. from Leh on the Leh-Manali Road. It is not visible from the road as it is located in a side valley. Unfortunately, the monastery authorities had a bad experience with visiting tourists as some of its precious exhibits were pilfered. Now, they have hidden many of these. In June, a great festival is celebrated every year for three days. Many visitors come to watch it.

There are other monasteries too in the Ladakh countryside. About 3 km. from Leh is the GOMPA OF KAUSHIK BAKULA. It contains numerous small statues of pure gold and many interesting *Tanakas* (paintings). It should be visited in the evening when it is well-lit.

SPITUK is yet another interesting monastery, several kilometres short of Leh on Srinagar road. It has a totally new Gompa within the monastery as well as the old Gompa which has been restored. Higher up in the hill is a chamber housing the enormous statue of goddess Kali. Its face is covered and uncovered only once in a year in a mela which takes place in the month of January.

A Happy People

The Ladakhi Buddhists are a very happy people who love dancing, music and sports. Their favourite sports are archery and polo. They make a special kind of beer from barley which is called "Chang".

Most Ladakhis are farmers and they make their living by ploughing their small, dry plots with sturdy *Dzos* — cattle crossbred from yaks and hill cows. People living in villages survive on a simple diet of roasted barley or buck-wheat flour called *Tsampa*. They drink green salt tea mixed with yak butter.

EXPLORING JAMMU

If you travel by car, taxi or train to the State of Jammu and Kashmir, you have to pass through Jammu. Jammu is also the terminal station for the Indian railway system. Most visitors stay in Jammu for the night and take off for Kashmir early morning. The city has a Tourist Reception Centre where you can stay for the night. A few other reasonably good hotels are also there in Jammu.

Jammu, the summer capital of the State, is the home of the sturdy Dogras who ruled over the entire State in recent times till 1947. Little is known of the early history of Jammu. According to legend, the city was founded by the 9th century king Jambu-lochan, after whom it is named. This king is believed to have built the monumental BAHU FORT overlooking the Tawi river. In 1730, the region came under the control of war-like Dogras who continued their sway in the entire state till India's independence and its subsequent merger in the Indian Union. During the 18th and 19th centuries, there was a revival of arts, particularly in the field of paintings, under the Dogra rulers. Artists created exquisite miniature paintings of courts and other scenes. These miniatures are referred to as belonging to the Pahari School. Although Jammu is considered to be only a stopover point for moving to higher regions of the Himalayas, it has some interesting places to visit. If you have time, a two-day stopover may be rewarding, particularly during the cooler months.

As part of your sightseeing, it should be interesting to visit the two ART GALLERIES of Jammu. The better one is located opposite the New Secretariat. The Gallery has a rich display of Dogra art belonging to the Pahari and Basholi schools. Only a limited selection is on display, but to see more you can request the curator who is willing to oblige. Among other exhibits are terracottas, medieval weapons, sculptures and ancient manuscripts.

The AMAR MAHAL MUSEUM, built by the Dogra Raja, Amar Singh, in 1907 has a very large collection of royal miniature paintings and manuscripts. It overlooks the Tawi river. The portraits of past Dogra Rajas tell you more about their life and times than any other contemporary book. The museum is open every day except on Sundays when it is open for half a day only.

A 10-minute drive from the museum takes you to the ancient BAHU FORT, located over a hill. The fort is in ruins. Its ramparts, however, swarm with devotees who come to pay their homage to goddess Kali. There is temple dedicated to her in the fort.

But, the most outstanding landmark in Jammu is the RAGHUNATH TEMPLE, built by Maharaja Gulab Singh in 1835. The temple is dedicated to Lord Rama and is an impressive structure put up by a devout king in the now crowded bazar area. The temple is only a few minutes walk from the Tourist Office in Jammu. Around the temple are the shopping areas.

Jammu-Srinagar Road

On the road leading to Srinagar, there are interesting places. Most of them can be reached from Jammu only. Buses do not stop at any of these places. First comes AKHNOOR, the place where the Chenab river enters the plains. It is only 32 km. to the north-west of Jammu. This was the route which the Mughal kings took to reach Srinagar. Emperor Jahangir died here and was temporarily buried at a place called CHINGAS.

BASHOLI, fairly close to Dalhousie in Himachal Pradesh, is the home of BASHOLI SCHOOL OF PAINTINGS.

SURINSAR and MANSAR LAKES are located east of Jammu in picturesque settings. There is a religious festival held here annually.

VAISHNO DEVI, the famous Hindu shrine, attracts million pilgrims every year. The devotees take an arduous route, 12 km. uphill to reach the shrine to prove their devotion. The trek starts from KATRA where buses terminate.

At RIASI in Jammu district, 80 km. beyond Katra, are the ruins of the fort built by General Zoravar Singh who valiantly fought the Chinese over the control of Ladakh

KUD, a popular stop for luncheon on the way to Srinagar, is a hill resort in its own rights. Several Indian visitors prefer to spend their holidays here. BATOTE, another 12 km. ahead, was an overnight stop for buses on the way to Srinagar before the construction of the Jawahar Tunnel, which has made it possible for buses to reach Srinagar in 10 hours. Otherwise, the trip took almost two days.

PATNITOP is yet another hill resort in the Jammu region. It has become the nucleus of tourist developments in the area, with a tourist bungalow, tourist huts and some small hotels.

SANASAR at 2079 metres is set in a beautiful valley. It is a centre of nomadic Gujjar tribes. The place has a tourist bungalow and some tourist huts for accommodation. Off the Jammu-Srinagar Road, KISHTWAR is a beautiful place. You can trek from here to Srinagar. Another trekking path from Kishtwar leads you to ZANSKAR. There are many waterfalls in the area.

The Jawahar Tunnel which links Jammu province with the Kashmir valley, is 2500 metres long. It is 200 km. from Jammu and 93 km. from Srinagar. It has two passages for incoming and outgoing traffic. Before its construction, visitors had to take the longer route and during winter months, Kashmir was often cut off from the rest of India as the road was snowbound.

In the region before the Tunnel, you will hear people speaking Kashmiri as well as Dogri and, beyond the tunnel, is the green Kashmir valley and you hear the Kashmiri tongue. The road passes through long poplar avenues which have welcomed visitors for centuries.

Accommodation with basic amenities is available at most of these places for visitors. Check with the Tourist office.

SRINAGAR — STD Code 0194

GENERAL INFORMATION
Population: 900,000 (1991 census)
Altitude: 1586 metres (5281 ft)
Climate :

	Temperature	
	Max.	Min.
Winter	16^0 c	-2^0 c
Summer	31^0 c	7^0 c

Season: Throughout the year
Clothing
Summer : light woollens.
Winter : heavy woollens.

HOW TO GET THERE

By Air : Srinagar is connected to Delhi, Bombay, Ahmedabad, Amritsar, Chandigarh, Jammu and Leh by Indian Airlines Services.

By Rail: The nearest railhead is Jammu Tawi (305 km) from Delhi which has direct connections with Agra, Amritsar, Bhopal, Bombay, Calcutta, Cochin, Delhi, Kanyakumari, Lucknow, Madras, Pune, Trivandrum, Varanasi, etc.

By Road: Srinagar is connected by road and is
    305 km. from Jammu
    434 km. from Leh
    548 km. from Amritsar
    741 km. from Chandigarh
    892 km. from Delhi.

There are regular bus services to Delhi, Jammu, Gulmarg, Pahalgam, Leh and Kargil. There are fixed rates for hiring taxi, jeep and *jongas* (6-seaters) on these routes.

LOCAL TRANSPORT

Tourist taxis, metered taxis, tongas and coach services are available for road travel and shikaras as taxis for sightseeing by boat. The J&K Tourism Directorate has laid down fixed rates for specific tours and for point-to-point travel.

CONDUCTED TOURS

1. Full-day tour to Pahalgam.
2. Full-day tour to Gulmarg.
3. Half-day tour of the Moghul Gardens.
4. Special evening tour to Shankaracharya Hill and Chashma Shahi Gardens.
5. Cruise on Dal Lake.
6. Full-day tour to Daksun, Achabal and Kokarnag.
7. Full-day tour to Sonamarg.
8. Full-day tour to Wular.
9. Full-day tour to Kokarnag.

(Contact the Tourist Reception Centre, *Phone : 76298* (From 6 A.M. to 6 R.M.).

WHERE TO STAY

Deluxe
1. Centaur Lake View Hotel
   Phone : 77601, 73135
   Telex : 375-205 CLVH IN
   Cable : CENTAUR
2. Oberoi Palace
   Phone : 71241-42, 75651
   Telex : 375-201 LXSR
   Cable : OBHOTEL

Standard
4. Hotel Boulevard
   Phone : 77089
   Cable : YASHMIN
4. Hotel Nehrus
   Phone : 73641, 79471
   Cable : NEHRUGUEST
5. Hotel Tramboo Continental
   Phone : 73914, 71718
   Cable : HOST
6. Asia Brown Hotel
   Phone : 73856, 73844
   Cable : ASIAOTELS
7. Ahdoo's
   Phone : 72593
8. Hotel Broadway
   Phone : 75621, 22, 23
   Telex : 375-212 B'WAY
   Cable : BROADWAY
9. Hotel Sabena
   Phone : 78046
   Cable : SABENA
10. Hotel Jehangir
    Phone : 71830, 31
    Cable : JEHANOTEL

Houseboats
1. Hotel Shangrila
   Phone : 72422
   Cable : SHANGRILA
2. Hotel Zamrud
   Phone : 75263, 75614, 15
   Cable : ZAMRUD
3. Meena Bazar Group of Houseboats
   Phone : 74044, 77662, 75051
   Telex : 375-358
   Cable : FABULOUS
4. M.S. Baktoo Group of Houseboats
   Phone : 78698, 79612, 13
   Telex : 0375-274 KHE IN
5. Welcomgroup Gurkha Houseboat
   Phone : 75229

WHAT TO SEE

1. DAL and NAGIN LAKES. Fed by natural springs. Attractive houseboats are moored alongside. Shikaras(small boats) criss-cross the lakes presenting a unique picture.
2. The MUGHAL GARDENS of SHALIMAR, NISHAT BAGH and CHASHMA SHAHI are beautifully laid out with fountains and cascading streams in their midst.
3. PARI MAHAL, once a Buddhist monastery, was converted into a School of Astrology by Emperor Shahjahan's son, Dara Shikoh.
4. SHANKARACHARYA TEMPLE, on top of a hill, offers an excellent view of the valley.
5. HARI PARBAT, a hill believed to have appeared at the spot where Goddess Parvati killed a demon.

EXCURSIONS

1. GULMARG (56 km), the meadow of flowers. Has the highest green golf course in the world and is a convenient base for treks to the Himalayas. Offers an excellent view of the peak, Nanga Parbat. Has winter sport facilities. Also worth visits are KHILANMARG (4 km) and ALPATHAR LAKE (13 km from Gulmarg).
2. PAHALGAM (96 km.), through which flows the Lidder and Sheshnag streams, is the take-off point for treks to the Kolahoi Glacier and to several high altitude lakes, to the AMARNATH CAVE and to SONAMARG, the meadow of gold.
3. AVANTIPUR (29 km.), where there are ruins of a 9th century Hindu Temple.
4. The DACHIGAM WILDLIFE SANCTUARY (21 km). Can be visited with special permits from the Chief Wildlife Warden.
5. ACHABAL (58 km) was once the pleasure retreat of Empress Noorjahan. Has a trout hatchery.
6. DAKSUM (85 km). A peaceful forest glade girdled by mountains.
7. MARTAND (64 km) has the ruins of a Sun Temple built in the 7th century.
8. GANDARBAL (19 km), a camping site, KOKARNAG (70 km), with its botanical and rose gardens, MANASBAL (32 km), the deepest lake in Kashmir, VERINAG (80 km), the source of River Jhelum, WULAR (60 km), India's second largest fresh water lake and YUSMARG (40 km), a valley in the Pir Panjal mountains, are excellent excursions spots.
9. LEH (435 km), the capital of Ladakh. This is a land of high mountains and Buddhist monasteries.

Note: Because of the fear of terrorism, Kashmir valley is not very safe to visit at present.

GULMARG

WHERE TO STAY
Standard accommodation is available at
1. Highlands Park Hotel
   Phone: 207, 230
   Cable: HIGHLANDS
   Telex: 0375-320 HHPF IN
2. Hill Top
   Phone: 277, 245
3. Hotel Ornate Woodlands
   Phone: 68
   Cable: ORNATECLUB

PAHALGAM

WHERE TO STAY
1. Pahalgam Hotel (3-star)
   Phone: 26, 52
   Cable: PAHALGAM HOTEL
2. Hotel Woodstock.
   Phone: 27
   Cable: WOODSTOCK

There are also several Tourist Huts, a Tourist Bungalow and Dormitory (Contact the Tourist Reception Centre, Srinagar).

SHOPPING

Kashmir has innumerable handicrafts. Carpets, embroidered woollen caps and jackets, articles made of beaten and carved silver, articles made of walnut wood and papier mache, silks and embroidery are a few of the wide range of handicrafts available. The famous embroidered shawls, the Jamawar, silk-soft Pashmina shawls, crewel embroidery, *namdahs* (rugs), embroidered and gold and silver dresses, capes, boleros and ponchos, stone-studded jewellery, filigree, enamelware and many other artifacts make Kashmir a shopper's dream.

ENTERTAINMENT

A sound and light show is held every night in season in the Shalimar Gardens, recreating the love of Emperor Jahangir and his queen, Noorjahan.

Sports Facilities

Trout fishing in the ice-cold waters is a popular pastime (Contact Director of Fisheries, Tourist Reception Centre, *Phone*: 76298 for permits).

Hiking and Trekking are the best ways to see the mountains and the valleys of Kashmir. There are any number of treks. Popular treks are to the Kolahoi Glacier from Pahalgam, to several Himalayan lakes from Sonmarg, etc. (For information on treks contact the Tourist Reception Centre, Srinagar.)

Water sports, such as water skiing, surfing and swimming are best at Gagribal, part of the Dal Lake. River-running on the Indus through Ladakh in rubber rafts over rapids is a new adventure sport.

Gulmarg offers excellent facilities for winter sports. Ski instructors give training in skiing, ice skating, ski-bobbing, tobogganing and sledging (season for winter sports ... December to March, sometimes up to mid-April).

Golfing at Gulmarg, the highest golf green in the world, attracts many visitors.

LEH (STD CODE: 01982)

GENERAL INFORMATION
Population : 10,000 (1991 census)
Altitude : 3514 metres (11702 ft)
Climate :

	Temperature	
	Max.	Min.
Winter	8^0 c	-14^0 c
Summer	25^0 c	-1^0 c

Season : May to November
Clothing
Summer : light woollens.
Winter : heavy woollens

HOW TO GET THERE

By Air: Leh is connected to Srinagar, Delhi and Chandigarh by air.
Note: Those over 50 years of age or with heart trouble should check with a doctor before flying to such a high altitude.
By Rail: The nearest railhead is Jammu (739 km)
By Road: Leh is
    434 km. from Srinagar and
    739 km. from Jammu by road.
There is a motorable road between Srinagar and Leh via Kargil. Regular coach and ordinary bus services are available during the tourist season.

There are fixed rates laid down by the J&K Government for the Srinagar-Leh and Kargil-Leh journeys for taxi-cars, jeeps and *jongas* (6-seaters).

There are also fixed rates for jeeps for the Leh-Zanskar Valley route.

WHERE TO STAY

There are several hotels which can be booked through the Tourist Reception Centre, Srinagar, or the Assistant Director, Tourism, Leh.

Tourist Bungalaws can be booked through the above offices.

Tented accommodation set up by the J & K Tourism Corporation at Choglamsar, Leh, can also be booked here.

Continental food is available at the hotels.

Reservation can also be made through Mountain Travel India Pvt. Ltd. i/1, Rani Jhansi Road, New Delhi. *Phones: 7525357/ 7771055. Fax: 7777483.*

WHAT TO SEE

1. LEH KHAR PALACE, built in the 16th century. There are wall paintings on the life of the Buddha. It has a collection of 100-year old tankhas, statues etc.
2. The LEH MONASTERY which houses a solid gold statue of the Buddha.
3. The LEH MOSQUE of Turko-Iranian architecture, built in 1594.

4. TSEMO GOMPA, one of the royal monasteries.

EXCURSIONS

1. SHANKAR GOMPA (3 km.) has an outstanding collection of small statues of pure gold and paintings.
2. SPITUK MONASTERY (8 km.) has a collection of tankhas and face masks.
3. SHEY PALACE AND MONASTERY (15 km.), the summer palace of the former Raja of Leh. The monastery has a 2-storeyed statue of the sitting Buddha (visit to be arranged through the Lama beforehand).
4. THIKSEY MONASTERY (19 km.) en route to Hemis, presents a panoramic view of the Indus Valley and a collection of art in its chambers.
5. FIANG GOMPA (20 km.), the monastery of the red sect of Buddhist, has an exquisite collection of statues and tankhas.
6. HEMIS GOMPA (49 km.) has an impressive collection of tankhas, gold statues and stupas embedded with precious stones.
7. LAMAYURU (125 km.), Ladakh's oldest monastery. These are caves carved into the mountains.
8. ALCHI and LIHIR GOMPAS (135 km.), have 1000-year-old wall paintings.
9. MULBEKH MONASTERY (190 km.) has a huge standing Buddha carved out of rock.

FESTIVALS OF LOCAL INTEREST

1. HEMIS FESTIVAL (in June) commemorates the birth of Guru Padmasambhava, who fought with demons to protect his people. For 3 days there is gaiety, joy and worship. Masked dances are part of the celebrations.
2. LOSAR dating back to the 15th century, it is celebrated in the 11th month of the Buddhist year. There are several more festivals.

SHOPPING

Hand-woven carpets with dragon designs, copper and silver trinkets set with turquoise tankhas or scrolls. (Buying and selling of antiques is forbidden by law.)

SPORTING PASTIMES/TREKS

1. Archery contests are held in the season.
2. Trekking in Ladakh is spectacular as it goes through high mountains. However, it is advisable to be fully equipped before setting out, and to take a porter and ponies from Leh, Lamayuru or Padam, from where the treks commence. Some famous treks are — Leh-Kargil, Kargil-Suru-Zanskar-Kishtwar-Manali and Kargil-Suru-Wardwan-Kishtwar-Pahalgam. There are also many short treks.

Note: Take a tent, a good sleeping bag, tinned food and juices, cotton and warm clothing, essential medicines, lotions and creams (for sunburns).

Photography

Photography by still cameras is permitted free of charge, and nominal charges levied for movie cameras used for non-professional purposes. For documentary and feature films, there are higher charges.

Typical wayside line Ladakh

Rafting down the Jhelum

Chapter 10

HIMACHAL PRADESH
The Himalayan Retreat

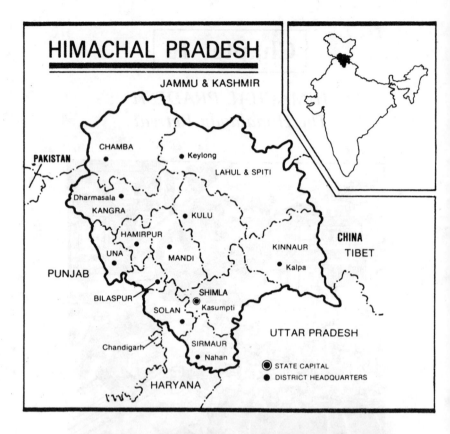

The mighty Himalayas

Nestling in the northern lap of Himalayan ranges, Himachal Pradesh, literally translated, means the land of the snows. It abounds in exotic valleys, green hill slopes, snow-capped peaks and gushing rivers and streams. Sparsely populated and essentially a rural country, Himachal Pradesh is for those seeking a quiet and cool holiday.

The State straddles the Himalayas from the foothills over LAHAUL and SPITI and beyond. Its capital, SHIMLA, was once the summer capital of the British Empire in India. The State is accessible by road from Pathankot (Punjab) in the west, Chandigarh in the south and Dehradun (UP) in the east. It is connected by rail from Kalka to Shimla. There is another rail link between Pathankot and Joginder Nagar. Besides, a regular air service operates between Delhi and Shimla and Delhi and Kulu.

Most people of Himachal Pradesh are Hindus and there are some small pockets with Buddhist influence. The arrival of His Holiness the Dalai Lama in DHARAMSALA has made Himachal Pradesh a second home for the Tibetan Buddhists. The State can boast of some 6,000 temples. People of Himachal live through a cycle of rituals and ceremonies all their life. They are happy and have colourful folk-dances. Every occasion is an occasion for dance. The traditional house of the Himachali people in the rural areas is an interesting structure of three storeys—the lowest for the household cattle, the middle for storage of grains and the top floor for living.

SHIMLA

The most famous city of Himachal Pradesh is SHIMLA, its capital city. The cool mountain air bears the fragrance of wild flowers in the surrounding hills. And, as the melting snows temper the heat, the honeymooners promenade along the Mall, the main street of the capital. It was once the summer capital of the British Raj. The setting of Rudyard Kipling's *Plain Tales from the Hills,* the city derives its name from Shimla — a name for goddess Kali, revered by the local people. Shimla was discovered by some British Officers who were chasing the Gurkhas from this region during their war with the Nepalese in 1814. In 1822, Major Kennedy started a new trend by building a permanent residence at this place. Others soon followed.

The British developed a special attachment with Shimla which amounted almost to an obsession. They developed what used to be called the "Punjab Head". They found it impossible to work in the intense heat of Punjab during summer months and take correct administrative decisions. Shimla soon became a glamorous summer bolt-hole for the British and Anglo-Indian elite. There were endless rounds of dinners, parties, picnics, amateur theatricals and furtive meetings between young British Officers and the so-called "grass widows" whose husbands sweated in the plains. Shimla gained respectability in 1864 when the Viceroy, Lord Lawrence, visited the hill resort and announced that Shimla would henceforth be the summer capital of the British Empire in India.

Thus began the annual exodus of Government of India with all the paraphernalia that goes with it — the guards, private staff, public servants, senior officers and their families, Army headquarters and an entourage to serve all of them followed. Cart-loads of files were despatched. Access to Shimla became a little easy when Kalka-Shimla rail link was opened in 1904. The Viceregal Lodge built in Shimla was so lavish that the Government of India had to invent Income Tax to pay for it ! Before that there was no Income Tax Act in India.

No carriages except for the Viceroy and his staff were allowed to ply on the Mall. All others had to use rickshaws drawn by four hefty coolies or use curtained sedan chairs carried on the shoulders of the coolies. Indians, even the rich ones, were not allowed to walk on the Mall except the coolies who carried the master race. The Indians were required to walk on what is even now called the Lower Bazaar. The Viceregal Lodge had a staff of 400 — not including 100 cooks. In 1913, when Sir Edward Lutyens visited Shimla, he was appalled by the architecture of Shimla and said : "If one was told that it was built by monkeys all one could say was, 'What wonderful monkeys!' But they must be shot if they tried to do it again...."

Despite the devastating comments of Sir Edward, the builder of the Imperial capital in Delhi, Shimla remained popular and nostalgically an "English" town. It is a perfect place to indulge in the fantasies of the Raj.

From the Ridge at Shimla, you can have spellbinding views of the Himalayan peaks and valleys; and more so, from the highest point where the JAKHU TEMPLE is located. Apart from the rambling on the MALL, you can enjoy quite a few excellent walks through the surrounding dense woods. The Shimla suburb, Summer Hill, has pleasant enjoyable walks and a little ahead lie the CHADWICK FALLS, 67 metres high and simply glorious. Shimla's ice-skating facilities are within the city itself and the ski slopes only a few kilometres away. While you are on your way to the ski slopes of KUFRI, do not forget to stop by the WILD FLOWER HALL, now a functioning hotel run by the Himachal Government Tourism, for a view of Shimla and out to Badrinath and Pir Panchal peaks of the Himalayas.

As Shimla changes its moods with every change of season, it holds you enthralled in a spell.

KULU AND MANALI

The Kulu-Manali region in the Himachal State has been described as the Valley of Gods. The road from Kulu to Manali runs along the swift, rushing torrents of the mighty Beas River, flanked by lofty mountains and dense forests.

MANALI leaves you spellbound with its scenic grandeur, girdled as it is by beautiful glades of deodars and flowering horse chestnuts. A short trek through rocky ranges leads you to the 13,123 feet (3915 metres) high ROHTANG PASS, the gateway to the enchanting LAHAUL and SPITI VALLEYS. Jawaharlal Nehru took his quiet holidays always in Manali.

Trekking to Rohtang Pass

In the town of NAGGAR, 20 kilometres from Manali, the medieval world still survives, untouched by time. The Russian artist Roerich who made Naggar his home was inspired by its surroundings.

The Kulu Dussehra Festival in October every year is a great gathering of more than 200 gods from across the valley. All of them descend in their chariots to pay homage to the principal god, Raghunathji, the presiding deity of Kulu Dussehra.

At VASHISHT, the famous waters of hot sulphur are captured in specially dug sinks for your bath. You can spend lazy afternoons trying your luck with Beas river trout.

KULU is also accessible from Shimla — 205 kilometres. The route is known for its beautiful scenery, apple orchards and lively tribal dances. Encircled by the last snow ranges of Himalayas — the DHAULADHAR and the PIR PANCHAL running parallel to the south — the narrow terraced valley runs north from MANDI through Kulu and Manali all the way up to Rohtang Pass. The Beas river is everywhere flowing through the flower-bedecked valley.

LAHAUL AND SPITI

Beyond Rohtang Pass (13,200 feet) are the twin valleys of LAHAUL and SPITI. Their height ranges from 9,800 feet to 15,700 feet. Both valleys remain cut off from the rest of India for much of the year. The Rohtang Pass remains open only during May to October. That is the time when visitors can enter the valleys to enjoy their beauty and charm. To enter the Spiti valley, one has to cross another higher pass, KUNZAM, from a height of 14,800 feet. Only the young and the young at heart can try this in summer.

The people of the two valleys are also unique and have a distinct culture of their own, predominantly Buddhist. It is also called the Little Tibet in the Himalayas. Their songs and dances are pure as the snow around them and their "Gompas" are the repositories of Buddhist treasures. It is altogether a new world unknown to the West.

Coming back to our base, the little town of Kulu, it is also an excellent base for walks, trout fishing and gentle treks up through the pine and cedar forests. The Himalayan Institute of Mountaineering located at Manali can help you plan your treks.

They can provide you the services of experienced Sherpa guides and also hire you the equipment for trekking. Fishing licences can be obtained through the local Tourist Office.

Good two-day trekking excursions could be undertaken to HANUMAN TIBBA (19,452 feet) and the Rohtang Pass (13,123 feet). Other interesting treks are MALANA, PARBATI, SOLANG VALLEYS and up to DEO TIBBA.

In Kulu, BIJLI MAHADEV is a remarkable temple worth a visit. It is built of large blocks of stone without the use of cement. It has a 65-feet-high flagstaff which is reputed to attract lightning and it often does. People believe that lightning reflects divine blessing. Every time the lightning strikes, the Shivalingam inside the temple is also shattered. It is put together again for another strike.

Beyond the Kulu Valley is the KANGRA VALLEY with its famous KANGRA FORT and many Hindu temples. The two hill resorts of DHARAMSALA, where His Holiness the Dalai Lama lives, and DALHOUSIE are located in this region. Both Dharamsala and Dalhousie have good budget hotels — offered by Himachal Tourism.

SHIMLA STD Code - 0177

GENERAL INFORMATION
Population: 6,15,000 (1991 census)
Altitude : 2202 metres (7333 ft)
Climate :
Temperature

	Max.	Min.
Winter	15⁰ c	2⁰ c
Summer	24⁰ c	11⁰ c

Season : Throughout the year, except the rainy season of July to August.
Clothing :
Summer : light woollens.
Winter : heavy woollens.

HOW TO GET THERE

By Air: Shimla has its own airport at Jabbarhatti. (17 km). Small Dornier planes connect Delhi with Shimla.
By Rail: Shimla is connected by a narrow guage line with Kalka (90 km.), which is connected with the major cities of the north.
By Road: Shimla is connected by road with all the towns and resorts of Himachal Pradesh, Punjab and Haryana and with Delhi and Chandigarh. It is 117 km. from Chandigarh (nearest major town). It is

274 km. from Manali
234 km. from Kulu
354 km. from Delhi.
There are luxury and ordinary bus services to Delhi, Kalka and Chandigarh as also to Kulu, Manali, Dharmasala, Chail, Jammu, etc.

LOCAL TRANSPORT

Taxis and mini-buses can be hired.
Local bus services available.

CONDUCTED TOURS

Full-day tours to
1. Wildflower Hall, Kufri, Fagu etc.
2. Mashobra, Naldehra etc.
3. Kufri, Theog and Narkanda.
4. Chail, Kufri etc.
(Contact the Tourist Information Office, *Phone: 77646, 78311*)

WHERE TO STAY

STANDARD
1. Oberoi Clarkes
   Phone : 212991/95
   Fax: 211321
   Cable : OBHOTEL

2. Asia the Dawn
   Phone : 77522/3142/43
   Telex : 205 ASIA IN
   Cable : ASIOTEL
3. Himland Hotel East
   Phone : 213043-213044

BUDGET
4. Woodville Palace
   Phone : 372763
5. Holiday Home
   Himachal Tourism
   Phone : 212890-94

Note: Shimla has scores of budget hotels. Tariff depends on the time of the year.

WHAT TO SEE

1. JAKHU HILL (2455 metres) offers an excellent view of the snowclad Himalayas.
2. HIMACHAL STATE MUSEUM. Has a collection of Pahari miniature paintings of this region.
3. The erstwhile VICEREGAL LODGE.
4. THE GLEN, SUMMER HILL, PROSPECT HILL, TARA DEVI and SANKAT MOCHAN are picnic spots from where excellent views can be had of Shimla and the mountains.

EXCURSIONS

1. WILDFLOWER HALL (13 km), now a hotel, has wonderful mountain flowers and magnificent views of the Himalayas.
2. MASHOBRA (13 km), has picturesque walks through forests of oak and pine.
3. KUFRI (16 km) and NARKANDA (65 km) are excellent skiing bases in winter.
4. FAGU (22 km), at a height of 2510 metres, has interesting views of the valley.
5. CHAIL (45 km), former summer capital of the Maharajah of Patiala, is a peaceful haven in the mountains.
6. TATTAPANI or hot springs on the banks of the Beas river.
7. KASAULI (77 km) is a hill resort of special interest to bird-watchers.
9. ROHRU (104 km) is ideal for a fishing holiday.
10. KULU (234 km) and MANALI (274 km), in the VALLEY OF THE GODS, are two of the most beautiful hill resorts of the Himalayas.

SHOPPING

Shawls, embroidered woollens, handmade shoes, wooden toys and other articles made of wood.

SPORTS

1. Shimla is the base for treks to the Kulu Valley via Jalori Pass or via Bashieo Pass and to the Kalpa and Kinnaur Valleys.
2. Golfing is popular in the scenic golf course at Naldehra.
3. Fishing for trout in the Pabbar river is allowed from February to October.
(Contact District Fisheries Officer, Shimla, for permits.)
4. Skiing at Kufri and Narkanda Ski Resorts from December end to early March.
5. Ice skating in winter and roller-skating in summer.

KULU and MANALI

GENERAL INFORMATION
KULU
Population : 30,000 (1991 census)
Altitude : 1219 metres (4059 ft)
Climate :

	Temperature	
	Max.	Min.
Summer :	31⁰ C	18⁰ C
Winter :	16⁰ C	5⁰ C

Season : Through the year except July-August
Clothing
Summer: cottons and light woollens.
Winter : heavy woollens.

HOW TO GET THERE

By Air : Vayudoot and Jagson Airlines flights connect Kulu (Buntar airport 10 km) with Delhi and Chandigarh.
By Rail: The nearest railhead is Jogindernagar, but the most convenient railheads are Chandigarh (259 km) and Pathankot (285 km).
By Road: Good roads connect Kulu with the states of the north. It is

    40 km. from Manali
    233 km. from Shimla
    259 km. from Chandigarh
    285 km. from Pathankot
    501 km. from Delhi.

Regular bus services connect Kulu and Manali with Chandigarh, Delhi, Hardwar, Pathankot, Dharamsala, Shimla, Mandi, etc. During the high tourist season, air-conditioned luxury coaches operate from Delhi to Kulu/Manali thrice a week.

LOCAL TRANSPORT

Cars and station wagons are available at Pathankot Tourist Bureau and at Kulu Tourist Bureau.

CONDUCTED TOURS

Available from Manali to Rohtang Pass, Naggar, Manikaran and Chandigarh in the season.

WHERE TO STAY

KULU (STD Code - 01902)
Deluxe
1. Span Resorts
   Phone : 83138-40
   Cable : SPAN RESORTS
2. Apple Valley Resorts
   (5 kms from Airport)
   Phone: 5270/75

Standard
3. Sarvari (Himachal Tourism)
   (8 kms from Airport)
   Phone: 2471
4. Hotel Silver Moon (Himachal Tourism)
   (7 kms from Airport)
   Phone: 2488

Budget
5. River View (Himachal Tourism)
6. Hotel Parvati (Himachal Tourism)
7. Hotel Castle Naggar (Himachal Tourism)

MANALI - STD Code 01901
Standard
1. Ambassador Resorts
   Phone: 2173, 2237
   Fax: 01901-2178

2. Quality-Inn Snowcrest Manor
   Phone: 3188, 3351-52
3. Hotel Piccadily
   Phone: 2149, 2152, 2114
   Fax: 01901-2113
4. Holiday Inn Manali
   Phone: 2262
   Fax: 3312

BUDGET

5. Hotel Manali Ashok (ITDC)
   Phone: 2331
   Cable: Tourism
6. Benon Resorts
   Phone: 2490, 3026
   Fax: 2378
7. Pankaj
   Phone: 2744, 2492
8. Log Huts (Himachal Tourism)
   Phone: 2360, 2325
9. Hotel Beas (Himachal Tourism)
10. Hotel Rohtang Manalsu (Himachal Tourism)

WHAT TO SEE

KULU

1. There are several shrines in and around Kulu like the RAGHUNATHJI TEMPLE, VAISHNO DEVI (4 km.) and the BIJLI MAHADEV SHRINE (14 km).
2. RAISON (16 km) where there is a camping site on the banks of the Beas.
3. KATRAIN (20 km), en route to Manali, has apple orchards and a trout hatchery.
4. NAGGAR (27 km). Located above the River Beas, it commands an excellent view of the valley. It was the capital of the Rajas of Kulu for 1400 years.
5. ROERICH ART GALLERY (housing the paintings and sculptures of the famous Russian artist, Nicholas Roerich) 1 km. from Naggar.
6. MANIKARAN HOT SPRINGS (45 km) is also a place of pilgrimage for Hindus and Sikhs.

MANALI

1. VASISHT Baths and HOT SPRINGS.
2. DHOONGRI TEMPLE dedicated to Hadimba Devi (wife of Bhima of the *Mahabharata*).

3. JAGATSUKH, ancient capital of Kulu.
4. TIBETAN MONASTERY, Tibetan carpet weaving can be seen here.
5. SOLANG VALLEY, for winter sports. There are good skiing slopes with an excellent ski lift.

6. MOUNTAINEERING INSTITUTE which organises courses in hiking, trekking, mountaineering, etc.
7. ROHTANG PASS (51 km) at an altitude of 4112 metres(13,700 ft) on the route to Keylong is the only access to the Lahaul Valley (open June to September).
8. LAHAUL VALLEY is near the Indo-Tibetan border and is primitive and rugged, surrounded by high mountains and massive glaciers.
9. KEYLONG (117 km) is reached by a motorable road from Manali. There are several Gompas or Buddhists monasteries which are repositories of Buddhist art.

SHOPPING

Fine Kulu shawls, the most famous being the Pashmina, embroidered scarves from Chamba, and embroidered footwear are real works of art. Miniature paintings from Chamba and Kangra are also available. A popular craft is wood-carving out of the wide range of wood like birch, walnut, black mulberry, etc., made into articles of daily use. Dolls of Himachal, woven rugs in bright colours (called *namdahs*), Tibetan carpets, Kulu caps, Tibetan curios, *tankhas* (tapestries) to metalcraft.

FESTIVALS OF SPECIAL LOCAL INTEREST

1. *Festival of Hadimba Devi Temple*, Manali (May). Nearly every temple in the valley has a festival during some part of the year.
2. *Dussehra* (September-October) is the biggest festival at Kulu with festivities going till the Dussehra day. About 200 deities of the hill people are brought to pay homage to Lord Raghunathji, who is taken in a procession in a large *rath* (chariot). There is great celebration with music and dance.

ADVENTURE SPORTS

1. Trekking. Himachal is a trekkers' paradise. Popular treks are:
   (a) Manali—Vashist—Bhrigu—Manali.
   (b) Manali—Chikka—Hamta Pass—Sarotu—Bhanara—Jagatsukh—Manali.
   (c) Raison—Malana—Chandrakhani—Raison.
   (d) Manali—Solang Nullah—Dundi—Shagara Dugh—Marrhi—Kothi—Manali.
   (e) Manali—Rohtang—Keylong—Gispat—Patsea(Lahaul Valley).
2. White river runs, riverside camping, swimming, nature walks, angling and bird watching have ample scope in this region as do mountaineering and rock climbing.

3. Skiing on the snow-covered slopes of Manali and Rohtang are popular winter sports. A winter sport festival is organised by the Mountaineering Institute at Solang near Manali, every winter.

Temple at Baijnath

Chapter 11

PUNJAB AND HARYANA
The Fertile Land

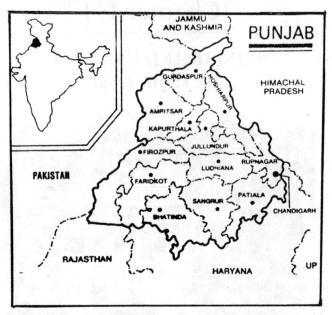

Punjab extended from Attock in the north-western part of India under the British down to Yamuna River in Delhi. The five rivers of Punjab were Jhelum, Chenab, Ravi, Beas and Sutlej. It was a fertile land which always attracted the greedy eyes of the invaders from Afghanistan and Central Asian Republics. The region suffered the most under repeated attacks. Punjab was inhabited by Rajputs, the brave warriors of India. Towards the middle of the 11th century, the Muslims were able to overcome the resistance of the Rajputs and Punjab came under their domination. The Mughals came to Punjab in the 16th century and took over the region and since then Punjab never rested in peace. Two centuries later, the Sikhs under Maharaja Ranjit Singh defeated the Mughals and took over the entire country up to Afghanistan. After the death of Ranjit Singh, the valiant Sikhs were defeated by the British in 1846 and 1849 resulting in annexation of Punjab by the British.

Another century later, in 1947, independence came, but Punjab had to be divided into two parts on the basis of the predominant religion in each district. The districts where Muslims were in majority went to Pakistan while those with Hindu and Sikh majority came to India. It was assumed that the people of both the religions would be allowed to stay where they were. But, it did not happen and the atmosphere became so tense that movement of people took place. In the process, atrocities were committed on both sides of the border on the fleeing population and at least a million died. The people from both sides of the border came from the same ethnic and social stock and spoke the same language. The tragedy was caused by the religions they professed.

After independence, the Indian part of Punjab thrived both in agriculture and in the field of industry. Punjab became the most prosperous state of India. That led to a political struggle. The Akalis, a dominant section of the Sikhs felt that they were losing their identity in the sea of Hindu majority and demanded a separate province where Sikhs would be in majority. The Indian part of the Punjab was once again divided and the Punjabi-speaking areas were separated and the Hindi-speaking part of Punjab became Haryana. Hilly areas of Punjab like Kangra and Shimla went to Himachal Pradesh as these areas were non-Punjabi speaking.

CHANDIGARH

Before the second division, Chandigarh, the most modern city of India, was created under the guidance of Le Corbusier, the French architect, as the new capital of Punjab in place of Lahore, the original capital of undivided Punjab. But, the city too became a centre of controversy. The two heirs to the Punjab legacy demanded it as their own. Ultimately, the Central Government made it the capital of both the states, retaining Chandigarh as a Central Territory under its own administrative control.

High Court

Rock Garden (Chandigarh)

The two states share the Secretariat as well as the High Court - an economical way to run an administration. But, it may not last long as the Punjab claims that it is the rightful owner of Chandigarh and the capital should come directly under their rule and that Haryana should build a new capital.

For the visitors, more interesting than the wrangle over the ownership of the city is the city itself. It is beautifully located at the foot of the Shivalik Hills. Two mountain torrents were canalised to form a beautiful large lake called SUKHNA LAKE with a wide boulevard. The lake has become a halting place for birds migrating from Central Asia to India and vice versa. The city of Chandigarh was designed by a team of French architects — Le Corbusier and his cousin Jeanneret. Corbusier himself designed some of the important public buildings like the Secretariat, High Court and the Legislative Assembly. Several of these buildings are on 'stilts' — a design which has become popular in India for public buildings.

Chandigarh is a very beautiful city with a large variety of flowering trees specially selected by a renowned civil servant and botanist, Dr. M. S. Randhawa, who later became its Chief Commissioner. You can often identify a street from the type of trees grown on its two sides. It has a very extensive 'ROSE GARDEN' — perhaps the largest in Asia. Another tourist attraction of Chandigarh is a huge, special Park, called the ROCK GARDEN, which a Chandigarh man, Nek Chand, has developed from broken pieces of cups and saucers and other waste materials. It is a statuary which is unique in the world, a whimsical fantasy, if one could describe it.

AMRITSAR

An important tourist attraction of Punjab is Amritsar, the most sacred city of the sturdy Sikhs. THE GOLDEN TEMPLE, the holy Sikh shrine, is in the old part of the town. The temple is surrounded by a pool, which gives it the name 'Amritsar', the pool of nectar. The high priest reads from *Granth Sahib*, the holy book of the Sikh Gurus, and the hymns are broadcast through a loudspeaker. The temple domes are covered with gold leaf, 400 kilograms of gold was used for it. The gold was donated by Maharaja Ranjit Singh. It should be worthwhile to spend an hour or two in the temple and witness the spirit that brings people to worship in this temple. Around the temple are several other historical buildings.

When in Amritsar, do not forget to visit the JALIANWALA BAGH, where the British General Dyer, massacred 300 innocent people who had gathered there for a meeting in 1919. The tragic event later led to the strengthening of the movement for total independence. Nearby is also the famous Hindu temple, DURGIANA MANDIR.

There are many other Sikh temples in Punjab and the most notable among them being the one at ANANDPUR SAHIB. It was here that the last Sikh Guru, Gobind Singh, baptized the Sikh community in 1699 and transformed them into a martial fraternity. The Sikhs made the Mughal empire tumble down like a pack of cards.

Golden Temple

Punjab as constituted today is predominantly a homeland of Sikhs, who are the most easily recognizable people. Their religion does not allow them to trim their hair or to shave. They normally also wear a steel bangle. They are very enterprising and are represented in all walks of life — as soldiers, farmers, mechanics, engineers, drivers of taxis or buses and also as successful industrialists. The other major towns of Punjab are Ludhiana and Jullundhar — both known for their industry. Patiala, former capital of an erstwhile princely state, is home of the Punjabi University.

HARYANA

Punjab and Haryana have been the cradle of the early Aryan civilisation. It was on the banks of the Punjab rivers that ancient Hindu sages had sung the Vedic hymns and authored the *Vedas*. It was at KURUKSHETRA, now in Haryana that the epic battle of Mahabharata was fought and Lord Krishna gave his advice to Arjuna, which is now part of the *Bhagavad Gita*. This sacred book spells out the essence of Hinduism.

Haryana has been the battleground for the control of the throne of Hindustan. PANIPAT, 92 kilometres north of Delhi, was the venue of the battle that changed the course of Indian history. In 1526, Babur defeated Ibraham Lodhi, the Sultan of Delhi, and founded the Mughal empire. Later in 1556, Akbar defeated the Pathans at the same place to retain the empire. Again, the Marathas who had succeeded the Mughals were defeated by the Afghan forces of Ahmed Shah Durrani. Not far from here at KARNAL, Nadir Shah took the Peacock Throne from Delhi after defeating the Mughal Emperor Mohammad Shah in 1739.

Tourist Complexes

Haryana does not have many tourist attractions to boast of, though Haryana Tourism has one of the most successful tourism departments in the country. Taking advantage of its location, it has built a series of tourist complexes with lakes, restaurants, motels, and shopping centres to attract motorists driving to other major attractions like Agra, Jaipur, Kashmir and Punjab. It makes travel a pleasure and many tourists stay overnight in these complexes. The accommodation and food in these places are very reasonably priced.

A few of the well known tourist complexes are listed below. Many of these are named after exotic birds. Distances shown are from Delhi.

1. Badkhal Lake, Faridabad (*Phone* 216901-3, 32 km)
2. Rajhans, Surajkund (*Phone* 8275357, 8 km)
3. Magpie, Faridabad (*Phone* 288083, 30 km)
4. Dabchick, Hodal (*Phone* 91, 92 km)
5. Barbet, Sohna (*Phone* 56, 56 km)
6. Jungle Babbler, Dharuhera (*Phone* 2225, 70 km)
7. Rosy Pelican, Sultanpur (*Phone* 42, 46 km)
8. Shama Restaurant, Gurgaon (*Phone* 20683, 32 km)
9. Uchana Oasis, Karnal (*Phone* 4279, 124 km)
10. Parakeet, Pipli (*Phone* 250, 152 km)
11. Blue Jay, Samalkha (*Phone* 2110, 60 km)
12. Yadavindra Gardens, Pinjore (*Phone* 2855, 281 km)
13. Kingfisher, Ambala (*Phone* 58352, 55 km)
14. Skylark, Panipat (*Phone* 25051, 90 km)
15. Tilyar, Rohtak (*Phone* 3966, 70 km)
16. Myana, Rohtak (*Phone* 77117, 72 km)
17. Flamingo, Hissar (*Phone* 75102, 160 km)
18. Bulbul, Jind (*Phone* 2293, 127 km)
19. Kala Teetar, Abubshehr, Sirsa (*Phone* 39, 325 km)
20. Sohna, Gurgaon (*Phone* 2256, 56 km).

AMRITSAR

GENERAL INFORMATION
Population: 750,000 (1991 census)
Altitude: 234 metres (779 ft)
Climate :

	Temperature	
	Max.	Min.
Winter	28^0c	5^0c
Summer	40^0c	16^0c

Season: Throughout the year. During the months of May and June, the days are hot.
Clothing
Summer : cottons,
Winter : woollens.

HOW TO GET THERE

By Air: Amritsar is connected by air with Delhi, Jammu and Srinagar.

By Rail: Amritsar is directly connected by rail with Agra, Bhopal, Bombay, Calcutta, Delhi, Lucknow, Patna, Varanasi, etc., and all parts of India. It is also connected to Lahore (Pakistan) by rail via Attari Border.

By Road: Amritsar is connected by road with all important centres. It is

    29 km. from Wagah, on the India-Pakistan border
    216 km. from Jammu
    240 km. from Chandigarh
    435 km. from Delhi.

There are regular bus services to Jammu, Dehradun, Chandigarh, Kulu, Manali, Pathankot and Attari Road.

LOCAL TRANSPORT

Taxis, scooters and buses are available.

CONDUCTED TOURS

Nil.

WHERE TO STAY

STANDARD
1. Mohan International Hotel
   Phone: 227801-8
   Fax: 226520

BUDGET
2. Ritz Hotel
   Phone: 26606, 26657
3. Amritsar International Hotel
   Phone: 31991-92, 32234
4. Hotel Astoria
   Phone: 66046, 66414
5. Hotel Airlines
   Phone: 64848

WHAT TO SEE

1. The GOLDEN TEMPLE, the most important shrine of the Sikhs, is also known as Hari Mandir (Temple of the Lord). The glittering golden domes of the temple are reflected in the pool, and a marble pathway leads to the temple.
2. DURGIANA MANDIR, a temple with a gold dome and silver portals. It is a place of pilgrimage for Hindus.
3. JALLIANWALA BAGH, a memorial where 300 victims, all unarmed, were massacred by the British.
4. BABA ATAL RAI TOWER, built in the memory of the 9-year-old son of Guru Hargobind, who martyred himself.

EXCURSIONS

1. TARAN TARAN (22 km). The pool near this shrine is believed to have curative properties.
2. GOBINDWAL SAHEB (30 km). The final resting place (*samadhi*) of Guru Angad Devji, is nearby.
3. AMANAT KHAN SERAI (38 km) has an ornamental gateway and glazed tile decorations.
4. BABA BAKALA (45 km), dedicated to the ninth Guru, Tegh Bahadur, has a magnificent gurudwara.
5. PATIALA (67 km from Chandigarh). The museum here has a rare collection

of weapons. The old Patiala Fort has fine examples of the Patiala school of painting.

6. Dharamsala (185 km), a popular hill station, is the present home of the Dalai Lama.
7. Dalhousie (191 km), at a height of over 2000 metres, has pine and oak forests and a bracing climate.
8. Kangra (194 km) is a lush green valley with fruit orchards and farms.
9. Chandigarh (240 km), the capital city, was designed by the French architect, Le Corbusier and 108 km. beyond is the beautiful hill resort of Shimla.

SHOPPING

Phulkari-worked fabrics and articles of traditional embroidery, woodcraft, gold and silver threaded footwear, cut-glass, silver work, carved bracelets, ivory combs, jewellery, handloom, textiles, woollens, shawls, durries and carpets. Amritsar is a whole-sale market for textiles and shawls.

FESTIVALS OF SPECIAL LOCAL INTEREST

1. Baisakhi (April 13) is the Solar New Year's Day and the Harvest Festival. It was also on this day that the Khalsa was founded by Guru Gobind Singh, converting the Sikhs into a martial community. It is an occasion for great celebration-dances and rejoicing.
2. Gurpurab (October-November), the birth anniversary of Guru Nanak, the founder of the Sikh religion, and of Guru Gobind Singh, the last Guru (in December-January) are important celebrations.
3. A four-day festival and fair are held at Ram Tirath (10 km) around the full moon night of November.

CHANDIGARH STD Code: 0172

GENERAL INFORMATION

Population: 500,000 (1991 census)
Altitude: 335 metres (1116 ft)
Climate

	Temperature	
	Max.	Min.
Summer	37^0 C	23^0 C
Winter	24^0 C	5^0 C

Season: Throughout the year. May-June are hot months.

Clothing
Winter: Woollens
Summer: Cottons

HOW TO GET THERE

By Air: Chandigarh is connected by air with Delhi, Srinagar, Jammu, Leh, Kulu etc.
By Rail: Chandigarh is connected by rail with all major cities of India. Two new Shatabdi air-conditioned train connects it with

Delhi twice a day besides other trains.

By Road: Chandigarh is best connected by road and buses are an important link. It is
- 452 km. from Amritsar
- 248 km. from Delhi
- 380 km. from Jammu
- 507 km. from Jaipur
- 586 km. from Nainital
- 276 km. from Rishikesh
- 666 km. from Srinagar

LOCAL TRANSPORT

Tourist taxis are available for prices which are negotiable. Auto-rickshaws and cycle rickshaws are the common mode of transport.

CONDUCTED TOURS

To visit places of interest in and around Chandigarh there are conducted tours by coaches and Matador vans organised by Chandigarh Tourism, (CITCO), Sector 17 *Phone*: 543839) Currently no regular daily tour is available.

WHERE TO STAY (STD CODE: 0172)

STANDARD

1. Hotel Shivalik View
   Phone: 544651/544012
   Telex: 395 584 CITC IN
   Cable: CITCO
   Fax: 0172-32094
2. Hotel Mount View
   Phone: 541120
   Telex: 0395-337 CITY IN
   Cable: MOUNT VIEW
   Fax: 0172-547120
3. Hotel Piccadily
   Phone: 43112, 43118
   Cable: PICCOTEL

BUDGET

4. Hotel Maya Palace
   Phone: 600547-48
5. Hotel Sun Beam
   Phone: 41335
   Telex: 0395-444 SUN-IN
   Cable: SUNBEAM
6. Rikhys International
   Phone: 531733
   Cable: RIKHYS
7. Kapil
   Phone: 533366
8. President
   Phone: 40840
   Fax: 0172-43410
   Telex: 0395-490 HYG IN
   Cable: COMFORTS
9. Pankaj
   Phone: 41906
   Telex: 0395-367
   Cable: HOTPANKAJ

WHAT TO SEE

1. The ROCK GARDEN is a special feature of the city and a must for every visitor. It has been built largely out of city garbage by a local man, Nek Chand.
2. The ROSE GARDEN. It is spread over 30 acres of beautifully landscaped gardens containing nearly 1,600 varieties of roses.
3. SUKHNA LAKE offers sports like boating, yatching, water-skiing, etc.
4. YADAVINDRA GARDENS at Pinjore (24 km) are on the road to Shimla. These 17th century gardens, designed by Nawab Fidai Khan are a pleasant blend of Mughal and Rajasthani styles.

Chapter 12

DELHI
A Tale of Seven Cities

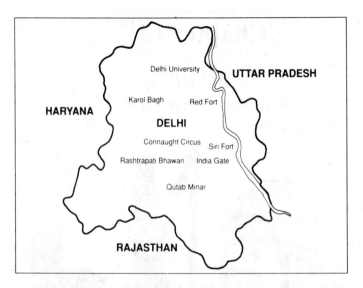

Teen Murti

Memorial pillar to George V

Delhi is one of the oldest of the old and the newest of the new cities of the world. It is at once the most oriental, a modern and green progressive city. Modern India's history is synonymous with Delhi. It was from the ramparts of the Red Fort that India's first Prime Minister, Pandit Jawaharlal Nehru, unfurled the national flag on August 15, 1947, signifying the end of 300 years of the British Raj. Today, it is India's capital and the seat of the Parliament, the Supreme Court and the President of India. The city boasts of tourism infrastructure that is one of the best in Asia.

Delhi is a highly political city. Politics and political scandals — real or unreal — are talked about at cocktail parties and dinners. Social rank is measured often by one's political power.

Another status symbol is owning a farm outside Delhi, like a countryhouse in England set in several acres of tilled land.

AN ANCIENT CITY

Nobody really knows the age of Delhi. Some stone inscriptions date it to the third century B.C. Pieces of earthenware and pottery have been discovered that could be traced back to 3,000 B.C. Historians differ about their perceptions of the number of cities built by different rulers over hundreds of years— some say there were seven cities while others think there were 15. But, there are visible ruins of at least seven cities. The eighth one, New Delhi, was built during the 20th century by the British.

The earliest references to Delhi are in Buddhist and Jain scriptures but these sources cannot be dated precisely. In the great epic *Mahabharata*, the city has been called Indraprastha which was founded by the Pandavas on the banks of river Yamuna. The epic was written in about 900 B.C. In the 11th century A.D., Raja Anangpal of Kanauj, a Tomar king, established Lalkot as his capital in the vicinity of present-day Qutab Minar area. Historically, this was the first city of Delhi and we can see its ruins. Anangpal's successors ruled from it for almost a century until Vishaldeva, a Chauhan Rajput from Ajmer, conquered it.

Towards the end of the 12th century, Mohammad Ghori, an Afghan king, came down to Delhi and defeated Prithviraj Chauhan, the grandson of Vishaldeva, and occupied Delhi. He, however, did not make Delhi his home and left his new kingdom in the hands of his trusted slave, Allauddin Khilji. Lalkot continued to be Khilji's capital till he built a new one after defeating the invading Rajputs at Siri where he built his own capital. That happened in 1303.

Next on the list of many Delhis are the cities of Tughlaqabad, which took four years to build, and Jahanpanah. The first built by Ghyas-ud-din Tughlaq had to be abandoned due to scarcity of water, and Mohammad, his son built another capital, Jahanpanah — quite close to the Qutab Minar. Founded by Feroz Shah Tughlaq, Delhi's fifth city was named after him as Ferozabad. It was located in the vicinity of Ferozshah

Qutab Minar

Kotla area. Delhi's sixth city was founded by Emperor Humayun between A.D. 1533 and 1534 in the old Indraprastha site where Purana Quila stands. Humayun could not enjoy his new capital for a long time as the invading Afghan warrior, Sher Shah Suri (1530-39), made him flee from his capital. Sher Shah, also a builder, gave India its Grand Trunk Road, and added a beautiful hall and a mosque in the old Fort. He ruled from there till 1555 when Humayun recaptured it and returned to power.

Shahjahanabad — what is now called Old Delhi—was built by Emperor Shahjahan as Delhi's seventh city between 1638 and 1649. This city comprised the well-known Red Fort, Jama Masjid and several Mughal monuments. Delhi's eighth city — now known as New Delhi — was the contribution by the British who had Calcutta as their capital. They decided to move the capital to a more central place and Delhi was the obvious choice as the city had the privilege of having been the nation's capital for several centuries. Decision was taken in 1911 and the capital was formally inaugurated in 1931. Two famous British architects, Sir Edward Lutyens and Sir Herbert Baker, were commissioned to design the new capital.

THE NEW CITY

Lutyens, assisted by Baker, designed a city to reflect the power and glory of the British Empire, with scope for much expansion to accommodate 70,000 people. Viceroy, Lord Hardinge, who was behind the transfer of the capital from Calcutta to Delhi, took a keen interest in this project. His successors, Lord Chelmsford and Lord Reading, watched it being realised. Lord Irwin who became the Viceroy in 1926, saw its completion and inauguration. About 30,000 labourers worked to build the capital, levelling land and building roads; 100,000 trees were planted. The capital reflects the synthesis of Hindu, Muslim and European architecture.

EXPLORING DELHI

The Viceregal Palace, now named RASHTRAPATI BHAWAN, the residence of the President of India, covers 330 acres of Raisina Hill and dominates the city. It looks down over the administrative buildings along the broad green vista of Rajpath to India Gate and, originally to beyond PURANA QUILA — a view obliterated by the next Viceroy of India, Wellington and his interfering wife's zeal to build a stadium. Rashtrapati Bhavan's famous MUGHAL GARDENS are open to public for five weeks following the Republic Day (January 26). You can find the exact dates from the Tourist Office if you happen to be in Delhi during this period.

CONNAUGHT PLACE, the main shopping centre for New Delhi, was designed to connect Old and New Delhi. It is now the haunt of jean-clad and hamburger eating young men and women. But Connaught Place has multi-storey buildings coming up in its periphery. Delhi, built in only 1900s, cost U.S. $ 11.25 million, but today a single highrise building alone is worth more than that. The city is changing its profile. Built to accommodate a few thousand people, it now houses almost 10 million! New Delhi is still in the shape as originally planned, but one cannot say anything about its future.

A famous Urdu poet of Delhi, Asad-ullah Ghalib, has described his city in the following verse —

"I asked my soul, what is Delhi? She replied: The world is the body and Delhi is its soul." Old Delhites still feel the same way. Some 40 year ago, it was possible to see all the seven cities of Delhi as the old ones had clung to their individuality and it was easy to retrace their history. One had only to visit them from south to north, for Delhi's growth has been a steady march northward to gain from the cool breeze that comes down from the hills. Today, Delhi engulfs the seven historic cities. An honest attempt has been made to protect what has been left of the old cities of Delhi. They all are still here. Here are the most important historical sites to see in India's capital.

Qutub Minar

The origins of QUTUB MINAR are shrouded in controversy. Some believe that it was built as a tower of victory to signify the beginning of the Muslim rule in India. Others say it served as a minaret to the adjoining mosque and was used by the muezzins to call the faithful to prayer. However, no one disputes that the tower is not only one of the finest monuments in India, but also in the world.

Qutub-ud-din Aibak, the first Muslim ruler of Delhi, commenced the construction of the Qutub Minar in A.D. 1193, but could only complete its basement. His successor, Iltutmush, added three more storeys, and in 1368, Firoz Shah Tughlak constructed the fifth and the last storey. The development of architectural styles from Aibak to Tughlak are quite evident in the minar. The relief work and even the materials used for construction differ.

The 238 feet high Qutub Minar is 47 feet at the base and tapers to 9 feet at the apex. The tower is ornamented by bands of inscriptions and by four projecting balconies supported by elaborately decorated brackets. Even in its ruin, the Quwwat-Ul-Islam (Light of Islam) Mosque in the Qutub complex is one of the most magnificent in the world. The main mosque comprises an inner and outer courtyard, of which the inner one is surrounded by an exquisite collonade, the pillars of which are made of richly decorated shafts. Most of these shafts are from the 27 Hindu temples which were plundered to construct the mosque.

Close to the mosque is one of Delhi's most curious structures — the Iron Pillar. Dating back to 4th century A.D., the pillar bears an inscription which states that it was erected as a flagstaff in honour of the Hindu god, Vishnu, and in the memory of the Gupta King Chandragupta II (375-413). How the pillar moved to its present location remains a mystery. The pillar also highlights ancient India's achievements in metallurgy. The pillar is made of 98 per cent wrought iron and has stood 1,600 years without rusting or decomposing.

Purana Quila

The old fort is said to have been constructed at the historic site of Indraprastha (900 BC) by Humayun and Sher Shah. Covering a circuit of about two kms the fort has three gates once is surrounded by a moat fed by the Yamuna. Its wall was built by Humayun while the buildings inside the fort are attributed to Sher Shah. The notable buildings that have survived are the Sher Mandal and the Quila-i-Kholina Mosque.

Sher Mandal is a two-storeyed octagonal tower which was used by Humayun as his library. The mosque, built around 1541-42, is a landmark in Indo-Islamic architecture.

Humayun's Tomb

The Mughals brought with them their love for gardens, fountains and water. The first mature example of Mughal architecture in India, HUMAYUN'S TOMB, was built by the Emperor's grieving widow, Haji Begum, in AD 1565. Designed by Persian architect, Mirza Ghyas, Humayun's Tomb shows a marked shift from the Persian tradition of using coloured tiles for ornamentation. Located in the midst of a large square garden, screened by high walls, with gateways to the south and west, the tomb is a square tower surrounded by a magnificent marble dome. The dome stands 140 feet high from the base of the terrace and is topped with a copper pinnacle.

Jantar Mantar

At first sight, Jantar Mantar appears like a gallery of modern art. It is, however, an observatory. Sawai Jai Singh II of Jaipur (1699-1743), a keen astronomer and a noble in the Mughal Court, was dissatisfied with the faulty working of brass and metal astronomical instruments. Under patronage from the emperor, he set on himself the task of correcting existing astronomical tables and updating the almanac with more reliable instruments. Jantar Mantar is the first of the five observatories he built with large masonary instruments.

Red Fort

It gets its name from the red stone with which it is built. The Red Fort is one of the most magnificent palaces in the world. India's history is also closely linked with it. It was from here that the British deposed the last Mughal ruler, Bahadur Shah Zafar, marking the end of the three centuries of Mughal rule. It was also from its ramparts that the first Prime Minister of India Pandit Jawaharlal Nehru, announced independence of India.

The Mughal emperor, Shahjahan, after ruling from Agra for eleven years, decided to shift to Delhi and laid the foundation stone of the Red Fort in 1618. For its inauguration in 1647, the main halls of the palace were draped in rich tapestry and covered with silk from China and velvet from Turkey. With a circumference of almost one and a half miles, the fort is an irregular octagon and has two entrances, the Lahore and Delhi Gates.

The DIWAN-I-AAM is the Red Fort's hall of public audience. Built of sandstone and covered with shell plaster polished to look like ivory, the 80 x 40 feet hall is sub-divided by columns. The Mughal emperors held court here and met dignitaries and foreign emissaries. The most imposing feature of the Diwan-i-Aam is the alcove in the back wall where the Emperor sat in state on a richly carved and inlaid marble platform. In the recess behind the platform are fine examples of Italian pietre-dura work.

The *piece de resistance* of the fort, the DIWAN -I-KHAS was the hall of private audience. The most highly ornamental of all Shahjahan's buildings, the 90 x 67 feet Diwan-i-Khas is a pavilion of white marble supported by intricately carved pillars. So enamoured was the emperor of the beauty of this pavilion that he engraved on it the following words: "If there is paradise on the face of this earth, it is this, it is this." Richly decorated with flowers of inlaid mosaic work of stones, the Diwan-i-Khas once housed the famous PEACOCK THRONE, which, when plundered by Nadir Shah in 1739, was valued at six million sterling.

Residence of the senior queens, the RANG MAHAL (Palace of Colours) has a central hall surrounded by six apartments. The apartments are assured privacy by intricately carved screens which do not hinder the free flow of fresh air and light. The stream of paradise flows through the main hall, and is marked by a huge lotus-shaped marble basin with an ivory fountain.

Moti Masjid

Constructed by Emperor Aurangzeb in 1662 as his private mosque, it is built with highly polished marble. The mosque is a good example of the Mughal fetish for symmetry with arches, sinuous decorative designs, carved cornices and bulbous domes.

Jama Masjid

Work on the Jama Masjid mosque was begun in 1650 by the Mughal Emperor Shahjahan to complement his palace at the Red Fort. More than 5,000 workers toiled for six years to complete the largest mosque in India. Every Friday, the Emperor and his retinue would travel in state from the fort to the mosque to attend the congregational prayers.

A fine example of Mughal architecture, the Jama Masjid has three gateways. The largest and the highest in the east was reserved exclusively for the emperor. The main courtyard of the mosque is 408 square feet and is paved with redstone. In the centre is a large marble tank in which the devout wash before attending prayers. The main mosque is crowned by three onion-shaped domes made of white marble and inlaid with stripes of black slate. On the north and south of the complex are two 130 feet high minarets which offer a spectacular bird's-eye view of the city. Jama Masjid is not only architecturally beautiful, but it is also a place of great religious significance as it houses a hair from the beard of the Prophet, as well as a chapter of the *Holy Quran* written by him.

Safdarjung's Tomb

Representing the last phase of the Mughal style of architecture, Safdarjung's Tomb stands in the centre of an extensive garden. Built in 1753 by Nawab Shauja-ud-Daula to house the remains of his father, who was a minister in the Mughal Court, the tomb is referred to as the "last flicker in the lamp of Mughal architecture".

India Gate

Built as a memorial to commemorate the 70,000 Indian soldiers killed in World War I, India Gate was designed by Sir Edward Lutyens and completed in 1931. Located on Rajpath, the road which leads to the magnificent Rashtrapati Bhawan, the gate is 160 feet high with an arch of 138 feet. Built from sandstone, the arch also houses the Eternal Flame, a gesture in memory of the brave Indian soldiers who laid down their lives in the 1971 war with Pakistan.

Rashtrapati Bhawan

Formerly known as the Viceregal Lodge, Rashtrapati Bhawan is the highlight of Lutyen's New Delhi and was completed in 1929 at a cost of £ 12,53,000. Located in an area of 130 hectares, the palace has 340 rooms. At one time, 2,000 people were required to look after the building and serve the Viceroy's household. It has an impressive garden called the Mughal Gardens, which is open to public twice in a year, usually in February and March.

Rajghat

The mortal remains of Mahatma Gandhi were cremated on this spot on the west bank of the Yamuna in the evening of January 31, 1948. A simple open platform inscribed with the Mahatma's last words, 'Hey Ram' (Oh God) it is set in a garden with fountains and a variety of exotic trees.

Lakshmi Narayan Temple
Built in 1938, this temple is an ideal introduction to some of the gods of the Indian pantheon. The temple contains a large number of idols. Visitors can watch priests performing ritualistic prayers.

SHOPPING PLEASURES

A walk through any of Delhi's markets is an unforgettable experience. It's a journey into history, tradition, art and culture, a trip to a treasurehouse which mirrors the very best of India's craftsmen. What, however, makes shopping in Delhi unique, is that the visitor has the option of walking into modern airconditioned stores or through narrow alleys to traditional shops where the artisan himself often is present to explain the intricacies of his craft. As the capital of Mughal rulers, known for their good taste, it is obvious that Delhi attracted the best of India's craftsmen who worked in the shadows of the Red Fort to

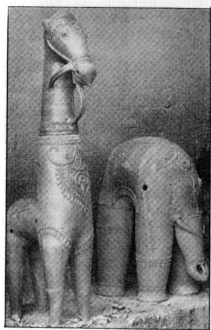

Terracotta figurines

create masterpieces that would assure them royal patronage. The Mughals have gone, but the craftsmen have stayed, and passed on their talents from generation to generation, making Delhi the show-window of India's craftsmanship. The tradition of creating unusual and fine crafts did not die with the Mughals. Delhi is the home of some of India's finest designers who have blended traditional styles with the latest international trends to create garments, jewellery, fashion accessories and furnishings that find place in some of the most prestigious stores all over the world. Be it sarees from Varanasi, leather from Agra, brass from Moradabad, silk from Madras, carpets from Kashmir, or pearls from Hyderabad, Delhi has them all. And what's more, a dollar still goes a very long way in Delhi's markets — the bargains are unbelievable. Devaluation of the Indian Rupee has made it even better!

The CENTRAL COTTAGE INDUSTRIES EMPORIUM on Janpath is a one-stop shop for Indian handicrafts. The multi-floors of this government-owned emporium offer an unbelievable variety; textiles, leather, jewellery, carpets, ceramics and furniture, all in airconditioned comfort and at prices fixed to make them amongst the most reasonable in Delhi. Then there are several STATE GOVERNMENT EMPORIA on nearby Baba Kharak Singh Marg dealing exclusively with the handicrafts of the region they represent. Here, too, the prices are fixed by the Governments. At POOMPUHAR, the Tamil Nadu emporium, you can pick up lustrous Kanchipuram silks; famous Madras plaids to make a dress, skirt, or a couple of tailored shirts; and ornate gilded Tanjore paintings. The KASHMIR EMPORIUM, features rugs, patterned papier-mache boxes and bowls, wool and silk caftans and robes, and a range of elegant carpets in silk or wool. Some of the states represented in the Baba Kharak Singh emporia complex are Gujarat, Rajasthan, Maharashtra, Kashmir, Bihar, Orissa, Nagaland, Assam, Himachal Pradesh, Haryana, Punjab, Uttar Pradesh, Andhra Pradesh, Madhya Pradesh, Tamil Nadu, Kerala, Karnataka, West Bengal, Tripura and Manipur.

The variety in Indian jewellery is mind-boggling. From intricately set necklaces in an array of precious stones to inlaid gold anklets to simple silver bangles, India has them all. Delhi's gold and silversmiths are the most famous in the country and, in fact, an entire street in Old Delhi is still called the 'Silver Street'. Besides gold and silver, Delhi offers a variety of precious gems—rubies, emeralds, sapphires and diamonds—and a number of semi-precious stones like cornelian, lapis lazuli and garnets. Delhi's jewellery shops are spread all over the city but Karol Bagh, Connaught Place, South Extension and Greater Kailash have the maximum number of shops in the New Delhi area.

For those interested in traditional Indian designs in gold and inlay jewellery, DARIBA KALAN at Chandni Chowk, Delhi's traditional jewellers street, is worth a visit. Here, in shops located in a narrow lane, visitors will be able to witness craftsmen at work and see designs which are still worn by traditional Indian women. What makes jewellery from Delhi so special is not only its quality of metal and stone but its fine and intricate workmanship.

Shoppers in Delhi have the option of either picking up fabric from the rich array of cottons, silks, woollens or synthetic materials, or buying readymade garments in the trendiest of the world fashions. Be it a traditional Indian saree or an evening dress, the bargains are many. PALIKA BAZAR, an underground shopping complex in Connaught Place, has a number of shops that specialise in inexpensive cotton readymades. The Janpath market also has a wide selection of mostly export quality cottons. Private emporia in Connaught Place have a dazzling selection of silks and brocades and less expensive shirts and scarves. For formal men's clothing, there are a number of famous garment stores. Women's boutiques are in almost every market. Custom-made tailoring is a luxury which is still affordable in Delhi. The city's tailors, considered to be amongst the best, will assure you a perfect fit in the shortest of time. Many of Delhi's tailors have a special 24-hour service and will deliver you a suit or a dress in just one day in your room.

Another enjoyable places to shop in Delhi is the SUNDER NAGAR MARKET. Collectors from all over the world come here to hunt for antiques and rare art objects like miniatures and bronzes, antique jewellery, wood carvings and unusual household objects.

India's leather is soft and fine, and its craftsmen have perfected the art of fashioning good quality footwear, bags and garments. Besides the chain stores, there are several establishments in different markets that feature trendy but inexpensive footwear. Other shopping bargains in Delhi include furniture and furnishings, carpets and durries, spices and tea and wide range of fashion accessories.

Delhi Haat

New Delhi's latest tourist alteraction is *Delhi Haat* an innovative shopping centre opposite the famous INA Market offering arts and crafts from different states of India and also the varied cuisines of India in some two dozen restaurants.

GENERAL INFORMATION

Population: 8,800,000 (1991 census)
Altitude: 239 metres (796 ft)
Climate:

	Temperature	
	Max.	Min.
Winter	33^0 c	7^0 c
Summer	41^0 c	21^0 c
Rainfall	534mm	37mm

Season: Throughout the year, except in the months of May and June, when the days are hot.

Clothing
Summer: cottons
Winter: woollens.

HOW TO GET THERE

By Air : Delhi is both a major international and a domestic airport and is connected with cities all over the world. Indian Airlines, Vayudoot and several private airlines connect Delhi with all important centres in India. Among these are: Jet Airways, *Phone*: 372472 8/29; East-West, *Phone*: 3721510; Modiluft, *Phone*: 3712222; Damania, *Phone*: 6881125 and Sahara India, *Phone*: 3326851/52. 25 International Airlines fly to Delhi.

By Rail: Delhi is connected with most of India by rail.

By Road: Delhi is connected by an extensive network of roads with all the main cities in India.

It is 203 km. from Agra,
603 km. from Allahabad,
373 km. from Almora,
190 km. from Bharatpur,
238 km. from Chandigarh,
297 km. from Corbett National Park,
250 km. from Jaipur,
596 km. from Khajuraho,
269 km. from Mussoorie,
318 km. from Nainital,
348 km. from Shimla,
876 km. from Srinagar,
663 km. from Udaipur and
147 km. from Mathura.

There are bus services to Agra, Ajmer, Amritsar, Bharatpur, Chandigarh, Dehradun, Gwalior, Hardwar, Jaipur, Jammu, Kulu, Mathura, Mussoorie, Nainital, Rishikesh, Shimla and several other places of interest.

LOCAL TRANSPORT

Luxury taxis (limousines), tourist taxis and coaches (air-conditioned and ordinary) can be hired. There are also metered taxis, auto-rickshaws and local bus services.

CONDUCTED TOURS

Conducted tours of Delhi, Agra and the Golden Triangle are operated by ITDC and Delhi Tourism (DTDC). Reservations can be made at the following addresses:

I.T.D.C., L Block, Connaught Place, New Delhi, *Tel*. 352336
D.T.D.C., N-36, Connaught Place, New Delhi, *Tel*. 3313637, 331-4229.

The following tours are available:

1. Half-day tour of OLD DELHI.
2. Half-day tour of NEW DELHI.
3. Evening tour of BIRLA TEMPLE, RAJPATH, INDIA GATE, PURANA QILA followed by SON-ET-LUMIERE show at RED FORT and dinner.
4. Full-day tour to AGRA.
5. Two-day tour to AGRA and FATEHPUR SIKRI.
6. Full Moon tour to AGRA, FATEHPUR SIKRI, MATHURA and DAYALBAGH (2-day tour).
7. Full-day tour to JAIPUR.
8. Two-day tour to JAIPUR.
9. GOLDEN TRIANGLE tour (2 nights and 3 days), visiting Agra, Fatehpur Sikri, Jaipur.
10. Full-day tour to PANIPAT, KURUKSHETRA, KARAN LAKE (Sundays).
11. Full-day tour to HODAL, BADHKAL, SURAJKUND (Saturdays).

TRAIN TOURS

There are special trains to Agra and Jaipur.

1. The Taj Express to Agra leaves early in the morning and returns the same night. (Travel time is 3 hours).
2. Shatabdi Express - another fast train, covers the distance in two hours. Leaves Delhi at 6.30 a.m. and leaves Agra for return journey at 8.10 pm.
3. The Pink City Express to Jaipur leaves in the morning and returns the same night.

WHERE TO STAY (STD CODE: 011)

Deluxe

1. Ashok Hotel
   Phone: 600121
   Telex: 031-82075 ASOK IN
   Cable: ASHOKA HOTEL
   Fax: 91-11-6873216
2. Centaur
   Phone: 5481411
   Telex: 031-62744
   Cable: CENTAUR
3. New Delhi Hilton
   Phone: 3320101
   Telex: 031-61186
   Fax: 332-5335, 331-6163
4. Hyatt Regency
   Phone: 609911
   Telex: 031-61512
   Fax: 678833
5. Le Meridian
   Phone: 3710101
   Telex: 031-63076, 4397
   Cable: MERIDHOTEL
   Fax: 3714545
6. Maurya Sheraton (Welcom Group)
   Phone: 3010101
   Telex: 031-61447
   Cable: WELCOTEL
   Fax: 3010908
7. Taj Mahal
   Phone: 3016162
   Telex: 031-66874
   Cable: TAJDEL
   Fax: 3017299
8. Taj Palace Intercontinental
   Phone: 3010404
   Telex: 031-62756, 62761
   Fax: 3011252
9. The Oberoi
   Phone: 62118, 4363030
   Telex: 031-622118 OBCL IN
   Cable: OBHOTEL
   Fax: 4360484
10. Park Hotel
    Phone: 3732477
    Telex: 031-6531
    Cable: PARKOTEL
    Fax: 011-3732025
11. Park Royal New Delhi
    Phone: 6223349
    Fax: 011-6224288

Standard

12. Vasant Continental
    Phone: 678800
    Telex: 031-72263
    Cable: CONTIHOTEL
    Fax: 6873842
13. Claridges
    Phone: 3010211
    Telex: 031-71266
    Cable: CLARIDGES
    Fax: 301-0625
14. Kanishka
    Phone: 3324422
    Telex: 031-62788
    Cable: KANISHOTEL

15. Imperial
    Phone: 3325332
    Telex: 031-62603
    Fax: 3314542
16. Qutab
    Phone: 660060
    Telex: 031-62537
    Cable: QUTABOTEL
17. Samrat
    Phone: 603030
    Telex: 031-73122
    Cable: HOTELSAMRAT
18. Siddharth
    Phone: 5712501
    Telex: 031-77125
    Cable: IRONHOTEL
    Fax: 5729581
19. Ambassador
    Phone: 690391
    Telex: 031-74045
    Cable: HOTEL AMBASSADOR
20. Connaught Place
    Phone: 4632600
    Telex: 031-74045
    Cable: INDIAFAME
    Fax: 310757
21. Diplomat
    Phone: 3010204
    Telex: 031-61041
    Cable: DIPLOMATIC
    Fax: 3018601
22. Hans Plaza
    Phone: 3316861
    Telex: 031-3126
    Cable: HANSTEL
    Fax: 3314830
23. Janpath
    Phone: 3320070
    Fax: 332-8073
    Cable: RESTWELL

ECONOMY
24. Marina
    Phone: 3324648
    Telex: 031-62969
    Cable: MARINA
25. Nirula
    Phone: 3322419
    Telex: 031-66224
    Cable: NIRULABROS
26. Oberoi Maidens
    Phone: 2525464
    Telex: 031-66303
    Cable: OBMAIDENS
    Fax: 2929800
27. Rajdoot
    Phone: 699583
    Telex: 031-74129
    Cable: RIVERVIEW
28. Best Western Surya
    Phone: 6835070
    Telex: 031-66700
    Cable: SUROTEL
    Fax: 6837758
29. Alka
    Phone: 344328
    Cable: HOTELALKA
30. Broadway
    Phone: 3273821
    Telex: 031-66299
    Cable: LUXURY
31. Lodhi
    Phone: 4362422
    Telex: 031-74068
    Cable: LIVEWELL
32. President
    Phone: 3277836
    Telex: 031-62422
    Cable: BHAISONS
33. Ranjit
    Phone: 3311256
    Telex: 031-66001
    Cable: STAYWELL

34. Sartaj
   Phone: 663277
   Telex: 031-73009
   Cable: DAAWAT
   Fax: 6864240
35. Sobti
   Phone: 5729035
   Cable: STAYFINE
36. Vikram
   Phone: 6436451
   Telex: 031-71161
   Cable: HOTELVIKRAM
37. York
   Phone: 3323769
   Telex: 031-63031
   Cable: YORK HOTEL
38. Flora
   Phone: 3273634
   Cable: FUSEE
39. Manor Hotel
   Phone: 6832171, 6832511
40. Metro
   Phone: 3313856
   Cable: HOTEL METRO
41. Y.M.C.A.
   Tourist Hotel
   Phone: 311915
   Telex: 031-62547
   Cable: MANHOOD
42. Ashok Yatri Niwas
   Phone: 3324511
   Telex: MANHOOD
   Cable: YATRINIWAS
43. Host Inn
   Phone: 3310704, 3310523
44. Hotel Neeru
   Phone: 3278522, 3278756
   Cable: FREEHOME
45. Hotel Nest
   Phone: 526614, 526429
   Telex: 031-62416
   Cable: HOTELNEST
46. Sheila
   Phone: 525603
47. Asian International
   Phone: 3321636
   Telex: 031-61258
   Cable: HAIHOTELS
48. Bright
   Phone: 3320444
49. Central Court Hotel
   Phone: 3315013
   Cable: CENTRAL COURT HOTEL
50. India International Center
   Phone: 619431
51. Y.M.C.A. International
   Phone: 311561, 311970

Guest House

52. Y.W.C.A.
   Phone: 3361915
53. Vishwa Yuvak Kendra
   Phone: 3013611
54. Youth Hostel
   Phone: 3016285

Camping Park

55. Tourist
   Camping Park
   Phone: 2523121, 2522507

RAILWAY RETIRING ROOMS

Railway retiring rooms are available at both New Delhi and Old Delhi Railway Stations. They are allotted to railway passengers on first-come-first-served basis.

AIRPORT RETIRING ROOMS

A few retiring rooms are also available at the airport.

WHAT TO SEE

1. JANTAR MANTAR, an observatory with astronomical instruments built of stone by the great royal

astronomer, Maharaja Jai Singh of Jaipur in 1724.
2. The modern LAKSHMI NARAYAN TEMPLE, also known as the Birla Temple after the business family, who built it.
3. SAFDARJUNG'S TOMB built in the 18th century by Nawab Shuja-ud-Daula, the last monument of the Mughal style.
4. The QUTAB MINAR, the tallest stone tower in India. Its construction was started by Qutb-ud-din Aibak in 1199. The attached mosque, also built by him, was started by pulling down 27 Hindu and Jain temples and using their columns. The IRON PILLAR, originally a standard of Lord Vishnu, is now in the courtyard of the mosque.
5. PURANA QILA, believed to be the ancient city of Indraprastha. The fortress was built in the 16th century.
6. HUMAYUN'S TOMB, built by the widow of the second Mughal Emperor, Humayun's tomb is an outstanding monument in the Indo-Persian style, a precursor of the Taj Mahal.
7. FEROZSHAH KOTLA, the ruins of the city founded by Ferozshah Tughlaq in 1354.
8. RAJGHAT. A black marble platform marks the site where Mahatma Gandhi, the Father of the Nation, was cremated.
9. RED FORT, built by the great Mughal Emperor, Shahjahan, when he shifted his capital from Agra to Delhi. This fabulous fort houses the Diwan-i-Aam, the Hall of Public Audiences and the Diwan-i-Khas, the Hall of Private Audience, the Moti Masjid or Pearl Mosque, Rang Mahal, Khas Mahal and Hammam (royal baths).
10. JAMA MASJID, built by Shahjahan can accommodate as many as 20, 000 worshippers. The courtyard is enclosed by pillared corridors and domed pavillons.
11. INDIA GATE, RASHTRAPATI BHAVAN (President's residence) and the avenues and gardens of New Delhi can be seen as part of a drive around the city.

EXCURSIONS
1. Picnic spots in Haryana (excellent accommodation put up by the Haryana Tourism Department is available at each centre as also recreation facilities). (See details under Haryana.)
2. Mathura (147 km. from Delhi and 56 km. from Agra) is associated with Lord Krishna who spent his childhood at

Vrindaban, 10 km. from here. It has many temples on the river bank. The Mathura Museum has sculptures and icons going back to the 5th century B.C.
3. HARIDWAR (214 km.), the holy city on the banks of the Ganges, and Rishikesh, 24 km. beyond (the base for pilgrimages to Kedarnath, Badrinath, the Himalayan shrines), are pilgrim centres with a great atmosphere of reverence.

SHOPPING

Delhi is a shopper's paradise. It has not only the local handicrafts available, but nearly every State of India has its handicrafts emporium at Delhi. Almost everything is available at Delhi. Some of the special handicrafts available are silver work, filgree, Indian perfumes, saris and fabrics embroidered with gold and silver, curios and paintings, semi-precious jewellery, brass and copperware, Indian musical instruments, etc.

SPORTS

1. Horse Show (mid-February) with equestrian feats, show-jumping, etc.
2. Polo matches held in the winter season.
3. The Defence Services Sailing Club holds races on Sundays from October through May.

ENTERTAINMENT

All the year round and especially during the winter months, there are music and dance recitals and theatrical performances. Newspapers and weekly magazines cover all types of programmes, including yoga demonstrations, Indian and foreign films, etc. There is a regular weekend theatre in winter and a play festival before summer.

The Ram Lila dance drama on the Ramayana is performed open-air during Dussehra.

Music and dance programmes are held regularly during autumn and winter.

There are two sound-and-light shows, one at the Red Fort and the other at Teen Murti House. An interesting evening of cultural entertainment and dining can be spent against the background of a 14th century Fort and Village right in the heart of Delhi. Called the Hauz Khas Village, it features restaurants specialising in different cuisines including the continental. You can eat anywhere and later see an hour's programme of Indian dance and music. The total tab is US$ 10 or Rs. 350 There are many shops in the village selling fashionable garments and handicrafts of the country.

The restaurant complex is called BISTRO
Phone: 6853857 / 6852226

Chapter 13

RAJASTHAN
The Land of Palaces, Forts and Camels

Jaisalmer Fort

Hawa Mahal, Jaipur

One out of every four foreign visitors to India visits the state of Rajasthan. The state apparently seems to have a great fascination for foreign travellers. Jaipur, Rajasthan's capital, along with Delhi and Agra is part of India's Golden Triangle.

Known as Rajputana under the British, it came to be called Rajasthan after the integration of some 100 princely States, into a new administrative unit created after independence. It is a region of rock and desert interspersed with fertile belts, enchanting lakes and dense jungles full of wildlife.

From a tourist angle, Rajasthan is a country which is still living in the historic past, cherishing old values and retaining old loyalties. Although the erstwhile rulers have no longer any legal status, they are still revered and respected by people who often elect them to Parliament or the State Legislature.

Gone are the days of pomp and ceremony that outdid Croesus in their mad extravaganza. A story is told about the Maharajah of Jaipur who visited England to participate in the Coronation of Edward VII in 1902. He chartered a ship, built a temple in it for worship. He threw bags of gold, silver and silks into the sea to invoke the blessings of gods for his safe journey. And he took enough Ganges water to drink to last him during his stay in England. He did not want to drink the impure English water!

Now, the Maharajahs have come to terms with the new realities of India. They still live in palaces or in parts of them but some of the larger palaces have been leased out to hoteliers. Visitors can still indulge in the luxury of living like Maharajas and Maharanis in Rajasthan with modern comforts in palaces converted into hotels.

Most of the newer palaces were built during the British Protectorate in the 19th and 20th centuries, except for a few which are ancient, like the

Amber Fort near Jaipur. These palaces with their massive size and grandeur, dazzle the visitors. They are the creations of an extravagant era when life was peaceful under the British suzerainty and they did not expect danger from one another. Before the British took them under their protection, war was their game and pastime. Proud, tall and moustached Rajputs were great warriors and horsemen. They made no bones about their pedigree and claimed descent from the Sun and the Moon via the heroes of the *Ramayana* and *Mahabharata* epics. They were constantly at war with one another if they were not fighting an invader. Each one had too much of ego.

The Rajputs' feats of valour and sense of honour have few parallels in world history. When faced by overwhelming odds, they preferred death to defeat. They donned saffron robes of immolation, went to battle and died in war. Their women threw themselves on flaming pyres to avoid dishonour. Thirteen thousand Rajput women died in this way along with Maharani Padmini when King Alla-ud-Din Khilji came down to Udaipur to abduct the Maharani, who he had heard, was the most beautiful woman in the world.

After the Mutiny in 1857, when British India came under the direct rule of the Crown, Rajput princes were allowed to remain independent. To encourage loyalty, the British heaped on them privileges, titles, medals and honours. They were also allowed to retain their army units which they used in defence of Britain during World War I and II. However, Maharajahs were encouraged to modernise. Their children went to Public Schools specially opened for the aristocrats. The British ploy worked — the princes forsook war for peace. To live in peace was to live and build as ostentatiously as possible which they did with a fervour.

Colour and gaiety abound everywhere. The Maharajahs of Rajasthan patronised art. The Rajput School of Miniature Painting, which flourished during the 17th and 18th centuries, bears testimony to it. The miniatures of their womenfolk reflect the Indian ideal of feminine beauty. Its architectural traditions are best represented in the Palace of Amber which has been described as a 'sleeping beauty'. The Lake Palace in Udaipur is another good example of Hindu architecture. The State presents some of the finest examples of Hindu traditions, manners, fashions, colour and pageantry.

Before the Muslims came to India, the princes of Rajasthan never allowed anyone from outside to subjugate them, though they fought constantly among themselves to establish their hegemony. During the Mughal rule, Akbar succeeded in winning the loyalty of a few of the Rajas by marrying Rajput princesses. Others did not yield, notably the great Maharana Pratap of Udaipur. Emperor Jahangir, Akbar's son, was the son of a Rajput Princess from Jaipur. Man Singh, who was the maternal uncle of Jahangir, was the Commander-in-Chief of Akbar's army. So were a few other Rajput princes who fought for the Mughals.

Their colourful costumes reflect the joy with which the people of Rajasthan enliven their lives. Their distinctive headgear is a pink or yellow turban. The costumes of women are even more colourful. These consist of a full skirt and a half-sleeved bodice. The dopatta or the head cover is two and a half yards long.

JAIPUR

Entering Jaipur by road from Delhi, the visitor first encounters the relics of the region's martial past. As the winding road snakes through the hills, a fortified gate looms ahead, set in a tall ridge. A little ahead, you are greeted by a delightful contrast — the sight of the city idyllically cocooned in the distance below.

Further along, there are more reminders of history — on the ridge, the JAIGARH FORT perches on craggy heights, symbols of the Rajputs and their fierce pride. These brave warriors lived and died in accordance with an inviolable code of honour and chivalry, and have inspired much of Rajasthan's romantic legend.

Entering the main city, the title of 'pink' becomes quite apparent. The entire old sector of Jaipur is built of pink muted walls clamped alike with this rich, earthy colour that traditionally signifies welcome. The old city, with its surprisingly modern grid layout stands in perfect harmony with the newer Jaipur — a progressive centre of commerce, industry, learning, arts. Busy streets and colourful markets depict much of Jaipur's vibrancy and charm.

Amer, the Fortress Capital

Before Jaipur, the State capital was the Amer Fortress. The Kachwaha Rajput clan are believed to have founded the city around the 10th century. The dynasty continued to rule through the 16th century and forged close ties with the Mughals. The old capital, Amer, displays unmistakable Mughal influences. The climb to the fort can be made on the back of an elephant, the preferred vehicle of medieval royalty. Once at the top, a spectacular view of the gorge and the land surrounding hills is revealed. Entering through the imposing SINGH POL (Lion Gate) one comes upon a sprawling complex of courtyards, halls, palaces and apartments separated by several gates. The DIWAN-E-AAM is the first building you encounter. Meant for public audiences, this hall shows a distinctly Mughal style — expertly copied with its double rows of columns and latticed galleries.

Opposite this hall stands an ornate gate, the GANESH POL. The painted facade of the gate with its arcades, shows a rich harmony of Hindu and Mughal styles. Beyond the courtyard lie the main palaces and other buildings.

The Maharaja's apartments on a higher terrace, feature rooms that are a riot of exquisite wall paintings and mirror-work inlay. Here, too, are the JAI MANDIR (Hall of Victory) and the SUKH NIWAS (Hall of Pleasure), which was cooled by a stream of water.

Most fascinating, perhaps, is the SHEESH MAHAL (Hall of Mirrors), where even a single lamp is replicated in thousands of glittering mirrors.

Companion Forts

Beyond Amer, commanding the surrounding country, stands the impregnable JAIGARH FORT. When illuminated by night, it becomes a fairy-tale castle floating in the air far above the city. In daylight, its forbidding exterior becomes more apparent. The walls of Jaigarh were never breached. In fact, the prospect of besieging it must have been so daunting that few tried to do it. And JAIVAN — the huge 8-metre cannon with its ornate barrel — was never called into action. For visitors, however, a toy cannon is let off from time to time.

NAHARGARH FORT, smaller and less imposing, than its two companions, makes up by offering the most panoramic view of all. By night, you can look through one of the Jharokhas (windows) and see the lights of Jaipur spread out below.

Within the Walled City

This story is a popular favourite with people of Jaipur. The mighty Mughal emperor Aurangzeb sat in state. Before him stood the young successor to the Amer throne. The Emperor gently admonished him for his ancestors' resistance, asked him what fate he deserved. The lad, not quite 11, yet shot back, "Your Majesty, when the groom takes the bride's hand, he is conferring lifelong protection on her. Now, that the Emperor has taken my hand, what do I need to fear?"

The Emperor was impressed and bestowed on him the title of Sawai (one and a quarter) presaging that the boy when he grows up would be a giant among other men. He went on to become Sawai Jai Singh II, a man of many parts. Master diplomat, tactician, astronomer, he was the one who founded the city of Jaipur 250 years ago. For its time, Jaipur must have been a remarkably advanced city. It was built in accordance with ancient Hindu tenets of town planning with broad avenues in a grid, and a logical division of the area into nine zones.

The pink came in 1853, when Prince Albert paid a visit. The city was daubed in the traditional colour of welcome, and the practice endures to this day.

The walled city is the soul of Jaipur. The sharp and picturesque contrasts in the marketplace are typical of the city. The men's bright turbans and women's skirts stand out boldly against the muted pink background. Nippy cars and stately camels match their paces. Puppeteers brush past trendy young people in the streets. And glittering, neon-lit shop windows show off traditional colour and craftsmanship.

Among all these, the CITY PALACE holds much in store for the visitor. The former Maharaja still resides in a part of it, but the rest serves as a museum. One of the first exhibits to catch the eye stand outside the building. These are two enormous silver urns in which a former ruler carried a six-months' supply of holy Ganga water to England.

There is the SILEH KHANA (armoury) with its collection of Rajput weapons and battle gear. And the DIWAN-E-AAM and the DIWAN-E-KHAS, where the treasures of the royal house are on display. The collection is exquisite, and consists of textiles, carpets, miniature paintings and precious manuscripts.

At the rear of the City Palace is one of Jaipur's most interesting monuments, the HAWA MAHAL (Palace of Winds), a five-storey facade which overlooks the walled city's main thoroughfare. The quaint pink sandstone structure is studded with 953 little windows, balconies, and fine screen work. The ladies of the royal household used to sit here to catch the breeze (*hawa*, hence the name) and watch the world go by.

Close to the City Palace is a fascinating complex called JANTAR MANTAR. Sawai Jai Singh's abiding passion was astronomy. He built 5 observatories, with huge masonry instruments for plotting the seasons, the stars, eclipses, and of course for astrology. The observatory at Jaipur is the most ambitious of them all.

Jantar Mantar. An observatory of outsized astronomical instruments.

The RAM NIWAS GARDENS, south of the old city, hold out varied promises for the visitor. Here, housed in the ALBERT HALL is the CENTRAL MUSEUM, a superb gallery of miniature portraits, and other works of art. Within the garden complex is also JAIPUR ZOO. Its star attraction is the crocodile breeding farm. And close at hand is the GALLERY OF MODERN ART.

The traditional markets of Jaipur are a voyage of discovery for the adventurous shopper. Most of the main markets are within the old walled city and are interconnnected.

Gold, precious and semi-precious stones are traded in the traditional JOHARI BAZAR (Goldsmiths' Market). MANIHARON KA RASTA

(Street of the Lac Bangle Makers) is known for its multicoloured lacquer bangles. Costume jewellery is the hot item at TRIPOLIA BAZAR. In the BAPU and NEHRU BAZARS textiles are in abundance, printed in the typical styles of Rajasthan. And, so inexpensive.

In a country renowned for its handicrafts tradition, Rajasthan and Jaipur have their unique place. Perhaps the most popular craft is *Bandhani*, a local name for the tie-and-dye technique. Young girls work with strings on fabric, tying a series of little knots which bunch up the fabric according to a pattern. When the whole is dyed, the knots keep the tied-up part clear, while the rest takes on the dye. This gives rise to bright patterns of dots in circles, spirals or clusters.

A variation in the knot-tying method produces stripes. This is called *Lahariya* (waves). At SANGANER, close to Jaipur, another folk art is alive and thriving. This is the block-printing of textiles. Woodblocks, along with vegetable dyes in orange and red (with a few occasional colours) are used to turn out bedspreads, skirts, and a variety of products.

Another exquisite craft practised here is *Meenakari*, the art of enamelling on silver or gold. The designs are engraved on the object to be enamelled, the metallic colours then being deposited in the depressions.

The famous blue-art pottery of Jaipur.

Jaipur's blue pottery is well known. The motifs and designs have been handed down over the generations. In addition, stoneware, brassware, ivory and wood carving, handmade paper, and carpets are flourishing handicrafts.

An easier and the most comfortable way to see Rajasthan is to buy one-week trip on PALACE ON WHEELS, the luxury train from Delhi. You will not only visit Jaipur but also Udaipur, Jodhpur, Jaisalmer, Bharatpur and Taj at Agra.

ALWAR

Craddled by several small hills, Alwar has had a turbulent past. It is today muted by its rich forests and glass-like lakes.

Ride a jeep up the road which winds through tall grass, past black crags across precipices. Soon you reach SALIM MOSQUE, and further up, SALIM MAHAL, named after Emperor Akbar's hedonist son who spent three years here.

An 8 km drive through thickly wooded hills brings you to SILISERH LAKE, once a source of Alwar's water supply. Remains of the old

Alwar Palace

aqueduct can be seen on the way. The lake is teeming with fish and water birds.

Moving eastward, you come to two fascinating wildlife and bird sanctuaries. SARISKA, 37 km from Alwar, a thickly wooded reserve, is inhabited by cheetal, sambhar, tiger, porcupine and wild boar. Tourist facilities include a tourist bungalow at the edge of the woods with a bar and transport facilities.

BHARATPUR—
Colour On Wings

Once the stronghold of a fierce rebel Jats and the curse of the Mughal rulers, Bharatpur today is famous for the KEOLADEO GHANA NATIONAL PARK, a sanctuary for several indigenous bird species and migratory fowl which come here annually to nest and breed, some from as far away as Siberia. It is a delight for wildlife enthusiasts. Spend a leisurely morning with some of the rarest birds, greyleg geese, Siberian cranes, the barheaded goose from China and winged beauties from Afghanistan, Central Asia and Tibet. The native birds include pelican, ibis, egret, painted stork and darter. Other animals like the blue bull, spotted deer and wild boar inhabit the dense woods.

The vast fortifications of the BHARATPUR FORT speak of the builder's determination to secure safe retreats for his fiercely loyal Jat peasants. Suraj Mal, the arch enemy of the Mughals, made frequent inroads into the capital of Delhi and once carried away the gates of the Agra Fort to strengthen his retreat at Bharatpur. Within the massive fort of Bharatpur are two victory towers: JAWAHAR BURJ which celebrated the victory over the Mughals, and FATEH BURJ, marking the defeat of the British in 1803. Not far from Bharatpur is DEEG, an 18th century stronghold whose massive fortifications are surrounded by luxuriant woods and pools.

AJMER—On Pilgrim's Trail

Driving 132 kms southward from Jaipur, taking the camel trail to Ajmer, thousands of Muslim pilgrims are seen walking up to Ajmer from many parts of the world.Their destination is the tomb of Sufi SAINT MOINUDDIN CHISTI. The tomb, it is believed, fulfils the desires of all the devotees. Ajmer has also the placid green. PUSHKAR is one of the holiest of Hindu pilgrim centres. In the month of November every year, it is suddenly alive with colours, sounds and excitement of one of India's biggest cattle fairs, where over 1000,000 people gather. The festival is very popular with foreign visitors from Europe, USA and Japan,who pitch in their tents to participate in the festivities.

South-east of Ajmer lies BUNDI. A luminous white fort shelters the quaint houses; a steep paved carriage way leads up to a complex of lovely palaces iridescent with exquisite murals; everything reflected in a deep, lapping lake in the centre.

Further away (38 km), KOTA on the Chambal river is fast becoming an important industrial centre. It has a busy air about it in contrast to the medieval and somewhat sleepy appearance of other cities of Rajasthan. RANA PRATAP SAGAR DAM is well worth a visit.

On the road between BUNDI and CHITTORGARH **are two sites renowned** for their temple architecture. MENAL, a complex of 9th century temples, is set amidst wooden remains near a river that flows over a bed of granite slabs and plunges into a gorge. The main temple, dedicated to Lord Shiva, has expressive carvings of Lord Shiva and his consort, Parvati.

BIJOLIA is 16 km from Menal on the road to Chittorgarh. Of the 100 ancient temples only three stand mute witnesses to the zealous fury of Muslim invaders.

CHITTORGARH—The Heroic City

From Bundi the road curves westwards towards the proudest of Rajput fortresses, Chittorgarh. If ever there was a city which witnessed bloody carnage and rare sacrifices, it was this. Sacked three times, Chittorgarh represents the quintessence of Rajput chivalry and valour. The ruins of the great monuments here depict innumerable deeds of heroism and sacrifice and an endless struggle of Maharana Pratap against the forces of the Mughal emperor Akbar. Maharana never gave up!

On the crest of the enormous grey hill, girdled by massive walls and seven majestic gateways, one stumbles upon shattered palaces, a TEMPLE OF MIRABAI — the mystic poetess—and the intricately carved nine-storeyed TOWER OF VICTORY rising into the sky. Near a Jain temple stands the TOWER OF FAME, built in the 12th century in honour of Lord Adinath, the first Jain Tirthankara.

UDAIPUR—The Serene Vale

In the midst of this romantic land you come upon Udaipur, a beautiful city of lakes, palaces and fountains. Serene in the shadows of dark green hills, Udaipur's three lakes — PICHOLA, FATEH SAGAR and UDAI SAGAR — are shimmering jewels from the opal surfaces of which rise fairy-tale white palaces. Maharana Udai Singh, son of Maharana Pratap, sought shelter here from the Mughal hordes and then tried to fashion a city out of the silent vale.

Overlooking the Lake Pichola, the CITY PALACE is accessible through three gateways. Within are the SHEESH MAHAL with inlaid mirror work, and the KRISHNA VILAS, the most beautiful enclosure with four rows of painted scenes in miniature. It was here that the beautiful princess, Krishna Kumari, drank poison and saved the kingdom from the wrath of two rival suitors.

Once the refuge of Prince Khurram (later Emperor Shahjahan, who built the Taj Mahal), JAG MANDIR is a yellow sandstone tower inlaid with marble and dedicated to the Lord of the Universe. The black and white marble tiles of the floors form a striking mosaic. Other places worth a visit are SAHELIYON KI BARI, the fountained and flowered 'garden of maidens', PRATAP SMARAK, a memorial to the legendary warrior Rana Pratap, and the BHARATIYA LOK KALA MANDAL MUSEUM, a museum of folk art and craft.

Around Udaipur

Just 3 kms outside Udaipur are 4000-year old ruins at AHAR, the most ancient city of the region. North of Udaipur, 21 kms away, is the EKLINGJI TEMPLE dedicated to Lord Shiva. Originally, this was a complex of 108 temples with bathing terraces leading to the edge of a lake.

Further 27 km. north of Eklingji, lies NATHDWARA, one of the wealthiest temples of India enshrining the remarkable image of Lord Krishna. The image, almost 1,600 years old and sculptured out of one piece of black marble, seems to radiate power and is highly revered.

JAISAMAND, 51 km from Udaipur, is the largest artificial lake in Asia framed by mountains. The vast stretch of water is broken by hilly islands. Perched on a cliff overlooking the lake is a white marble palace built for a favourite queen There is a 65 sq kms forest area which has deer, wild boar and panther. Once a royal game reserve, the forest is a protected wildlife sanctuary today, and has *machans* or watch towers for viewing the wild animals.

Hire a jeep and head for KUMBHALGARH, 64 km north-west of Udaipur. The winding road climbs steeply as you pass through one imposing gate after another. Within the fortress there are some interesting temples, a palace, BADAL MAHAL, with pastel-tinted chambers, unexpected in the surrounding grimness.

JAGAT AMBIKA MATA, 58 km from Udaipur, is a 1000-year-old temple, pentagonal in shape, with 17 turrets. It has a pagoda-like roof. The road from Udaipur leading into the desert is paved with temples. The most remarkable are the profusely carved Jain temples at RANAKPUR, 98 km from Udaipur — one of the holy places of Jain pilgrimage. The CHAUMUKHA TEMPLE here is a three-storeyed building and has four subsidiary shrines, 80 domes supported by 1,444 columns.

MOUNT ABU—Hymns in Marble

Further west is the quaint hill-station of Mount Abu where shaded woods shelter temples, shrines and clusters of dwellings. The air is cool and bracing at this 1,220 metres high resort. You can see the 1000-year-old JAIN DILWARA TEMPLES, exquisitely cut and carved in pure marble. Elaborate arches embellish the hall of Adinath temple, its pillars carry a stunning profusion of nymphs and musicians in snowwhite marble. The NEMINATH TEMPLE, the other shrine, honours the 22nd Tirthankara. Once again, the profuse carvings seem to flow out of the marble everywhere. Mount Abu has many Hindu temples as well the beautiful NAKKI LAKE and a developing wildlife sanctuary. DILWARA TEMPLES are some of the most beautiful in the world.

JODHPUR—The Desert City

Travelling north 250 kms, the cool blue and green of Mount Abu give way to the burning sands of the Thar desert — untamed, sun-scorched and inhospitable. Yet, to this harsh terrain came Prince Jodha, a Rajput scion, and founded the city of Jodhpur in 1459.

A bleak scrap rears up 120 metres from the desert valley. Straddling the rocky eminence is the JODHPUR FORT, its sheer walls reflecting the strength of its warrior-builders. Entered through seven gates, each a formidable barrier, the fort encloses several palaces interspersed with vast courtyards. Arched windows crown overhanging balconies and display fine lattice work in sandstone. Pierced stone screens protect the royal ladies' chambers. The craftsmanship in stone at its finest is manifest here — MOTI MAHAL (Pearl Palace) and MAN MAHAL (Palace of Honour). Not to be missed is the SILEH KHANA which houses an armoury containing the fabulous treasures of the royal household.

The city is a walled habitation with seven gates at the foot of the citadel, studded with lakes, palaces and temples.

JAISALMER—City within a Fort

Jaisalmer, 287 km westwards, is an architectural dream set in the lonely yellow silence of the desert. The citadel city provokes wonder at what could have induced Jaisal, a Bhatti prince, to settle right in the heart of a desolate desert.

In the narrow, cobbled alleys of Jaisalmer — no wider than a stretched arm — lie a cluster of *havelis* or the mansions of the rich, with stone carving and lattice work of breathtaking intricacy.

The JAISALMER FORT, built on the highest point of the TRICUTA HILL, is entered through the SURAJ POL GATE. The MEGH DURBAR or Hall of Clouds and THE KING'S WELL must be seen.

There are several superbly carved Jain temples in and around Jaisalmer. The entrance to the 15th century RISHABDEOJI TEMPLE is through a beautifully carved arch.

The ruins of Lodurva, original capital of the Bhatti rulers of Jaisalmer, lie 16 km north of Jaisalmer.

BIKANER—The Camel Country

Bikaner, a true desert city in a camel country, was founded by Bikaji, a son of Jodha Singh, founder of Jodhpur, on the ancient caravan routes that originated from Africa and West Asia. The fortified town stands on a slight eminence.

The Bikaner Fort, founded by Raja Rai Singh, is distinguished by its long range of 37 pavilions. A line of balconies and soriel windows of varying designs lend it a graceful dignity. An enormous arched doorway leads to the Joramal Temple in a spacious courtyard. Tar Mandir is the royal chapel where royal weddings and births were once solemnised

A visit to the Camel Breeding Farm, 10 km from Bikaner, is a unique experience. Here, you can ride on a gaily caparisoned camel and have perhaps the first taste of camel's milk.

Just 8 km away is an unexpected oasis of greenery in the barren desert, alive with birds and animals. There are thick woods surrounding a lake on the shores of which the kings built themselves luxurious palaces.

A drive of 32 kms on the Jodhpur road takes you to Deshnoke, famous for its temple, dedicated to Karnik Devi, the tutelary deity of the Rajas of Bikaner. Thousands of rats, held sacred here, scamper freely in the temple.

JAIPUR

GENERAL INFORMATION

Population: 1,510,000 (1991 census)
Altitude: 390 metres (1299 ft)
Climate:

	Temperature	
	Max.	Min.
Winter	31°c	8°c
Summer	41°c	21°c

Season: Throughout the year. The months of April to June, are hot.

Clothing
Summer: cottons.
Winter: woollens

HOW TO GET THERE

By Air: Indian Airlines and some private airline services connect Jaipur with Ahmedabad, Aurangabad, Bombay, Delhi, Jodhpur and Udaipur.

By Rail: Jaipur is connected by rail directly with Ahmedabad, Abu Road, Agra, Bharatpur, Delhi, Jaisalmer, Jodhpur, Udaipur, etc. The Pink City Express is a fast train running between Delhi and Jaipur.

By Road: Jaipur has good road connections. It is
230 km from Agra,
174 km from Bharatpur,

306 km from Delhi,
340 km from Jodhpur and
406 km from Udaipur.
There are regular bus services to Agra, Ahmedabad, Ajmer, Bharatpur, Bhopal, Delhi, Jodhpur, Udaipur, etc.

LOCAL TRANSPORT

Tourist taxis, metered auto-rickshaws, tongas, cycle-rickshaws and bus services are available.

CONDUCTED TOURS

Half-day and also full-day tours of local sightseeing are available. Rajasthan Tourism Development Corporation (RTDC) is a very active agency of tourism development in the State. Convenient bus tours with trained guides are available for sightseeing not only in Jaipur but also to the neighbouring cities. Contact for more information

India Tourist Office
Tel.: 372200

Rajasthan Tourist Office
Tourist Hotel
Tel.: 575466

WHERE TO STAY (STD Code: 0141)

Deluxe

1. Welcomgroup Rajputana Palace Sheraton
   Phone: 360011
   Fax: 367848
2. Rambagh Palace
   Phone: 381919
   Fax: 381098
   Cable: RAMBAGH
3. Jaimahal Palace
   Phone: 371616
   Telex: 365-2250 JMPH IN
   Cable: JAIMAHAL JAIPUR
   Fax: 365237
4. Rajmahal Palace
   Phone: 381676
   Fax: 381887
   Cable: RESIDENCY

Standard

5. Jaipur Ashok
   Phone: 75121
   Fax: 67923
   Cable: ASHOKOTEL
6. Clarks Amer
   Phone: 550616-21
   Fax: 550013
   Cable: CLARKSAMER
   Fax: 091-141-550013
7. Mansingh
   Phone: 378771
   Fax: 377552
8. Jaipur Palace
   Phone: 512961
   Fax: 512966
   Cable: HOTELMERU
9. Megh Niwas
   Phone: 74018, 75661
   Telex: 3652110
10. Meru Palace
    Phone: 371111-16
    Fax: 563767
    Cable: COMFORTS
11. Aditya
    Phone: 381720
    Cable: ARTAGE

Budget

12. Narain Niwas
    Phone: (141)563448
    Cable: NARAINIWAS
13. Bissau Palace
    Phone: 74191, 67728
    Telex: 365-2644 REGIIN
    Cable: HOBL

14. Lakshmi Vilas
    Phone: 381567
    Cable: LAKSHMI
15. Mandawa House
    Phone: 385398
16. Khasa Kothi
    Phone: 375151-5
    Fax: 374040
    Cable: KHASAKOTHI
17. Gangaur (RTDC)
    Phone: 371641-42
18. Tourist Hotel (RTDC)
    Phone: 360238
19. Swagatam (RTDC)
    Phone: 310595
20. Teej (RTDC)
    Phone: 374206, 374373

Paying Guests

Jaipur is one of the first cities in India where paying guest accommodation is available to visitors in about 250 houses. A copy of the *Directory of Paying Guest Accommodations* is available from the tourist office. Similar accommodation is also available in other cities of Rajasthan. Price ranges from Rs. 200 to Rs. 250 per night.

WHAT TO SEE

1. CITY PALACE and MUSEUM. Within the walled city are several glittering palaces and a museum resplendent with collections of the princely era.
2. JANTAR MANTAR OUTDOOR OBSERVATORY. Built in 1726, it is one of the five such astronomical wonders built by Sawai Jai Singh and makes accurate predictions to this day.
3. HAWA MAHAL, Palace of the Winds, the landmark of Jaipur, stands 5 storeys high. The cool wind blows through its facade of windows and latticed screens through which the queens of the court once viewed the streets of the city.
4. GOVIND DEVJI. Temple of Krishna inside the City Palace.
5. CENTRAL MUSEUM, RAM NIWAS GARDEN.
6. DOLL MUSEUM with dolls of all nationalities.

EXCURSIONS

1. AMBER PALACE and FORT (11 km.). Perched on a hill, it has a marble palace, Temple of Victory and Sheesh Mahal (hall of mirrors) which are marvellous examples of ancient Rajput architecture.

    Elephants are available to take you up to the Fort.
2. SISODIA PALACE and GARDENS (8 km.), built for a Sisodia queen.
3. GAITOR (8 km.), where there are the cenotaphs of the kings of this region, the most beautiful being that of Sawai Jai Singh II.
4. NAHARGARH FORT (7 km.), atop a hill offers excellent views of Jaipur city.
5. SANGANER (16 km.) known for its Jain temples and carvings, besides being

famous for its handmade paper and block-printed fabrics.
6. AJMER (138 km.). The tomb of the Sufi saint, Khwaja Moinuddin Chisti, the Dargah Sharif. The annual festival, the URS MELA, attracts Muslims from all over the world.
7. PUSHKAR (11 km. from Ajmer), a place of pilgrimage for Hindus, is famous for the sacred Pushkar Lake.
8. SARISKA GAME SANCTUARY (37 km. from Alwar which is on the route of the Pink City Express), is the site of one of the Project Tiger reserves. Apart from the tiger, there are the panther, leopard and varieties of deer in the sanctuary. Can be visited on the journey from Jaipur to Delhi.
9. BHARATPUR BIRD SANCTUARY (174 km.), venue for seeing thousands of water-birds.
10. RANTHAMBOR (162 km.), the game sanctuary, is one of the tiger preservation projects. There are tigers, leopards, sloth bear and deer of various kinds.

SHOPPING

Tie-and-dye fabrics and sarees, Sanganer prints, brocades, cottons and silks, marble statuettes, kundan-work (stone-set) jewellery, ivory carvings, enamel work on articles and jewellery, blue pottery, semi-precious stones, handicrafts in brass, *pichwai* (painted wall hangings), folk paintings, bangles inlaid with mirrors, handwoven blankets, etc.—Jaipur is a shopper's paradise.

FESTIVALS OF SPECIAL LOCAL INTEREST

1. ELEPHANT FESTIVAL during Holi, when bedecked elephants race take part in polo grounds. A riot of colour of the Spring Festival greets the visitor (in the month of March).
2. GANGAUR FESTIVAL dedicated to Goddess Parvati, when gaily dressed women, with rows of brass pots on their heads, sing on their way to the temple praying for husbands like Shiva (in the month of March or April).
3. TEEJ FESTIVAL—with the coming of rains, women and young girls swing amidst green groves singing folk songs (in the month of July or August).
4. PUSHKAR FESTIVAL (11 km. from Ajmer), a camel and cattle fair attracting thousands. Camel races and pilgrims bathing in the lake are some of the attractions (in the month of November).

SPORTS

1. Rajasthan is the home of POLO, called the sport of kings. Polo is played here not only on horses but

there is Elephant Polo, Camel Polo and even Bicycle Polo. Spring (March) is the Polo season. In Jaipur, five Polo tournaments are held at this time.
2. BOATING at Ramgarh Lake where there are boating events. There is boating available at the adjoining Jheel Tourist Village.

UDAIPUR

GENERAL INFORMATION

Population: 300,000 (1991 census)
Altitude 582 metres (1938 ft)
Climate

	Temperature	
	Max.	Min.
Winter:	32°c	8°c
Summer:	39°c	20°c

Season: Throughout the year, except that, during the months of April to June, the days are hot.
Clothing
Summer: cottons.
Winter: woollens.

HOW TO GET THERE

By Air: Udaipur is connected by air with Aurangabad, Bombay, Delhi, Jaipur and Jodhpur.
By Rail: Udaipur has rail connections with Chittorgarh, Ahmedabad, Jaipur, Delhi, etc.
By Road: Udaipur has convenient road connections and is
  112 km from Chittorgarh,
  185 km from Mount Abu,
  262 km from Ahmedabad,
  275 km from Jodhpur,
  406 km from Jaipur,
  630 km from Agra,
  670 km from Delhi and
  730 km from Bombay.
There are regular bus services to Ahmedabad, Bombay, Jaipur, Jodhpur, Mt. Abu, etc.

LOCAL TRANSPORT

Taxis, autorickshaws, tongas are available.

CONDUCTED TOURS

Conducted tours of the city and also to Eklingji, Haldighat and Nathdwara are available. The tours are operated by Rajasthan Tourism Development Corporation (RTDC).
Tourist Information from:
Rajasthan Tourist Office
Kajari Tourist Bungalow
Tel.: 29535

WHERE TO STAY (STD Code: 0294)

PALACE HOTELS
1. The Lake Palace
   Phone: 527962
   Fax: 525804
   Cable: LAKEPALACE
2. Laxmi Vilas Palace
   Phone: 529711
   Fax: 525536
   Cable: TOURISM
3. Shikarbadi Hotel
   Phone: 83200-04
4. Shiv Niwas Palace
   Phone: 528016
   Cable: PALACE
   Fax: 528006
STANDARD
5. Anand Bhavan
   Phone: 523256
   Fax: 523247
   Cable: ANANDBHAVAN

6. Lake Pichola
   Phone: 29387
   Cable: PICHOLA
7. Hill Top Palace Hotel
   Phone: 28764-66
   Fax: 525106
   Cable: HILL-TOP
8. Hotel Rajdarshan
   Phone: 526601
   Fax: 524588
   Cable: DARSHAN

BUDGET

9. Hotel Lake End
   Phone: 23841,28008
   Cable: LAKEND
10. Hotel Fountain
    Phone: 28291-92
    Cable: FOUNTAIN
11. Hotel Vinaya
    Phone: 26166
    Cable: VINAYAK
12. Kajri Tourist Bungalow
    Phone: 29509,25122
13. Hotel Airpalace
    Phone: 23898
    Cable: AIRPALACE
14. Hotel Gulab Niwas
    Phone: 523644
15. Hotel Kalpana
    Phone: 27485

WHAT TO SEE

1. The CITY PALACE MUSEUM is of granite and marble with filigreed balconies, ornate windows and craftsmanship in glass. Each palace within is an outstanding creation of art.
2. JAGDISH TEMPLE built in 1657.
3. BHARATIYA LOK MANDAL, a folk art museum.
4. SAHELIYON KI BARI, a garden with fountains, once used for the enjoyment of royal ladies.
5. PRATAP MEMORIAL, overlooking FATEH SAGAR LAKE, a homage to the great king, Maharana Pratap.
6. JAG MANDIR PALACE, where once Emperor Shahjahan, then only a prince, was in hiding. Some of the designs of this Palace were copied in the Taj Mahal at Agra. (The film, *Octopussy* was filmed here.)
7. AHAR MUSEUM where, in the ruins of the ancient city of Ahar, there are cenotaphs of the Maharanas of Mewar.

EXCURSIONS

1. EKLINGJI (22 km). Built in the 8th century, it is the family temple of the Maharanas of Udaipur.
2. RANAKPUR (98 km). The 15th century Chaumukh Jain Temple is noted for its outstanding sculptures and the tremendous height of its carved pillars. No two of its 1,444 pillars are alike. A must for lovers of art.
3. CHITTORGARH (115 km from Udaipur and 98 km from Udaipur airport), reached the pinnacle of Rajput courage and chivalry.

Some of the monuments to be seen are the VICTORY TOWER, FORT, KIRTI STAMBH, RANA KUMBHA'S PALACE, RANI PADMINI'S PALACE, etc.

JODHPUR

GENERAL INFORMATION

Population: 600,000 (1991 census)
Altitude: 224 metres (746 ft)

Climate

	Temperature	
	Max.	Min.
Winter:	33^0c	10^0c
Summer:	42^0c	22^0c

Season: Throughout the year except the hot months of April to June.
Clothing
Summer : cottons.
Winter : woollens.

HOW TO GET THERE

By Air : Indian Airlines services connect Jodhpur to Ahmedabad, Aurangabad, Bombay, Delhi, Jaipur and Udaipur.
By Rail: Jodhpur has direct rail connections with Agra, Ahmedabad, Bharatpur, Delhi, Jaipur, Jaisalmer and Udaipur.
By Road: Jodhpur is connected by road with the north and west of India. It is
  275 km. from Udaipur,
  290 km. from Jaisalmer,
  300 km. from Jaipur,
  603 km. from Agra and
  592 km. from Delhi.
There are regular bus services to Bikaner, Jaipur, Jaisalmer, Ranakpur, Mt. Abu, Udaipur, etc.

LOCAL TRANSPORT

Unmetered taxis, autorickshaws and tongas are available.

CONDUCTED TOURS

There are two half-day tours of Jodhpur.
Contact RTDC, Hotel Ghoomar Jodhpur
Phone: 45083/44010).

WHERE TO STAY (STD Code: 0291)

Deluxe
1. Ratanada Polo Palace
   Phone: 31910-14
   Fax: 35373
   Cable: POLO
2. Welcomgroup Umaid Bhavan Palace
   Phone: 33316
   Fax: 33118

Standard
3. Ajit Bhavan
   Phone: 37410
   Fax: 37312
4. Hotel Karni Bhawan
   Phone: 32220
   Fax: 33495
5. Hotel Anand Bhawan
   Phone: 523256
   Fax: 528957

Budget
6. Hotel Ghoomar (RTDC)
   Phone: 44010
7. Marudhar Hotel
   Phone: 27429
8. Arun Hotel
   Phone: 20238

WHAT TO SEE

1. The remarkable Meharangarh Fort which has a high stone wall protecting the well-fortified city. Within the palace inside the Fort are rooms with rich collections of palanquins, elephant howdahs,

musical instruments, costumes, furniture and armoury. The display of cannons here is one of the rarest in India.
2. JASWANT THADA. White marble memorial built in 1899 in memory of Maharaj Jaswant Singh II.
3. UMAID BHAWAN PALACE. This huge Palace was built by Maharaja Umaid Singh. Part of the palace has been converted into a hotel.
4. The GOVERNMENT MUSEUM has exhibits, armoury, textiles, local arts and crafts, miniature paintings, etc.
5. THE MAHAMANDIR TEMPLE is supported by 100 pillars and has carvings depicting yoga postures.

EXCURSIONS

1. BALSAMAND LAKE and PALACE (7 km.). An artificial lake with a summer palace on the embankment.
2. MANDORE GARDENS (9 km.). The ancient capital of Marwar lies here in ruins. The highlight of Mandore is the Hall of Heroes, which houses 16 gigantic figures chiselled out of a single rock.
3. SARDAR SAMAND LAKE and PALACE (55 km.).
4. DHAWA WILDLIFE SANCTUARY (45 km.). The largest number of Black Indian antelopes can be seen here roaming freely.
5. OSEAN (65 km.). The ruins of an ancient city which was the cradle of Rajasthan temple art but was destroyed by early Muslim invaders. There are now only 16 Hindu and Jain temples dating from the 8th to 11th centuries.
6. SAILA (74 km.). Here the Shiva Temple has a unique Sabha Mandap or meeting hall with beautifully carved pillars.
7. NAGAUR (135 km.). An impregnable fort and a grand palace rich in murals of the Nagaur style.

SHOPPING

Jodhpur is famous for its bazars which sell tie-and-dye fabrics and garments, linen and mirror work, embroidery, zinc water bottles, ivory curios, carved wooden handicrafts and embroidered footwear.

ENTERTAINMENT

There are cultural tourist organisations putting up cultural shows regularly during the seasons — September to March.

Enquiries

Tourist officer or your hotel counter.

FESTIVALS OF SPECIAL LOCAL INTEREST

1. MARWAR FESTIVAL of Jodhpur when an old world atmosphere is recreated by the music and folk dances of the desert. (October)

2. The NAGAUR FAIR held at Nagaur (135 km.) is one of the largest cattle fairs where thousands of camels, bullock and horses are for sale. Camel races and other sports provide entertainment. (January or February)
3. NAG PANCHAMI (July-August) dedicated to snake worship. Crowds visit the Mandore Gardens to honour folk heroes of Jodhpur.

SPORTS

For those interested in horses, there are several stud farms and stables. Also horse riding can be arranged.

JAISALMER

GENERAL INFORMATION

Population: 35,000 (1991 census)
Altitude: 242 metres (806 ft)

Climate:

	Temperature	
	Max.	Min.
Winter:	32⁰c	8⁰c
Summer:	42⁰c	21⁰c

Season: Throughout the year, except during the hot months of April to July
Clothing: *Summer* : light cottons. *Winter*: woollens.

HOW TO GET THERE

By Air: The nearest airport is at Jodhpur. Indian Airlines serves Jodhpur.
By Rail: Jaisalmer is connected to Jodhpur by rail.
By Road: Jaisalmer is
  285 km. from Jodhpur,
  330 km. from Bikaner,
  638 km. from Jaipur,
  897 km. from Delhi and
  663 km. from Udaipur.
Bus services are available to Jodhpur, Bikaner, Delhi, Ajmer and Udaipur.
RTDC operates a coach service between Jodhpur and Jaisalmer. Reservation—Moohal Tourist Bungalow, *Phone*: 2392.

LOCAL TRANSPORT

Unmetered taxis, camel and camel-carts.

CONDUCTED TOURS

Nil.

WHERE TO STAY (STD CODE: 02992)

STANDARD
1. Gorbandh Palace
   Phone: 52749
   Telex: 5501-203 GOP
2. Hotel Himmatgarh Palace
   Phone: 52002
   Fax: 52005
3. Heritage Inn
   Phone: 52769
4. Hotel Narain Niwas
   Phone: 52408
   Fax: 52101
BUDGET
5. Hotel Moomal
   Phone: 52392
6. Hotel Jaisal Castle
   Phone: 52362
7. Hotel Forview
   Phone: 52214

There are several budget hotels in town.

WHAT TO SEE

1. THE CITADEL, the fort built by Rawal Jaisal. A fourth of the population live inside the fort. Exquisitely carved balconies, *havelis* or mansions, palaces and towers present a feast to the visitor.
2. JAIN TEMPLES of the 12th to the 15th centuries with intricate and delicate carvings. The GYAN BHANDAR (Library) has rare manuscripts.
3. PATWON KI HAVELI, a five-storey spectacular mansion with carved pillars and painted murals.
4. SALIM SINGH KI HAVELI, noted for its arched blue roof and peacock brackets.
5. NATHMALJI KI HAVELI, built in two parts by two brothers. Interiors are covered with paintings.

EXCURSIONS

1. SAM SAND DUNES (42 km.). The vast expanse of the Thar Desert, with its endless vista of the golden sands, is a sight to behold. Camel rides in the desert, arranged through the Tourist Bungalow, are an unforgettable experience.
2. AMAR SAGAR (5 km.), a lake set amongst fruit trees, on the way to Lodurva.
3. BADA BAGH (6 km.), where there are cenotaphs of former kings, with elaborate carved images of kings on horse-back.
4. LODURVA (17 km.), the ancient capital of Jaisalmer.
5. WOOD FOSSIL PARK (17 km.), where there are 180 million years old fossils of this desert area.
6. DESERT NATIONAL PARK (40 km.) spread over 3000 sq. km. It is a breeding ground for the Great Indian Bustard. The gazelle, chincara and desert fox can be seen here.
7. BARMER (153 km.), especially noted for its handicrafts such as block-printing, wood-carving, carpets and embroidery.

SHOPPING

Mirror-work embroidery, rugs, blankets and shawls of colourful Rajasthani weave, peasant silver jewellery, carved wooden trinket boxes and curios in stone, carpets and block-printed fabric.

FESTIVALS OF SPECIAL LOCAL INTEREST

1. THE DESERT FESTIVAL (January-February). A unique annual event when Jaisalmer revives its bygone culture in full glory. Folk music and dancers with their swirling skirts, camel rides and races, and camel acrobatics are part of the festival.
2. HOLI, the spring festival (February-March).

Jaisalmer reverberates with special celebrations in the Mandir Palace.

MOUNT ABU

GENERAL INFORMATION

Population: 16,000 (1991 census)
Altitude: 1195 metres (3979 ft)

Climate:

	Temperature	
	Max.	Min.
Winter:	27^0c	9^0c
Summer:	32^0c	18^0c

Season: Throughout the year
Clothing
Summer: light tropicals and cottons.
Winter: woollens.

HOW TO GET THERE

By Air: Nearest airports are Udaipur (185 km) and Ahmedabad (222 km).
By Rail: Nearest rail-head is Abu Road (27 km), which has direct rail connections with Ahmedabad, Jodhpur, Jaipur, Agra, etc.
By Road: Mt. Abu is connected by good roads. It is
  185 km. from Udaipur,
  222 km. from Ahmedabad,
  264 km. from Jodhpur,
  509 km. from Jaipur,
  764 km. from Delhi,
  782 km. from Bombay.
There are bus services to Abu Road, Achalgarh, Ranakpur, Ahmedabad, Udaipur and Jaipur.

LOCAL TRANSPORT
Unmetered taxis and tongas available.

CONDUCTED TOURS
Half-day tour of Abu, Achalgarh and Guru Shikhar. Information RTDC - *Phone*: 3151.

WHERE TO STAY (STD CODE: 02974)

BUDGET
1. Cama Rajputana Club
   Phone: 3163
2. Palace Hotel
   Phone: 3121, 3133
3. Hotel Hill Tone
   Phone: 3112, 3113
4. Hotel Savera Palace
   Phone: 3354
5. Hotel Shikhar (RTDC)
   Phone: 3129-77
6. Bikaner Palace
   Phone: 3121

DORMITORY
7. Hotel Purjan Niwas
   Phone: 185

WHAT TO SEE

1. DILWARA JAIN TEMPLES. These temples built between the 11th and 13th centuries and dedicated to the Jain Tirthankaras (saints), are famous for their rich and intricate carvings in marble of a type that can rarely be seen elsewhere. They are masterpieces of marble sculpture, especially the Vimal Vishahi and the Tejpal temples.
2. ADHAR DEVI (or Arbudha Devi) TEMPLE. A beautiful temple chiselled out of a

huge rock on top of a hill.
3. NAKKI LAKE. The placid lake is studded with little islets. Boating is available on the lake.
4. GAUMUKH TEMPLE, where a little stream flows from the mouth of a marble cow. It is believed that the four Agnikula clans of Rajputs were born here from the sacrificial fire of Sage Vasishtha.
5. SHRI RAGHUNATHJI TEMPLE. The image of Shri Raghunathji was placed on this spot by Saint Ramananda in the 14th century.

EXCURSIONS

1. ACHALGARH (11 km) is famous for its Shiva Temple.
2. GURU SHIKHAR (15 km) is the highest peak of Mt. Abu, 1722 metres (5740 ft) high.
3. UDAIPUR (185 km) is a fairy tale city of lakes and palaces.
4. RANAKPUR (197 km). The Chaumukh Jain Temple here is outstanding for its architecture and sculpture.

FESTIVALS OF SPECIAL LOCAL INTEREST

SUMMER FESTIVAL. Summer seeps into Mt. Abu with colour, fragrance and exuberance. Classical and folk music and Rajasthani folk dances are the highlights (in the month of June).

BHARATPUR BIRD SANCTUARY

GENERAL INFORMATION

Altitude: 250 metres (833 ft)

Climate:

	Temperature	
	Max.	Min.
Winter:	45^0c	37^0c
Summer:	32^0c	22^0c

Season: October to February. October - November is the breeding season.
Clothing
Summer: Cottons
Winter: Woollens.

HOW TO GET THERE

By Air: Agra is the nearest airport (54 km)
By Rail: Bharatpur has rail connections with Agra, Ahmedabad, Bombay, Delhi, Jaipur, etc.
By Road: Bharatpur is
54 km. from Agra,
36 km. from Mathura,
182 km. from Delhi and
174 km. from Jaipur.
Bus services connect Bharatpur to Agra, Ajmer, Delhi, Jaipur etc.

LOCAL TRANSPORT

Tongas (horse carriages), cycle rickshaws are available. Also jeeps and mini buses can be hired from the Tourist Officer, RTDC. However, vehicles are not allowed inside the Park. One can go either by foot or by cycle rickshaws.

WHERE TO STAY

Bharatpur Forest Lodge, on the edge of the Sanctuary, owned by ITDC, has 17 double rooms.
Tel: 2760, 2722, 2864.
Cable: FORESTOUR.
SARAS, a tourist bungalow owned by Rajasthan Tourism Development Corporation offers good budget accommodation.
Tel: 23700

WHAT TO SEE

1. BHARATPUR (Keolodeo Ghana) BIRD SANCTUARY. Covering 52 sq km, it once used to be the royal hunting preserve of the Bharatpur royal family. Walking on the banks of the marshes, being driven in cycle-rickshaws or punting through the bushes is the best way of seeing the birds.
   The wild boar, sambar, nilgai and spotted deer are also seen in plenty.
2. LOHAGARH FORT, or the Iron Fort, was built by Maharaja Suraj Mal, the founder of Bharatpur, in the 18th century. There are several monuments worth seeing inside this once invincible fort.
3. THE PALACE, a blend of Rajput and Mughal architecture.

EXCURSIONS

DEEG (32 km). Once the second capital of the Maharaja of Bharatpur, it served as a summer resort of the rulers. There are gardens and fountains much like the Mughal gardens, as also forts and palaces well known for their architectural splendour.
   The Deeg Fort and the palaces, Gopal Bhavan, Suraj Bhavan and Purana Mahal are worth a visit.

Parshvanath temple, Ranakpur

Chapter 14

UTTAR PRADESH
The Heart of Hindustan

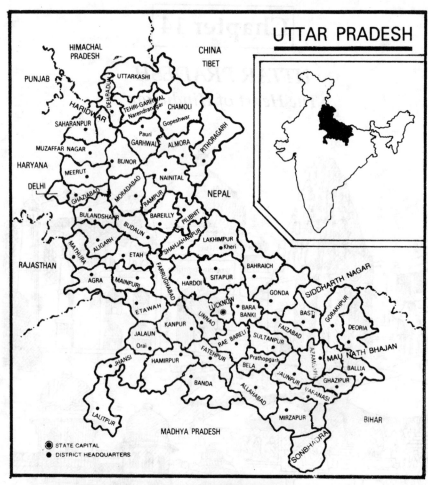

Hemkund

In this part of the book, we plan to deal with a very large part of India, one of the two largest states of the country — Uttar Pradesh the most populous state. It forms more than one-eighth of India and constitutes its heartland. Uttar Pradesh literally means northern province.

With an area of 294,411 sq kilometres and a population of 139 million, Uttar Pradesh is the most populous state of India, 16.4 per cent of total population of the country. It has also some of the most well-known tourist centres of the country like AGRA, the city of the Taj, and VARANASI, one of the most ancient cities of the world on the banks of the Ganges. The State borders Tibet (China) in the north and the north-east; it meets five Indian states — Himachal Pradesh, Haryana, Delhi, Rajasthan and Madhya Pradesh in the west—and it borders Bihar in the east.

The antiquity of the state can be traced back to stone age. Archaeologists have discovered stone tools like hand axes and choppers in some parts of Uttar Pradesh. By 600 B.C., Uttar Pradesh had a thriving agricultural economy based on money exchange. There were eight well known republics and kingdoms at that time like Kashi the modern Varanasi, Kosala, the present day OUDH, and Vatsa, today's ALLAHABAD region, etc. The State was the birthplace of two major religions. It was in Uttar Pradesh where both—Gautama, the Buddha, and Mahavir, the founder of Jainism, found their first disciples. Prasenjit, the ruler of Kosala, and Udayan, the king of Vatsa, were early followers of Lord Buddha. It was in this region that fusion of cultures took place— originally Vedic Hinduism followed by spells of Buddhism and Jainism. Islam came here in the 10th century. The Mughals replaced the early Muslim Sultanates in the 16th century. After initial hostility against the invaders, the Hindus and Muslims settled down to develop a composite culture. Urdu — which is Hindi written in Arabic script—was developed in this part of India and is now a popular language of the entire Indian subcontinent. It is the official language of Pakistan and the State of Jammu and Kashmir in India.

The vast territory of Uttar Pradesh can be divided into three distinct physiographical regions : the Himalayan region in the north, the vast Gangetic plains in the centre and the Vindhya range and plateau on the south.

EXPLORING THE GARHWAL AND KUMAON HIMALAYAS

The Himalayan region with valleys and hills of varying altitudes and colder climates is the area where most of the sacred rivers of India rise. The Himalayan forests rich in cedars, oaks, pines, rhododendrons and other varieties of trees and flowers together with gushing rivers and snowclad mountains make it one of the most beautiful regions of the world. The entire region is called UTTARAKHAND and covers an area of about 25,000 square kms. It encompasses the area of GARHWAL and KUMAON HILLS in Uttar Pradesh or, Uttarakhand.

GANGOTRI, YAMNOTRI, KEDARNATH AND BADRINATH

Temple at Badrinath

High up in the Garhwal Himalayas, in the company of awesome snow-covered peaks lie the holy shrines of GANGOTRI, YAMNOTRI, KEDARNATH and BADRINATH. Here melting glaciers give rise to sacred Ganga and Yamuna rivers. For thousands of years, pilgrims, Sadhus and mystics walked the tracts of Garhwal to meditate and pray. Garhwal has many peaks over 7,000 metres including India's second highest peak, NANDA DEVI, named after Parvati, Lord Shiva's consort. Inner Garhwal is a land of stark grandeur, steep cliffs, gushing rivers, snow-covered peaks. Here the Valley of Flowers is at its best in July-August. Just one valley offers 500 species of flowers. Among fauna, the area is rich in birds, different species of wildlife depending on the climate of different regions. Tigers and elephants are found in Shivalik range, black bear, wild sheep and goats and musk deer in the Himalayan range and the snow leopard and brown bear in Himadri region. The area has three national parks and two high altitude sanctuaries.

The people of Garhwal are Hindus. Two of the most important shrines of Hinduism — KEDARNATH, the highest temple of Shiva, and BADRINATH of Vishnu—are located here. Also, the very famous Sikh pilgrimage site, HEMKUND, believed to be the spot where Guru Gobind Singh meditated in a previous incarnation. Hindu mythology and religion originated from these mountains. Higher up live the Bhotias and Marchas, nomadic tribes of Indo-Tibetan origin. In Western Garhwal ritual as well as polyandry are practised.

The principal occupation of the villagers is agriculture and grazing. It was in Garhwal that a people's movement "Chipko" was started by women with a view to saving its forests from greedy commercial interests. The women clung to trees willing to sacrifice their life for trees. They succeeded in the end and today, felling of trees in these mountains is banned.

Prominent Peaks
The most prominent peaks of the Garhwal Himalayas (over 7000 metres) are NANDA DEVI (7817 metres), KAMET (7756 metres), W. IBBI GAMIN (7376 metres), MANA (7272 metres), MUKUT PARBAT (7242 metres), CHAUKHAMBA

(7138 metres), TRISHUL (7120 metres), SATOPANTH (7084 metres) and DAULAGIRI (7066 metres). Then there are over 20 other peaks higher than 6000 metres.

HILL RESORTS OF UTTAR PRADESH HIMALAYAS
The U.P. Himalayas or Uttarakhand, as the region is called, nestle in their bosom two exciting hill resorts where Indians move during summer. One of them is MUSSOORIE (2000 metres), often described as the Queen of Indian Hill Stations. It lies past DEHRADUN. Mussoorie could be your base camp for a trip to GANGOTRI and YAMNOTRI — sources of the

Har-ki-doon, Garhwal

Ganga and the Yamuna respectively. HARIDWAR, the Hindu pilgrim centre is also close by. At Haridwar, you can witness every evening, the river Goddess Ganga being worshipped in her small temple mid-stream. To get away from the crowded temples of Hardwar, you have an option to move to the quiet and peaceful Ashrams (Retreats) of RISHIKESH. As you walk on the bridge at Rishikesh, you will find it hard to decide which is more memorable: the beauty of the gushing waters of the Ganga or the beautiful expression on the face of the worshippers.

Nainital—Almora - Ranikhet - Corbett Park
The other hill resort is NAINITAL (2000 metres), the summer capital of Uttar Pradesh Government. It is a popular resort in the Kumaon Hills with a sparkling lake in the centre of the city. Every year during summer, Nainital has a national level regatta on its famous lake.

About 65 kilometres from Nainital is the town of ALMORA. Perched on a 5 km ridge, the hill station offers a majestic view of the snowclad Himalayas. Nearly 54 kilometres from Nainital is RANIKHET, an idyllic hill station with a year-round bracing climate. The resort attracts the tourists throughout the year.

On your way to Nainital is the famous CORBETT NATIONAL PARK at RAMNAGAR. The pug marks of a tiger are fresh and your guide motions you to follow him in silence as the slightest sound might scare away the magnificent beast. As you peer through the edge of the elephant grass, you spot a golden hue in the grass... the camera clicks and you have got a tiger by his tail!

The dawn sees you climbing up the CHINA HILLS near Nainital town. And your labour is rewarded with an eternal sight of the sun rising above the snow-capped Himalayas.

And as the cool bracing breeze wafts over in the evenings, the yachts sail out their sails billowing in the wind on the waters of Nainital Lake.

ADVENTURE POSSIBILITIES

Uttar Pradesh Himalayas offer tremendous opportunities for an exciting adventure holiday. Among the things you can do are: Cycling on village and forest trails; going on a Wildlife Jeep Safari in Rajaji National Park and reserved Forest Blocks; white-water rafting on the River Ganga; going on easy treks on the foothills of the Himalayas through forests; seeing wildlife nature camps; mahaseer fishing, yoga and meditation camps, enjoying elephant rides for photo-safari through forests. And there are many other possibilities including a motor cycle trip through river valleys, GOMUKH GLACIER and the sacred temples of Badrinath and Kedarnath.

White-water rafting on the Ganges

SUMMER ACTIVITIES

Trekking in the Inner Himalayas for 7 to 20 days with an experienced outfitter and modern camping equipment. Each group is accompanied by an English-speaking trained guide and experienced kitchen staff to serve fresh meals. Among the popular treks are those through the KUARI PASS to the VALLEY OF FLOWERS. The maximum height reached in this trek is 3658 metres.

A view of the Himalayas in Garhwal

The trekkers do not have to carry their backpacks more than 3 to 5 kilograms — the rest of the equipment is carried by porters who accompany them. The price ranges from US $ 150 per person to $ 1000 depending on the length of the trip.

We can recommend Captain K.J. Singh, a native of the Garhwal Himalayas who knows the land like the palm of his hand. Address
   Himvat Camps and Tours, Pvt Ltd.,
   11, Post Office Road, Clement Town,
   Dehradun, 248002.
   Phone: 23772. *Fax*: 0135-28392

Any major tour operator of the country will plan a trip for you in the U.P. Himalayas with all the usual facilities.

Garhwal's mountains, rivers, valleys and forests make it an "Adventure Tourism" paradise for the whole year. DEHRADUN, a modern city is the principal entry point for the Garhwal valleys. With an airport and a railway station, it lies in a valley (at 640 metres) bounded by the rivers Ganga and Yamuna in the east and west, the Himalayas in the north and the Shivalik Hills in the south. This fertile valley of the Doon boasts of spring-fed perennial streams and dense forests of sal. It naturally abounds in wildlife. Dehradun is also a city of research institutions, philanthropic organisations and residential schools, where children come to study from far corners of India. To name a few — Forest Research Institute (one of the largest in India), Institute of Petroleum Exploration, Wadia Institute of Himalayan Geology, and Wild Life Institute of India, and many others.

EXPLORING THE GANGETIC VALLEY
The Gangetic Valley has some of the world's most renowned tourist attractions — AGRA, the city of the Taj, and VARANASI, one of the world's

most ancient cities. Agra forms part of the Golden Triangle of India, the other two cities being Delhi and Jaipur.

Most tourist Cities of Uttar Pradesh are easily accessible from Delhi — by air as well by comfortable surface transportation. Let us take a trip by car. On leaving Delhi, the first city on the Grand Trunk Road is MEERUT — a nondescript city known as the cradle of the Indian Mutiny of 1857, the first war of Indian independence. The revolt may be considered as the first stirrings of a nationalist movement. Indian soldiers of the British Army, irrespective of their religious affiliations, had revolted against their British masters and transferred their loyalty to the ageing Mughal Emperor of Delhi, Bahadur Shah Zafar, whose jurisdiction did not go beyond the city of Delhi. After many battles the insurrection was contained. The British East India Company was liquidated and the Queen of England took direct charge of the administration of India by appointing a Viceroy or Governor General for India.

AGRA

Travel by road to Agra 204 km from Delhi takes more than four hours due to a crowded 2-way highway. There is, however, a new fast train— Shatabdi Express—which takes exactly two hours to cover the distance.

But, few trips in India or anywhere else in the world could offer you such a rich fare of history and architecture as this short journey through time. Tradition ascribes the foundation of the present city of Agra to Raja Badal Singh around A.D. 1475. However, mention of Agarbana (Paradise) in the Mahabharata proves that it was the sister city of Mathura—a much older city like Varanasi. Sikandar Lodhi made Agra his capital when the Lodhis ruled Northern India. The invasion of Mughals led by Babur in 1526 changed the scene and a new epoch started which contributed greatly to art and architecture in India. Agra reached its zenith between 1556 and 1658 under the three Mughal emperors, Akbar, Jahangir and Shahjahan.

The excursion into the past takes us not only to Agra but also to other interesting regions around Agra. We have, for instance, a trip to FATEHPUR SIKRI, the deserted ghost city built by Akbar the Great. There are nearby places with great historical significance—GWALIOR, SHIVPURI and JHANSI, the home of Rani Luxmibai of Jhansi, India's Joan of Arc who fought the British for the independence of her country.

VRINDABAN, a city of thousand temples where every house appears to be a temple. The biggest of them all is the Gobind Deo — only half of it remains now.

Another ten km. down the road is another holy town - MATHURA - on the west bank of the Yamuna river. Mathura was the birthplace of Krishna and is sacred to every Hindu and thousands of pilgrims come here the year-round. Its history can be traced back to the Maurya dynasty which ruled India from 325 to 184 B.C. Its famous MATHURA

MUSEUM proudly displays artistic wealth left by foreign conquerors like the Greeks and Parthians — a museum you should not miss. It is perhaps the richest museum in India. It may be interesting to drive another 60 km. to west and see DEEG, the home of the 18th century Palace built by the Jat ruler SurajMal.

Ten kilometres north of Agra is SIKANDRA, named after Sikander Lodhi, the dynasty from whom the Mughals snatched the empire of Hindustan. It is the site of the tomb of the Emperor Akbar, the Great. In 1566, the 26-year old Akbar ordered the construction of a red sandstone fort beside the Yamuna river. The Fort was the Mughal dynasty's first major architectural venture. It remained the centre of imperial activity during the early years of Mughal rule. At its peak, stories of Agra's opulence and splendour spread all over the world and attracted a large number of traders, missionaries, musicians, scholars, artists, painters, physicians and craftsmen to this great city. Akbar created an environment of tolerance which encouraged fine arts including the newly developing Mughal school of paintings which flourished under him and his progeny. The Fort is like a big city. Within its walls are palaces, mosques, bazars, royal audience halls, gardens and parks — all executed with a finesse which was rare among kings and emperors.

Diwan-i-Aam
The most impressive part of the Fort is the DIWAN-I-AAM — the Hall of Public Audience, where the people including foreign emissaries came to plead their petitions before the Emperor. A large Throne Room overlooks the Audience Hall, below where stood the Wazir, the Prime Minister on a platform across a silver railing. Bernier, the famous French traveller who was visiting India, has left a detailed account of the Court.

Diwan-i-Khas
Not far from Diwan-i-Aam is the DIWAN-I-KHAS, the Hall of Private Audience, where the Emperor met foreign ambassadors and other distinguished dignitaries of the realm. The Throne Terrace here had two thrones, one of black marble, made from one piece of rock and the other of white marble. Inscriptions tell us that the black throne was built by Akbar for his son Jahangir and the white throne for Shahjahan. In the area around the Hall of Public Audience was also the mysterious MEENA BAZAR where ladies of the court went shopping for jewellery and other luxury goods. When the grand Mughal was in a playful mood, those close to him played store, a game in which wives of noblemen acted as vendors and the emperor amused himself by haggling with the lady vendors! Near Diwan-i-Khas is the tall MUSEUM BURJ, originally built by Shahjahan for his queen Mumtaz Mahal — the exalted of the Palace — who now lies buried in the Taj Mahal. It is an octagonal tower with a courtyard on the lower floor decorated with octogonal marble slabs. The delicate lattices of marble were used by the ladies of the Palace to look

out on the Fort without being seen. In the centre of the Tower, is a beautifully carved fountain.

Jahangir Mahal

The biggest private residences in the Fort is the JAHANGIR MAHAL, the Palace of Emperor Jahangir. It is an excellent blend of Hindu and Mughal architecture. The palace has a hall which is called Jodhabai's Dressing Room. Jodhabai was Jahangir's Hindu mother. Its design and layout is essentially Hindu. Later, the Palace was used by Jahangir's queen — Noorjahan — the Light of the World. Jahangir was very fond of wine as well as his queen whom he adored even more. The love of wine interfered in the day-to-day running of the Government. To help him out in administering imperial justice, Noorjahan sat with her husband to advise him in taking decisions. She was an iron lady and never tolerated opposition. Those who came in her way ended mysteriously in the Yamuna river.

Shahjahan's Residence

Shahjahan's palace called KHAS MAHAL (Private Palace) — it consists of three pavilions overlooking the Yamuna. The white marble walls were decorated with designs containing precious and semi-precious stones. But, they were looted in the 18th century when the Palace was pillaged. A staircase of the Palace leads to the air-conditioned quarters — cool underground rooms, where the king relaxed with the ladies of the harem.

In the north-eastern courtyard of Khas Mahal is the SHEESH MAHAL or Palace of Mirrors. This was the Bath of the Khas Mahal where water was fed through marble channels.

Apart from these private and public buildings, other interesting areas in the Fort are the two main gates — AMAR SINGH GATE and the DELHI GATE. There is also the intriguing HAUS-I-JAHANGIRI — the bath carved out of a huge block of stone 5 feet high and 25 feet in circumference.

The Taj Mahal

By far, the greatest contribution of Shahjahan to Indian architecture was the Taj Mahal, which took 20,000 labourers working for 22 years to build it. The white marble building was created in the memory of his beloved queen Mumtaz Mahal.

Noorjahan was the second wife of Shahjahan whom she married at the age of 21 in 1612 and took the name of Mumtaj Mahal — the exalted of the Palace. Stories are told of her beauty, magnanimity and wisdom.

When she died, Shahjahan was terribly upset. He decided to build a memorial for his beautiful queen which no other building in the world could surpass. Mumtaz Mahal was taken out of her temporary burial place in Burhanpur in a massive procession to Agra to be buried in her new resting place in the Taj Mahal. During his seven-year imprisonment in the Agra Fort, the aging emperor watched the changing moods of his creation during different hours of night and day — nothing could, surpass its beauty during a full moon night.

The Taj Mahal is built on two bases — one of sandstone and above it, a marble platform, worked into a black and white chessboard design. A slender marble minaret stands on each corner of the platform.

Standing on a central marble plinth, the mausoleum is balanced with two subsidiary buildings — one a mosque and the other an assembly hall.

Fifty years after Taj Mahal was constructed, the famous French historian Bernier visited it. He was stunned by its beauty and exclaimed, "I must say that I believe it must be reckoned amongst the wonders of the world rather than those unshapen masses of Egyptian Pyramids which I was weary to see after I had seen them twice....". Rudyard Kipling described it as "the embodiment of all things so pure, all things holy and all things unhappy". Mark Twain who came to India in 1807 said he felt himself "drunk on someone else's cork".

Jama Masjid

Among Agra's other attractions are the JAMA MASJID built by Shahjahan in 1648. It faces the Delhi Gate of the Fort. A 15-minute taxi ride takes you across the Yamuna to see what is popularly called the "Baby Taj" - ITMAD-UD-DAULA. It is the resting place of Mirza Ghyas Beg (alias Itmad-ud-Daula) the Pillar of the State. He was the father of Noorjahan. It was completed in 1628 by his doting daughter. The monument was in a way a forerunner of the Taj Mahal — smaller yet more delicately beautiful. It was the first Mughal building in India built entirely of white marble.

Itmad-ud-Daula

Itmad-ud-Daula was the first Mughal monument where the Persian techniques of pieta dura was used and later repeated in Taj Mahal. Further north is the CHINI-KA-ROZA, a memorial dedicated to the famous scholar of Jahangir's court, Allama Afzal Khan Malkah Shukrfullah of Shiraz. He left this monument for posterity.

To the north along the river-side lie the RAM BAGH GARDENS laid by the founder of the Mughal dynasty Babur in 1528.

FATEHPUR SIKRI—The Ghost Capital

No visitor to the Taj should miss a trip to Fatehpur Sikri, 37 kilometres west of Agra. When Elizabethan Englishmen came to Fatehpur Sikri in 1583 to meet Emperor Akbar, their eyes bulged out of their heads. They saw a city exceeding London both in size and population. And, they lost count of the rubies, the diamonds, the silks and the other clothes spread before their eyes. Today, Fatehpur Sikri is still beautiful though a ghost city. The Emperor abandoned the capital and returned to Agra as the newly built capital did not have enough water-supply to meet the needs of the growing population.

In Sikri, a small village in Akbar's time, lived a holy man called Sheikh Salim Chisti. Akbar had heard about the miraculous powers of the Saint. He fell at the feet of the Saint and prayed to him to bless him a much craved son and within a year his heir Salim was born who later became Emperor Jahangir. To express his grateful thanks, Akbar moved his capital to Sikri and called it Fatehpur — the city of Victory. The sandstone metropolis was filled with magnificent palaces, pleasure domes, gardens, mosques, courtyards and fountains in a circumference of 14 kilometres.

The Gateway

The graceful buildings of Fatehpur Sikri seem barely touched by the ravages of time. Although the periphery of the town is in ruins, the main capital complex is safe showing its perfect harmony. There are two main entrances to the town — SHAHI DARWAZA — where you can hire licensed guides to accompany you and tell you many stories connected with this ghost town—and the BULAND DARWAZA. The tall GATE OF VICTORY is visible for miles. The Gateway has a Koranic inscription. It is 176 feet high from the ground level and 134 feet high from the platform. Below the Gateway, there are many stairs enhancing its beauty.

Chisti's Tomb

The Gateway leads to the Friday mosque or the JAMI MASJID. It is believed to be a copy of the main mosque at Mecca. Nearby is the small white marble tomb of SHEIKH SALIM CHISTI. It is ornamented with latticed screens and serpentine brackets. Shahjahan added exquisite pieta dura work later as a mark of respect for the saint. The tomb was built over the exact spot where the holy man sat in meditation during his lifetime. Even, today, childless couples come to the tomb to seek the blessings of Sheikh Salim Chisti.

Palace of Jodhabai

The SHAHI DURWAZA is only five minutes walk from here. Within this complex are seemingly endless number of palaces, one better than the other. First looms the casket-like Palace belonging to Raja Birbal — Akbar's Hindu advisor known for his wit and wisdom. The PALACE OF JODHABAI is the most prominent one. Within the Zanana (Female Quarters), there were fountains, gardens and a mosque. His Christian wife Mariam lived in the so-called golden Palace and his Turkish wife Sultana Begum lived in a marble pavilion once studded with precious stones. Favourite wives had favoured treatment.

Panch Mahal
PANCH MAHAL, a five-storey structure is an architectural marvel. It was Akbar's personal citadel for pleasure and relaxation. Each storey is pillared and is smaller than the other. The building resembles a Buddhist temple. It tapers from the ground floor with 84 columns to its domed top supported by only four columns.

Diwan-i-Aam
Other principal public buildings of Fatehpur Sikri are the DIWAN-I-AAM. It is over 350 feet long. It consists of cloisters surrounding a courtyard which contains the Hall of Judgement. It was here that Akbar dispensed imperial justice. Near the Diwan-i-Aam is the PANCHISI courtyard where Akbar is believed to have played chess using slave girls as living pieces.

Diwan-i-Khas
The Hall of Private Audience, DIWAN-I-KHAS, in this town is far more interesting than in the Agra Fort. Here Akbar received foreign Ambassadors and other dignitaries. The Diwan-i-Khas was an important cog in the functioning of the Mughal Empire. Akbar became interested in astrology. He appointed a court astrologer — and provided a seat for him. One of his functions was to advise the Emperor what colour he should wear on a given day. Emperor's favourite colours were yellow, purple and violet. Another building - ANKH MACHOLI - has an interesting history about it. The Emperor is believed to have played the game of blindman's bluff here with the ladies of the harem. An amazing feature of this building is an upper storey room called the "PALACE OF WINDS". It may have been the cool vantage point for the ladies of the harem to see without being seen.

ALIGARH
The next interesting place on the road is Aligarh which has a historic fort SEMDIA — scene of many battles with the Afghans, Jats and the British. It is now the seat of the internationally known Aligarh Muslim University. Muslim students from several countries in the Middle East come here to study.

KANAUJ
KANAUJ, the ancient Kanyakubja, comes next. It was for centuries the capital of the legendary Raja Bhoj, a wise king. Founded by Emperor Harsha, it remained the symbol of imperial power for five centuries till it was devastated by the Muslim invaders. Thereafter, it quickly passed into oblivion. Nothing remains today in Kanauj to remind us of its glorious past except the melancholy ruins of a few ramparts and temples.

KANPUR—the Pittsburg of India

Some 75 kilometres further, you enter Kanpur — a major industrial city of the country. It is the centre of textile and leather industries. Among the historical remains is the MEMORIAL CHURCH built in 1875 in romanesque style. It bears the names of British soldiers who died in the revolt against the British East India Company in 1857. There is a 16th-century brick temple at BHITARGAON, a village not far from Kanpur.

LUCKNOW—The City of Gardens

Lucknow is the capital of Uttar Pradesh with a history going back to the *Ramayana* days. It derives its name from Lakshman — Lord Rama's valiant younger brother. It straddles both banks of the Gomati river, a tributary of the Ganga. It witnessed the rise and fall of many dynasties. But the city owes a lot of its elegance to its good ruler, Asif-ud-Daula who moved his capital in 1775 from Faizabad to Lucknow and shaped it into a city of gardens and great buildings. The rulers of Oudh were great connoisseurs of music and poetry. It remained an imperial capital city and even during the British Raj it remained a centre of political and cultural activities. The tradition of 'Ghazal' singing, 'Mushairas' (recital of poetry) and 'Kathak' dance forms are significant contributions of Lucknow to India's cultural legacy.

Lucknow is also a gourmet's city — it is known for good food. 'Lucknavi Parathas' (unleavened bread) with 10 layers are soft and crisp. The 'Dam Kababs' fish and 'Biryani' are other popular dishes of Lucknow.

Bara Imambara

An interesting attraction of Lucknow is its BARA IMAMBARA — 'Bara' means big and there is another 'chota' or small Imambara. It has a charming accurate labyrinth supporting the roof of the edifice, locally called 'Bhul-Bhulaiyan'. Here many a visitor can be totally lost and is always advised to go with a guide. One could wander through narrow zigzag galleries for hours without finding the way out. It certainly is a very eerie sensation — moving towards the semi-lit corridors that seem to be going out but actually take you deeper and deeper into the labyrinth. The RUMI DARWAZA is the massive

gateway of the BARA IMAMBARA which is presumed to be a facsimile of one of the gateways of Constantinople in Turkey. HUSSAINABAD IMAMBARA or 'Chotta' (small) Imambara has numerous domes and minarets. The 67-metre high clock tower opposite the Imambara was built between 1860 and 1887. Nearby is the PICTURE GALLERY containing portraits of Nawabs of Oudh.

Other Interesting Places to Visit

Residency Building

The RESIDENCY BUILDING, connected with the events of Mutiny, still bears the scars of destruction. The gardens around the Residency are beautifully kept and are peaceful.

LAKSHMAN TILLA on the right bank of the river Gomati was the original site of Lucknow in the 15th century. Now, Aurangzeb's mosque stands there — an example of vandalism practised by the invaders.

In the centre of Lucknow are perfectly proportioned tombs of Nawab Ali Khan and Queen Khurshed Begum built in the beginning of the 19th century. The KAISER BAGH which adjoins the tombs contains rows of yellow structures. These were the royal harems. Close to the river is SHAH NAJAF, the early 19th century tomb of Nawab Ghaziuddin Haider and his queen.

On the outskirts of the city in a park close to a lake rises an architectural jumble built in the 18th century by a Frenchman called Claud Martin. Gargoyles rub shoulders with Cornthian columns. Rounded arches standing side by side with oriental turrets. Interestingly, this architectural hotch-potch was built for a boys' school!

While in Lucknow, you should not miss the CHAWK, the main bazar in the old city. Here flourish the arts and crafts — 'saris', gold and silver brocades, clay figures, pottery and folk embroidery. It was the haunt of the feudal aristocracy in the old days and is still the place for good bargains. Old 'Nawabi' dwellings abound — some still inhabited by patrician families. It is here that the old culture and gracious 'Nawabi' manners still persist, reminding you of the 18th century culture of the elite of Lucknow.

AROUND LUCKNOW

On leaving Lucknow, you can drive east to FAIZABAD, the old capital of Oudh. The Nawabs of Oudh shifted their capital to Lucknow in the 18th century. Adjoining Faizabad is AYODHYA — now the focus of a controversy surrounding the BABRI MASJID, which Hindus believe was built by the invading Mughal emperor Babar in 16th century after demolishing a Rama temple at the exact site of Lord Rama's birthplace. The dilapidated monument has since vanished.

Ayodhya, located on the banks of Saryu river, is believed to be the capital of Kosala, a kingkom ruled by Rama — God-king of the *Ramayana*. It is one of the most sacred cities of the Hindus. There are some 300 temples in it. Buddha also preached his 'Dharma' in Kosala. Hieun Tsang, the indefatigable Chinese traveller, visited Ayodhya in the 7th century and described it in glowing terms.

Not very far from Lucknow, are two very ancient cities connected with the life of Lord Buddha — SRAVASTI and KUSHINAGAR. Buddha came to Sravasti to preach and it was also the place where he performed some miracles to convince the non-believers about the truth of his religion. At Kushinagar, at the age of 80, he achieved "Parinirvana" — he passed away. The last rites were performed with all the honour that is due to a universal monarch (Chakravartin), as he was held in reverence by all people. The kings of eight Indian states of the Gangetic basin came for the funeral rites and divided his ashes in eight parts. Each king carried these back to his kingdom and built a 'Stupa' over the mortal remains of Lord Buddha. At Kushinagar temple, a sculpture showing the dying Buddha is visited by thousands of Buddhist pilgrims every year from all parts of the world. It is always part of a Buddhist itinerary along with LUMBINI where he was born, BODH GAYA where he attained wisdom and VARANASI, where he gave his first sermon.

ALLAHABAD

About 137 kms west of Varanasi lies the ancient city of Prayag, renamed Allahabad by Akbar, the great Mughal, in 1583. The city is very sacred to the Hindus and devout Hindus are enjoined to have a bath at the 'Sangam' at Allahabad which is the confluence of the Ganga and the Yamuna rivers. Its importance is even greater as the legendary Saraswati river of the *Vedas* is believed to have joined the two rivers at this very place. Every year thousands of devout Hindus congregate here for pilgrimage. But once in twelve years, there is a special pilgrimage for the 'Kumbh' Fair when about five million people assemble at the 'Sangam' to have the sacred bath at this place.

Allahabad is a quiet and peaceful city, the site of one of the great Universities of India — Allahabad University. It was built on the site of an ancient Ashram where sage Bhardwaj taught 10,000 students. The great Indian patriot, Motilal Nehru, father of India's first Prime Minister, Jawaharlal Nehru, lived in this city, and their residence, ANAND BHAVAN, is now a national monument open to visitors.

After conquering Prayag, Akbar built a fort which stands majestically at the confluence on the Yamuna side. The FORT is most impressive when you view it from the river. Apart from the fort, there is no other Mughal building in the city, though there are many temples.

The ASHOKA PILLAR re-erected in Akbar's Fort, dates back to 232 B.C. It was found lying on the ground of the Fort in 1837 and was set up at the present site. Inscribed on its polished 10.6 metres high sandstone shaft are Ashoka's inscriptions. There are also later inscriptions by Emperor Samudragupta (A.D. 326-375) This is the only historical record of the great monarch's life - a monarch who ruled over a large part of India. Later, Mughal Emperor Jahangir added his own inscription on the pillar.

The KHUSRAU GARDEN close to the railway station contains the tomb of Prince Khusro, who was executed by his own father Jahangir for his rebellion. The tombs of his Rajput mother and sisters are close by.

A small door in the east wall of the Fort, near the river, leads to the undying banyan tree which is believed to have existed for thousands of years. The Chinese Traveller, Hieun Tsang, in A.D. 650 described it as Akshyaya Vatt, the Undying Banyan Tree.

Visitors on a low budget can plan to travel from Allahabad to Khajuraho in Madhya Pradesh. One can take a train from here to Satna where buses are available for Khajuraho.

Between Lucknow to Varanasi, there is a town called BAHRAICH where a nephew of Mahmud Gazni, the scourge of India, was killed in 1033. There is a shrine to him, 3 kilometres from the town.

Next, SAHET-MAHETH is a centre of Buddhist pilgrimage attracting national and international visitors. The town is also known as Sravasti and can be reached from GORAKHPUR. At Sahet-Maheth, Lord Buddha performed the miracle of sitting on a thousand petalled lotus, multiplying himself a thousand times. The town has extensive ruins and some modern Buddhist temples.

GORAKHPUR AND LUMBINI

Gorakhpur (population 2,50,000) is a thriving town on the Indo-Nepal border and provides easy access to some of the most important places connected with the life of Lord Buddha. KUSHINAGAR, 5 km. to the east, was the place where Buddha died and was cremated. This is also the town from where you can have 'backdoor' entry into Nepal on the way to Pokhra, the beautiful Himalayan resort in Nepal. While on the way to Pokhra, you pass by the greatest pilgrimage centre of Buddhists — Lumbini, the sacred place where Gautama the Buddha was born. If you want to visit Lumbini only, take a cycle-rickshaw from the border town of KAKARHWA. It may cost you not more than ten rupees. Visa is given to you for a nominal fee at the border itself. Indians do not need a visa to enter Nepal.

VARANASI

Varanasi was known as Kashi in ancient times long before Christ was born. When Buddha came here to deliver his first sermon to five disciples at Sarnath — around 500 B.C. — Kashi was already an old settlement. Comtemporary with Babylon, Nineveh and Thebes, it is perhaps the oldest living city in the world. Varanasi is the restoration of an another old name of Kashi which means the City between Two Rivers, Varuna and Asi. Since the British could not pronounce it, they called it Benaras.

All Hindus wish to visit Varanasi once in their lifetime and revisit it over and over again in the evening of their lives. River Ganga holds to them the powers of salvation. Each year Varanasi welcomes millions of pilgrims and some even stay back to die there.

The earliest inhabitants of Varanasi were the Aryans. They contributed to its growth as a great centre of culture and education, commerce, craftsmanship and learning. The city represented the best thoughts of Vedic religion and culture. Students from all over the country, and from other countries came to visit the city or to study here. The divinity and the fame of Varanasi grew and flourished, attracting patronage from the rich, and the knowledge of the wise. Stretching from the 3rd century B.C. to the seventh century A.D., Varanasi, as recorded in texts, consisted of houses, big and small, built along narrow streets with temples interspersed between them.

Its fame as a great religious centre of the Hindus invited the wrath of the Muslim invaders. The city was ransacked and looted in succession from the 11th century to the 18th century. Temples were razed and mosques built in their places. Varanasi's fame lies beyond mere intellectual and religious curiosity. Once it exported its silks and textiles to Burma and Ceylon, China, Malaya, Indonesia and Central and Western Asia, Babylon, Greece and Rome. Today, the same craftsmanship characterises its industry; brocades, silks, handicrafts and carpets are among its important commercial products.

Another activity — an offshoot of religious ceremonies — was the development of music and dance. The Varanasi 'gharana' has contributed to the growth of the graceful, supremely melodious styles of singing, called the 'thumri' and the 'dadra', in north Indian classical music. It was here, in Varanasi, that Goswami Tulsidas enacted the first Ram Lila in the 17th century, considered by art historians to be the first attempt to stage dramas in Hindi. The Benaras Hindu University (one of India's more prestigious universities), was founded here in 1916, following sustained efforts of Pandit Madan Mohan Malviya. In 1921, the Kashi University was established.

The Ghats

The principal attraction of Varanasi is its long string of bathing ghats — over 100 in all. The ghats are the steps leading to the river where pilgrims take their dip. The DASAWAMEDH Ghat can be the best starting point from where you can hire a boat to see the other ghats. Raja Man Singh of Jaipur built an unusual Observatory at the Ghat in 1710.

The Temple

Among the temples, every pilgrim's destination is the GOLDEN TEMPLE, dedicated to Shiva-Vishwanath, the Lord of the Universe. It stands across the road from its original temple. Mughal emperor Aurangzeb destroyed the original temple and built a mosque over it. Traces of the temple can be seen behind the mosque. The present temple was built in 1776 by Maharani Ahalya Bai of Indore in 1776. Gold-plating on the towers was provided by Maharaja Ranjit Singh, the valiant Sikh ruler of Lahore. Next door is GYAN KUP, the well of knowledge. It is said to contain the Lingam of the original temple hidden from Aurangzeb. Non-Hindus are not allowed into the temple but can see it from a vantage point.

Around the Vishwanath temple, there are an incredible number of shops.

Aurangzeb built a great mosque in Varanasi using the columns of Biseswar temple which he destroyed. It has minarets towering 71 metres around the Ganga. Armed guards protect the mosque as many Hindus now resent the vandalism practised by the Muslim rulers.

DURGA TEMPLE is another interesting temple to visit. It is commonly known as the Monkey Temple due to the presence of a large number of monkeys around it. It was built in the 18th century by a Bengali Maharani and is stained red with ochre. It is one of the best known temples, but not open to non-Hindus.

Near the Benares Hindu University, a beautiful modern Hindu temple, a replica of the original Vishwanath Temple destroyed by Aurangzeb, has been built.

BHARAT MATA TEMPLE is dedicated to Mother India. It has marble relief map of India instead of the usual images of gods and goddesses and is open to all.

On the other side of the river, the 17th century RAMGARH FORT is the home of the Maharaja of Benares. It has an interesting museum containing old silver and brocade palanquins for ladies of the court; elephant 'howdahs' made of silver; an armoury of swords and old guns and many other unique objects. The fort offers a panoramic view of the city.

SARNATH

After roaming the streets of Varanasi, you must pay a visit to a very peaceful and serene place, less than ten kilometres from the city. It is Sarnath, the cradle of Buddhist faith. Buddha preached his first sermon here. He revealed his Eightfold Path that would lead to the end of sorrow, attainment of inner peace; enlightenment and Nirvana. He established the Middle Path — the golden path between extremes of ascetism and self-indulgence.

Three hundred years later, Ashoka, the great emperor, adopted Buddhism and built a vast 'Stupa' at the site where the great Master preached. He also erected a stone pillar containing Buddha's teachings. His famous LION CAPITAL, which is now India's state emblem, is preserved in the SARNATH MUSEUM. Another six centuries later, Sarnath reached the zenith of its glory. The Chinese traveller, Fahian, who visited Sarnath, informs us that 1500 priests were in daily attendance at prayers round the Banyan Tree, close to the VIHARA TEMPLE. The BANYAN TREE was believed to be the original Bo tree from BODH GAYA under which Buddha had meditated.

Five great monuments still survive in Sarnath. Among them the DHUMEKH-STUPA (A.D. 500) is the largest survivor. It has geometrical designs on its wall. Although constructed during the Gupta period, remains of Mauryan bricks (200 B.C.) have been discovered. DHARMARJIKA STUPA, built by Ashoka, is believed to contain the bodily remains of Lord Buddha. Then there is the main shrine where Ashoka sat in meditation. Finally, the CHANKAMA marks the sacred promenade where Buddha would sit while preaching.

In recent times, Sarnath has seen Buddhist revival through the International Mahabodhi Society. The Society built a new temple in 1931 over the old foundations of several sundry Stupas. The MAHABODHI TEMPLE stands close to the Dhumekh Stupa. It contains rare Buddhist relics from different parts of India. The walls are decorated with hundreds of paintings of a Japanese artist. The MAHABODHI SOCIETY LIBRARY contains a rare collection of Buddhist literature.

Buddhist monks and lay devotees from all parts of the world meet in Sarnath once a year, on full moon day in November.

A little to the east of the new temple is a Chinese temple. It contains a marble image of the Great Master.

The MUSEUM at Sarnath should be a 'must' for every visitor. It contains many figures and sculptures from various periods of history of Sarnath - Mauryan, Kushan, Gupta and later.

At Sarnath, you will meet Buddhist preachers from many countries of Asia. A visitor feels the aura of peace all around him at this sacred place.

AGRA

GENERAL INFORMATION

Population: 1,000,000 (1991 census)
Altitude: 169 metres (563 ft)

Climate

	Temperature	
	Max.	Min.
Winter	30°c	7°c
Summer	42°c	24°c

Season: Throughout the year. April to June the days are hot.

Clothing
Summer: cottons
Winter: woollens.

HOW TO GET THERE

By Air: Agra is connected by air with Delhi, Bombay, Jaipur, Khajuraho, Kanpur and Varanasi. Daily flights from Delhi-30 mts.
By Rail: Agra is connected by rail with all major cities of India. Daily Shatabdi train takes only two hours.
By Road: Agra is connected by good roads.
It is 204 km. from Delhi,
237 km. from Jaipur,
54 km. from Bharatpur,
54 km. from Mathura and
395 km. from Khajuraho.
There are frequent bus services to Mathura, Bharatpur, Delhi, Jaipur, Gwalior and Hardwar.

LOCAL TRANSPORT

Tourist taxis, unmetered taxies, autorickshaws, tongas (horse carriages), cycle-rickshaws and bus services available. Air-conditioned cars available from hotels.

CONDUCTED TOURS

1. Full-day tour to Fatehpur Sikri, Taj Mahal and Agra Fort.
2. Half-day tour to Fatehpur Sikri.
   (Contact UPSTDC Office,
   Phone: 360140 and
   UPSRTC office
   Phone: 72206)
   Tourist office
   Phone: 66438
   Similar tours are available from various travel agencies.

WHERE TO STAY (STD CODE: 0562)

Deluxe

1. Hotel Agra Ashok
   Phone: 361223-32
   Fax: 361620
   Cable: ASHOKOTEL
2. Welcomgroup-Mughal Sheraton
   Phone: 361701
   Fax: 361730
   Cable: WELCOTEL
3. Taj View - Taj Group
   Phone: 361172-78
   Fax: 361179
   Cable: TAJVIEW
4. Clarks Shiraz
   Phone: 361421-29
   Fax: 361428
   Cable: SHIRAZ
5. Novotel Agra
   Phone: 68282
   Fax: 360217

Standard

6. Mumtaz
   Phone: 361771 (6 lines)
   Telex: 0565-222 MMTZ IN
   Cable: MUMTAZTEL

7. Amar
   Phone: 360695-99
   Fax: 366999
8. Mayur Tourist Complex
   Phone: 360302-360310
   Cable: MAYUR

BUDGET
9. Taj Khema UPSTDC
   Phone: 360140
   Cable: UPTOURISM
10. UPSTDC Tourist Bungalow
    Phone: 77035, 72123
    Telex: 0565-322
11. Youth Hostel
    Phone: 65812
12. Agra Deluxe
    Phone: 360110
    Fax: 360185
    Cable: SHAHNSHAH
13. Laurie's Hotel
    Phone: 364536
14. Grand Hotel
    Phone: 364014

WHAT TO SEE
1. The TAJ MAHAL is the world's greatest monument dedicated to the love of an Emperor for his queen. It took 22 years to build and was completed in 1653 A.D.
2. AGRA FORT, built by Emperor Akbar in 1565 A.D. Inside are several palaces and the largest of pure marble mosque, the MOTI MASJID.
3. ITMAD-UD-DAULAH'S TOMB, built by Empress Noorjahan in memory of her father. Pieta dura inlay work, later used in the Taj, was used here for the first time.
4. AKBAR'S MAUSOLEUM at Sikandra (10 km.) is a fusion of Muslim and Hindu architectural styles which was characteristic of that period.
5. RADHASWAMI SAMADHI (8 km.) where the ashes of the revered founder of the Radhaswami faith are preserved. Congregational services are held daily.

EXCURSIONS
1. FATEHPUR SIKRI (37 km.), the deserted ghost capital of Emperor Akbar. This exquisite city designed by Akbar, with its forts, palaces and mosques, was abandoned after a few years due to scarcity of water.
2. MATHURA (54 km.), associated with the life of Lord Krishna. The Mathura Museum has excellent collections dating back to 600 B.C.
3. VRINDABAN (63 km.), associated with the childhood of Lord Krishna. It has many temples of the 14th to the 19th centuries.
4. GWALIOR (118 km.), famed for its ancient fort, one of the largest in the country, and palaces, temples and the cenotaphs of its rulers.
5. SHIVPURI (112 km from Gwalior), the summer capital of the Scindia dynasty, has a National Park which is famed for

the chinkara deer, the Indian gazelle, and the chital deer.

SHOPPING
Marble inlay on trinket boxes, carved teak-wood figures, marble curios, ivory statuettes, semi-precious stone inlay, metal and leather work, carpets and cotton rugs, gold and silver embroidery, ready-made garments and semi-precious jewellery.

Most markets open at 10 am and close after 7 pm.

Porcelain pottery design

CUISINE
Agra is known for its Mughlai food. The best known dishes include the *burra kabab*, succulent meat cubes marinated in yoghurt-based sauce and roasted over a slow charcoal fire. Other specialities include *tandoori* chicken, *seekh* and *bote kababs*.

LOCAL FESTIVALS
1. SHEETLA FAIR (July-August). It is held near Delhi Gate at Agra.
2. KAILASH FAIR (August-September), held at the temple at Kailash, 12 km. from Agra. The spot is sanctified by the belief that Lord Shiva appeared here.
3. SHARAD POORNIMA (October). This famous fair takes place at the Taj on the full-moon night of October.

Information: Govt. of India Tourist Office, the Mall, Agra, *Tel*: 72377.

LUCKNOW

GENERAL INFORMATION
Population: 1,650,000 (1991 census)
Altitude: 111 metres (370 ft)
Climate

	Temperature	
	Max.	Min.
Winter	33^{0}c	9^{0}c
Summer	41^{0}c	22^{0}c

Season: Throughout the year. The months of April to June are very hot.

Clothing
Summer: light cottons.
Winter : woollens.

HOW TO GET THERE
By Air: Lucknow is connected by Indian Airlines flights to Delhi, Bombay, Calcutta, Allahabad, Gorakhpur, Patna, Ranchi and Kanpur. Vayudoot and private services also operate.
By Rail: Lucknow is on the trunk line and has direct express rail

connections with Agra, Ahmedabad, Amritsar, Bombay, Cochin, Delhi, Gorakhpur, Jammu, Puri, Varanasi, etc.
By Road: Lucknow is connected to the north and east by road. It is
  79 km. from Kanpur,
  128 km. from Ayodhya,
  314 km. from Agra,
  314 km. from Varanasi,
  480 km. from Corbett National Park,
  260 km. from Dudhwa National Park and
  300 km. from Gorakhpur.

LOCAL TRANSPORT
Unmetered taxis and scooters are available as also bus services, tongas (horse-drawn carriages) and cycle-rickshaws.
  It is advisable to confirm the fare in advance.

CONDUCTED TOURS
There are conducted tours of the city and also to the Dudhwa National Park and to the Nawabganj Bird Sanctuary.
Information: UP Government Tourist Information centre
Tel: 52533

WHERE TO STAY (STD CODE: 0522)
DELUXE
1. Clarks Avadh
   Phone: 236501-06, 240131
   Cable: AVADH
   Fax: 636507
STANDARD
2. Carlton Hotel
   Phone: 224201
   Fax: 249793
   Cable: CARLTON

BUDGET
3. Kohinoor
   Phone: 232716
   Cable: SAPNA
4. Deep Avadh
   Phone: 236521-25
   Telex: 0625-216
5. Gomte (UPTDC)
   Phone: 232291
6. Asif Castle
   Phone: 221313-17
   Fax: 231360
7. Deep Hotel
   Phone: 236441
   Cable: DEEP
8. Capoor's Hotel
   Phone: 243958
9. Mohan Hotel
   Phone: 54283
   Fax: 51955
10. Charans International
    Phone: 247219-21

WHAT TO SEE
1. The great IMAMBARA. Built in the 18th century, it was constructed to provide employment during a famine. The absence of beams and pillars in the huge main hall is an architectural wonder. It is also famous for the BHUL-BHULAIYAN, a maze of labyrinths with unusual acoustics. You can get lost here without a guide.
2. The RUMI DARWAZA or Turkish Gate at the entrance to the Great Imambara.
3. HUSSAINABAD (CHHOTA) IMAMBARA built in a florid Saracenic style with a dome, turrets and

minarets. The Tazias (replicas of the tomb of Imam Hussain) are its great attractions.
4. LUCKNOW RESIDENCY where the British Resident lived. A historical building, as it was the site of the famous siege of 1857.
5. SIKANDARABAGH built by Wajid Ali Shah with buildings and a pavilion set in a pool.
6. PICTURE GALLERY. There are excellent full-sized portraits of the Nawabs of Oudh.

EXCURSIONS

1. KUKARAIL RESERVE FOREST (9 km.), where crocodiles are reared.
2. CHINHAT PICNIC PAVILION (13 km). Boating available.
3. NAWABGANJ BIRD SANCTUARY (45 km)
4. SRAVASTI, the present Saheth-Maheth (170 km), site of a great miracle performed by the Buddha. It is a Buddhist pilgrim centre.
5. SANKASYA (249 km), another important place of Buddhist pilgrimage.

SHOPPING

Lucknow is the home of the *chikan* work (delicate embroidery on fine cotton fabric) perfumes (with a base of sandalwood oil, agar, saffron and other herbs), zari (silver and gold thread embroidery), clay toys, velvet slippers, block-printed fabrics and glazed pottery.

FESTIVALS OF SPECIAL LOCAL INTEREST

MOHARRAM. This is really not a festival but a period of mourning when huge tazias (replicas of tombs of the son-in-law and grandsons of the Prophet) are taken out in procession by Shia Muslims amidst beating of breasts, and the pageantry of the Nawabi days is re-enacted. Fire-walking takes place on one of the nights.

ENTERTAINMENT

1. The LUCKNOW FESTIVAL is held in early February every year.
2. Regular music and dance performances are presented at local theatres.

VARANASI

GENERAL INFORMATION

Population: 1,020,000 (1991 census)
Altitude: 76 metres (253 ft)

Climate:

	Temperature	
	Max.	Min.
Winter	33^0c	9^0c
Summer	42^0c	22^0c

Season: Throughout the year. During the months of April, May and June, the days are hot.

Clothing

Summer: light cottons.
Winter: woollens

HOW TO GET THERE

By Air: Varanasi is connected by Indian Airlines flights to Kathmandu, Delhi, Calcutta, Agra, Bhubaneshwar, Khajuraho, Lucknow, Patna and Raipur. Private airlines (Modiluft and Sahara) are also operating.
Indian Airlines *Tel*: 43746 (City) 43792 (Airport)
Transfers for Airport to city provided by Indian Airlines - charges Rs. 25 only per seat.

By Rail: Varanasi is connected by rail with Ahmedabad, Amritsar, Bombay, Calcutta, Delhi, Gorakhpur, Jammu, Lucknow, Madras, Puri, etc. Several express trains are available.

By Road: Varanasi is connected by roads to the northern and eastern regions. It is
- 252 km. from Patna,
- 243 km. from Bodh Gaya,
- 259 km. from Kushinagar,
- 320 km. from Lucknow,
- 613 km. from Agra,
- 678 km. from Calcutta and
- 819 km. from Delhi.

There are bus services to Gorakhpur (for Kushinagar), Sunauli (for Kathmandu), Lucknow, Allahabad, etc.

LOCAL TRANSPORT

There are tourist taxis, unmetered private taxis, autorickshaws, cycle-rickshaws and local bus services.

CONDUCTED TOURS

1. RIVER TRIP (visiting bathing ghats on the riverside, temples and Benaras Hindu University); half-day tour.
2. SARNATH and RAMNAGAR FORT, half-day tour.

(*Contact* U.P. Govt. Tourist Office, Parade Kothi (*Phones*: 43486, 42018) or Govt. of India Tourist Office, Mall. *Phone*: 43744).
Local sightseeing as well as excursion tours are operated by ITDC-Ashok Travels and Tours - from Hotel Varanasi, the Mall, *Tel*: 46020-30, *Fax*: 42141.

WHERE TO STAY (STD CODE: 0542)

DELUX

1. Clarkes Varanasi
   Phone: 348501-10
   Fax: 348186
   Cable: CLARKOTEL
2. Taj Ganges
   Phone: 42481, 42495
   Fax: 348067
   Cable: TAJBEN

STANDARD

3. Varanasi Ashok
   Phone: 46020-30
   Fax: 42141
   Cable: TOURISM
4. Hindustan International
   Phone: 57075-82
   Fax: 352374
5. Hotel de Paris
   Phone: 46601-08
   Cable: HOTEL PARIS

6. Hotel Ideal Tops
   Phone: 42591-92
   Fax: 355785
BUDGET
7. Sidharth
   Phone: 352001
   Fax: 352301
8. Malti
   Phone: 352001
9. Tourist Bungalow (UPTDC)
   Phone: 43413, 43486, 42368
10. India
    Phone: 45127-43261

WHAT TO SEE
1. The RIVER FRONT. At dawn, pilgrims standing waist-deep in water, pray to the rising sun. At dusk, lighted lamps and flowers are offered to the flowing River Ganga.
2. GOLDEN TEMPLE OF VISHWANATH. The original temple was destroyed by the Mughal Emperor, Aurangzeb, and the present temple was built by Rani Ahalyabai of Indore in the 18th century. The gold plating of the spires was done in the 19th century by Maharaja Ranjit Singh of Punjab.
3. 18th century DURGA TEMPLE.
4. BHARAT MATA TEMPLE.
5. TULSI MANAS TEMPLE on the spot where Saint Tulsidas composed the *Ramayana* in Hindi (The *Ramacharitamanas*).
6. BENARES HINDU UNIVERSITY, believed to be the largest residential university in Asia.
7. NEW VISHWANATH TEMPLE and BHARAT KALA BHAVAN MUSEUM on the University Campus.

EXCURSIONS
1. SARNATH (10 km). It was here in the Deer Park that the Buddha delivered his first sermon and set in motion the Wheel of Law of the Buddhist faith.
2. The ARCHAEOLOGICAL SITE MUSEUM at Sarnath has interesting sculptures of the life of the Buddha. The lion capital, which is the national emblem of India, can be seen here.
3. RAMNAGAR FORT (16 km). The residence of the former Maharaja, it has unique collections of furniture, palanquins, costumes, arms and weapons.
4. CHUNAR FORT (37 km) of the Afghan ruler, Sher Shah Suri.
5. JAUNPUR (58 km), the 14th century capital of Sharqui Kings. It is known for its perfumes and incense, tombs and buildings.
6. MIRZAPUR (75 km), famous for its carpets.
7. CHANDRAPRABHA FOREST (70 km) and the RAJDARI and DEODARI WATERFALLS.
8. KUSHINAGAR or Kasia (265 km), where the Buddha left his mortal body.

SHOPPING

The famous Benaras silks and brocades woven with silver and gold thread, brass and copperware, carpets, wooden and clay toys, ivory, beads, glass bangles, etc.

FESTIVALS OF SPECIAL LOCAL INTEREST

1. BUDDHA PURNIMA (May), the day of the birth, enlightenment and death of the Buddha. Relics of the Buddha are taken in procession at Sarnath.
2. DUSSEHRA (September - October). Special celebrations are held at Ramnagar. It is also celebrated as DURGA PUJA when, after four days' worship, images of the goddess are immersed in the river with great eclat.
3. BHARAT MILAP (October - November) celebrating the reunion of Rama, the hero of the *Ramayana*, with his brother Bharat. The former Maharaja of Benaras attends the celebrations, seated on an elephant.
4. NAGNATHAIYA (November) at Tulsi Ghat, celebrating the conquest of the serpent king, Kaliya, by Lord Krishna.
5. In addition, there are several temple festivals like the CHAITRA NAVARATRI (March-April), PANCH KROSHI YATRA (holy travel around Kashi in April-May), RATH YATRA (June-July), DURGA MELA (July-Aug.), SARNATH BUDDHIST MELA (July-Aug), SORHIYA MELA (Aug.-Sept.), RAMNAGAR RAMLILA (Sept.-Oct.), and GANGA DUSSEHRA (June).

NAINITAL

GENERAL INFORMATION

Population: 30,000 (1991 census)
Altitude: 1933 metres (6437 ft)
Climate

	Temperature	
	Max.	Min.
Winter	16.6°c	2.8°c
Summer	26.7°c	10.6°c

Season: April to July and mid-September to mid-November.
Clothing
Summer: light woollens or cottons.
Winter: heavy woollens.

HOW TO GET THERE

By Air: The nearest airport is Pantnagar (7 km) which is connected by irregular air services to New Delhi. Pantnagar is connected to Nainital by bus/taxi services and is about two hours' drive.
By Rail: The nearest railhead is Kathgodham (35 km) which is connected by metre gauge from Agra, Bareilly and Lucknow.

By Road: Good motorable roads connect Nainital with the following cities. It is
277 km. from Agra,
65 km. from Almora,
303 km. from Badrinath,
137 km. from Bareilly,
113 km. from Corbett,
373 km. from Dehradun,
277 km. from Delhi,
306 km. from Hardwar,
380 km. from Lucknow,
155 km. from Moradabad and
54 km. from Ranikhet.

LOCAL TRANSPORT
Cycle-rickshaws, ponies and taxis.

CONDUCTED TOURS
The Kumaon Mandal Vikas Nigam; the Mall, conducts various tours in and around Nainital. *Phone*: 2656.
There are several private tour operators.

WHERE TO STAY (STD Code: 059427)
STANDARD
1. Arif Castles
   Phone: 2801-01-03
   Telex: 05703 201
2. Everest
   Phone: 2453
3. Claridges Naini Retreat
   Phone: 2105-8
   Cable: Retreat
4. Shervani Hilltop Inn
   Phone: 3298, 3128
5. Grand
   Phone: 2406-2008
6. Swiss
   Phone: 3013
7. Vikram Vintage Inn
   Phone: 3177

8. Belvedere
   Phone: 2802
9. Langdale Manor
   Phone: 2858, 2447
10. Holiday Inn, Nainital
    Phone: 2531, 3031
BUDGET
11. Silverton
    Phone: 2249
12. Alka
    Phone: 2220
13. Pratap Regency
    Phone: 2866

UP Tourism offers excellent budget accommodation at fixed rate. Contact: UP Tourism, The Mall, *Tel*: 2337.

WHAT TO SEE
1. At the centre of Nainital is NAINI LAKE around which the city has grown. Boating is available here.
2. STATE ASTRONOMICAL OBSERVATORY can be reached by foot or pony-back. Views of the distant plains from here are spectacular.
3. SANJAY PARK is a botanical garden.
4. GUFA MAHADEV is a cave temple dedicated to Shiva and close to the Sepoydhara spring.
5. The last motorable point is LAND'S END. A little distance from here is TIFFIN TOP, a popular picnic spot.

EXCURSIONS
1. SAT TAL (25 km) is a complex of five natural lakes with good angling prospects.

2. BHIMTAL (23 km) is larger than Naini Lake and has a beautiful island and a restaurant.
3. RAMGARH (26 km) is well known for its orchards.
4. MUKTESHWAR (52 km) is a celebrated scenic spot overlooking the Himalayan ranges.

MUSSOORIE

GENERAL INFORMATION

Population: 40,000 (1991 census)
Altitude: 2005 metres (6677 ft)
Climate

	Temperature	
	Max.	Min.
Winter	7.2°c	1.0°c
Summer	25.6°c	7.2°c

Season: April to July and September to October.
Clothing
Summer: woollens
Winter: heavy woollens.

HOW TO GET THERE

By Air: The nearest airport is Jolly Grant (60 km) from Mussoorie which is connected by Vayudoot services from Delhi.
By Rail: Dehradun (34 km) is the nearest railhead which is connected to all major cities in India.
By Road: Mussoorie is connected by road with the following cities. It is
  442 km. from Agra,
  269 km. from Delhi,
  103 km. from Hardwar,
   77 km. from Rishikesh,
  314 km. from Shimla,
  139 km. from Yamnotri.

There are regular bus services to Dehradun, Roorkee, Saharanpur, Tehri and Muzaffarpur.

LOCAL TRANSPORT
Ponies, taxis and jeeps.

CONDUCTED TOURS
Garhwal Mandal Vikas Nigam organises tours to Gangotri and Yamnotri during season. Tours to Kempty Falls, Dhanolti, Sarkhanda Devi Temple are also available.
Information: Tourist Office, the Mall. *Tel*.: 632863.

WHERE TO STAY (STD Code: 013563)
STANDARD
1. Claridge Nabha Palace
   Phone : 632525
2. Savoy
   Phone: 632120, 632010
   Telex: 585 302 SAVY IN
   Cable: SAVOY
3. Solitaire Plaza
   Phone: 632164/65
   Fax: 532166
   Cable: SOLITAIRE
4. Shilron Hotel
   Phone: 632983
5. Hakman's Grand Hotel
   Phone: 632559
   Cable: HAKMAN'S

6. Filigree
   Phone: 632380
   Cable: SAMOVAR
7. Hotel Shining Star
   Phone: 632323
   Cable: SHINING STAR
   Mussoorie has several budget hotel. Please contact UP Tourist Information Office at the Mal-*Tel*: 632863.

WHAT TO SEE

1. GUN HILL (2 km) the highest point in the city, surveys the surrounding hills and snow-covered ranges further away. A ropeway operates between the Mall and the Gun Hill.
2. KEMPTY FALLS (5 km).
3. JHARIPANI FALLS (8.5 km).
4. KATHGODAM TIBBA (5 km) and LAL TIBBA (6 km).
5. NAG DEVTA TEMPLE (6 km).
6. BHATTA FALLS (10 km).
7. DEPOT HILL (11 km) and BENOG HILL (6 km).

EXCURSIONS

YAMUNA BRIDGE (27 km), NAG TIBBA (35 km), DHANOLTI (25 km), SURKHANDA DEVI (35 km), LAKHA MANDAL (75 km).

CORBETT NATIONAL PARK

GENERAL INFORMATION

Altitude: 400 to 1100 Metres (1333 to 3667 ft.)
Climate *

	Temperature	
	Max.	Min.
Winter	30^0c	8^0c
Summer	44^0c	22^0c

Season: Mid-November to mid-June. (The Park is closed from mid-June to mid-November.) In the nearby Nainital and Almora, it is cooler.
Clothing
Summer: cottons
Winter: woollens.

HOW TO GET THERE

By Air: Pantnagar, the nearest airport (135 km) with irregular flights.
By Rail: Ramnagar is the nearest railhead (51 km). It is connected with Moradabad on the main line.
By Road: Dhikala, the base for the Corbett National Park, is connected by motorable road to important tourist centres. It is
300 km. from Delhi,
134 km. from Ranikhet,
144 km. from Nainital,
180 km. from Almora and
480 km. from Lucknow.
There are regular bus services from Dhikala to Ramnagar, and from Ramnagar to Pantnagar, Delhi, Lucknow, etc.

LOCAL TRANSPORT

Mini-buses, station wagons, jeeps and elephants are available for sightseeing. (Contact Assistant Wild Life Warden, Dhikala.)

CONDUCTED TOURS

There are tours to Corbett from Delhi, Nainital, etc. (Contact the nearest Tourist Office for information).

WHERE TO STAY

1. Quality Corbett Jungle Resort
   Phone: 85520, 85230
2. Tiger Tops Corbett Lodge
   Phone: 85946

The other accommodations at Dhikala vary from 3-roomed cabins (air-conditioning provided on request) with attached baths to Forest Rest Houses, three-bedded hutments, Swiss cottage tents and log hut dormitories. Dining facilities available.

WHAT TO SEE

ANIMALS: Elephant, tiger, panther, sloth bear, wild bear, nilgai, sambar, chital, antelope, barking deer, hog deer, monkeys, etc.

REPTILES: Crocodile, python, king cobra.

BIRDS: Bulbul, heron, woodpecker, kingfisher, weaver bird and hundreds of other species.

FISH: Mahseer, trout and goonch.

EXCURSIONS

1. KANDA (18 km from Dhikala). A scenic spot.
2. RANIKHET (134 km from Dhikala), is a hill resort surrounded by Himalayan peaks like Nanda Devi, Trisul.

NAINITAL

3. NAINITAL (144 km from Dhikala Altitude: 1938 metres), a popular hill resort surrounding a lake. There are conducted tours during the season from here to BHIMTAL, a 2-day tour to CORBETT, a 2-day tour to KAUSANI, ALMORA and RANIKHET and a 3-day tour of the Kumaon area. There is also a 4-day tour to the famous Hindu pilgrim centre of BADRINATH. For tours contact Kumaon Mandal Vikas Nigam, Nainital. *Phone*: 2656. New Delhi-3322251. For treks and mountaineering, contact Nainital Mountaineering Club.
   Phone: 2543, 2509

4. ALMORA (180 km from Dhikala) Altitude 1646 metres. Bordered by the Himalayas, Almora is an important starting point for treks in the Kumaon region, the most exciting being to the PINDARI GLACIER. Others are to the SUNDARHUNGA GLACIER and MILAM GLACIER. There are many shorter treks too.

The 2-star Westview Hotel (Tel: 61196) and Tourist Cottages run by KMUN (Tel: 2297) are available for stay in Ranikhet. At Almora there are also the U.P. Govt. Holiday Home and Forest Rest Houses.

SPORTS

Angling for mahseer, trout and goonch in the streams is a popular sport of the region.

Chapter 15

MADHYA PRADESH
India's Tribal Province

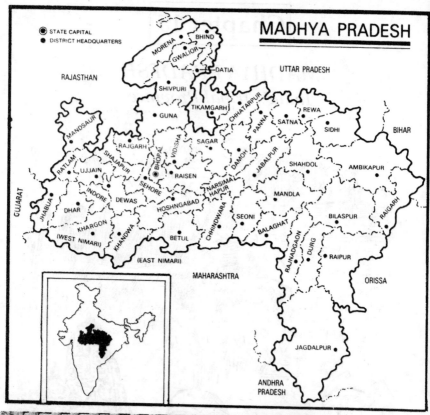

A frieze, Sanchi temple

India's largest State is Madhya Pradesh. Literally, it means Central Province. Its land area is 4,50,000 km. and population about 66 million. Most people speak Hindi or some dialect of Hindi. One can imagine the size of the State when you are told that if India had a system of time zones as in other large countries, the time would be 40 minutes ahead in Ramanujganj (a town on the eastern border of the State) of Jabhua (on the western border).

Geographically, but for the valleys of Narmada and Tapti rivers, the entire State is a plateau, 500 metres above the sea level. Its northern part, with GWALIOR as its major city, lies in the Indo-Gangetic Plains. Much of the State consists of upland plateaus and hills interspersed with deep valleys and rivers flowing into the Bay of Bengal. Its hills have dense forests. In fact, one-third of India's forests are in Madhya Pradesh. The forests are rich with some of the finest varieties of wood in the world — teak, sal, Indian ebony and rosewood. There is plenty of bamboo in the forests, as also magnificent fruit and flowering trees.

MAHADEO HILLS of the Satpura range are home to the tiger, panther, Indian bison and many other species of wildlife. The countryside has not changed much since Kipling roamed about in these jungles.

The written history of Madhya Pradesh goes back right up to Emperor Ashoka in the 3rd century B.C., who built a great Buddhist Stupa at Sanchi not far from present-day BHOPAL, its capital. A thousand years later the Parmars ruled over the south-west Madhya Pradesh. They are often remembered for some of their great rulers - wise and great patrons of arts like Raja Bhoj who gave his name to Bhopal. Between A.D. 950 and 1050, the Chandellas ruled the north-eastern parts of Madhya Pradesh and gave India its famous temples of KHAJURAHO — a place which remained hidden from the world for a few centuries. Today, Khajuraho is one of the most frequented tourist attractions of the country. Visiting Khajuraho is not difficult. It lies on the main tourist air route of Delhi-Agra-Khajuraho and Varanasi. Another tourist attraction JABALPUR, known for its marble rocks, is also on the air-map of India. To visit GWALIOR, a more convenient mode of travel is the Shatabdi Express, India's fastest train from Delhi which touches both Agra and Gwalior. From there, it is easy to reach SANCHI, BHOPAL, UJJAIN, INDORE and MANDU - other interesting historical places in Madhya Pradesh.

KHAJURAHO—The Temples of Love

Khajuraho, undoubtedly, is the most popular destination for foreign visitors for its exotic, beautiful and erotic temples. These temples show Indian sculptural art at its best. They were built 500 years before the discovery of America. Of the nearly 85 temples, now some 20 remain.

These temples show the creative part of life—men and women hunting, feasting, enjoying music and dancing. The other side of life which may have been taboo to the western mind 50 years ago is also shown in its glittering beauty. Here the Khajuraho artists portrayed with no false modesty and even less prudery, handsome men and voluptuous women in the most intimate postures making love to each other. One begins to wonder what made the people of Khajuraho to build such fine temples with sculptures which have no equal in the world. One reason that comes to our mind is that India at that time was an Asian eldorado. The land was fertile. It produced plenty of food. The population was not too large. The Chandellas provided peace and stability. Islam had not come to this part of India and women were free to move about and enjoyed perfect equality with men. Women dressed simply, wore ornaments and joined their men in hunting, feasting, and attending fairs and festivals. The peace and abundance in life provided a perfect environment for creative arts as temple construction became one of the most vocal form of expression. In themselves, the temples were meeting places, clubs, dance halls, news or gossip centres. The offerings made by the devout were enough for the King and the priests to build more temples and take care of the existing ones. The Chandellas ruled over this part of India for five long centuries and the people lived in harmony. History has a way of changing the life of the people. Just as the Barbarians destroyed Rome, Mahmud of Ghazni invaded India and started his holy war against the idol worshippers. By 1200, the Chandella kingdom had vanished and so were many of the temples built by them. Some did survive and have survived till today because the Chandella capital was destroyed and the people disappeared from it. Even today Khajuraho is a small village. The remote isolation of temples guaranteed protection.

The temples of Khajuraho were just not the outcome of the imagination of some creative artists. The temple construction had a philosophical base. As you approach the temples, they look like 'soaring' masses culminating in a series of mountain peaks. Just as medieval Christian churches were built pointing towards heaven so were the Hindu temples. The soaring top is the Heaven. The sculptures relating to everyday joys of flesh and wealth are at eye level. You have to keep your mind off these matters and rise above the profane. As you move your eyes upwards, there are signs of spiritual awakening. The joys of flesh give place to meditation. You see spiritual upliftment - Yogis meditating and praying.

Khajuraho temples belong to the 'Nagara' or North Indian style of architecture. But, they are perfect in proportions and design. One wonders at the patience of the artists involved in this work. The figures are almost alive, turning and twisting, dazzling in their profusion and astounding in detail.

Stonework panel

The portrayal of erotic fantasies was perhaps connected with the Tantric philosophy - which was anti-thesis of asceticism. It emphasised woman as the dominant force of creation and taught that senses were not less important than spirit. And creative indulgence could also lead to God — a theme that gives Khajuraho its dubious reputation. The 'Mithuna' couples on the walls are those rioting figures of love and lust. Other similar figures portray tenderness and tranquillity of human love fulfilled. A visitor has to draw his own conclusions.

The temples are located within an area of eight square kilometres. These can be divided into three groups — the western group being the largest and the most important. The KHAJURAHO MUSEUM is located within this area. It comprises the largest temple — Kandriya Mahadeva Temple, Devi Jagdamba — the oldest, the Chaunsath Yogini temple — the temple of 64 nymps and a few others. All the temples in this group are within a fenced enclosure which is also a Park and are well maintained. Enclosure is open from sunrise to sunset, and the best time to see the temples is at sunrise as the rays of the new sun fall on the sculptures.

Kandariya Mahadeva Temple

Kandariya Mahadeva Temple is not only the largest in this group they also architecturally and artistically the most perfect. Built during the period A.D. 1025-1050, it represents Chandella art at its finest. Although its five other subsidiary shrines have disappeared, the main temple stands majestically with the typically five-part design of Khajuraho temples.

The main spire of the Kandariya Mahadeva Temple soars 31 feet high in its majesty and the temple is lavishly carved. The British archaeologist Cunningham counted 226 statues inside the temple and another 646 outside it — making a total of 872. Most of these are one metre high. The statues are carved around the temple in three bands and include among them gods, goddesses, musicians, dancers, beautiful women showing off their body and the famous Maithuna poses. The sexual exercises depicted are mind-boggling and a conservative visitor could get the shock of his life.

There are two other temples which stand on the same platform as the Kandariya Mahadeva Temple. One is MAHADEV TEMPLE and the other DEVI JAGDAMBA TEMPLE. Although small compared to its mighty neighbour, the Mahadev Temple contains one of the finest sculptures of Khajuraho — an excellent figure of a person (it is difficult to decide whether it is a man or a woman) caressing a lion.

The third temple on the common platform is Devi Jagdamba, slightly older than the Kandariya Mahadev. It is considered by some as the most erotic. Relatively simpler in construction, it has only a three-part design instead of the usual five parts as in Khajuraho temples. It was successively dedicated to Vishnu, Parvati and Kali — who also is a manifestation of Parvati. The three-headed and eight-armed statue of Shiva in this temple is an excellent piece of sculptural art.

Chitragupta Temple

The fourth temple at the back of the western enclosure is called CHITRAGUPTA TEMPLE and does not share the common platform with the other three temples mentioned above. Its design is similar to Devi Jagdamba temple.

A unique feature of this temple is that it is dedicated to the Sun god (Surya) driving his chariot with seven horses. On the central niche, you can see an 11-headed statue of Lord Vishnu — the central head is of Lord Vishnu and the others 10 are of his various incarnations. It has many other fine sculptures of dancing girls, elephant fights and processions, etc.

Lakshmana Temple

One of the earliest of Khajuraho temples (A.D. 930-950), the large Lakshmana Temple, is dedicated to Lord Vishnu. Its design is similar to that of the Kandariya Mahadev Temple. It is one of the well-preserved temples. Around the shrine, there are two rather than three bands of sculptures. There are some very good sculptures of Apsaras (nymphs) and erotic scenes. On the subsidiary shrine, we see an architect working with his students. He was perhaps the master builder himself. Around the base of the temple, there is a continuous frieze with scenes of battle, hunting and processions.

Facing the large Lakshmana Temple are two small shrines — LAKSHMI and VARAHA TEMPLES. The Varaha Temple is dedicated to

Vishnu's boar incarnation or the Varaha Avtar. Inside this small shrine is a huge, solid and intricately carved figure of the boar.

Walking around the enclosure we see another small shrine — PARVATI TEMPLE. It has an image of Ganga riding over the back of a crocodile.

The VISHVANATH TEMPLE is a major temple in the western group. It was built in 1002 and has the five-part temple design similar to that of the Kandariya Mahadev Temple. At least two of its four subsidiary shrines are still intact. Since the shrine has Shiva's vehicle, the bull Nandi, it was obviously dedicated to Lord Shiva. Steps lead up to its high terrace, flanked by lions on the northern side and elephants on the southern side. The sculptures around the Vishwanath Temple include the usual Khajuraho scenes but the sculptures of women in this temple are remarkable for their delicacy and beauty. The women write love letters, fondle a baby, play music and linger provocatively in interesting poses. Inside the temple is a polished 2.5 metre high Lingam.

Chausath Yogini Temple

This is the oldest temple in western group built around nine hundred A.D. and perhaps earlier. It is also the only temple which is built entirely of granite — and the only one oriented north-east instead of the usual north-south. Chausath means 64 and the shrine contains the cells of 64 Yakshinis (nymps) who attended to Goddess Kali - only 35 survive.

Another half kilometre west, you can see the LALGUAN MAHADEV TEMPLE, a shrine dedicated to Shiva and built of stone and granite.

Khajuraho Museum

Within the area of western group of temples is the rich archaeological museum of Khajuraho. The museum is small but worth a visit. Opposite the museum is the ARCHAEOLOGICAL SURVEY OF INDIA compound. It has many more rescued sculptures.

Eastern Group of Temples

The eastern group of temples can be further sub-divided into two groups. The first group is located in a walled enclosure having Jain temples. The second group is scattered in the village of Khajuraho itself.

One way of looking at these temples is to hire a cycle-rickshaw and see them all. These temples can also be seen on your way to the southern group of temples.

Not all the temples are Jain temples — three of them are Hindu temples — which shows the religious tolerance of the people of those days. The VAMANA TEMPLE, for instance, is a Hindu temple dedicated to Vamana, the Dwarf incarnation of Vishnu but it has Buddha's statue too. Outside this temple, two tiers of sculptures are mainly carved with the nymphs of Paradise. They strike charming poses under their private awnings. The artists of Khajuraho apparently enjoyed creating so many full-blown female bodies with ornaments and beautiful coiffures to delight the onlookers.

Slightly to the south is the BRAHMA TEMPLE. Made entirely of granite and sandstone, it is dated as one of the earliest shrines. Its general outline makes it distinct, even different from the normal run of the Khajuraho temples. It was originally dedicated to Shiva but the idol in the shrine was miscalled Brahma and the name has stuck. Nearby is the JAVERI TEMPLE in a simple three-part design. Its exterior bands boast of hosts of heavenly nymphs.

Sculpture work of Parsvanath temple

The Jain temples are located south of the above group. The most beautiful among them is the GHANTAI. Only a shell has been left of what was once a great temple. Its open colonnaded structure is known for its classicism and details of the pillars. Adorning the entrance is a Jain goddess riding a mythical bird. There is a relief illlustrating 16 drawings of mother of Lord Mahavira, founder of Jainism.

The ADINATH TEMPLE stands east of Ghantai. It is a minor shrine containing the statue of Adinath. Its apex and base are richly carved.

The largest and the finest among Jain temples in this group is called PARSVANATH TEMPLE. Kandariya Mahadev undoubtedly is the best designed temple in Khajuraho but Parsvanath is larger, architecturally perfect and has some great sculptures. Some of the best known classic sculptures of Khajuraho temple art can be seen here — a woman removing thorns from her foot; another woman applying her eye make-up, etc. Originally dedicated to Adinath, an image of Parsvanath was substituted some centuries later. And the temple, therefore, takes its name from the image of Parsvanath.

SANTINATH is another relatively modern Jain temple here, but contains many components from very old temples around Khajuraho. It also has a small museum.

Southern Group
There are only two temples in this group. The first one, DULADEO TEMPLE, is a major attraction of Khajuraho while the second, the CHATURBHUJA TEMPLE, is small and about 2 km. from the first. The Duladeo Temple was built on the traditional 5-part design. It looks flatter and more massive than the typical Khajuraho shrines. It appears to be of a later period when Khajuraho temple art had passed its peak. The sculptures are now wooden and stereotyped. The decorations are still very graceful — particularly the bracket capitals inside and the flying wizards on the highest carved band outside.

The CHATURBHUJA TEMPLE has an attractive collonnaded entrance. This ruined temple has a very fine and large image of Vishnu. It is three metres high.

The present day village of Khajuraho is a cluster of hotels, restaurants, shops and stalls around the bus station. Within this area is the GOVERNMENT OF INDIA TOURIST OFFICE and the museum. Even the airport is at walking distance. The western temple complex is also in this area. Other temples are not far away. Everything is easily accessible.

Khajuraho is a nice place to linger on and have an interesting time. Small statues of gods and charming couples can also be purchased from the stalls at unbelievably low prices.

GWALIOR—The Legendary City

Gwalior, the northernmost city of Madhya Pradesh, is the most easily accessible one from Delhi and Agra by car or by train. It is known for its historic massive 15th century fort. Rajput valour and chivalry are redolent in the stories of this most redoubtable fort in the world.

Gwalior Fort

The great city of Gwalior had a legendary beginning. Story goes that a great saint, Gwalipa, lived on the hill-top where the fort stands. King Suraj Sen who ruled over the region, approached the holy man for cure of his leprosy. The holy man gave him a drink of water from the SURAJ KUND — a water tank — and the king was cured. Suraj Kund is still in the fort. The king established a town here and it was named after the saint Gwalipa. The saint gave the king a new name, Suhan Pal and directed him that so long as his descendants would retain the Pal name they would rule uninterruptedly. This lasted for 84 generations. The 85th descendant changed his name to Tej Karan and lost his throne.

In more historical times, Gwalior came into limelight when Tomar Rajputs took power in 1398. Gwalior rulers became involved in wars with neighbouring kings. Man Singh Tomar who came to power in 1486 was the greatest of the Tomar Kings. He defeated the Lodhis of Delhi. When Sikandar Lodhi attacked again, Man Singh died but his son held on to the fort for one year. During the Mughal period, Babur defeated Gwalior but Man Singh's grandson continued to fight till Akbar became the Emperor. After the Mughals, the Marathas took over Gwalior and they were followed by the British. Maharaja Scindia sided with the British during the Mutiny but his forces did not. Gwalior was the scene of many bloody battles with the British in 1857.

The HILL-TOP FORT dominates the Gwalior city. Its houses TELI-KA-MANDIR, an ancient temple, dating back to 9th century A.D. It has an interesting design, the roof is in Dravidian style while the rest of the temple is covered with Indo-Aryan sculptures. Another ancient temple has an interesting name, the SAS BAHU TEMPLE (Mother-in-law, Daughter-in-law temple). The palace within the fort was built by Man Singh between 1498 and 1516 for his favourite queen Mrignayani. The palace has four storeys, two of them underground.

Jai Vilas Palace
Located in the new town called LASHKAR, the Jai Vilas Palace was built in early part of the 19th century by the family of the Scindia Maharaja. Lashkar means army camp which Maratha chief Daulat Rao Scindia had set up in 1809 to take control of Gwalior and the town that sprang up on the site came to be called Lashkar. The present Maharaja still occupies a part of the palace but a larger part of it is used as a museum. It has an interesting collection of European goods collected by the luxury-loving Maharajas during the British time. The *piece-de-resistance* is a model railway that used to carry brandy, liquor and cigars around the dining table to the guests after dinner. Gwalior has the distinction of being a centre of Indian classical music. Mian Tansen, one of the nine jewels in the court of Emperor Akbar, belonged to Gwalior and is buried here. An annual music festival is held every December in Gwalior to commemorate the memory of the great classical singer.

Around Gwalior
Gwalior is a good take-off point for some very interesting areas around. The old summer capital of SHIVPURI is 117 km. south-west of Gwalior or 51 km. east of JHANSI. The road runs through a national park where sometimes you see wild animals on the road. Near Shivpuri, there is a pleasant lake with gardens around its perimeter. The road from Gwalior passes through NARWAR — the beautiful old capital of Gwalior state

made famous recently by India Tourism Development Corporation (ITDC) by setting up tented accommodation at this beautiful place and offering package tours to domestic and international tourists. Narwar has also a very large, old fort.

JHANSI

About 100 km. south of Gwalior is the famous Jhansi, whose queen Lakshmi Bai played a major role in the fight against the British in the Indian War of Independence in 1857. The British called it a mutiny. Jhansi is actually in Uttar Pradesh and a tiny finger of that State extends into Madhya Pradesh and for all tourism purposes, it is more convenient to travel to Jhansi via Madhya Pradesh. In the 18th century, Jhansi was a power to reckon within the region. Under the pretext that the Maharaja of Jhansi had died leaving no heir, the British intervened in the affairs of Jhansi. The East India Company took over the State of Jhansi and pensioned off the Maharani. When the Indian Mutiny burst into flames, the Maharani was in the forefront of the rebellion. The British Resident posted at Jhansi was wiped off. In a subsequent battle, the Maharani disguised as a man led her army against the British and died fighting. Since then she is adored as a great heroine for India's struggle for independence.

The JHANSI FORT offers excellent views from its ramparts. The British ceded the fort to Maharaja Scindia in 1858 but later exchanged it for Gwalior in 1866.

DATTIA AND ORCHA

Two other places in the area are hauntingly beautiful but forlorn. These are the Palace cities of DATTIA (69 km.) from Gwalior and ORCHA (11 km. south of Jhansi). Orcha was once a powerful State in the region. Bir Singh Deo ruled from Orcha from 1605 to 1627 and built the present Jhansi Fort. At Dattia, the seven-storey hill-top GOBIND PALACE (1614) awed even the British architect Lutyens who was never an admirer of

Orcha fort and temples

Indian architecture. He went as far as describing it as "one of the most interesting buildings architecturally in the whole of India". The palace is a fabulous maze of latticed corridors, verandahs, pillared cupolas and rooms with frescoes. Once these rooms were studded with semi-precious gems. The palace is surrounded by a 17th century stone wall. Both Dattia and Orcha palace complexes were built by Bir Singh who was then the ruler of this entire region.

Till the 1930s, Dattia was always on the standard itineraries of the British Viceroys. In 1902, Dattia hosted Lord Curzon. Today, it is a forgotten masterpiece and gypsies camp in its extensive ruins with their sheep. Orcha is more magnificent and less spoiled of the two fort cities. Its palaces and temples rise from overgrown foliage. Around here, you can see deer roaming about and nesting birds from afar. Its most impressive structure is JAHANGIR MAHAL, combining lofty walls with the delicacy of many meshed screens and ornate carvings. You can stay within the palace garden as Madhya Pradesh Tourism authorities have converted a part of it into a delightful hotel called SHEESH MAHAL. It can be easily booked through the Madhya Pradesh Tourist Office i Delhi's Kanishka Hotel.

INDORE

An old historic city, it is today a major textile centre of India. Indore is on the air and rail map of India. It is also a convenient take-off point for the exotic Mandu and ancient Ujjain.

Indore is the western metropolis of Madhya Pradesh. Here you are well on the Malwa Plateau, a region where cotton is produced from fertile black soil. It looks like a very affluent city.

Since 1733, Indore State has been ruled by the Holkar family which remained loyal to the British during the Mutiny of 1857. On its periphery is the city of DEWAS, made famous by Forester in his book *The Hill of Devi*.

MALWA is sacred to the Hindus. Two of the 12 Jyotirlingas of Shiva are found in this land, one at MAHABALESHWAR TEMPLE at UJJAIN and the other at MANDHATA at OMKARESHWAR. These two places enjoy sanctity equal to that of Varanasi. Every twelve years, Ujjain has the great Kumbh Fair or Simhastha as it is locally called.

UJJAIN

Ujjain, 60 kilometres from Indore, is not only one of the holiest cities of India but also a town known for industry and crafts. The sacred river Sipra flows through it and people come here in millions every year to take a holy dip — the congregation at the last Kumbha (1995) exceeded 3 million.

Legend has it that the gods and the *asuras* (demons) churned the ocean for Kumbha (a pot of divine nectar). First emerged a pot of *vish* or poison. Shiva drank it down. The poison was so strong that his divine neck turned blue — giving him the name Nilkantha or the Blue-necked one. It all happened at Ujjain and that is the reason for its sacredness.

According to historical records, Chandragupta II (A.D. 380-414) transferred his capital from Pataliputra to Ujjain. Kalidas, the great Sanskrit poet, has described the city as the "town fallen from Heaven to bring heaven to earth." Later in history, Ujjain was involved in many political upheavals. Places to see in Ujjain are the river-side temples Ghats, and Maharaja Scindia's Palace. Outside the city, we can see yet another observatory built by Maharaja Jai Singh of Jaipur. It is not as good as the one in Delhi.

Ujjain is known for its dyers and printers of BHERUGARH, a suburb of the town. The Chipas, as they are called, produce the most exquisite and colourful block-printed cloth for saris, tapestries, hangings, bed-sheets and floor coverings.

MANDU — The City of Joy

Any tour of Malwa would be incomplete without a visit to Mandu — 90 kms from Indore. Mandu's other name, Shadibad, means the "city of joy." The former magnificent capital of the central Indian kingdom of Malwa, is now a romantic ghost city remarkably intact over an area of 12 sq. km. Its atmosphere has been described as "dormant rather than dead". There is an abundance of mango, tamarind and banyan trees. The city is particularly beautiful immediately after the monsoons — emerald green landscape full of waterfalls.

Mandu is situated on an isolated hill-top which is separated from the tableland to the north by a deep and wide valley over which a natural causeway runs to the main city-gate. There is a chasm, a deep wooded ravine, which is crossed by a narrow bridge. Piercing the skyline is the largest standing fortified town in the world. The walls of Mandu have a circumference of 75 km. The walls look the same as they did some 300 years ago.

There are some 70 Hindu or Muslim monuments built during the heyday of Mandu from the 11th to the 16th centuries. Its construction activity was at its peak under its two rulers Mohamud Shah (1436-1468) and Ghiasuddin (1469-1500). The latter is reported to have been very fond of women and had a harem of 15,000 pretty girls.

Mandu saw its greatest spectacle on March 13, 1617 when it heralded the entry of Jahangir with a procession of 500 elephants.

Britain's first Ambassador to India, Thomas Roe, had followed Jahangir to Mandu from Ajmer. He gives interesting details of what he saw and experienced. He found a lodging in an old building. His little white Iceland pet dog was carried away by a lion. On November 11, he attended Jahangir's birthday party where the Emperor was weighed in gold and jewels. But dysentery and piles had prevented him from seeing Prince Khurram's triumphant entry and ceremonial weighing in gold. A year later a healthier Roe succeeded in getting at Ahmedabad from Emperor Jahangir what he had come for. And that started the long relationship between India and England.

Mandu was founded by Raja Bhoj in the 10th century as a fortress and retreat. It was taken over by Afghan rulers in the 14th century. The Mughals took it from the Afghans and the Marathas from the Mughals. The Marathas moved their capital to neighbouring Dhar, leaving Mandu deserted as it is today.

Mandu is also known for a very romantic love story between its last King Baz Bahadur and his love Rani Rupmati — a lovely Rajput peasant girl. He fell in love with Rupmati as he heard her singing in a forest and brought her to his palace. He was so involved with her that he built several buildings for his queen but had to flee in the face of Akbar's army. Rupmati was captured for the pleasure of the Mughal General. But, before he could touch her, she committed suicide by swallowing ground diamonds.

Jahaz Mahal

You enter Mandu through the BHANGI GATE, a portal obviously designed for defence. It would be foolhardy for any enemy to make a frontal assault. Once inside the gates, vistas of a fairyland open up. There are lakes, groves, gardens and palaces. The JAHAZ MAHAL, a palace shaped like a ship, floats serenely on the bosom of the lake. It looks like a heavenly ship sailing into eternity. Ghiasuddin, the pleasure-loving king of Mandu, built this palace to follow his interesting pursuits with women. At the northern end of the ship is a beautifully designed bath where one can imagine the king watching the ladies of the harem rolling around seductively in the pool. HANDOLA MAHAL is built like a swing with massive stones. It appears to sway gently in the breeze. Mandu's JAMA MASJID has so perfect acoustics that even a whisper from the pulpits is heard clearly in the farthest corner of the courtyard. The NILKANTH TEMPLE is a standing monument to Akbar's respect for all religions.

To the west of two royal palaces is another interesting building called CHAMPA BAOLI on the north shore of the lake. Its subterranean levels feature cool wells and paths — obviously a popular retreat during hot, summer days.

As you wander around through the green valleys of Mandu, you see the romantic lake of REWA KUND, a gem-like lake. It is said to be filled by the waters of the Narmada river, 90 km. away and 600 metres lower down.

Legend has it that Rupmati agreed to marry Baz Bahadur on the condition that he would bring the Narmada to Mandu and Rewa Kund was the fulfilment of that promise. On the bank of the lake, he built a Palace for himself, and further down a Pavilion for Rupmati. From here, the peasant girl could see the Narmada as a silver screen on the horizon.

BHOPAL—The Madhya Pradesh Capital

The present capital of Madhya Pradesh, Bhopal, is situated in Malwa region. The city has a moderate climate. Like Rome, it is built on seven hills. The town has three lakes.

Bhopal takes its name from its famous founder Raja Bhoj who built it in the 11th century. He is believed to have created the three lakes by constructing a dam (*pal*) around which the city developed. That is how the city got its name Bhopal.

The present town was laid out by an Afghan chief, Dost Mohammad Khan. During Aurangzeb's rule, Dost Mohammad was the Governor of Bhopal. He took advantage of the confusion following the death of the Mughal emperor in 1707 and carved out a kingdom for himself.

The capital city of Bhopal is 157 km. from Indore and 290 km. from Mandu. It is also the city where the devastating Union Carbide explosion took place in 1984, killing thousands of people.

The city apparently inspired the famous architect, Charles Correa, to design its unique multi-art centre, BHARAT BHAWAN. Bhopal is a great centre of art and culture. A visitor could spend days in its art galleries, museums, theatres, poetry centre and library. It is India's leading centre for performing arts and for the preservation of traditions of tribal and folk arts.

Although Bhopal is a modern city, its surrounding areas are full of ancient remains. Only 30 km. away is BHIM BAITHAK where over 500 caves with neolithic rock-paintings have been discovered. The oldest paintings are at least as old as those of the Pyrenees.

You can commence your tour by seeing the largest mosque of India called TAJ-UL-MASJID. It is a huge, pink mosque with two massive white-domed minarets and three white domes over the main building.

There are several other mosques. A mosque built by Qudsia Begum in 1837 is now surrounded by a bazar. Another mosque, MOTI MASJID, was built in 1860 by Qudsia Begum's daughter, Sikandar Jahan Begum. Though smaller than Delhi's Jama Masjid the style is the same with two dark minarets crowned by golden spikes.

Lakes
Bhopal is also a city of lakes. The larger upper lake has an area of 6 km. A bridge separates it from the lower lake. You can do boating in the picturesque lakes. They look prettier at night with lights of the houses around the lake reflected in water.

A fine view of the city can be had from SHAMLA HILL or Idgah Hill. You may be able to see the minarets of the city's mosques towering over the lesser buildings.

SANCHI

Sanchi is an important Buddhist pilgrim centre of India. Sixty-eight km. north of Bhopal on a hill rising from the plains, it is topped by some of the oldest and most interesting Buddhist shrines in the country.

The site had no direct connection with the life of Lord Buddha. But, the Buddha's greatest disciple Emperor Ashoka came and built the first Stupa here in the 3rd century B.C. During the succeeding years, a great number of other Stupas and Buddhist buildings were added. (Stupa is a mound where Lord Buddha's relics are enshrined).

With the decline of Buddhism, the monuments of Sanchi were totally forgotten. It was only through chance that Sanchi was rediscovered in 1818 by a British officer, General Taylor. During the following years, amateur archaeologists and greedy treasure hunters did great damage to the monuments. One Ashoka Pillar was used to build a sugarcane press. Between 1912 and 1919, the structures were carefully repaired and restored through the efforts of an archaeologist and historian, Sir George Marshal.

It may be easier to see and enjoy the monuments at Sanchi if you buy a guidebook on Sanchi published by the Archaeological Survey of India available at their office at Sanchi itself.

The Great Stupa

Originally constructed by Ashoka in the third century B.C., the Great Stupa I was later enlarged. The original brick stupa was enclosed within a stone one. At present it stands 16 metres high and 37 metres in diameter. A railing encircles the Stupa. There are four magnificently carved gateways or Toranas. These Toranas are among the finest works of Buddhist art in India. The four gateways were erected around 35 B.C. They fell down during restoration. The scenes carved on the pillars are from the *Jataka Tales* about previous lives of Lord Buddha. The northern gateway is the best preserved. At that time, the Buddha apparently was not worshipped in human form. His presence was often indicated by the Bo tree or his footsteps. Interesting scenes from Buddha's life — his present and past incarnations — are shown. In one scene he is seen ascending a road into the air as in the Miracle of Saravasti. He is represented by a Bo tree. In another scene, a monkey offers a bowl of honey to Buddha. Elephants in four directions support the architraves above the columns while horses with riders and elephants fill the gaps between the architraves.

Buddha's life and teachings are conveyed through symbols in early Buddhist art. The lotus represents the birth, the tree is enlightenment, the wheel his first sermon, the Stupa is Nirvana. His footprints, throne or riderless horse, indicates his presence.

The buildings at Sanchi span the whole range of Buddhist art in India from its beginning in the third century B.C. till its decay in the 12th century A.D.

Scattered around the side of Stupa I are a number of pillars or remains of pillars. The most important among these is Pillar No.10 which was erected by Ashoka and stands close to the south entrance of the Stupa. Only the base of this beautifully proportioned shaft now stands. The three back-to-back lions which once topped the column are a good example of Greek-Buddhist art of that period. They now form part of India's national emblem and can be seen on every bank-note. There are a few more interesting pillars to be seen here.

Other Stupas
Of the eight Stupas built by Ashoka, only three remain, including the Great Stupa. There are many other Stupas on the hills, some of them are tiny — only one metre high.

Stupa II is one of the most interesting of the lesser Stupas. There are no gateways here but the medallions which decorate the surrounding walls are interesting. Flowers, animals, people and some mythological creatures adorn the walls.

Stupa III stands north-east of the Great Stupa. It has only one gateway. It is smaller in size and similar in design to the Great Stupa. It is believed that this Stupa was built soon after the Great Stupa was constructed.

Besides these ancient Stupas, Sanchi has ruins of several Buddhist temples and monasteries. The earliest monasteries here were built of wood and have since vanished. The usual plan is of a central courtyard surrounded by monastic cells from the monasteries 45 and 7 which are on the higher eastern edge of the hill top, you can have a good view of the Sanchi village down.

After having seen the Sanchi magic, let us make a day trip out to VIDISHA and its surrounding country. The first stops are UDAYPUR and BARETH. At Udaypur, we are stunned to see a magnificent and splendidly preserved temple — UDAYESHVARA (A.D. 1080). It is one of the finest monuments of the Parmar dynasty comparable to Khajuraho temples built by the Chandellas.

At Bareth, 5 kms east, we discover something different — a 15th century mosque and several other Islamic monuments. A little further, at CHANDERI, there is a huge fort. It was the citadel for the northern capital of Malwa. It has not changed much since Babur took it in 1528.

KANHA NATIONAL PARK
South of Bhopal is the Kipling country with river Narmada flowing through it like a cord which binds the Satpura and Vindhya Hills. One of

the great rivers of India, the Narmada rises from its source at Amarkantak through the gorges and cataracts that it has carved out of the Satpura hills. The waters of the Narmada are still unpolluted, its banks well defined and the hills around the river densely forested.

Ranging from the low hills of HOSHANGABAD and rising into the Mahadeo Hills at PANCHMARHI, BATUL and CHHINDWARA, the forests explode into exuberance at Kanha, India's best known wildlife sanctuary. It has been popular with distinguished visitors to India. In 1983 Prince Phillip and Duke of Edinburgh visited it. The Kanha National Park has an area of 7000 square kilometres with 1000 sq. km. of core-area. To reach the core area, you have to drive through hundreds of km. of unbroken forests.

The jungles of Kanha National Parks teem with a large population of leopards, bear, deer and wild cats. Thousands of deer roam around these forests with spotted deer alone numbering over 17,000. The number of tigers is about 100. It is a true haven for its animal and avion population.

Here you can see the famous Indian bison, the gaur. Even the tiger makes a long detour when he suspects the presence of a gaur.

Kanha is home to that unique species — the 12-horned swamp deer, called Barasingha. It is the only swamp deer which has adopted to dwelling on hard ground. This species was facing extinction sometime back but thanks to the efforts of the Government it is now prospering in this park. Forest Department guides accompany visitors around.

Jabalpur—City of Marble Rocks

The list of places worth seeing in the Madhya Pradesh is endless. Among these, PANCHMARHI is a well-known hill resort. It lies up in the Satpura Hills. It is a great place for adventure, travel, trekking, rock-climbing and nature walks. Another beautiful place is Beraghat, not far from Jabalpur, the city of MARBLE ROCKS. At Beraghat, the Narmada flows through a 5-km. long gorge. On its both sides are towering white marble cliffs. Below the gorge are the DHUANDHAR FALLS, literally meaning smoky falls. It is an exciting and unforgettable experience to row past the Marble Rocks on a full-moon night. The silence of the night is only broken by the

soft plop of the boatman's oars. The waters of the river reflect the moon at night. Recently the Marble Rocks have been flood-lit by the Department of Tourism.

Marble rocks are about 24 kilometres from Jabalpur which is today the second largest city of Madhya Pradesh. En route, there are many shops where you can buy inexpensive marble carvings. Jabalpur was once the capital of the Gond kings in 12th century A.D.

THE TRIBAL TERRITORY

Madhya Pradesh is the largest tribal country. From the graceful Marble Rocks to CHITRAKOOT FALLS on the Indiravati river in BASTAR DISTRICT, it is a long journey of 600 km. But remote Bastar opens your eyes. It is a world in itself. It is one of India's largest districts covering an area of 40,000 square kilometres — as large as the entire Switzerland.

The sheer inaccessibility of Bastar lends charms to travel. It is the home of many aboriginal tribes of India. Among them are the bison-horn-wearing Madias who have participated in several folk-dance festivals in India and abroad. It is also the home of the little hill mynah who imitates the voice of man.

In Bastar, the hills march in serried ranks and the forests are primeval. The KANGER VALLEY in the district has the largest national biosphere reserves. Here Nature has been left totally undisturbed. TEERATHGARH FALL decorates the hills with 820-feet of white froth.

South and East Madhya Pradesh are jungle-clad and remote. Below the surface lie some of the richest mineral deposits in the world. It contains huge reserves of iron ore, copper, tin, limestone, dolomite, bauxite and coal. The district is now waking up and large factories are coming up in this region.

BHOPAL

GENERAL INFORMATION

Population: 1.06 million (1991 census)
Altitude: 523 metres (1742 ft)
Climate:

	Temperature	
	Max.	Min.
Winter	34^0c	10^0c
Summer	41^0c	21^0c
Rainfall	969 mm	32 mm

Season: Throughout the year. The months of April to June are hot.
Clothing
Summer: cottons
Winter: woollens.

HOW TO GET THERE

By Air: Indian Airlines connect Bhopal with Bombay, Delhi, Gwalior, Indore, Jabalpur and Raipur. Private Airlines too have flights.
By Rail: Bhopal has rail connections with Amritsar, Bangalore, Cochin, Delhi, Lucknow, Madras, Pune, etc.
By Road: Bhopal is connected by road to northern and western India. It is 188 km. from Indore,
  186 km. from Ujjain,
  290 km. from Mandu,
  197 km. from Panchmarhi,
  46 km. from Sanchi,
  387 km. from Khajuraho and
  525 km. from Agra.
There are regular bus services connecting Bhopal to Indore, Mandu, Ujjain, Panchmarhi, Gwalior, Jabalpur and Khajuraho.

LOCAL TRANSPORT

Madhya Pradesh Tourism Development Corporation (MPTDC) has luxury cars (limousines), air-conditioned and ordinary tourist taxis, coaches and mini buses available for hire. Information: M.P. State Tourism Development Corporation, Gangotri, TT Nagar, *Tel*: 554340/43, *Fax*: 552384. There are also metered and unmetered taxis, metered auto-rickshaws and horse-drawn tongas.

CONDUCTED TOURS

MPTDC organises conducted tours within the State for groups of 12 to 35 persons. They also operate tours from outside the state.

WHERE TO STAY (STD CODE: 0755)

STANDARD

1. Hotel Palash
   Phone: 553006, 553076
   Fax: 552384
2. Hotel Panchanan
   Phone: 551647, 553076
3. Lake View Ashok
   Phone: 541600, 541075
   Fax: 541606
   Cable: ASHOKOTEL BHOPAL
4. Jehan Numa Palace
   Phone: 540100
   Fax: 540720
   Cable: JEHANUMAL BHOPAL
   Fax: 91-755-551912

5. Hotel Taj
   Phone: 747690
   Telex: 705-366 HITAJIN
   Cable: HTLTAJ
6. Hotel Residency
   Phone: 556001

BUDGET

7. Hotel Mayur
   Phone: 77323
   Cable: PEACOCK
8. Hotel Ramsons International
   Phone: 555298-99
   Telex: 705-354HTAJIN
   Cable: SETHIBROS
9. Hotel Siwalik Gold
   Phone: 74242, 76000, 76001
10. Hotel Rajdoot
    Phone: 75271, 75272
11. Hotel Red Sea Plaza
    Phone: 75551, 72252, 76979
12. Amer Palace
    Phone: 557197, 557127
    Fax: 553309

WHAT TO SEE

1. TAJ-UL-MASJID, the huge mosque begun by Shahjahan Begum, (1868-1901) was completed after her death. Its main hall, large courtyard and marble floors are impressive. It is reputed to be the largest mosque in India.
2. JAMA MASJID built by Kudsia Begum in 1837 on the site of an ancient temple. There are gold spikes on the minarets of this mosque.
3. MOTI MASJID built in 1860.
4. BHARAT BHAVAN, a national institute for the performing and visual arts. Has a museum of fine arts, ROOPANKAR, an art gallery, theatres, auditoria, etc.
5. GANDHI BHAVAN, with its collection of photographs of the Father of the Nation, and GANDHI MUSEUM.
6. LAXMI NARAYAN TEMPLE and MUSEUM.
7. SHAMLA and IDGAH HILLS from where you get good views of the city.
8. UPPER AND LOWER LAKES, most attractive in the evenings.

EXCURSIONS

1. ISLAMNAGAR (11 km), the palace of the Afghan rulers built by Dost Mohammed Khan. Formal gardens, palaces in Hindu-Muslim style and Rani Mahal are worth seeing.
2. BHOJPUR (28 km), founded by Raja Bhoja, has the ruins of a Shiva temple. The symbol of Shiva, the Lingam, is a huge monolith.
3. BHIMBETKA (40 km). About 700 rock shelters, belonging to the neolithic age, have been recently discovered. Over 500 caves have paintings of pre-historic man.
4. PANCHMARHI (210 km) is a hill resort 1067 metres high ringed by the Satpura ranges. Forests, glades, pools, waterfalls, ravines and gorges make this an attractive summer resort.

SHOPPING

Bhopal is known for its zari (silver thread) work on velvet, evening bags, filigree work, jewellery, inlaid leather, bead and sequin-embroidered bags, glass-encrusted bags and richly decorated shoes. Handicrafts and handlooms from all over Madhya Pradesh are available in Bhopal.

Terracotta figurine

SANCHI

GENERAL INFORMATION
Population: 1,564
Altitude: 427 metres.
Climate: Same as Bhopal

HOW TO GET THERE
The nearest airport is at Bhopal (46 km).
Sanchi is a station on the Central Railway where trains stop at the request of 1st class passengers.
It is connected by road to Bhopal and from there to the other places.
Sanchi is
    46 km. from Bhopal
    232 km. from Indore.

LOCAL TRANSPORT
All monuments are within walking distance. However tongas can be hired.

WHERE TO STAY
BUDGET
1. Ashok Travellers' Lodge
    Phone: 23
2. Mahabodhi Buddhist Guest House
    Phone: 39

WHAT TO SEE
1. The GREAT STUPA is the earliest existing stone structure in India. Begun by Ashoka himself in the 3rd century B.C., the massive dome dominates the countryside. Thousands of Buddhists from all over the world visit it as a place of pilgrimage.
2. The four gateways or TORANAS around the Great Stupa are the finest expressions of Buddhist art. Every inch is carved with events from the life of the Buddha. According to Buddha's wish, his image is never shown and he is represented only by symbols.
3. STUPAS 2 AND 3. In the latter, the relics of Sariputta and Mahamogallana, disciples of the Buddha, were found.

4. ASHOKA PILLAR (3rd century B.C.). Its glazed polish has remained untarnished throughout the centuries.
5. GUPTA HINDU TEMPLE of the 4th century A.D., one of the earliest specimens of temple architecture.
6. SITE MUSEUM.

EXCURSIONS
1. VIDISHA (10 km) where Emperor Ashoka ruled as a viceroy. A 2nd century B.C. Hindu shrine shows bricks cemented together with lime mortar, the earliest known use of cement. The Heliodorus Pillar nearby, a monolith, was erected in 140 B.C. by a Greek who embraced the Hindu religion.
2. UDAYPUR CAVES (90 km) has a colossal 11th century temple of Neelkanteshwar.

KHAJURAHO

GENERAL INFORMATION

Population: 6,000
Altitude: 217 metres (723 ft)
Climate:

	Temperature	
	Max.	Min.
Winter	27^0c	4^0c
Summer	42^0c	21^0c

Season: Throughout the year, except the hot months of May and June.
Clothing
Summer: Light cottons
woollens: Winter.

HOW TO GET THERE

By Air: Khajuraho is connected by air with Delhi, Agra and Varanasi.
By Rail: The nearest railhead is Harpalpur (94 km.) on the Central Railways. Other convenient railheads are Jhansi (172 km.) and Satna (117 km.).
By Road: Khajuraho is connected with major tourist centres of the north by road. It is

287 km. from Lucknow,
395 km. from Agra,
372 km. Bhopal
598 km. from Delhi and
420 km. from Varanasi.
There are regular bus services to Bhopal, Harpalpur, Jhansi, Satna, Indore and Jabalpur.

LOCAL TRANSPORT

Tourist taxis (contact MPTDC, *Phone*: 2051), unmetered taxis, tongas and cycle-rickshaws.

CONDUCTED TOURS

The Government of India Tourist Office (*Phone*: 2047-48) can be contacted for trained guides to take tourists around the monuments.

WHERE TO STAY (STD CODE: 76861)
DELUXE
1. Hotel Chandela (Taj Group)
   Phone: 74250
   Cable: CHANDELA
   Fax: 74255

2. Jass Oberoi
   Phone: 2085, 2086, 2087, 2088
   Cable: OBHOTE
   STANDARD
3. Khajuraho Ashok (ITDC)
   Phone: 2024
   Fax: 2042
   Cable: TOURISM
4. Holiday Inn, Khajuraho
   Phone: 2178
   BUDGET
5. Hotel Payal (MPTDC)
   Phone: 2076
   STANDARD
6. Hotel Rahil (MPTDC)
   Phone: 2062
7. Tourist Village
   Phone: 2128

WHAT TO SEE
1. The Western Group of temples of which the most famous is the KANDARIYA MAHADEV TEMPLE - 31 meters high. It has a fantastic range of sculptures including sensuous erotic themes.
   THE CHAUSATH YOGINI is a granite temple and the Devi Jagadamba, a temple to the Mother Goddess. The CHITRAGUPTA TEMPLE is dedicated to Surya, the Sun God. Other interesting temples are the VISHWANATH, VARAHA and MATANGESHWARA, the last named being a shrine where worship goes on even today.
2. In the Eastern Group the PARSVANATH JAIN TEMPLE is the finest of the structures, with its exquisite figure carvings. Other Jain temples are the GHANTAL and the temple dedicated to ADINATH. The Hindu monuments in this group are the BRAHMA, VAMANA and the JAVARI TEMPLES.
3. In the Southern Group (5 km.) are the CHATURBHUJ TEMPLE with its carved image of Vishnu and the DULADEO TEMPLE.

EXCURSIONS
1. Interesting and picturesque spots are the BENISAGAR DAM (7 km.), RANEH FALLS (20 km.) and RANGAUN LAKE (25 km.).
2. RAJGARH PALACE (25 km.), a 150-year-old deserted palace and the DHUBELA PALACE (64 km.) which houses a museum of sculptures, period garments, paintings and weapons.
3. PANNA NATIONAL PARK (32 km.) is a wildlife sanctuary.
4. PANNA DIAMOND MINES (46 km.), with the PANDAV FALLS enroute.
5. BANDHAVGARH NATIONAL PARK (210 km.) where wildlife such as tiger, leopard, bison, sambar, etc., can be seen.

FESTIVALS OF SPECIAL LOCAL INTEREST
1. Khajuraho Festival (March). A dance festival is

held every year when leading classical dancers from all over India perform against the backdrop of the temples. A unique event.
2. MAHASHIVARATRI FAIR (February-March). The great night of Lord Shiva when pilgrims by the thousand pour pots of water over the Lingam, the symbol of Shiva, as part of worship in the Matangeshwara Temple.

INDORE, MANDU & UJJAIN

GENERAL INFORMATION
INDORE

Population: 1.17 million (1991 census)
Altitude: 564 metres (1878 ft)
Climate:

	Temperature	
	Max.	Min.
Winter	34°c	10°c
Summer	40°c	20°c
Rainfall	804 mm	13 mm

Season: Throughout the year
Clothing
Summer: cottons
Winter: woollens.

HOW TO GET THERE
By Air : The nearest airport is at Indore which is 100 km. from Mandu and 53 km. from Ujjain. Indian Airlines services connect Indore with Bombay, Delhi, Bhopal and Gwalior.
By Rail: Indore and Ujjain have direct rail connections with Delhi, Agra, Bhopal and Jabalpur. Indore is the nearest railhead for Mandu.
By Road: Indore is
186 km. from Bhopal and
398 km. from Ahmedabad.

Mandu is
149 km. from Ujjain,
100 km. from Indore and
475 km. from Bombay.
Regular bus services connect Indore with Bombay, Ahmedabad, Aurangabad, Bhopal, Mandu and Sanchi.

LOCAL TRANSPORT
Unmetered taxis, metered autorickshaws, tempos and tongas are available at Indore and Ujjain. Tourist taxis can be hired from MPTDC, Indore. At Mandu tongas, cycle-rickshaws and bicycles are available for local sightseeing.

CONDUCTED TOURS
(Tours organised on request by MPTDC for groups of 12 to 35 persons).

WHERE TO STAY
INDORE (STD CODE: 0731)
Mandu
1. Tourist Cottage MPTD
   Phone: 63235
2. Travellers Lodge
   Phone: 63221

UJJAIN (STD Code: 20734)
1. Hotel Shipra (M.P. Tourism)
   Phone: 29628, 29629
2. Yatri Niwas (M.P. Tourism)
   Phone: 51498

INDORE (STD Code: 0731)
1. Amaltas International
2. Ambassador
   Phone: 33216-19
3. Balwas
   Phone: 39938
4. Central
   Phone: 385417
5. Embassy
   Phone: 36574-76
6. Indore Manor House
   Phone: 322122

WHAT TO SEE
Indore
1. BADA GANAPATI, a colossal image of Ganesh.
2. KANCH MANDIR, the famous Jain temple with its walls, roof and floors lavishly inlaid with mirrors, glass, mother-of-pearl and coloured beads.
3. CHHATRI BAGH, with its majestic cenotaphs of the Holkar rulers.

EXCURSIONS
1. MAHESHWAR (91 km.), an ancient town mentioned in the *Ramayana* and the *Mahabharata* and revived by Ahilya Bai of Indore. Has beautiful temples and a fort complex. Also ghats where pilgrims bathe.
2. OMKERESHWAR (77 km.), an important place of pilgrimage. The Omkar Mandhata temple has beautiful carvings.
3. BAGH CAVES (155 km.) have paintings which are comparable to Ajanta.

Mandu
1. JAHAZ MAHAL, the 'ship palace' built between two lakes resembles a pleasure boat.
2. HINDOLA MAHAL designed with its sloping walls to look like a swing. Has graceful archways.
3. BAZ BAHADUR'S PALACE with a superb view of the countryside.
4. ROOPMATI'S PAVILION, a retreat built by Baz Bahadur for his queen Roopmati, from where she could see the sacred Narmada flowing at a distance and also BAZ BAHADUR'S PALACE.
5. HOSHANG SHAH'S TOMB, India's first marble edifice. Shahjahan is believed to have taken the concept of the marble for Taj Mahal from this beautiful monument.
6. JAMA MASJID, inspired by the great mosque at Damascus.
7. ASHRAFI MAHAL, planned as a school with study cells for young boys.

UJJAIN
1. TEMPLE OF MAHAKALESHWAR, an important pilgrim centre for Hindus.

2. BHARTRIHARI CAVES where the great Sanskrit scholar poet Bhartrihari lived.
3. SANDIPANI ASHRAM where Krishna studied at the ashram of Guru Sandipani.
4. The Observatory, JANTAR MANTAR, built by Maharaja Sawai Jai Singh of Jaipur, is still in use.
5. VIKRAM KIRTI MANDIR, a cultural centre with rare manuscripts, built to perpetuate the memory of the great King Vikramaditya.
6. BATHING GHATS on the Shipra river.
7. GOPAL MANDIR, a 19th century temple of Maratha-style architecture.

EXCURSIONS
Mandu
1. DHAR (35 km), capital of the Parmar kings of whom Raja Bhoja was the best known. Later conquered by Muslims, the monuments are a combination of Hindu, Afghan and Mughal architecture.

SHOPPING
This region is famous for Maheshwari sarees, a unique weave introduced to Maheshwar by Rani Ahilyabai. They are mostly woven in cotton with reversible borders.

FESTIVALS OF SPECIAL LOCAL INTEREST
Indore
ANANT CHATURDASHI (September) when there is great festivity.

Ujjain
1. KARTIK MELA (November). Lasting a month, the fair is attended by a large number of people from nearby villages.
2. KUMBHA MELA (in April once in 12 years). Millions from all over the country flock here for a dip in the holy river.

KANHA NATIONAL PARK

GENERAL INFORMATION
Area: 940 sq. kms.
Altitude: 450 metres (1499 ft)
Climate

	Temperature	
	Max.	Min.
Winter	24⁰c	1⁰c
Summer	41⁰c	24⁰c

Season: Feb to June. The park is closed from end June to beginning of November due to rains. However, the animals are also seen in the cool season (November to February).

Clothing
Summer: cottons, but a sweater and scarf are advisable for early morning and evening drives through the forest.
Winter: woollens.

HOW TO GET THERE

By Air: Jabalpur (169 km) is the nearest airport. Indian Airlines services connect Jabalpur with Bhopal and Raipur.

By Rail: Jabalpur is the most convenient railhead. It has direct rail connections with Bombay, Calcutta, Madras, Patna, Varanasi, Agra, Bhopal, etc.

By Road: The park can be reached by road. It is
- 169 km. from Jabalpur,
- 330 km. from Nagpur,
- 469 km. from Khajuraho and
- 537 km. from Bhopal.

A bus service operates between Kisli and Jabalpur.

LOCAL TRANSPORT

Tourist taxis can be hired at Jabalpur from ITDC c/o Jackson's Hotel. Jeeps and elephants can be hired for rides inside the park area.

WHERE TO STAY

STANDARD
1. Kanha Safari Lodge
   Phone: 233
2. Baghira Log Huts, Kishi (MP Tourism)
3. Jungle Camp, Khalia (M.P. Tourism)

WHAT TO SEE

KANHA NATIONAL PARK, famous for the richness and variety of its wildlife. The vegetation ranges from grassland to thick jungles of evergreen trees. Rivers and small streams flow through hill gorge into the valleys.

1. There are 22 species of mammals seen in the park as given below.
   - (1) Common Langur Monkey ***
   - (2) Indian Hare **
   - (3) Indian Crested Porcupine *
   - (4) Jackal ***
   - (5) Indian Wild Dog or Red Dog (Dhole) **
   - (6) Bengal Fox *
   - (7) Sloth Bear *
   - (8) Stripped Hyena *
   - (9) Grey Mongoose **
   - (10) Jungle Cat *
   - (11) Tiger **
   - (12) Wild Pig ***
   - (13) Mouse Deer *
   - (14) Chital (Spotted Deer) ***
   - (15) Barasingha (Swamp Deer) ***
   - (16) Sambar **
   - (17) Barking Deer **
   - (18) Black Buck ***
   - (19) Chausingha (4-horned antelope) *
   - (20) Nilgai (Blue Bull) *
   - (21) Gaur (Indian Bison) **

   The star guides are:
   - *** very good chance of sighting.
   - ** sighting possibilities are good, given time and luck.
   - * chances of sighting are slim.

2. There are over 200 species of birds. They are hard to see in the thick forests. They are best seen in the grassy clearings, near the streams, and in the

hills in the bamboo forests. There are water birds near large pools of water.

EXCURSIONS
1. JABALPUR (169 km.). The flood-lit marble rocks at Bheraghat, 23 km. beyond Jabalpur, stand on either side of a 1.5 km. gorge through which the Narmada flows. The jagged cliffs of limestone are more than a hundred feet high and gleam in moonlight like marble. Boating in the gorge on a moonlit night is a great experience. Standard accommodation available in Hotel Kalchuri M.P. Tourism, *Tel*: 321491-93.

Teli ka mandir

Chapter 16

GUJARAT
The Land of Gandhi and Merchant Princes

The West Coast State of Gujarat is not on popular tourist itineraries of foreign and Indian tourists. Although it is easy to travel to Gujarat during your trips to Bombay or Rajasthan, few people pause to explore this very interesting part of India. It has a population of over 41 million and an area of 195,984 sq. km. Gujaratis are reputed to be a successful business community. You can see the hardworking Gujaratis operating hotels and motels in California, running stores in Australia and New Zealand and newspaper kiosks in England. The most distinguished son of Gujarat was Mahatma Gandhi who won for India its independence through non-violence. His Ashram (retreat) on the banks of the Sabarmati river near Ahmedabad reveals the stuff this man was made of—his austere mode of living and his great ambition to free his country from the foreign yoke. His spinning wheel symbolised India's goal of self-reliance and independence.

Parsis too belong to this State where they had landed at a place called Saijan in A.D. 745 and many of them still live here. Thousands of them have migrated to Bombay. The money-making Jains of Gujarat are also a very important community. There are families owning textile and chemical mills. As the Jains earn, they spend lavishly on building new temples and on charities like schools and religious trusts. Most Gujaratis are vegetarians as Jainism strictly prohibits meat-eating.

The contradictions of Gujarat are revealed in another shape — the attempt of the people to harmonise their cultural pattern. With modern changes in technology, wading through the congested roads of Ahmedabad, you may see a motor-cycle rider with large milk cans hanging on both sides of his vehicle while he wears a brilliant red turban and flashes golden earrings and a fierce moustache. He is the traditional milkman of Gujarat who has adopted the modern transportation but sticks to his traditional wear. This is how Gujarat lives, changing yet changeless.

HISTORY

The archaeological finds at LOTHAL near Dhandauka in Ahmedabad district and RAZDI in Saurashtra carry the history of Gujarat back to 3,500 years — to the times of Harappa and Mohenjodaro. Legend tells us even more. The story goes that the Somnath shore temple in the south was built by Soma, the moon god, himself to mark the creation of the Universe. Legend also places Lord Krishna's kingdom at DWARAKA on the west coast of Gujarat. Gujarat also features in the exploits of the great Buddhist emperor Ashoka and his Rock Edicts can be seen near JUNAGARH.

Later, Gujarat suffered incursions from Mahmud of Ghazni who demolished the SOMNATH TEMPLE and carried away with him its riches. Gujarat became a battlefield between the Mughals and the Marathas. It was also the earliest contact point with the West at SURAT where the British set up their first commercial outpost in the 16th century. Two small Portuguese enclaves - DAMAN and DIU - survived within Gujarat for over 450 years till 1961 when these were liberated by the Indian Army. During the British Raj, Gujarat was part of the larger Bombay Presidency and ruled from Bombay, but it became a separate State in 1956 when the Indian States were demarcated on a linguistic basis.

GEOGRAPHY

Geographically, Gujarat can be divided into three areas. The mainland region includes the major cities of Ahmedabad, Surat and VADODARA (Baroda). The Gulf of Bombay divides the mainland strip from the flat, often barren, plains of the Kathiawar Peninsula - also known as Saurashtra. During pre-independence India, the Saurashtra region was ruled by some 200 Rajas and Maharajas who had continued to rule it as they had made peace with the British. These tiny States were amalgamated in the larger State of Bombay Presidency after independence and subsequently merged in the new Gujarat State. Finally, the Gulf of Kutch separates Saurashtra from KUTCH. Kutch is virtually an island cut off from the rest of Gujarat — wedged between Pakistan to its east and the low-lying Ranns of Kutch to its north.

Gujarat offers a variety which is bewildering to a visitor.

ACCESS

Being an industrially advanced State — recent surveys have indicated that Gujarat has done better than Maharashtra — it is very well connected with all parts of India. Indian Airlines flights link Ahmedabad daily with many cities of India. Several new private airlines link Ahmedabad with Bombay and Delhi. Ahmedabad is also on the main rail network. The roads in Gujarat are in excellent condition and travel by car can be fun.

Accommodation in major cities is good and in out-of-way tourist spots satisfactory. Tourist accommodation has been provided by the Gujarat State Tourism Development Corporation a very active organisation.

The mild winter months from November to March are certainly the best time to visit Gujarat. The monsoon period has its own charm when the air is cool and the sky overcast. Most Gujaratis come on home leave during the rainy season.

Gujarat has an abundance of fairs and festivals. The Gujaratis are a fun-loving people and there are festivals for every month. But, if you are coming in January, try to make it on January 14, the Kite festival on

Makar Sankranti, or during the nine-day Navaratri Festival during September-October. The celebrations include impromptu street dances and Bhavai folk theatres.

GUJARATI FOOD
Gujarati food is essentially vegetarian though non-vegetarian cuisine patronised by the Muslims is available in major hotels. European, Chinese and American food are also available in better class hotels.

A great experience in Gujarati food can be had by ordering a THALI feast at Vishala - 5 km. from the centre of Ahmedabad. It is a restaurant, part of a complex described as a Gujarati village with a museum, local crafts and performing arts. Here you can have exclusively vegetarian Gujarati food and also a variety of entertainment. You have to order the food before 8.30 p.m. and wait for the call (costs about Rs. 100 for two). In the village complex, you will see craftsmen weaving and making earthen pots. The puppeteers recount legends with huge string puppets while musicians and dancers play. As you watch all this, your turn for dinner comes.

The meal is taken sitting cross-legged on the floor, the knees resting on the wooden leg-rests. The stiff-limbed need not worry, they will have chairs. The waiters converge bearing steaming hot pans and pots laden with freshly cooked array of vegetables, pulses and yoghurt. Food is served on platters of leaves stitched together. Among the breads are those made with millet and other flours. There is rice too. A dozen varieties of chutneys follow; and salads are served separately. There are mugs of buttermilk to wash down the food.

Dinner is overwhelming and the rich homemade ice-creams that follow are irresistible. Ice-cream eating in Gujarat is a lucrative business and it is advisable to try some. A good ice-cream parlour in Ahmedabad compares favourably with the American Baskin and Robins.

Although Vishala is unique, Gujarati vegetarian food is available in many other good restaurants of Ahmedabad - Hotel Chetna or Hotel Saba, for instance.

SHOPPING
Like Gujarati cuisine, Gujarati handicrafts are unique. Handicrafts have been given a fillip by the Government and some private individuals like Mrinalini Sarabhai, widow of the brilliant scientist Vikram Sarabai and a well-known dancer by her own right. Craftsmen and women who had left their villages to work as stone crushers for a living have been brought back to practise their traditional arts. Their products can be seen and purchased in Gujarat emporia in cities like Ahmedabad, Delhi or Bombay.

Gujarat has also a rich tradition of high quality weaving and hand-block printing. Tie-and-dye fabrics are its greatest strength. In

Ahmedabad, apart from the Government emporium, you can look for good shopping for nut-crackers, silver, wood, brass and other treasures in the tiny shops in the back streets.

Of course, fabrics are synonymous with Ahmedabad. For variety and prices, these are the best buys. At the top end of this field are the Patola silk saries - extremely fine and quite expensive. They are still made by a handful of master-craftsmen at Patan.

From Surat comes the zari or gold thread embroidery work. Surat is also a centre for silk saries. More mundane but still very beautiful are the block prints of Ahmedabad. From here, you can take along hand-painted cloth in traditional black, red, maroon and ochre colours. It is inexpensive too.

JAMNAGAR in Saurashtra is known for its woollen shawls, blankets and rugs. Wooden chests and traditional furniture are a great attraction. Kutch embroidery has unique qualities. Samples can be seen in the Gujarat State Emporium (Gurjari) or Handloom House — both at Ashram Road in Ahmedabad. Delhi too has a Gurjari Emporium.

EXPLORING GUJARAT

Just over the State boundary as you go from Bombay to Ahmedabad is a historic place, SIJAN. A masonry flame-topped pillar marks the landing place of India's progressive community called the Parsis in A.D. 745.

Heritage Hotels of Gujarat

There has been a new development. During your travels in Gujarat, you will come across some unusual hotels — palaces of the erstwhile princes or the feudal homes (*Havelis*) converted into deluxe hotels. It will be a great experience to stay in one of them or some of them. A few such accommodations are listed below.

1. The Palace Utelia, Lothal Burkhi
   Booking in Ahmedabad, *Tel*: 079-441511
2. Nilambagh Palace, Bhavnagar
3. Riverside Palace, Gondal
   Tel: 079-441511
4. The Royal Oasis, Wankaner
   Wankaner, *Tel*: 2000
5. Hingolgadh Castle
6. Darbargadh Poshina
   Booking: 079-441511
7. Balaram Palace
   Booking: 079-76288
8. Rajwant Palace Resort - Rajpipla
9. Laxmi Vilas, Mote Bagh Palace, Vadodara

More information can be obtained from the Gujarat Government Tourist Office in Ahmedabad.

Earlier, they had spent 19 years in the small island of Diu in Saurashtra. Why they left Diu for the mainland of Gujarat is not known. They moved in the same ships they had brought with them from Persia. Now, the Parsis are scattered all over Gujarat and Maharashtra. Often, they take their names from the town they belong to.

SURAT

Along the palm-fringed coast of Gujarat are many old ports — now no more. The only important modern port now left is Surat, also a thriving industrial city. It is still known for its silks, cottons and gold and silver brocades, which originally attracted the British and the Dutch to set up their commercial outposts here in the 17th century. But in course of time Surat lost its importance to Bombay as the British moved their headquarters to the fast developing new harbour.

The FORT at Surat is in ruins. It was first built in the 14th century by Mohammad-bin-Tughlaq to keep the Bhils away from overpowering the city. Akbar recaptured the Fort from the Portuguese and at that time it became the principal port from where the Haj pilgrims departed for Mecca. Shivaji raided Surat four times to plunder the city. The number of Dutch and English tombs at Surat indicates the enormous wealth of Surat, which apparently, the Europeans were keen to protect with their lives. Then comes BROACH, overlooking the wide Narmada river. The town was known to travellers 2500 years back, even before Lord Buddha's time. It was well-known for its fine muslin exported to Europe in ships built in Broach itself. The Narmada was the right place for bleaching the cloth.

It was at Broach that the British first set up a post in 1616 with permission from the Mughal Emperor. Commercial activities are again reviving on this coast since oil was discovered at ANKLESHWAR near Broach as well as CAMBAY.

VADODARA (BARODA)

Located 120 km. south-west of Ahmedabad, Vadodara (population 1.12 million) the former capital of the erstwhile Baroda State ruled by the Maratha Maharaja Gaekwad, is a beautiful city of sprawling parks, lakes, palaces, museums and is also a major university town. In Buddhist texts, Vadodara has been described as a town "in the heart of the Banyan Trees".

History and literature of the region can be studied in its well arranged MUSEUM and in the INSTITUTE OF ORIENTAL STUDIES. The Art School at Vadodara led to the development of the BARODA SCHOOL OF INDIAN ART. The ART GALLERY has a rich collection of Mughal miniatures as well as paintings of European masters.

The flamboyant LAKSHMI VILAS PALACE offers a large collection of armour and sculptures. The Palace itself is a conglomeration of domes, towers and spires, a wonderful example of an architecture that strayed from the Indo-Saracenic style.

A fine example of antiquity is an old town, DABHOI, a ruined city, dating back to 13th century. It succumbed to the raids by a succession of Muslim, Maratha and British invaders. Its temples remind us of the Gujarat style of Hindu architecture.

Among the fertile fields of Gujarat planted by farmers all in white and harvested by women wearing flared red skirts is the busy town of ANAND. It was here that Operation Flood started to produce more milk by an enterprising visionary, Dr.Kurien. Much of Bombay's milk and India's butter comes from a cooperative dairy organisation based here. The organisation was helped by Danish experts. The country is now self-sufficient in milk products and exports them to the Middle East.

Vadodara Municipal Corporation offers local sightseeing tours. *Tel:* 329656.

AHMEDABAD

Founded on the banks of the Sabarmati river by Ahmed Shah I in 1411, it was ranked as the greatest city of India until Fatehpur Sikri and Delhi were built by the Mughal kings. Sir Thomas Roe, the British envoy at Jahangir's court, described Ahmedabad as a "goodly city as large as London, the handsomest town in Hindustan, perhaps, the world". Even the fun-hating Aurangzeb called the city "the beauty and ornament of India". Shahjahan spent the early years of his romantic marriage to Noorjahan in this city. Under its many cruel but culture-oriented Sultans, Muslim ideals of architecture were blended with local arts. Ahmed Shah's JAMA MASJID used a great many pillars, carvings and inscriptions of demolished Hindu and Jain temples to build his mosque. There are 260 columns supporting the roof of the mosque with its 15 cupolas. But during the earthquake of 1819, the two shaking minarets lost half their height and another quake in 1957 completed the demolition.

It is said that a large black slab by the main arch is actually the base of a Jain idol buried upside down for the Muslim faithful to tread on.

The Shaking Minarets

A little south of the railway station is SIDI BASHIR MOSQUE famed for its shaking minarets — an architectural wonder. When one minaret is shaken, the others rock in sympathy. This was said to be for protection against earthquakes. The RAJ BIBI MOSQUE also had shaking minarets, one of which was dismantled by an inquisitive Englishman to discover its secret.

Ahmed Shah's ornamental mausoleum can be seen in MANAK CHOWK. Also in Manak Chowk rests the last Hindu ruler of Junagarh who was forcibly converted to Islam.

To most Indian minds, Ahmedabad is associated inextricably with Mahatma Gandhi and his SABARMATI ASHRAM: the music of hymns, charkha spinning and the march to Dandi for salt.

But all around Gandhi's ashram now bustles a city with an eminently modern profile, a model city in terms of growth. New mansions and high rise monuments of magnificent proportions, and of different eras and styles, synthesis into a whole — a city that is now the design and textile centre of India.

Ahmedabad's cotton industry received patronage under its Sultans. The first mill was established by Rancholal Chotalal in 1859, and today Ahmedabad boasts of as many as 80 mills with the most modern processing plants for bleaching, finishing, mercurising, sanforising, dyeing and printing, producing nearly 25 per cent of India's total cloth.

The origin of Ahmedabad can be traced to the ruined township of Karnavati, founded on the left bank of the Sabarmati by Karna Solanki between A.D. 1063 and 1093. It was re-established in 1411 by Sultan Ahmed Shah I who named it after him. It was a city created with love and an excellence of design.

The city's rich and prosperous historic past has bequeathed it an architectural legacy that is a happy blend of Hindu and Muslim schools of architecture.

A miniature painting

Ahmedabad grew under the patronage of the Ahmed Shahi and Solanki rulere and today the JAMA MASJID, the SARKHEJ MONUMENTS, SIDI SAYYID'S MOSQUE, and the SHAKING MINARETS of Ahmedabad are excellent idioms of the architectural excellence of the past.

Ahmedabad is unusual in more ways than one. Within its precincts are housed four unique museums. The SARABHAI CALICO MUSEUM is the only good museum in India devoted entirely to textiles — now housed in the gardens of the Sarabhai family mansion. There are three others: N.C. MEHTA MUSEUM which has the finest collection of Indian miniature paintings, and it is housed in the SANSKAR KENDRA MUNICIPAL MUSEUM designed by, the French master Le Corbusier. VEECHAAR is a large collection of rare Indian utensils housed in a newly constructed traditional Gujarat village called VISHALA — mentioned earlier for its famous restaurant. Another worthwhile museum is SHREYAS FOLK ART MUSEUM holding traditional mirror work, distinctive tribal clothes and decorations — located off Circular Road in Ahmedabad.

Kankaria Lake

In the south-east of Ahmedabad city, an artificial lake Kankaria was constructed in 1451 which has 34 sides, each 60 metres long. It still survives and is now a popular picnic spot. The ZOO and a CHILDREN'S PARK in the area are excellent.

Cambay

Cambay, the old seaport of Ahmedabad is situated to the south-west at the northern end of the Gulf of Cambay. At the height of Muslim power, the entire region was called Cambay. When the first ambassador to the Mughal Court arrived in Ahmedabad, he carried with him a letter to the Mughal Emperor from the King of Cambay.

The rise of Surat, however, eclipsed Cambay and when the port was silted, the decline was inevitable.

LOTHAL

About 80 km. south of Ahmedabad, archaeologists have discovered at Lothal the remains of the earliest known urban civilisation in the Indian subcontinent. What the archaeologists have actually excavated is part of an ancient port - complete with dockyards, streets, houses, underground drains and a well. This was perhaps India's most ancient port having maritime contacts with Mesopotamia and Egypt. From all accounts, it appears that when Mohenjodaro fell into decay,Lothal and its surrounding areas continued to prosper till these were assimilated by the Aryans.

MODHERA

The ruins of the SUN TEMPLE at Modhera are 106 km. north- west of Ahmedabad. There are bus services direct to Modhera or you can take a train to MEHSANA, from where it is only 40 kms.

The Sun Temple was built by King Bhimdev I in 1026-27. It bears some relationship to the Sun Temple at Konark, built later in Orissa. Like the Konark, this temple was also designed to let the sun shine on the image of Surya, the Sun God, at dawn at the time of equinoxes. The main hall and shrine are reached through a pillared porch. The exterior of the temple is intricately and delicately carved.

As at Somnath temple, it was Mahmud of Ghazni who also destroyed this temple.

UNJHA

A little north of Mehsana on the way to Modhera, there is an interesting town called Unjha, known for its peculiar marriage customs of the Kadwakanbis who live in this area. Marriages occur only once in 11 years and on that day every unmarried girl over 40 days old must be married. If no husband can be found for some girl, a proxy marriage takes place and the girl immediately becomes a "widow" to be remarried when a suitable husband shows up. The custom is now disappearing under government laws.

PATAN

North-west of Ahmedabad 120 km., this town was sacked by Mahmud of Ghazni in 1024. Now a pale shadow of its past glory, it is a centre for the manufacture of beautiful Patola silk saris.

SAURASHTRA

The bleak and flat region you will visit now was probably once a river bed. Perhaps the legendary Saraswati river or even the Indus cut Saurashtra off from the mainland. The strip is still known as Nal or stream.

The Dwaraka peninsula which looks like a mango on the map, is very sacred to the Hindus. It was here that Lord Krishna ruled with his capital at Dwaraka - a very important place of Hindu pilgrimage. It is believed that the original Dwaraka, which was an island, was submerged in the sea. Attempts are being made to rediscover the lost Dwaraka from the sea.

On the extreme western tip of Kathiawar peninsula, Dwaraka is one of the four holy places of the Hindus. It was here that Lord Krishna set up his capital after his flight from Mathura. The present temple has a 5-storey spire supported by 60 columns.

RAJKOT

In Saurashtra, all good roads lead to Rajkot, a very pleasant provincial town. Mahatma Gandhi spent a few years of his life in this town - his father was the Dewan (Chief Minister) of Rajkot, a small princely State.

JAMNAGAR

The Jains of Nawanagar are Jadeja Rajputs who built this town in 1540. They were progressive rulers and opposed the Marathas when they came to collect taxes from the rulers of Jamnagar. On independence, Jamnagar was the first State to join the Indian Union.

Right in the centre of the city is a romantic lake. Its Lakhota Fort and the museum with its rich collections of sculptures and archaeological finds from this region are well-worth a visit.

PALITANA

Palitana, 215 km. from Ahmedabad, is a sacred city of the Jains. It provides access to Shatrunjaya Temple, the most sacred temple on the hill. GIRNAR, near Junagarh, comes next.

Jainism developed in the 6th century B.C. Like Buddhism a century earlier, it broke away from the caste-ridden Hinduism under the guidance of Prince Mahavir (599-527 B.C.). He renounced his pampered life and lived as a naked ascetic for 12 years before achieving the supreme knowledge. They believe in reincarnation and salvation which they assert can be achieved by Ahimsa (non-violence) and by building temples. That is why you see thousands of Jain temples all over India. It takes about 2 hours to climb the 4 km. of steps to SHATRUNJAYA (place of victory over worldliness). You arrive through a white marble jungle of 863 temples, each with its own enclosure. The final destination is 591 metres up. If climbing is hard, sturdy labourers can haul you up in a *doli* (string chair). There are hundreds of white-robed pilgrims trekking their way to the hill. The rich, despite their renunciation, come on richly caparisoned elephants.

There is a stunning view from the top of the hill and the air is filled with the scent of jasmine trees. The biggest temple, CHAUMUKH, was built by a wealthy merchant in 1618 to save his soul. The most sacred temple is devoted to the first Tirthankar, Shri Adishwar. Temples groan with gold, silver and jewels donated by rich merchants — anyone may add a necklace to the treasure. A donation of Rs. 900 brings you the honour of dressing the deity with jewels. The donor also gets a pass from the priest which may get him, many steps down, a free breakfast of *ladoos* (sweets) and steaming sweet tea.

Also on the top of the hill is a Muslim shrine where childless women offer tiny cradles in the hope of conceiving.

JUNAGARH AND GIRNAR

The second most sacred hill for the Jains is GIRNAR near Junagarh. There is a motorable road between Palitana and Junagarh which passes through a desolate landscape. If you travel via RAJKOT, you will come to JETPUR, an old walled town. After Jetpur the sleepy JUNAGARH and its remarkable FORT UPARKOT (Upper Fort) comes in view. Over the centuries, enemies had laid siege to this fort but it remained impregnable. An Anhilwad Patan king once attacked Junagarh to win the Raja's wife. He won the battle only because one of the Raja's Ministers betrayed him, but he could not win the wife of the Raja as she committed *Sati* (burnt herself on the funeral pyre)—an irony of the fate because it was the Raja's affair with the wife of the traitor that led to his revenge.

In places, the walls of this fort are as high as 70 feet. Ruins of buildings — some three-storey high — lie nearby. The only structure which is intact is a mosque built from an earlier Hindu temple. Some Buddhist caves show that there might have been a monastery here before its regal history began.

The town itself is surrounded by the walls of the old Junagarh Fort and is today a beautiful city with cool gardens. In the SAKERBAGH GARDEN ZOO, you can meet some of the Gir lions, if you cannot make it to the GIR FOREST to have a look at them.

Emperor Ashoka began the stone-written history of Junagarh on a boulder on the road from Junagarh to Mount Girnar. His 14 edicts in Pali are exhortations to virtue and assurances that he, "the Beloved of the Gods", is looking after all his subjects.

Thick woods surround the road to one of the fine peaks which is sacred to the Jains. This hill has 2,000 steps rising 600 metres. The temple on the top is called AMBA MATA. Couples come here to worship, praying for a happy marriage. Below this temple is the biggest and the oldest temple (12th century) dedicated to the 22nd Tirthankar — NEMINATH. When a traveller to Gujarat, Joss Graham, climbed up the hill for the festival of Shivaratri, he slept there overnight. He woke up on hearing the praying murmurs of the great mass of devotees — 100,000 of them, in their communities and tribal groups. There is an image of Neminath in each of the courtyard colonnade's 70 cells.

The town of Junagarh is beautiful — with wide streets, arches leading to piazas and shopping arcades. Its splendour is more like an English factory city than a city in a remote corner of Gujarat.

GIR FOREST FOR ASIAN LIONS

From the hill-top of Girnar, you can also have a grand view of dark green woods stretching out to the sea. One is, therefore, not surprised that the rulers of arid Saurashtra always vied with one another for the control of

Asiatic Lions (Gir Forest)

Junagarh which was an oasis in the desert. From Junagarh, you can drive to VERAVAL for the last bastion of Asian lions. But, you must make advance arrangements for accommodation and jeeps with the Regional Manager of Tourism Development Corporation of Gujarat at Junagarh or do it through your travel agent in Bombay or Delhi.

SASAN GIR is the name of the place from where the expedition into the forest begins. SASAN GIR NATIONAL PARK is one of India's finest wildlife sanctuaries set in an area of 1295 sq. km. of lush deciduous forests. It is the final refuge of the rare Asian lions which roamed freely two centuries ago throughout Middle East and North and East of India. Over the years, specially during the British Raj, lions were hunted mercilessly by the British officers assisted by the obliging Maharajas and Nawabs. Every Maharaja was proud of the number of lions or tigers he killed during his lifetime. The famine of 1899 decimated the lion population so badly that Lord Curzon cancelled his shoot in Gir where he had been invited by the Nawab for a 'Shikar'. Curzon also advised the ruler to protect the remaining lions. Although the number of lions increased by the time India became independent, they were once again hunted mercilessly by the 'New Maharajas' — the foreign tourists who were guaranteed trophy of a dead lion by the Shikar-outfitters who organised their Shikar. It became a major tourist attraction of India. The Government of India came to the rescue of the lions when it banned lion hunts altogether in the mid-1960s. Now the Gir Forest is open only for photo-safaris. You can shoot the lion only with your camera.

The sanctuary is open from mid-October to mid-June. November, January and February are the best months to see the lions. They retreat to the interior of the forest during the summer months.

This forest has a wide variety of wildlife. Among them, besides the lion, are wild boar, bear, panther, antelope, hyena, leopard and the Indian Chawsingha — the 4-horned antelope.

During monsoons, you can see in the forest some 200 varieties of birds.

The Gir Forest Department organises "Lion Shows" as part of its conducted tours by jeeps. They make sure that you can see the lions at close range as they send trackers early morning on a mission to locate large groups and tempt them with live baits. Advance arrangements are necessary, preferably through your Indian travel agent.

If you wish to explore the Sanctuary on your own, jeeps can be hired with a guide. The cost is reasonably low, including per kilometre for the hire of the jeep with the driver.

Within the forest are the TULISHYAM HOT SPRINGS in a scenic setting. Here you can bathe in natural sulphur springs. It is about 90 km. from the entrance to the sanctuary.

SOMNATH

Veraval, mentioned earlier, is a port city and has a shipbuilding yard to manufacture coastal ships. It is also the city nearest to the great SOMNATH TEMPLE which had an extremely chequered history. Legend has it that the original temple was built by Somraj, the moon-god himself, out of gold. Later, Ravana made it with silver, then Krishna in wood and finally King Bhimdev in stone.

What is more certain is that the description of the richness of the Somnath temple by Al Biruni, an Arab traveller, brought in the most unwelcome guest of all — Mahmud of Ghazni in A.D. 1024. At that time the temple was so rich that it had 300 musicians, 500 dancing girls and 300 barbers to shave off the heads of pilgrims. After a 2-day battle, Mahmud destroyed the temple and carted off its fabulous wealth to his homeland. This started a tradition of Muslims destroying the Hindu temples and Hindus rebuilding them as soon as they got an opportunity in the following centuries. The Somnath Temple was razed again in 1297,

1394 and finally in 1706 by the notorious Mughal emperor Aurangzeb who did the most damage to Hindu-Muslim relations in India. It was rebuilt by the Hindus again in 1950. The present temple was built to traditional pattern on the original site by the sea.

Between Somnath and Veraval is the BALAK TIRTH TEMPLE which contains a reclining statue of Lord Krishna, signifying death here while resting over a deer-skin. A Bhil hunter mistook him for an animal and killed him accidentally. Also, near Veraval is the site of his cremation — a three-river Sangam. It is a sacred spot of great antiquity.

The Ahir women in this area — the members of the same tribe as his consort Radha still wear black — in what must be the longest mourning in the history of mankind.

AHMEDPUR MANDVI — The Beach Resort

Ahmedpur Mandvi, 298 km. from Ahmedabad, and connected by state transpsort buses, this is one of the country's finest beaches. The SAMUDRA BEACH RESORT is ideal for a holiday, for swimming, water sports or just lazing around on the beach. Book rooms with the Tourism Development Corporation of Gujarat. Tariff is around Rs. 500 to 575 for cottages. Across the resort is Diu, former Portuguese enclave, which can be approached by ferry or by a bridge connecting the mainland with the island.

DAMAN AND DIU

Although geographically a part of the Gujarat State, Daman and Diu, the two tiny former Portuguese enclaves, are a centrally administered territory. Till recently, these were administered from Goa. When Goa achieved Statehood in 1987, Daman and Diu retained their status as Union Territories to be administered locally

The two enclaves are right in the south of Gujarat. These areas were liberated from the Portuguese in 1961 along with Goa. The Portuguese had seized Daman, 380 sq. km. in area, in 1531. The territory still retains some Portuguese flavour with imposing buildings, churches and an old fort.

Although like Goa, Daman is by the sea, its beaches bear no relationship with the golden beaches of Goa. Daman beaches are drab and dirty.

VAPI station on the main railway line is the jumping off point for Daman, 90 km. from Surat. Not all trains stop here. Daman is only 10 km. from Vapi.

While Daman has no good beaches, Diu has excellent golden beaches — yet to be discovered. The India Tourism Development Corporation (ITDC) had recently set up tented accommodation to introduce to visitors the charm of Diu beaches. Tourism development did not take place here because access to the Island is difficult.

Diu is an island — 11 km. long and 3 km. wide — separated from the coast by a narrow channel. You reach Diu through the town of UNA.

The island has beautiful, though a small, bazar and a massive fort built by the Portuguese in 1536.

Once Diu was an opium exporting centre. It still is an important centre for smuggling goods into India or out of it. There is a PWD resthouse where visitors can stay.

Diu, in the Gulf of Cambay, is close to Junagarh, BHAVNAGAR, PORBANDAR (the birthplace of Mahatma Gandhi), Somnath and the Gir forest. Diu was the first settlement in India of the Parsis fleeing from Persia in the 7th century.

Diu is one of the few places where the endangered great Indian bustard is still seen.

DADRA AND NAGAR HAVELI

Dadra and Nagar Haveli, made up of 72 predominantly tribal villages, is yet another former Portuguese enclave, liberated alongwith Goa in 1961. Its area is 491 sq. km. and population about 1,25,000. Forty per cent of the land is under forests on which tribal population depends heavily.

The area is a Union Territory which means centrally administered. It lies between two highly industrialised cities in Gujarat — Surat and Vapi—interrupted by the Gujarat State territory. Assigned to the Portuguese by the Marathas under a Friendship Treaty in 1779, it was under Portuguese rule till 1961.

The economy of the Territory is essentially agrarian. The main crops are paddy, sugarcane, mango and apple.

Dadra and Nagar Haveli are a quick getaway from Bombay (180 km.), Surat (150 km.) and Vapi (17 km.). The tribals of Nagar Haveli believe that once upon a time, their king had built in it a great 'mansion of peace', because peace is God's own precious gift.

The Union Territory of Dadra and Nagar Haveli is located between Gujarat and Maharashtra and is about 30 km. from the west coast. The nearest railway station is Vapi, which is about 15 km. from SILVASSA, the headquarters of the union territory. Silvassa is situated midway between Bombay and Surat. Dadra and Nagar Haveli are linked with National Highway No.8.

Since 1986, attempts have been made to identify tourist spots and develop some infrastructure. The emphasis is on tourism development that does not affect ecology. For instance, Government has developed a tourist spot, VANVIHAR, 20 km. from the capital, Silvassa, at a place called KHANVEL. It is in the heart of a lush green forest. The Forest Rest House overlooks the rolling lawns and terraced gardens resplendent with flowers. Adjoining the Rest House is the TRIBAL MUSEUM where you can see tribal outfits, hunting tools, identifying the area where different tribes live in the territory. Another tourist spot is MADHUBAN — 10 km. from Silvassa where a dam has been built across the Damanganga river. A rest house for tourists stands on the top of the hill giving them a panoramic view. Local tourism authorities plan to develop a garden on the lines of Brindavan Gardens near Mysore.

Dadra has its VANGANGA PROJECT. An artificial lake has been created with a Japanese garden in the centre of the lake. The project attracts a lot of local tourists from the Gujarat State.

Since Dadra and Nagar Haveli have a wonderful terrain, there are opportunities for forest walks and hiking. Natural trails of 2 to 5 km. have been laid for this purpose. For entertainment, tribal dances can be arranged on request.

The territory has a modest hotel — RAS RESORT HOTEL — in the capital Silvassa. It has a swimming pool, health centre and other facilities.

AHMEDABAD

GENERAL INFORMATION
Population: 3,280,000 (1991 census)
Altitude: 55 metres (183 ft.)
Climate

	Temperature	
	Max.	Min.
Winter	36^0 c	12^0 c
Summer	41^0 c	23^0 c
Rainfall	24 mm	12 mm

Season: Throughout the year, except from April to June, when days are very hot.
Clothing
Summer: cottons
Winter: light woollens in the evenings.

HOW TO GET THERE
By Air: Ahmedabad is connected by air with Bombay, Calcutta, Madras, Delhi, Jaipur, Jodhpur, Aurangabad, Hyderabad, Patna, Srinagar, Vadodara and Bangalore. Private Airlines also fly to Ahmedabad.
Air India provides an international connection from Ahmedabad to London and New York. (twice weekly)
By Rail: Ahmedabad has direct rail connections with Bombay, Delhi, Calcutta, Madras, Agra, Bhopal, Jaipur, Jodhpur, Veravel (for Gir), Porbandar.
By Road: Ahmedabad is connected by road with all the major cities in India. It is
531 km. from Bombay,
1076 km. from Delhi,
664 km. from Jaipur,
253 km. from Udaipur and
112 km. from Vadodara.
There are regular bus services to Bombay, Indore, Mt. Abu, Udaipur, Vadodara and to other cities in Gujarat.

LOCAL TRANSPORT
Tourist taxis, metered taxis, autorickshaws and bus services. The flagdown fare for a taxi is Rs. 3.50.

CONDUCTED TOURS
1. Half-day tour of the city (twice daily).
2. On Sundays, half-day tour to Adalaj Vav, Gandhi Ashram, Calico Museum. Shreyas Folk Arts Museum, Sunderban and Vishala restaurant.
3. 5-day tour of the Saurashtra area.
4. 5-day tour of North Gujarat and Rajasthan tour.
5. 5-day of South Gujarat and Ajanta-Ellora tour.
6. 2-day tour of Udaipur and Nathdwara.
7. 2-day tour of Mount Abu.

(The above tours operated by the Tourism Corporation of Gujarat (TCGL) are good value. For Information: Tourist Office (*Tel.* 449683)

WHERE TO STAY (STD CODE: 0272)
STANDARD
1. Cama Hotel
   Phone: 305281
   Fax: 305285
   Cable: HOTELCAMA
2. River Hotel
   Phone: 304201
   Fax: 302327
   Cable: RIVERHOTEL
3. Hotel Karnavati
   Phone: 402161
   Telex: 0121-6519-CSCO IN
   Cable: SHREEHOTEL
4. Holiday Inn
   Phone: 305505
   Fax: 305501
   Cable: ATITHI
5. Hotel Kanak
   Phone: 467291
   Telex: HOTEL KANAK
6. Inder Residency
   Phone: 425050
   Cable: HOTAMBASS
7. Hotel Nalanda
   Phone: 426262
   Fax: 426090
8. Quality Inn Shalin
   Phone: 426967
   Fax: 46002

BUDGET
9. Hotel Ambassador
   Phone: 352245
10. Moti Mahal
    Phone: 339091/92/93
11. Hotel Shakunth
    Phone: 345614-15
12. Hotel Mahal
    Phone: 339096
13. Hotel Paradise
    Phone: 401520, 410805
14. Dimple International
    Phone: 341849

WHAT TO SEE
1. GANDHI ASHRAM, SABARMATI. Mahatma Gandhi set up his first Ashram here in 1915. It is now a national monument and preserved as it was in Gandhi's lifetime. THE GANDHI MEMORIAL CENTRE, LIBRARY and a SON-ET-LUMIERE show give a glimpse of the life and work of the Father of the Nation.
2. THE SHAKING MINARETS (Jhulta Minar). When one

minaret is shaken the other also vibrates.
3. SIDI SAIYYID'S MOSQUE, famous for its exquisite stone window tracery of lace-like filigree.
4. The richly ornamented RANI RUPMATI'S MOSQUE.
5. SARKHEJ ROZA, the tomb of Mohammed Begada.
6. DADA HARI VAV, a step-well, a unique feature of Gujarat architecture.
7. HUTHISING JAIN TEMPLE, built of white marble and profusely carved.
8. THE CALICO TEXTILE MUSEUM, probably the finest textile museum in the world.
9. The SHREYAS FOLK ART MUSEUM presenting the most attractive folk art of Gujarat.
10. N.C. MEHTA COLLECTION of rare miniature paintings.
11. VEECHAR UTENSIL MUSEUM with its collection of brass, bronze and metal vessels.
12. NATIONAL INSTITUTE OF DESIGN.

EXCURSIONS
1. ADALAJ VAV (19 km.), a decorated step-well.
2. MODHERA (106 km.), where one can see a temple dedicated to the Sun God, built in 1026.
3. LOTHAL (80 km.), the site of archaeological ruins of the Harappan civilisation of the 2nd millennium B.C.
4. VADODARA or BARODA (118 km.), city of gardens, palaces and educational institutions.
5. PATAN (133 km.), famous for the weaving of Patola silk saries.

SHOPPING
Tie-and-die fabrics, khari work with gold and silver thread embossing, textiles printed and woven, gold and silver thread embroidery, patola saris from Patan are some of the highlights. Sankheda lacquered furniture, mirror-work embroidered skirts and blouse material, bead-work, handicrafts, woodwork, brass articles and appliqued work are some of the popular items available.

FESTIVALS OF SPECIAL LOCAL INTEREST
1. KITE-FLYING FESTIVAL (Jan. 14). Kites of various shapes and sizes are flown by young and old. After dark, kites lighted with candles sparkle in the sky.
2. SARKHEJ FAIR (July-August), This is held near the mausoleum of the mentor of Sultan Ahmed Shah, Shah Ahmed Khattu.
3. TARNETAR FAIR (July-August), a most colourful village fair, not to be missed. Conducted coach tours are operated to Tarnetar from Ahmedabad during the fair.
4. NAVARATRI, the festival of nine nights (September-October) devoted to the

three goddesses of the Hindu Trinity. Garba dances are performed when women dancers clap hands and dance on the streets in every town and village, late into the night.

Ranjit Vilas Palace at Wankaner

GIR NATIONAL PARK

GENERAL INFORMATION
Altitude: 157 metres (523 ft)
Climate

	Temperature	
	Max.	Min.
Winter	31^0 c	14^0 c
Summer	32^0 c	22^0 c
Rainfall	77 mm	57mm

Season: Mid-October to mid-June. However, the best season is December to mid-June. (The Sanctuary remains closed during the monsoon months.)

Clothing:
Summer: Cottons
Winter: Woollens

HOW TO GET THERE
By Air: The nearest airport is at Keshod (90 km). There are air services from Keshod to Porbandar and Bombay.
By Rail: Sasan Gir is the nearest railhead.
By Road: Gir is
43 km. from Veraval,
127 km. from Junagadh,
400 km. from Ahmedabad and
882 km. from Bombay.
Regular bus services are available to and from Junagadh and Veraval.

LOCAL TRANSPORT
Jeeps and a mini-bus are available to take visitors around the forest.

CONDUCTED TOURS
1. 2-day package tour of the GIR SANCTUARY.
2. Lion Shows.
a) General Show — Sundays.
b) Special Shows — for parties of up to 8 persons.
c) Exclusive Shows — (Apply 15 days in advance to the conservator of Forests, Wild Life Circle, Junagadh *Tel.* 362-001 or Sanctuary Superintendent, Sasan Gir, Dist. Junagadh).

Lion shows are arranged to ensure that you do not miss the King of the Forest. These are not circus shows, but it is ensured that visitors see lions by placing a kill to tempt them. The name Lion Show is actually a misnomer.

WHERE TO STAY
1. Lion Safari Lodge
2. Saurashtra Safari Gir Jungle Camp.

WHAT TO SEE
1. Beside the Asiatic lion there are other animals such as the panther (a rare sight), large Indian deer, sambar, chital (spotted deer), nilgai (blue bull), chinkara, chowsingha (4-horned antelope), bear and long-tailed langur monkey.
2. Other attractions are a Crocodile Farm and Sirvan Village where tribals of African origin live. Besides, a large number of birds are seen. The peacock is a common sight.

EXCURSIONS
1. SOMNATH TEMPLE (45 km), believed to have been built by Soma, the moon-god is a famous centre of pilgrimage. The temple famed for its wealth, was sacked seven times by Mahmud of Ghazni, but has risen each time like the phoenix from the flames. The ruins of the ancient temple can be seen in the nearby museum.

Lioness with her cubs

2. BALAK TEERTH (39 km), where Lord Krishna was accidentally shot by the arrow of a hunter.
3. DEHOTSARGA (39 km), the holy spot where Krishna spent his last hours on this earth.
4. PORBANDAR (197 km), the birthplace of Mahatma Gandhi.
5. TULSISHYAM HOT SPRINGS (96 km).
6. CHORWAD (35 km. from Keshod), a picturesque beach resort.
7. PALITANA (50 km. from Bhavnagar, the nearest airport). There are 863 exquisitely carved Jain temples on top of a hill.
8. DIU (142 km. from Keshod) was once a Portuguese territory. It has a Portuguese fort and a good beach.
9. AHMEDPUR MANDVI BEACH RESORT (18 km. from Diu and 120 km. from Sasangir). A beautiful beach, with accommodation in cottages. Offers water sport facilities.

Temple at Dwarka

Chapter 17

MAHARASHTRA
The Land of Caves, Forts and Temples

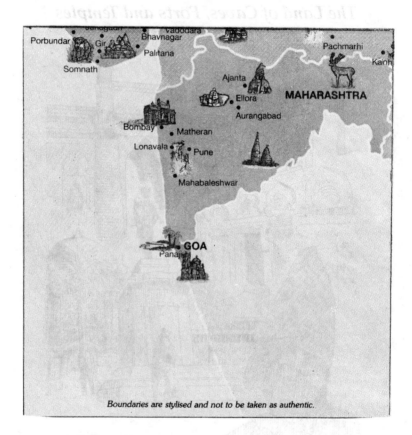

Boundaries are stylised and not to be taken as authentic.

Bombay is the capital of the Maharashtra State, India's fourth largest State, but it does not reflect the spirit of Maharashtra. The city is Maharashtra's avaricious heart, its soul lies in the interior of the State in cities like Pune, Kolhapur and Nagpur. Mumbai contains a cross-section of the people of India - it is like a mini India. If you walk in Bombay, you will hear a babble of languages you cannot understand, but all Bombayites communicate in their Mumbai Hindi. In cities like Pune, you will find proprietary pride in the Maratha hero, Shivaji, who shook the Mughal empire. Many of Shivaji's forts are around Pune. But, this glorious past — not just from the Shivaji period — has left behind treasures for the visitors in the form of forts, temples and other great works of ancient art and architecture. The best approach to see Maharashtra is to use five cities — Pune, Kolhapur, Aurangabad, Nagpur and Nashik — as bases for exploratory trips to nearby places. But, if you are short of time and have to choose only one, choose just Aurangabad. The cave temples of Ajanta-Ellora offer riches which may, depending on your preference, excel even the Taj Mahal. Let us explore the various cities and towns to get a flavour of the Maharashtrian culture, including the city of Bombay.

The course of Mumbai's history would have been different had the Portuguese not given the tiny island of Bom Bahia in dowry to their Royal Princess, Catherine of Braganza, when she married Charles II of England. The British had no idea what they had got. While Pepys believed that it was a poor little island Lord Clarendon thought it had "towns and castles thereon which were very little distance from Brazil". The name came from the Goddess Mumba - the patron deity of the Kolis—the earliest inhabitants of the island. Coming full circle, it was suggested that the name of the city revert to its original vernacular term, i.e., Mumbai. In 1981, the name was officially changed, but the world at large still calls this city - Bombay.

The State of Maharashtra has an area of 301,672 sq. km. and its population now exceeds 60 million - same as that of France. In Maharashtra, you can find relics of some 175 forts - big and small. Most of them are directly or indirectly connected with Shivaji who is credited to have built some 111 of them.

MUMBAI—Maharashtra's Crowning Glory

The city to begin with, was spread over seven lush, green islands. While the British got one island as dowry gift, they took over other six by force. Though the area was part of Shivaji's empire, he was too busy chasing Aurangzeb or being chased by him. They, therefore, had a freer hand. The East India Company had received trading rights from Queen Elizabeth I in 1600 and had already set up a base in Surat which was then an important post on the Arabian Sea. They moved their headquarters to

Bombay. They defeated the Marathas in the Fourth Maratha War in 1818 and that paved their way for their further expansion into India.

Mumbai's progress has been slow but steady over the three centuries since the East India Company started administering it in 1668. The first Governor of Bombay was Gerald Aungier (1672-77) who was known as the Father of Bombay. He established Courts of Justice as well as the Company Militia - which later shaped into the Army of East India Company. He encouraged people of all communities to come and settle down in Bombay — Gujaratis, Parsis, Hindu Banias and Arab traders fleeing from the oppression of Jesuits in Goa. Since then the cosmopolitan composition of Bombay's population has been its strength.

However, life for the British in India was pretty dull - there were not many British women around. There was only a little racing and a lot of Bombay Punch - a local toddy to amuse them. By the end of the 18th century, there were only 1000 Europeans in Bombay while Indians numbered 1,20,000. In the beginning of the 19th century, life began to change for the better. With the East India Company losing its monopoly of trade to India, the new P & O Steamers began regular services between the two countries and many women came from England in search of husbands. These were known as the 'fishing fleet'. Railway started in 1853 - first in the east of Suez - and telegraphs followed in 1865.

A view of Mumbai

In the second half of the 19th century, new streets were laid and great victorian Goethic buildings came up which still dominate Central Mumbai. The city needed land for expansion. Once the seven islands were joined, the city expanded towards the sea by reclaiming land. By 1950, its total area had increased by a third through various reclamation projects which still continue. Maps of Mumbai city have to be constantly redrawn and revised.

Since possibilities of acquiring more land through reclamation are now limited, a new twin city called New Bombay is coming up across the harbour. It has been designed by a well-known architect, Charles Correa, but has not proved very popular so far.

Mumbai's wealth came from trade over the centuries. First it was export of cotton to China and Great Britain. India also became a major supplier of opium to China through British merchants. The British even fought an opium war to force China to buy opium. The Civil War in America in the 1860s helped India to fill the gap for the loss of American cotton to Manchester mills. But, it was only a short-term gain. As the war ended in 1865, the cotton markets crashed.

Mumbai has been built by small communities and strong individuals. The best known among them are the Parsis who westernised their lifestyle in tune with the ruling class. Immigrants from Persia in the 8th century A.D., Parsis had remained a distinct community as they did not allow their children to inter-marry. They were the first Indians to send their children to Oxford and Cambridge and it was a Parsee, Jamshedji Jeejeebhoy (1783-1859), who was created a baronet by the British. Many streets of Mumbai are named after successful Parsi businessmen, industrialists and philanthropists. The Tatas have been the most successful business family among them during the current century—almost every field of industry in India has something to do with them. Air India was set up by the legendary J.R.D. Tata and the Hotel Taj Mahal stands as a great memorial to his visionary father. Another strong individual who set up home in Mumbai was David Sasoon, a Sephardic Jew from Baghdad. From Mumbai, he spread his wings to Britain and the USA and finally settled there.

After independence, other hard-working communities like the Sindhis and Punjabis have added to the wealth of the city.

Mumbai's gleaming skyscrapers have an air of Manhattan or Osaka about them. Its streets are crowded by the little Marutis acquired by the newly emerging middle class in India. Its air is no longer so pure and its sky no longer blue as it was even a decade ago. It is difficult to say what course the city of Bombay will take during the years to come.

Trade has fed Mumbai's progress from a 7-island swamp to a single island city of ten million today.

Mumbai is India's financial, commercial, industrial and trading centre. It has 40 per cent of India's textile industry. Its port handles over

50 per cent of exports and the citizens of Bombay pay one-third of India's income-tax. An unusual phenomenon of Mumbai's economy is the large scale prevalence of the cash economy called "black money". Hardly anything is done without it cash payment - whether you buy a house or business, rent premises or do any other transaction, cash payment - not subject to tax - is unavoidable.

Mumbai is also India's most expensive city as far as the cost of living is concerned. The real estate prices are comparable to New York, London and Tokyo. The rent laws favour the tenants who live in large houses paying rents they paid 50 years ago and the owners cannot get them ejected. Now Bombay has added another feather to its cap. It has emerged as the largest state in India with a population of 12.57 million in 1991 census.

Mumbai claims to be the world's largest production centre for films. About 150 Hindi films are produced annually in this city - an average of three releases every week. The cost of production is very high, largely due to the 'stars' system which allows popular film stars to charge fees as high as 30 to 40 per cent of the total cost of the film. However, few films make a hit, the majority of them bomb out at the box office. Indian films are a peculiar potpourri of dance, music, violence, revenge, intrigue and humour. It is not surprising that Indian films seldom win awards at International Film Festivals.

Because of its cosmopolitan character, the Mumbai Municipal Corporation imparts primary education to children at least in ten languages of India including English. But the people of Mumbai have developed a lingua franca which is uniquely its own, called Mumbai Hindi. It is understood by all residents of Mumbai and it is often caricatured in Hindi films.

Mumbai has good weather most of the year. Bombayites love to talk about their beautiful winter (December-March) which is more like the continental summer. The winter does not last very long - heat and humidity start rising in March. The monsoon starts in June and have a cooling effect. Weather improves from September-October and lasts till March.

The city boasts of some of the finest hotels in Asia and you should, if you can afford, stay in the best. The best may not cost what a 'standard' hotel costs in USA and Europe. The top hotels are the Taj, the Oberois, Leela Kempinsky, Holiday Inn, etc.

The monsoons need not dampen your enthusiasm to come to India during the rainy season. They pour large quantity of water in short time and when it is over let you move about in peace. In fact, this is the time for rich Arab travellers. They come to Bombay to see the rains. The hotels are full with Arab visitors.

Winter-October-March is also the time for major festivals like Ganapati Puja in September - and Diwali, Holi and Christmas. Bombay has also a very busy social calendar during this part of the year — sports like cricket matches, as well as regular music and dance festivals are held during this period.

To explore Mumbai, it is best to start from the GATEWAY OF INDIA by water's edge at APOLLO BUNDER. It was built to commemorate the visit of King George V to India in 1911 and was designed by an architect George Wittet. The design of this splendid arched gateway is similar to that of the Arch de Triomphe in Paris, with touches of Moorish architecture. King George had come to India with Queen Mary to hold a Durbar in Delhi. It was the highest watermark of the British Raj in India - after which the British power started its decline. Not far from the Gateway, is a village of the Kolis - one of the original tribes of fishermen. Here, the men ride to sea to collect fish and the women sell fish all over the town. The Kolis are a very interesting tribe, they love dance, music and spend lavishly on weddings.

The southern tip of the Mumbai island is under the control of Army and Navy. Within the military area is Saint John's Church popularly called AFGHAN CHURCH. It was built to commemorate the death of soldiers killed during the Afghan War. In the churchyard, you can read the gruesome price the British had to pay to hold on to the golden jewel in the British Empire in India. As soon as they used to enter the harbour in the old days, British families suffered from cholera, malaria and plague, to name but a few diseases.

At low tide you can walk up to the LIGHTHOUSE off the tip of the island.

The CHURCH GATE, the most crowded area in Central Mumbai, is known for the Gate in the old Fort wall near ST THOMAS' CATHEDRAL. The area is part of the reclaimed land. It is also popularly called the Fort area. The MANTRALAYA STATE SECRETARIAT which houses many government offices faces an inlet of the sea. Nearby is the stunningly beautiful modern TATA THEATRE, National Centre of Performing Arts. Here, you can see regular performance of Indian classical dance, music and plays. Acoustics are perfect — perhaps the best in India.

NARIMAN POINT is a beautiful complex of high rise buildings on the reclaimed land, each having a view of the sea. It is the business and commercial centre of Bombay. Most Airlines offices including Air India and the Oberoi Hotel are located here. The Government of India Tourist Office is located opposite the main Church Gate railway station from where it is amazing to see thousands of people emerging every 5 minutes after the offices close.

Along the Marine Drive
Between Nariman Point and FLORA FOUNTAIN are some of the Mumbai's most interesting buildings. The PRINCE OF WALES MUSEUM, a good example of India Saracenic architecture, is perhaps one of the finest museums in India. The JEHANGIR ART GALLERY is also right there. Nearby are the UNIVERSITY BUILDINGS and RAJABAI CLOCK TOWER. From this Tower, you can have an overview of Mumbai's 'Manhattan'. The Mumbai Mint too is close-by. Then, there is the famous TOWN HALL. The University Buildings stand between the HIGH COURT and the OLD SECRETARIAT. Designed by Sir Gilbert Scott, the University Buildings were completed in 1874 in a florid and highly decorative French Goethic style.

The University Library and Clock Tower were commissioned in 1880 - the bells and clock followed two years later.

Skirting along Back Bay is Mumbai's picturesque MARINE DRIVE, popularly called the Queen's Necklace. Its best view at night can be had from the HANGING GARDENS of MALABAR HILLS. The Drive is a promenade in the evening - hawkers from Kerala on the parade selling you fresh coconuts.

From time to time the sea-wall of the Marine Drive has to be strengthened as the monsoon sea swings in with great fury. Across the Bay is MALABAR POINT which has important buildings like the residence of the Governor - the RAJ BHAVAN.

To the right of the Marine Drive is the large Maidan on an open space. This Maidan houses the Aquarium and several sports clubs. In the evening, the Maidan becomes the site of folk dances and music by groups of common folks.

CHAWPATTY BEACH is a beach right in the centre of the town where Mumbai's citizens come for a breath of fresh air from the sea. The beach has many foodstalls selling popular Indian snacks like *Bhelpuri*. It is worth a try.

Malabar Hills

Upon the Malabar Hills and below them are the bungalows of the rich people. To the east side of the Malabar Hills is the green-topped KAMALA NEHRU PARK - named after the wife of Jawaharlal Nehru. B.J. Kher Road, named after the first Chief Minister of Mumbai, runs along the top of the Malabar Hills. The beautiful gardens and bungalows are proof of how Mumbai could be - if there were less people and more money spent on tree planting. The Chief Minister's present residence "Varsha" is on this road.

Malabar Hills, COLUMBIA HILLS and areas as far as the RACE COURSE have the most fashionable parks of the city. You can find here ladies dressed in the latest Paris or London designs.

Tucked away in the corner below the hill and on the sea is Bombay's famous DHOBI GHAT where washermen wash clothes by pounding them on the stones. The business is slower now as people have realised that the washermen do not wash clothes on stones but 'break' stones with clothes. Nearby is the WALKESHWAR TEMPLE and also a JAIN TEMPLE.

Then one can visit the famous HANGING GARDENS of Mumbai. It is a quiet place away from the din and noise of the city. You can also have a sweeping view of the city from the sea to the mountains in the background.

As you go beyond the gardens, you see the PARSI TOWER OF SILENCE. It is the place where they dispose of their deads. A park surrounded by high walls conceals the Tower. Even the relatives of the dead are not allowed to go beyond a particular point. The body is taken by bearers to the top where it is devoured immediately by the waiting vultures. The skeletons subsequently are disposed of in a well.

Among the other places to see in and around Mumbai are TARAPOREVALA AQUARIUM on Marine Drive. It has an interesting collection of acquatic plants and fish.

VICTORIA TERMINUS STATION is architecturally one of the finest stations in the world. This Italian Goethic building has a frontage of 1500 feet. The most prominent feature of V.T. (as the station is popularly called) is its high 160 feet dome crowning the centre. Designed by F.W. Stevens, the construction of the building commenced in 1878. FLORA FOUNTAIN - another Mumbai landmark - was an exquisite fountain laid in honour of Sir Henry Bartle Edward Frere who was responsible for many public buildings in the city.

Mumbai has a National Park within the city itself, the SANJAY GANDHI NATIONAL PARK, which is located towards the hill ranges around the Borivili suburb. Wildlife includes panther, antelope, moose, deer and wild boar.

The well-known religions shrines of Bombay are:

Jama Masjid
The construction of the present Jama Masjid started in 1775 but work on it could not be completed till 1802. The Masjid is a quadrangular pile of brick and stone encircled by a ring of terraced roofed and double-storeyed buildings. The main eastern gate leads to an ancient tank filled with about 10 feet of water.

Mahalakshmi Temple
The Mahalakshmi Temple in Beach Candy is one of the most popular temples in the city. During Navaratri celebrations, devotees stand for hours in long queues awaiting their turn to worship the goddess. The temple is devoted to the goddess of wealth. An interesting thing about Mumbai's shrines is that people belonging to different faiths visit them and ask for some favour or the other.

The Beaches of Bombay
Chowpatty on Marine Drive is perhaps the most popular beach in the city. Efforts are under way to clean it and provide better amenities. The popular *chaat* and *pani-puri* stalls have been moved to one end of the beach and a large sandy portion left clear. Palms and other trees are also being planted as a part of the beautification programme.

JUHU BEACH, about 30 km. from the city, is a long stretch of sandy beach. Foodstalls, merry-go-rounds and tumble boxes are clustered together at a midway point on this sandy strip. This part of the beach tends to get very crowded, especially on weekends when families come out to spend a whole day at the beach. The sea at Juhu is relatively safe during high tide. At the Ramada Inn Palm Grove Hotel at Juhu, visitors may hire surf boards and go out wind-surfing. Further north, Bombay has the beaches of GORAI, MARVE, MANORI and MADH. These beaches are unspoilt stretches of golden sand. The sea at Marve and Madh, however, is treacherous in places and it is important to look out for signboards that indicate the dangerous points. Maori and Gorai are easily approachable by ferries. Cars may be parked at Marve, and thereafter a 10-minute ride in a small ferry takes you across to Manori. At the other end you may hire a horse or bullock cart to take you to the beach, or else enjoy a leisurely walk down. The sea at Manori is relatively calm. Across from Apollo Bunder, by ferry, is ALIBAUG - a quiet uncrowded beach resort. Alibaug is still relatively undeveloped and good hotels and adequate facilities are not easily available. Most people who visit Alibaug use private cottages or company shacks and bring along a picnic hamper. Alibaug is also approachable by road but this involves a two hour drive.

Elephanta Caves
From the modern Mumbai, the ancient is not far away. An hour's ride from the Gateway of India, there lies the small but celebrated island of Elephanta. The island rises near its centre into two conical hills. The

excavations for which Elephanta is so celebrated are situated about two-thirds up the higher of the two hills. Rock temples were hewn out of the hill sometime towards the end of the Buddhist period in India, probably in the 8th century.

The outside of the main cave consists of a columned verandah 30 feet wide and 6 feet deep, approached by steps flanked by sculptured elephants. The Portuguese are said to have named the place after the stone elephants they found in the caves. The main sculptures decorate the southern wall at the back. Three square recesses contain giant figures of *dwarapalas*. Four rows of massive columns cut in the solid rocks from three magnificent avenues lead to the outstanding three-headed sculpture representing Brahma, the Creator, Vishnu the Preserver and Shiva the Destroyer. The idol is over 16 feet tall and is guarded on each side by a colossal figure leaning on a dwarf. There are several other interesting sculptures on the island, including some depicting the marriage of Shiva and Parvati, Ravana the demon king, and lesser male and female divinities.

At the other end of the city and almost 40 km. from the Gateway, lie the 2nd century Buddhist hill caves of KANHERI. Built in the early stages of rock-cut architecture, the sculptures are executed on a large scale and match those of the better known Ajanta and Ellora caves. At Kanheri, there are no actual representations of Buddha himself, only the symbols of his religion.

Where to Shop in Mumbai

The island of Mumbai is one big 'bazar'. With its myriads of tiny narrow streets or gullies, crowded with people and shops alike, the city is a shopper's paradise. Whether the goods are manufactured here or imported from other parts of the country or abroad, the variety available speaks volumes for the people who patronise these outlets.

The harbour areas of Mumbai have the oldest markets around. COLABA, where the British lived, still bears names of the old shops on some of the buildings of Army and Navy Stores. The Gujaratis and Jains who lived in Bhuleshwar created an ethnic market to suit their needs, while the predominantly Muslim areas located in the Mohammad Ali Road portray a distinctly Muslim flavour.

The 70 odd bazars that the city has, are not just a market for the local population,but they cater to the whole country as wholesalers. Running parallel to the area is FASHION STREET, opposite BOMBAY GYMKHANA. This new bazar (only six years old) offers its export surplus garments - the focus of popular attention. The Bombayite today swears by the wares that are available on the side-walls.

Into the lanes of Mohammad Ali Road, past the colourful fruit and vegetable laden stalls of CRAWFORD MARKET, are a variety of merchandise. Fabric markets for the city are centred around this area. MANGALDAS MARKET is the fabric wholesale market for both synthetics and cotton whilst the COTTON EXCHANGE offers mainly pure cotton.

A couple of twisty lanes away is one of the wealthiest bazars: JHAVERI BAZAR or the Jewellers Market. In the tiny cubbyhole, stamp-sized shops is available some of the most exquisite diamond and gold jewellery. All the big jewellery stores have their main branches in Jhaveri-Bazar. Around the corner is the silver market.

Nobody can visit Mumbai and skip the CHOR-BAZAR. The market, nick named thieve's market, is not really one, but is a second-hand market. It is a good place to pick up antique replicas and hunt for other exotica. Furniture, old chandeliers, gramophones, brass curios abound in these shops. You may get lucky if you may find a few plates from your broken Royal Doulton set. Two streets away is the leather market.

Leaving the South Mumbai area, and heading north to the suburbs into the Bandra and Juhu areas is the LINKING ROAD — a shopping belt. Linking Road is suburban Mumbai's answer to Colaba Causeway, Flora Fountain and Fashion Street rolled into one. The road is so popular that most large shops located in South Bombay have branches on this road.

If walking on foot and exploring the best bargains is not your cup of tea you do have another way out to arcades or malls. Yes, Mumbai does have them and most are air-conditioned to keep you comfortable. Most are found in the 5-star hotels. One of the best arcades is located at the Oberoi Towers at Nariman Point.

The TAJ MAHAL HOTEL also has some nice boutiques. Burlingtons is one. Malabar is a fabric shop with some unusual fabrics. Joy Shoes, an exclusive shoe store, is located in this hotel.

Another arcade well worth visiting is at the WORLD TRADE CENTRE. Amidst the boutiques are state emporia. Do not get misled by that term for some of them have fascinating handicrafts. Punjab, Kashmir, U.P., MP are well represented here. Trimurti handicrafts shops is one of the few shops in Mumbai to have the local fare, such as Himroo shawls and exotic Paithani saris.

There are some shops that are a must on any shopper's list, and these include Shyam Ahuja and Chimanlal's. Both these shops are one of a kind. The Duree king Shyam Ahuja's warehouse shop located at Worli has furnishings for the whole house. This exclusive shop has branches in Juhu and now at the Oberoi also. Chimanlal's, the stationery store, located on D.N. Road, has ethnic stationery, giftwrappers, and bags, made of coarse, handmade paper.

The Playing Fields of Mumbai

Who says there are no sports facilities in Mumbai? Agreed there are more high rises than 'maidans' and more people than place, but the sporting spirit the Bombayite has makes him find the time and space to exercise. Do not forget the city produced Sunil Gavaskar, Ajit Wadekar, Michael Fereira and Anita Sood to name a few.

Congested Mumbai offers practically all kinds of sports - from Tennis, squash and swimming to Angling, wind-surfing, sailing and horse riding. Your hotel reception or tourist office will provide you all the information if you have the time to play.

PUNE

Visitors to Mumbai, if they can find time, should not miss Pune — only 170 km. away. It is accessible by road, rail and train. One of India's better known trains — the DECCAN QUEEN — takes you to Pune in four hours. The British called it Poona, but the Maharashtra Government has restored to it its original Marathi name, Pune.

Pune, once the capital of the Maratha empire and childhood home of Shivaji, was captured by the British in 1818 and they decided to develop it on the lines of an archetypal army town. Over the decades, it shaped into a beautiful town with its usual cantonment, broad and uncluttered roads - very different from the old Pune town. India's NATIONAL DEFENCE ACADEMY is located near Pune at a place called KHADAKVASLA.

During the British Raj, Pune became the centre of many Hindu reform movements and during the heyday of Bal Gangadhar Tilak and G.K. Gokhale, the two maralte references it was the epicentre of Indian independence movement.

Rapid industrialisation is changing the face of Pune. Among the places of interest here are the

Aga Khan Palace

AGA KHAN PALACE where Mahatma Gandhi and his wife Kasturba were detained by the British before India became independent. Kasturba died in this Palace during detention and a memorial has been built in her honour. RAJA KELKAR MUSEUM, a private one-man museum with 36 sections, is well worth a visit.

Today, Pune has been brought on the international tourist map by the disciples of Bhagwan Shri Rajneesh. RAJNEESH ASHRAM is the sole reason for a large population of Westerners in this city. The Ashram is in KOREGAON PARK, a spacious suburb of Pune. At any one time, there are three to four thousand of his followers from overseas in the town.

OTHER PLACES OF INTEREST

It was the hill fort of TORNA (Prachandgad as it was known then) that was Shivaji's first major conquest. This hill fort is located about 35 km. northwest of BHOR. On capturing it, Shivaji repaired the fort and made it his base for the early years of his campaigns. But, realising that Torna was vulnerable as it had a large and open summit, Shivaji abandoned it for RAIGAD.

Raigad - located in the district of the same name - was the ancient capital of Shivaji. It can be approached from PACHAD, a sleepy village that lies near the base of the mountain. Raigad got its name from the mountain Rairi and in ancient times it was so inaccessible that it was called the Gibraltar of the East by the early Europeans. It was at Raigad that Shivaji was coronated amidst great pomp and splendour in 1674.

Prominent among other hill forts are PURANDAR one of the strongest of the hill forts, and PANHALA. Legend has it that Panhala was the residence of Sage Prashara. Pretty close to KOLHAPUR, it is situated about 273 feet above sea level; the hill-stop is pleasantly broken by cliffs and pools with the result that Panhala is also a popular hill station for vacationers.

A few of the other forts are remembered for different reasons. PRATAPGAD has the honour of being an authentic Maratha fort, practically untouched by other hands. VISHALGAD was one of the grandest and most coveted of hill forts, crowning as it did the Gajapur hill, about 112 km. from Kolhapur. SAJJANGAD is remembered on account of its being hallowed by the hands of Ramadas Swami, the spiritual guru of Shivaji. And the fort of AHMEDNAGAR has been praised by experts for its well planned layout.

Apart from the forts of the Deccan, there are many forts in Maharashtra's Konkan region.'Konkan' is the region between the Western Ghats on the east and the Arabian Sea on the west. Of these, are some sea forts built by the Bijapur kings and later captured by Shivaji.

One of the most important of the sea forts is BASSEIN, located about 55 kms from Bombay. Built by Bahadur Shah, Sultan of Gujarat, it was initially one of a chain of forts intended to guard the coast against the

Portuguese. The Portuguese captured the fort and remodelled it, building a citadel inside. In course of time, Bassein became a flourishing shipbuilding centre and the famous Bassein stone was very much in demand.

SINDHUDURG, which is located on a low island, a short distance out in the sea, was Shivaji's capital on the coast. The 18-acre enclosure, once full of buildings, is now empty. This fort is a popular tourist attraction, not only on account of its location, but also because of a statue of Shivaji found there. Slightly different from the rest, the blackstone image shows Shivaji with a slightly rotund face sporting a sailor's cap.

In the Raigad district there is the famous FORT OF JANJIRA, undoubtedly one of the most impregnable forts on the western coast. Close by on the mainland is MURUD, the former capital of Janjira state. Situated about 165 kms from Bombay, its nearest railhead is PANVEL. Yet another important fort in this area is ALIBAUG which is situated on a small hill in the sea.

A hilltop fortress par excellence is DAULATABAD. Located between AURANGABAD and ELLORA, Daulatabad, the impregnable fort has had a chequered history. It was plundered many times in the course of the 13th century. It was made the second capital of the Delhi Sultanate.

With the passing of time, the rise and fall of dynasties and the inevitable flux of political fortunes, the forts began to gradually lose their earlier grandeur and significance.

AJANTA-ELLORA — Maharashtra's Timeless Art

The "Black" Princess stands frozen in a timeless moment on the wall of cave No.17 at Ajanta. Attended by her *sakhis*, with flowers strewn on the floor of her inner apartment, she is lost in contemplation of her own image in a golden mirror.

Despite the ravages of time, there is no mistaking the absolute mastery of the unknown artists who created these stunning images for their royal patrons, of the Vakataka dynasty, in the 5th century A.D. These paintings were executed when the ancient Indian civilisation was at its zenith. Nothing comparable from this glorious era survives. The wall paintings have, therefore, been rightly included in the *World Heritage List of Monuments*.

They illustrate the major events from the life of Buddha and tales from the *Jatakas* — a large collection of stories about the previous incarnations of Buddha, both animal and human.

The paintings are valuable because they bring to life what works like the Jatakas and the poems of Kalidasa describe in words - the gem-set jewellery, rich furniture, imposing architecture, natural scenery and fleeting expressions on the faces.

Kailasa Temple, Ellora

The story of how the 30 caves at Ajanta were discovered is equally fascinating. Early in the 19th century, a party of British officers, scrambling over the thickly wooded slopes of the Sahyadri hills, accidentally stumbled on to this treasure-trove. Rescued from a long period of obscurity (which no doubt helped preserve the wall paintings for the modern generation), Ajanta is today an important landmark on the tourist map of the world. Aurangabad, the city founded by the Mughal Emperor Aurangzeb as his viceregal capital in the Deccan, serves as the base to explore Ajanta.

AURANGABAD

Aurangabad itself has a number of monuments: the BIBI KA MAQBARA, the tomb of Begum Rabia Durani, Aurangzeb's wife, the PAN CHAKKI, an intricate 17th Century water-mill by which the Mughals using the concept of the Persian water-wheel, managed to channelise water from a spring on a hill some distance away and generated energy to turn large grinding stones; and the cluster of caves in the hills just outside the city.

DAULATABAD

Excursions from Aurangabad include Daulatabad, an old Hindu fortress that was taken over by the Muslims. It became the second capital of the Delhi Sultanate in the 14th century. A few kilometres away is KHULDABAD, the austere, plastered masonry tomb of Aurangzeb. In stark contrast to monuments like the Taj Mahal, the tomb was built according to the wishes of the emperor, who directed in his will that it should be as simple as possible.

Also accessible from Aurangabad (30 kms) are the cave temples of ELLORA. In all there are 34 caves - 16 Hindu, 13 Buddhist and five of the Jain faith.

The KAILASA TEMPLE, named after Siva's celestial mountain stronghold, is undoubtedly one of the greatest glories of Indian architecture. It is the very antithesis of the cave temple. Carved out by master craftsmen during the reigns of the Rashtrakuta king, Krishna, the

The Kailasa Temple

whole temple was cut out of the hill from the top downward to the base. The entire work progressed exactly as the plan visualized by the architect without paper and quill! The Rashtrakutas were fully aware of the stupendity of their artistic achievement because the beauty of the KAILASANATHA TEMPLE is recorded on a later Rashtrakuta copper plate grant. This records an imaginary conversation of celestials, who are shown to have paused here in their journeys through the clouds.

Besides Ajanta and Ellora, Maharashtra has many other beautiful cave sculptures to offer, such as PITALKHORA, BEDSA, KARLA, BHAJA and PANDAVLENI. The Elephanta Island, just off Bombay, is famous for four rock-cut cave temples, which are dedicated to Shiva. The Kanheri caves are located within the KRISHNAGIRI UPAVAN NATIONAL PARK, about 42 km. from Mumbai. These are a series of 109 Buddhist caves lining the side of a rocky ravine.

Those curvaceous craggy ranges that spine along the coast of Maharashtra, the Western Ghats, are the home of several little known but charming hill stations. In fact, they almost belong to the colonial era, when people travelled up to these stations to escape the heat of the plains. Many of them still retain some of that old world charm and would make an ideal holiday even if it be only the weekend.

MATHERAN

The nearest of these hill stations from Bombay is Matheran. You can catch any Pune-bound train from Victoria Terminus which will take you up to NERAL, in about two hours. From there you travel uphill in a delightful little toy train. Take in the panoramic view of the plains below as the train chugs uphill. It makes several stops en route, where the local tribals will sell you forest fruits such as *jambouls* and *karvandas*.

This is the only hill station in the country which is out of bounds for vehicular traffic throughout the year. Matheran market is where you could pick up some good bargains, especially cane and leather goods made by the tribals.

KHANDALA AND LONAVALA

Sitting atop the Western Ghats on the Bombay-Pune highway are the twin resorts of Khandala and Lonavala. By train, the tracks snake in and out of several tunnels, offering you fleeting glimpses of the gaunt hills and their valleys.

Suddenly you sense a freshness in the air and feel a levelling of the tracks on which the train has been travelling and you realise that you have reached Khandala. By road, you would take the Borghat road at KHOPOLI. The ghat is indeed steep, but the climb faster and shorter and it is only an 8 km. distance before you reach the top.

Khandala is especially beautiful during the monsoons; clouds literally envelope the entire town giving you the ethereal feeling of walking on them. Look out onto the hills and you will notice a thousand waterfalls that gush from its sides and flow into the ravines below. Do not miss the sun going down over the hills at SUNSET POINT.

Further up the road, you come to Lonavala. Over the last decade this town has developed rapidly and it is here that both the rich and the

A frieze—Karla Caves

powerful have their farm-houses and holiday villas. Several of these fancy structures are out of place with the rural surroundings. While at Lonavala, do visit the VALVAN and the BUSHY DAMS. They are usually full during the monsoons and attract hordes of tourists.

On the Pune road, about 12 km. from Lonavala, are the KARLA CAVES. Belonging to the 2nd century B.C, they bear a striking resemblance to those at Ellora. The Stupa inside the cave and the rock sculptures at the entrance are an eloquent testimony to the skill the artisans of that time.

Today Karla moves out of its ancient past to provide sport and adventure to tourists. Maharashtra Tourism provides courses in rock and fort climbing here.

PANCHGANI AND MAHABALESHWAR

Among the hill resorts of the state, Panchgani and Mahabaleshwar are the most frequented because several travel agencies, as well as the government tourist department, offer package tours to these places. Tucked away in the Satara district, they are best approached from Pune, Panchgani, at a lower height derives its name from the five hills that surround it. This is an ideal base for some good trekking.

Mahabaleshwar was the erstwhile summer capital of the old Bombay Presidency, which despite the increasing crowds that come there, still retains its quintessential charm. Numerous majestic mansions built during the days of the British, still stand as monuments of the Raj.

Shopping at Mahabaleshwar

At both Panchgani and Mahabaleshwar, Maharashtra Tourism has accommodation that caters to the needs of all categories of tourists.

AMBOLI

Further down the coast, Amboli, on the southern ranges of the Western Ghats, is a quiet and pleasant hill resort. The SEA VIEW POINT offers you a panoramic view of a good part of the Konkan coast. Facilities are scarce here, but you can enjoy a restful holiday away from the crowds.

Maharashtra has a long tradition of tolerance and symbolc interaction with different religious faiths.

To the south lies the basin of Godavari and the territory from NASHIK to NANDED which is regarded as sacred. A majority of saints and poets were born here. TRIMBAKESHWAR, the place from where the Godavari originates, has a sanctity of its own. Nanded is a pilgrim point for the Sikhs as it has a *samadhi* of Guru Gobind Singh.

Besides HAJI ALI, HAJI MATANG, churches of Bassein and Bombay, synagogues of PEN and ALIBAUG, Jain and Buddhist temples, Maharashtra alone has five of the twelve jyotirlingas, located at CHRISNESHWAR near Ellora, AUNDH NAGNATH in Parbhani, PARLI VAIJNATH in Beed, TRIMBAKESHWAR in Nashik and BHIMASHANKARA in Pune.

Maharashtra imbibed the cultural and religious influences of the northern Aryans and southern Dravidians. Thus, both Vaishnavism and Shaivism, flourished in the region.

Shaivism extened its ambit to the worship of Ganesha, son of Shiva. In fact the elephant-headed god is one of the most popular deities worshipped by the people here.

NASIK

Nashik has 2000 temples, both big and small. The Simhastha fair is held once in twelve years at Nasik and thousands of devotees from all over India come here to take a dip in the sacred waters of the Godavari.

NANDED

Nanded, an important Sikh pilgrim centre, is about 663 km from Mumbai and 272 km from Aurangabad. Guru Gobind Singh, the 10th and the last of the Sikh Gurus, lived here during the last days of his life. His ashes are buried at the famous SACH KHAND SHRI HUZUR SAHIB GURUDWARA, on the banks of the river Godavari.

SHIRDI

296 km from Mumbai, Shirdi has attracted pilgrims from different faiths who come to worship the mystic saint Sai Baba. The Shirdi Sai Baba is said to have attained *samadhi* on Dussehra day in 1918. Fairs are held regularly at Shirdi on Ram Navami, Guru Purnima and Dussehra.

SEASIDE EXCURSIONS

Maharashtra has a 720 km long coastline, bordering waters that are relatively safe during high tide. The beaches, a little out of the city limits, are quiet, clean and unspoil.

Ganpatipule

Located off the Mumbai-Goa Highway, and approximately 375 km. from Bombay, is Ganpatipule, one of the most beautiful beaches on the coast of Maharashtra. At Ganpathipule, clean silver sands and a gentle sea bathe the roots of tall swaying palms. Besides being a seaside resort, Ganpatipule is also a pilgrim centre where people come to worship at the famous Lord Ganesh temple.

Murud-Janjira

The capital of the former state of Janjira, Murud-Janjira is 216 km from Mumbai. The sea here is relatively placid and safe for swimmers. About a kilometre across the waters is the famous 17th century sea fort of Janjira.

Kihim
Situated 136 km from Mumbai and 12 km. from Alibaug is the beautiful beach of Kihim. Kihim, like Alibaug can be reached by sea - a 90-minute boat ride from the Gateway.

Nagaon
Nagaon, in Raigad district and not far from Alibaug and Kihim, is another beautiful and unspoilt beach resort.

WILDLIFE SANCTUARIES
Maharashtra has a fair share of national parks and wildlife sanctuaries which, thanks to the general awareness about wildlife preservation, are now being cared for and conserved.

Tadoba
This national park has been maintained as a game preserve since 1931. Taboda is 995 km from Mumbai. Nagpur (137 km from Tadoba) is the most convenient base to visit this park.

Karnala
Just 60 km from Mumbai, the Karnala Bird Sanctuary on the Mumbai-Goa road is within easy access from the city. Though essentially a bird sanctuary, antelope and African monkeys are also seen at Karnala.

MUMBAI

GENERAL INFORMATION
Population: 12,570,000 (1991 census)
Altitude: Sea level

Climate

	Temperature	
	Max.	Min.
Summer	33^0c	19^0c
Winter	32^0c	21^0c

Season: Throughout the year.
Clothing: Cottons throughout the year.

HOW TO GET THERE
By Air: Major international airlines touch Mumbai and connect it with the important cities of the world. Indian Airlines and several private airlines connect Mumbai with all parts of India.
By Rail: Regular train services connect Mumbai with all the major cities of India.
By Road: Mumbai is connected by good motorable roads with important tourist centres. It is 163 km. from Pune,
392 km. from Aurangabad,
545 km. from Ahmedabad and
597 km. from Panaji (Goa).
By Ship: There is a daily service by ship between Mumbai and Goa except on Tuesdays. These are suspended during the monsoons

(June to September). A new luxury cruise ship has been launched between Mumbai and Goa - taking only 9 hours each way.

LOCAL TRANSPORT

Luxury taxis (limousines), tourist taxis and good coaches, metered taxis, autorickshaws (which ply only in the suburbs), electric trains and city bus services available.

CONDUCTED TOURS
1. Half-day tour of the city.
2. Half-day tour to Elephanta by boat.
3. Harbour cruise by launch.
4. Full-day tour to the suburbs.
5. Aurangabad-Ajanta-Ellora tour (2 days and 3 nights).
6. Shirdi-Nashik tour (1 day and 1 night).
7. Mandu-Ujjain-Indore tour (3 days and 4 nights) every fortnight during season.

WHERE TO STAY (STD Code: 022)

Deluxe
1. Centaur Juhu Beach Resort
   Phone: 6143040
   Telex: 011 78081THJB
   Fax: 61 16343
2. The Leela Kempinski
   Phone: 8363636
   Telex: 011 79236, KEMP IN
3. The Oberoi Towers
   Phone: 2024343
   Telex: 84153, 82340 OBBY IN
   Fax: 2043282
4. The Oberoi, Nariman Point
   Phone: 2025757
   Telex: 011-84153/4
   Fax: 2043282
5. Taj Mahal Inter Continental
   Phone: 2023366
   Telex: 011-82442/83837 TAJC IN
   Fax: 022-2023366
6. Welcomgroup SeaRock Sheraton
   Phone: 6425454
   Telex: 011-71230
   Fax: 022-6408046
7. Holiday Inn
   Phone: 6204444
   Telex: 011-71266, 71432
   Fax: 6204452
8. President
   Phone: 2150808
   Telex: 11-84135 PRES IN
   Fax: (022)215-1201

First Class
9. Ambassador
   Phone: 2041131
   Telex: 011-2918
   Fax: 2040004
10. Centaur Bombay Airport
    Phone: 6116660
    Telex: 011-71171
    Fax: 91-22-6113535
11. Nataraj
    Phone: 2044161
    Telex: 011-2302
    Fax: 2043864
12. Ramada Inn Palm Grove
    Phone: 6112323
    Telex: 011-71419

Standard
13. Fariyas
    Phone: 2042911
    Telex: 011-3272
    Fax: 287-1441
14. Grand
    Phone: 2613558, 2618211
15. Kamats Plaza
    Phone: 6123390
    Telex: 011-71365
    Fax: 022/612-7564

16. Ritz
    Phone: 220141
    Telex: 011-2520
    Fax: 91-22-2850494
17. Sun-n-Sand
    Phone: 6201811
    Telex: 011-71282
    Fax: 91-22-6202170
18. Hotel Horizon
    Phone: 6148100, 6148217
    Telex: 011-71218 HORZ IN
    Cable: BEACHREST
    Fax: 022-6116715

BUDGET

19. YWCA International Guest House
    Phone: 2020445
20. Bombay Central
    Phone: 3077292

Railway Retiring Rooms
Note: Mumbai has good paying guest accommodation for foreign visitors. *Contact:* Govt. of India Tourist Office, 123, H. Karve Road. *Phone*: 293144

WHAT TO SEE

1. HANGING GARDENS and KAMLA NEHRU PARK on MALABAR HILLS. The former is built over Mumbai's water reservoir. From the Kamla Nehru Park, one can get a panoramic view of picturesque Marine Drive.
2. MANI BHAVAN (Gandhi Memorial), the house where the Father of the Nation stayed on his early visits to the city. The room in which he stayed, is preserved as it was. Scenes of his life in photographs and models are of special interest.
3. PRINCE OF WALES MUSEUM, one of the leading museums of the country.
4. THE GATEWAY OF INDIA, the landmark of Mumbai which was, before the advent of air travel, the only gateway to India. It is built in the Gujarat style of architecture and commemorates the visit of King George and Queen Mary to India in 1911.
5. The QUEEN'S NECKLACE, as the lights on Marine Drive are called a great attraction after sunset.
6. WEAVER'S SERVICE CENTRE. designing, weaving and hand-block printing of fabrics can be seen with permission.

Bombay has many other attractions like the NEHRU PLANETARIUM, NEHRU SCIENCE CENTRE, several gardens and parks, art galleries, TARAPOREVALA AQUARIUM, etc.

EXCURSIONS

1. ELEPHANTA CAVES (9 km). A one hour journey by launch takes you to the cave temples of Elephanta dating back to the 7th century. Dedicated to Shiva, the beauty and power of these sculptures is overpowering.
2. JUHU BEACH (21 km), with rows of beach hotels on the seafront. Other beaches further away and less crowded are VERSOVA, MADH, MARVE and MANORI beaches, MURUD JANJIRA and URAN.
3. KANHERI CAVES (42 km), where there are more than a hundred Buddhist cave temples. The LION SAFARI PARK is in the National Park nearby.

4. There are several lakes around Mumbai like the POWAI and VIHAR LAKES, TULSI, TANSA, VAITARNA. At Powai is Swami Chinmayananda's Sandeepani Sangrahalaya (Ashram).
5. VAJRESHWARI HOT SPRINGS and the MUKTANAND ASHRAM at Ganeshpuri (88 km.).
6. MATHERAN HILL RESORT (105 km) with shady walks, thick wooded areas and a lake.
7. LONAVALA (99 km) and the KARLA CAVES. Lonavala is a hill resort. The Buddhist rock-cut caves at Karla are over 2000 years old. The large Chaitya prayer hall here is considered to be the most perfect of its kind.
8. NASHIK (184 km) on the banks of the River Godavari, is an important place of pilgrimage associated with the Ramayana.
9. SHIRDI (309 km.), associated with the mystic saint Sai Baba, attracts pilgrims of all faiths.
10. BATTIS SHIRALE (371 km). During the festival of Nag Panchami (July-August), hundreds of snakes are fed here.

SHOPPING

Bombay has shops selling handicrafts made in all parts in the country. There are very interesting shopping areas in every part of the city. Readymade western dresses made of Indian fabric are sold at the various boutiques which are located in hotels and in shopping areas. Leather goods like jackets, handbags and shoes are also available as are silver, gold and diamond jewellery, carpets.

FESTIVALS OF SPECIAL LOCAL INTEREST

1. Janmashtami (July-August) celebrates the birth of Lord Krishna. Young men and boys form human pyramids and break pots of curds hung up high between buildings.
2. Coconut Day (August), when the angry monsoon seas are propitiated by devotees throwing coconut into the waters.
3. Ganesh Chaturthi (August-September), when massive figures of Ganesh are worshipped and immersed in the sea on several days following the festival.
4. Mount Mary's Feast (September), celebrated at St Mary's Church, Bandra. There is also a fair held at this time.
5. During Dussehra (September-October) there are group dances by Gujarati women in many auditoria. Also Ramlila celebrations at Chowpathy Beach.
6. Diwali, the festival of lights, when the business community celebrates its New Year and opens new account books.

ENTERTAINMENT

Music, dance and drama programmes are held all over the city every weekend. There are programmes of classical North Indian and South Indian music, all schools of dancing, classical and folk, and dramas in Marathi, Gujarati, Hindi and English. The daily engagement columns, newspaper advertisements and weekly and fortnightly publications provide information about programmes and venues.

Some of the popular theatres/auditoria are the Tata Theatre, Birla Matushri Sabagriha, Patkar Hall, Bharatiya Vidya Bhavan, Tejpal Auditorium, Sophia Bhabha Auditorium, Ravindra Natya Sabhagriha, Shivaji Natya Mandir and Shanmukhananda Hall.

Dramas in various languages are staged regularly at the Tata Theatre, Prithvi Theatre, the Tata Experimental Theatre and at other auditoria in the city.

Mumbai is considered as the Hollywood of India as the largest number of films are made here.

Tourist Plaza every Sunday (November to May). This is a unique festival of fun and entertainment. Tourist Plaza brings together a unique fair of snake charmers, palmists, bangle sellers, jugglers, 'mehendiwallas', tight-rope walkers, musicians-western and Indian, as well as dances - an enjoyable option for spending a Sunday evening.

The Elephanta Festival (Feb 19-21). The festival started in 1989 has become an annual event. The magic of the evening begins with a ferry ride from the majestic Gateway of India to the tiny island of Elephanta. Colourful Koli dancers welcome the visitors. The festival brings together some of the renowned classical musicians and dance for a morning of music and dance till the early hours of the evening. There are unique foodstalls in this 7th century island.

'Esselworld' at Gorai and 'Fantasy World' at Jogeshwari are popular amusement parks for kids and adults alike.

SPORTS

Horse racing is a popular sport on Sundays and public holidays all through the Bombay racing season.

Regular golf, tennis, swimming, yachting, sailing and other tournaments are held regularly. Fishing is available at Powai Lake.

PUNE

GENERAL INFORMATION
Population: 2,440,000 (1991 census)
Altitude: 559 metres (1861 ft)

Climate:

	Temperature		
	Max.	Min.	Rainfall
Summer	38^0c	12^0c	156 mm
Winter	32^0c	12^0c	134 mm

Season: Throughout the year

Clothing:
Summer: cottons
Winter: light woollens.

HOW TO GET THERE
By Air: Indian Airlines flights link Pune with Bangalore, Mumbai, Delhi and Hyderabad. Private Air Taxis too have regular services.
By Rail: Pune is connected by rail with Mumbai, Bangalore, Delhi, Jammu, Kanniyakumari, Madras, Secunderabad, Thiruvananthapuram, Vasco (Goa) and all parts of India.
By Road: Pune is connected by road to western and southern India. It is
163 km. from Mumbai,
120 km. from Mahabaleshwar,
195 km. from Shirdi,
226 km. from Aurangabad,
548 km. from Hyderabad,
493 km. from Goa and
835 km. from Bangalore.
Regular bus services are available to Mumbai, Goa, Aurangabad, Sholapur, Bangalore and Nagpur.

LOCAL TRANSPORT
Tourist taxis, taxis, auto-rickshaws, tongas and bus services.

CONDUCTED TOURS
1. Two half-day tours covering Pune.
2. Tours arranged to Ajanta-Ellora, Goa, Mahabaleshwar Shirdi, Karla-Lonavala etc. on request.

WHERE TO STAY (STD Code: 0212)
STANDARD
1. Blue Diamond
   Phone: 663755
   Telex: 0145-7369 BLUE IN
   Cable: BLUEDIAMOND
   Fax: 0212-666101
2. Aurora Towers
   Phone: 660130
   Telex: 0145-7547 MONA IN
   Cable: TOWERS
   Fax: 0212-664488
3. Executive Ashok
   Phone: 57391, 50463
   Telex: 0145-565 HEAP IN
   Cable: EXECOTEL
4. Hotel Regency
   Phone: 669411
   Telex: 0145-7609 HOTR IN
   Cable: REGENCY
5. Hotel Sagar Plaza
   Phone: 661880
   Telex: 0145-7645 SAGR IN
   Cable: STAYWITHUS

BUDGET
6. Hotel Woodland Plaza
   Phone: 661111
   Telex: 0145-4545 SAGR IN
   Cable: WOOD IN
   Fax: 660909
7. Hotel Gulmohar Plaza
   Phone: 661773
   Cable: GULMOHR
8. Dreamland
   Phone: 662121
9. Hotel Amir
   Phone: 661840
   Telex: 1045-7292
10. Hotel Ranjit
    Phone: 345012

WHAT TO SEE

1. RAJA KELKAR MUSEUM, an extraordinary collection of a venerable old gentleman, Dinkar Kelkar, who is often seen talking to visitors to the museum. It has an outstanding collection of musical instruments, nutcrackers, locks, lamps and other artifacts of the Mughal and Maratha periods, as also part of a palace of the courtesan of a ruler reconverted into a Museum.
2. KASTURBA SAMADHI in the Aga Khan's Palace. A marble memorial to Kasturba, wife of Mahatma Gandhi, who died when she and Mahatma Gandhi were imprisoned by the British Government here.
3. PARVATI HILL. 108 steps lead to this historical temple from where there is a panoramic view of the city.
4. SHANWARWADA. Once the palace of the Peshwa rulers - now only the fortified walls remain.
5. SHINDE'S CHHATRI, a memorial to Mahadaji Shinde.
6. BHANDARKAR ORIENTAL RESEARCH INSTITUTE which has a museum displaying 20,000 manuscripts.

EXCURSIONS

1. SINHAGAD FORT (25 km). Site of one of Shivaji's most daring battles.
2. SHIVNERI FORT (93 km), birthplace of Shivaji.
3. KARLA (40 km) and BHAJA CAVES (42 km). Karla has the largest Buddhist Chaitya cave. It is over 2000 years old.
4. LONAVALA, a charming hill resort, 10 km. from Karla.
5. MAHABALESHWAR (120 km), hill resort. It has the highest altitude (1350 metres) in the western mountain ranges.
6. MATHERAN (126 km), a scenically beautiful hill resort, popular with trekkers.
7. PRATAPGARH FORT (137 km), one of the most invincible of Shivaji's forts.
8. MUMBAI (163 km), India's commercial capital.
9. SHIRDI (195 km), associated with the saint, Sai Baba.
10. NASHIK (202 km), a holy city associated with the life of Rama, hero of the epic, Ramayana. Scenes of pilgrims worshipping knee-deep in the Godavari are a moving sight.
11. BATTIS SHIRALA (224 km). Here hundreds of snakes can be seen during the Nag Panchami festival.
12. AURANGABAD (226 km), from where the magnificent Ajanta and Ellora caves can be visited.

SHOPPING

Pure silk and cottons sari, handlooms, jewellery, metalware and handicrafts.

FESTIVALS OF SPECIAL LOCAL INTEREST

1. Shiv Jayanti (April-May), the birth anniversary of Chatrapati Shivaji. A big fair

is held and colourful processions taken out.
2. Nag Panchami (July-August) dedicated to the great cobra - Ananta. Snake charmers with snakes can be seen in plenty.
3. Ganesh Chaturthi (August-September). Huge figures of the god, Ganesh, are taken out in procession and immersed in rivers or the sea.

SPORTS/YOGA
1. Horse Racing. Pune has a fine turf and races are held from July to October.
2. Gliding at the Gliderdrome (12 km).
3. Yoga Classes at the Ramamani Iyengar Memorial Yoga Institute (Pune) and the Kaivalyadham Yoga Institute, Lonavala (64 km).

AJANTA & ELLORA (AURANGABAD)

GENERAL INFORMATION
Population: 480,000 (1991 census)
Altitude: 581 metres (1935 ft)

Climate:

	Temperature		
	Max.	Min.	Rainfall
Summer	40^0c	14^0c	165 mm
Winter	32^0c	14^0c	103 mm

Season: Throughout the year. During months of April and May, the days are very hot.
Clothing:
Summer: light cottons
Winter: light woollens.

HOW TO GET THERE
By Air: The nearest airport for Ajanta-Ellora is Aurangabad which is 106 km. from Ajanta and 29 km. from Ellora. Aurangabad is linked by Indian Airlines flights to Ahmedabad, Bombay, Delhi, Hyderabad, Jaipur, Udaipur, etc.
By Rail: Aurangabad is on the Manmad-Secunderabad metre guage line. Jalgaon is the nearest rail head for the Ajanta Caves (50 km.). Manmad and Jalgaon are linked with Bombay, Calcutta, Madras, etc.
By Road: Aurangabad is connected by road to many places. It is
136 km. from Shirdi
221 km. from Nashik
229 km. from Pune
389 km. from Mandu
392 km. from Mumbai
539 km. from Hyderabad
There are regular bus services to Ajanta, Ellora, Bijapur, Mumbai, Hyderabad, Indore, Nashik, Pune, Shirdi.

LOCAL TRANSPORT
Tourist taxis, metered taxis, coaches, autorickshaws, tongas (horse-carriages) and city bus services.

CONDUCTED TOURS
1. Full-day tour covering the Ellora Caves, Daulatabad Fort, Girishneshwar Temple, Aurangzeb's Tomb and Aurangabad.
2. Full-day tour to the Ajanta Caves.

WHERE TO STAY (STD Code: 02432)

DELUXE
1. Welcomgroup Rama International
   Phone: 82241-82340
   Bombay contact: 6225454
   Cable: WELCOTEL
2. Taj Residency
   Phone: 20411/20123
   Bombay contact: 202-3366
3. Ajanta Ambassador
   Phone: 82211-82215
   Bombay contact: 2041131

STANDARD
4. Aurangabad Ashok
   Phone: 24520-29
5. Quality Inn Vedant
   Phone: 26785, 25844

BUDGET
6. Youth Hostel
   Phone: 23801

WHAT TO SEE

Aurangabad
1. PANCHAKKI, an ancient water-mill. There are cool underground rooms which served as a hostel for students in the hot summer. Also the shrine of a saint, Baba Shah Musafir.
2. BIBI-KA-MAQBARA, the mausoleum of Rabia Daurani, wife of Aurangzeb, patterned on the Taj at Agra.

Ajanta (106 km.)
1. The AJANTA CAVES, 30 in number, are magnificent rock-cut Buddhist cave temples dating from the 2nd century B.C. to the 7th century A.D. the wall paintings, pulsating with life, recount the life of the Buddha, his previous lives, as also the court life of kings and the commoners. Although there are many sculptures, Ajanta is noted for its paintings.

Ellora
The ELLORA CAVES are rock-cut temples of three religions, Hinduism, Buddhism and Jainism. Of the 34 caves, the most remarkable is the magnificent KAILASA TEMPLE carved out of a mountain-side, out of a single rock - an engineering marvel.

EXCURSIONS

1. DAULATABAD FORT (13 km. en route to Ellora from Aurangabad). Built by the Yadava kings as Deogiri, it was renamed Daulatabad by the Tughlaq king who moved his capital here. It was considered an impregnable fort.
2. JAIKWADI PROJECT (60 km.), is 4 km. from the ancient city of Paithan. The area around the dam is being developed into a tourist complex with beautiful fountains playing at night. (Best season for bird watching here is October to March.) At Paithan visitors can see the weaving of the famous Paithani silk and gold saris.
3. SHIRDI (136 km.), where Sai Baba spent his life as a mystic saint, attracting pilgrims of all faiths.

SHOPPING
Bidri art objects (zinc and copper alloy) with silver inlay. Himroo shawls with designs taken from Ajanta paintings.

FESTIVALS OF SPECIAL LOCAL INTEREST
1. Paithan Fair (March-April). Pilgrims gather on the banks of the Godavari to pay homage to saint Eknath. The fair lasts 10 days.
2. Shivaji Jayanti (May), when colourful processions preceded by dancers, celebrate the birth anniversary of Shivaji.
3. Buddha Jayanti (May) celebrated with processions and floats at Aurangabad.
4. Pola (August), a festival when cattle are decorated and displayed, as thanksgiving for their help to the farmer.
5. Ganpati Festival (Aug-Sept.). Huge figures of Ganesh are installed and worshipped for 10 days.
6. Khuldabad Urs when, for five days, Muslims gather at the tomb of the saint of Khuldabad.

Chapter 18

GOA
India's Tourist Haven

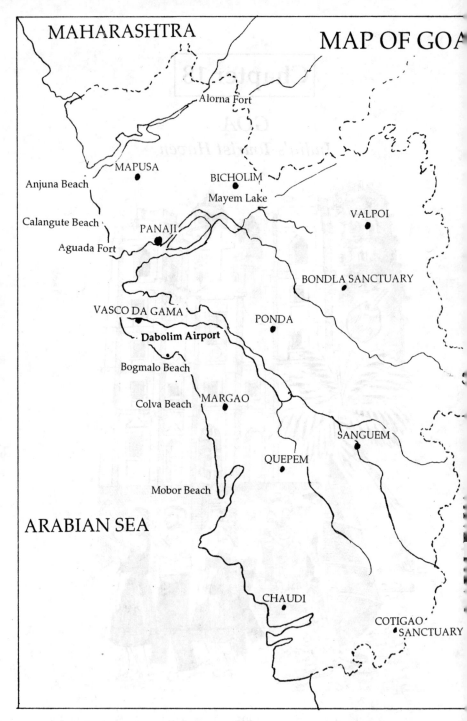

The tiny 25th State of India, Goa is the country's tourist haven attracting over 1.2 million visitors every year — almost equal to the population of the State which is 1.2 million. Nestling between Karnataka and Maharashtra and fringed by the Arabian Sea on the west, Goa has an area of 3813 sq. km. It is justifiably famous for its dazzling 105-km. sweep of palm-fringed coastline on the Arabian Sea. Unspoiled and rustic, Goa's fertile green palms are covered with cashew, mango and jackfruit groves. The countryside is criss-crossed by the Mandovi and Zuari rivers from which rise forested hills to the mountain ranges of the Western Ghats. Goa was under Portuguese rule for over 450 years and was liberated by the Indian Army in 1961. It has a Latin atmosphere. It combines old Portuguese architecture with a Portuguese flavour to the lifestyle of its people which Goa has managed to retain despite 35 years of independence. Alongwith Goa, four other small Portuguese enclaves were liberated - Daman and Diu, and Dadra and Nagar Haveli in the Gujarat region.

Goa supplies the best of everything, making it tops for pure beach enjoyment. There are good hotels, good food, good beaches and good water and sports. But for someone who gets itchy feet after a few hours lolling in the sun, the Portuguese sights of Goa do not compare with the Hindu glories on the east coast of Tamil Nadu. Here, the Coromandal Coast just south of Madras has much less of resort atmosphere, but a quality hotel and fascinating nearby sights. An American Guide Book on India has described it as "The Hindu Catholic Gold Coast."

Goa today, is a surprising place. In the midst of India, you suddenly come upon the Mediterranean. Charming little towns have been built around the whitewashed churches. There are sunny plazas splashed with bougainvillea. Roads bear names like Rua del Conda, Torres Nova and Avenida Sagrado Coracao del Jesus. Each afternoon, almost for four hours siesta is observed when practically everything comes to a halt.

The blending of two cultures — Portuguese and Indian—is apparent everywhere. You find little wayside crosses at every turn erected by Christian Goans — just as their Hindu forefathers built little temples wherever they moved. The figures of saints carved into the altars of Goan cathedrals are Christian in subject, but their faces and expressions are wholly Indian. The girl in the church may be wearing a black lace mantilla and carrying a fan, but the language of the Mass is pure Konkani. The flowers that she offers at the wayside cross are the perfumed mogrins — the same that are offered to Hindu gods in the neighbouring temples. The two communities live in perfect harmony with each other. On the issue of official language of the State, both Hindu and Christian Goans opted for Konkani in preference to Marathi, which is now one of the 17 national languages enshrined in the Constitution of India.

Ensconced on the slopes of the Western Ghats (Sahyadri ranges), Goa is bounded on the north by Sindhudurg district of Maharashtra, on the east by Belgaum, on the South by the Karwar district of Karnataka, and on the west by the Arabian Sea. It is interspersed with extensive paddy fields and has fine a network of waterways. Its rivers, the Tiracol, Chapora, Mandovi, Zuari, Sal and the Talpona, are navigable throughout the year. They have their origin in the Sahyadri ranges and flow westward into the Arabian Sea, 60 km. away, the rivers break the long coastline covering a length of 105 km. into enchanting estuaries and bays which mark off idyllic palm-fringed beaches like Arambol, Vagator, Anjuna, Baga and Calangute in the north and Colva, Betul and Palolem in the South.

HISTORY

Goa has a long history going back to the 3rd century B.C. when it was part of the Mauryan empire. Later, it was ruled by the Satavahanas of Kolhapur at the beginning of the Christian era and then passed on to the Chalukyas of Badami who controlled it from A.D. 580 to 750. During the next few centuries, it was ruled successively by the Shilharas, the Kadambas and the Chalukyas of Kalyani. Goa fell to the Muslims for the first time in 1312, but they were forced out by Harihara I of Vijayanagar in 1370. Goa was under the rule of Vijayanagar kings for 100 years. During this period, the Vijayanagar rulers imported Arabian horses through the harbours of Goa to strengthen their cavalry. Subsequently, Goa was taken over by the Muslim Bahmani Sultans of Gulbarga and later by the Adil Shahis of Bijapur. They made GOA VELHA their second capital. The present Secretariat building in PANAJI is the former Palace of Adil Shah. Later, it was occupied by the Portuguese Viceroys as their residence.

Goa had been the envy of kings and emperors; Portuguese, bankers and merchants Arabs, Venetians, Jews among others; and a meeting place for all kinds of people: adventurous travel writers saints and none-too-few sinners. A Brazilian adventurer came to Goa when she was 18 in 1700 disguised as a man—Baltazar de Couto Cardozo—and fought for the Portuguese against the Marathas. She was found out when she was seriously wounded in combat. And she married the captain of the Fort who made the astounding discovery and fell head over heels in love with her.

The Portuguese came to Goa in 1510 under the command of Alfanso de Albuquerque. Initially, they had tried to find a foothold on the Malabar Coast. But, they faced stiff opposition from the Turks who controlled the sea lanes in the Arabian Sea. Goa proved to be an ideal base for the seafaring Portuguese to carry on their trade in spices and started expanding their foothold. It reached its present size in the 18th century as a result of more annexations — first in 1763 and later in 1788.

It was only in 1961 that the Portuguese were ejected from Goa in a bloodless operation by the Indian Army.

Most visitors come to Goa in the winter months—October-March. Although the rainy season is not popular with Western visitors, it has its charm for the Indians. During monsoons (June to September), visit Goa, if you are a nature-lover. Goa then is at its greenest, all hues of it, a grand carpet running from hill tops to rice fields. The rivers are then full and brimming with fish. If you are lucky, you might even sight an otter backstroking or leap-frogging as the occasion requires, in pursuit of mackerels heading from the sea to their traditional spawning grounds on the silted banks of the rivers.

From August to November is the time of harvest festivals, of Lord Ganesha (the Great Provider), and of 'Novidade' (Portuguese for new crop). In late August/early September there will be an *Adao* at TALEIGAO; where the villagers will recall the deal they made with the Portuguese 500 years ago.

There will be a Sangod at Sinquerim, to mark the most important cyclic life of the event in the fishing community. Every year at the beginning of the south-west monsoon, a sand bar is formed across the mouth of the Mandovi and the river is closed for navigation. The Sangod celebrates its reopening. A priest draped in bright vestments is taken on a raft to the sand bar and he cuts it open with a centuries-old golden sword, amid hymns, music and fireworks

There will be a Bonderam at the island of Divar. Bonder, from Bandeira (Portuguese for flag) is a new version of the tribal rituals to reconnoitre village boundaries. Elsewhere, women will dance the Fugadi, the men will play the flute and the ghumat and children will feast at tea time on sweets made of raw sugar, tender coconut and parched rice.

Anytime between mid-February or early March, there will be Carnival, a popular festival. And Holi which in Goa is known as *Shigmo*. *Sugrishimak* is Sanskrit for rainbow, and that is what Shigmo is: a festival of colour. And also of friendship and bonhomie. Once it was a peacetime frolic of professional warriors.

March to May is the time for cashew and mango, jackfruit and all the bounty of summer. It is a time for happy family reunions, when Goan emigrants from all over, Bombay, Africa, the Arabian Gulf, Europe, Canada, return to their primal village. Literally, a time for jubilations and celebrations.

ACCOMMODATION AND TRANSPORT

An interesting aspect of Goa is the availability of a wide range of accommodation to suit every budget. On the top end are some of the finest 5-star deluxe hotels like the Taj's Fort Aguada Beach Resort, Goa Renaissance and Leela Beach. There are several small hotels and motels run by the Goa Tourism Development Corporation offering excellent value for money.

If you happen to be a budget traveller, Goa Tourist Office at PANAJI, the capital, is your best bet to recommend you accommodation most suitable for your requirements.

Although Goa looks like a small dot on the map of India, a visitor has to cover long distances if he wants to see the real Goa and have a feel for it. Taxis are freely available for day hire on a charge which is one of the lowest in the world. Hiring a motorcycle can be far more exhilarating and the rates may be less than US $ 5 for the whole day.

Your hotel can help you find a good motorcycle. But make sure you wear a helmet as the Police in Goa has made wearing of helmets compulsory for all drivers.

HOW TO GET TO GOA

By far the most enjoyable way of reaching Goa is by a steamer from Bombay which operates daily except on Tuesdays during October to May. During monsoons, it does not ply.

The steamer is full of jubilant families returning home to Goa. Till late into the night, the decks echo the strumming of guitars and the tapping of feet. Since winter of 1994, a new luxury cruise ship operates regularly between Bombay and Goa and takes only seven hours each ways.

For people opting for a speedier mode of transport, Indian Airlines has daily flights from Delhi as well as Bombay. Some private airlines also connect Goa with Delhi and Bombay daily. Goa is also connected by bus-services and trains.

The Goans are basically a simple and God-fearing people, happiest when they are celebrating the feast of their saints, attending marriages, singing their Mandos or devouring vast quantities of their favourite dish, *Vindaloo* with fiery *Tequila*-like Feni — a speciality drink of Goa.

HINDU TEMPLES WITH PORTUGUESE NAMES

The temples of Goa are like temples nowhere else in India. Once in the 16th century, Hindu temples stood prominently by the rivers. Razed by the fanatical Portuguese, the temples were moved to the interior where they now lie hidden among the paddy fields and dark area forests.

Visit the temples of MUNGESH and SHANTI DURGA. The buildings bear the influence of cathedral culture, which crystallised in their dome-shaped shikharas and octagonal chandeliers. Below these chandeliers, sit the shaven-headed priests praying to their deity. Even the names of the temples reflect the curious blending of the Orient and the Occident. In Portuguese manner, these temples are often called 'Manguexi' or 'Xanta Durga'.

FESTIVALS

The most famous celebration of Goa is the EXPOSITION OF SAINT FRANCIS XAVIER'S RELICS. It generally takes place once every ten years. Thousands come to India to participate in the Exposition. The last one was held in 1995.

Carnival
It is celebrated in true Latin style for three days before Lent each year, with much music, dancing and masquerading in the streets.

Reis Magos—The Three Kings
Celebrated on January 6 to commemorate the visit of the Three Wise Men to infant Christ.

Diwali
The Hindu festival of lights falls in October or November depending on the lunar calendar.

Apart from these, there are numerous colourful ZATRAS (temple festivals) and feasts dedicated to Christian saints throughout the year.

Carnival dance

THE TAVERNA SPIRIT OF GOA

A unique institution of Goa is its many taverna. You may wander through a sleepy village deep in Goa or visit a bustling town or move to a secluded beach, you are sure to find a taverna or a bar. It may be a thatched hut with a few benches, tables and a refrigerator. Larger towns may have taverna with gleaming fittings and fancy names. The traditional taverna, small but friendly, retains a certain rustic charm. But, all these bars, big and small, breathe the atmosphere of relaxation that pervades Goa. These tavernas give you an opportunity to meet a cross-section of the people.

There are, of course, the newer beach bars, where you can cool off after a swim or an afternoon in the sun. Toss down a sundowner and watch as the sea and sky are ignited by the setting sun, turning the horizon into a vivid palette of colours. Here you will also encounter members of Goa's large floating population of expatriates, all on an extended sojourn in this idyllic land.

Traditionally, Goa has always had a fairly open policy on liquor compared to the rest of the country. The local produce seems to provide ample justification going by the quality. Goan wines going by its quality, specially the port, are particularly good and inexpensive. The tradition of brewing country liquor has also been well nourished. The most prevalent form is one drink which is uniquely, inimitably Goan: Feni. Made from cashews or from the palm tree, Feni is a typical Goan brew, the stuff that local legend is made of. 'Feni' comes from the Konkani fen, meaning froth, which is what characterises it. Clear and with a distinct bouquet, Feni is admittedly not for the faint-hearted. But once you have acquired the taste for it, it is hard to be weaned off it.

PANAJI, the capital of Goa, is a charming city on the banks of the Mandovi river, with broad avenues spilling into cobbled squares, grand public buildings, narrow lanes and tavernas. It was only a sleepy village till Portuguese decided to move their capital nearer to the shore. The only monument dating back to pre-capital days is the SECRETARIAT BUILDING — once a Muslim palace and later a Portuguese fort.

Fairytale - like cottage

The best way of having a good look at Panaji to catch its flavour, is to take a cruise over the wide Mandovi river. There are cruises on the river during day time and also in moonlight.

Panaji could be your base for travel within Goa unless you decide to base yourself at one of the several modern beach resorts. The scenery around the capital is lush green with rice paddies and palm groves of mango and jackfruit. Your first excursion will probably be Velha Goa, the 16th century old capital under the Portuguese. Old Goa is an interesting study in splendour and decay. If you travel by boat, you may pass through the VICEREGAL ARCH as each Viceroy had done in the past before taking charge of his office. The arch marked the symbolic entry into the city as well as served as the gateway from the harbour. Vasco da Gama in full regalia gazes out from his niche.

The shell of the old Goa is about one and a half sq. km. only. Once upon a time, it was the greatest commercial centre east of the Suez and was ranked equal to Lisbon in grandeur. Now the great square — the site of the trials of Inquisition — lies totally neglected and in ruins.

OLD GOA

Old Goa was deserted after a series of virulent plagues in 1534, 1635 and 1735 that wiped out nearly 80 per cent of its population. The survivors created Panaji — some 9 km. away — as the new Portuguese capital.

Among the Churches of old Goa, the BASILICA OF BOM JESUS, completed in 1604, is perhaps the oldest and the most well-known all over the world. It contains a remarkable boroque gilded altar. In an airtight silver and glass casket lie the sacred remains of St. Francis Xavier who spent his lifetime in spreading the message of Christ in the Portuguese colonies.

Beneath the Basilica is a beautifully sculpted mausoleum. St. Xavier died in China in 1552 and his mummified corpse was brought to Goa in 1613. For a small fee, you can see his silver encased feet. The Basilica is open daily from 9 a.m. to 6 p.m.

Across the road is the majestic CHAPEL OF ST. CATHERINE. It was completed in 1610 and is dedicated to St.Catherine of Alexandria. She was a pagan girl who became an ardent Christian.

The Cathedral is regarded as Asia's largest and most significant church. It is a grand renaissance structure with an ornate gilded interior. Detailed panels around the centre altarpiece depict St. Catherine's life. The Cathedral has five bells, one of which is the "Golden Bell" — the biggest in the world. It was used to announce the burning of pagans and heretics, during the Inquisition.

Not far from this Church is another Cathedral, the CONVENT OF

Church of St. Francis of Assissi

CHURCH OF ASSISSI. Built originally as a small Franciscan chapel, it was later remodelled in 1661 with gilded, beautifully carved woodwork and exquisite frescoes. The church houses the ARCHAEOLOGICAL MUSEUM which displays portraits of Portuguese Viceroys over the years and also ancient Indian Hindu sculptures and art works discovered from this region.

The CHURCH OF ST. CAJETAN near old Goa's ferry wharf, was built by Italian friars to resemble St. Peter's Basilica in Rome. On MONTE SANTE, (the holy hill)is the ST. AUGUSTINE TOWER. It is the only remains left of what was once Goa's biggest church. Opposite the tower is the fortress-style CONVENT OF ST. MONICA, once India's largest nunnery. A gate leads you to the CHURCH OF OUR LADY OF THE ROSARY, one of the earliest in Goa. It contains the tomb of Dona Caterina, wife of the 10th Viceroy of Goa and the first woman to venture out to Goa.

Only 38 per cent of Goa's population is Christian. But, the number of churches is far in excess of the needs of the population. Over 60 per cent of Hindus have only a few temples. One reason is that the Portuguese in their religious zeal destroyed all symbols of Hindu or Muslim religions. Hindus moved their temples to the interior and only those have survived. The Portuguese followed their policy of destruction of mosques with equal fervour. The only remaining mosque dates from 1560 and is known as SOFA SHAHOURI MASJID.

Anyone interested in military architecture could see the AGUADA FORT on the way to CALANGUTE BEACH. For those interested in economic development of Goa, a visit to mining operations near SIGAO may be interesting.

OTHER IMPORTANT TOWNS

Among other important towns of Goa is, MARGAO, 33 kilometres from Panaji in South Goa district. It is a thriving commercial town linked to the rest of India by rail and road and also with the MORMUGAO HARBOUR.

VASCO DA GAMA is a modern, well laid-out city close to Mormugao harbour. DOBOLIM, Goa's airport, lies on the outskirts of this town. It is only 30 km. from Panaji

BEACHES OF GOA

Goa has many attractive beaches, with miles and miles of sun, sand and surf. If you are not committed to one particular resort hotel, you have a tremendous choice. Generally, the southern coastline is popular for its hotels, beaches and restaurants. Southern beaches are not so well developed though two major resort hotels are located in the southern coastline.

North of Fort Aguada are the twin beaches of Calangute and CANDOLIM, with a beach stretch of 7 km. There are dozens of good hotels and guest houses in the beach front. Besides, there are makeshift bars and restaurants, built with wood and palm leaves. The fishermen can be seen unloading their catch after a hard day's work.

During the 1960s when the hippies thronged to the Goan beaches, Calangute was their favourite beach. There are small stalls on this beach doing roaring business in hessian trousers, ethnic sandals, kurtas, etc

Two kilometres further north is BAGA BEACH, with a steep hill in the background. It is perhaps one of the best and is totally uncluttered. You can see traditional fishing boats hauled past the high-tide mark. Nuns escorting school children can be seen having their siesta under the coconut palms. Baga also has a good wind-surfing school.

From Baga beach, another 10 minutes walk brings you to the ANJUNA BEACH. This beach is adjacent to CHAPORA FORT. It has a magnificent ALBUQUERQUE MANSION flanked by octagonal towers and attractive Mangalore tiled roofs

It is a 'faded paradise' of the 'love generation' who live in crude matting shacks along the cliff face.

Nude bathing, though not legally permitted, attracts squads of Indian men. Daily life at this beach centres around exhibitionist yoga, frisbee games and 'smoking' of lots of 'hashish'. There is a Friday market which attracts both locals and foreigners.

The beaches of Chapora and Vagator are 3 km. further north. Chapora faces the ruins of a Portuguese fort built in 1717. One can have a fine view from the ramparts of the fort.

Vagator has idyllic and secluded setting, with only one hotel.

The local people here rent out rooms to visitors. It is also possible to rent out a full house for a month in the village.

In the south, BAGMOLA is known for its luxury beach resort, the erstwhile Oberoi Hotel. The management has changed. It is the only multi-storeyed hotel in Goa. The beach is relatively small by Goan standards.

COLVA BEACH is a secluded beauty. This 40 km. stretch of powdery sand and pristine, warm waters make it a mini paradise. Away from the main cluster of tourist lodges and cafes, you can have the entire beach to yourself.

Goa's 115 km. long coastline (with 40 beaches) is the delight of swimmers, anglers, water-sports, buffs and the sun-bathers.

Less than 50 km. across, the whole new cosmos is waiting to be discovered. It has some of the best preserved mangroves in South East Asia with unspoiled ecosystem — waterfalls cascading from the Western Ghats, and, probably the largest King Cobra habitat in the world at CARANZOL on Goa's border with Karnataka and also its three wildlife sanctuaries. Bondla Forest is one of these with good facilities. The DUDHSAGAR WATERFALLS, 60 km. from Panaji, is a spectacular sight with water cascading from a height of 30 metres.

However, Goa's best asset is its people — polite, cultured and modern. Its ethnic food is a blend of many cultures, foreign and Indian.

There is a lovely song for every occasion and the Goans do not need a reason to sing and dance. Its folk dances are graceful. The architecture of Goan houses is based on a fine sense of aesthetics and deep knowledge of what is best for good living - high ceilings, natural light, ventilation and greenery all around.

GOA

GENERAL INFORMATION

Population: 11,69,793 (1991 census)
Altitude: Sea level to 1022 mts.
Climate:

	Temperature	
	Max.	Min.
Winter	32⁰ c	19⁰ c
Summer	33⁰ c	24⁰ c
Rainfall	77 mm	2 mm

Season: Throughout the year except that in the monsoon months of June to September sea-bathing is not recommended.

Clothing: Tropical clothing throughout the year.

HOW TO GET THERE

By Air: Dabolim (29 km. from Panaji) is connected by Indian Airlines with Bangalore, Bombay, Cochin, Delhi, Hyderabad, Trivandrum and Cochin. Private airlines also provide regular services to Goa.

By Rail: Vasco-da-Gama station is connected by a metre-guage line with Londa junction which is on the Miraj-Bangalore line. The convenient railhead for Panaji is Margao, 34 km. away. Konkah Railway project when completed in 1996 will provide fast services to Goa from different cities of India.

By Road: Goa has good road connections. Panaji is
594 km. from Bombay,
598 km. from Bangalore,
315 km. from Hospet (for Hampi),
359 km. from Badami,
371 km. from Mangalore and
494 km. from Pune.
There are several luxury and regular bus services to Bangalore, Bombay, Belgaum, Hubli, Mangalore, Miraj, Mysore, Pune.

By Ship: A coastal cruise ship operates daily between Bombay and Goa. Time - 7 hours only.

LOCAL TRANSPORT

Tourist taxis, ordinary taxis, motorcycle taxis, bus services and auto-rickshaws available. Water transport is available between Panaji and Mormugao. There are motorboat, launch and ferry services to various parts of Goa.

CONDUCTED TOURS

1. Full-day tour around South Goa (9 a.m. to 6 p.m.).
2. Full-day tour around North Goa (9 a.m. to 6 p.m.).
3. Half-day Pilgrim Special Tour (on demand).
4. Half-day tour covering beach resorts (on demand).

5. Full-day tours to Bondla Wildlife Sanctuary, Terekhol Fort and Tambdi Surla (subject to demand).
6. Evening cruises along the Mandovi from River Navigation Jetty, opposite Tourist Hotel, Panaji.

For information: Goa Tourism Development Corporation, Trinora Apartments, Panaji. *Tel* : 225583/225715or any of the Resorts/Hostels run by GTDC. Government of India Tourist Office *Phone*: 43412.

WHERE TO STAY (STD CODE: 0832)
DELUXE
1. Fort Aguada Beach Resort & Hermitage
   Phone: 276205
   Fax: 276044
   Cable: FORT AGUADA
2. The Taj Holiday Village
   Phone: 276205
   Fax: 276044
3. Sarover Park Plaza Beach Resort
   Phone: 512191
   Fax: 512510
   Cable: OBHOTEL
4. Majorda Beach Resort
   Phone: 720025/26
   Telex: 0196-234
   Cable: MBR GOA
5. Cidade de Goa
   Phone: 221301
   Fax: 223303
   Cable: WELCOTEL
6. The Leela Beach Goa
   Phone: 746363
   Telex: 0196-258

Cable: KEMPIN
Fax: 08344-6352
7. Goa Renaissance Ramada Inn Resort
   Phone: 745200-20
   Fax: 745225
STANDARD
8. Holiday Inn Hotel
   Phone: 746303-4
9. Fidalgo
   Phone: 226291-9
   Fax: 225061
   Cable: MABEREST
10. Mandovi
    Phone: 224405
    Fax: 225451
    Cable: MANDOVIT
11. Keni's
    Phone: 224582
    Cable: MANDOVIT
12. Golden Goa
    Phone: 46231-39
13. La Paz Gardens
    Phone: 512121
    Fax: 513302
    Cable: LAPAZ
14. Metropole
    Phone: 721552
    Cable: METROPOLE
15. Delmon
    Phone: 226847
    Telex: 0194-252
    Cable: ALCON
16. Nova Goa
    Phone: 46231-39
    Fax: 224958
    Cable: KAMBROS
17. Old Anchor
    Phone: 736337
18. Dona Paula Beach Resort
    Phone: 227955
    Fax: 221371
BUDGET
19. Tourist Hostel, Panaji
20. Tourist Hostel, Mapusa

21. Tourist Hostel, Margao
22. Tourist Hostel, Vasco da Gama
23. Tourist Resort, Calangute
24. Tourist Cottages, Colva Beach
25. Tourist Rest House, Terekhol Fort
26. Lake Resort, Mayem
27. Tourist Cottages, Farmagudi
28. Yatri Niwas, Miramar Panaji
29. Tourist Home, Palto Panaji

Information
1. Goa Tourism Development Corporation, *Tel*: 225583/225715
2. Government of India Tourist Office *Tel*: 43412

Paying Guest Accommodation available in Goa. Information: Director of Tourism, *Tel*: 224757, 225535

WHAT TO SEE

Panaji
The STATUE OF ABBE FARIA (said to be the father of hypnotism), colonial homes, gardens and taverns, ALTINHO (the residential hill), the River Mandovi, the CHURCH OF OUR LADY OF IMMACULATE CONCEPTION, MIRAMAR and DONA PAULA BEACHES.

EXCURSIONS
1. The BEACHES OF GOA are unbelievably beautiful. The popular ones, and hence often crowded, are Calangute, Colva, Dona Paula and Miramar. Quieter and isolated beaches are also many, such as Siridao, Aguada, Vagator, Baga, Mandrem, Morgim, north of the airport, and Bogmalo, Majorda, Betul, Palolem to the south. In fact, the Goan coastline is one continuous stretch of beaches.
2. OLD GOA (10 km). Founded by the Adil Shahi King in the 15th century, it was conquered by the Portuguese who made it their capital. They called it Velha Goa. It became the seat of conversions to Christianity and a court of Inquisition was set up in 1560. The city was abandoned in 1738. There are many churches of interest, such as the Basilica of Bom Jesus where the body of Saint Francis Xavier is kept in a silver casket. The Church of St. Cajetan, built over a Hindu temple, is a treat for lovers of art. It is patterned on St. Peter's Basilica in Rome.
3. The MAPUSA MARKET (13 km. from Panaji). On Fridays everything that a Goan needs is sold here.
4. PONDA. Its Hindu temples were set within the hilly, thickly-wooded areas and escaped the wrath of Portuguese zealots. The tall lamp tower or sthhamba is a unique

feature. The temples often visited are those of Shri Mangueshi, Shri Shanta Durga, Shri Ramnath, Shri Mahalsa, Shri Gopal Ganapati, Shri Nagesh, Shri Saptakoteshwara and Shri Mahalakshmi.
5. Temple or TAMBDI SURLA (12th c.) in Sanguem (70 km. from Panaji).
6. MAYEM LAKE (35 km. from Panaji), a popular picnic spot.
7. BONDLA FOREST and SANCTUARY en route to Belgaum.
8. DUDHSAGAR WATERFALLS (60 km.), accessible only by train. A spectacular sight.

SHOPPING

Interesting brass lamps with lights and articles of clay are the specialities of the region. Also carved furniture, handicrafts made of sea-shells, coir mats and other crafts.

FESTIVALS OF SPECIAL LOCAL INTEREST

1. The EXPOSITION OF THE BODY OF ST. FRANCIS XAVIER, once every 10 years. Catholics from all over India and the world flock to Goa.
2. REIS MAGOS ZATRA to celebrate the Feast of the Three Kings (January).
3. THE CARNIVAL is a joyous 3-day festival celebrated all over Goa in February-March. There is a lot of music and dancing, and masquerades and processions led by the legendary King Momo.
4. JATRAS (or temple processions) are held in various parts of Goa every year at the temples of Shri Shanta Durga, Ponda (January), Shri Hanuman, Panaji (January), Shri Mangueshi, Ponda (January-February), Mardol (February). Also the Narve Jatra, Bicholim (September), Dindi at Margao (September), Nageshi Jatra (November), Shri Datta Jayanti, Sankhali (December).
5. The LAIRAI JATRA in April, where the highlight is the fire-walking spectacle in the early morning.
6. VASCO SAPTAK when there is the singing of songs and processions of floats with stories from the Hindu PURANAS.

7. FEAST OF ST. FRANCIS XAVIER (December) in Old Goa.

ENTERTAINMENT
Goans love music and dance. Goa is famous for its music (a combination of eastern and western music) and its lively dances. These are performed at all festivals. Goan bands are found at hotels all over India. Every street corner in Goa has a bar and major hotels have floor shows, music and dance.

SPORTS
Most of the 5-star hotels have facilities for swimming and watersports like water-scooters, water-skiing and wind-surfing.
Equipment is available on hire here.

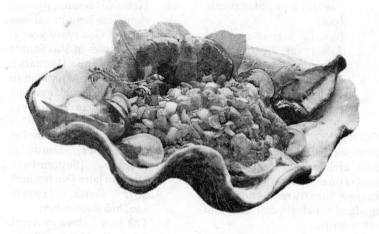

Chapter 19

KARNATAKA
The Land of Great Monuments and National Parks

Fresco at Badami

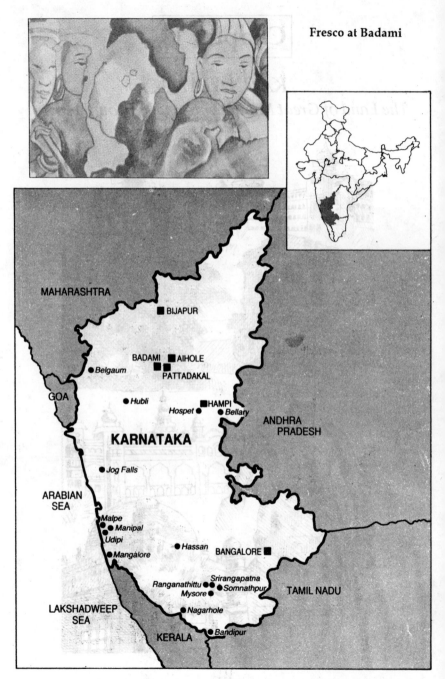

Karnataka is one of the most toured States of the country. Accounting for a sixteenth of the total landmass of India, it has a population of over 40 million and an area of 192,000 sq. km.

It has three distinct regions — a narrow, fertile coastal strip comprising two districts of North and South Kanara along the Arabian sea; the hilly uplands dominated by the Western Ghats, and the Deccan plateau east of the Ghats, where the landscape becomes rock-strewn and bare. No three regions could be more strikingly different.

Coastal Karnataka is 65 km. broad at its widest, with some of the loveliest yet uncrowded beaches along the west coast. The sudden upthrust of Western Ghats, comprising densely forested mountain ranges with horseshoe-shaped peaks and verdant greens reminds one of the English downs. Then there are the fantastic age-old formations, defying the law of gravity on the Deccan Plateau. The plateau is reputed to be one of the oldest formations on earth — the so-called Gondwana Plate is believed to have — emerged at the very beginning of the geological times.

The State can boast of some of the best wildlife national parks and bird sanctuaries. It has India's most spectacular waterfalls — the Jog Falls — where the water leaps down 800 feet into an awesome gorge. There are other waterfalls too in this area, but Jog is the most popular one visited by thousands of people, specially in winter months when the flow of water is at its full and the sun paints a complex of rainbows.

As varied as the land are the people of Karnataka. In southern corners of the State live the tall and sinewy Kodagu people amidst the hills and valleys of Coorg. Their striking costumes are in marked contrast to the simpler lifestyle of the rest of the people in Karnataka.

In the flatlands, north of Coorg live the Vokkaligas who farm their rich lands watered by the Cauvery river. Northern Karnataka is inhabited by Lingayats - followers of the great saint, Basava (12th century). Coastal Karnataka is inhabited by, among others, the simple fisherfolks who have plied their boats for centuries and had contacts with Mesopotamia and Greece in pre-Christian era. In this area, both Kannada - the official language of Karnataka — and Konkani are spoken. The Christians of the Kanara region were among the earliest converts. The CHURCH OF THE MOST HOLY ROSARY at BOLAR was established in 1526.

A land so rich, naturally, became the cradle of mighty dynasties like the Kadambas, the Chalukyas, the Gangas and the Rashtrakutas. The Rashtrakutas built the massive monolithic Kailasa Temple carved out of solid rock at Ellora in the present-day Maharashtra.

The State's history is intimately interwoven into the great epic *Ramayana*. India's first great emperor, Chandragupta Maurya, retired to SRAVANABELAGOLA, 90 km. from MYSORE. He had become a Jain monk and gave up all his worldly possessions including his large empire. His grandson Ashoka who ruled over most parts of India raised edicts carved on stone pillars in RAICHUR and CHITRADURGA. By the 1st century B.C.,the Satavahanas succeeded the Mauryas and they built Buddhist Viharas and Stupas. Around fourth century A.D., the Ganga dynasty which came to power erected the massive statues of Lord Gomateswara and the Jain temples at Sravanabelagola. The 6th century ushered in the Chalukyas of BADAMI who evolved the Chalukya style of architecture. Then followed the Rashtrakutas who encouraged art and poetry. The Hoysalas, who followed them at their capital DWARASAMUDRA built the great temples of SOMNATHPUR, HALEBID and BELUR.

All these great dynasties have left behind a mind-boggling vista of temples and forts, palaces and ruins which represent a 900-year span when Hindu art and architecture reached its zenith, during a most dazzling epoch of South Indian history. With the destruction of the mighty Vijayanagar empire came the Muslim influence which continued during the next few centuries. During this period, Karnataka gave birth to many saints and singers. After the downfall of the Vijayanagar empire, Karnataka did not emerge on the Indian national scene till Hyder Ali and his son Tipu built a strong kingdom of their own and galvanised the people against the British. Tipu Sultan was killed in the battle of Srirangapatana in 1794. The victors parcelled out the empire of Tipu among so many claimants leaving its core to an earlier deposed Hindu dynasty with their capital in Mysore.

Even before the advent of Hyder Ali, Muslim rulers had themselves set up what is now known as Northern Karnataka. BIJAPUR was their capital. Yusuf Adil Shahi of Constantinople founded the kingdom of Bijapur. His successors enriched Karnataka by building mosques which could be better than any which Muslims built elsewhere in the world. Outstanding among these is the GOL GUMBAZ in Bijapur whose dome is comparable to that of Saint Peters in Rome. GULBARGA has remnants of a fort built by Raja Gulchand which was later developed by Allaudin Bahmini, the founder of the Bahmini Kingdom. The GULBARGA FORT is very large and includes a Jami Masjid with 35,000 square metres of

Gol Gumbaz

built-up area in the style of the mosque at Cardova in Spain. The interior arches and pillars are so placed that the pulpits can be seen clearly from any part of the hall. The acoustics are perfect.

Before the Kannada-speaking areas of India were merged to make a greater Karnataka State, it was called Mysore State with its capital in Mysore. The now enlarged State of Karnataka has its capital in BANGALORE, a city known for its mild climate. This fast emerging metropolis of India with strong industrial base is one of India's leading tourist cities.

BANGALORE, The Garden City

Bangalore can boast of Winston Churchill's unforgettable experiences recounted in his *Memoirs*. It is the city where weather is delightful most of the year. The old stately bungalows with eucalyptus-lined drives and the gentle noise of church bells are fast giving way to multi-storeyed complexes and utilitarian residential blocks.

If you are an airborne traveller, your most convenient jumping off city to see Karnataka State will be Bangalore. The city is connected with all major towns of India by Indian Airlines and several private airlines. For Indian Railways too Bangalore is a major stopover. It is a flourishing city of some 5 million inhabitants, an industrial town as well as a beautiful garden city. The absence of ancient monuments in the city is adequately compensated by a beautiful planned city.

Bangalore's charm peeps through tree-shaded gardens, lawns and ever-fragrant blooming flowers. The beautiful 240-acre botanical LALBAGH GARDENS have been well-cared for since the Muslim period. The gardens have been landscaped with a large variety of century-old trees, fountains, lotus pools, terraces and an assortment of tropical and sub-tropical herbs. Its floral clock is worthseeing.

Lalbagh Garden and Cubbon Park

Developed by Hyder Ali to please his son Tipu Sultan, the Lalbagh ranks among the finest gardens of its kind in Asia. It has an amazing variety of over 1,800 species of herbs, plants and tropical trees. In the 'Glass House' the most enchanting and colourful flowers are exhibited on 15th August and 26th January. The floral clock is another highlight.

The Cubbon Park in the heart of the city houses the STATE LIBRARY, an impressive Gothic structure in red, and the KARNATAKA HIGH COURT.

It includes the magnificent post-Independence Government Building, the VIDHANA SOUDHA, which houses the State Legislature and the Secretariat. Built in the 1950s, its architecture is a combination of several styles, including that of South Indian temples.

Cuisine

Bangalore offers a rich fare of Indian, Chinese and Western food. Small cafes still serve the old type of English cuisine complete with "curries" and Mulligatawny soup. A whole host of fast food joints offers "sit down" and "carry-away" meals. The city can boast of some of the finest hotels in the country belonging to major hotel chains.

Karnataka has the largest machine tool factory, the oldest and the largest aircraft manufacturing complex in India. The city of Bangalore can boast of INDIA'S SPACE RESEARCH CENTRE as well as many multinational companies manufacturing consumer products.

In shopping, Bangalore silks excel and are a good buy. It is also the centre of sandalwood carvings — very beautiful replicas of some temples can be bought in the town.

Looking for the ancient, it is not far away. Only 68 km. from Bangalore are the famous NANDI HILLS, the scene of many savage battles in the past. It is now a health resort. Two 1,000-year old temples grace the landscape — one at the foot and the other on top of the hill. The better one is at the bottom of the hill. Not so ancient is the 16th century mud-brick fort built by a Hindu king which was later rebuilt by Tipu Sultan.

Among other interesting things to see in Bangalore is the BULL TEMPLE, built by the founder of Bangalore, Kempegowda over a monolithic bull. TIPU'S PALACE within the Fort is a 2-storeyed ornate structure in wood. The ground floor houses a museum tracing the life and times of Hyder Ali and Tipu Sultan.

The GOVERNMENT MUSEUM and VISVESWARAYYA INDUSTRIAL ART GALLERY are worth a visit. India has its KOLAR GOLD MINES — the deepest in the world — only 100 km. east of Bangalore. It is possible to visit the pit with special arrangements.

MYSORE AND PLACES AROUND IT

An excellent 140 km. road leads from Bangalore to Mysore, the City of Palaces. On the way, you pass through a picturesque country and some interesting places to stop by. First is RAMPUR - site of the experimental centre of rural health, CHANNAPATNA, a place where enchanting lacquered toys and excellent silks are produced, and the FRENCH ROCKS, headquarters of the French Army who were the allies of Tipu Sultan in India. From here a short detour leads to ancient temple towns of TONNUR and MELKOTE and then to SRIRANGAPATANA.

Srirangapatana is an island between the two branches of the Cauvery river and was the capital of the Mysore Rajas from 1610 to 1790, only 16 km. from the Mysore city. Later, Hyder Ali and Tipu Sultan were its famous denizens. It is here that Tipu Sultan died fighting against the British for the control of Mysore State. Outside the ruins of the old fort is DARYA DAULAT — splendour of the River. It is Tipu's summer palace set in exquisite gardens is still in good shape, though it was built in 1784.

A visit to TIPU'S FORT and its surrounding areas is rewarding. The Muslims lived cheek by jowl with the Hindus. Proof is the existence of two 1,000-year old temples — one is the SRI RANGANATHA TEMPLE. Tipu

Sultan's favourite mosque, JUMA MASJID with its twin towers, is worth a visit. From the top of its minarets, you can have a view of the fort and the first glimpse of Mysore city.

Mysore, the sandalwood city, is a fascinating tourist centre of India. In this city, you will find yourself enveloped with the lingering aromas of sandalwood, jasmine, rose, musk and frangipani. After you leave Mysore, you will always recall their beautiful fragrances. The city is one of the major centres of incense manufacturing in India. Mysore incense products are exported all over the world. Each of these incense sticks is made by hand and a good worker can turn out some 10,000 in a day. You can see them being made at the Government sandalwood oil factory.

Mysore is also a centre of arts and crafts — an incredible range of ivory, sandalwood, rosewood and teakwood goods — especially furniture, can be seen in the Government Emporium called KAVERI ARTS, a popular shopping centre.

If shopping is an important reason to see Mysore, there are several others too. The city was the capital of the erstwhile Mysore State ruled by the Hindu Maharajas. The city can boast of a walled Indo-Saracenic PALACE in the centre of the town. The PALACE is open to visitors. The Maharaja used to lead one of the most colourful processions in India during the 10-day Dussehra Festival in October. Richly caparisoned elephants, liveried retainers, cavalry, bands and flower bedecked deities form part of the procession every year.

Mysore Maharaja Palace

Just south of Mysore lies CHAMUNDI HILL, 1062 metres above sea level, on top of which stands an impressive South Indian temple with 7-storey gopurams visible from all sides. The hill is climbed by a flight of 1,000 steps, or you can drive up along the winding road. On the way to Chamundi Hill — named after the patron goddess of the royal family— you can see the famous 16 ft high NANDI (Shiva's bull) — a huge

Nandi bull, Chamundi Hill

monolithic statue, perhaps the largest in the world. It is a Hindu pilgrim centre.

Other places worth a visit in Mysore city are the GOVERNMENT SILK WEAVING FACTORY and SRI CHAMARAJENDRA ART GALLERY housed in the JAGMOHAN PALACE. It displays paintings, particularly of Ravi Verma, and also handicrafts, historical objects and old musical instruments.

TOURS OUT OF MYSORE

A number of tours can be taken out of Mysore, the most covering Mysore city, SOMNATHPUR, Srirangapatana, BRINDAVAN GARDENS and RANGANATHITTOO BIRD SANCTUARY (only in season). Brindavan Gardens are ornamental gardens laid out below the KRISHNARAJASAGAR DAM across the Cauvery River, 19 km. from Mysore. The Gardens present a glorious

Somnathpur temple

view at night with numerous lighted fountains turning the landscape into a fairyland. An overnight stay at the Krishnarajasagar, a western style beautiful bird lovers, Ranganathittoo Bird Sanctuary will be a fascinating experience, the best time to visit it being June-September. The site of the Bird Sanctuary is on one of the three islands on the Cauvery River, only 3 kilometres from Srirangapatana.

60 km. north of Mysore, there is an opportunity to see wild elephants roaming about freely. A company called Jungle Lodges and Resorts Limited (same as the one running Tiger Tops in Nepal) operates a tented camp and lodge by the lake at KARAPUR. From here, trips can be arranged to the NAGARHOLE NATIONAL PARK where elephants roam freely. An unusual feature of this jungle safari is a chance to paddle along the waterways in *Caracles* - round basket-shaped boats lined with buffalo hide. These boats are so slow and quiet that one can reach very close to the families of wild elephants as they graze on the river banks. Other animals like the Indian gaur (bison), wild boar, sambar and barking deer can be seen in plenty. The elusive tiger and leopard also lurk by. Adjacent to the tented camps is the Kabini River Lodge, incorporating the original hunting lodge built specially by the Maharaja for the Viceroy.

100 km. north of Mysore by road is SRAVANABELAGOLA presided over and dominated by the colossal statue of Jain saint - Gomateshwar. The monolithic image, 57 feet tall, has been watched over by millions of

Panel on temple wall, Belur

pilgrims during the last 1,000 years since it was built by a Ganga king. The religion may have lost its touch now, but the principles that it enshrines are eternal. The nakedness of the statue portrays renunciation of all wordly goods and the stiff posture indicates perfect self-control. There are several smaller Jain statues in the vicinity of this temple. Every 12 years, Jains from all parts of the world gather here for a bathing festival. A special scaffolding is erected to bathe the statue with pots of milk, honey and fruit.

Between Sravanabelagola and HASSAN (60 km.), the green countryside may remind the visiting Englishmen of the countryside back home. From Hassan, BELUR is only 50 km. away. It was a flourishing city 800 years ago under the Hoysala kings.

Somnathpur temple is 45 km. from Mysore. Built in A.D. 1260 during the heydays of the Hoysala kings, it is considered to be one of the most beautiful and interesting buildings in the world. The walls of the star-shaped temple are literally covered with sculptures in stone depicting various events in the *Ramayana* and *Mahabharata* epics. No two friezes are alike.

A visit to Somnathpur will encourage you to see two more temples built by Hoysala kings north of Mysore.

Of the three major temples in Belur, the CHANNAKESAVA stands almost as perfectly as it was when it was built — a tribute to the great builders of the Hoysala era who followed the Chalukyas. The Moslem invaders did not destroy it.

The design of Belur temples is similar to that of Somnathpur — a star-shaped plan. The temple itself is squat, set on a platform and flat on the top. It does not have a spire.

In Belur you find intricate sculptures of gods and goddesses in their various incarnations and sages. The life as in the Hoysala period is portrayed intimately — hunting, war scenes, agricultural activities, stylised animals and birds. There are also sensual scenes — beautiful temple girls in various poses, decorating themselves or dressing. Nothing is taboo. Figures are beautiful and erotic. No outer wall or interior without intricate sculptures and no two sculptures have been repeated. The patience and dedication of these anonymous artists has only to be believed till we see their worth. Events of the *Ramayana* and *Mahabharata* epics are also portrayed there.

The Hoysala temples can be compared favourably with the temples at Khajuraho and Konark. They can rival the best in Goethic art found anywhere in Europe. In fact, these temples could outrank any contemporary art.

Some 16 km. from Belur is its sister temple at HELEBID. The HOYSALESWARA TEMPLE at Helebid was built by the same king, but has remained incomplete despite 180 years of labour.

Hoysaleswara temple, Helebid

Here, the virtuosity of Hoysala artists reached its peak. One cannot give a rational explanation for such richness of carvings, except saying that these artists could treat the stone like wood or ivory. Their patience was unlimited. Another reason was that the stones they worked on were somewhat soft which hardened over the centuries when exposed to rain and sun.

The friezes are breathtaking — first comes a row of elephants, then a lordly lion, then swift horses. Above are scenes from the epics. Here are the Apsaras — the heavenly maidens clothed in jewels with bracelets on each arm — and they may have as many as six arms. Sitting or standing in graceful poses — the young damsels are 800 years old but look as fresh as ever. There are 280 figures — mostly feminine — that can rival the best in Goethic art.

BANDIPUR WILDLIFE SANCTUARY

South of Mysore, 80 km. on the Mysore-Ootacamund road, BANDIPUR is part of a larger national park which includes the neighbouring wildlife sanctuaries of Madumalai in Tamil Nadu and Wynad in Kerala.

The sanctuary is known for its herds of bison, spotted deer, sambar, elephants and tigers. The Forest Department offers you jeeps on hire to go for a photo safari. One can also see the sanctuary on elephant back. The best time to visit the sanctuary is October-March.

Accommodation can be reserved through Field Director, Project Tiger, Government House Complex, Mysore or through your havel agent.

NORTHERN KARNATAKA

Having seen the most recent and the not so 'ancient' part of Karnataka, we move to the north taking you back to the 6th to 14th century A.D. Travelling north, it may be advisable to have robust walking shoes which can have easy grip of the rocky surface. A headgear to protect you from the sun will come in handy and binoculars to have a closer look at the temple details.

HAMPI

From Bangalore, travelling by road, it should take about 6-1/2 hours to reach Hampi. So one should leave after an early breakfast so as to reach Hampi by lunch time.

Another way of travelling would be by India's second airline Vayudoot which has on and off flights from Bangalore to BELLARY, a short distance away from Hampi.

Ruins of a Golden Age

Hampi, once a flourishing capital of the Vijayanagar Empire, is today a small village. Exhibiting vast relics of a great empire, Vijayanagar, the "City of Victory", was the seat of an empire that extended from the Arabian Sea to the Bay of Bengal and from the Deccan Plateau to the tip of the peninsula. It was built as a showpiece of imperial magnificence. Besides being lovers of art and architecture as is evident from the carved temples, monuments and sculptures in Hampi and all over the South, the rulers also introduced new techniques in warfare, buildings, waterworks and agriculture. In fact, some of the irrigation networks constructed by them are in operation to this day.

The Vijayanagar rulers patronised a variety of Hindu cults and also permitted the practice of other religions. Under their enlightened leadership, the city became rich and a cosmopolitan blend of peoples with a wide variety of linguistic, ethnic and religious background. The most outstanding of these rulers was Krishnadeva Raya, who raised his empire to the zenith of its glory during 1509-1529. But in 1565, the combined armies of the Muslim Sultanates defeated the Vijayanagar Military Commander. Plundering, burning and sacking the abandoned city mercilessly, they left it in ruins for the treasure seekers. Today, the temples and palaces lie scattered over an area of 25 sq. km.

VIRUPAKSHA TEMPLE is one of the few temples amidst the ruins, still in worship. At the heart of the complex are several minor shrines dating back to Chalukya and Hoysala periods, completely engulfed by Vijayanagar extensions. The eastern gateway which is 50 metres high, is a marvel of engineering skill. The hall leading to the sanctum sanctorum has finely carved columns of animals. The ceiling is painted with scenes from mythology.

VITTALA TEMPLE, despite its ruined state, represents the highest achievement of Vijayanagar art. The temple stands on a rectangular courtyard. Its 56 columns are richly carved with fantastic beings and rampant animals. One is overwhelmed by the elaborate, delicately chiselled brackets, supporting the columns and the ceiling. The slender columns echo with music when tapped. Ceilings are decorated with foliage and geometric designs.

Most impressive is the celebrated stone chariot fashioned like a miniature shrine but with wheels. The elongated columns of this structure are sculptured with animals and figures and are intricately ornamented.

HAZARA RAMA TEMPLE, the family temple of the rulers, is surrounded by enclosures containing buildings and ruins associated with the king, court and military. Finely carved basalt pillars depict the incarnations of Vishnu. The exterior walls are sculptured with events from the *Ramayana*.

Colossal monoliths in the south of the Virupaksha Temple are of two Ganesha images carved on boulders. One of them is enclosed in a temple with unusually tall columns. The other stands within an open hall.

Further south, carved out of a single boulder is another badly damaged STATUE OF NARASIMHA

LOTUS MAHAL, inspired by the beauty of a woman, is a two-storeyed pavilion on a stepped plan. Hindu and Islamic architectural elements are skilfully blended displaying the best possible Vijayanagar courtly style. The tower which today is in a dilapidated state, was guarded by eunuchs, as royal maidens watched the festivities from this tower.

The QUEEN'S BATH, a water pavilion exposed to the sky, was built in an Islamic style. It consists of a square water basin surrounded by a vaulted corridor. A lotus-headed fountain once sprouted perfumed water into the pool. The overhanging filigreed balconies were for the ladies of the court to watch the fun and frolic in the bath.

AROUND HAMPI

TUNGABHADRA DAM is South India's largest stone masonry dam across the river Tungabhadra. The reservoir has a storage capacity of 132,559 million cubic feet of water. It contributes 99000 KW of electric power.

AIHOLE

To reach Aihole, it takes approximately 12-1/2 hours by road from Hampi. Since Aihole and PATTADAKAL have to be seen in a day, it would be convenient to leave Hampi early in the morning.

Whatever you have seen at Hampi is derived from what you will see at Aihole, Pattadakal and BADAMI. The temple architecture of Hampi belongs to the 13th-15th centuries, that of these three places belong to the 6th, 7th and 8th centuries.

Aihole was once the capital of the early Chalukyan dynasty. It is a picturesque village on the banks of the Malaprabha river. On entering Aihole, you see a whole lot of temples. There are about 125 temples divided into 22 groups scattered all over the village and the fields nearby, with 30 in a single enclosure surrounded by crenated walls. Most of the temples were built between the sixth and 8th centuries. Nearly every day more and more temples are being excavated bearing witness to the vigorous experimentation in temple architecture which went on in Aihole fourteen centuries ago.

The DURGA TEMPLE derives its name from Durgadagudi meaning temple near the fort. Dedicated to Lord Vishnu, it is the largest and most elaborately decorated monument, noted for its apsidal ended plan. Standing on a high platform, its columns at the entrance and within the porch are carved with figures and ornamental reliefs.

The LADH KHAN TEMPLE was the abode of a Muslim prince, Ladh Khan. It is one of the earliest temples, belonging to the 5th century. You have to climb through the roof on a stone ladder, to come upon a shrine bearing 'Vishnu' and 'Surya' on its walls. From here, you get a panoramic view of the village bordering on the temples.

The MEGUTI TEMPLE, the only dated monument in Aihole, was constructed atop a small hill in A.D. 634. Built of 630 small stone blocks, it is one of the last of its kind in Aihole. Though partly in ruins now, it provides important evidence about the development of the South Indian temple style.

We have covered only the main temples. However, there are a number of other temples of interest in Aihole bearing witness to the prolific temple building activities under the Chalukyas.

PATTADAKAL

As mentioned earlier, there is no other route to visit Pattadakal except by road. So the drive from Aihole to Pattadakal should take you about 30 minutes.

Pattadakal is a small village on the banks of the Malaprabha river. It was the commemorative site for the Chalukyan kings from the 17th to the 19th centuries.

As you enter Pattadakal, you are greeted by a cluster of temples at the foothills. Here you will see experiments in architecture, even small-scale models. Delicately chiselled, rich in detail, the stone used is sandstone with a pink tinge that flames in the sunset.

The temples represent the climax of the Chalukyan architecture, providing one of the most striking illustrations in India, of the co-existence of different building styles and art traditions. The evolution is toward the high-towered, much sculptured structure. The sculpture, however, is not so much representative as decorative. Pattadakal is unique in having temple architecture of the Northern Nagara and Southern Dravidian styles.

The oldest temple is the SANGHAMESWARA TEMPLE built by King Vijayditya (A.D. 696-733). The MALLIKARJUNA TEMPLE has pillars depicting the birth and life of Krishna. The ceiling has panels of Gajalakshmi and Nataraja with Parvati. There are also sculptures of Mahishasura Mardhini and Ugranarasimha. The largest of the temples, the Virupaksha has beautiful sculptures and panels depicting scenes from the *Ramayana* and *Mahabharata*. The PAPANATHA TEMPLE is unique. Two columned halls lead to the sanctuary. Built in the northern style, it has impressive carvings on pillars and ceiling, illustrating episodes from the two great Indian epics.

BADAMI

After visiting Aihole and Pattadakal in one day, you must leave Pattadakal the same evening to reach Badami by night. The drive should take you approximately 130 minutes.

When you enter Badami, you are drawn to its gold-rust sandstone cliffs. The fort walls rise up from the cliffs as if born from the stone. The natural gorge embellished with temples and gateways, leading to this hill city is one of the highlights.

Badami, founded by Pulakesin I, was once the capital of the Chalukyas, reflecting the Chalukyan art's maturity in style, grace and strength. The sculptures at the famous cave temples seem to come alive under your eyes. It is as if stone begins to breathe.

The CAVE TEMPLES at Badami were hewn out of solid rock as early as A.D. 550. They follow a set pattern: a verandah with pillars, a hall with columns and a small cell to enshrine the deity. Though the exterior is quite plain, the interior has been lavishly adorned.

These are a group of four temples opposite the BADAMI FORT. Of these, three are Hindu and one is Jain.

The first cave burrows deep into the rock. Dwarfs decorate the front of the verandah with a Nandi bull on the left and an 18-armed Shiva on the right who strikes 81 dance poses. There is an image of Vishnu in the vestibule and the goddess Durga beating the demon Mahishasura on the farthest wall. The second temple is the smallest and is also dedicated to Vishnu. Its sanctuary depicts the god's various incarnations.

The third temple, the largest and the best of them, has a double row of pillars with carvings pertaining to both Shaivite and Vaishnavite themes.

Inside the fourth temple which is exclusively Jain sits Mahavira in a uniquely comfortable pose. The other carvings are of Padmavati and other Tirthankaras.

BADAMI FORT, situated on top of the hill, encloses large granaries, a treasury, watch tower and impressive temples on the hill. MALLEGITTI SHIVALAYA, the oldest temple, is built of stone, finely joined without mortar, with a Dravidians tower.

BIJAPUR

When you look back on the visual images of Hampi, Badami, Pattadakal and Aihole, you experience the golden age of Hindu temple architecture. However, in the battle of Talikota on 25 January, 1565, the mighty Vijayanagar ruler was defeated by the combined forces of five Muslim Sultanates bringing to an end the pomp and glory of the Vijayanagar Empire. From here on, all the architectural monuments become naturally Islamic in character. One does see a little bit of Hindu architecture but all the domes, minarets, archways are Islamic in style and structure.

You should either drive up to Bijapur from Badami, which would take you less than 2-1/2 hours. The nearest airport is BELGAUM which is connected with Bombay by Indian Airlines flights.

The Deccan Plateau was a rich prize for the Muslim invaders. Thus, within the same scenario, you visit one of the golden cities of the Muslim kings, Bijapur - "The City of Victory".

500 years ago Bijapur was described by foreign historians as a flourishing city with a vast army. Located on one of the ancient trade routes, it was visited by scholars and historians of both the East and the West.

It was the capital of the Adil Shahi kings who left a wealth of monuments. A walled, medieval and wholly Muslim city, Bijapur boasts of Islamic architecture at its best. The Adil Shahis encouraged building activity to such an extent that Bijapur itself has over 50 mosques, more than 20 tombs and an equal number of palaces.

The GOL GUMBAZ, literally meaning 'the round dome', is the most dominant building. It has a magnificent tomb of Mohammad Adil Shahi and boasts of being the second largest dome in the world, unsupported by pillars. Even a pin dropping is distinctly heard from across a space of 38 metres in the WHISPERING GALLERY. The sound is echoed 11 times over.

Under the dome are the tombs of the Sultan, his two wives, his mistress, his daughter and grandson.

Jama Masjid

The JAMA MASJID is the finest mosque, remarkable for its harmonious proportions and graceful minarets, ornamental details. Emperor Aurangzeb later added a grand entrance and painted the floor. The sacred alcove has the Quran daintily painted on it in letters of gold.

The IBRAHIM RAUZA is a palatial mosque and tomb. With its richly decorated walls and perforated stone windows, it is very beautiful and symmetrical. It has many delicate minarets. Panels decorated with crosses, lotuses and wheels, signify the tolerance of the Adil Shahi dynasty.

The other buildings to see are the GAGAN MAHAL, BARA KHAMBA, TAJ BAWDI, MALIK-I-MAIDAN, etc.

BANGALORE

GENERAL INFORMATION
Population: 4,110,000 (1991 census)
Altitude: 921 metres (3067 ft)
Climate

	Temperature	
	Max.	Min.
Winter	32^0 c	15^0 c
Summer	33^0 c	19^0 c
Rainfall	68 mm	10 mm

Season: Throughout the year.
Clothing
Summer: cottons
Winter: light woollens in the evenings.

HOW TO GET THERE
By Air: Indian Airlines links Bangalore with most major cities of India. Private airlines also link Bangalore with many cities of India.

By Rail: Bangalore has direct rail connections to Madras, Bombay, Delhi, Ahmedabad, Mysore, Pune, Secunderabad, Trichy, Trivandrum and all important places en route.
By Road: Bangalore has very good roads reaching all parts of the south and Bombay. It is
140 km. from Mysore,
220 km. from Bandipur,
299 km. from Ooty,
334 km. from Madras and
353 km. from Hampi.
There are regular bus services to Madras, Mysore, Ooty, Mangalore, Tirupati, Coimbatore, Madurai, Hyderabad, Bombay, Goa, Pune, etc.

LOCAL TRANSPORT
Taxis, metered taxis, auto-rickshaws, cycle-rickshaws and city buses.

CONDUCTED TOURS
1. Half-day tours of the city.
2. Full-day tour to Srirangapatna, Mysore and Brindavan Gardens.
3. Full-day tour to Sravanabelagola, Belur and Halebid.
4. Full-day tour to Nandi Hills.
5. Week-end tour to Mantralaya, T.B. Dam and Hampi.
6. One-day tour to Tirupati.
7. Three-day tour to Ooty, Srirangapatna, Mysore, Bandipur Wildlife Sanctuary.

Information: Government of India Tourist Office, Church Street Bangalore. *Tel*: 5585917. Karnataka State Tourism Development Corporation, Mitra Towers, Queens Circle, Kasturba Road, *Tel*: 2212901

WHERE TO STAY (STD CODE: 080)
Deluxe
1. Taj Residency
   Phone: 5584444
   Fax: 558-4748
   Cable: RESIDENT
2. West End
   Phone: 2269281
   Cable: WESTEND
   Fax: 220-0010
3. Gateway Hotel
   Phone: 5584545
   Fax: 584030
4. Welcomgroup Windsor Manor Sheraton & Tower
   Phone: 2269898
   Cable: WELCOTEL
   Fax: 2264941
5. Oberoi
   Phone: 5585858
   Fax: 5585960
6. Ashok (ITDC)
   Phone: 2669462
   Cable: ASHOKOTEL
   Fax: 2250033
7. Holiday Inn
   Phone: 2269451
   Cable: MACHARLES
   Fax: 267676

Standard
8. Comfort Inn Ramashree
   Phone: 2225152
   Cable: RAMCOMFIN
9. Ashraya International
   Phone: 2261921
   Cable: ASHRAYAINT
10. Harsha
    Phone: 5574024
    Telex: 0845-2561 HH IN
    Fax: 563249
11. Cauvery Continental
    Phone: 2266966
    Telex: 0845-8112 HCC IN
    Cable: TELCAUVERY
12. Bangalore International
    Phone: 2268011
    Telex: 0845-2340HOBIINN
    Cable: SWEETOME
13. St. Mark's Hotel
    Phone: 2219090
    Fax: 2215700
14. Central Park
    Phone: 5584242
15. Maurya
    Phone: 2264111
16. Chalukya
    Phone: 2265055

WHAT TO SEE
1. LALBAGH (Botanical Gardens) and Cubbon Park. Extending over 240

acres, Lalbagh has a wide variety of exotic trees and plants. Many public buildings and the magnificent post-independence Government building, the VIDHAN SOUDHA, are located in Cubbon Park.
2. BULL TEMPLE, built in the Dravidian style over a monolithic bull.
3. TIPU'S PALACE and FORT. This was the summer residence of Tipu Sultan.

EXCURSIONS
1. WHITE FIELD (16 km). The Sri Satya Sai Baba Ashram here attracts visitors from all over the world.
2. BENNARGHATTA (21 km), has a Lion Safari Park, Crocodile Farm and a Snake Park.
3. NANDI HILLS (60 km), a hill-resort with a commanding view of the plains below.
4. MYSORE (140 km), the former capital of the princely State. It is a city of fine buildings and palaces. The Brindavan Gardens nearby and its illuminated fountains are its great tourist attraction.
5. BELUR and HALEBID (222 and 216 km), where there are exquisite carvings in temples of the Hoysala dynasty.
6. SRAVANABELAGOLA (160 km). The 1000-year old colossus, the 17-metre high monolithic statue of the Jain saint, Gomateshwara, attracts Jain pilgrims especially at festival time.
7. BANDIPUR (220 km) and MUDUMALAI (239 km) are Wildlife Sanctuaries en route to Ooty. Elephant rides can be arranged to see wildlife.
8. OOTY (299 km). A beautiful hill-resort in the Nilgiris (Blue Mountains).
9. LEPAKSHI TEMPLE (104 km), has a huge monolithic Nandi bull and a massive Naga (Cobra) sculpture in stone.
10. NAGARHOLE WILDLIFE SANCTUARY (240 km) and Elephant Camp. New Jungle Top forest accommodation.
11. MANGALORE (357 km). Nearby are beaches at Ullal, Marawanthe, Malpe, Coondapur and Karwar.

SHOPPING
Brass and copper temple carvings and figurines, woodcraft (sandalwood and rosewood), ivory and coloured wood inlay on wooden articles, stone carvings and stone friezes in granite and soapstone, perfumes of jasmine, rose, sandalwood, musk and lavender, incense sticks, sandalwood oil and soaps, laquerware, clayware, ceramics, carpets, durries, silk, crepe, cotton, georgette and chiffon fabrics and saris, silverware and jewellery. Bangalore is a shopper's paradise.

FESTIVALS OF SPECIAL LOCAL INTEREST

1. KARAGA FESTIVAL (April). A series of pots are balanced on the head to test one's strength of mind. Draupadi, the daughter of fire, is worshipped as Shakti, the Mother Goddess.
2. KADALEKAYE PARIKSHE, the Groundnut (peanut) fair (November-December), held at the Bull Temple. There are groundnut eating competitions during the fair.

SPORTING EVENTS

Bangalore is famous for horse racing and its stud farms. The racing season is from May to July and from November to March.

BANDIPUR WILDLIFE SANCTUARY

GENERAL INFORMATION
Area: 231 sq. kms.
Altitude: Sea level
Climate:

	Temperature	
	Max.	Min.
Winter	29^0 c	17^0 c
Summer	33^0 c	19^0 c
Rainfall	64 mm	39 mm

Season: March to August. However wildlife can be seen in the winter season also.
Clothing:
Summer: cottons
Winter: light woollens

HOW TO GET THERE
By Air: The nearest airport is Mysore which is connected by Vayudoot flight with Bangalore. The other air connection is with Coimbatore.
By Rail: The nearest railheads are Ooty and Mysore. Ooty is connected by rail with Madras and Mysore (which has rail connections with Bangalore and Hassan).
By Road: Bandipur is 14 km. from Mudumalai, 80 km. from Mysore, 78 km. from Ooty and 220 km. from Bangalore.

LOCAL TRANSPORT
Forest Department jeeps and vans are available to take visitors around the sanctuaries. However, it is more interesting to take an elephant ride through the jungle.

CONDUCTED TOURS
1. There are daily conducted tours in season from Ooty which include a visit to Mudumalai (operated by KSTDC and private agencies).
2. The 7-day package tour by coach of South India operated by KSTDC covers Mudumalai in the itinerary.

WHERE TO STAY
1. Forest lodges, cottages, tourist rest houses (BUDGET).

DELUXE
Accommodation available in Kabeni River Lodge in Bandipur. Reservation from their Bangalore Office. *Ph*: 5586163, 5597021 *Fax*: 080-5586183 *Cable*: JUNGLE LIFE.

Information:
For Bandipur
Field Director, Bandipur Tiger Reserve, Mysore, 570004.

WHAT TO SEE
Some of the common animals seen here are wild elephant herds, chital deer, sambar, gaur, barking deer, wild dog, jackal, sloth bear, four-horned antelope, langur monkey, wild boar and, if lucky, the tiger and the panther. There is a wide range of bird life.
Note: Visitors to the forest must hire a forest guide to accompany them.
The best time to view wildlife is from 6 am. to 9 am. and from 4 pm. to 6 pm.

EXCURSIONS
1. ELEPHANT TRAINING CAMP at Abhayaranyam (5 km. from Mudumalai) where elephants are tamed and trained for timber work.
2. OOTY (64 km. from Mudumalai). Known as the Queen of Hill Stations, it is a beautiful mountain resort in the Nilgiris.
3. COONOOR (19 km. from Ooty), a hill station surrounded by tea plantations.
4. KOTAGIRI (29 km. from Ooty), another hill resort of the Nilgiri mountains.
5. MYSORE (80 km. from Bandipur) is a well planned city of palaces and boulevards. Excellent hotels including the famous Lalitha Mahal Palace Hotel.

BADAMI-AIHOLE-PATTADAKAL

GENERAL INFORMATION
BADAMI:
Population: 16,000 (1991 census)
Altitude: 177 metres (589 ft)
Climate:

	Temperature	
	Max.	Min.
Winter	29⁰ c	15⁰ c
Summer	38⁰ c	23⁰ c

Rainfall 500 mm annually.

Season: Throughout the year, except that the months of April to June are very hot.

Clothing
Summer: light cottons
Winter: cottons with a light sweater for the evenings.

HOW TO GET THERE
By Air: Belgaum, the nearest airport for Badami (192 km) is connected with Bombay by Indian Airlines services. The nearest airport for Hampi is Bellary (77 km) which is connected by Vayudoot flights with Bangalore.

By Rail: Badami is on the Hubli-Sholapur metre gauge line and is connected to Bangalore, Bijapur and Bagalkot.

By Road: Badami is connected by road to all nearby centres. It is 22 km from Pattadakal, 44 km from Aihole, 189 km from Hampi, 163 km from Bijapur, 359 km from Panaji, and 499 km from Bangalore. Bus services operate from Badami to Aihole, Pattadakal, Bagalkot, Hospet (for Hampi), Hubli, Belgaum and Bangalore.

Hampi is connected with all parts of Karnataka and to Hyderabad by bus.

LOCAL TRANSPORT
Private taxis, vans and horse-drawn tongas.

CONDUCTED TOURS
Nil at Badami

WHAT TO SEE
1. BADAMI CAVE TEMPLES dating back to the 6th century. Of these three are Hindu and one Jain. Sculptured out of solid rock they are adorned with carvings.
2. BADAMI FORT, on top of a hill, encloses large granaries, a treasury and a watch tower. The famed MALLEGITTI SHIVALAYA TEMPLE, set on the summit of a hill, is built of stone joined together without mortar.
3. The SCULPTURE GALLERY of the ARCHAEOLOGICAL SURVEY OF INDIA with many old pieces found in this area.

EXCURSIONS
1. AIHOLE (44 km) is the cradle of stone temple architecture of the southern Dravida school; the oldest temple, the Ladh Khan, goes back to the 5th century A.D. There are 70 temples in this group. The Durga Temple is noted for its sculptures. The Meguli temple is built of 630 small stone blocks. The Ravanaphadi Cave has some beautiful carvings.
2. PATTADAKAL (22 km) was well known even in the 1st century A.D. when Ptolemy referred to it as Petrigal. It reached its pinnacle of glory under the Chalukya kings from the 7th to 9th centuries. The queens Lokamahadevi and Trailokyamahadevi brought sculptors from Kanchipuram and created fantasies in stone.

Pattadakal is unique in having temple architecture of the northern Nagara and southern Dravida styles. The oldest temple in this group is the Samghameshwara Temple. The Mallikarjuna Temple has pillars depicting the birth and life of Krishna. The largest of the temples, the

Virupaksha has sculptures and panels depicting scenes from the *Ramayana* and the *Mahabharata*. The Papanatha Temple in the northern style has impressive carvings on its pillars and the ceiling. Students of temple architecture should visit Badami-Aihole-Pattadakal for visual lessons in the origin and early development of Hindu temple design and form.

3. HAMPI (77 km from Bellary, the nearest airport. 189 km from Badami and 353 km from Bangalore). The Vijayanagar Empire of medieval India spread from the Arabian Sea to the Bay of Bengal and covered all of the Deccan Plateau (Peninsular India). The greatest of its rulers, Krishnadeva Raya, has few equals in history. His patronage of the visual and performing arts, and the

Ruins of Virupaksha temple

strength and power of the ruined monuments at Hampi are evidence as are the temples all over the south, built or expanded in this period. The five Muslim Sultanates of the south joined together in 1565 and razed the capital, Hampi (known for its magnificent palaces, baths, temples and sculptures) for 6 months, giving it the name, the Pompeii of India.

Some of the interesting ruins remaining are the Virupaksha, Vittala and Hazara Rama temples, huge Ganesha and Narsimha images, elephant stables, the Queen's Bath, carvings on the Ramachandra Temple, Lotus Mahal, stone chariot etc.

4. BIJAPUR (163 km from Badami) was the capital of the Adil Shahi kings who have left a wealth of monuments. The most famous is the Gol Gumbaz, whose dome is the second largest in the world.

2. At Aihole: The famous Irkali handloom, art silk and silk saris are available near here.
3. At Bijapur: Handlooms from Gulekgud and Irkali, toys and Lambadi gypsy jewellery.

SHOPPING
1. At Badami: Woven choli (blouse) material of Gulekgud.

FESTIVALS OF SPECIAL LOCAL INTEREST
Temple festivals are held at Badami, Pattadakal, Alihole, Hampi and Bijapur.

Budithi Planters – vase and pots

Chapter 20

KERALA
India's Tropical Paradise

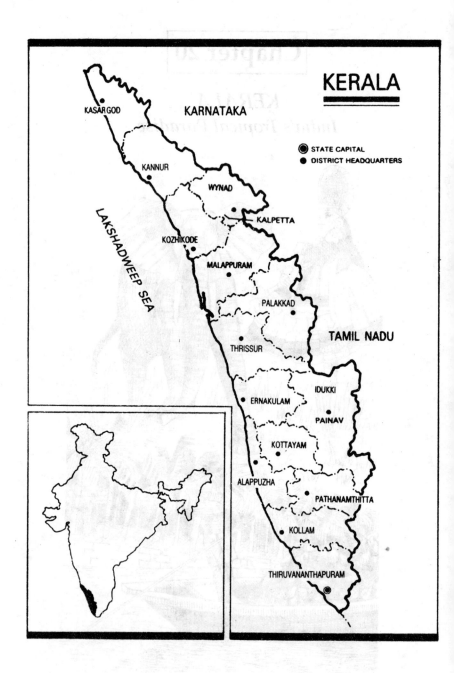

Kerala (population 29 million), the land of Green Magic, is one of India's smallest States. It is a narrow fertile coastal strip, 583 km. long and seldom wider than 120 km., offering to the visitors an unusual panorama of palm-fringed beaches, and high mountains. One of its peaks, ANAMUDI, is 2690 metres, the highest south of the Himalayas. It has centuries-old backwaters and a warm and hospitable people who have welcomed foreigners for over 5000 years.

Its mountain sides are full of rubber, coffee, tea, cocoa, pepper and cardamom plantations. The word cardamom had its origin from the hills where it is grown — CARDAMOM HILLS. These mountains look down on contrasting landscape of coconut palms and grey farm-houses in the plains of Kerala. One-fourth of its land is covered with thick forests sprouting some six hundred varieties of trees including valuable timber.

The vast sea around it yields as much as 400,000 tons of fish every year — 30 per cent of India's total catch. Its shrimps and frog legs are exported to Europe, USA and Japan. The State produces over 4000 million coconuts — more than any other State of India. It has rich fauna—elephant, leopard, bear, gaur, sambar and the Nilgiri ibex.

Land and water share an extraordinary kinship in Kerala. The land, according to legend, is believed to have sprung forth from the womb of the sea with the blessings of Lord Parsurama. It continues to bask in the tender life-giving care of waters that lap gently on its coast, and cascade down the hills and valleys. Later, these waters collect into exotic backwaters and lagoons. The backwaters stretch over 1900 kilometres and snake their way across the entire state. Sometimes, they melt into the sea, then emerge again and flow on, fertilising the soil. At times, these waters shoot up right in a busy marketplace. Many colourful tales have been woven around these backwaters when merchant ships in ancient times carried valuable cargo of ivory, gold, coconut, rubber and spices of Kerala to foreign shores and were raided by pirates.

HISTORY

Although Kerala was protected from the northern invaders in the past because of its high mountains, at no time was Kerala isolated. The Malabar coast was open to the ancient world through the sea and that is why Kerala has remained cosmopolitan all these centuries and open to religious and cultural influences. Long before Vasco da Gama landed in CALICUT in 1498, the Phoenicians came here to trade in ivory and spices. The Biblical Ophir visited by King Solomon's ships around 1000 B.C. is believed to have been in Kerala - the village PAVAL - not far from today's THIRUVANANTHAPURAM, the present-day capital of Kerala. They were followed by Greeks and Romans who travelled in small dhows and ships from Arabia. The Chinese had a flourishing trade with COCHIN and QUILON. The Chinese have left a lasting influence in Kerala in the shape of the houses on the Malabar coast and fishing nets used by the local fishermen. These fishing nets even to this day are known by the name of the country of their origin.

Among the earliest immigrants to Kerala were the Jews, believed to have fled to Kerala when Nebuchadnezzar occupied Jerusalem in 587 B.C. Later, more Jews came to Kerala persecuted by Romans, and they settled down at CRAGANORE. The Jewish synogogue at MATTANCHERI at Cochin displays an ancient copper plate containing the orders of King Bhaskar Ravi Verma in the fourth century A.D. awarding the village of ANJUVANNAM to Joseph Rabban and his descendants in hereditary possession "so long as the world and moon exist." This principality was later razed by the Arab traders who had problems with the Jews. The Jews moved to Cochin and built a synogogue which reminds us of the tolerance of Indian people. Now, most of the young Jews have migrated to Israel for better opportunities and only the old people have been left at Cochin.

Among 24 per cent Christians in Kerala, some claim their descent from the people who were converted to Christianity by St. Thomas who came to Kerala in A.D. 50. He is believed to have landed near Craganore. In this town, there is still a 4th century Church with carved Hindu style columns. There is a Syrian Church VALIA PALLI built in 9th century. Kerala's Syrian Christians were here as early as A.D. 190. An emissary from Alexandria found that the local Christians had a copy of the Gospel of St. Mathew in Hebrew. Today, the Syrian Christians still chant the liturgy which was brought by their forefathers 1900 years ago. They pray in churches that must be some of the oldest in the world. They are concentrated in the central districts of Kerala and are well integrated with the local communities — some of them have distinguished themselves as scholars of Sanskrit and Malayalam languages.

Like other religions, Islam too came to Kerala not with the proselytising zeal of swordsmen. It came to Kerala through Arab traders, many of them settling down here. Interestingly, Kerala had never the types of communal riots that have been the bane of the northern States.

The presence of Christians in Kerala was quite a surprise to Portuguese who followed Vasco Da Gama to the Malabar coast. The local Christians told the newcomers that they had never heard of the Pope, which upset the Portuguese who were ardent followers of the Pope. Therefore, the local Christians had to face the wrath of the Portuguese zealots as much as the Hindus.

The profitable spice trade had attracted many adventurers from European countries. The Dutch were the first to come although their stay was short and uneventful. They were followed by the Portuguese who signed a treaty with the Rani of Quilon in 1516. The Dutch came back again and forced the Portuguese out. The British appeared on the scene, and opened their first settlement at ANJENGO, south of Quilon. They succeeded in winning over the Maharaja of Travancore, forcing the Dutch to move out.

The present-day State of Kerala appeared on the map of India only in 1956. After independence, the States of India were reorganised on the basis of linguistic affinity of the people. The Malayalam-speaking areas were merged into the new State of Kerala which included earstwhile Travancore and Cochin State. The Tamil-speaking district of Kanyakumari was ceded to the State of Tamil Nadu. The new State is 11 times smaller than the largest Indian State of Madhya Pradesh. It is almost of the same size as Switzerland.

Even before independence, the erstwhile State of Travancore and Cochin had emerged as one of the most advanced States of India under its enlightened rulers and progressive Dewans (Chief Ministers). After independence, Kerala made quick progress by harnessing its water and mineral resources and by the enterprise of its hardworking people who made the best of the opportunities available in the Gulf States. Half a million Malayalese live and work in the Gulf. The State is relatively rich where average per capita income is one of the highest in India. Kerala has also been recently proclaimed as the first 100 per cent literate State in India.

Kerala's another claim to fame—it was the first State which democratically elected a Communist Government. But, paradoxes do not end here. It was not uncommon for Marxist Ministers to prostrate in reverence before the Hindu idols.

CASTE SYSTEM IN KERALA

Despite universal literary, the caste system of Kerala is complicated and has lot of influence on all religions. Among the Hindus a prominent section belongs to the Nair caste - traditionally governed by matriarchal system under which property is inherited through the female side of the family. The Nair women, therefore, always had a proud position in the society. The system is now changing. The Nairs are of Kshatriya (warrior) caste who often decided their disputes by duelling. They gave it up only under British pressure. A Nair family used to be a huge unit who lived in a large home called Tarawada. Kerala countryside is dotted with such beautiful homes. Another important caste which has played a key role in the Kerala society are the Namboodiri Brahmins who are said to have been brought by Saint Parsurama to this land. They settled in 64 different centres. Apparently, they were Aryans and were responsible for Sanskritisation of the Malayalese language. Until recently, the Namboodiris were a dominant class among the landowners. They devoted their life to the study of the *Vedas* and were among the most orthodox Brahmins of India. Other castes lived in awe of them — the Shudras would not wear the upper garment before them and addressed them as Tirumeni — a venerable body. The Namboodiris had a peculiar custom — only the elder son married in his own caste. The younger ones were supposed to remain celebate but they contacted alliances or moganatic marriages with Nair women whose children could not inherit property. Many Namboodiri women had to remain unmarried resulting in social tension. The system is now changing.

Another important caste of Kerala are the Ehavas, believed to be of Polynesian origin. They came to Kerala via Sri Lanka. They belong to the depressed classes but lately they have advanced economically and socially. Many Tamil Brahmins have also settled down in Kerala.

Hindus, Christians, Jews and Moslems form part of the great kaleidoscope of Kerala. Most men wear impeccable white clothes and carry black umbrellas to ward off the ever-present tropical sun. Their beautiful women dress in colourful saris and decorate their hair with flowers.

The people of Kerala have their own way of relaxing and entertainment. The religious fervour of the people of this state finds its expression in the dance-drama of Kathakali - a classical dance form which originated in Kerala. It took shape in the 17th century under the patronage of princes and landowners. Once confined to temples, it has now travelled to all parts of the world. Traditionally, the roles of women are also played by men. They wear interesting and colourful costumes. Dances more often relate to religious and epic stories and themes.

The people of Kerala are very God-fearing and you can see the young and the old visiting temples every morning and evening.

Festivals are a common sight and a way of relaxation. They come regularly except perhaps during the months of heavy rains. The most picturesque festival of all is the ONAM - a four-day harvest celebration with races of giant snake boats manned by over one hundred oarsmen as the climax. It comes in August. Then, every temple has its own festivals which is often led by elephants in procession.

WHEN TO VISIT KERALA

By far the best time to visit Kerala is from October to March when the rains' fury has subsided. The weather is pleasantly cool and breezy. But, if you want to see Nature in all its fury, turmoil and glory, see Kerala in June and July. For weeks together, the sun, moon and the stars are blotted out. The rains come pounding — the red earth and keep tapping the tiled roofs and broad leaves of plantains. The ponds are full and rivers turbulent. The skies are menacingly dark. Under the dark canopy, there is an uproarious burst of green in every nook and corner of the State. In August, the sun re-emerges and the rain-washed foliage glimmers in light presenting the green magic of this State. The rice is ready for harvest and people look forward to celebrating their most important festival - Onam - with all the zeal and gusto.

Being rain-fed, there is hardly any wasteland in Kerala. In some areas rain is as high as 500 cms annually.

Not many people even in India know that India's second-ranking seaport on Arabian sea is in Kerala. Here in Cochin, the mainland is pierced by the flowing backwaters creating the WELLINGTON ISLAND. The new town on one side is ERNAKULAM. The twin-city across the water is Cochin. It was called the British Cochin when the British ruled over India.

In terms of shopping, Kerala offers its own specialities of handicrafts. You could take home handicrafts in wood, ivory, horn or metal. There are brass lamps, coir mats, wall hangings, handloom fabrics and gold jewellery of exquisite designs.

Although two or three days' stay in Kerala, looking at its well-known wildlife sanctuary PERIYAR and travelling through the countryside, may be all right for the hurried foreigners, Kerala is really for travellers who can journey through the countryside leisurely. You will certainly enjoy Kerala if you take some cruises and boat rides, travel through the countryside by trains and buses. The State has an excellent network of metalled roads and many trains criss-cross the land.

THIRUVANANTHAPURAM

It may be better to start from the capital. Trivandrum (Pop: 700,000) is the anglicised form of the original name Thiruvananthapuram which means the town of Ananth, the serpent on which Lord Vishnu reclines. The city has been the seat of rulers of Travancore who trace their ancestry to A.D. 849. There is a temple dedicated to Vishnu - Shri Ananthapadmanabhaswamy. The town takes its name from this temple.

TRIVANDRUM INTERNATIONAL AIRPORT is a useful jumping off point for Air India, Air Lanka or Indian Airlines for journey to Sri Lanka, the Maldives or the Gulf countries. Indian Airlines connects the capital of Kerala with all major cities of India including Delhi, Bombay, Madras, Goa, Bangalore, Cochin, etc.

Kerala offers some of India's most enjoyable train journeys, riding past spectacular palm-fringed coastal backwaters and vast rice plantations. Tourists travel up Kerala's coastline to Cochin — a distance of 219 km. — by a unique combination of train, backwater trails and buses.

From the State capital, Kerala State Transport Corporation operates frequent long-distance services not only to towns within the State but also to major towns in Tamil Nadu and Karnataka. For wildlife enthusiasts, there is a daily bus service to THEKKADY (PERIYAR) WILDLIFE SANCTUARY, a distance 272 km. It takes eight hours to reach the sanctuary.

The buses, unfortunately, do not have English signboards - an independent foreign tourist has to do some effort to find out which bus goes where. But, there are helpful people who go out of the way to assist foreign visitors and many people in Kerala speak English.

If you happen to be interested in Indian art, you must visit the city's MUSEUM and CHITRALAYAN ART GALLERY. It displays paintings from all parts of India. Its walls show the paintings of Rajput, Mughal and Tanjore Schools, copies of Ajanta and Sigirya frescoes in Sri Lanka and works from China, Japan, Tibet and Bali along with the works of modern Indian painters. A section of the gallery is devoted entirely to the works of Raja Ravi Verma - a great and eminent painter of Kerala.

In the same precincts is situated the Museum housed in a rambling palace with a rich collection of ancient bronzes.

For travellers who want to enjoy Nature in easily digestible form, there is a ZOO nearby and an excellent AQUARIUM. The aquarium is used by marine biologists, fisheries experts and visitors.

Trivandrum is a beautiful city built on seven hills. The pagoda-style tiled roofs show the architectural influence of South East Asia with which Kerala had close contacts.

The PADMANABHASWAMY TEMPLE, the famous temple in the city, however, is built in the Dravidian style.

Padmanabhaswany Temple

This temple, with huge pylon-like gopurams, heavily decorated and gilded finials, is dedicated to Vishnu. The shrine is very ancient, though the structure as it is seen today is the result of renovation and additions by king Martanda Verma of Travancore.

Three hundred and sixty-eight carved granite pillars mark the corridors. Only Hindus can go into the temples wearing a dhoti - an unstitched garment. Non-Hindus can admire it from the outside. Hindu women are also not allowed.

To see what life was in the princely times, a visit to KAVADIYAR PALACES is recommended. It is the residence of the former Maharaja. Since it is the private property of the scions of the ruling family, permission is necessary to visit it.

KOVALAM BEACH

Inviting beachscape at Kovalam

Sixteen km. away spread on silk-soft sand, this calm and quiet resort has one of the finest beaches in India.

Apart from ITDC's fine Kovalam Beach Resort and a cluster of cottages at Kovalam Grove, there are facilities for aquatic sports, yoga and oil massage-treatment according to the Ayurvedic system and an open-air theatre for the performance of the Kathakali dance. Since Kovalam is not far from the capital, tourists visiting the city may like to stay at the Beach hotels.

Padmanabhapuram Palace

Fifty-three kms on the way to Kanyakumari or Cape Comorin - the Land's End - one can stop to marvel at this ancient palace of the Travancore rulers. It is rich with unique murals, and exquisite carvings in bronze and stone.

It is said that in the making of its floor, an ancient technique, using charred coconut husks, was applied.

PONMUDI or the golden peak is a one and a half hours' drive from the city. The road is lined with fruit and mango trees.

Varkala

Thirty-two km. north from Trivandrum on the way to Quilon lies Varkala. It offers a breathtaking scenery of the cliff looming over the beach and spurting mineral water springs. It has the JANARDHAN TEMPLE where Hindu pilgrims go in thousands.

QUILON

Ninety km. from Trivandrum, this ancient town, girdled by inland waterways, is within easy reach of the Kerala capital. Marco Polo visited this sea coast kingdom ruled by a Queen in the 13th century. Sailing, you can see Chinese style barges with pagoda-curled roofs. It is Kerala's answer to Venice — it is often described as the 'Venice of the East'.

LAKE ASTAMUDI (so named because of eight creeks) can give you a pleasant boating experience. The Lighthouse area at THANGASSERI bears traces of Dutch, Portuguese and the English presence in bygone days. The THEVALI PALACE on the sea is another attraction.

If you have time, take a 9-hour northward boat trip along the coastal backwaters to ALLEPPEY.

The old RESIDENCY of the Viceroys, now turned into a Tourist Bungalow offers accommodation in an old world charm.

ALLEPPEY

Eighty-five km. from Quilon (64 km from Cochin and 155 km. from Trivandrum) Alleppey is a water-borne town criss-crossed by a network of canals cutting through the town. A boat journey from Quilon takes about nine hours.

Home of Kerala's famous coir industry, it is interesting to see coconut husks being beaten into fibre for mats or coir carpets. A stroll along the busy wharf markets with barges laden with local produce can be a memorable experience.

Many of the famous snake boat races of Kerala are held on Alleppey's shallow, Vembanad Lake generally during August.

COCHIN

Cochin is one of the finest natural harbours in the world. This ancient city has an eventful history. A cluster of isles, it bears the stamp of foreign influences.

The first Europeans to form a colony here were the Portuguese coming in the wake of Vasco da Gama's voyage. The peaceful Jewish colony believed to have been established before the beginning of the Christian era has its old synagogue, the floor of which is paved with hand painted willow-patterned Chinese tiles, blue and white.

Synagogue

The CHURCH OF ST FRANCIS was the first European place of worship in India. The Portuguese built it as a Roman Catholic Church. Under Dutch occupation, between 1644 and 1804, it became Protestant. The British made it Anglican. Now, it is a constituent of the Church of South India.

The DUTCH PALACE is neither Dutch nor a palace. It was a house built by the Portuguese in the mid-16th century, as a gift to the king of Cochin. Later, the Dutch renovated it so thoroughly that it came to be known as the Dutch Palace. Its walls have murals depicting scences from Hindu mythology. WILLINGDON ISLAND, where the airport and the railway terminus

Church of St. Francis

Krishna Temple

are situated, is a man-made island with land dredged out of the sea for improving the Cochin harbour.

The largest city in Kerala with a population of about one million, Cochin is well connected by air, rail and road with all major cities of India. It is 218 km. from the capital, Trivandrum.

The tourist bungalow called BOLGHATTY PALACE, on BOLGHATTY ISLAND, was originally a Dutch residence. Chinese fishing nets in the backwaters are a familiar sight and remind you of the centuries gone by when Kerala and China had flourishing trade.

KOTTAYAM

Sixty-nine kms. from Cochin and 154 km. from Trivandrum, Kottayam was the high centre of the Syrian Christian Church. It is also the nearest railway station to the Periyar Wild Life Sanctuary.

The VALIA PALLI or the Big Church here is famous for its ornate altar and the Persian frescoes cut in relief on the side altars.

The 400-year old CHERIA PALLI CHURCH is rich in murals, blending western Coptic tradition and oriental colour. There are impressive carved multiple altars. The boat races are held at nearby ARANMULA.

PERIYAR WILDLIFE SANCTUARY

Periyar National Park, 208 km. from Cochin, 258 km. from Trivandrum, and 32 km. from PEERMADE, surrounds the uneven Periyar Lake. The Lake is 26 km. long and the park is over 675 sq. km. in area. There is a man-made reservoir behind a dam on Periyar River. Like a placid river, it winds around capes and hills. Some hills rise 1,000 metres above the surface of the Lake.

This is the best sanctuary in the country for closely watching the Asiatic wild elephant. There are motor boats to take the visitors around the Lake and along its creeks.

Periyar offers one of the most sybaritic ways of seeing big wildlife in the whole world. There are no tiring trips or long safaris. You just have a leisurely cruise on a motor launch around the bends of the Lake. Wild elephants in herds come for a drink. So do deer or bison. During the dry season when the water holes within the forest are dry, tiger and leopard too trek to the lake for a drink.

From the safety of the boat, one can closely watch wild elephants coming down to the lake in small herds. Occasionally, a lone bull too. Gaur are also to be found in a few herds and may be seen in the open flat

Periyar Lake

of AIYAPPAN-KURUKKU, EDAPALAYAM. They are very big in size though they may not look so in the vastness of the setting. One may see sambar early in the morning or in the evening. Pig, dhole (wild dogs) are seen occasionally. The monkey of the area is the black Nilgiri langur. Other animals include bison, wild boar, leopard and sloth bear. Fresh water tortoises bask on low stumps. Herons, egrets, darters and kingfishers perch on deadwood.

Apart from the Tourist Bungalow, there are some hotels at Periyar.

OTHER ATTRACTIONS

KOZHIKODE or CALICUT (218 km. from Cochin) is the city that was the capital of the Zamorins. Kozhikode is famous for its cotton fabrics. The word Calico was derived from Calicut.

At SULTAN'S BATTERY stands a fine ancient Jain Temple in a grove which is a short trip north-west of Kozhikode

CANNANORE, about 235 km. from Cochin, was the premier seaport on India's west coast. It was the capital of Cheraman Perumal. Vasco da Gama called in here in A.D. 1498 and the Portuguese built a settlement and a fort. The fort stands to this day.

MUNNAR, 136 km. from Cochin at 1,525 metres above sea level is a tea plantation centre. Tribal people are the neighbours here to the planters still living in the Victorian style. A beautiful golf course is at nearby KUNDALE.

KALADI, 54 km. from Cochin, is the birthplace of Adi Shankaracharya, India's most renowned 8th century saint and philosopher. He was the founder of the Advaita doctrine of monotheistic Hindu philosophy. He gave unity of thought to Hinduism and travelled to the nooks and corners of India, propounding his thoughts. He set up Hindu centres called Maths at major pilgrim centres and to this day, the Gurus at these centres - also called Shankracharyas - guide the Hindu mind.

CRAGANORE, 77km. from Cóchin, is a drowsy seaside town that sheltered colonies of Greek and Roman traders and Jewish and Christian immigrants over 2000 years ago.

TRICHUR, well-known for the VADAKKUNATHAN TEMPLE, is among the other places worth a visit.

GURUVAYOOR, 32 km. further, is an important pilgrim centre with its famous KRISHNA TEMPLE.

WOMEN FIRST IN KERALA

Kerala women have many firsts to their credit. The latest is the appointment of Miss M. Fathima Beevi (former Judge of the Kerala High Court) as the Judge of the Supreme Court of India. She is the first-ever woman to become a member of the country's highest judicial body.

Kerala contributed India's first woman Magistrate (Mrs. Omanakunjamma), first woman High Court Judge (Mrs. Anna Chandy), first woman Chief Engineer (Ms. P.K. Thresia), first woman I.A.S. officer (Mrs. Anna George Malhotra) and first woman Director of Animal Husbandry (Annamma Jacob).

NAME CHANGES IN KERALA

Names of major cities of Kerala have been changed recently.

New Name	Old Name
Thiruvananthapuram	Trivandrum
Kollam	Quilon
Alappuzha	Alleppey
Kochi	Cochin
Thrissur	Trichur
Palakkad	Palghat
Kozhikode	Calicut
Cannoor	Cannanore

THIRUVANANTHAPURAM

GENERAL INFORMATION
Population: 700,000 (1991 census)
Altitude: Sea level
Climate

	Temperature	
	Max.	Min.
Winter	33^0 c	22^0 c
Summer	32^0 c	23^0 c
Rainfall	75 mm	3 mm

Season: Throughout the year, except during the months of heavy rain (May, June, July, November).
Clothing: Light cottons throughout the year.

HOW TO GET THERE
By Air: Thiruvananthapuram is an international airport from where flights operate to the Middle East, Europe, Sri Lanka and the Maldives. Indian Airlines operates flights to major cities.

By Rail: Thiruvananthapuram has direct rail connections with Ahmedabad, Bangalore, Bombay, Delhi, Ernakulam (Cochin), Guwahati, Jammu, Madras, etc.

By Road: Thiruvananthapuram is connected by good roads with all parts of the South. It is
87 km. from Kanyakumari,
223 km. from Cochin,
272 km. from Periyar (220 km. by a shorter route) and
320 km. from Madurai.
There are direct bus services to all parts of Kerala as also to Kanyakumari, Madras, Madurai, etc.

Information:
Government of India Tourist Office, Airport. *Tel* 451498
Government of Kerala Tourist Office, Park View. *Tel* 61132
Fax: 62279

LOCAL TRANSPORT
Luxury cars (limousines) and tourist taxis, yellow-topped taxis, auto-rickshaws and city bus services.

CONDUCTED TOURS
1. Full-day tour by Kerala Tourism Corporation covering the city and beaches as also NAYYAR DAM and other picnic spots. All days except Mondays from 0800 to 1900 hrs.
2. Full-day tour to KANYAKUMARI via Kovalam, Padmanabhapuram palace and Suchindram Temple. (Daily)
3. Full-day tour to PONMUDI, a health resort in the hills, 61 km. away.
4. Week-end 2-day tour to the PERIYAR GAME SANCTUARY, including a cruise to see wildlife.
5. Tours are also available to KODAIKANAL and Courtallam.

WHERE TO STAY (STD CODE: 0471)

DELUXE
1. Kovalam Ashok Beach Resorts
   Phone: 480101
   Fax: 0471-481522

STANDARD
2. Luciya Continental
   Phone: 73443
   Fax: 73347
3. Mascot (KTDC)
   Phone: 438990, 438976
4. Pankaj
   Phone: 76667
   Fax: 76255
   Cable: PANKAJ

BUDGET
5. Chaithram
   Phone: 75777
6. Silver Sand
   Phone: 70318
   Cable: HAPPYSTAY
7. Amritha
   Phone: 63091
   Telex: 0435-205 AMRTHA IN
8. Highlands
   Phone: 78440, 78466
9. Paramount Tourist Home
   Phone: 63474
10. Lal Tourist Home
    Phone: 68477
11. Ammu
    Phone: 79906, 77937
12. Horizon
    Phone: 66888
    Cable: HORIZON
13. Geeth
    Phone: 71941, 71987
    Cable: GEETHHOTEL
14. Jas
    Phone: 64881
    Cable: JASHOTEL
15. Samudra Kovalam
    Phone: 480242
    Cable: SAMUDRA

WHAT TO SEE
1. NAPIER MUSEUM built on the pattern of an ancient Kerala family homes.
2. SRI CHITRA ART GALLERY which has an excellent collection of paintings.

EXCURSIONS
1. KOVALAM BEACH (16 km), one of the most beautiful beaches of the world, where the surf is ideal for surf-riding and the waters invite the visitor to ride a catamaran (log) with the fishermen, or to swim. ITDC's Kovalam Beach Resort has the Kovalam Hotel built on the side of a hill. Along the beach is Kovalam grove with 'kudis' (cottages) set amidst palm trees and nearby is the Beach Centre for acquatic sports. At the Yoga and Health Centre are held classes in Yoga and transcendental meditation. Ayurvedic oil massages and oil baths are given by experts.
2. PADMANABHAPURAM PALACE (53 km). The seat of the ancient rulers of Travancore, it has beautiful mural paintings and elaborate woodwork.
3. SUCHINDRAM (74 km). The temple here is known for its intricate stone carvings.
4. KANYAKUMARI (87 km) in Tamil Nadu state is the land's-end of India. Here the three oceans meet. It is famous for its fabulous

sunrises and sunsets, the rock on which Swami Vivekananda meditated and the new temple built on it which draws visitors throughout the year. Boat trips operate to the rock regularly.
5. NAYYAR DAM (29 km). An International Yoga conference is held here every year.
6. PONMUDI (61 km), a quiet hill resort known for Nature treks. KTDC's Ponmudi Tourist Complex has cottages, rooms, etc.
7. KUMARAKOM (10 km from Kottayam), is a typical Kerala village on Vembanad Lake.
8. PEERMADE (75 km from Kottayam). Plantation country and a hill resort, it is a good halting point on the way to Periyar.
9. PERIYAR WILD LIFE SANCTUARY (272 km). A Project Tiger Sanctuary where a boat-ride takes you to see wildlife on the banks of Periyar Lake, especially elephant herds.
10. MUNNAR (302 km)—a hill resort.

FESTIVALS OF LOCAL INTEREST
1. USAVOM (March-April and October-November). A 10-day festival when processions of elephants are taken out and music performances and folk dances are held.
2. ARAT FESTIVAL (March-April and October-November). A 10-day festival. On the concluding day, a procession with caparisoned elephants is taken down to the beach.
3. ONAM FESTIVAL (Aug.-Sept.) is the harvest festival and is the most important celebration in Kerala. Floral decorations, cultural shows and snake boat races and processions are part of the programme.

ENTERTAINMENT
The Thiruvananthapuram Kathakali Club, and organisations like Drysyavedi and Margi organise regular Kathakali programmes.

KOCHI (COCHIN)

GENERAL INFORMATION
Population: 700,000 (1991 census)
Altitude: Sea level
Climate

	Temperature	
	Max.	Min.
Winter	31° c	23° c
Summer	31° c	24° c
Rainfall	99 mm	22 mm

Season: Throughout the year except during the months of heavy rains - June and July.
Clothing: Light cottons throughout the year.

HOW TO GET THERE

By Air: Indian Airlines and private airlines flights daily connect Cochin to Madras, Bombay, Delhi, Bangalore, Goa, Madurai and Trivandrum (Thiruvananthapuram).

By Rail: Cochin has direct rail connections with Ahmedabad, Bangalore, Bombay, Delhi, Guwahati, Kanyakumari, Jammu, Madras, Ooty, Trichy, Trivandrum, etc.

By Road: Cochin is accessible by road. It is
190 km. from Periyar,
223 km. from Trivandrum,
312 km. from Ooty and
565 km. from Bangalore.
There are regular bus services to all parts of Kerala, as also to Mysore (for Ooty), Madurai, Madras, Pondicherry and Kanyakumari.

LOCAL TRANSPORT

Luxury taxis (limousines), tourist taxis and regular taxis are available. Boat services operate on the waterways within the city and to the suburbs.

CONDUCTED TOURS
1. A half day tour by boat.
2. THEKKADY WILDLIFE TOUR — 2 day tour on week-ends, including a cruise to see wildlife at Periyar. *Reservation*: Kerala Tourism Development Corporation. *Tel*: 353234.

Information: Government of India Tourist Office, Wellingdon Island *Phone*: 666045

WHERE TO STAY (STD CODE: 0484)

DELUXE
1. Hotel Malabar
   Phone: 666811
   Fax: 0484-668297
   Cable: COMFORT

STANDARD
2. Hotel Casino
   Phone: 666822
   Fax: 0885-668001
   Cable: CASINO
3. Hotel Abad Plaza
   Phone: 361636
   Fax: 0885-370729
4. Hotel Presidency
   Phone: 363100, 360103
5. Bolgathy Palace Hotel (KTDC)
   Phone: 355003
   Cable: RELAX

BUDGET
6. Hotel International
   Phone: 353011
   Fax: 0885-5698
   Cable: TURISTOME
7. Hotel Abad
   Phone: 28211
8. Hotel Grand
   Phone: 353211, 352560
   Cable: GRAND
9. Hotel Woodlands
   Phone: 351372
   Cable: WOODLANDS
10. Hotel Bharat
    Phone: 353501, 361415
    Telex: 0885-6366
    Cable: BHARATHOME

WHAT TO SEE
1. DUTCH PALACE, Mattancherry. In the centre is the Coronation Hall of the Cochin Maharajas. 17th

century murals on the events of the *Ramayana* can be seen in the adjacent rooms.
2. JEWISH SYNAGOGUE, Mattancherry. Built in 1568, it contains Grand Scrolls of the Old Testament, and copper plates containing the privileges granted to the Jews by the Cochin Maharajas.
3. ST. FRANCIS' CHURCH, the oldest church built by Europeans in India. Vasco da Gama was originally buried here.
4. GUNDU ISLAND. The highlight of a visit to Cochin is a boat ride through the backwaters to various islands where coir mat-making and other cottage industries can be seen. At Bolghatty Island, KTDC, has a medium-priced hotel.
5. Chinese fishing nets still in use going back to ancient days when there was brisk trade between India and China.

EXCURSIONS
1. ALWAYE (21 km). An ideal place for swimming in the Periyar river. The annual Shivaratri Fair is held on the banks of the river.
2. ALAPPUZHA (64 km). It is from Alleppey that backwater cruises take off through a network of canals. On the shores of these canals are villages against the backdrop of coconut trees. Allow a full day for this interesting excursion. Colourful Snake-Boat Races are held every August.
3. KOTTAYAM (78 km) is surrounded by rubber, tea, coffee, pepper and cardamom plantations.
4. KUMAKAROM (86 km), an idyllic village set amongst paddy fields and Vembanad Lake. Backwater trips can be taken from here also.
5. MUNNAR (136 km) is a hill resort, 1,524 metres high, in the midst of cardamom and tea plantations. Nearby is ANAMUDI PEAK (1,695 metres), the highest point in South India.
6. KOTTAKAL (168 km). Famous for its oil massages and Ayurvedic Indian medicinal treatments.
7. PERIYAR WILDLIFE SANCTUARY (190km) is ideal for seeing wild elephants and other wild animals while cruising on PERIYAR LAKE. It is spread over an area of 777 sq. km.
8. LAKSHADWEEP (LACCADIVE) ISLANDS are coral islands of the Arabian Sea. Ships of the Shipping Corporation of India make several trips every month from Cochin. Journey time 18 hours. These islands are excellent for swimming and viewing underwater

corals. Individual foreign tourists require permits from the Ministry of Home Affairs, Delhi. Tourist groups can obtain permits through their travel agent in Cochin.

SHOPPING

Ivory, sandalwood, rosewood and white cedar carvings, inlay work on wood, horn products, lace work, articles made of coconut and coir, pineapple, banana and coconut fibre articles, bell-metal lamps, etc., are some of the local handicrafts. Delicate gold jewellery is a speciality of the region.

FESTIVALS OF SPECIAL LOCAL INTEREST

1. UTSOVAM (festival) at the Shiva Temple, Ernakulam (January-February) held for 8 days. It includes a procession of elephants and staging of folk dances and music.
2. MALAYATTOOR PERUNNAL (March/April), a festival celebrated in the Shrine of St. Thomas at Malayattoor (45 km. from Cochin).
3. POORAM FESTIVAL (April-May) at Trichur (74 km from Cochin). A spectacular pageant of caparisoned elephants, fireworks, etc.
4. CHAMPAKKULAM VALLOMKALI (June-July) at Ambalapuzha (16 km from Alleppey) when a snake-boat procession is held.
5. BOAT RACES at Alleppey (usually on the second Saturday in August). Exciting races for the Nehru Trophy are held here.
6. ATHACHAMAYAM (August-September), a procession at Thiruppunithura, near Cochin, marks the commencement of the 10-day Onam festival.
7. ONAM (August-September) is the harvest festival and is the most important celebration of Kerala. Floral decorations, folk dances, cultural shows and snake-boat races and processions are part of the programme.

ENTERTAINMENT

Several organisations stage the classical colourful Kathakali and Mohiniattam, Ottamthullal and Koodiyattam dances daily in various parts of the city - some specially for tourists.

SPORTING EVENTS

Snake boat races are major events in Kerala.

(THEKKADY) PERIYAR WILDLIFE SANCTUARY

GENERAL INFORMATION
Area: 775 sq. kms.
Altitude: Sea level
Climate

	Temperature	
	Max.	Min.
Winter	28^0 c	16^0 c
Summer	30^0 c	19^0 c

Rainfall: Heavy between June and September.
Season : September to May (October to April).
Clothing
Summer: light cottons
Winter — evenings: light woollens.

HOW TO GET THERE
By Air : Nearest airports are Madurai (145 km.), Cochin (190 km.) and Thiruvananthapuram (272 km.).

By Rail: Nearest railhead is Bodinayakanur but the more convenient railheads are Madurai and Cochin/Ernakulam.

By Road: Periyar is connected with Madurai, Cochin, Trivandrum and Kodaikanal by road. Regular bus services connect Periyar with these cities.

LOCAL TRANSPORT
Metered taxis are available at the nearest city of your arrival.

CONDUCTED TOURS
There are conducted tours of Periyar from Cochin, Trivandrum and Alleppey.

WHERE TO STAY (STD CODE: 04863)
STANDARD
1. Aranya Niwas
   Phone: 04869-22023/22283
2. Lake Palace
   Phone: 22223/22283
3. Periyar House
   Phone: 04809-22026

WHAT TO SEE
Wild life can be seen on the banks while cruising on Periyar Lake in a motor boat. Amongst the animals are wild elephants, which can be seen and photographed at close quarters, wild boar, sambar, tiger, leopard, wild dog and langur monkeys. The king cobra and other reptiles are in plenty.

EXCURSIONS
There are several beautiful spots which can be reached by motor launch or by bridle paths, like MANAKAVALA (10 km.), PERIYAR DAM (15 km), CRUSOE ISLAND (19 km), MULLAKKUDI (29 km) and THANIKKUDI (38 km).
Forest guides can be hired to accompany tourist groups.

Chapter 21

TAMIL NADU & PONDICHERRY
Land of Sculptural and Architectural Beauty

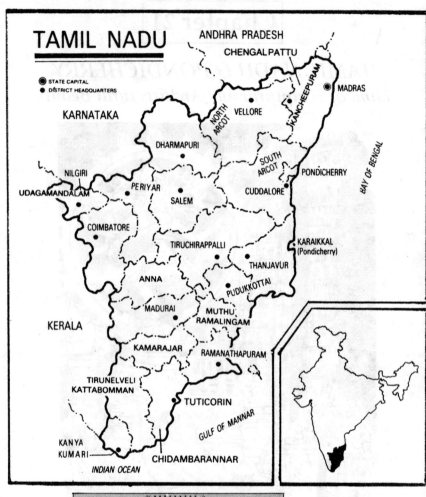

Rameshwaram Temple

Deep south is the fascinating State of Tamil Nadu, the home of the Tamils. Founded by the Dravidians over 5,000 years ago, the State is also the home of some of the most ancient architectural beauties and sculptures in the world. Its capital, MADRAS, is the most 'Indian' of the Indian cities where you can still see glimpses of the traditional way of life that has all but disappeared in northern cities. Although the pace of life is not hectic anywhere in the Indian subcontinent, it is certainly leisurely in Tamil Nadu — all the way from Madras to KANYAKUMARI (Cape Comorin). The climate of the State is varied. When it is hot in Madras, there are opportunities to relax in the cooler climes of Tamil Nadu's great hill resorts of OOTY and KODAIKANAL.

Despite numerous invasions into India from the northern passes, Tamil Nadu remained relatively unaffected by the turmoils of the early history of northern India. The early Muslim invaders and later Mughals seldom made it to deep South. Even the British influence was only marginal, although the early Europeans set their foot first on the soil of Tamil Nadu.

Tamil Nadu had its own early Dravidian kingdoms which patronised and encouraged fine arts. First, there were the Pallavas with their capital at KANCHIPURAM, followed by the Cholas who ruled from TANJORE. Further south, the Pandyas ruled from MADURAI. The neighbouring Karnataka, with some parts of present Tamil Nadu, was ruled by the Chalukyas who brought the temple art of the South to the pinnacle of its glory.

Although relaxed and easy-going on their home-turf, one finds enterprising Tamils in all parts of the world. They are in a considerable strength in Singapore, Malaysia , Sri Lanka and now in the Middle East.

Tamil Nadu's special attractions are its many temple towns, amazing and ornate with their soaring towers called GOPURAMS. A trip through the State takes you through several interesting places like RAMESHWARAM, THIRUCHIRAPALLI, CHIDAMBARAM, Madurai and Kanchipuram. There are more ancient temples at places like MAHABALIPURAM and Kanchipuram. The State is blessed with some of the finest beach resorts and wildlife sanctuaries. Tamil Nadu is a perfect place to have a relaxing holiday.

An advantage of Tamil Nadu holiday is the modest tariff of hotels and food services compared to hotels in the north. If you are tired of the usual inexpensive vegetarian thali, you have a vast choice of Western and Indian food in better hotels and restaurants.

The people of Tamil Nadu speak Tamil, one of the oldest and most developed languages of India. Tamil has greatly influenced the other three major South Indian languages — Telugu, Kannada and Malayalam.

The economy of Tamil Nadu is predominantly agrarian though the State is one of the most industrialised in India. Thanks to its rich mineral resources, it is a leading producer of cement, fertilisers and other chemicals in the country. Textile and leather industries provide employment to thousands of people. Tamil Nadu is reputed for its fine handicrafts and silk saris. Kanchipuram silks are known all over India. Among other shopping ideas are temple lamps in brass and copper, metal bells, idol carvings in wood, stone, metal and leather products.

RELIGION

Religion is second nature to Tamilians, intricably mixed with day-to-day life. Their marriages are a colourful blend of secular practices and religious observance. Following the Vedic injunctions concerning various stages of man's life, Tamilians attach great importance to the wearing of the sacred thread by the Brahmins and MANGALSUTRA (a special necklace) by women after marriage. Many men often wear the religious marks over their forehead — the auspicious TILAK (vermilion). Another common practice is bathing every day in nearby river, stream or tank. No wonder, therefore, houses in the countryside often do not have a regular bathroom as both men and women go out for their daily bath to the river or a stream nearby.

Before we set out on a tour of the temple towns of Tamil Nadu, a word about two important areas of interest: the temple architecture of Tamil Nadu and the traditional Bharatanatyam dance — a rich cultural heritage. During a visit to Madras, try not to miss a Bharatanatyam performance. Many of these dance recitals relate to Lord Krishna, the most popular and playful god who expounded the sermon of practical wisdom in *Bhagavad Gita*—the Hindu Bible. The dancers seem to express their infatuation with the Lord who has been described in one of the prayers as Lord Krishna, with eyes like lustrous pearls, heads bedecked with peacock feathers and body the hue of Heaven. During performance, the dancers show complete control of every muscle in their lithe bodies. They execute their movements with clockwise precision.

The other great and creative achievement of the Tamils is, undoubtedly, their magnificent temple architecture. The temple was the hub of social activities in the past. It served as a school, a university, hospital, a small court dealing with local problems, a granary, a bank, and above all, a guardian of people's moral and social relationships.

Although the broad designs of temples have been laid down and preserved in the ancient treatises, those of the Tamil temples were slightly refined. The general pattern of temples is characterised by a rectangular ground plan with the pyramidal form of the *vimana* (the wall and tower over the main shrine) and the *gopuram* (gateway). The tower consisted of a series of horizontal bands that grow smaller as they rise to the finial top, giving it a pyramidal shape. Another important feature is that a Tamil temple lies in the heart of the city and it is enveloped within its concentric walls and corridors. The walled enclosure around the temple has a place for markets, workshops, educational centres and residential quarters for the priests. It was a city within a city — an all-purpose institution.

The temple invariably had within it a Parikrama (walled enclosure) where the devotees could go round in prayers. Each temple has its own ablution tank, *nandanvana* (flower garden) and temple chariot. On the annual festival day, the *ratha* (chariot) is drawn out and taken through the town with the deity mounted on it and thousands of devotees following in a procession.

MADRAS

Madras is now attracting more tourists from Europe. In an effort to provide convenient services to Europeans coming to South India, British Airways have started direct London-Madras services with a brief halt at Dubai. Other European Airlines are exploring similar direct services to Madras. Recently, the British Airways acquired rights to make two landings in India — one at Bombay and Madras, and the other at Calcutta.

Lufthansa too has started direct services to Madras. Madras is also a major seaport of India. This artificial harbour serves almost the entire South. It is a centre for textile, leather, engineering and automobile industry. It has a RAILWAY COACH FACTORY too.

Spread over an area of 80 sq. km., Madras has developed into a magnificent metropolis of 5 million inhabitants with gardens, palms and a broad esplanade along the shore. It feels airy and open, specially after your visit to the more crowded Calcutta or Bombay. The luxury of space has resulted in relatively few tall buildings in Madras city.

While the rest of Tamil Nadu is dominated by the temples built by the great Hindu kings of the past, Madras is dominated by an old English fort built by the British and the decaying colonial houses and soaring Goethic public buildings. The city has an interesting history. The British East India Company arrived in 1639. A friendly and kind Raja of Chandragiri gave land to the Company to set up shop at Madraspatnam (that was the name of the place then). The British built the FORT SAINT GEORGE in 1641 which had about 400 weavers working for them to export cloth to England. Two separate settlements came into existence — one for the white men, later called Goerge Town and the other for the coloured Indians. The colour bar was strictly enforced in those days.

After a couple of decades' struggle with the French, the British were in complete control of the city. They expanded the city further into the countryside and developed gardens, clubs and churches.

Fort St. George

Today, the old buildings in Fort St.George house the Secretariat of the Tamil Nadu Government and the Legislative Assembly. Within the Fort, a number of other early buildings stand out. St. Mary's Church, the first Anglican Church in India, is most interesting. It was at this Church that Robert Clive, who laid the foundations of the British Empire in India, was married in 1753. Elihu Yale, who later lent his name to a major University in USA, was also married in this church. Yale rose from a Company Writer to the Governor in 15 years. He stayed in Madras to augment his fortune and donated books worth 560 pounds to the Collegiate School in Connecticut where his father had emigrated. As a token of gratitude, the University was named after him. It is now called Yale University. The Fort St. George Museum displays some of the fascinating items belonging to the early days of the East India Company. The Museum has everything from prints of terrified Europeans landing through the surf on to the beach to portraits of Queen Victoria and Edward VII.

Other interesting buildings in the Fort are the old Government House, the splendid Banqueting Hall now called Rajaji Hall. It was built for official entertainment of the Governor. The hall's structures drew inspiration from classical Greek and Roman styles.

Just north of the Fort are the Lighthouse and the High Court (1888-92) which is considered to be the second largest judicial building in the world after the one in London.

George Town, the original Madras city, lies to the north . It overlooks the man-made harbour — a good example of English planning. Its streets still bear such exotic names as China Bazar Road, Evening Bazar, Portuguese Church Street and Armenian Street reminding us of the past history of Madras. Since Madras did not have a natural harbour, the first Europeans had to come ashore on an exposed beach—a frightening experience. Madras was the centre of international trade. Two other buildings in the area are noteworthy: the Southern Headquarters of the State Bank of India and the General Post Office designed by R.F.Chisholm (1845-84).

Marina Beach and its Environs

The glorious Marina Beach is 13 km. long and very wide offering excellent walks. Along the shore, there are many buildings built during the British Raj. The South Beach Road runs past the Madras University, the Senate House, the Chepauk Palace (Nawabs of Carnatica once held their court here).

The Marina of Madras is the second longest beach in the world. It is an elegant promenade with flower beds along its lanes. It easily resembles the coasts of the French Riviera or Italy with its glistening sand beaches. Its width is upto 300 metres. But the Riviera crowds are not in

Madras and there is a reason for it. The sea waters have sharks and swimming is not recommended. As a consolation, perhaps, there is a swimming pool at the Marina next to the MADRAS AQUARIUM.

Near the Aquarium in the same area, there is another interesting building called ICE HOUSE - a memento of the East India Company days. Here the Americans brought ice all the way from New England in USA and stored it for the comforts of the rich English businessmen during the pre-airconditioning days.

The SAN THOME CATHEDRAL was the house of the great Tamil poet Tiruvalluvar who lived in the 2nd century A.D. and wrote the *Tirukural* - the greatest work in Tamil literature. His poems are still recited reverently in Tamil Nadu.

Kalakshetra

Kalakshetra, in a rural setting, is an internationally known institution devoted to the revival of ancient dance forms. It is also a school for Bharatanatyam classical dance.

OTHER ATTRACTIONS

Mylapore is the site of the famous Hindu temple KAPALEESWARA, dedicated to Lord Shiva. The temple is a traditional unified complex — it has the market, the Tank and nearby Brahmin residential houses. Every year, a festival is held at this temple. The pyramids of the Gopurams on entrance rise majestically in the horizon making the temple a landmark of Madras. Another ancient temple in Madras is PARTHASARATHI, dedicated to Lord Vishnu in the Triplicane section of the city. It was built in the 8th century by an early Pallava king.

On the Pantheon Road is the NATIONAL ART GALLERY. Nextdoor is the GOVERNMENT MUSEUM. It houses superb bronzes, sculptures and architectural beauties of the Dravidian dynasties. There are also some of the best examples of collections from the Indus Valley Civilisation and specimens of Gandhara art.

On MOUNT ROAD in the heart of Madras, RAJAJI HALL is the place where the Governors of Madras stayed and still do. It has an impressive collection of portraits of the past Governors.

As we move into the immediate outskirts of Madras, we discover the CHURCH OF OUR LADY OF EXPECTATIONS on SAINT THOMAS MOUNT. It is believed that Saint Thomas came to India in A.D. 52, barely a few years after the crucification of Christ. He was martyred here. A church was built in his memory in the 16th century.

A short drive beyond the Marina and near the Adyar river are the headquarters of the THEOSOPHICAL SOCIETY. The grounds of the Society contain one of the largest banyan trees in the world. 500 people can sit under the shade of its branches.

MADRAS SNAKE PARK is a charming spot. It was set up by an American, Romulus Whitaker, as a conservation project. It is located in

Holy Cross Church, Manapadu

the beautiful Guindy Deer Park. About 500 different types of snakes can be seen moving in natural surroundings. Other reptiles on show are crocodiles, alligators, monitor lizards and chameleons. Over half a million visitors come to the Snake Park every year. The entrance fee collections are used for the upkeep of the park, which also receives some financial support from the World Wildlife Fund.

Madras has some of the finest hotels and restaurants in India. Several major chains of Indian hotels are represented in Madras — the Taj, the Welcomgroup and the Oberois. The Welcomgroup Hotels have their Sheraton link. A Holiday Inn, too, has come up in the town to offer the demanding foreigners a wider choice.

Madras offers comfortable tourist cars for sightseeing. Both India Tourism Development Corporation (ITDC) and Tamil Nadu Tourism Development Corporation (TTDC) offer city tours of Madras. These provide the best value for money.

For more information contact the Government of India Tourist Office on Mount Road, *Phone* 8269685/8269695 or the Tamil Nadu Government Tourist Office *Phone:* 830390/830498.

EXCURSIONS

If you happen to be in Madras city as a tourist, you cannot miss a trip to the nearby ancient cities of MAHABALIPURAM (Mamallapuram) and KANCHIPURAM. These cities reflect the glory of the ancient Pallavas who ruled over this part of India. You can visit these cities either in a hired car or by bus. Fortunately, there are good roads linking Madras with the two cities.

Mahabalipuram which comes first is exactly 37 km. from Madras and Kanchipuram, the Pallava capital, another 40 kms.

CHINGLEPUT AND COVELONG

Covelong is a beautiful beach on the main Madras Mahabalipuram Road where the Taj Group of Hotels have developed an excellent beach resort. If you need a beach holiday nearest to Madras city, Covelong is the place to go. It is a fishing settlement and you will enjoy the rural environment.

Chingleput on the same road has the ruins of an ancient Vijayanagar Fort.

TIRUKALIKUNDRAM

This pilgrimage centre is 14 km. from Mahabalipuram with a hill-top temple, known for the legendary two eagles who come here to be fed by priests every day. It is believed that they come from Varanasi. The temple complex has an enormous *gopuram* at the base of the hill. One can also visit the temple from Mahabalipuram by hiring a bicycle.

Crocodile Farm

Fourteen kms from Mahabalipuram on the road to Madras this Crocodile Farm is engaged in breeding crocodiles. This reptile is on the list of endangered species. You can see here crocodiles of all sizes.

MAHABALIPURAM (MAMALLAPURAM)

Mahabalipuram on the Bay of Bengal was once the main harbour and naval base of the great Pallava emperors with its capital in glittering Kanchipuram - the Golden City. Kanchipuram was known to the Phoenicians, the Greeks and Arab traders.

Mahabalipuram was established by Narasimha Verman nicknamed Mamalla or great wrestler. Hence the original name, Mamallapuram.

The Pallavas have left here an astonishing legacy of unique monolithic rock-cut temples, caves, massive bas-reliefs and the lonely SHORE TEMPLE.

The landmark of Mahabalipuram is a large but lonely Shore Temple which has stood the test of time braving the waves of the ocean for 1200 years. Once, it is believed, there were 7 such temples. Six of them have been lost to the sea, unable to protect themselves against the erosion by the sea. Attempts are now being made to protect the existing temple for future generations.

Built by King Rajasimha in the 7th century A.D., the Shore Temple comprises three shrines: one to Vishnu and the other two to Shiva. It is a good example of the finest stage of Dravidian architecture. The temple is surrounded by a row of bulls carved out of a solid rock. The temple stands with its back to the sea rising starkly against the white foam of the waves.

The two-spire Shore Temple is unique in that it houses shrines to both Shiva and Vishnu. In the Vishnu temple, you can see an 8-foot long bas-relief of Vishnu reclining on his serpent conch. Another chamber contains remnants of a 16-sided granite phallic lingam which once touched the ceiling. Rows of stone bulls guard the temple courtyard.

The beach around the temple is excellent and there are half a dozen good hotels offering accommodation to visitors. It is worthwhile spending a night here and seeing the temple in moonlight. The sea is excellent for swimming.

After an exciting visit to the Shore Temple, you can start your discovery of the most famous of the bas-reliefs — the immense ARJUNA'S PENANCE. It is a huge 88 feet long and 30 feet high frieze, crammed with birds, beasts, mythological figures including life-size elephants. The entire frieze has been sculpted across a whale-back shaped rock. It was sculpted during the reign of King Narsimhavarman (A.D. 630-670).

Archaeologists differ about the theme of the frieze. Some believe that it depicts a *Mahabharata* story where a mortal Arjuna does penance to Lord Shiva for having killed his fellow humans during the war. Others are of the view that it tells the story of Ganga River coming down to the earth. One can see Lord Shiva letting the flood waters flow through his hair.

Either ways, the panel is a brilliant piece of artistry with some realistic and humorous touches. For instance, a deer scratching its face with its hoof and an emaciated hermit doing penance while standing on one foot mocked by a cat who strikes a similar pose.

The nearby hillside is dotted with eight *mandapams* — shallow rock-cut cave temples. Each temple is sculpted with five bas-reliefs depicting scenes from Hindu mythology — a couple of these have been left unfinished. One of the finest is the Krishna Mandapam. The bas-relief here depicts the story of Krishna using an umbrella to save shepherds and animals from the wrath of Indra, the Rain God. To the left of the penance relief, you can climb up the Hill to discover several other scattered Mandapams and Krishna's BUTTERBALL, a massive boulder precariously balanced on the hill's slope.

Bas-relief

In the rear of the hill is the tall lighthouse. You can have a fantastic view of the entire region from its top. Below the lighthouse is MAHISHASURA MARDHINI CAVE which has exquisitely beautiful reliefs. In one of these, Lord Vishnu is seen sleeping over the coils of the serpent Adishesh.

Another 15 minutes walk and you see the monolithic 7th century FIVE RATHAS (Five Chariots) named after the five Pandava brothers of *Mahabharata*. These rathas are guarded by three stone guardians — a lion, an elephant and the Nandi Bull. These temple chariots are also covered with ornate porches, pillars and statues. One has to admire the patience of the artists.

Back in town, there is a good open-air Museum and a School of Sculpture run by the Government. Here sculptors recreate excellent replicas of ancient masterpieces in marble, soapstone and granite. Prices are tempting.

Stone Monolith

KANCHIPURAM, The Golden City

Translated in English, Kanchipuram means the Golden City, which indeed it is. Kanchipuram first flourished as the capital of the Pallava dynasty — the great builders. In the 7th and 8th centuries A.D. the Pallavas were not only great builders but they also encouraged the tradition of silk weaving as well as the Bharatanatyam dance. "Kanjeevaram" saris (the English name for Kanchipuram) still maintain their reputation. The colonies of weavers are seen in the backlanes of the city. The Bharatanatyam dance was performed within the pillared halls of temples by *devadasis*, young women who had dedicated themselves to the service of God.

Kanchipuram is one of the seven most sacred pilgrim centres of Hindus, others being Varanasi, Mathura, Ujjain, Haridwar, Dwaraka and Ayodhya. A special feature of Kanchipuram pilgrimage is that it offers worship to both Lord Shiva and Vishnu rather than one or the other. Shankaracharya, the 6th century saint who travelled all over India to promote Hinduism, set up an episcopal seat here.

After the fall of Pallavas, Kanchipuram was taken over by a succession of dynasties — the Cholas, the Chalukyas and later the Vijayanagar kings. All of them have left their artistic stamps in elaborate temples built over 12 centuries.

An interesting feature of Kanchipuram is that it is a city of festivals. There is always one or the other festival taking place in the city connected with its many temples. It may be advisable to coincide your visit with a major temple festival. One such festival is the CAR FESTIVAL held at the KAMAKSHIAMMAN TEMPLE. It is held sometimes in February or March. On this occasion, deities are taken out on elaborately decorated wooden chariots against an extravagant backdrop of fire-crackers, fairs, street acrobats and folk theatre. Similar festivals are celebrated by other temples during April to coincide with the Tamil New Year.

Once called a 'City of a Thousand Temples', Kanchipuram still has 124 temples. Some of the temples are great examples of massive architecture. For instance, the entrance Gopuram of the EKAMBARESWARA TEMPLE built in the 16th century, stands 188 feet high with no less than 10 storeys of intricate sculptures. Similar but more pleasing to the eye is the 100-feet tower of the VARADARAJASWAMY TEMPLE. This temple is known for its hall of 96 pillars decorated with interesting sculptures.

VELLORE

From Kanchipuram, it is a short run to Madras. But if you have time and patience, travel another 55 kms west to Vellore on the banks of the Palar river. The heart of Vellore is its FORT, built in the 13th century which is still in good condition. It has seen many bloody battles including a Sepoy Mutiny by Indian soldiers in 1806, a prelude to the Indian War of Independence in 1857.

There is an exquisite 14th century SHIVA TEMPLE within the fort. It was not in use till 1981 but has since been activated. Regular worship is conducted now.

VEDANTHANGAL BIRD SANCTUARY

Seventy-five km. from Madras city, the Vedanthangal Bird Sanctuary is the oldest retreat of migratory birds in India. Here, the birds have been protected by the local people for more than 250 years. The sanctuary gets its name from a nearby village. A grove of *Barringlonia acutangula* trees and a relatively small pond which is submerged during rains constitute the sanctuary. A great number of aquatic birds — both migratory and resident—flock to this place. Peak time is immediately after the end of the rainy season. There is a REST HOUSE and OBSERVATORY TOWER in the sanctuary. The best time to see the birds is between 3 pm and 6 pm.

TIRUVANNAMALAI

The main road South from Madras towards Pondicherry brings you to this temple town - there are over 100 temples in it. It has one of South India's largest temples sprawling over an area of 25 acres. ARUNACHALA TEMPLE is dedicated to Tejo Lingam, the fire incarnation of God. A gopuram rises up to 200 feet with 11 sculptured stones. Behind the temple is a magnificent courtyard of 1000 pillars.

CHIDAMBARAM

Sixty km. from Pondicherry towards Thanjavur along the coast is the magnificent 9th century TEMPLE OF NATARAJA at Chidambaram. Dedicated to Lord Shiva, this temple sprawls over 32 acres of flat land between two rivers. The Nataraja temple complex of Chidambaram is said to be the oldest in the South. There are four gopurams — the north and south ones soaring 49 metres in the sky. Two of its gopurams are carved with 108 classical poses of Nataraja — Shiva, the Cosmic dancer.

Other notable features of the temple are a 1000-pillared Hall, NRITYA-SABHA COURT—carved out like a giant chariot and the image of Nataraja in the central sanctum. There are other smaller temples in the complex devoted to other gods.

The Nataraja temple in this city was built during the reign of Vir Chola Raja (927 to 997). Chidambaram was the Chola capital from tenth to 14th century.

TANJORE (THANJAVUR)

Another 110 km. down the coast from Chidambaram is Tanjore (now called Thanjavur).

On way to this place is a Danish settlement, TANQUEBER, built by the Danish East India Company with a DANSBORG FORT (1620), and the usual churches and colonial houses by the sea.

There is a tourist bungalow to stay in case you want to fully discover this Danish township.

On the same route but with some diversion, we head off to GANGAIKONDACHOLAPURAM - a tongue twister. The name means "Ganga brought by Chola King City". The city was built by King Rajendra (1002-44) to commemorate his trip to the sacred Ganga and the waters of the river he brought back to the city.

It is a vast building modelled on the Brihadeshwara temple built by his father at Thanjavur. There are excellent sculptures and a huge tank where vassal kings brought Ganga water when they visited his Court

Then comes KUMBAKONAM, a centre for gold and silversmiths. Its betel leaves are very much sought after.

There are 12 temples in the city, some of them of great merit. NAGESHVARA (9th century) has very good sculptures, SARANGPANI (13th-17th centuries) the largest with a ten-storey gopuram second only to Meenakshi temple in Madurai and Kumbheshvara (17th century), a large NAYAK TEMPLE housing remarkable silver *vahanas* (transport) required to move deities.

Every twelve years the Ganga is believed to flow into the MAHAMAKHAM TANK. Water level rises automatically and thousands of people come to bathe here, the last being in 1992.

Finally, on road to Thanjavur, 40 kilometres away, is the PULLAMANGIS TEMPLE. Temple historian Christopher Tedgill called it, "most wonderful, one of my favourites."

Thanjavur town is 158 km. from Madras and only 50 km. from TIRUCHIRAPALLI.

This temple city bears a lot of impact of the Chola rulers who followed the Pallavas. The Cholas were mere chieftains from the first to the 8th century. One of them took over Thanjavur and declared it as his State — the ruler claiming descent from the Sun. Expansion and consolidation followed. They acquired vast territories, moved into Kerala, Sri Lanka and the Maldives. They conquered the area up to Orissa. From there, the seafaring Cholas landed into neighbouring territories of Malaysia and Indonesia. They had trade links with China, Russia and Arabia.

The Cholas encouraged the cult of god kings through image worship of past kings. They built temples to the memory of past kings. They ran a complex but efficient system of administration guided by the Raj Guru who combined temporal and spiritual powers. During their rule, India became a major exporting country, with plenty of surplus food, textiles, ivory, sandalwood, camphor, etc. Trade was controlled by merchants and guilds who naturally became very rich. They donated their earnings to the temples, so did the common folk making temples centres of all social activities.

The system of *devadasis* (slaves to God) originated during the rule of Chola kings. Parents dedicated one of their daughters to the service of the temple on birth to avoid perceived calamity to her family. The girls spent their lives in worship and in learning Bharatanatyam. But in course of time, the system degenerated and these innocent girls became victims of carnal desires of the priests.

The biggest and the richest temple in Thanjavur is BRIHADESHWARA—monumental in design, concept and execution and the greatest architectural achievement of the Chola rulers. Built by Rajaraja (985-1014), it is dedicated to Lord Shiva as a temple fortress with a moat. A huge Nandi Bull guards the *gopuram* - its *vimana* is 64 metres high.

The rich carvings of the temple are still fresh. There is also a portrait of the king with his Guru, Karur Thevar. There is a picture of royal visit to Chidambaram, and Lord Shiva riding a chariot drawn by Brahma.

Off the inner courtyard of the temple is an ARCHAEOLOGICAL MUSEUM.

During its heydays, temple annual income included 250 kilograms of gold, 300 kilograms of silver and many precious stones. Revenue also came from hundreds of villages donated for the upkeep of the temple.

In Thanjavur town, there are 70 more temples. If your curiosity is not satisfied with this magnificent temple, you can discover some more.

The town is known for its arts and crafts. Among these are stone, wood, brass and bronze carvings. Its speciality is the repousse work, tapping a design in the relief from behind and copper work inlaid with brass and silver. There are silk weavers, makers of musical instruments specially veena and mridangams. The bazars are buzzing with activity and one can see craftsmen at work. To buy crafts of good quality, the State Government Emporium "Poompuhar" on Gandhi Road is the best place.

TIRUCHIRAPALLI (TRICHY)

Fifty-three kms from Thanjavur is Tiruchirappalli - Trichy for short. Tiruchirapalli has always been a seat of power over the centuries. It also bears the scars of wars fought to control it by the British and the French.

Right in the centre of the town and visible from all directions is the ROCK FORT TEMPLE (7th century). To reach the fort, you have to climb a tunnel of 437 steps to the top when you are rewarded with a view of the countryside as well as two major temples — the massive RANGANATHA TEMPLE and the smaller Sri JAMBUKESWAR TEMPLE on SRIRANGAM ISLAND in the Cauvery river.

A very important landmark of the city is the SRIRANGAM TEMPLE built on an island in the middle of the river. It covers a staggering 250 hectares. It is surrounded by seven concentric walls and has 21 *gopurams*. The Sri Jumbukeshwara Temple is surrounded by 5 concentric walls and has a total of 7 *gopurams*. The top of the Fort is shrouded in coconut palms.

It is worth spending at least a day discovering the great and ancient city. It is a pleasant experience to roam around this ancient town.

Tiruchirappalli has a long history going back to pre-Christian era. During the first millennium, it changed hands from the Pallavas and the Pandyas when it was taken over by the Cholas in the 10th century. After the Chola rule, it fell into the hands of Vijayanagar rulers and then the Deccan Sultans. The English, and the French also, tried their strength for the control of this city.

MADURAI

Madurai is 130 km. from Tiruchirapalli and 440 km. from Madras. It is yet another temple town, throbbing with life and teeming with thousands of pilgrims who pour in the city every day. This is one place in the south where the temple continues to live almost at the same scale of action and activity for which it was originally designed ten centuries ago. The pattern of life has remained unchanged and appears at the same time changeless. There is never a dull moment. The lotus shaped Madurai is an ancient city dating back to 2600 years. It was constructed by a Pandyan king, Kulashekhra, on the banks of River Vaigai. The name of this city emerges from a legend. In a forest near a lotus pond, Indra - the Rain God—worshipped Lord Shiva. A drop of *madhuram* (nectar) fell from the locks of Lord Shiva at this place. Since then it has been called Madhurapuri, now Madurai.

The MEENAKSHI SUNDARESHWARA TEMPLE (17th century) constitutes the hub of Madurai. At its head, there are two temples - one dedicated to Shiva (Sundareshwara) and the other dedicated to Devi (Meenakshi).

bazars around the temple sell everything from temple offerings to spices and garlands of jasmine — anything you wish to buy. The temple serves as the granary, kitchen and the store. Every facet of Hindu ritual is practised here and you can see the faithful sitting, chatting, praying, meditating and performing puja rituals. The *gopurams* (gateways) are the tallest (48.8 metres) in Madurai temple dwarfing the *vimana* (central shrine). If you climb up the *gopurams*, you will have a splendid view of the city. The most fascinating part of the temple is a 1000-PILLARED MANDAPAM (Hall) linked with sculptures. Within the Mandapam is a museum of temple art with photographs and paintings on display. The city has been a centre of Tamil culture, sponsoring literature, art, dance, music and other cultural events over the centuries.

There is an interesting legend about the temple. The daughter of one of the Pandyan rulers was born with three breasts. It was supposed to disappear when she met her spouse. The miracle did happen when the girl saw Shiva on Mount Kailash. Eight days later they were married in Madurai when Shiva appeared in the form of Sundareshwara.

The present temple was built during the reign of Tirumalai Nayak (1635-55), the original temple having been destroyed. It is a unique example of Dravidian architecture where *gopurams* are covered from top to bottom with a profusion of multi-coloured images of gods, goddesses, animals and mythical figures.

Most of the hotels and restaurants used by visitors are within walking distance of the Meenakshi Temple. Outside the city is the Cantonment area where a tourist lodge is run by ITDC. The Pandyan Hotel - the best in town—YWCA, Circuit House, etc., are all here. The Tourist Office is on the West Weli Street.

About a kilometre from the Meenakshi Temple, THIRUMALAI NAIK PALACE was built by Thirumalai in 1636. Much of it has fallen into ruins. The pleasure gardens as well as the defensive wall had disappeared but was later partially restored by Lord Napier, the Governor of Madras in 1866-72. Restoration work is still on. There is a GANDHI MUSEUM too in the city containing memorabilia of Mahatma Gandhi as well as a Gandhi Library.

A few km. to the east of the city is the MARIAMMAN TEPPAKULAM TANK. It covers an area as large as the Meenakshi Temple itself. A major festival (Teppam or Float Festival) takes place in January and February when images of Meenakshi and Lord Sundareshwara are mounted on floats and taken to the Tank.

The festival attracts thousands of pilgrims from all parts of India. The Tank was built by the same king Thirumalai Naik and is connected to the Vaigai with underground channels. Indeed, Madurai is a city of festivals and there is one almost every day.

RAMESHWARAM

Rameshwaram (pop: 30,000) is the Varanasi of South India - a major pilgrim centre. The sacred island of Rameshwaram is 173 km. from Madurai - Sri Lanka is only 80 km. away. It is an island hallowed by Lord

Thousand Pillared Corridor

Rama who worshipped Shiva here after he won the war against Ravana. It is, therefore, sacred to devotees of both Vishnu and Shiva.

The temple at Rameshwaram, RANGANATHSWAMY TEMPLE, is believed to have been built on the site where Rama worshipped Shiva in order to do penance for killing the ten-headed Ravana, King of Sri Lanka. Rameshwaram is so intimately linked with Rama that to a Hindu every grain of this sand is sacred. The highest point of the island has the footprints of Lord Rama.

The temple of Rameshwaram is one of the most beautiful shrines in terms of sculptures. It rises above a lake as a vast rectangle about 1,000 feet long and 650 feet wide and covers an area of 15 acres. It dates back to the 17th century though the process of building spanned three centuries. A remarkable feature of the Temple is its corridor — the longest in the country extending to 1200 metres and is flanked on either side by ornate pillars. Each pillar is an individual composition carved out of solid granite. Leading authorities on temple architecture have described the temple as the most evolved of all Dravidian temples.

Another famous temple at Rameshwaram is the KOTHANDARAMASWAMY TEMPLE which has idols of Rama, Sita, Lakshman, Hanuman and Vibhishan — all central characters of the epic *Ramayana*.

Close to Rameshwaram is the KURUSADAI ISLAND, one of a cluster of 16 islands in the region. The waters surrounding the lands are a biological paradise with rich and rare marine life and coral reefs.

If time permits, try to visit DHANUSHKODI at the tip of Rameshwaram islands. Here the waters of the Bay of Bengal and Indian ocean meet. Bathing at this place is considered very auspicious by the Hindus.

Rameshwaram is also a place from where the ferry to Sri Lanka (Talaimannar) departs.

KANNIYAKUMARI (CAPE COMORIN)

At Dhanushkodi, only two seas meet. At Kanniyakumari (Cape Comorin) three seas — the Indian Ocean, Bays of Bengal and the Arabian Sea — converge into one another. Indians call this point Kanniyakumari, though in most western geography books it is mentioned as Cape Comorin. It was known to the ancients too. Ptolemy called it Comaria Akon and Marco Polo knew it as Comori.

Kanniyakumari is Land's-end of India and also a well-known pilgrimage centre for the Hindus. For non-Hindu foreigners, it is an interesting place to watch the sun rise and set. It is the only place in India where you can enjoy the unique experience of sunset and the moon rising over the ocean simultaneously on full moon day.

There are some five beaches. A 16th century CATHOLIC CHURCH and the 18th century DUTCH FORT remind you of its recent past.

The main temple in Kanniyakumari is dedicated to goddess Kanniyakumari— an incarnation of Parvati, consort of Lord Shiva. The temple is very picturesquely located.

A MEMORIAL TO SWAMI VIVEKANANDA — the Indian philosopher and teacher—is another popular tourist attraction. Vivekananda came here in 1892 and meditated on a rock before setting out on the most important religious crusade propagate Hinduism. The memorial was built on two rocky islands which project from the sea about 200 metres from the shoreline. It has used architectural styles from all parts of India. A boat service is available to reach the island.

Kanniyakumari is more easily accessible from Thiruvananthapuram. From Madurai, Kanniyakumari is 200 kms. The journey can be broken comfortably at Courtalam.

COURTALAM

Courtalam lies on the western Ghats mountain ranges and you will certainly appreciate this stopover after a hectic journey through south Indian temples. The main charm is the 300 feet waterfalls on the Chittar river. There is an interesting temple nearby. The falls also have their reputation as a spa — bathing here is considered good for body and soul. With all these assets, Courtalam has developed into a pleasant hill resort. From here, it takes another four hours to reach Kanniyakumari.

KODAIKANAL

Within the borders of Tamil Nadu, you can find some very fine hill resorts: Kodaikanal — only a short distance from Madurai—and Ootacamund, Conoor and Yercaud — delightful places in the Nilgiri Hills further north.

Kodaikanal is about 120 kms from Madurai, a quiet hill resort at an altitude of 2133 metres. The nearest railway station is some 80 kms. away on the main line from Madras. It is a highly scenic drive, climbing upto over 2300 metres and runs through coffee plantations and forests. Europeans first discovered this spot in the PALANI HILLS in 1821. Fifteen years later, one of the British District Magistrates of Madras built a house there followed by many others.

Today, Kodaikanal is popular with everybody who can afford to take a holiday at a nice hill resort. The best time to come here is April-June, and September-October when the climate is temperate and the sun shines all the 12 hours. It is just not the weather that brings people into Kodaikanal. A wiseman, Sir Vere Levenge, changed the landscape of the hill resort by putting up a dam on the stream to form an exquisite lake reminiscent of Switzerland. Boating on the lake is a popular pastime. Walkways and riding trails keep visitors occupied. Nearby are several other interesting cascades and falls.

Kodaikanal is the site of an OBSERVATORY built in 1899, 850 feet above the lake. It is mainly used for research in meteorology and solar physics.

OOTACAMUND, The Queen of the Hill Stations

Kodaikanal's main rival as a premier hill resort is Ootacamund (Ooty for short) which has often been described by Guide Book writers as the "Queen of the Indian Hill Stations".

Set at 2600 metres above sea level, Ooty's name is derived from "Ooty ka mandu" which means the village with a lake. Ooty nestles among the hills at a point where the Eastern and Western Ghats meet, giving the visitor a glimpse of both.

The first Britisher came here in 1812 and was followed by other missionaries, educationists and civil servants. Later, it became the summer capital of the vast Madras Presidency. This also attracted many of the south Indian ruling families to build their summer residences.

Ooty offers to the visitor an unending array of walks and heights to conquer, not to mention the scenic beauty to be enjoyed in the most pleasant of climates.

Ooty is also the home of Todas, one of the earliest aboriginal tribes living in the hills. Only a thousand of them are still left.

The downs of Ootacamund could well be in Devon or Yorkshire. There are 80 km. of them, offering golf, tennis and other sports. The BOTANICAL GARDEN here was laid 125 years ago and boasts of 650 varieties of plants. Like Kodaikanal, its artificial lake adds to a charm of this hill resort. Conceived by Sullivan in 1823, it measures only 2 km. but it offers good boat rides and excellent fishing. Near the lake's shore is the HERBERT PARK for weekly horse racing which brings the elite of India to this town.

OTHER HILL RESORTS

Besides Ootacamund, there are other hill resorts in the Nilgiri Hills. KOTAGIRI is 2200 metres above sea level, and only 20 kms. from Ootacamund. Kotagiri is an island of green fields, surrounded by thick forests. It is one of the quietest spots in the Nilgiris.

COIMBATORE, a large industrial city of Tamil Nadu, is the gateway to the Nilgiri Hill Resort of Ootacamund and other places. The little mountain train to Ooty starts from here. COONOOR, 26 kms down the mountain railway line, is at an altitude of about 2000 metres. The climate is pleasant throughout the year. Conoor is surrounded by tea plantations, pleasant walks and provides opportunities for hikers.

Another quiet hill resort in Tamil Nadu is YERCAUD, situated in the Servaroyan Hills of SALEM DISTRICT. The hills provide panoramic view. Yercaud has a mild climate and is pleasant throughout the year. It is only an hour's drive from Salem.

WILDLIFE SANCTUARIES

Although Tamil Nadu can boast of 6 Wildlife Sanctuaries-MUDUMALAI SANCTUARY is the most popular with full roll call of Indian wildlife.

Mudumalai is at the foot of the Nilgiris in the extreme north-western tip of the State. It is the largest sanctuary in Tamil Nadu and is contiguous with BANDIPUR SANCTUARY in the neighbouring Karnataka and WYNAD SANCTUARY in Kerala. Its main attractions are the herds of spotted deer, gaur (Indian bison), elephant, tiger, panther, wild pig, sloth bear and others, as well as crocodiles which live in the river.

Another important sanctuary is CLIMERE WILDLIFE SANCTUARY. Located on the east coast just south of Pondicherry territory of Karaikog, it is noted for congregations of black buck, spotted deer, wild pigs and vast flocks of migratory birds.

ANAMALAI is a Wildlife Sanctuary located in the mountains along the Tamil Nadu-Kerala border. It lies south of Coimbatore. Major wildlife attractions are tiger, panther, spotted deer, wild boar, bear, etc. Nilgiri Tahir commonly known as Ibex can also be seen here.

There is a tiny wildlife sanctuary within the metropolitan boundaries of Madras. It is GUINDY DEER PARK. This is the only place in the world where it is possible to see fairly large numbers of fast dwindling species of the Indian antelope (black buck). It has also other species of animal life, like the spotted deer.

PONDICHERRY — The French Ambience

Pondicherry, the former French Colony is 160 kms from Madras. We are due for quite a change — the atmosphere of a sleepy small French town. The tiny enclave was voluntarily returned to India as early as 1954, after 250 years of French rule.

War Memorial

Matri Mandir, Auroville

It is now a Union Territory of the Indian Republic and not part of the Tamil Nadu State. Other French enclaves in India were Karaikal (Tamil Nadu), Mahe (Kerala) and Yenam (Andhra). Near the beautiful Government House by the sea in Pondicherry is the STATUE OF DUPLEX, the French Governor who ruled Pondicherry for 40 years in the 18th century. He lost to his more successful English rival Robert Clive. The French touch is complete with a STATUE OF JOAN OF ARC and the MONUMENT OF POLIUS of World War I.

Pondicherry was founded by Francois Martin in 1674 and rebuilt by Jean Law in 1750-77. Today, it is more known for the Indian philosopher Sri Aurobindo, poet and patriot who sought shelter in Pondicherry after a political trial by the British lasting two years. He alongwith a French woman established in 1926 an ASHRAM (Retreat) in Pondicherry which has attracted worldwide following. Sri Aurobindo's philosophy is based on synthesis of Yoga and modern science. After Aurobindo's death, spiritual authority passed on to his French disciple who was called 'Mother'. In 1968, she founded the nearby futuristic universal town of AUROVILLE, designed by the French architect Roger Anger for people of all religions, politics and cultures. It was meant to be an experiment in international living and took off with great fanfare in February 1968 when the President of India inaugurated it. Some 200 foreigners still reside here.

MADRAS

GENERAL INFORMATION
Population: 536,000 (1991 census)
Altitude: Sea level
Climate

	Temperature	
	Max.	Min.
Winter	33⁰ c	20⁰ c
Summer	38⁰ c	25⁰ c
Rainfall	715 mm	46 mm

Season: Throughout the year, except that the months of May and June which are hot.
Clothing: Light cottons throughout the year.

HOW TO GET THERE
By Air: Madras is an international airport with flight connections with all parts of the globe. Indian Airlines, Jet Air, Modiluft and East West connect it to all important tourist centres of India. Several international airlines including British Airways and Lufthansa fly into Madras.

By Rail: Madras has direct rail connections with Ahmedabad, Bangalore, Bombay, Cochin, Delhi, Guwahati, Calcutta, Hyderabad, Madurai, Trichy, Thiruvananthapuram, Varanasi, etc.

By Road: Madras is connected by excellent roads with all parts of the south. It is
143 km. from Tirupati,
162 km. from Pondicherry,
334 km. from Bangalore,
469 km. from Mysore,
535 km. from Ooty,
620 km. from Hyderabad
Madras is connected by express bus services to every tourist centre in the south.

LOCAL TRANSPORT
There are tourist taxis, metered taxis, auto-rickshaws, cycle-rickshaws, city bus services and electric trains.

CONDUCTED TOURS
There are several conducted tours by coach run by the ITDC, TTDC etc.
1. Half-day CITY SIGHTSEEING tours.
2. Full-day excursions to KANCHIPURAM, TIRUKKALIKUNDRAM and MAHABALIPURAM.
3. Daily trips to TIRUPATI (an important Hindu pilgrim centre).
4. 7-day tour of Tamil Nadu visiting TRICHY, SRIRANGAM, KODAIKANAL, MADURAI, KANNIYAKUMARI, SUCHINDRAM, TIRUCHENDUR, RAMESHWARAM, THANJAVUR, MADRAS run by TTDC. (Saturday 0630 hours to Friday 1630 hours).
5. 7-day South India tour visiting MADRAS, BANGALORE, SRAVA-

NABELAGOLA, BELUR, HALEBID, MYSORE, SRIRANGAPATNA, BRINDAVAN GARDENS (MYSORE), MADHUMALAI SANCTUARY, OOTY, COONOOR, COIMBATORE, HOGENAKKAL, TRIVANNAMALAI, run by the TTDC.

Information
India Tourism Development Corporation,
Commander-in-Chief Road.
Tel: 8278884/8272186

Tamil Nadu Tourism Development Corporation. (TTDC),143, Mount Road
Tel: 830390, 830498

WHERE TO STAY (STD CODE: 044)

DELUXE

1. Taj Coramandel
   Phone: 8272827
   Fax: 8270070
2. Welcomgroup Chola Sheraton Hotel
   Phone: 8280101
   Fax: 8278779
   Cable: CHOLA MADRAS
3. Welcomgroup Park Sheraton and Tower
   Phone: 4494101
   Fax: 4997201
   Cable: ADYARHOTEL
4. Hotel Connemara
   Phone: 8260123
   Fax: 8257361
   Cable: CONNEMARA
5. The Trident
   Phone: 2344747, 2344751
   Fax: 044-2346699
   Cable: TRIDENT HOT
6. Ambassador Pallava
   Tel: 8268584
7. Quality Inn Arun
   Tel: 8259090
   Fax: 8258282

STANDARD

8. Abu Palace
   Phone: 6412222, 6411313
9. Hotel President
   Phone: 832211
   Telex: 041-6699
   Fax: 044-832299
10. Hotel Madras International
    Phone: 8261811
    Fax: 861520
    Cable: HOTEINTER
11. Dasaprakash
    Phone: 8255111
    Cable: DASPRAKASH
12. Shrilekha Inter-Continental
    Phone: 543131
    Cable: LEKHA
13. Hotel Palmgrove
    Phone: 8271881
    Cable: PALM
14. Ganpat
    Phone: 8272165
15. Savera Hotel
    Phone: 8274700
    Cable: SAVERA
    Fax: 044-473475
16. Hotel Breeze
    Phone: 6413334-7, 6412931
    Cable: Open BREEZE
17. The Sindhoori Hotel
    Phone: 8271164
    Cable: SINDOTEL
18. Hotel Residency
    Phone: 8253434
    Fax: 044-8250085

BUDGET

19. Swagath
    Phone: 868422
    Cable: SUBASWAGAT

20. Imperial
    Phone: 8250377
    Cable: MAJESTIC
21. Hotel New Woodlands
    Phone: 8273111
    Cable: WOODLANDS
22. Hotel Maris
    Phone: 470541
    Telex: 041-6380 MARS IN
    Cable: HOTELMARIS
23. Hotel Kanchi
    Phone: 471100
24. Hotel Peacock
    Phone: 5322981

Note: TTDC has a network of neat and clean tourist accommodations at all major tourist centres. Tariff is very low. Budget travellers are advised to have this information from the Tourist office.

WHAT TO SEE

1. FORT ST. GEORGE. The British East India Company built this fort in A.D. 1653. ST. MARY'S CHURCH inside the fort is the oldest Anglican church east of Suez.
2. PARTHASARATHI TEMPLE (A.D. 8th century). It has finely carved sculptures.
3. MARINA BEACH, one of the longest beaches in the world. Crowds of people gather here in the evenings to enjoy the cool sea-breeze.
4. SAN THOME CATHEDRAL, built on the site of a chapel originally believed to have been built by St. Thomas, an apostle of Christ.
5. KAPALEESWARA TEMPLE, Mylapore. This ancient Shiva temple was destroyed by the Portuguese in 1566 and rebuilt 300 years ago.
6. SNAKE PARK.
7. World headquarters of the THEOSOPHICAL SOCIETY, Adayar.
8. VALLUVAR KOTTAM, an auditorium built in the form of a temple chariot, dedicated to Saint Thiruvalluvar.
9. ANNA SAMADHI, where lie the remains of a much-loved leader of the people who was Chief Minister of Tamil Nadu.

EXCURSIONS

1. Mamallapuram or MAHABALIPURAM (64 km), was the main port of the Pallava dynasty (6th to 10th centuries). It had trade and cultural relations with Rome in the west and with South-east Asia. Now a beach resort, it has exquisite rock-cut monuments, monolithic structures and bas-reliefs.
2. KANCHIPURAM, the Golden City (76 km). One of the 7 sacred cities of India, it once had 1,000 temples. Now only 200 temples are left to see. It was a great centre of learning. It is famed for its hand-woven cottons and silks.
3. THIRUKKALIKUNDRAM (15 km, from Mahabalipuram). Two kites, believed to be two sages halting on their

daily flight from Varanasi to Rameshwaram, stop here on the hill top everyday at noon and are fed by the priests.
4. CHOLAMANDAL (20 km from Madras), a village of artists and sculptors.
5. COVELONG BEACH (38 km en route to Mahabalipuram) has a fine beach and an excellent resort hotel run by the Taj Group.
6. CROCODILE BANK (42 km) where several species of crocodile are housed.
7. VEDANTHANGAL BIRD SANCTUARY (85 km), a water-bird sanctuary where nearly 30,000 birds come from different parts of the world to breed.

FESTIVALS OF SPECIAL LOCAL INTEREST

1. PONGAL, the 3-day harvest festival of Tamil Nadu (January 13 to 15) when the products of the harvest and a cooked sweet dish, Pongal, are offered to the Sun-god. A Tourist Fair is also held in the city. It is a time of great rejoicing.
2. FLOAT FESTIVAL in January-February, when the deities of the Kapaleeswara Temple are taken out at night in colourfully lit floats around the temple tank.
3. FESTIVAL OF THE 63 SAINTS (Nayanmars), a 11-day temple festival. On the 8th day, images of the saints are taken in procession around the Mylapore temple.
4. ANNUAL MUSIC AND DANCE FESTIVAL held between December 15 and January 15. It attracts visitors and artistes from all parts of the world.
5. Every temple has its own festival. There are festivals practically throughout the year.

ENTERTAINMENT

Madras is a centre of classical music of the Carnatic School and the home of Bharatanatyam, the oldest classical dance form of India. There are several institutions/theatres like the Kalakshetra, Music Academy, Krishna Gana Sabha, Rasika Ranjani Sabha, Raja Annamalai Hall, Vani Mahal, Narada Gana Sabha where regular programmes are held throughout the year. The Tamil theatre is equally active. The newspapers list daily programmes.

SPORTS

There are facilities for swimming, golf, badminton and other games and water sports at Mahabalipuram and Covelong Beach Resorts. Also annual motor rallies.

MADURAI

GENERAL INFORMATION
Population: 1,000,000 (1991 census)
Altitude: 133 metres (443 ft)
Climate: Same as Madras.
Season: Throughout the year. The months of May and June, are hot.
Clothing: Light cottons throughout the year.

HOW TO GET THERE
By Air: Madurai is connected by air with Madras, Bangalore and Cochin.

By Rail: There are direct rail connections with Madras, Bangalore, Trichy, Thanjavur and Rameshwaram.

By Road: There are excellent roads connecting Madurai with all parts of the south. It is
140 km. from Trichy,
158 km. from Thanjavur,
136 km. from Periyar,
232 km. from Kanniyakumari and
480 km. from Madras.
There are regular bus services to Bangalore, Madras, Periyar, Thanjavur, Trichy, Trivandrum and other cities.

LOCAL TRANSPORT
Tourist taxis, unmetered taxis, auto-rickshaws, cycle-rickshaws and city bus services.

CONDUCTED TOURS
Information: Tamil Nadu Tourist Office, Hotel Tamil Nadu Complex-*Tel*: 4757. Railway Station *Tel*: 33888

WHERE TO STAY (STD CODE: 0452)
STANDARD
1. Taj Garden Retreat
   Phone: 601020, 602300
   Fax: 88601
2. Madurai Ashok
   Phone: 45521
   Fax: 42530
   Cable: TOURISM
3. Pandyan Hotel
   Phone: 42470
   Fax: 42020

BUDGET
4. Hotel Supreme
   Phone: 36331
   Fax: 36637
5. Hotel Tamil Nadu
   Phone: 42460-69
   (Algarkoil Road)
6. Hotel Tamil Nadu
   (West Vali Street)
   Phone: 37470
7. YWCA
   Phone: 24763

WHAT TO SEE
1. MEENAKSHI TEMPLE. A superb example of the Dravida School of architecture, this temple is famous for its gigantic gateways or Gopurams profusely carved and reaching out to massive proportions — the most famous gateway being 49 metres high. The temple has exquisite sculptures, ornate pillars and painted ceilings.

2. TEMPLE MUSEUM. The 1000-pillared hall in the same temple now houses a large collection of icons.
3. TIRUMALAI NAIK PALACE. Built in the 17th century, it is in the Indo-Saracenic style.
4. MARIAMMAN TANK. A square temple tank 305 metres long on each side. It attracts pilgrims during the 'Float Festival'.
5. GANDHI MUSEUM and GOVERNMENT MUSEUM.

EXCURSIONS
1. GANDHIGRAM (51 km). Centre for propagating Gandhian thought and ideals.
2. ALAGAR KOLI (21 km). Famous Vishnu Temple.
3. VAIGAI DAM (69 km). Beautiful picnic spot on the way to the Periyar Game Sanctuary.
4. KODAIKANAL (120 km), a beautiful hill resort noted for its lake and pine forests.
5. PERIYAR GAME SANCTUARY (136 km). Well-known game reserve of Kerala state, particularly famed for its elephant herds.
6. RAMESHWARAM (152 km). A famous pilgrim town renowned for its 1220 metre long corridors of carved pillars.

FESTIVALS OF SPECIAL LOCAL INTEREST
1. PONGAL, the harvest festival (January 13 to 15) is a time of great rejoicing. The Jellikkattu (bull fight) held in nearby Alanganallur draws crowds.
2. FLOATING FESTIVAL in the Mariamman Tank. Temple deities are carried in a lighted floats at night (January-February).
3. WEDDING OF GODDESS MEENAKSHI. The wedding of Lord Sundereswara and Goddess Meenakshi is celebrated in April-May with great pomp and colour.
4. AVANI MOOLAM FESTIVAL (August-September). The coronation of Lord Shiva as Sundereswara in the Meenakshi Temple.

ENTERTAINMENT
1. A Sound-and-Light show is presented by the Tamil Nadu Tourism Department at the Tirumalai Nayak Palace every evening (first show in English and the second in Tamil).
2. The Sri Satguru Sangeetha Samajam holds regular music and dance programmes in its auditorium.

TRICHY

GENERAL INFORMATION
Population: 400,000 (1991 census)
Altitude: Sea level
Climate:
Same as Madras
Season: Throughout the year. During April to July, the days are hot.
Clothing: Light cottons throughout the year.

HOW TO GET THERE
By Air: Trichy is an international airport with flights to Colombo. Indian Airlines flights connect it to Madras and Thiruvananthapuram.
By Rail: There are direct rail services to Madras, Madurai, Thanjavur, Rameshwaram, Tirupathi, etc.
By Road: Excellent roads connect Trichy with all of south India. It is 140 km. from Madurai, 302 km. from Ooty and 320 km. from Madras.
There are regular bus services between Trichy and Coimbatore (for Ooty), Madurai, Rameshwaram, Kanniyakumari, Madras, etc.

LOCAL TRANSPORT
Tourist taxis, unmetered taxis, auto-rickshaws, cycle-rickshaws and city bus services.

CONDUCTED TOURS
Nil.
Information: Tamil Nadu Tourist Office - Tel: 4601136

WHERE TO STAY (STD CODE: 0432)
(No deluxe hotels available)
STANDARD
1. Hotel Sangam
   Phone: 44700
   Fax: 0431-41779
   Cable: SANGU
2. Femina Hotel
   Phone: 41941 (10 lines)
   Fax: 0431-40615
   Cable: FEMINA
BUDGET
3. Gajapriya
   Phone: 41144
   Cable: GAJAPRIYA
4. Ramyas Hotel
   Phone: 411653
   Cable: RAMYAN
   Fax: 0431-42750
5. Rajali Hotel
   Phone : 25925/25251
6. Hotel Sevana
   Phone: 41201
7. Hotel Aristo
   Phone: 41818, 26365
   Telex: 0455-256ARISIN
8. Hotel Anand
   Phone: 40545
9. Ashby Hotel
   Phone: 40652, 23653
10. Hotel Tamil Nadu
    Phone: 40383
    (Unit 1)
11. Hotel Tamil Nadu
    Phone: 23498
    (Units 2)

WHAT TO SEE
1. The ROCK FORT rises abruptly to a height of 83 metres. At the end of the climb, a magnificent view

of the city as well as of Cauvery river looms in focus.
2. SRIRANGAM ISLAND (10 km). This is a living example of a temple town where all life centres round the temple. This massive temple complex has 21 magnificent gateway towers (*gopurams*) and a 1000-pillared hall with beautiful carvings, all within the 7 walls of the temple town. The 22nd gateway tower, 236 ft. high, has just been completed. It is the tallest temple tower in Asia.
3. JAMBUKESHWARA TEMPLE (9 km.). Has some very beautiful carvings.

EXCURSIONS
1. GRAND ANICUT (24 km). This dam originally built by a Chola king in the 2nd century is an engineering marvel, as it functions as a dam to this day. It was expanded by the later Chola kings.
2. THANJAVUR or Tanjore (54 km). The beautiful Chola temple of Brihadeshwar and its bronzes and handicrafts make Tanjore one of the highlights of a visit to the south.
3. SITTANNAVASAI (72 km. via Pudukottai). An 8th-9th century Jain temple where paintings are similar to those at Ajanta.

SHOPPING
Trichy is famous for its cigars and cheroots. Amongst its handicrafts are brassware, handloom textiles, pith models of temples and the Rock Fort, wood and clay toys, jewellery, ornamental carved brass and copper plates inlaid with silver (Tanjore plates), silks, carpets and musical instruments.

FESTIVALS OF SPECIAL LOCAL INTEREST
1. In December-January several festivals, including a FLOWER FESTIVAL and a CAR FESTIVAL, are celebrated at the Srirangam Temple.
2. FLOAT FESTIVAL (March) in the Teppakulam Tank.

PONDICHERRY

Climate: Same as Madras

HOW TO GET THERE
To reach Pondicherry from Madras bus rides are most economical. There are frequent services.

Taxi - up and down costs about Rs. 700 only

WHERE TO STAY (STD CODE: 0413)
STANDARD
1. Pondicherry Ashok
   Tel: 460-468

BUDGET
2. Ajantha Guest House
   Tel: 28927
3. Hotel Ram International
   Tel: 27230-39
4. Government Tourist Bungalow
   Tel: 226376
5. Yatri Niwas
   Tel: 29474
6. Youth Hostel
   Tel: 23495

Gandhi Memorial

Chapter 22

ANDHRA PRADESH
Land of Silks, Spices and Temples

Bas relief, Simhachalam temple

Across the Deccan, the southern States have an altogether different environment. The four major States in the South are Andhra Pradesh, Karnataka, Tamil Nadu and Kerala — each has its own traditions, language and colour. But, there is the underlying unity of culture, dance, music and religion. The people of South India are devoted to religion. The countryside is cleaner than the northern States and the standard of living a little higher. Andhra, the largest of the four southern states is the home of the Telugu-speaking people. It has an area of 275,068 sq.kms and population of 66 million.

HYDERABAD - A City of Thousand Faces

When Sultan Mohammed Quli Qutb Shah laid the foundation of Hyderabad in 1591, he prayed, "Let millions of men and women of all castes, creeds and religions make it their abode, like fish in the ocean".

The present capital of Andhra Pradesh is relatively a modern city. It recently celebrated its 400th anniversary. The Qutb Shahis who ruled the area in 16th and 17th centuries had GOLCONDA, the nearby fortress city, as their capital. Mohammad Quli, the fourth of the Qutb Shahis, built his new capital on the southern bank of the Musi river as alternate capital to his cramped, disease-ridden fortress capital of Golconda, 11 km. to the West. The extensive ruins of this Fort, which has its roots going back to the earlier Hindu kingdoms of the Yadavas and Kakatiyas together with nearby tombs of Qutb Shahi kings, are the principal attractions of Hyderabad. Golconda is also known for its diamond mines. Several historical diamonds including the Koh-i-noor, now belonging to British Crown, were mined here. Qutb Shahis themselves were benevolent

rulers and encouraged arts and crafts. The states' present claim to fame goes to Golconda wines manufactured here.

According to legend, Sultan Mohammad Quli Qutb Shah built Hyderabad for the love of his beautiful Hindu wife Bhagmati when he had given her the title of Hyder Mahal. Hyderabad was named after her. Strategically placed, Hyderabad was a gateway to the southern kingdoms.

This thriving trading centre with its rich diamond mines lured the wily, Emperor Aurangzeb who invaded the Golconda kingdom. The king retreated to Golconda Fort when he fought the Mughal army. The fall of the city in 1687 marked the end of the Qutb Shahi dynasty. After Aurangzeb's death in 1707, his Viceroy in Hyderabad, Asaf Jah, declared independence. He founded the Asaf dynasty which spanned seven generations and the last of his successors, Osman Ali Khan, was reported to be the richest man in the world.

In the giant PALACE OF THE LAST NIZAM, there were 11, 000 servants — 38 were required to dust the chandeliers. Others did nothing except grind spices. Entire wings of the palace were used to store bullion and jewellery. The Nizam used egg-sized diamonds as paperweights. His parsimony was equally well-known. He used the same oil-streaked fez cap and jacket for 30 years and bargained over the price of local Charminar cigarettes. At times, he ordered jewellery and forgot to pay for it. The locals have numerous stories to tell about their last Nizam

The Asaf Jahi Nizams ruled till 1948 when the State was merged in the Indian Union. Till 1948, the original Hyderabad State ruled by the Nizam from Hyderabad city was the largest State of India ruled by an Indian prince. It included the whole of Telangana, Vidarbha and Marathawada, now belonging to Maharashtra. It also included in its domain the districts of Bidar and Gulbarga which now form part of the Karnataka State. Because of the Nizam's steadfast loyalty to the British Crown, the British treated him well and

A statuette at Salar Jung Museum

gave him the title, "His most Exalted Highness', a title not given to any other Indian ruler. Although the then Hyderabad State had about 90 per cent of Hindu population, the Nizam, a Muslim, toyed with the idea of founding an independent kingdom outside the Indian Union or joining the newly created Pakistan. In a swift action, the Indian Army brought the State under Indian control. The present State of Andhra Pradesh was constituted in 1956 including all areas where Telugu is spoken.

One of the early generals of the Asaf Jahi clan, Salar Jung, was noted for his voluminous collections of antiques and rare art treasures. These are housed in a landmark of Hyderabad called SALAR JUNG MUSEUM which has been given the status of a national museum. It is India's answer to Victoria and Albert Museum in London. It has since been shifted to a new building. Among its unique collections are miniature paintings, illuminated manuscripts of the Quran, armour and weaponry, clothing of Mughal emperors and many other interesting exhibits. It is one of the finest museums of India.

OSMANIA UNIVERSITY, founded in 1918, is well worth a visit. It is among the most important centres of learning in the Deccan. The language used in Hyderabad is an interesting blend of Urdu and some of the other Indian languages spoken with a peculiar accent, which sets a Hyderabadi apart. During the reign of Asaf Jahi rulers, Hyderabad city developed a distinct style in every facet — its richly flavoured cuisine, its etiquettes, its handicrafts and its festivals and fairs.

Hyderabad's first major monument, the CHAR MINAR, remains its most magnificent emblem. It is as much a signature of Hyderabad as is Taj Mahal of Agra or Eiffel Tower of Paris. Romance appears to be the motive behind the building of the new city of Hyderabad. Mohamad Quli Qutb Shah loved his Hindu wife Bhagmati very much. To perpetuate her memory, when the foundations of the city were laid, he reserved the location of its central monument, Char Minar, near the site of his beloved queen's village, Chickalam. Around Char Minar, he laid the new city. He called it BHAGYANAGAR after his queen's name. When she was given the title of Hyder Mahal, the town was renamed Hyderabad.

Char Minar

Built in 1591, the Char Minar arch straddles the city's original grid of broad intersecting boulevards. Legend has it that the Char Minar was built as a charm to ward off a deadly epidemic which was raging at that time. Four graceful minarets soar to a height of 48.7 metres above the ground. Within the Char Minar complex are 45 prayer spaces and a mosque.

Just beyond the Char Minar, you will see the colossal MECCA MASJID, one of the largest in the world. It was so named because it is said that Mohammad Quli Shah who built it, had bricks from Mecca used in the construction of the Masjid. The Qutb Shahis could not finish the Masjid as Aurangzeb defeated them. It was completed by Aurangzeb in 1694.

Mecca Masjid is poetry in stone with a hall measuring 67 metres and soaring to a height of 54 metres. The roof is supported by 15 graceful arches, five to each of three sides. Towards the southern end of the mosque lie the marble GRAVES OF NIZAM ALI KHAN and the families of the Asaf Jahi dynasty. The mosque can accommodate 10, 000 kneeling devotees. During Ramadan, many thousands more spill over the streets outside the mosque.

From the Char Minar, any number of cobbled lanes will plunge you into the bustling, medieval pantomime of Hyderabad's OLD BAZAR. Wind your ways through the crowds of men and burqa-clad women. Shops on both sides sell you pearls, carpets, jewellery, glass bangles, Indian scents and every other conceivable product. There are traditional Himroo brocades, delicate silver jewellery, lacquered sandalwood toys and distinctive Bidri work.

Lacquered glass bangles

Hyderabad is particularly known for its two crafts: Bidriware and Pearls. Bidriware is a technique of decorated metal work unique to India. It was developed under the Mughals and named after Bidar in Karnataka where it originated. Various utility goods like dishes, boxes, hooka bases, etc., are cast from an alloy of zinc, copper, tin and sometimes even lead. Each piece is then decorated with very fine arabesques, flowers,

Bidriware

geometric patterns. Designs are inlaid with silver and brass. In the past, designs were also inlaid with gold but now the buyers cannot pay the price. You can see craftsmen working on it in bazars around Char Minar.

Jewellery making with pearls have been one of the oldest crafts of India. The market is concentrated in a row of shops near Char Minar. Here millions of pearls come from Japan. Supplies from the Middle East have since dried up. These are then sorted, pierced, sorted again and sold in India and exported overseas. You can see shoppers coming from all parts of India to buy pearls or jewellery made of pearls.

Several old and decaying city palaces are within walking distance from the bazar area. Among these are PANCH MAHAL, CHOW MAHAL, KING KOTHI and BARADARI PALACES — later known for a battalion of Amazonian female sepoys, who patrolled and protected the Nizam's harem.

The most extravagant of these palaces is the FALUKNUMA PALACE, 5 kilometres south, which was used by the Nizam to house his important guests such as the Viceroy. It was built in 1897. Now, more or less deserted, the Nizam's successor lives in Australia with his Australian wife. It can be seen by obtaining permission from the Tourist Office.

On the other side of the Musi river lies the former BRITISH RESIDENCY, a fine Greco-coloured building built in 1803. The front has two crouching sphinxes. It is now used as a college. Other nearby architectural relics are the ochre-red HIGH COURT and OSMANIA HOSPITAL, both built in the Indo-Saracenic style in the late 19th century.

GOLCONDA is one of the most famous forts in South India. The name originates from the Telugu words "Golla Konda", meaning "Shepherd's Hill". The origin of the fort can be traced to the Yadava dynasty of Deogiri, and the Kakatiyas of Warrangal. Golconda was originally a mud fort, which passed to the Bahmani dynasty, and later, to the Qutb Shahis who held it from A.D. 1518 to 1687. The first three Qutb Shahi kings rebuilt Golconda, over a span of 62 years. The fort is famous for its acoustics, palaces, factories, ingenious water supply system and the famous Fateh Rabben gun, one of the cannons used in the last siege of Golconda by Aurangzeb, to whom the fort ultimately fell. Eyewitness accounts by Marco Polo and 17th century French traveller Jean-Baptiste Tavernier spread the legend about the enormous wealth and splendour of Golconda as well as its decadence which led to its fall. It is also a place to ramble about at will and make one's own discoveries. The one-hour halt at Golconda provided by the organisers of the city tours is not adequate to see this great wonder.

The legendary QUTB SHAHI TOMBS lie to the north of Golconda, about a kilometre away from the BANJARA DARWAZA of the Golconda Fort. Planned and built by the Qutb Shahis themselves, these tombs are said to be the oldest historical monuments in Hyderabad. They form a large group and stand on a raised platform. The tombs are built in Persian,

Qutb Shahi Tombs

Pathan and Hindu architectural styles using grey granite with stucco ornamentation.

Hyderabad has several beautiful, gardens, one of the most popular being the PUBLIC GARDENS. It also encloses the STATE LEGISLATURE, STATE ARCHAEOLOGICAL MUSEUM, JUBILEE HALL, JAWAHAR BAL BHAVAN and TELUGU LALITHA KALA THORANAM, an open air theatre.

This shimmeringly ethereal TEMPLE OF LORD VENKATESWARA, built in sculpted white marble, floats on the city skyline on the KALA PAHAD. The idol in the temple is a replica of the one at Tirupati.

BIRLA PLANETARIUM is India's most modern planetarium, and the first of its kind in the country. It is equipped with the most advanced technology from Japan and is built on the NAUBHAT PAHAD, adjacent to the Kala Pahad.

Sprawling across 300 lush green acres, the NEHRU ZOOLOGICAL PARK is a must for nature lovers. The biggest zoo in India, it has over 1500 different kinds of animals and birds, most of which are kept in conditions as close to their natural habitats as possible.

Statue of Lord Buddha

OSMAN SAGAR is a jewel-like lake, formed by the damming of the Musi, in 1920 to maintain a regular supply of drinking water for Hyderabad. Beautiful gardens laid out on either side of the Osman Sagar Bund, and a guest house, make this a popular picnic spot.

HUSSAIN SAGAR LAKE was constructed during the time of Ibrahim Quli Qutb Shah, by Hussain Shah Wali, in A.D. 1562. Today the road across the bund is a busy thoroughfare connecting the twin cities of Hyderabad and SECUNDERABAD. Boating and water sports are a regular feature at the Hussain Sagar. Another major attraction of Hussain Sagar is the 18 metre high, 350-ton monolithic STATUE OF LORD BUDDHA on the Rock of Gibraltar in the middle of the lake.

Dinner with Founder of Hyderabad
Andhra Pradesh Tourism organises special entertainments for groups of tourists on request. These include "Dinner with the Founder of Hyderabad". During the dinner, visitors can travel back in time and enjoy a traditional Hyderabadi Chowki dinner with a typically Hyderabadi menu, meant for kings.

An interesting SOUND AND LIGHT SHOW has been mounted at Golconda Fort which brings to life the glory and splendour of Golconda.

For all practical purpose, Golconda is now part of the Hyderabad city.

The people of Hyderabad are warm and hospitable and welcome the visitor with an old world charm. There is music in their language and a gentleness of life that permeates beyond Hyderabad's recent industrial boom.

BEYOND HYDERABAD

Hyderabad is not Andhra Pradesh. Andhra Pradesh reserves some of its best attractions beyond Hyderabad. It is one of India's large States population over 60 million.

Geologically, it is one of the most ancient parts of the peninsular India. There are three distinct geographical tracts. The first is the rich and fertile riparian and deltic parts of the Godavari and Krishna rivers. The second is the forested and hilly tracts of the north, between the Vindhya ranges and the Godavari river. The third is the south-western part of the Lower Deccan. It includes the districts of CUDDAPPAH, KURNOOL, CHITTOOR and ANANTPUR hilly plateau land. This is TELANGANA, the core region of Andhra.

The Telugu language has the richness of classical Sanskrit. Despite its basic Dravidian matrix, it is overwhelmingly "spoken Sanskrit"in its style as well as embellishments. It has rich literature created by a galaxy of poets like Potana, Vemana, Srinatha, Nannaya and many others.

Andhra also produces great craftsmen. They make excellent laquer toys, Anakapalli articles, Nirmal painted pottery, bidri work, palm leaf and slate articles. Andhra silk products are also well-known.

In the cultural sphere, Kuchipudi is Andhra's prominent classical dance form. Essentially, a narrative dance relating to the Pauranic legends, it derives its gesture and essential grammar from the pristine Bharatanatyam of Tamil Nadu. Andhra was a major Buddhist centre during the times of Ashoka in the third century B.C. In the 14th century when Muslim power reached Andhra regions, it marked the blending of Hindu and Muslim cultures.

Beyond Hyderabad, the ancient can be discovered at NAGARJUNAKONDA, 150 km. towards southeast. It remained the most important Buddhist centre in South India for 5 centuries. It takes its name from Nagarjuna - one of the most respected monks of Buddhism who was the founder of the Madhyamika School. It was originally called VIJAYPUR.

The site was discovered in 1926. Excavations have revealed remains of stupas, viharas, chaityas and mandapas. There are some outstanding examples of marble carvings about the events in the Buddha's life. These have been moved to an Island Museum following the construction of the NAGARJUNA SAGAR DAM which will submerge the whole area. The dam will be one of the largest masonry constructions creating the world's third largest artificial lake.

Excavations at nearby centres like AMARAVATI, Nagarjunakonda, BHATTIPROLA, GOLI, GHANTASALA and several other places have unearthed Buddhist settlements. Here Buddhist students came from Kashmir, Gandhara, China, Sri Lanka and Kamrup (Assam).

The academic and medical services were on par with other major Buddhist universities like Nalanda, Valabhi and Vikramshilla. Brahmanical Hinduism and Buddhism flourished in harmony as is evident from the several Hindu temples existing side by side with Buddhist temples at Nagarjunakonda.

Stupa at Amaravati

The earliest and the biggest Stupa site was at AMARAVATI. This was vandalised by building contractors who used it as source for stones - especially marble. Only remnants were salvaged and have been carted off to the Government Museum in Madras and to Albert Museum in London.

The sculptures of the Buddhist sites of Andhra are in a class by themselves. Their rich representation of Jataka tales and Buddha's life is extraordinary.

To visit Nagarjunakonda, there are regular coach tours from Hyderabad, organised by the Andhra Pradesh Tourism Development Corporation as well as India Tourism Development Corporation(ITDC). If you cannot travel all the way to Nagarjunakonda from Hyderabad, take a local tour by launches to NAGARJUNAKONDA ISLAND MUSEUM which houses the remains from the Buddhist sites. The Museum also has full-scale model placements of the excavated remains. It can be a rewarding experience.

WARRANGAL

North-east of Hyderabad in Telangana region, Warrangal, an ancient city, was once the capital of the Kakatiya kingdom which ruled over much of the present-day Andhra State from the 12th to the early 14th centuries. The Kakatiya kings were great builders. It was during their time that the Chalukyan style of architecture reached the pinnacle of its glory.

Notable examples of this architecture are the THOUSAND-PILLARED TEMPLE on the slopes of the HANANAKONDA HILL. One of its shrines is still in use. There are other temples too in the area around Warrangal.

Ramappa Temple at Palampet

The RAMAPPA TEMPLE at PALAMPET, 77 kilometres from Warrangal, represents a combination of Chalukyan and later Hoysala art. It is one of the finest examples of temple architecture in South India.

Another attraction of Warrangal is the mud-brick FORT built by the Kakatiyas. The Kakatiyas kings had earlier built Golconda Fort which was later improved by the Muslim rulers. Warrangal has a massive fort which was reputed to be impregnable. It was under continuous attack from the Delhi Sultans from the 13th to 14th centuries.

If your interest is in the various streams of Hindu temple architecture, try to visit Badami, Aihole and Pattadakal in the neighbouring Karnataka. In those days the region was part of the Chalukya Empire. (see chapter on Karnataka.)

SOUTH OF HYDERABAD

Going south of Hyderabad, the first tour of any importance is to KURNOOL at the confluence of two rivers. It has a pleasant climate, specially in winter months. Kurnool is the gateway to an important Hindu pilgrimage earlier — the SHRINE OF SRISAILAM. Although this place of pilgrimage is only accessible by foot, thousands of people make the long trek to MALLIKARJUNA TEMPLE, a Shiva temple. The rich and old are carried by palanquins.

Kurnool has also fragments of its old fort and several mosques built by Muslim rulers.

TIRUPATI

In the extreme South of Andhra Pradesh, lie three other important temples. One is TIRUPATI, where every Hindu wants to go for the blessings of the Lord. Tirupati is the abode of the "Lord of the Seven Hills" and is the richest temple in the South. The Temple Trust runs several educational institutions. The shrine is a good example of early

Thousand Pillars Temple

Dravidian art. While ascending, you can see several *gopurams* (monumental gates) above.

The temple surrounded by mango and sandal trees stands on top of a 2500-feet peak. In front of it is the HALL OF PILLARS, an attractive stepped-way leads you to the temple gate. Worship inside the Hindu temple follows elaborate rituals while outside the souvenir crafts and flower shops do a roaring business.

Non-Hindus are allowed to ascend up to the temple and see it from the outside but are not allowed to participate in the worship rituals.

Sixty km. south of Tirupati lies TIRUTTANI, a hill shrine of great antiquity. Three hundred and sixty steps lead to the top of the hill — one for each day of the year.

Tirupati lies on the main railway line from Madras and there are regular bus services linking the two cities. Air services connect Madras with Tirupati.

KALAHASTI is yet another pilgrimage centre, 60 km. east of Tirupati and on the border of Tamil Nadu. The holy temple which attracts thousands of devotees every day stands on the banks of a river and looks up to the hills of the Eastern Ghats.

Closer to Tirupati is CHANDRAGIRI MAHAL and FORT. It was here that the last Vijayanagar king, Ranga Raya, approved of the sale to the East India Company of the land on which Fort Saint George was built in Madras.

In the opening centuries of the Christian era the entire coastal belt, and more especially the Krishna River in its deltic and lower reaches hummed with activity. Seafaring vessels reached as far as Amaravati and Nagarjunakonda. Now, only the ruins of those great cities are visible.

VIJAYAWADA

Sixty-six km. from Amaravati, Vijayawada lies between the Krishna and Badanmeru rivers. A large lake has been created near the city with the construction of PRAKASHAM BARRAGE on the Krishna River. Three canals from the lake run through the city giving it a Venetian look.

With a history of two thousand years, Vijayawada is often considered to be the gateway to the South. Lying in the midst of Telugu heartland, the city, today, remains true to its age-old character. Part of the great Vijayanagar empire, the city is one of the major railway junctions of India linking Andhra with all parts of India.

The birth of Vijayawada is traced to Hindu mythology. According to legend, Arjuna, the third of the Pandava brothers, prayed to Lord Shiva at the top of INDRAKILA HILL for victory (Vijaya). He was blessed and that gave the settlement its name Vijayawada. The presiding deity of the town — Kanakdurga—is also locally called Vijaya. The KANAKDURGA TEMPLE, on a hill-top is synonymous with Vijayawada. On the way to the temple are the rock-cut caves dedicated to Akkanna and Madanna — ministers in the court of Qutb Shahi rulers.

The city was visited by the great Chinese traveller Hieun Tsang and he has described the town in glowing terms. Remains of its past, preserved in its cave temples are reminders of the importance of Vijayawada over the centuries.

After the fall of the Mauryan empire, nearby Amaravati became the principal centre of Buddhism in South India under the Satavahanas. Adi Shankara blessed the city by installing a 'Sri-Chakra' at the temple here. Two Jain temples recall 1000-year old heritage of Vijayawada. The HAZARAT BAL MOSQUE in this town is credited to have a relic of the Prophet Mohammad.

About 60 kilometres from Vijayawada is the small town of KUCHIPUDI from where the famous classical dance Kuchipudi of Andhra Pradesh originated. The dance was created by Sidhendra Yogi who was born here. Today, the Dance School here offers a five-year programme to prepare master dancers in Kuchipudi.

Mangalgiri temple **Kondapalli toys**

Twelve km. south of Vijayawada is MANGALGIRI, the site of the temple of Lord Narasimha — one of the nine incarnations of Vishnu. KONDAPALLI, 16 km. from Vijayawada, is the place where Kondapalli wooden toys were first made. These toys have characteristic Indian themes of mythological figures, birds, animals, fruits and vegetables. The town has also a seventh century fort.

VISHAKHAPATNAM (VIZAG)

Named after the God of Valour, Vaishaka in the 11th century, it is one of the finest sea-resorts on the eastern sea board of India. For its fine beaches and verdcurt country-side, it is often compared to Goa.

Apart from Vishakhapatnam's (vizag for short) image of sea resort, it is a growing identical and one of India's finish sea-ports.

The British, during then colonial tenure set up a resort town here on a rise near the sea shore. Waltair uplands as it is called still retains its original character with beautiful lags language and a panoramic view of the bayer well on the below it.

Vizag is connected by air to major cities of India and has excellent hotels including a Taj Regency and a Park Hotel. The part at her plenty of budget hotels also.

HYDERABAD

GENERAL INFORMATION
Population: 4,270,000 (1991 census)
Altitude: 545 metres (1815 ft)
Climate

	Temperature	
	Max.	Min.
Winter	35⁰ c	13⁰ c
Summer	37⁰ c	22⁰ c
Rainfall	475 mm	26 mm

Season: Throughout the year. During the months of April and May the days are hot.
Clothing
Summer: Light cottons
Winter: Light woollens for the evenings

HOW TO GET THERE
By Air: Indian Airlines flights operate to most of the major cities of India. Also now private airlines East West and Jet Airways.
By Rail: Hyderabad and its twin city, Secunderabad, are connected by rail with Ajmer, Bombay, Bangalore, Bhubaneswar, Delhi, Madras, Manmad (for Aurangabad), Vishakhapatnam, etc.
By Road: Hyderabad is connected by road with all parts of India. It is 539 km. from Aurangabad (for Ajanta-Ellora),
567 km. from Badami,
590 km. from Bangalore,
667 km. from Vishakhapatnam,
671 km. from Madras,
698 km. from Goa and
713 km. from Bombay.

LOCAL TRANSPORT
Tourist taxis, metered taxis, metered auto-rickshaws and rickshaws. Also city bus services.

CONDUCTED TOURS
1. Full-day tour including the CITY SIGHTS, QUTB SHAHI TOMBS and GOLCONDA. (Daily)

2. NAGARJUNASAGAR — full-day tour.
3. MANTRALAYAM tour (full-day) twice a month.
4. WARRANGAL and RAMAPPA tour (full-day) once a week.
5. TIRUPATI tour (once a week).

Information: Andhra Pradesh Govt. Tourist Office. Gagan Vihar M.J. Road, Hyderabad Tel: 577531-32.
Cities Tours operate from Yatri Niwas Complex, S.P. Road, Secunderabad. Tel: 843943-1-2.
Govt. of India Tourist Office. Tel: 666870

WHERE TO STAY (STD CODE: 040)

DELUXE
1. Gateway Hotel on Banjara Hills
   Phone: 399999
   Cable: GATEWAY
   Fax: 392218
2. The Krishna Oberoi
   Phone: 392323
   Cable: OBHOTEL
   Fax: 0842-393079
3. Bhaskar Palace
   Phone: 226141
   Fax: 222712
4. Quality Inn Green Park
   Phone: 291919
   Fax: 291900
   Cable: GREENPARK
5. Krishna Holiday Inn
   Phone: 223347

STANDARD
6. Baseraa
   Phone: 823200
   Cable: BASERAA
7. Asrani International
   Phone: 842267, 842320-21
   Fax: 811529
   Cable: ASRANIS
8. Nagarjuna
   Phone: 237201

BUDGET
9. Golkonda
   Phone: 226001
10. Deccan Continental
    Phone: 840981-80
    Cable: HOTDECON
11. Parklane
    Phone: 840466, 840399
    Cable: HIARCHES
12. Karan
    Phone: 840190
    Cable: MALWALA
    Fax: 842-844533
13. Sarovar
    Phone: 237638
    Cable: SAROVAR
14. Sampurna International
    Phone: 40165-66
    Telex: 0425-2132 JOY IN
    Cable: SAMPURNA
15. Jaya International
    Phone: 232929, 237483
    Cable: NEERA HOTEL
16. Blue Moon
    Phone: 35815
    Cable: BLUMOON
17. Ashoka
    Phone: 230105
    Cable: PROHOTEL
18. Emerald
    Phone: 202836
    Cable: STAYFINE
    Fax: 0842-233901
19. Siddhartha
    Phone: 557421
    Cable: HOMELY
20. Yatri Niwas
    Phone: 847603

WHAT TO SEE

1. The CHAR MINAR, called the Arc de Triumph of the East, stands in the centre of the city, a gateway-shaped sentinel. (It is floodlit in the evenings.) It is surrounded by bazars where the famous Hyderabadi bangles can be bought.
2. The SALAR JUNG MUSEUM, a collection of a former Prime Minister of the State. A unique one-man collection of antiques from all over the world.
3. MECCA MASJID, one of the most impressive mosques, with four domes, lofty colonnades and arches.
4. FALUKNAMA PALACE of the Nizams can be visited with prior permission.
5. GOLCONDA, once famed for its diamond mines (from which the famous Kohinoor diamond of the British Crown was mined), is the site of a strategic fort dating back to the 13th century. An invincible fort, it has an extraordinary acoustical system and massive battlements.
6. QUTB SHAHI TOMBS, graceful mausolea of seven sultans who lie buried here.

EXCURSIONS

1. OSMAN SAGAR (23 km), a beautiful man-made lake.
2. HIMAYAT SAGAR (23 km), a vast lake 85 sq. km. in area.
3. NAGARJUNASAGAR DAM (149 km), named after a great Buddhist teacher of the A.D. 2nd century, is the highest masonry dam in the world. The ruins of this great city have been removed and reconstructed on top of the hill, a work of modern-day genius. Eleven km. downstream are the 21 metre high ETHIPOTHALA WATERFALLS.
4. BIDAR (130 km), an ancient fort with tombs of the Bahmani and Barid Shahi kings.
5. WARRANGAL (157 km.), the thousand-pillared temple of the 12th century is notable for its richly carved pillars. The Ramappa Temple, 64 km. away, is considered to be the brightest star in the galaxy of medieval temples.
6. PAKHAL (217 km.), a lake 60 km. from Warrangal, also boasts of a wildlife sanctuary.

FESTIVALS OF SPECIAL INTEREST

1. BATKAMMA FESTIVAL celebrated after a harvest. Starting on Ganesh Chaturthi day, it goes on for a month ending on Dassehra day. OCTOBER CELEBRATIONS take place around a mound of flowers.
2. JATRAS or processions and fairs take place at all the main temples around Hyderabad at different times of the year.

3. URS at the tombs of the various Muslim saints are part of the cultural life of the city.
4. UGADI FESTIVAL (March-April), celebrates the New Year.

ENTERTAINMENT
There are many cultural organisations which organise music and dance programmes on weekends in the city. See newspapers for listing.

VIJAYAWADA

GENERAL INFORMATION
Population: 750,000 (1991 census)
Altitude: 3 metres (10 ft)
Climate

	Temperature	
	Max.	Min.
Winter	31^0 c	18^0 c
Summer	34^0 c	26^0 c
Rainfall	79 mm	31 mm

Season: Throughout the year.
Clothing
Light cottons throughout the year. Light woollens during nights from December to February.

HOW TO GET THERE
By Air: Indian Airlines operates flights to Calcutta, Hyderabad and Madras.
By Rail: Vijayawada has direct rail connections with Calcutta, Madras, Delhi, Guwahati, Hyderabad, Puri, Thiruvananthapuram, etc.
By Road: Vijayawada is well connected by road. It is 638 km. from Hyderabad, 801 km. from Madras, 1107 km. from Calcutta. Regular bus services operate to the major towns of Andhra Pradesh.

LOCAL TRANSPORT
Unmetered taxis, auto-rickshaws, cycle-rickshaws, bus services.

CONDUCTED TOURS
1. There is a full-day tour of the city and SIMHACHALAM as also of BHIMILI operated by Andhra Pradesh Travel and Tourism Corporation starting from Krishnaveni hotel.
2. Once a week there is a full-day tour to ARAKU VALLEY.
3. Once a week there is a full-day tour to SRIKAKULAM.

Information: APTTDC. Tel : 75382

WHERE TO STAY (STD CODE: 0866)
BUDGET
1. Manorama
   Phone: 77221
   Cable: BLISS
2. Anupama
   Phone: 61224, 61243
   Cable: HOTEL ANU
3. Srilekha International
   Phone: 61270
   Cable: HOTEL ANU
4. Mamata
   Phone: 61251 (10 lines)
5. Raj Towers
   Phone: 61311 (10 lines)

Cable: RAJ TOWERS
6. Krishnaveni Hotel
Phone: 75382

WHAT TO SEE
1. LAWSON BAY, an attractive beach for swimming.
2. RAMAKRISHNA MISSION BEACH, one of the loveliest beaches in the area.
3. DOLPHIN'S NOSE, 358 metres above sea level, a promontory which shelters the port.
4. MOUNT KAILAS, 304 metres high, overlooks another fine beach.
5. SRI VENKATESHWARA KONDA, a temple built by an Englishman, Capt. Blackmoor, in 1886.

EXCURSIONS
1. SIMHACHALAM (16 km.) - the Hill of the Lion, a famous pilgrim centre dating back to the 11th century. Situated on top of a hill, it has interesting architecture and sculptures.
2. BHEEMUNIPATNAM (24 km), or BHIMILI, once a Dutch settlement, has a very beautiful beach. Specially interesting is the coastal drive from Vizag.
3. ARAKU VALLEY (112 km) at an altitude of 950 metres above sea level. A cool hill resort, it is also home for many tribal sects whose dances and festivities are of great interest. The drive to Araku is through coffee plantations. A high altitude railway line with 46 tunnels presents an unusual journey. En route, 90 km. from Vishakhapatnam, are the limestone BORRA CAVES with stalagmite and stalactite formations.

SHOPPING
Kalamkari printed fabrics and wall hangings, saris from Venkatagiri, Narayanpet, Padampuram and Pochampalli, ivory horn products, Kondapalli, Nakkapalli and Yetikippaka toys.

FESTIVALS OF SPECIAL LOCAL INTEREST
1. CHANDANAYATRA FESTIVAL (March-April) at the Simhachalam Temple.
2. CHAITRA FESTIVAL (March-April) in the Araku Valley. The tribals have very attractive dances called Dimsa and Mayura performed at this festival.
3. NARASIMHA JAYANTHI TEMPLE FESTIVAL (May).

Chapter 23

ORISSA
Past Splendours & Contemporary Expressions

Konark temple

Orissa, one of the most interesting States of India, lies on the shore of Bay of Bengal, and has an area of 1,56,000 sq km and population of 31 million. In the west are the tablelands of the Eastern Ghats, part of the central plateau and in their midst are the green valleys of five big rivers which flow into the Bay of Bengal.

In the upland region and on the upper slopes are lush green forests abounding in wild elephants, Bengal tiger and other rare species.

In Orissa, you will find India in a capsule form—from the India lost in the depth of history before the birth of Christ, to the tribes that still live in the hunting stage of civilisation, through the golden age of Hindu temple builders to the very modern India grappling with problems of a great industrial revolution. Everything is present in Orissa. A gentle, smiling people meet you everywhere during your travels.

The principal tourist attractions of Orissa are the temple towns of PURI and BHUBANESWAR and the great SUN TEMPLE OF KONARK. These three tourist attractions form a convenient and compact little triangle. Bhubaneswar is on the main Calcutta-Madras rail route and the other two places are easily accessible by car. The State is predominantly rural but industrialisation is changing its face.

The origins of Orissa are hidden in the dawn of history. The State, known in the ancient times as Kalinga, is often mentioned in Hindu epics. Legend has it that Kalinga — one of the five sons of a sage— travelled as far as the hills of the Eastern Ghats, looked down on the valleys below, was fascinated and decided to settle down here with his people. Orissa has since been called Kalinga. Outside the hazy past, Orissa's recorded history begins from 260 B.C. Emperor Ashoka installed carved ROCK PILLAR at DHULI, only 5 km. from the present capital of Bhubaneswar. The pillar has stood the test of time for 23 centuries. The carved inscriptions carry the message of Buddhist principles. Having fought a bloody war with the people of Kalinga and having won it, he repented at the loss of life and the devastation caused by him. He accepted the faith of the people of Kalinga who were Buddhists.

The zenith of Orissa civilisation was reached between the 4th and 13th century under the great builders — Kesari and Ganga kings. During their rule, thousands of temples and monuments were built all over the country. Fortunately for Orissa, the State remained outside the power of Muslim invaders till late in the 16th century. And, when Muslims invaders reached Orissa they destroyed most of the 7,000 temples that once lined the banks of the sacred lake of Bhubaneswar. Today only 500 temples survive.

And finally the British took over Orissa in 1803. Since Orissa was not strategically important for them, they did little to improve its economic conditions. It was divided into some 26 vest-pocket sized states ruled by Rajas leaving little scope for economic development. The Independence of India led to the amalgamation of the State into a compact province of

Orissa. Now, a democratically elected State Government is trying to bring about changes by using the State's immense water and other natural resources.

BHUBANESWAR, The City of Temples

If you fly to Orissa, Bhubaneswar — the capital of Orissa — is the first town you arrive at. And it is also the right place to start a tour of the State from where you can move on to the other two angles of Orissa's Tourist Triangle — PURI and KONARK.

Bhubaneswar has two aspects — a 20th century garden city and what the visitors would like to see most — its monuments and temples. Within a radius of ten sq. km., the city presents a panorama of Orissan art and history from the third century B.C. till A.D. 16th century. With hundreds of temples Bhubaneswar can well be described as the "Cathedral City of India". BINDU SAGAR — the sacred lake in old Bhubaneswar, once claimed 7,000 temples; now only 500 survive in varied stages of preservation

The golden age of temple construction in Orissa stretched from the 8th to the 13th century but it achieved the pinnacle of glory in the 10th and 11th centuries. The shrines of Orissa taken together represent the development of the "Nagara" style of Indo-Aryan architecture. Orissan temples consist almost entirely of a vaulting spire thrusting upwards in a pinnacle among much lower replica turrets which are reduced to a role of mere surface decoration. The plan of the temple is simple. First come the Jagmohan or porch which is usually square with a pyramidal roof. Immediately follow the Daul, the cubical inner apartment, which enshrines the deity. It is surmounted by soaring towers. Sometimes one or two more halls are built in these temples. These are set in front of the porch. They are called Natmandir and Bhogmandir.

The sculptures in these temples is not easy to describe. The statues represent everything from the sacred to the profane, but every stone used in temple construction has been carved. Birds, animals, flowers and plants, human beings alone or together in amorous postures — each can be seen in chiselled details.

The largest and the most interesting temple in the city is the 11th century LINGARAJ TEMPLE which exhibits the temple art of several centuries. Shiva is the presiding deity but almost all Hindu gods are represented here. It is set in a huge walled-in compound with dozens of votive shrines. It really forms a world of its own. Although entry to the temple is restricted to Hindus, there is an excellent vantage point from where you can see the entire temple. Pilgrims flock to the neighbouring Bindu Sagar Lake where it is believed that water from all the sacred rivers of India is gathered and it is, therefore, considered a very purifying experience to have a dip in the lake.

The compound of the temple measures 520 by 465 feet. Its curvilinear tower (*vimana*) rises to a height of 127 feet. The tower has been built without mortar. It is hollow inside and you can reach its top by an internal staircase below out of the 7-feet thick walls. While the interior of the shrine is without any adornment the exterior is profusely decorated with beautiful sculptures of gods and goddesses, some couples clinging to each other in amorous poses which may shock the first time Western visitors. Along the eastern side of the Lingaraj Temple, there are several small temples of a similar shape as the original Lingaraj Temple.

One of the most delightful temple built on a more human scale is the 11th century RAJA RANI TEMPLE — standing alone in the green rice fields. It is perhaps the most harmoniously planned temple. Its decorations are beautiful and enchanting — the naked, smiling nymphs, the embracing couples, etc. Here the feminine form is the subject of glorification and incredibly seductive. It has been suggested that some pleasure-loving king of Orissa may have built it more as his pleasure retreat than as a prayer hall. It is perhaps the latest in date and the most refined.

About a kilometre to the east of the Lingaraj temple is the "Grove of the Perfect Being". More than 20 temples remain here intact. Some of these are described below.

Mukteswar Temple

This 10th century gem of a temple is an important transition point between the early and later phases of the Kalinga school of temple architecture.

Many elements of the older order have been blended with new designs and conceptions. Many of the innovations etched here became essential features of all later temples.

Richly sculpted, the temple offers pride of place to tales from the *Panchatantra*. The niches on the outer face of the compound wall include Buddhist, Jain as well as Hindu images, pointing to the synthesis which was so much a part of Orissan religious life.

The temple gateway, an arched masterpiece, is worth a visit. Beautiful sculptures, include elaborate scrolls, graceful female figures, and excellent decorative details characterise the archway.

Parasurameswara Temple
Lavishly decorated, this small Shiva temple has friezes depicting amorous couples, animal life, human figures and floral motifs. Specially appealing are the ornate lattice windows and the busts of Shiva.

Vaital Temple
The Vaital Temple represents the Khakhora order of the Kalinga style of temple architecture, devoted to tantric cults.

A very definite style of decoration through sculpture is evident. As is the practice in tantric worship, elements from certain sects of Hinduism and Buddhism centred around the female life force, Shakti, have been combined. The presiding deity, the eight-armed Chamunda (Kali)represents Shakti.

The first erotic sculptures of Orissan art are found here. In course of time, temple builders may have considered these images as an integral part of temple decoration and adapted them to their skills and techniques.

Behind the Mukteshwar Temple stands KEDARESWAR where ground plan is almost circular. It has a 8-feet statue of Hanuman (the Monkey God) and another of Goddess Durga standing on a lion.

The SIDHESWAR TEMPLE northwest of Mukteswar is not very different. It has the traditional five parts.

Dhaului Edicts
Only a few kilometres from Bhubaneswar, Emperor Ashoka carved his famous edicts into a five metre by three metre rock. He related the horrors he experienced in the Kalinga wars which he won and his subsequent conversion to Buddhism. These inscriptions are still remarkably clear after 2000 years of exposure to weather. The rock is at the base of the small hill. The adjacent large hill is topped by a new Peace Pagoda built by the Japanese in early 1970s.

Other Attractions
The partly excavated ruins of SISUPAL GARH are believed to be the remains of an ancient Ashokan city.

PURI

Fifty-five kilometres from Bhubaneswar is the beach town of Puri, one of the four holiest cities of the Hindus known for its JAGANNATH TEMPLE.

The city revolves round the great Jagannath temple known for its famous RATH YATRA or "Car Festival".

Most tourists love the place for its beaches and consider getting up before sunrise to see fishing boats leave for the sea.

Jagannath Temple

Even before one enters the town of Puri, the 65 metre-high JAGANNATH TEMPLE makes its presence felt. The sense of devotion heightens in Puri with nearly every aspect of the place touched by the aura of the magnificent temple. The whole universe is framed within its huge compound, as it were. And the central deity, Lord Jagannath, has become the focus of religious life across Orissa. Because of its great religious importance and hallowed traditions, non-Hindus are not allowed within the temple complex. But, they can see the temple from a specified point.

The maintenance of the temple, caring for the millions who throng it, and the performance of the various rituals have made every citizen of Puri a part of the temple in his own way.

On the main road leading to the temple is a fascinating market place, filled with small stalls selling paintings, wooden images of the deities, art and craft works from the whole region, items for the rituals and more.

A walk down the bazaar, with its colour and energy and pilgrims milling around each stall, is a good experience for visitors.

KONARK

Konark is on the sea coast, 64 kilometres from Bhubaneswar and only 33 km. north of Puri. It is known for its SUN TEMPLE on the sea.

The Sun Temple

One of the most stunning symbols of religious architecture, the Sun Temple is the crowning glory of Orissan temple art. Centuries of myth and legend shroud its past. Built in the 13th century, the entire temple was designed in the shape of a colossal chariot, carrying the Sun god, Surya, pulled by seven horses. The 24 giant wheels of the chariot symbolise the division of time. The temple is a brilliant chronicle in stone, with thousands of images including those of deities, the Surasundaris, heavenly damsels, and human musicians, lovers, dancers, and different scenes from courtly life. Besides, birds, animals and a plethora of intricate geometrical decorative designs adorn the walls.

The temple was conceived to be a true microcosm of the world. This, however, would not have been complete without depiction of the union of love. Hence, erotic art covers a major part of the temple area.

CUTTACK

The Cuttack District has also temples worth visiting. Situated on an island on the banks of the Mahanadi river is the SIMHANATH TEMPLE. The temple reflects the influence of old and new experiments, and offers interesting images of the Shaiva, Shakta and Vaishnava cults of Hinduism.

Cuttack was the capital of Orissa before the new capital at Bhubaneswar was built. The city had a great BARABATI FORT built in the 14th century. Only the gateway and the moat remain. The stone rivetment which protects it from seasonal floods was built in the 16th century.

The MADHAVA TEMPLE, built in the 13th century, is located on the banks of the Prachi river. Madhava, the four-armed Vishnu, is the presiding deity, with a small image of Durga next to him. This is yet another example of the synthesis so unique to Orissan religious process. A place of active worship, the temple draws thousands of devotees to its sacred portals.

BUDDHIST MONASTERIES

Buddhism had considerable presence in some parts of Orissa. North-east of Cuttack, the three hills of RATNAGIRI, LALITGIRI, and UDAYAGIRI provide an immense Buddhist monastic complex.

Buddha Shanti Stupa

Ratnagiri has the most extensive of ruins. Excavations have unearthed sculptures dating back to the 8th and 9th centuries. A recent excavation had led to the finding of inscriptions dating back to the Kusahan period in the 2nd century A.D. Lalitgiri is known for the discovery of an ancient stupa containing relics preserved in caskets of stone. Its antiquity and silver and gold contents have led to speculation that these are relics of the Buddha. From the main stupa of Ratnagiri, one can see a limitless panorama of greenery, with the Brahmani River gently flowing nearby and the other two hills clearly visible. Udayagiri, the third of these hills, is known for the Lokeshwara image, with 8th century inscriptions.

Seven km. west of Bhubaneswar, the strong Jain influence is evident in the twin hills of KHANDAGIRI and Udayagiri, where caves cut from rocks seem to form a honeycomb. Udayagiri has the famous RANI GUMPHA or Queen's Cave, a two-storeyed structure with a spacious courtyard and elaborate sculptural friezes. Popular legends, historical scenes, religious functions and dancers have been carved on stone with singular grace.

The 18 caves of Udayagiri include the HATHI GUMPHA—the Elephant Cave. Recorded here on rock is the life chronicle of King Kharavela, the first known Orissan ruler, responsible for the expansion of the Kalinga empire.

SUN, SEA AND SAND

Orissa is more than a land of religious architecture, warm people and fascinating traditions. It is a land blessed with quiet beaches that invite the traveller to share their charm.

GOPALPUR-ON-SEA, an ancient seaport, is one of the most beautiful, unspoiled beaches one can see. Today, it is a modern, luxurious beach resort, and offers excellent facilities for surfing and sailing.

Still relatively undiscovered is CHANDIPUR, where the sea retreats several kilometres everyday, and life is serene and unhurried. And then there is the superb beach of BALIGHAT, where the river merges with the ocean.

Just south of Puri lies CHILKA LAKE. A place of enchanting beauty, where one sees the largest mixed salt and fresh water lake in Asia. Marshes, lowlands and islands dot the shallow waters.

A crane at Chilka Lake

Chilka is 70 km. long and 15 km. wide on an average. It is separated from the sea by a narrow sand bar. Power boats or yachts are available on hire.

Chilka is heavenly, particularly in winter. Millions of migratory birds, ducks, cranes, golden plovers, sandpipers, ospreys, flamingoes, hawks, and more, fly in from their harsher natural climes to make Chilka their home. One can enjoy the wondrous sight while boating down the gentle waters or fishing for the abundant fish. For anyway one looks at it, Chilka is a total experience.

ABUNDANT WILDLIFE

The natural abundance of Orissa has made it an ideal place for wild animals and birds to thrive without fear of man.

Where necessary, man has built boundaries around them with the idea of protecting them. NANDANKANAN, set in the natural wilderness, about 20 km. from Bhubaneswar, is an example. A delightful zoo, it is renowned the world over for its white tigers and for its success as the first breeding ground in captivity of black panthers and gharial. Leopards, rhinoceros, elephants, bear, monkeys, and several other types of mammals can also be seen at close quarters, in near-natural surroundings.

Orissa has excellent wildlife sanctuaries. The SIMILIPAL NATIONAL PARK is the most famous. Established as one of India's Project Tiger reserves, the sanctuary has rich valleys, rolling hills, grand waterfalls and majestic mountains.

Besides tigers, there are panthers, antelopes, Indian bison, deer, sloth bear, and over 200 species of birds that make this sanctuary truly irresistible.

One can visit smaller sanctuaries on day-visits to see the tigers of USHAKOTHI near SAMBALPUR, the deer of SAPTASAJYA near DHENKANAL, and the crocodiles of SATKOSIA GORGE, situated between ANUGUL and Dhenkanal.

For a glimpse of the truly unusual, the wildlife sanctuary of GAHIRMATHA, 130 km. from Bhubaneswar, is the place to be in. Beginning in September each year, hundreds and thousands of Pacific Ridley sea turtles swim in from as far away as South America to make this their nesting ground, making it an important Pacific Ridley nestling ground in India.

ORISSAN DANCES

The many Orissan dance forms are a study in the near-total synthesis of rhythm and movement, devotion and its expression.

The Odissi dance particularly proves this, giving the viewer an experience that goes beyond words. Traditional poses are woven to the accompaniment of *talas* (cycles) of sung poetry to present a highly stylised and graceful dance genre.

The tribal dances such as the 'Godha', the Praja wedding dance, and the colourful Gond dances, performed in mirrored and shelled turbans are fascinating.

The most active time of the year for the dances is usually October-November and March-April.

FESTIVALS

India is a land of festivals and fairs. Orissa has its own way of celebrating them. Some of the more famous of the Orissan festivals and fairs are the Makar Mela on Kalijal Island, Chilka Lake, the Tribal Fair of Bhubaneswar, the Car Festival of Lord Lingaraja of Bhubaneswar and the most popular of all, the Rath Yatra in Puri.

The Rath Yatra has a special significance to pilgrims who throng Puri from within India and overseas. The three deities, Jagannath, Balabhadra and Subhadra, are taken in a chariot procession to their summer temple for a week. Prior to this, the three deities have a ritual boat ride after a refreshing bath in fragrant sandalwood-scented water. This is followed by Sanana Yatra, literally the festival of bathing in which the main images are bathed ceremoniously. The deities then retire to their garden home. New attires are donned by them everyday, and after eight days, they return to the main temple riding their magnificent chariots drawn by devotees.

The Bali Yatra of Cuttack on the Kartik Purnima day in October/November is another memorable event. In memory of the traders who had set sail for the islands of Bali, Java and Sumatra in the olden days, people go to the river Mahanadi, bathe and sail tiny boats made of pith and paper. From daybreak till late in the evening, a huge fair is held on the river-bank, in front of the Barabati fort for four days.

SHOPPING

It can be a delight to shop in Orissa. Choices are many. Cigar boxes, jewellery, and decorative trays with extremely intricate silver filigree work, Pattachitra, the folk painting of Orissa, brassware, papier mache masks, colourful canopies, awnings and umbrellas with applique work from Pipli—not very far from Puri.

Orissa is also the home of exclusive silk and cotton handloom saris and fabrics that can be made into dresses, bedspreads, table linen and furnishings.

BHUBANESWAR-PURI-KONARK

GENERAL INFORMATION

Population: 300,000 (1991 census)
Altitude: 45 metres (150 ft)
Climate

	Temperature	
	Max.	Min.
Winter	35^0 c	16^0 c
Summer	38^0 c	25^0 c
Rainfall	943 mm	54 mm

Season: Throughout the year, except the rainy season (June to September) for those who wish to go swimming to the sea at Puri.
Clothing
Summer: light cottons.
Winter: light woollens.

HOW TO GET THERE

By Air: Indian Airlines (City Booking Office - *Tel.* 400533) operate from Bhubaneswar to Bombay, Calcutta, Delhi, Hyderabad, Varanasi, Nagpur and Raipur.

By Rail: Bhubaneswar has direct rail links with Agra, Calcutta, Delhi, Guwahati, Hyderabad, Gaya, Madras, Puri, Thiruvananthapuram, Varanasi, Vishakhapatnam, etc.

By Road: Bhubaneswar is connected by road to all parts of India. It is 470 km. from Calcutta and 1020 km. from Varanasi.

There are regular bus services to Puri, Calcutta, Vishakhapatnam, etc.

LOCAL TRANSPORT

Luxury taxis (limousines), tourist taxis and good coaches are available for hire. Also auto-rickshaws, cycle-rickshaws and bus services.

CONDUCTED TOURS

1. Tour of Bhubaneshwar, Khandagiri-Udayagiri, Dauli, Nandan Kanan and Museum — full day.
2. Puri and Konark — full day.
3. Chilka — full day.

(Bookings: Orissa Tourism, Panthrivas. *Tel.*: 50009) Swoste Travels: *Tel.*: 408738
Information: Government of India Tourist Office *Tel*: 54203

WHERE TO STAY (STD CODE: 0674)

D<small>ELUXE</small>
1. The Oberoi
   Phone: 56116
   Cable: OBHOTEL
   Fax: 0674-56269

S<small>TANDARD</small>
2. Kalinga Ashok
   Phone: 53830/53318
   Fax: 410745
   Cable: TOURISM

3. New Kenilworth
   Phone: 411723
   Cable: NEKEN
   Fax: 411561
4. Swosti
   Phone: 404178-79, 404359
   Fax: 0407524
   Cable: SWOSTI
5. Prachi
   Phone: 402366, 402728
   Fax: 403287
   Cable: DESTINY

BUDGET
6. Safari International
   Phone: 480550-2
   Cable: SAFARI
7. Meghdoot
   Phone: 405802
8. Natraj
   Phone: 57648
   Cable: NATRAJ
9. Anarkali
   Phone: 404031
   Cable: ANAR
10. Panthaniwas
    Phone: 54515, 55314
    Telex: 0675-335

WHAT TO SEE
1. LINGARAJ TEMPLE (11th century), dominates the landscape rising to a height of 45 metres. It is the finest representation of Kalinga art.
2. MUKTESHWAR TEMPLE (10th century), with its profusion of wall carvings.
3. PARASURAMESHWAR TEMPLE (7th century), famous for its latticed windows.
4. RAJA RANI TEMPLE (11th century), with its exquisite carvings of the feminine form.
5. BRAHMESHWAR TEMPLE (11th century), typical of the Orissan temple.
6. MUSEUM. Has interesting exhibits, especially of tribal art.

EXCURSIONS
1. UDAIPUR-KHANDAGIRI CAVES (8 km). Dating back to the 2nd century. B.C. these were the abode of Jain monks.
2. DAULI (10 km). On top of a hill is a Peace Pagoda (Shanti Stupa) near Ashoka's ancient rock edict.
3. NANDANKANAN (23 km). A park in which animals are kept in a zoo like a natural jungle. Also has a Lion Safari Park.
4. PIPLI (21 km). Village where applique handicrafts are made.
5. PURI (62 km). A Hindu religious centre famous for the massive chariot-cars used in the annual Rath Yatra procession. Also a popular beach resort.
6. KONARK (65 km). Famous for its Sun Temple built symbolically like the Chariot of the Sun.
7. CHILKA LAKE (106 km). Ideal for bird-watching. It is the biggest salt water island lake in the country.
8. GOPALPUR-ON-SEA (196 km), a beautiful beach resort.

9. SIMILIPAL NATIONAL PARK (368 km), one of the sites of Project Tiger, has a large variety of animals, birds and a crocodile sanctuary. (Jeeps and spotlights available.)

SHOPPING
Silver filigree, stone carvings and statuettes, applique work, lacquer-ware, Pattachitra folk paintings, jari (brocade) work, tie-and-dye cottons and silks, tussar silks, shell-work and wooden inlay are some of the good buys. Brasswork of Ganjam, coir mats, carpets and handloom fabrics are also available.

SPECIAL FESTIVALS OF LOCAL INTEREST
1. ASHOKASTAMI (March-April). Car festival of Lord Shiva at the Lingaraj Temple, celebrated like a mini Rath Yatra.
2. RAJA SANKRANTI (June). A 3-day festival welcoming the first showers, celebrated mainly by women.
3. DURGA PUJA (September-October), when images of the Mother Goddess are worshipped and immersed in rivers.
4. BALI YATRA (October-November) at Cuttack (29 km), in memory of ancient

traders who set sail for Bali several centuries ago. (Indonesia)
5. RATH YATRA at Puri (June-July). Three gigantic chariots carrying the images of Jagannath, Balabhadra and Subhadra are taken in procession through the streets of Puri followed by a million people. The chariots are drawn by devotees from all over India, accompanied by devotional music. A similar procession brings back the deities after a week.
6. CHANDAN YATRA at Puri (April-May) when the deities of the Jagannath temple are taken in decorated barges for a boat ride after being bathed in sandalwood paste, accompanied by music and dancing. It is a 21-day festival.

PURI

GENERAL INFORMATION
Population: 1,50,000 (1991 Census)
Altitude: Sea level.

HOW TO GET THERE
Nearest airport is Bhubaneswar (62 km).
Puri is a railway terminus with rail connections to Bhubaneswar, etc. It is connected with Bhubaneswar (62 km) and Konark (35 km) both by very good roads. It is 532 km. from Calcutta and 1082 km. from Varanasi. Bus services operate to Bhubaneswar and other places in Orissa.

WHERE TO STAY (STD CODE: 06752)
STANDARD
1. Nilachal Ashok
   Phone: 23639, 23551
   Cable: NILASHOK
2. Toshali Sands
   Phone: 22888/22999
   Cable: YELLOW SAND
   Fax: 0674-57365
3. Hotel Mayfair
   Phone: 24041/24313
   Fax: 06752-24242
4. S.E. Railway Hotel
   Phone: 22063
BUDGET
5. Vijay International
   Phone: 23705/22702
   Cable: MANISA
6. Holidiny Resort
   Phone: 22440/22430
   Cable: SANDY
   Fax: 06752-23968
7. Samudra
   Phone: 22705
8. Panthnivas
   Phone: 22562

WHAT TO SEE
1. JAGANNATH TEMPLE. Standing 65 metres high, this 12th century temple is an important place of pilgrimage for the Hindus. The adjoining ANANDA BAZAR or food market, where tens of thousands

buy cooked food, is astounding.
2. PURI BEACH. The excellent surf and shallow waters are great attraction as are the brilliant sunrises and sunsets on the beach.

KONARK

GENERAL INFORMATION
Population: 4760
Altitude: Sea level

HOW TO GET THERE
Nearest airport is Bhubaneswar (65 km).
The nearest rail-head is Puri (35 km).
It is connected to Puri and Bhubaneswar by good roads.

LOCAL TRANSPORT: Only cycle-rickshaws are available.

WHERE TO STAY
BUDGET
1. Panthnivas
   Phone: 8823
2. Travellers Lodge
   Phone: 8831

(Both operated by Orissa Tourism)

WHAT TO SEE
1. SUN TEMPLE. The massive ruins of the original monument and its intricate carvings are of unbelievable beauty. The temple is illuminated in the evenings.
2. A long stretch of quiet BEACH fringed with casurina and palm trees is very close to the temple.
3. The ARCHAEOLOGICAL SITE MUSEUM has a rare collection of sculptures from the ruins of the main temple.

Chapter 24

WEST BENGAL
The Land of 24 Parganas

Bounded on the north by Sikkim and Bhutan, on the east by Assam and Bangladesh, on the south by the Bay of Bengal, and on the west by Orissa, Bihar, and Nepal, West Bengal geographically consists of two parts : the northern districts of Darjeeling, Jalpaiguri and Cooch-Behar and the rest of the State. Its area is 88752 Sq. km. and population over 68 million.

Bengal is the anglicised form of Banga, the ancient name of one part of the State. The other part was known as Gauda.

After a long phase of uncertainty and rule by different dynasties within and outside Bengal, the region experienced a period of peace and prosperity under the Pala Kings, from the 8th to 12th centuries. In the early 13th century a Turkish general, Muhammad Bhakhtiyar, invaded Bengal. The Buddhists of Bengal, persecuted by him, fled to Nepal with their valuable books and images. Intrigues and murders marked the Muslim rule over Bengal for a long time, with a brief spell of Hindu rule in the country.

In the 15th century Sri Chaitanya, the great Vaishnav prophet, appeared on the scene. In the 16th century, Bengal came under direct Mughal rule. In 1757, the young Nawab of Bengal, Siraj-ud-daula, who was disgusted with the behaviour of the British East India Company, clashed with it on the field of Plassey. Under Robert Clive's leadership, the army of the Company won, due to Siraj-ud-daula's Commander-in-Chief, Mir Jaffar's betrayal. Siraj was soon assassinated by the treacherous Mir Jaffar's henchmen. With the Company's support, Mir Jaffar occupied the throne of Bengal and was soon deposed. From his weak successors, the Company snatched more powers and privileges. Later Warren Hastings forced the Nawab to retire and he himself became the administrator of Bengal, and then the Governor-General of British India, in 1773.

The sons of Bengal played a prominent role in the resurrection of India. English education in India started from Bengal, and at the suggestion of the great Indian reformer, Raja Rammohan Roy, the first English college was set up in Calcutta in 1817.

CALCUTTA—The City of Palaces

A vast network of airways, railways and highways originate from Calcutta, the gateway of eastern India. Places of historical, ethnic and cultural interest and also wildlife sanctuaries can be easily and conveniently planned and reached from Calcutta. The West Bengal Tourist Bureau organises conducted tours in the State. Bookings at tourist lodges and forest bungalows can be made from these offices three months in advance. Other states too have tourist offices in the city and conduct package tours originating in Calcutta.

By Indian standards Calcutta certainly is a new city, only 300 years old. It is a European city, planted on the soil of Asia, though the inhabitants are brown and clad in white *dhoti* and *kurta*. They are also too many of them crowded in an area of 1380 square metres which was not meant even for half of them.

The first recorded mention of Calcutta was found in the *Ain-i-Akbari* in 1596. The Bysacks, traditional weavers of Bengal, and the Seths, merchant bankers, had established SUTANATI which, as the name implies, was the 'Cottonopolis' of Bengal. Calcutta grew around the villages of KALIKATA, SUTANATI, GOVINDAPUR, and CHITPORE on the east bank of the Hooghly river and SALKIA and BETOR on its west bank. On the south fringe was the SUNDERBANS, the world's largest estuarine forests. The old Fort was safe from the Dutch, the French and the Danes on the opposite bank of the river. Eastwards extended the protective SALT LAKES, the draining board of Calcutta.

Job Charnock was Calcutta's first Governor. Looking back, it may be said that Calcutta's existence hangs on a doctor's prescription. In 1640, Gabriel Boughton, an English surgeon, effected a royal cure for which the fee asked for and granted was the Mughal Emperor Shahjahan's concession of free trade in Bengal. Permission was granted to the East India Company to purchase the three villages of Sutanati, Kalikata and Govindapur in the immediate neighbourhood of the Fort. The negotiation price, we are told, was Rs.16, 000 and the purchase price in 1690 was Rs.1, 300. This single transaction was of great importance. The Company, till now just an adventurous group, became landowners with a landlord's prerogatives. The Union Jack was hoisted for the first time in 1702 on FORT WILLIAM.

The Maharatta invasion of Bengal broke the monopoly of life in Calcutta and led to the digging of the five km Maharatta Ditch, the present CIRCULAR ROAD, from whence the sobriquet 'Ditcher' came to be coined and applied to the Anglo-Indian. Of greater consequence was the defeat of the British by the then Nawab of Bengal, Siraj-ud-daula, in 1756. The town was rescued a few months later by Robert Clive and Admiral Watson from Madras, and the Battle of Plassey in 1757 was a victory of British diplomacy and intrigue. In 1773, the capital was transferred from Madras to Calcutta and it grew into the second city of the Empire.

In 1803, Lord Wellesley constituted an Improvement Committee for the city that a decade later became the Lottery Commission which by running lotteries raised funds for buildings such as the TOWN HALL (1813), which still stands today, and a number of roads. New buildings and institutions burgeoned. The European settlement moved out from the fortified quarter in TANK SQUARE, now BENOY BADAL DINESH BAGH (BBD Bagh), and CHOWRINGHEE took shape.

It was James Atkinson who in 1824 first gave Calcutta the epithet "City of Palaces" Calcutta was likened by his contemporaries to

St. Petersburg and London. The climate had its effect and the buildings have since crumbled and nothing looks new.

From the mid-19th century, the age of laissez faire brought individual free traders to Calcutta. At the turn of the century, Municipal markets were a regular feature. Tramways and street lighting appeared. The town of Howrah was linked to Calcutta by a pontoon bridge in 1874.

When the British strengthened Fort Williams in 1780, they cleared the vast jungles for target practice from the Fort and to prevent any sneak invasion. An interesting fact is that not a single angry shot was fired from this Fort. It was around and near the Maidan that the city started coming up. It was also here that they decided to build a memorial to the British Empire, called VICTORIA MEMORIAL. Gradually, the whole of India came under the British rule and Calcutta continued to be the capital of India, even when the Company forfeited the empire to the British throne.

Politically conscious Bengal was always a tough nut to chew for the British empire. It was one of the important reasons for the transfer of the capital from Calcutta to Delhi. In order to weaken Bengali solidarity, Lord Curzon partitioned the State into two parts, East and West Bengal, in 1905. But the resultant agitation forced him to withdraw the order 5 years later. However, the British did divide Bengal at the time of their departure, though with the consent of the feuding Congress and Muslim League parties. Partition in 1947 left only 88,000 square kms with Calcutta as its capital, and East Pakistan, now Bangladesh, got an area of 1,44,000 square kms and Dhaka became the capital of Bangladesh.

From a 10,000 strong trading centre 200 years ago, Calcutta Metropolitan District is today eight times the size of Washington and is the largest urban centre in India and the second largest city in the British Commonwealth after London. It houses more people than the entire population of Sweden.

Its hinterland encompasses the eastern and north-eastern zones of India. The rich mineral deposits of iron ore, manganese and limestone find their way to other parts of the world through Calcutta Port, Chittaranjan in West Bengal. Calcutta's role in the national economy is crucial as the gateway to Eastern India.

Today Calcutta is a weird combination of good and bad - palaces and slums, theatre, dance, art and all-around pollution. Despite all these contrasts, Calcutta certainly has a vibrant soul.

The normal sightseeing tours of the city often start from the West Bengal Tourist Office in the historic DALHOUSIE SQUARE - the new name is difficult to pronounce - BENOY BADAL DINESH BAGH (BBD Bagh). A city bus tour organised by the West Bengal Tourist Bureau offers good value for money. A trained guide escorts the tours. However, you are free to see the city independently in a hired tourist car with a guide who speaks your language. It is also a bargain considering the prices in Europe and America. We start with SAINT JOHN'S CHURCH where Job Charnock, founder of Calcutta, is buried. The mausoleum over his grave was perhaps the first piece of masonry erected by the British in Calcutta which is still standing.

A brass line inlaid on the steps of the General Post Office (GPO) marks the position of the south-eastern bastion of the OLD FORT WILLIAM (1707) where the imposing modern Post Office, Customs House and Eastern Railway building now stand. Calcutta's oldest building — the sole relic of the old Fort—stands beside the GPO and it houses the Collectorate.

WRITERS BUILDING, once plain squat barracks for the East India Company's writers (clerks), has been extended, docorated and refronted with a Corinthian facade and fills the northorn end of BBD BAGH. The state government machinery operates from here and has spilled over into a 14-storeyed building, the NEW SECRETARIAT, on the extension of the Strand, not far from No. 7 Hastings Street, the one time residence of Warren Hastings.

Old Calcutta had its theatres and as the city expanded, the theatre followed, to CHOWRINGHEE and PARK STREET. A part of ST. XAVIER'S COLLEGE is the mid-19th century SANS SOUCI THEATRE where during World War II the troops were entertained.

ST. JOHN's, the first Anglican Cathedral, was consecrated in 1787. Built of chuna stone in Doric order, it resembles St. Martin-in-the-Fields.

High Court

Puncturing the city scape on Old Court House Street is the spire of ST. ANDREW'S CHURCH opened in 1818, the Scots Kirk, Grecian in style.

Through RED CROSS PLACE we step at GOVERNMENT HOUSE (1803), now RAJ BHAVAN, the residence of the Governor of West Bengal. An adaptation of Kedleston Hall by Wyatt, this splendid Georgian building in Palladian style was the centrepiece and model for the 'City of Palaces'. The imperial design of its monumental gateways catches the eye of the passerby.

Further west and almost on the river which once flowed along Strand Road, the HIGH COURT catches the eye. Impressive replica of the original Stadd-Haus at Ypres in Belgium, it was designed by Walter Granille.

Opposite the High Court is the LEGISLATIVE ASSEMBLY where the local representatives meet. It is open to the public at the annual Chrysanthemum Shows which herald in the "season".

The Imperial Library occupied METCALFE HALL (1844) at the junction of Strand Road and Hare Street erected to commemorate Lord Metcalfe and his great achievement the emancipation of the press. Designed after the portice of the Temple of Winds at Athens, the building is raised on a solid ornamental basement and its 30 columns rising up to 36 feet give the appearance of a Greek temple. The library has since moved to BELVEDERE in ALIPORE.

The STATUE OF NETAJI SUBHAS CHANDRA BOSE with arm outstretched commands RED ROAD is renamed INDIRA SARANI. Lord Curzon saw Calcutta as an imperial city and erected statues in memory of British Indian heroes on both sides of the road, now replaced by heroes of the freedom struggle. The former have been retired to the Victoria Memorial and to BARRACKPORE, once a military cantonment and summer residence of the Governor-General. At the intersection of the Victoria Memorial gardens and Red Road extension, Jatin Mukherjee, a freedom fighter, is mounted on a horse. During World War II, Red Road was used as a runway for British army fighter planes. For the last four deçades, Republic and Independence Day ceremonial parades are held here.

The CHOWRINGHEE GATE of the new Fort William opens to Red Road. Started by Clive in 1757 and completed 16 years later, Fort William altered the entire plan for Calcutta. A large open space for an unrestricted field of fire gave birth to the Maidan. Around it grew a magnificent collection of public buildings and "garden houses".

One of the earliest garden settlements was in Alipore. Belvedere, of uncertain antiquity, now the National Library, was the residence of the Lieutenant Governors of Bengal for some time. After the victory at Plassey (1757), the city grew without restriction southwards along the pilgrim's road Chowringhee - presently Jawaharlal Nehru Road - to the KALI TEMPLE at KALIGHAT. Here the presiding deity, Ma Kali, draws the largest number of devotees, especially on festive occasions such as the Bengali New Year (April) and Diwali (October-November) better known as Durga Puja.

Returning to Chowringhee, the INDIAN MUSEUM or "Jadu Ghar", designed by the architect of the High Court, Walter Granville, presents a 300 foot frontage rising two storeys in Italian architectural style dating to 1814. The central portice has elegant Corinthian columns. Adjoining the museum is the GOVERNMENT ART SCHOOL. Outside, on its Edwardian railings, young artists often display their works of art.

The GEOLOGICAL SURVEY OF INDIA, once the United Services Club, is another colonial construction. It conjures up an old Calcutta social scene of crinolined ladies and gallant braves in lace and ruffles tripping lightly through the halls of the club till the wee hours of the morning.

Multistoreyed office buildings rise from the pavement. Part of the BENGAL CLUB (1827), the oldest club in India, is the office of the Metro Rail.

Early morning or late afternoon is an ideal time to visit the MAIDAN. Once a dense forest infested with tigers, jackals, snakes and dacoits, it is today the city's playground. Calcutta, like many other cities, also has its column. Rising over 150 feet at the northern end of the Maidan, it is an Egyptian plinth crowned by a Turkish cupola. It was built to commemorate the hero of the Indo-Nepalese war, Maj-General Sir David Ochterlony, and has been renamed SAHEED MINAR to remember those who died for the freedom of the country.

Victoria Memorial

The VICTORIA MEMORIAL dominates the Maidan. Its marble bricks came from the quarries of Makrana in Jaipur, Rajasthan, the suppliers for the Taj Mahal. The extensive gardens with canna beds and tanks are a favourite place for morning jogs or leisurely walks by the senior citizens. Its hybrid architecture, surmounted by a crowning dome, has a huge bronze revolving ANGEL OF VICTORY which functions as a weather cock. Opened by the Prince of Wales in 1921, the Victoria Memorial houses within its spacious galleries some of the memorabilia of the Raj and personal effects of Queen Victoria.

The eye travels from the dome to the tower of ST. PAUL'S CATHEDRAL besides the Victoria Memorial — the steeple fell in the earthquake of

1897. Outside the gates of St. Paul's is the post-independence BIRLA PLANETARIUM (1962), another of India's firsts in Calcutta.

A drive around its 4 km. perimeter at the RACE COURSE evokes the racing scenes when His Highness, the late Haile Selassie, Emperor of Ethiopia, and Queen Elizabeth II among other distinguished visitors watched the classic events with the enthusiastic Indian crowds.

And now to PARK STREET, best described as downtown Calcutta. This street, vibrating with life, was once called Burial Ground Road because it was the way to God's Little Acre, on the outskirts of the town. The focal point of executive life in the city, Park Street's shops and restaurants are well stocked and well appointed. Besides Kwality Restaurant, retiring behind iron gates and tall palms, is the BENGAL MASONIC LODGE, the headquarters of Free Masonry in the East, dating back to 1728. Close in Ezra Street is the Parsi Agiaree or FIRE TEMPLE and the HEBREW SYNAGOGUES.

The ARMENIAN CHURCH off Brabourne Road has the oldest gravestone (1630) which has presented an enigma: Who came to Calcutta first, the English or the Armenians?

The Portuguese residences in MANGO LANE and TIRETTA BAZAR, ornate villas with cast iron railings enclosing narrow projections, can still be seen amidst the changing topography of this area — once the Grey Town. From ESPLANADE we will explore the Grey Town to the east along the broad D'Oyley Avenue, Dharamtalla, now LENIN SARANI, featuring the Portuguese CHURCH OF THE SACRED HEART OF JESUS (1834).

The layout of the town divided the European settlements and the native quarters. Over the jumble of house-tops, TV antennae and overhead tram wires, the great NAKHODA MOSQUE built in 1926 by Abdur Rahim, a Cutchee merchant, is visible. JORASANKE, the home of the merchant Prince Dwarkanath Tagore and his illustrious grandson Rabindranath, is the RABINDRA BHARATI UNIVERSITY and the museum.

The MARBLE PALACE (1855) in a narrow lane off Chittaranjan Avenue welcomes visitors to wander freely between the hours of 11 and 4 for nothing more than a signature in the visitor's book. Recently, it has been found necessary for visitors to get passes from the Tourist Bureau before proceeding to the palace.

Skirting LA MARTINIERE, Claud Martin's school, the only educational institution in the world with battle honours, we go further south to the lake area of RABINDRA SAROBAR. A JAPANESE BUDDHIST TEMPLE nestles in its environs. The dignified edifice of the RAMAKRISHNA MISSION INSTITUTE OF CULTURE and the BIRLA ACADEMY OF ART AND CULTURE are close by. Still further south, JADAVPUR UNIVERSITY spreads its sprawling campus.

A boat ride will not disappoint you for Calcutta looks her best when viewed from the river. Half a day may be set aside for a trip to the temples of BELUR and DAKSHINESWAR on opposite banks. Rani Rashmoni received divine directions in a dream to build the NAVRATNA KALI temple at Dakshineswar (1855). The saintly Sri Ramakrishna lived and worshipped here. Twelve monolith Shiv temples line the waterfront. As we cross the river to BELUR MATH on the western bank, there is a clear view of the river. Belur Math is the headquarters of the international missions of the monastic order of Sri Ramakrishna. The architecture represents a church, a mosque and a temple when viewed from different angles, truly symbolic of the founder's universality of belief.

Built in 1899, the mission was founded by Swami Vivekananda, the internationally known philosopher and disciple of Sri Ramakrishna.

In the city you are sure to notice ladies clad in blue and white saris. They are Mother Teresa's army, the Missionaries of Charity. Mother Teresa, the living saint of Calcutta, her SHISHU BHAVANS and HOMES FOR THE DYING are worth a visit.

Dakshineswar temple

A silver cantilever bridge is the only direct road link with Calcutta and the flow of traffic, like the river, is never ending. If you are caught on the bridge in one of its usual traffic snarls, look for the flower market below at the Calcutta end of the bridge — thousands of orange, marigolds and crimson hibiscus garlands, and the river craft, a wide assortment of unsophisticated launches, barges and dinghies will amaze you.

The outline of Greater Calcutta is like a giant's footprint with the toe pointing northwards to the only direction of expansion. The grand plans for Calcutta A.D. 2000 are off the drawing board and a 'Garland' canal for inland water transport and a circular railway has almost been completed. The tramways may still be there in the 21st century as they cause the least pollution. Two new flyovers are in South Calcutta and another near Esplanade are on the cards — one has since opened.

Business and Industry

Calcutta is still a major centre for business, industry, trade and exports. It accounts for over 80 per cent of the total production of jute goods in the country. The majority of 70-odd jute Mills of India lie on the two banks of the Hoogly, 48 km. north and south of Calcutta.

India is the world's largest producer, consumer and exporter of tea and the bulk of the country's exports of tea are shipped from Calcutta. The major quantum of high quality Darjeeling tea is sold through Calcutta.

The discovery of coal at RANIGANJ in the second decade of the 19th century was one of the most significant contributory factors behind the process of industrialisation of eastern India. Calcutta naturally developed into a focal point of the engineering industry in the country.

During the 1950s, the industrial importance of Calcutta grew with the rapid development of the DURGAPUR-ASANSOL belt. In quick succession came the integrated steel plant at DURGAPUR, the Alloy Steels Plant, the Chittaranjan Locomotive Works, the Mining and Allied Machinery Corporation, the first telecommunication cables manufacturing plant in India at RUPNARAINPUR and other large units to exploit the high mineral resources of this region. Above all, the mammoth Damodar Valley Corporation was modelled along the lines of the Tennessee Valley Authority in USA. As high as 70 per cent of the railway wagons produced in the country come from units located in and around Calcutta. Among the largest manufacturer of passenger cars in India Ambassador is only a short distance away from the city. One of the biggest suppliers of textile machinery is located near Calcutta. Leather tanneries located in the city account for over 25 per cent of the country's leather exports.

Eating out in Calcutta can be varied to suit the mood, the budget and the appetite for dinner. With the general throng that came to Calcutta came the chef, the hotelier and the tavern keeper. They influenced the adventurous Bengali to create his own version of the food for the Sahib. Hence the appearance of such mouthwatering creations as Kabiraji Cutlet, Bhekdi Machher Fry and vegetable chop, to be had at the small eating-houses around the University and Bengali theatre houses in north Calcutta. Today the fashionable Park Street restaurants and the five-star hotels provide the kind of eating that has become common to all India cities. There are elaborate menus offering a choice of Indian, Chinese and Continental dishes. On Park Street, FLURY'S is the only place where one can breakfast. It opens early, by 6.30 a.m.

SKYROOM has acquired the reputation of serving the best western food in Calcutta. Bengal's contribution to the gourmet world is 'smoked Hilsa'. OASIS, further down the street, is good for quick lunches at a reasonable rate. OLYMPIA BAR AND RESTAURANT is where the advertising world meets. The standard Indian restaurant, if there is one, is KWALITY.

TRINCA'S is one of two places which has a live band over Christmas week. MING ROOM, the Chinese restaurant, serves Schezwan food while THE OTHER ROOM is a moderately priced family restaurant.

At BLUE FOX, pre-prandial drinks are accompanied by teeny-weeny *samosas*, a happy departure from the usual sameness of chips and peanuts.

PETER CAT, hung with Tiffany lights, specialises in Fish Baroda Kabab and Chelo Kabab, a meal in a dish of chicken, egg and rice. MOULIN ROUGE advertises the best Nawabi food in town.

HOTEL HINDUSTAN INTERNATIONAL'S new venture, KALASH, offers ethnic food in a room full of copper tables lit with lamps, all very gracefully arranged. Eating in style is done at OBEROI GRAND'S LA ROTISSERIE where the service is divine and prices not talked about.

Calcutta has two garden cafes where one can dine alfresco on a cool summer evening or have beer with friends on a Sunday morning in December. Both are gardens of gracious houses turned into hotels on Shakespeare Sarani. KABAB-E-QUE on the lawn of the ASTOR HOTEL serves a variety of grilled foods, and the chicken legs are a real treat. White painted furniture dots the green grass at MAIKHANA, NEW KENILWORTH INTERNATIONAL'S outdoor restaurant and bar. The rooftop of DHABA near the Ballygunge PHARI is an ideal setting for eating Sarson-ka-saag and Makai-di-roti on a cold winter evening.

The best value for Indian food is at AMBER on Waterloo Street. No visit to Calcutta is complete without tasting the now ubiquitous Kattir Roll, pioneered by the Nizams on Corporation Street.

Shopping is not easy in Calcutta but it can be very rewarding. Bengali silver and goldsmithy is perhaps the best in the whole of India.

Calcutta is also known for its silk and cotton saris and fabrics. There is a huge variety of gaily striped cottons, embroidered bedspreads and woollen blankets. The Baluchari brocade saris are now collector's items. Once made in Murshidabad, it takes six months to one year to make one, The designs on the saris are beautiful and typically Bengali. Cheaper versions are now available.

It is also a centre for the manufacture of musical instruments. All kinds of musical instruments can be bought here.

Among Bengali crafts, traditional terracota figures are made in villages throughout the State. For handicrafts, the BENGAL HOME INDUSTRIES ASSOCIATION, 57 Chowringhee, and WEST BENGAL GOVERNMENT EMPORIUM at Lindsay Street are the best places. For fabrics, HANDLOOM HOUSE on Lindsay Street and KHADI GRAMODHYOG BHAWAN , Chittaranjan Avenue, are recommended.

CHANDARNAGORE

Thirty-nine km. north of Calcutta is yet another former French enclave, Chandarnagore. It was returned to India in 1951 alongwith Pondicherry in the south. The French settlers first came here in 1673 and set up a trading post. There are still several buildings dating back to the French era.

DARJEELING – The Place of Thunderbolts

Darjeeling (2,134 m above sea level) in North Bengal is about 650 km. from Calcutta. An overnight journey by rail or road brings you to SILIGURI/NEW JALPAIGURI at the foothills of the Himalayas. A daily Indian Airlines service from Calcutta gets you to BAGDOGRA in less than an hour.

Comfortable walking shoes, woollens and an umbrella are your best bet for a wonderful holiday. Hotels such as Oberoi Mount View, Sinclairs and Windamere are of international standards. Reasonable accommodation is also available at Tourist Lodges. Bookings can be made in Calcutta. The best seasons are October to December and April to June. The scenic beauty of Mount Everest and Kanchenjunga, the two highest peaks of the Himalayas, is something never to be forgotten.

Darjeeling lies on a spur on the GHOOM SANCHAL RIDGE with spectacular views across the Himalayan peaks. The journey up is part of the trip. First, you may fly to BAGDOGRA. Then either take the narrow gauge train from NEW JALPAIGURI or SILIGURI to Darjeeling along the 2-foot gauge line completed in 1881. It takes 7 hours of chugging and puffing on the part of the tiny train to cover a distance of less than 100 km. But your reward is the spectacular scenery on the way. Your eyes never get tired and the colourful hill people you see on the way up are an added attraction.

Trekking in the Himalayas

Darjeeling's past history is highly interesting. Until the beginning of the 18th century, the whole area between the present borders of Sikkim and the plains of Bengal belonged to the Raja of Sikkim. Taking advantage of a clash between the Sikkimese and the Nepalese, the British despatched in 1828 two officers on a fact-finding mission. The officers were quick to appreciate the value of the area then called Darjeeling — the Place of Thunderbolts — for a sanatorium and as a key to entry into Nepal and Tibet. The officers' observations were conveyed to Calcutta and the British authorities forced the Raja to cede this area to them for a small stipend of Rs. 3,000. Later developments enabled the British to annex the entire area to then empire.

Darjeeling, which was then completely under forests, shaped into a resort by 1840. A road was built and numerous houses and a sanatorium constructed. Hotels too followed in course of time. A toy train was constructed by 1881 at a cost of Rs.1,700,000 only! Darjeeling became the summer capital of the State of Bengal.

This 2,555 metre high TIGER HILL is approachable through GHEEM ROCK, a fine picnic spot. It is famous for the spectacular view it offers of sunrise over KANCHENJUNGA. The magnificent changes in colour, the snows and the sky have no parallel in the world. April and October are the right seasons to enjoy this view. Vehicles are always available to pick you up from your hotel at dawn.

Fifty-eight km. away and at a height of 3,656 metres, SANDAKPHU is an excellent trek from Darjeeling. A Youth Hostel and a Dak Bungalow at FALUT (21 km. further) are there if you wish to stay longer.

The Tibetan Buddhist monastery, the GHOOM MONASTERY with a 15-foot high statue of Maitreya Buddha, is 8 km. from the town. It is the most famous monastery of the town. The railway climbs to a height of 8,000 feet at Ghoom, making the station the highest railway halt in the world. There is another monastery nearby in Ghoom itself.

Close to Tiger Hill, SANCHAL LAKE and FOREST attractive picnic spot, 10 km. from Darjeeling. It is the source of water for the city. Permission has to be obtained from the Municipal Officer, Darjeeling, to visit the place.

Two km. from the Mall is the HIMALAYAN MOUNTAINEERING INSTITUTE (HMI) imparting the art of climbing hills to aspiring mountaineers. The institute has also a museum.

Close to the institute is the PADMAJA NAIDU ZOO, showing the Himalayan black bear, panda, deer, panther, leopard and the Siberian tiger, among other animals.

Three km. from the town, the RANGEET VALLEY ROPEWAY spanning 8 km. to SINGLE BAZAR passes over tea gardens and scenic fields.

Eight km. from the Mall, the LEBONG RACE COURSE is the highest one in the world. March to June is the racing season.

The Observatory Hill is a vantage point for a grand view of the Kanchenjunga ranges. On top of the Observatory is the CAVE TEMPLE OF MAHAKAL.

The TIBETAN REFUGEE SELF-HELP CENTRE is a workshop producing woollen carpets and a variety of items in wood and leather in traditional Tibetan craftmanship.

MIRK is a charming excursion that has been opened to the tourists.

KALIMPONG

This hill resort, at an altitude of 1, 250 metres, pleasantly cool throughout the year, is 51 km. from Darjeeling and 77 km. from Gangtok, the capital of Sikkim. The journey to Kalimpong is memorable. The descending road through tea estates has a beautiful spot that demands a halt - the *View Point* — showing the confluence of the Rangeet and Teesta rivers.

DR. GRAHAM'S HOME is a shelter for destitute children of European descent, and a centre for training them in a variety of crafts. It has also a sales wing.

KURSEONG

This charming hill station is 32 km. from Darjeeling on the highway to SILIGURI. Situated at a height of 1,482.5 metres above sea level, this hill resort in the district of Darjeeling offers a magnificent southward view of the plains spreading to the distant horizon more than 150 km. away. DAW HILL and EAGLE'S CRAG are two vantage points. There is a sericulture station here. The place is connected by railway with Calcutta and other cities via New Jalpaiguri.

COOCH BEHAR

Once a princely state capital, Cooch Behar is a charming town of north Bengal. Its palace, temples and parks are of tourist interest.

JALDAPARA WILDLIFE SANCTUARY

This sanctuary, spread over 100 sq km., is situated at a distance of 121 km. from Siliguri. The nearest railway station is HASIMARA, which can be reached from New Jalpaiguri on your way to Darjeeling from Calcutta.

The entrance to the forest at MADARIHAT is 6 km. from Hasimara. Nine tributaries of the Torsa river flow through the area which is shaded by tall grasses and clumps of green woods. The travellers can avail of elephants to take them round the forest. The sanctuary is remarkable for its treasure of one-horned rhinos. But there are tigers (Royal Bengal included), wild elephants, bear, sambar, leopard, hog-deer, bison, python, goyal and other animals. There is tourist bunglow inside the forest.

VISHNUPUR

Famous for its 17th and 18th century terracotta temples, Vishnupur is 201 km. by rail. Bus services and conducted tours are also available. The pomp and splendour of the Malla Rajahs is still visible in the ruins around and inside the FORT. Vishnupur is also well known for its silk and tussar industries, terracotta toys, brass and bell metal products and conch shells.

Air-conditioned accommodation at the Tourist Lodge is available.

DURGAPUR

Called the "Ruhr of Eastern India", Durgapur is 78 km. from Vishnupur. Buses are available for a visit.

SANTINIKETAN

This idyllic campus town founded by Rabindranath Tagore at the turn of the century is a great centre for higher studies in various arts. It is the seat of VISHWABHARATI UNIVERSITY. It is at a distance of 164 km. from Calcutta, both by rail and by bus. The whole place is steeped in the memory of the great poet and savant, Tagore.

The UTTARAYAN COMPLEX formed the residence of Tagore in his life time. In a house named VICHITRA his manuscripts, paintings, different editions of his works, his Nobel Prize Gold Medal, and other objects associated with him are kept.

The VISHVABHARATI UNIVERSITY, which is dedicated to cultivating lofty human ideals and cultural values in the students, has various faculties, including the KALA BHAVAN, the school of the arts, SANGEET BHAVAN, the institute for music; CHINA BHAVAN, dedicated to Sino-Indian studies; and ANDREWS MEMORIAL HALL, for western studies. The university is enriched by the works of the artist Nandalal Bose and sculptures by Ramkinkar.

The foundation day of the institution is celebrated on the 7th day of Paush with fairs, folk songs and folk dances. There is another festival to mark the advent of spring.

SRINIKETAN

Three km. away from Santiniketan is a sister institute, Sriniketan, dedicated to rural development programmes. It has a wide range of activities.

NABADWIP

Nabadwip is the birthplace of Sri Chaitanya Mahaprabhu, hence a great pilgrim centre of the Vaishnavas. There is an environment of devotion, marked by constant prayers.

MAYAPUR in Nabadwip has a new temple, the CHANDRODAYA MANDIR, built by the International Society for Krishna Consciousness, run mostly by western devotees of Krishna.

Nabadwip is in district Nadia. The district headquarters is KRISHNAGAR, 80 km. from Calcutta by train. It is famous for its clay modelling.

DIGHA

A charming resort where the sea looks tame and mild, Digha is 243 km. from Calcutta. It is a quiet place bordering Orissa, shaded by casuarina trees. From Calcutta tourist buses ply to Digha regularly.

MALDA

Regular bus and train services are available to Malda, 338 km. from Calcutta. Here the visitors will get glimpses of many medieval relics. Conducted tours are organised to nearby GAUR, the capital of ancient Bengal in the 7th century, and to PANDUA. The MALDA MUSEUM has a collection of stone images and coins retrieved from the ruins of Gaur and Pandua. Overnight airconditioned accommodation at the Tourist Lodge is available.

MURSHIDABAD

Bastion of Siraj-ud-daula, the last of Bengal's Muslim rulers, Murshidabad is full of relics of its regal past. It is 197 km. from Calcutta. Among the monuments are HAZARDUARI (1837), the palace with a thousand doors, the NIZAMAT KILLA, KATHGOLA, the mansion of Jagat Seth, and KATRA MOSQUE.

CALCUTTA

GENERAL INFORMATION
Population: 10,860,000 (1991 census)
Altitude: 6 metres (20 ft)
Climate

	Temperature	
	Max.	Min.
Winter	34^0 c	14^0 c
Summer	36^0 c	25^0 c
Rainfall	897 mm	65 mm

Season: Throughout the year
Clothing:
Summer: cottons.
Winter: light woollens.

HOW TO GET THERE
By Air: Calcutta is an international airport connected with all parts of the world. Indian Airlines connects Calcutta with all important airports in India. Major

private airlines also operate to Calcutta. About a dozen international airlines fly into Calcutta.
By Rail: Calcutta is connected by rail with all the major cities and towns of India.
By Road: Calcutta is connected by road to
Santiniketan (211 km.),
Sunderbans (131 km.),
Digha (185 km.),
Darjeeling (685 km.)
There are regular bus services to Puri, Bhubaneshwar, Konark in Orissa, Siliguri (for Darjeeling), Malda, etc.

LOCAL TRANSPORT
Tourist taxis, metered taxis, metered auto-rickshaws, tongas, cycle-rickshaws, city buses and the metro railway are available. Ferry services are also available.

CONDUCTED TOURS
Regular and guided tours of the city organised by ITDC and the West Bengal Tourism Corporation are available.
West Bengal Tourism Organises regular package tours to other states of India.
Booking : ITDC
   Phone: 2420901
   West Bengal Tourism
   Phone: 2488271
Information: Government of India Tourist office
Tel: 2421402

WHERE TO STAY (STD CODE: 033)
DELUXE
1. Taj Bengal
   Phone: 2483939
   Fax: 2481776

2. The Oberoi Grand
   Phone: 2492323
   Cable: OBHOTEL
   Fax: 291270

STANDARD
3. Park Hotel
   Phone: 297336-40
   Cable: PARKHOTEL
   Fax: 297343
4. Airport Ashok
   Phone: 5529111
   Fax: 5529137
5. Hindusthan International
   Phone: 2472394-97
   Fax: 2472824
   Cable: MODERN
6. New Kenilworth International
   Phone: 2428394-95
   Cable: NEWKEN
   Fax: 2425136
7. Rutt-Deen
   Phone: 2475240
   Cable: RUTTDEEN
   Fax: 2475210
8. Lytton
   Phone: 2491872-79
   Cable: LYTTOTEL
   Fax: 2481747
9. Astor
   Phone: 2429917
   Fax: 2427430
10. Holiday Inn
    Tel: 2430301
    Fax: 2486650

BUDGET
11. Great Eastern Hotel
    Phone: 2482331
    Fax: 2480289
    Cable: GRE*ASTERN
12. Fairlawn
    Phone: 2451510
    Cable: FAIRHOTEL
    Fax: 2441835

13. Astoria
    Phone: 249679
    Cable: ASTORIATEL
    Fax: 2450190
14. Minerva
    Phone: 263365
15. Swagath
    Phone: 756150
16. Carlton
    Phone: 288853
    Cable: BONCUISINE
17. The Shamilton
    Phone: 748279-80
    Fax: 0748809
18. Shalimar
    Phone: 284904
19. YMCA
    Phone: 292192
    Cable: MANHOOD
20. YWCA
    Phone: 297033, 292494

WHAT TO SEE
1. VICTORIA MEMORIAL, opened in 1921 by the Prince of Wales, is an impressive white marble building often called the Taj Mahal of the British Raj. Inside are the memorabilia of the British India.
2. INDIAN MUSEUM, the largest in India, with one of the best collections of Indian art.
3. JAIN TEMPLE. Mirror and coloured glass-encrusted and with multi-coloured chandeliers, this temple, built in 1867, sparkles in the sun.
4. RABINDRA SAROBAR, a lake with parks and rowing clubs where regattas are held.
5. RAMAKRISHNA MISSION INSTITUTE OF CULTURE, a magnificent building housing an institute promoting India's cultural heritage.
6. MARBLE PALACE, a one-man collection of art treasures.

EXCURSIONS
1. BELUR MATH (16 km.), headquarters of the Ramakrishna Mission, a Hindu service organisation set up by Swami Vivekananda, a disciple of the great saint, Ramakrishna Paramahansa.
2. BOTANICAL GARDENS (19 km.), an impressive oasis of green trees and plants, especially noted for its gigantic over 200 years old banyan tree.
3. DAKSHINESHWAR KALI TEMPLE, famous for its associations with Sri Ramakrishna.
4. GANDHI GHAT (25 km.), where the Hoogly river turns towards the sea. Beyond is Bakkhali (132 km.) with a good beach.
5. NABADWIP (114 km.), the birthplace of Saint Chaitanya, is the scene of many colourful festivals.
6. SUNDERBANS (131 km.), a forest in the river delta, where wildlife is in abundance.
7. SANTINIKETAN (211 km.), the site of the open-air school started by Rabindranath Tagore. It now houses the

Vishwabharati International University.
8. DIGHA (185 km.), a beautiful beach resort.

SHOPPING

Terracotta Bankura folk artifacts, painted clay and ceramics, bell metal and brass figurines, handicrafts made of pith, conch shell and shola (sponge wood), handloom silks, tussar and cotton, printed silks and intricately carved gold jewellery are a few of the wide range of shopping opportunities. In addition, handicrafts of Assam, Tripura and the north-eastern states are also sold in Calcutta.

FESTIVALS OF SPECIAL LOCAL INTEREST

1. GANGA SAGAR MELA (January) at Sagar (105 Km.), where the Hoogly joins the sea. A large number of pilgrims congregate here to take a dip in the holy waters.
2. MAHESH YATRA (June-July), a car festival, particularly famous at Serampore (25 km.).
3. DURGA PUJA (Sept-Oct) is the most important festival of Bengal celebrated with music, dance and drama lasting 10 days. Huge figures of the Goddess Durga are worshipped in beautifully illuminated and decorated shamianas. Images are immersed in rivers on the last day of the festivities.

ENTERTAINMENT

The classical and folk music of Bengal, Rabindra Sangeet (the music of Tagore's compositions), masked Chhau and tribal dances of the Santhals, the art cinema, and the Bengali theatre are all available to the visitor. Dramas and cultural shows are regularly held in theatres like the Rabindra Sadan, the Academy of Fine Arts, Kala Mandir, Vidya Mandir, Mahajati Sadan, Biswarupa, Star, etc.

DARJEELING

GENERAL INFORMATION
Population: 75,000 (1991 census)
Altitude: 2127 metres (7, 083 ft)
Climate

	Temperature	
	Max.	Min.
Winter	19^0 c	3^0 c
Summer	20^0 c	11^0 c
Rainfall	999 mm	101 mm

Season: April to mid-June and mid-September to November.

Clothing:
Summer: light woollens.
Winter: heavy woollens.

HOW TO GET THERE
By Air: The nearest airport is at Bagdogra (90 km.). Indian Airlines services connect Bagdogra with Calcutta, Delhi, Patna, Guwahati and Imphal.

By Rail: New Jalpaiguri (80 km.) and nearby Siliguri (90 km.) railway stations are the railheads which have connections with Calcutta, Guwahati, Patna, Delhi, Bhubaneswar, Madras, Thiruvananthapuram, etc.

By Road: Darjeeling is connected by road with all important centres of the eastern region. It is 100 km. from Gangtok, 513 km. from Guwahati and 651 km. from Calcutta.

LOCAL TRANSPORT

Tourist taxis, cars, jeeps, Landrover taxis and ponies.

CONDUCTED TOURS

(Operated during the tourist season.)
1. Half-day tours of DARJEELING visiting the Ava Art Temple, Dhirdham Temple, Himalayan Mountaineering Institute, Lebong Race Course, etc.
2. Full-day tour to MIRIK (43 km.).
3. Full-day tour to KALIMPONG (51 km.).
4. 2-day tour to KALIMPONG, GANGTOK, ORCHID SANCTUARY, etc.(96 km.).
5. TIGER HILL tour (early morning).

Information on tours from West Bengal Government Tourist Office, Nehru Road. *Tel*: 54050.

WHERE TO STAY (STD CODE: 0354)

STANDARD
1. Sinclairs Hotel
   Phone: 54355
   Fax: 54355
2. Windamere Hotel
   Phone: 54041-42
   Cable: WINDAMERE
   Fax: 54043
3. Central Hotel
   Phone: 2033, 2746
   Cable: CENTRAL
4. New Elgin Hotel
   Phone: 54114, 54082
   Fax: 54267
   Cable: NEWELGIN
5. Chancellor
   Tel: 2956
   Fax: 54330

BUDGET
6. Bellevue Hotel
   Phone: 54075, 54130
   Cable: BELLEVUE
7. Tourist Lodge
   Phone: 2611-2-3
8. Youth Hotel
   Phone: 2290
9. Lewis Jubilee Complex
   Phone: 2127
10. Valentine
    Phone: 2228
    Cable: VALENTINE

WHAT TO SEE

1. LLOYD BOTANICAL GARDENS with spectacular ferns, rhododendrons and multitudes of trees and plants. Also an ORCHID HOUSE.
2. OBSERVATORY HILL for a magnificent view of the Kanchenjunga ranges.
3. DHIRDHAM TEMPLE built in Nepali style.
4. HIMALAYAN MOUNTAINEERING INSTITUTE where mountaineers are trained. The late Tenzing Norgay, who was one of the first

two to conquer Everest, was its Director.
5. The ZOOLOGICAL PARK has high altitude animals.
6. BATASIA LOOP from where one can see the Toy Railway winding its way up.
7. DARJEELING-RANGEET VALLEY ROPEWAY. It links Darjeeling with Single Bazaar.
8. LEBONG RACE COURSE, one of the smallest and the highest race courses in the world.
9. HAPPY VALLEY TEA ESTATE (3 km.) to see tea being produced.

EXCURSIONS
1. GHOOM MONASTERY (8 km.). Built in Tibetan style, it enshrines a status of the Maitreya Buddha.
2. TIGER HILL (11 km.) to see sunrise over Mount Everest and the Kanchenjunga ranges.
3. TAKDAH (26 km.) where there are several nurseries growing Himalayan orchids.
4. KURSEONG (32 km.), a charming health resort.
5. MIRIK (49 km.) is a hill station 1800 metres high with a beautiful lake in the centre.
6. KALIMPONG (51 km.), another hill resort, is reached by a fascinating journey through tea estates, winding roads and several "View" (vantage) points from where the Himalayas can be seen in their panoramic glory.
7. SANDAKPHU (58 km.) at a height of 3,657 metres. A favourite with trekkers. Affords glorious views of the Himalayan peaks. (There are Trekkers Huts along the route.)
8. GANGTOK (139 km.), the capital of Sikkim, a state of great scenic charm.
9. JALDAPARA WILDLIFE SANCTUARY (224 km.) and the DOOARS. Trained elephants are available to take you around the sanctuary where the rare one-horned rhino can be seen.

FESTIVALS OF SPECIAL LOCAL INTEREST
BUDDHA JAYANTI (May), the birth anniversary of Buddha is a great event, colourfully celebrated at various Buddhist monasteries.

SPORTS
1. The Himalayan Mountaineering Institute holds demonstrations in season on mountain climbing, rock climbing, etc.
2. There are any number of Himalayan treks which can be undertaken from Darjeeling as the base. A popular one is to Sandakphu by different trekking routes. The best season for treks are April-May and October-November.

Chapter 25

BIHAR
The Land of the Buddha and Ashoka, The Great

A statue of Buddha

India is the land of Buddha and Bihar was the State where he spent the major part of his life. Most sacred places connected with his life are located in Bihar or the neighbouring Uttar Pradesh. Buddha's travels were confined to the region which now constitutes the two States of Bihar and Uttar Pradesh. Bihar, therefore, is sacred to Buddhists all over the world who come here for pilgrimage, specially to BODH GAYA, where the Buddha attained enlightenment.

It was also from his capital Pataliputra (PATNA) in Bihar that Emperor Ashoka, the great Buddhist emperor, ruled over the entire Indian subcontinent and spread the message of the Buddha not only in India but also beyond its shores. It was during Ashoka's time in the third century B.C. that Buddhism spread to the former Soviet Republics and Afghanistan in the West and Thailand, China, Japan and Indonesia in the East.

Most of the people in Bihar earn their living by cultivating rice. It is also one of India's most backward States. Yet, it possesses huge reserves of mica, high grade iron ore, coal, bauxite, chromite and kyanite which are now gradually being exploited. Irrigation and hydroelectric works like the Damodar Valley project are slowly changing the face of Bihar and the Bihari farmers are slowly adopting modern agricultural tools.

HISTORY

The present-day Bihar State has an area of 173,876 sq. km. and is surrounded by West Bengal, Orissa, Uttar Pradesh, Madhya Pradesh and Nepal. In ancient times, Bihar witnessed great empires rise and fall. Different parts of the State at different times in history were parts of Anga, Videh and Vaishali. Bihar was the core part of the famous empire of Magadha under the Maurya and Gupta dynasties. The Indian subcontinent was ruled from Pataliputra, at that time the capital of India.

The antiquity of Magadha is established from the *Vedas*. The kings of Magadha were so mighty that Alexander the Great decided to retreat from India apprehending defeat. In the closing years of the 4th century B.C., Magadha became a greater power under Maurya and his grandson, Chandragupta. Pataliputra at that time was as important as Rome in subsequent centuries.

Bihar was the State where two great religions of the world were born—Buddhism and Jainism. It was also the State where both the Buddha and Mahavira lived and preached.

PATNA — The City of Flowers

"The city of Pushpapur or Pataliputra (PATNA) is the capital of the Magadha country. It is the touchstone by which all other cities are judged. It has revealed the splendid vastness of the sea by securing from it numerous precious jewels and other objects, which are spread over its several markets", wrote Dundin, a renowned poet and storyteller of the

6th century A.D. To Fa-hien, the Chinese traveller, who visited Pataliputra a century earlier, it looked so magnificent that he thought it must have been built by supernatural beings.

Pataliputra had two older names, Pushpapur and Kusumpur, both meaning the City of Flowers. Patali also means the trumpet flower. King Ajatashatru built a fort at Pataliputra though the city was founded by his son Udayana.

"Modern researches have shown that this ancient metropolitan city of Pataliputra was situated on a long strip of land, half a mile to the north of the village Kumarhar. Ashok's palace extended from the mound called Chhoti Pahari to Kumarhar and it covered an area of 4 sq. miles. Bhikra Pahari, an artificial hill of brick debris, over 40 feet high and about a mile in circuit, on which stood the residence of one of the Nawabs of Patna, is identified as the hermitage-hill built by Ashoka for his brother Mahendra. In the Panchpahari are identified five great relic-stupas built by Ashoka." (Pataliputra by J.H. Dave, *Bhavan's Journal*, 26 August 1956).

Now Patna is connected by air with Calcutta, Varanasi and Delhi, and by train with all other major cities. Over a million people live in this city. Patna is also a convenient place to visit Nepal through a land route.

BODH GAYA

The most sacred place to the Buddhists is Bodh Gaya, a quiet township in Bihar State, where the Buddha attained enlightenment under the shade of a Bodhi tree in 533 B.C. Born as prince Siddhartha, he came to be known as the Buddha, the WISE one. The Mahabodhi tree under which he meditated is still there grown from its saplings again and again. Nearby is the Mahabodhi temple, perhaps one of the most ancient temples in the world. The Ashok Hotels chain has a hotel in Bodh Gaya for tourists.

BODH GAYA is 14 km. south of Gaya. The Buddha meditated under a peepul (Ficus religiosa) tree there and achieved enlightenment. The tree, known as the Bodhi tree, continues to live through replantation of its saplings. Emperor Ashoka had sent saplings of the tree to Sri Lanka. When the original Bodhi tree died in the 6th century, a sapling of the tree from Sri Lanka was brought back and planted at the very spot where the original tree stood. The tree again fell down during the last part of the 19th century while some repair work was under way. Two of its saplings were planted, one in place of the old tree and the other a little away from it. Thus the present Bodhi Tree is about a century old.

Nearby flows the Niranjana river where the Buddha bathed. The pyramidal MAHABODHI TEMPLE, 170 feet high, is unique in Buddhist architecture. It has a huge gilded image of the Buddha, and a richly carved gateway.

The ANIMESH-LOCHAN CHAITYA, near the Mahabodhi Temple, marks the spot where the Buddha stood gazing in gratitude after attaining enlightenment.

CHANKRAMANA or the Jewel Walk is a raised platform where the Buddha paced up and down as he pondered on whether to reveal his knowledge to the world or not. There is a Tibetan monastery with a large Dharma Chakra or the Wheel of Law inside it.

LUMBINI - The Birthplace

The Buddha was born in a small village called Lumbini in 561 B.C. while his mother Mayadevi was on her way to her parents' home. His father, King Shudhodhan, was the ruler of the kingdom of Kapilavastu. The village is

Mahabodhi Temple

now located in Nepal, 6 km. across the Indian border. The most convenient place to reach Lumbini is from Gorakhpur in Uttar Pradesh, a major railway station and also an airport. You can hire cycle Rickshaw to reach Lumbini.

The village Lumbini is no more, but the place of his birth was later identified by Lord Buddha's great disciple, Emperor Ashoka, who built an iron pillar in Lumbini to mark his visit to the Buddha's place of birth. A temple of Mayadevi, her mother, is close by.

Lumbini is now being rebuilt as a great pilgrim centre through international aid. It is shaping into a great Buddhist centre.

RAJGIR - Where Buddha Lived

Not far from Bodh Gaya, Rajgir is more easily accessible from PATNA, capital of Bihar State. It was at Rajgir, capital of the State of Magadh, that its great king, Bimbisara, was converted by Lord Buddha himself to the new faith. The Buddha liked Rajgir and spent most summers on one of its hills which is now the main pilgrim centre. Rajgir is also known for its natural hot springs.

NALANDA, the seat of the famous Buddhist University from the 5th to the 12th century, is nearby and worth a visit. The Buddha had preached here and Emperor Ashoka had built a monastery in his commemoration.

VAISHALI

Vaishali was one of the ancient Republican States of India. The Buddha visited Vaishali several times to preach his gospel. He gave his last sermons here and announced his impending *nirvana*.

Emperor Ashoka built a massive lion column here in memory of the Buddha. The lion is now India's national emblem, printed on all currency notes. Vaishali is 50 km. from Patna.

KUSHINAGAR

Kushinagar, also accessible from Gorakhpur, is the place where the Buddha went into *parinirvana* or died. A massive figure of the Buddha in the *nirvana* pose is there for the worshippers. The large figure was brought some 2,000 years ago all the way from Mathura. A large number of Buddhist monasteries testify to the fact that it must have been a great pilgrim centre in ancient times.

SARNATH

Sarnath is only a few kilometres from Varanasi, the ancient Hindu pilgrimage centre on the banks of the Ganga river. It was the place where Buddha delivered his first sermon and made five disciples.

Sarnath is an international Buddhist centre with monasteries built by people of different countries.

Lion column

SRAVASTI

The ancient capital of the Kaushal kingdom, Sravasti, is sacred to the Buddhists for it was here that the Buddha performed his famous Miracle, a millionfold self-manifestation on a 1,000-petalled lotus.

Sravasti is reached from Lucknow, the capital of Uttar Pradesh.

OTHER PLACES OF INTEREST

Bihar abounds in rivers, hills, lakes and forests. The most important of the rivers is the Ganga, flowing from the west to the east for 560 km. The three major dialects of the people are Maithali prevailing in the east, Magadhi in the south, and Bhojpuri in the west.

Eleven km. from the Patna railway station, is situated the village KUMARHAR. The road to reach it passes through crowded streets breathing a medieval air. It is here that the relics of some of the monuments of Pataliputra have been discovered. Megasthenes, the Greek ambassador to Chandragupta Maurya's court, wrote an account of India in the 4th century B.C. where he says that the royal palace excelled in splendour, being better than the palaces of the Egyptian, Babylonian and Cretan monarchs. Here polished sandstone columns have been found with decayed woodworks still clinging to some of them. The excavation site is open daily between 9.30 a.m. and 5.30 p.m. except on Mondays. A park has been created around the ruins of Pataliputra, the great Indian capital.

The 29 metre high hemispherical granary GOLGHAR, built in 1786, has two spiral staircases. From the top, it commands a panoramic view of the city and its suburbs.

In 1666, the last of the ten Sikh Gurus, Gobind Singh was born in HARMANDIR SAHIB. The site is one of the four most sacred Sikh shrines. A marble temple was built here by the illustrious 19th century Sikh monarch of Punjab, Maharaja Ranjit Singh.

PADRI-KI-HAVELI, the old Roman Catholic church, was built in 1751 by the Capuchin Fathers.

The PATNA MUSEUM contains beautiful ancient sculptures and bronze images, Tibetan antiques and paintings, a fine collection of coins and many relics of the Maurya period (4th and 3rd centuries B.C.).

An asset for scholars of medieval history, the KHUDA BAKHSH ORIENTAL LIBRARY is rich in rare Persian and Arabic manuscripts. A number of them are beautifully laminated.

A sculpture in Gandhara art

Across the river Ganga, SONEPUR is the venue of the world's largest, month-long cattle fair held in the month of November. From elephants to camels, sheep and birds are put on sale here. The fair attracts a large number of curious foreigners every year. The MAHATMA GANDHI BRIDGE across the Ganga is among the longest river bridges in the world.

Mughal Emperor Jahangir's son Prince Parvez built SAIF KHAN'S MOSQUE on the banks of the Ganga. Also known as Pathar-ki-Masjid or Chimni Ghat Masjid, it is worth a visit.

The SADAQUAT ASHRAM is the seat of Bharatiya Vidyapith, a national university, since 1921. Its museum displays the belongings of India's first President, Dr. Rajendra Prasad and the presents received in his lifetime. He lived in this house after his retirement.

MARTYR'S MEMORIAL, LAKSHMI NARAYAN MANDIR, PASCHIM DAROJA, QILA HOUSE, SHAHI MASJID and GANDHI MAIDAN are other places of interest in Patna.

MONGHYR was the seat of the ancient Anga kingdom and the capital of Mir Qasim before the British occupied Bihar. There is a MUGHAL FORT in the city with a beautiful Hindu temple inside it.

THE BETLA NATIONAL PARK, 200 km. north of Patna, is a tiger reserve. Located in PALAMAU, Betla is famous for its sal forests which are very hot during summer. The best time to visit the Park is between October and March. Fauna includes tiger, elephant, leopard, wild cat, hyena, gaur, sambhar and chital or axis deer.

GAYA

GAYA, 206 km. from Patna and 15 km. north of Bodh Gaya, is an ancient place of pilgrimage for Hindus as well as Buddhists. The sacred footprints of Vishnu are believed to have been preserved in the VISHNUPAD TEMPLE. The Hindus consider it a great honour to be able to perform the shraddha ceremony (offering of oblation) for their forefathers here. The sacred Phalgu river, generally invisible, flows by this spot. Gaya is considered second only to Varanasi in sanctity.

The town derives its name from Gayasur, a demon who was an ardent devotee of Vishnu.

VAISHALI

Vaishali, 44 Km. from the birthplace of Lord Mahavira, the Jain Tirthankar (527 B.C.) was a famous city in the days of the Buddha. Ruins of the old city have been discovered near the village BESARH on the north bank of the Ganga.

Vaishali derived its name from King Vaishala, a famous ruler mentioned in the *Ramayana*. Once this region, with Vaishali, belonged to the Lichchavis, a clan of Kshatriyas who ruled the territory as a republic.

It is said that once the city experienced a terrible plague. The citizens requested the Buddha to visit the city. With his arrival, the plague ended.

The Buddha took a liking for the place. Here, in the garden of the courtesan Ambapali, he delivered the last series of his sermons.

In A.D. 383 the Second Buddhist council met here and two stupas were erected to commemorate the event. An ASHOKAN COLUMN, ancient tanks, Jain shrines, Buddhist stupas, RAJA VISHAL KA GHAR and the MUSEUM are worth a visit. Most of the great Vaishali city is still underground.

NALANDA

Nalanda University

Ninety kilometres south of Patna once stood the world-famous Buddhist University, Nalanda, accommodating 10,000 students. The Buddha had preached here and Emperor Ashoka had built a monastery in commemoration of the event. Lord Mahavira too lived here. If Bodh Gaya marked the beginning of Buddhism, Nalanda was the continuation and intellectual nerve centre of Buddhism.

The excavated ruins of Nalanda are immensely impressive, with chapels, monasteries, and lecture halls spreading symmetrically over a large area. A museum exhibits rare examples of sculpture and archaeological finds.

The huge stupa standing at the centre of the site can be ascended by a steep flight of stairs. The hills of Rajgir can be seen at some distance. Below the stupa spreads a vast complex of the ruins of the various faculties of the ancient Nalanda — walled enclosures, pillars, shrines and tanks. The new building here is the NALANDA INSTITUTE, an international centre of postgraduate studies in Buddhology founded in 1951.

From Patna to Rajgir, the road meanders through a charming landscape. This ancient capital of the glorious Magadha empire is 103 km. from Patna and 19 km. from Nalanda.

Rajgir, the name derived from Rajagriha, the home of the king, has bewitching surroundings. Among the ruins to be seen are those of a fort, a chariot track, baths, stupas and mansions. Buddhist texts speak of two groves that were the Buddha's favourite retreats, and a hillock,

GRIDDHAKUTA, which he often climbed. The sites of the groves and the hillock have been located.

An aerial ropeway takes travellers to a marble stupa built by the Japanese Buddhists. The Centaur Hotel's Hokke Club caters to the needs of Japanese visitors for meals and accommodation. Burmese Buddhists have built their own temple to the east of the fort. Three kilometres away are the hot sulphur springs. The first Buddhist Council, immediately after the MAHAPARINIRVANA of the Buddha, was convened here at the SAPTAPARNI CAVE. Lord Mahavira also spent 14 years here. Nearby are SAPTADHARA and MAKHDUM KUND HOT SPRINGS.

PAWAPURI

104 km. from Patna and 25 km. from Nalanda is Pawapuri, the village where Mahavira, the Prophet of Jainism, attained NIRVANA. White marble temples dominate this holy place. JALMANDIR, a shrine amidst a lake, is a serene sight. During the Deepavali (the festival of lights in October-November), Jains from all over India gather here to discuss issues concerning their faith.

PARSHNATH HILL

Parshnath Hill is of great religious importance to the Jain as 21 out of the 24 Tirthankaras - the Masters of Jainism - attained their Nirvana here. Situated at a distance of 200 km. from Pawapuri and 8 km. from GIRIDIH, the hill, which is called Parshnath after the name of the 23rd Tirthankar, rises steep above the plains of DHANBAD to a height of 1,365 metres. The hill-top, with the temples is in sylvan setting. It is the first stop across the Bengal borders. The path to the hill-top passes through the village MADHUBAN from where it is an 11 km. trek. It takes almost a full day to reach the Parshnath Hill and to the temple and to come back. For those who want to stay overnight, there is a Dak Bungalow on the hill.

MANER

To the west of Patna, 29 km. away, is the earliest seat of Islam in Bihar, Maner. Here lived, in the 13th century, a famous Sufi Saint, Pir Hazrat Makhadun Yahiya Maneri. His tomb is known as the CHHOTI DARGAH. The designs and carvings on the mausoleum are beautiful.

BIHAR-SHARIF

About 64 km. from Patna, Bihar-Sharif flourished as an important seat of Muslim culture during the 13th-16th centuries. The tomb of a saint, Pir Makhdum Shah Sharifuddin, is a pilgrim centre for the Muslims.

SASARAM

Hundred and ninety-three km. from Patna, Sasaram is on the main railway line connecting Delhi and Calcutta. Here you can see the finest building of medieval India, the MAUSOLEUM OF SHER SHAH. Son of a chieftain, Sher Shah was the emperor of India from A.D. 1539 to 1545. He was a competent administrator. He had planned the mausoleum himself and had executed the construction barring only the last touches which were given by his son after his death.

The mausoleum stands amidst an artificial lake, the hills in the distant horizon forming an excellent background for the monuments, with reflections in the water adding to its grandeur.

RANCHI AND HAZARIBAGH

Ranchi, 338 km. from Patna, the former summer capital of Bihar, has lost much of its charm as a cool resort. Many of its trees have been felled to make room for a new industrial town. It was originally a tribal country with vast parts of forest lands. Ranchi is a large hill resort, the countryside around it boasts many beautiful waterfalls. The centre of the town is called RANCHI HILL, a surprising bare black outcropping in the midst of a flat land. It is crowned by a SHIVA TEMPLE. At the foothills is an artificial lake flanked by two temples and a pillared bathing ghat.

Ten km. south-west of Ranchi is JAGANNATHPUR VILLAGE. The JAGANNATH TEMPLE is a miniature replica of the large Jagannath temple at Puri in Orissa. The car festival is celebrated here with great abandon, but not on the scale of Puri.

HUNDRU FALLS, 40 km. north-east of Ranchi, are one of the world's largest waterfalls. When the Subarnarekha river is in spate, the Falls are spectacular and violent. There is a magnificent view of the river from top of the Falls. There are half a dozen other beautiful falls in the area.

NETRAHAT is the prize beauty spot of the Ranchi area. But its isolation (160 km. west) makes it possible only for visitors with plenty of time to reach it. The place itself and the road leading to Netrahat are surrounded by dense forests.

Ranchi and Hazaribagh, the two hill resorts, are situated on opposite sides of the Damodar Valley. Both are good places to relax and enjoy natural scenery. There is a wildlife sanctuary in Hazaribagh and accommodation is available in a tourist lodge or forest resthouse. Hazaribagh, the resort, is a quiet little place 67 km. from the railway junction of Hazari Bagh Road.

The wildlife reserve known by the same name covers an area of 186 sq. km. It is situated in a dense, forested plateau and has more sambar population than any other wildlife sanctuary of comparable size. Among other animals in the sanctuary are panther, spotted deer, wild boar and bear. There are observation towers located at strategic locations. Carefully nurtured over the last two decades, the forests in Bihar have once again started teeming with wildlife. There are about 12 wildlife sanctuaries in Bihar.

JAMSHEDPUR—The Steel City

South of Ranchi near the Bengal border is Jamshedpur, the Steel City, founded in 1907 by Sir Jamshedji Tata. It is often called the Pittsburgh of India. The gigantic factory complex of the Tata Iron and Steel Company dominates the well-planned city. Nearby is DIMNA LAKE, one of the popular beauty spots of the State.

The Damodar Valley Project area is an excellent attraction for tourists. The project impounds the flood water of the Damodar river and its tributaries through a number of dams and utilises it for purposes of power and irrigation. The States it serves are Bihar and West Bengal. The CHHOTA NAGPUR area of Bihar is now dotted with steel, coal and mica industries.

It is convenient to begin a tour of this area from KODARMA, a railway station of the main line between Calcutta and Delhi. A drive of 19 km. through sylvan surroundings brings you to the TILAIYA DAM, showing the reservoir flanked by two green hills. The circuit-house at Tilaiya is a peaceful retreat.

Hazaribagh at an altitude of 2,000 feet is an ideal summer resort. A few kilometres from the city is the HAZARIBAGH NATIONAL PARK mentioned earlier. Fifty-six km. from Hazaribagh is the KONAR DAM where flowering trees and shrubs surround the lake.

About 77 km. from MAITHON is SINDRI, the largest factory in Asia. In another direction, only 16 km. from Maithon, is the 6 km. long PANCHET DAM, the biggest in the Damodar Valley Project.

PALAMAU was once the seat of the Ghero kings and has a fort deep inside the forest. It is a charming forested hill station with waterfalls and hot springs.

BHAGALPUR

It is a university town, famous for the BARARI CAVES near the city and the rock-cut TEMPLE AT COLGANG. South of the city in a forest is the MANDAR HILL capped by a VISHNU TEMPLE.

SIMULTALA, a charming health resort, lies in secluded surroundings on the Calcutta-Amritsar rail route. JASIDIH, 25 km. from Simultala, is another charming hill resort. Jasidih connects DEOGHAR, also known as the Baidyanath Dham. TAPOBANA, KARAMIBAG, TRIKUT and NANDAN HILLS, ANUKIL THAKUR'S ASHRAM, are some of the attractions of Deoghar.

RAJARAPPA

89 km. from Hazaribagh, the RAJARAPPA WATERFALLS are enchanting. Believed to be one of the 51 sacred sites where a part of the body of Sati, the spouse of Lord Shiva fell, a temple has been dedicated to DEVI CHINNAMASTA on the top of the hill. TOPCHANCHI LAKE is an ideal resort, 37 km. from DHANBAD, the mining city of Bihar. GHAT SHILA is another

enchanting health resort of Bihar along the bank of the Subarnarekha river—the golden line.

PATNA

GENERAL INFORMATION
Population: 1,100,000 (1991 census)
Altitude: Sea level
Climate

	Temperature	
	Max.	Min.
Winter	34^0 c	10^0 c
Summer	41^0 c	23^0 c
Rainfall	847 mm	55 mm

Season: Throughout the year. April to June which are hot months

Clothing
Summer: cottons,
Winter: woollens

HOW TO GET THERE
By Air: Patna, the capital of Bihar, is well connected by air with all major cities of India. It is also the nearest airport for the Buddhist tourist attractions of Bihar.
Patna is a Railway Junction connected with all parts of India.
By Rail: Gaya (12 km) is the nearest railhead for Bodh Gaya.
By Road: Patna is connected by road to Bodh Gaya, Nalanda, Rajgir, Varanasi, Gorakhpur, etc. It is
90 km. from Nalanda,
102 km. from Rajgir,
186 km. from Bodh Gaya (via Rajgir) and
125 km. from Bodh Gaya,
653 km. from Calcutta and
252 km. from Varanasi.

There are bus services to places within the state of Bihar and to Siliguri (for Darjeeling), Gorakhpur (for Kushinagar), Calcutta, etc.

LOCAL TRANSPORT
Tourist taxis, unmetered taxis and auto-rickshaws are available at Patna and Bodh Gaya.
Unmetered taxis and cycle-rickshaws at Rajgir.

CONDUCTED TOURS
1. Full-day tour to RAJGIR, NALANDA and PAWAPURI.
2. Tour to RAXAUL (for Lumbini).
3. Tour to RANCHI.

Information: Bihar Government Tourist Office, Frasor Road, *Phone*: 225295
Government of India Tourist Office, *Tel*: 226721

WHERE TO STAY (STD CODE: 0612)
DELUXE
1. Maurya Patna
   Phone: 222061
   Cable: MAURYA
STANDARD
2. Patliputra Ashok
   Phone: 226270
   Fax: 223467
   Cable: TOURISM
3. Chanakya
   Phone: 223141-42, 220590-6
   Fax: 0612-220598

4. Samrat International
   Phone: 220560-67
   Fax: 226386
   Cable: SAMRAT

BUDGET

5. Avantee
   Phone: 221959, 220540-9
   Fax: 0612-220549
6. Jaysarmin
   Phone: 55573
7. President
   Phone: 220600-5
8. Republic
   Phone: 655021-24

WHAT TO SEE

1. PATNA MUSEUM. It has excellent collections.

2. JALAN MUSEUM, a private collection, can be seen with special permission.
3. KUMHRAR (5 km.) where excavations have found remains of the capital Pataliputra.
4. SHER SHAH MASJID, built in the Afghan style of architecture.
5. BIHAR INSTITUTE OF HANDICRAFT AND DESIGN.
6. HARMANDIR SAHIB TEMPLE built at the birthplace of Guru Gobind Singh, the 10th Sikh Guru.

EXCURSIONS

1. MANER (29 km). The Chhoti Dargah is considered one of the finest mausoleums in the region.
2. VAISHALI (55 km). Site of the oldest republic in the world, it is the birthplace of the great teacher-saint, Mahavira, the founder of Jainism, and the place where the Buddha preached his last sermon.
3. NALANDA (90 km).
4. PAWAPURI (90 km), where Mahavira, the founder of Jainism, attained enlightenment.
5. RAJGIR (105 km).
6. BODH GAYA (186 km via Rajgir)
7. SASARAM (148 km), site of the tomb of Sher Shah.
8. KUSHINAGAR (232 km), where the Buddha left his mortal remains.

SHOPPING

Painted decorations on wall-hangings, miniature paintings on paper and leaves, patchwork and wall hangings are some of the local handicrafts. The villages are also famous for stone pottery, bamboo artifacts, leather goods, white metal statuettes, applique work and wooden toys. Leather footwear are now exported in large quantities.

Bihar's most unique folk art, the Madhubani paintings, are now done on paper or on canvas, usually by the women of Mithila.

A Madhubani painting

FESTIVALS OF LOCAL INTEREST

1. MAKER MELA FAIR (January) held for 7 days at Rajgir.
2. VAISHALI FESTIVAL (March-April) is held on the birthday of Mahavira at Vaishali (55 km, from Patna).
3. BUDDHA JAYANTI (April-May) is a day of prayer and celebration at the Mahabodhi Temple.
4. SRAVANI MELA (July-August). Pilgrims gather water from the Ganges at Sultanganj and trek with it for 100 miles to Deogarh where it is offered in the Shiva temple.
5. PITRIPAKSHA MELA (September-October). Pilgrims gather at Gaya to pray for the souls of their ancestors.
6. CHATH, the Sun Festival (October-November), marks thanksgiving to the Sun god, after the harvest.
7. SONEPUR MELA (October-November). The largest cattle fair in the world, is held for a month here.

BODH GAYA

WHAT TO SEE

1. MAHABODHI TREE, believed to be the fifth in succession of the original Mahabodhi pipal tree, under which the Buddha attained enlightenment.
2. MAHABODHI TEMPLE, the Shrine of Supreme Enlightened, consecrating the spot where Buddha attained enlightenment. Other sacred spots are ANIMESHLOCHANA (from where the Buddha gazed at the Bodhi Tree for a week, in gratitude), VAJRASANA (the seat where the Buddha sat in meditation), CHANKRAMANA, RATNAGAR, LOTUS TANK, ASOKAN PILLAR, etc.
3. The Tibetan, Thai, Japanese, Korean and Chinese temples built in recent times.

WHERE TO STAY
STANDARD
Bodhgaya Ashok
Tel: 22708-9
ITDC Tourist Lodge
Tel: 25

EXCURSIONS
1. GAYA (15 km), a sacred place for Hindus who offer oblations to the dead and to their forefathers.
2. RAJGIR (80 km).
3. NALANDA (90 km).
4. PAWAPURI (105 km).

RAJGIR

HOW TO GET THERE
Rajgir is connected by rail to Patna and is also the nearest railhead for Nalanda. Patna is on the main line and is well connected by rail.

WHERE TO STAY (STD CODE: 0612)
STANDARD
1. Centaur Hokke Hotel
   Phone: 5231-5224
   Cable: CENTAUR, RAJGIR
   Fax: 5231

WHAT TO SEE
1. VISHWA SHANTI STUPA on top of a hill, constructed by the Japanese. An aerial ropeway connects the temple to Rajgir.
2. SAPTAPARNI CAVE, where the first Buddhist Council was held after the demise of the Buddha.
3. GRIDDHAKUTA, from where the Buddha used to preach.

EXCURSIONS
1. NALANDA (12 km)
2. PAWAPURI (33 km).

FESTIVALS OF LOCAL INTEREST
1. MAKER MELA FAIR (January) held for 7 days at Rajgir.

NALANDA

WHAT TO SEE
1. Ruins of NALANDA UNIVERSITY. Once 2,000 teachers and 10,000 students lived and studied here.
2. HIUEN TSANG MEMORIAL HALL, in memory of the great Chinese traveller who spent 12 years here and travelled all over India in the 7th century A.D.
3. NALANDA MUSEUM.
4. NAVA NALANDA MAHA-VIHIRA, set up for research in the Pali language and Buddhism.

EXCURSIONS
1. RAJGIR (12 km).
2. BIHAR SHARIF (13 km), where there is the tomb of a Muslim saint of the 13th century, Mukhdoom Shah. The annual Urs (fair) attracts great many pilgrims.

Chapter 26

ASSAM AND ITS SIX SISTERS

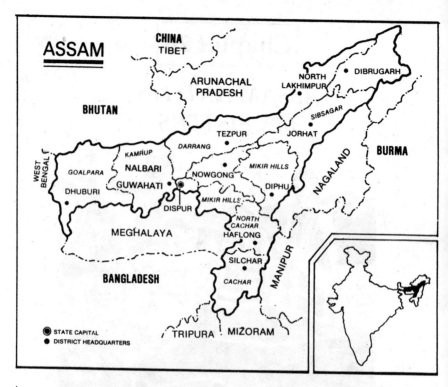

Coffee cultivation in Arunachal Pradesh

The north-eastern region of India is the most varied, but also the least visited by the foreign travellers. Before independence, the entire north-east was known as Assam Province. Various factors including ethnic and linguistic divides led to the formation of seven separate States, now popularly called the seven sisters. The following is the new set up of the former Assam Province after reorganisation:

NAME OF STATE	CAPITAL	AREA(km.)	POPULATION
ASSAM	Dispur	79,500	22,294,562
MANIPUR	Imphal	22,300	1,826,714
MEGHALAYA	Shillong	22,400	1,760,626
NAGALAND	Kohima	16,500	1,215,573
TRIPURA	Agartala	10,400	2,744,827
ARUNACHAL	Itanagar	83,600	852,392
MIZORAM	Aizawl	21,000	·686,217

Source: 1991 census

In many ways, north-east is very much unlike the rest of India. It is an area inhabited by a great number of tribes who speak a hundred different dialects and languages. In Arunachal Pradesh alone, over 50 distinct languages are spoken. In some ways, these hill tribes are similar to tribes found in other parts of the Himalayas. The tribal people here have more similarity with those found in Burma, Thailand and Laos. During the British period, the Christian missionaries found the tribesmen an easy prey for conversion under the State patronage. The missionaries were the only people to get Inner Line Permits to enter the tribal areas. Although predominantly Christians, these hillmen still follow their old customs and traditions.

For entry into this region, there have always been some restrictions on foreigners — partly to preserve the ethnic identity and culture of the tribal people and partly because India after the Indo-China War in 1962, had become

Tribal dancers of Arunachal Pradesh

very sensitive to the security aspects of this region.

The north-east is a vast fertile region of rice paddies, mountains and jungles and is not densely populated. Attracted by fertility of the soil and low population, immigrants from Bangladesh started pouring into Assam and other neighbouring States resulting in ethnic tensions and even attacks on immigrants. An uneasy peace has now been restored but attempts are being made to make sure that the flood of immigrants from across the border is stemmed. The region is wedged between Nepal and China to the north, Bangladesh to the west and Burma to the east. It is connected by road and rail with mainland India by a sliver of territory above Bangladesh. All the State capitals are connected by air. Tripura is bordered by Bangladesh from three sides, making surface transportation very difficult.

ASSAM

Geographically, Assam broadly comprises the Brahmaputra Valley where the Brahmaputra River with its numerous tributaries, flows over 700 km. through the State. The total length of the river from its source is 2,900 kms.

The ancient name of Assam is Kamarupa mentioned in the *Ramayana*. According to a popular legend, Kama - the God of Love— tried to arouse passion in the heart of Lord Shiva who was in meditation. Shiva opened his third eye and destroyed Kama Dev. The compassionate Lord later forgave Kama and revived him. The land where Kama got back his Rupa, the form came to be known as *Kamarupa*.

Later, the old tribes of Kamrupa were subdued by the fierce tribals who came from Burma's Iravady Valley in the thirteenth century. They were called Ahoms — the present name of Assam is derived from the new inhabitants of Kamarupa.

The Ahom rulers were so powerful that they thwarted attempts of the Mughals 13 times to annex Assam. When the Mughals failed to subdue the "the rats of Assam", the Ahom rulers expanded east establishing their authority over the Nagas of Cachar destroying their capital Dimapur.

Ahom power started weakening in the 17th century. In 1792, Burma invaded Assam and the Assamese king, Gaurinath, sought the assistance of the East India Company. The Burmese were repulsed but they came back in 1816. After the Anglo-Burmese War in 1824-26, Burma ceded Assam to East India Company and the British annexed it to their Indian empire.

During World War II, the Assamese helped the Allied forces in repulsing the Japanese invaders and kept open the supply route to China.

For travel in Assam, we must be ready to wear clothes in the regular boy-scout tradition. It is the wettest place in the world with waterfalls six times as high as the famous Niagara Falls. The temperature here can drop from 90^0 C to 50^0 C degrees in an hour of ascending into the hills. You may also find yourself riding an elephant into the forest, chasing wildlife, for that is the most convenient transport to see wildlife.

Assam is well-connected by air with the rest of India. Other State capitals within the region are also connected by air from where taxis and buses are easy to get.

GUWAHATI

Guwahati lies on the banks of the River Brahmaputra which is the prime attraction of this city as well as the State of Assam. Its name when translated into English means "Son of the Lord of the Universe." In a way, it is the Lord of Assam and like God it dispenses life and death. During rains, the river may rise up to 15 metres above its normal water levels flooding thousands of square kilometres in Assam and the neighbouring areas. Some years, this natural irrigation of the fertile lands of Assam may yield rich harvest of jute, rice and mustard while in other years, it may leave death and destruction in its wake.

An interesting way of seeing life in Assam is to embark on a steamer up the river to DIBRUGARH - 550 km. away.

Kamakhya Temple

Guwahati has other attractions besides the Brahmaputra which, of course, is unique among the great rivers of the world. Six km. from Guwahati is the new capital of the State - Dispur also called Pragjyotishpur..

It has many temples, the most important temple attracting pilgrims from all over India being the KAMAKHYA TEMPLE dedicated to Sati, the consort of Shiva. The deity was installed where the limb of Sati fell when, according to a legend, Vishnu cut asunder her body so that Shiva did not see her dead and start his dance of destruction. The temple, according to another legend was built by Narkasur — a king mentioned in the *Mahabharata*.

This temple stands on the NILACHALA HILL, 5 km. off Guwahati.

With its beehive-patterned top, the temple is an excellent specimen of old Assamese architecture.

Another interesting temple in Guwahati is the UMANANDA TEMPLE located right in the middle of the Brahmaputra on an island called PEACOCK ISLAND. Dedicated to Lord Shiva, the temple has several rock-cut figures of gods and goddesses on its walls, some of the finest examples of Assamese craftsmanship.

Located on the west of CHITRACHAL HILL is the temple of NINE PLANETS, Navagraha — once known as the seat of astronomical and astrological research. Because of this temple, Guwahati came to be known as Pragjyotishpur, the city of eastern astrology.

Another place worth a visit in Guwahati is the VASHISTHA ASHRAM. It is believed that the great seer Vashishta, the Guru of Rama, in the ancient times, had his *ashram* (retreat) here. It is a pilgrim and scenic spot with three streams — the Sandhya, Lalita and the Kanta flowing nearby.

Only 24 kilometres from Guwahati is HAJO, an important place of pilgrimage for Hindus, Buddhists and the Muslims. The Buddha, according to one version, achieved his NIRVANA here in HAYAGRIBA MADHAV temple.

There is a Muslim mosque, too, held in great esteem by Muslims. The mosque is called PAO MECCA, considered equal in sanctity to one-fourth of the piety that one acquires by Haj at Mecca.

SULAKSHI, a village 24 km. from Guwahati, is the principal centre of silk production in Assam. In this village, almost every household is busy producing silk and garments made of silk. It is also famous for its brassware.

KAZIRANGA WILDLIFE SANCTUARY

Marco Polo, the intrepid explorer, visited Assam in the 14th century. On seeing the Indian rhinoceros he imagined that he had spotted the fabulous unicorn. He was wrong but what he had seen was a rare animal in the world. The Indian rhinoceros (Rhinoceros unicornis) is one of Nature's last relic from the pre-historic world.

Kaziranga Wildlife Sanctuary, which is home to the one-horned rhinoceros, is an important tourist attraction of Assam. No lover of wildlife misses an opportunity to see this National Park which is a lovely spot on the banks of the Brahmaputra river. It is 233 km. north-east of Guwahati.

Once almost extinct, there are now more than one thousand rhinoceros in this park alone, thanks to the protection given to this animal by the Government of India. No one is allowed to kill the animal but despite the efforts of the Indian Government, some 40 rhinoceros are killed by poachers every year. Their horns are in great demand in Hong Kong, China and Taiwan for their presumed medicinal value.

In Kaziranga, visitors see wildlife riding on an elephant — that is the most suitable transport for viewing the rhinos, safe and secure. Kaziranga is less of a jungle and more of a marshy, grassy plain with 16 feet tall grass, justly called elephant grass. Rhinos are most comfortable in this environment. A *mahout* guides you comfortably through the fields to the heart of the sanctuary where soon a rumbling noise warns you that you are in the vicinity of the great rhino. The *mahout* knows where to stop and how to handle the situation in the face of an angry rhino.

Rhinos are not the only attraction of this great National Park, Kaziranga protects several other animal species. Among these are elephants, tigers, wild boars, wild buffaloes and jackals. The tigers are not often seen during day time but they are there.

To reach Kaziranga one has to use different kinds of transport. The easiest way is to fly to JORHAT airport from where it is only 56 km. From Jorhat, jeeps, taxis or landrovers can be hired to make a trip to the sanctuary. Within the sanctuary it is the elephant transport.

MANAS WILDLIFE SANCTUARY

To the north-west, 176 km. from Guwahati, is another wildlife sanctuary, its surroundings are even lovelier than those of the larger Kaziranga. Set in the thick jungle along the Bhutan border, the Manas wildlife sanctuary is home to a wide variety of wildlife: rhinoceros, elephants, buffaloes and many species of rare deer, apes and birds. It has been justly called the loveliest wilderness in the country. There is good accommodation in furnished bungalows and forest lodges.

OTHER ATTRACTIONS

Further north starts Upper Assam where 10 per cent of India's oil is produced and most of Assam's tea. DULIAJAN is a new well-planned city. Derricks and rigs can be seen right in the centre of tea gardens and paddy fields. This is, however, not a new phenomenon, oil was first struck in Assam as early as 1867.

Between Jorhat and Duliajan, we can discover the ruins of the old capital of Ahoms — SIBSAGAR. A few old monuments can be still found — the water tank dug by King Siva Singha in the 17th century. He also built three temples on its banks dedicated to Vishnu, Shiva and Durga. There is also a RANG GHAR, an original oval-shaped pavilion from where the king watched elephant fights. Besides, there is CHARAIDEO, the necropolis of Ahom kings and a palace at GURGAON. In this area, there are still some isolated village communities where Shan Thai is still spoken and Buddhism practised.

Another place of tourist interest in Assam is BARPETA, 145 km. from Guwahati known for its Vaishnava SHRINE OF SHRI MADHADEVA — the disciple of the great Hindu reformer, Sankardeva.

DURRANG, 80 kilometres from Guwahati, is known for a Bhutanese fair held during November to March. Here you can pick up interesting curios and handicrafts of Bhutanese origin.

TEZPUR, once known as Sonitpur, was ruled by the mythical Demon King Vanasur. There are several old temples here of remote antiquity. The ruins of the fort are attributed to Vanasur.

MEGHALAYA

South of Assam is one of the most visited touristic States of India, Meghalaya, the abode of clouds. Formerly part of Assam, it was created as a separate State in 1972, comprising the hilly regions which are very foggy in winter.

It is inhabited by three major tribal groups. the Garos in the west, the Khasis in the centre, and the Jaintias in the east. Before the British came to Assam, the region had tiny city kingdoms ruled by Rajas which were annexed one by one by the British in the 19th century.

The tribals in this State have a matrilineal and matrilocal family system. Christian missionaries have been very active in the area since its annexation by the British and a majority of the tribal population have been converted to Christianity.

Tribals in the State love their dance and music. A major festival, the Shad Suk Myasiem (Festival of Joyful Heart), is held in Shillong in April.

SHILLONG

A Cathedral

Shillong is the capital of Meghalaya and till it was separated from Assam, it served also as the capital of the whole of Assam. It is 100 km. from Guwahati — only three hours drive. There is also an air connection from Guwahati to Shillong.

The drive to Shillong is picturesque passing

Botanical Garden

through pineapple and betel plantations. It passes along the UMIAN LAKE, formed by a recently built dam.

The British described it as the "Scotland of the East" as the landscape reminded them of their home. It is located at a height of 1500 metres. The climate is temperate and the people very colourful and warm-hearted. From its top, you can have a good view of the orchard country and see the meadows and hamlets of Bangladesh and on a clear day, many of the snowclad peaks.

An artificial lake, WARD LAKE, near the RAJ BHAWAN has a beautiful bridge over it and the BOTANICAL GARDEN close by.

Shillong has many natural waterfalls. Only 2 km. from the city is CRINOLINE FALLS with a swimming pool. Five km. from the city are the BISHOP and BIDON FALLS: then there is one more, GUNNER FALLS.

Another popular place for visitors is CHERRAPUNJI, 56 km. from Shillong. It is the wettest place in the world, with an average rainfall of 1150 mms. It is amazing to see this place which looks so dry on a sunny day — the water comes in torrents and in a matter of minutes it falls on the cliffs and is absorbed in the gorges and the plains below. On the way back, the visitors stop at SHILLONG PEAK which offers a view of the neighbouring hills. Another interesting spot is ELEPHANT WATERFALLS.

JAKREM, a popular health resort with hot sulphur springs, is 64 km. from Shillong.

MAWSYNRAM is 55 kilometres from Shillong. It closely rivals Cherrapunji in annual rainfall. Its major attraction is a picturesque cave of vast and unexplored depth, featuring a giant stalagmite, in the shape of a natural Shivalinga, which is bathed the year round by water dropping from an overhanging stalactite. A place of pilgrimage Hindus, and a natural wonder for sightseers.

ARUNACHAL PRADESH

To the north of Assam lies the Union Territory of Arunachal Pradesh — the land of the Rising Sun. It is bounded on three sides by Bhutan, China

Tawang monastery

and Burma. The capital of the State is ITANAGAR. Because of its strategic location, an inner line permit from Government of India is needed to explore the area.

The 800,000 inhabitants of Arunachal Pradesh are divided into Mangoloid and Tibeto-Burmese tribes. Most of them practice Buddhism. At Tawang, there is over 350-year-old monastery at a height of 3,050 metres, the largest monastery in the country. The sixth Dalai Lama was born here.

Some of the areas of Arunachal are so remote that an Indian Army expedition recently found a tribe still living in caves and eating their food raw — not having yet discovered fire.

The westernmost district of Arunachal is KAMENG with its headquarters at BOMDILA, a town at an altitude of about 2800 metres, known for its scenic beauty. Bomdila has a famous Buddhist monastery and a museum of folk arts.

The Lohit District has the famous PARSHURAM KUND, a pilgrim centre. Parshuram was an incarnation of Lord Vishnu.

In the east, near the border with China and Burma, the Brahmaputra forms a lake called BRAHMAKUNDA before entering into the plains of Assam. Bathing here is believed to wash off one's sins and Hindus come in thousands on the day of Makara Sakranti in mid-January for pilgrimage.

At LEDO starts the old road to MANDALONG, crossing the Burmese border at PANGSO PASS. Beyond this is the "Lake of No Return", where the retreating British troops lost their way in 1942 and perished in quicksand.

NAGALAND

KOHIMA is the capital of Nagaland, a newly created State of India. The State is inhabited by a variety of Tibeto-Burmese tribes speaking over two dozen dialects.

Nagaland is a narrow strip of mountain territory between Assam and Burma with an area of about 17,000 sq. km. and a population of over one million . English is spoken here along with several tribal dialects. A majority of people are Christians.

DIMAPUR, the principal entry point for Nagaland has an airport. It is connected with Calcutta and Guwahati. It is an enchantingly beautiful hill city. Although Nagaland is almost entirely a State inhabited by tribal population, Dimapur is a prosperous trading centre and has a mixed population. It was once the capital of Cachar, a Hindu kingdom. The Cacharis, one of the Naga tribes, were strong enough to raid the neighbouring Assam and Burma. But by the end of the 17th century, the Ahoms of Assam were able to subdue them. When the British intervened in Assam, they set up a post at Kohima. This post too came under the Naga siege. But, a permanent peace was established between the two parties in 1889.

A Naga tribe in ceremonial dress

During World War II, the Japanese and the Indian National Army joined hands to attack Kohima and in 1943, they occupied more than half of the city. They also attacked Imphal. The objective was to take over Dimapur which was a vital rail-head for reaching supplies to British troops in the forward areas.

After independence, some Naga groups demanded autonomy, and later independence. For some years, a state of insurgency prevailed but in 1975, the Naga rebel groups agreed to accept statehood within the Indian Constitution.

Kohima has a war cemetery with Commonwealth graves and a memorial with the famous inscription, "When you go home, tell them of us and say for your tomorrow, we gave our today".

Naga villages are usually perched on hills and are surrounded by a stone wall. One such village, BARA BASTI, can be seen a few kilometres outside Kohima.

MANIPUR

IMPHAL, the capital of Manipur, can be reached by road from Dimapur(Nagaland) and by air either from Calcutta or from Guwahati.

Manipur was an ancient kingdom. It is mentioned in the *Mahabharata*. Arjuna, the third Pandava brother, had married the princess of Manipur and had subsequently suffered defeat at the hands of his son Babrubahan.

Lord Irwin British Viceroy and Governor-General of India, described Manipur as the "Switzerland of India". Nehru called it the Jewel of India, for "Mani" means jewel. The Manipur dance is known for its style and delicacy.

At Imphal the golden TEMPLE OF SHRI GOVINDJI offers a daily performance of dance on the Krishna theme.

About 27 kilometres to the south-west of Imphal is VISHNUPUR or Bishenpur, known after its historical VISHNU TEMPLE, built in the 15th century.

45 kilometres from Imphal is MOIRANG, a village that becomes festive in May with dance and music.

In Bishenpur Sub-Division is to be found Manipur's largest fresh-water lake, LOKTAK LAKE. A boat-trip to either THANGA or KARANG islet in the lake becomes a memorable experience.

KOINA, the hillock, 1,000 feet above sea-level has a temple dedicated to Shri Govindji. It is a drive of 29 km. from Imphal.

For a full view of the valley of Manipur, a drive to TENGNOUPAL at a distance of about 75 kilometres from Imphal, is recommended. It is the highest point on the Imphal-Tamu Road.

An ideal place for relaxation and for seeing and buying the arts and craft of the tribal people is the local market — NEW CHURACHUNDPUR.

The highest hill resort of Manipur is UKHRUL, about 72 km. from Imphal, famous for a kind of land-lily known as Siroi Lily growing on the SIROI HILLS.

The people of Manipur are reputed to be fierce warriors. They excel in martial arts like spear dance, sword fights and wrestling. They are also excellent riders. Polo, the sport that spread over the Mughal empire in the 16th century before becoming international through the British, originated in Manipur. They also enjoy dancing.

Over the centuries the Manipuris had battles for the suzerainty of Manipur with Burma. The British intervened and by the treaty of Yangdaboo on February 24, 1826, the Burmese recognised British sovereignty over Manipur. A revolt in Manipur later led to the hanging of Maharaja's brother. In 1930, there was one more attempt at freedom from the British. A self-styled prophet, Jodonang who announced the imminent departure of the British, was hanged. Another young freedom fighter, Rani Gaidiniliou, then aged 17, was sentenced to life imprisonment. She was released by Jawaharlal Nehru after independence and honoured.

Imphal was also under siege by the Indian National Army in World War II and part of it was captured. The city has two war cemeteries, a museum displaying tribal arts and crafts, ROYAL POLO GROUNDS and the RAJA'S PALACE.

The tribals live not far from the capital, some 60 km. to the northeast. The area is restricted due to occasional insurgency.

MIZORAM

Mi means the human being and Zo means the hill. So, Mizo is the human dweller of the hill. Mizoram means the land of the hill-dwellers. Mizoram is a state with AIZAWL as its capital.

A view of Aizawl

Aizawl is picturesque town built in tiers along the hill. In the markets, one finds typical local products for souvenirs. To stay here in the dak bungalow or a hotel is to experience the atmosphere of Aizawl—a unique world.

A hundred km. to the south of Aizawl is LUNGLEH, another Mizo town, approachable by jeeps. To the south of Lungleh is LONGTALAI, not far from the blue mountains overlooking the Bay of Bengal.

Mizoram, the former Lushai Hill District, is bordered by Bangladesh on one side and Burma on the other. The Mizos are a group of tribesmen related to the Shans, who came to India not too long ago. They started raiding the tea gardens in 1872. The British retaliated and established control by 1892. A system of Inner Line permit was introduced not allowing anyone into this region except the missionaries who converted a majority of the Mizos into Christianity. At present, Mizoram has almost cent per cent literacy in a population of over half a million.

TRIPURA

Raj Bhavan, Agartala

The oldest ruins of this region are found at UNKOTI TIRTHA, 189 km. from Agartala. Huge figures of the Hindu deities and epic characters have been found carved on both sides of a meandering hill-track, emerging from bushes. An awesome atmosphere fills the valley.

Tripura, a former princely State of India, joined the Indian Union after independence in 1949 and became a State of the Union in 1972. The population, mostly of Tibeto-Burmese origin, took up Vaishnava Hinduism very early in its history and the State was continuously ruled by Hindu Maharajas till independence. Tripura was often at war with its neighbours and the British took advantage to make it a Protectorate. They also divided the State into two parts — some areas were left under the Maharaja. The British took direct charge of the tribal belt.

Ujjayanta Palace

Well-connected by air from Calcutta is AGARTALA, the capital of Tripura. One can also take a 600-km drive by road from Guwahati, via Shillong (Meghalaya) and Silchar (Assam).

Tripura had been a kingdom since mythical times, ruled by various dynasties. The palace of the last ruling dynasty, the UJJAYANTA PALACE is now the Legislative Assembly. It is a lovely building with a tank and a garden in front of it.

The old palace is only eight kilometres away, at old Agartala. The town has a famous temple dedicated to 14 deities — CHOWDA DEVTA.

The 14 deities, consisting of brass heads, represent a combination of Hindu faith and tribal cults. They are attended upon by tribal priests and not Brahmins.

Udaipur (now RADHAKISHOREPUR, 55 kms from Agartala), was the ancient capital. The principal temple TRIPURESWARI is situated on a hillock. The deity is Goddess Kali. This is one of the 51 Pithas mentioned in the *Tantras*.

Beyond this age-old temple there is a big tank called DHANI SAGAR, the abode of old tortoises, sacred to pilgrims for food offerings. It is said that when any of these wise tortoises is to die, it approaches the altar of the temple and breathes its last.

The famous "roaring" DUMBUR FALLS is 100 kms from Agartala, near TIRTHAMUKH, a holy spot.

NEER MAHAL or the PALACE IN WATER, is 55 kilometres from Agartala. Standing at the centre of

Temple of Govindjee

LAKE RUNDRANAGAR, it is an attractive sight. You can always respond to its appeal by hiring a rowboat.

GUWAHATI

GENERAL INFORMATION

Population: 250,000 (1991 census)
Altitude: 55 metres (183 ft)
Climate

	Temperature	
	Max.	Min.
Summer	35^0 C	22^0 C
Winter	6^0 C	10^0 C

Rainfall: Monsoons — May to September
Season: Throughout the year, except during heavy rains from June to September.
Clothing:
Summer: light cottons
Winter: woollens.

HOW TO GET THERE

By Air: Guwahati is a major tourist centre of the East besides Calcutta. It is well connected by Indian Airlines to all important cities of India in the east and west. The airport is 25 kms from downtown.
Major private airlines too fly to Guwahati. Coach services are available for airport transfer.
By Rail: Guwahati is an important terminus on the North-western Frontier Railway and is connected with most parts of India by express trains. The railway station is only 1 km. from downtown.
By Road: Guwahati at the junction of National Highways 31, 37 and 40 is the hub of the road network in the eastern and north-eastern region.
State Transport Corporation of Assam, Meghalaya, Arunachal Pradesh, Nagaland and West Bengal operate scheduled bus services linking their own capitals and other cities.
Shillong (103 kms) is connected with Guwahati by frequent taxi and bus services. Taxis seat five passengers.
Enquiries: Assam State Transport Corporation, *Tel* 540208/546453.

LOCAL TRANSPORT

Unmetered Taxis and auto-rickshaws are available in plenty. Fares have to be negotiated.

CONDUCTED TOURS

1. Assam Tourism Corporation operate CITY SIGHTSEEING TOURS regularly.
2. Trips to SHILLONG are operated on Sundays and Wednesdays.
3. Two-day trips from Guwahati to KAZIRANGA WILDLIFE SANCTUARY are operated on Mondays, Wednesdays, Fridays and Sundays.

Reservations: Tourist Lodge, Station Road, *Tel*: 544475

Information: Tourist Office, Government of India, B.K. Kakate Road, Ulabasi, *Tel* 547407

WHERE TO STAY (STD Code: 0361)

STANDARD
1. Brahmaputra Ashok
   Phone: 541064-65
   Fax: 0361-540870
   Cable: BRAHMASHOK

2. Belle Vue
   Phone: 540847-48
   Fax: 44813
   Cable: BELLEVIEW
3. Dynasty
   Phone: 542868-69
   Cable: BELLEVIEW
BUDGET
4. Urvashi
   Phone: 84219
5. Rituraj
   Phone: 540853-54
6. Raj Mahal
   Phone: 541125
7. Nandan
   Phone: 540855-56
   Fax: 0361-542634
   Cable: NANDAN
8. Tourist Lodge (Assam Tourism)
   Phone: 544475

WHAT TO SEE
1. KAZIRANGA WILDLIFE SANCTUARY, home of the one-horned rhino.
2. SIBSAGAR, ruins of the old capital, three temples.
3. MANAS WILDLIFE SANCTUARY, home of a variety of wildlife.
4. GUWAHATI, a fascinating view of sunrise on the Brahmaputra river.
5. Tea gardens.

EXCURSIONS
1. KAMAKHYA TEMPLE, 8 km. away, famous for its Shakti worship.
2. BARPETA, 145 km, known for its Vaishnava monastery and Shri Madhavdeva Shrine.
3. DARRANGA, 50 km from Guwahati, has an exotic Bhutan mela in winter.
4. TEZPUR, a hill resort.
5. SIBSAGAR, 20 km, known for its monuments.
6. SHILLONG, Meghalaya's capital.
7. CHERRAPUNJI, 52 km away, the wettest place on earth.

FESTIVALS OF SPECIAL LOCAL INTEREST
The BIHU FESTIVAL in mid-April, which heralds the Assamese New Year, a week-long festival with songs and dances.

SHOPPING
Assam is noted for its handloom silks, bamboo and cane handicrafts and ivory products.

SHILLONG

GENERAL INFORMATION

Population: 1,50,000 (1991 census)
Altitude: 1500 metres (4995 ft)
Climate

	Temperature	
	Max.	Min.
Winter	22^0 C	4^0 C
Summer	24^0 C	14^0 C

Season: Throughout the year except during rainy season, May end to September.
Clothing
Summer: light tropical shawls and sweaters
Winter: woollens.

HOW TO GET THERE

By Air: Shillong is connected by Vayudoot air services with Calcutta, Guwahati and Silchar. Guwahati Airport (127 km. from Shillong) is connected by Indian Airlines services with major cities of India.
By Rail: The nearest railhead is Guwahati (104 km.) which is connected to all the major Indian stations.
By Road: Shillong is connected by good roads with all major tourist centres of the east. It is
104 km. from Guwahati,
295 km. from Kaziranga,
578 km. from Siliguri,
658 km. from Darjeeling and
1184 km. from Calcutta.
There are buses from Shillong to Silchar, Guwahati, Aizawl, Itanagar, Dimapur, Imphal, etc. Taxi takes 4 hours to reach Shillong from Guwahati.

LOCAL TRANSPORT

Taxis (unmetered) and bus services.

CONDUCTED TOURS

1. Half-day tour of SHILLONG.
2. Full-day tour to CHERRAPUNJI.
3. Weekly 2-day tour to KAZIRANGA WILDLIFE SANCTUARY. These conducted tours operate daily during season and twice a week in the off-season.
4. Full-day tour to JAKREM (Hot Springs).
5. Full-day tour to DAWKI (Bangladesh border) twice a week.

Reservation and Information: Government of Meghalaya Tourist Office, Police Bazaar. *Tel:* 226220

WHERE TO STAY (STD Code: 0364)

STANDARD
1. Hotel Pinewood Ashok
   Phone: 223081/223116
   Fax: 0364-224176
   Cable: PINEWOOD
BUDGET
2. Hotel Orchid (MTDC)
   Phone: 224933
3. Hotel Alpine Continental
   Phone: 225361
   Fax: 25199
   Cable: ALPOTEL
4. Polo Towers
   Phone: 222341/2
   Fax: 0364-22384
   Cable: MAGNUM

5. Orchid Lake Resort
   Phone: 224933
6. Shillong Club
   Phone: 226938

ENTRY FORMALITIES
Foreign tourists visiting Meghalaya require Restricted Area Permits from the Ministry of Home Affairs, New Delhi. Groups of four and more persons can get permits from
Liaison Office,
Govt. of Meghalaya,
9 Aurangzeb Road,
N. Delhi.
Tel: 3014417.
Also Russel Street,
Calcutta.
Tel: 290797/291775

WHAT TO SEE
1. WARD LAKE for boating.
2. LADY HYDARI PARK, gardens and waterfalls (ELEPHANT FALLS and others).
3. BARA BAZAAR. Crowds of tribal people in their traditional dresses can be seen here.
4. SHILLONG PEAK, 1960 metres high is revered as the 'abode of the gods'.
5. SHILLONG GOLF COURSE, one of the best in the region.
6. ARUNACHAL PRADESH, MEGHALAYA STATE MUSEUMS and the BUTTERFLY MUSEUM.

EXCURSIONS
1. CHERRAPUNJI (56 km.) at an altitude of 1300 metres is the wettest place in the world receiving 1140 cm. (450 in) of rainfall.
2. MAWPHLANG (24 km), rich in botanical wealth, especially orchids.
3. JAKREM HOT SPRINGS (64 km).
4. JOWAI (64 km) in the Jaintia Hills with excursions beyond to Thadlaskein Lake, Nartiang, Garampani, etc.
5. GUWAHATI (104 km), the gateway to Assam and the states of the north-east. It is a city surrounded by hills. Once the ancient city of Pragjyotishpur, "the light of the east", it is an important place of pilgrimage.
6. MANAS WILDLIFE SANCTUARY (273 km), home of the one-horned rhino. Animals and birds here can be seen from tree-houses or from the back of the elephants.

OTHER PLACES OF INTEREST IN THE EASTERN REGION
1. KOHIMA in Nagaland, where the Japanese army was halted in their invasion of India. Famous for its tribal culture and villages.
2. IMPHAL, the ancient capital of Manipur, rich in dances (of the classical Manipuri style), colourful festivals, handloom fabrics and handicrafts.
3. AIZAWL (in Mizoram), a hill station. Criss-crossed with ridges and valleys. Mizoram State has a great natural beauty.

4. AGARTALA (in Tripura) and its environs, rich in scenic beauty and old monuments.

Note: To visit Assam and Meghalaya, foreign tourists have to obtain Restricted Area Permits issued by the Ministry of Home Affairs, New Delhi. Inner Line Permits have to be obtained from the same Ministry for visits to the states of Arunachal Pradesh, Manipur, Mizoram, Nagaland and Tripura.

FESTIVALS OF SPECIAL LOCAL INTEREST

1. SHAD-SUK-MUNSIEM (April). This "Dance of the Joyful" held at Shillong, is a time for dancing and merry-making.
2. BEHDEINKLAM (June-July). It is a festival of the farmers, but spreads goodwill to all. For four days, there is continuous music, dancing and revelry (Held at Jowai—64 km).
3. NONG KREM DANCE (June-July), when sacrifices are made to ancestors and to the deity, U Shillong. Dancers wear their best dresses and jewellery.
4. WANGALA HARVEST FESTIVAL (November-December), also known as the Dance of the Hundred Drums. Held in the Garo Hills, 11 km. from Tura.

SPORTS

Golf tournaments in the season. Archery competitions are organised daily in Polo Ground. Bull fights are held at Mawsynram, 56 km. from Shillong, after the Behdeinklam festival.

KAZIRANGA NATIONAL PARK

GENERAL INFORMATION
Area: 430 sq kms.
Altitude: 67 metres (223 ft)
Climate:

	Temperature	
	Max.	Min.
Winter	24^0 C	7^0 C
Summer	35^0 C	18^0 C

Season: October to April. The Sanctuary is closed during the monsoons.
Clothing
Summer: cottons (a shawl or sweater and a scarf would be advisable for early morning visits to the forest).
Winter: woollens.

HOW TO GET THERE
By Air: Jorhat (97 km) is the nearest airport. However foreign tourist groups have to fly only via Guwahati (217 km).
By Rail: The convenient railhead is Furketing (72 km) on the mainline from where buses ply to Kaziranga.
By Road: Kaziranga is connected by good roads to Shillong,

Guwahati, Kohima and Imphal. It is 217 km. from Guwahati and 97 km. from Jorhat. Bus services operate to Jorhat, Guwahati, Dimapur, etc.

LOCAL TRANSPORT
Jeeps, minibuses and elephants are available for going round the forests. For those driving from Guwahati, tourist minibuses, tourist taxis, tourist cars, etc., can be hired.

CONDUCTED TOURS
1. From GUWAHATI (from October to May every weekend) there are four-day excursions to KAZIRANGA.
2. There are several conducted tours in and around Guwahati, cruises on the Brahmaputra, and excursions to MANAS, SHILLONG, SIBSAGAR, HAJO, etc.

Information: Assam Tourism, Guwahati.

ENTRY FORMALITIES
Foreigners Registration Offices of the Government of India at Delhi, Bombay, Calcutta and Madras are authorised to grant Restricted Area Permits to organised groups of foreign tourists for visiting Kaziranga. Tourists can, however, visit only Kaziranga on these permits. The other conditions are : (a) they have to travel in organised groups in tours organised by recognised travel agencies; (b) the duration of stay can be up to seven days; and (c) they will have to fly to Guwahati and drive from there and back.

To visit the rest of Assam and Shillong (Meghalaya) foreign tourists have to obtain Restricted Area Permits issued by the Ministry of Home Affairs.

WHERE TO STAY
BUDGET
1. Kaziranga Tourist Lodge Bungalow No.II (8 rooms with baths)
2. Kaziranga Tourist Lodge Bungalow No.I
3. Kaziranga Forest Lodge
Phone: 29
Cable: TOURISM

Information: Tourist Information Centre, Assam Government P.O. Kaziranga, District Jorhat, Assam: 78519 *Phone:* 23029.

WHAT TO SEE
1. Wild animals at KAZIRANGA. There are one-horned rhinos, Indian bison, swamp deer, sambar, hog deer, barking deer, wild pig, bear, tiger and leopard (rare) and others.
2. There are, besides, a pelicanry, and a large variety of bird life.
3. Gharial (long-snouted crocodile).

Note:
1. You can enter the National Park on elephant back and/or in a jeep or car.

2. There is a fee for still and cine photography.
3. Special film shows on wildlife are arranged on request.

EXCURSIONS
1. HILLS OF KARBI ANLONG to see coffee and rubber plantations.
2. KARBI VILLAGES.
3. TEA PLANTATIONS.
4. GARAMPANI (83 km), a hot spring.
5. JORHAT (97 km), the centre of Assam's tea industry.
6. NAMBOR RESERVE FOREST (60 km. from Jorhat).
7. GUWAHATI (217 km), on the banks of the Brahmaputra, was once the ancient city of Pragjyotishpur, "the Light of the East", the city of astronomy and astrology. It is an important place of pilgrimage and the centre of Tantric worship.
8. HAFLONG (355 km), a hill resort. At the nearby village, Jatinga birds land on the torch-bearing villagers at night. This is now called as the Jatinga bird phenomenon.

SOME OTHER PLACES OF INTEREST IN THE EASTERN REGION
1. MANAS WILDLIFE SANCTUARY (176 km from Guwahati), a tiger reserve and angler's paradise.
2. KOHIMA in Nagaland, where the Japanese army was halted in their invasion of India. Famous for its tribal culture and villages.
3. IMPHAL, the ancient capital of Manipur.

Woollen carpet of Arunachal Pradesh

Chapter 27

SIKKIM
India's Fairy-Tale State

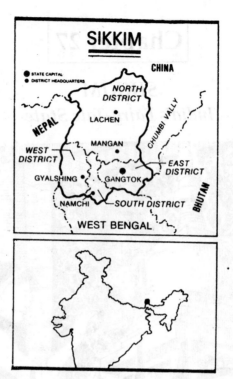

A view of the Himalayas

Sikkim is India's smallest State with some of the highest mountain peaks in the world. Till 1975, it was ruled by a semi-autonomous Raja called Chogyal. He had an American queen. In 1975, the popularly elected Legislature of Sikkim passed a unanimous resolution asking the Government of India to make Sikkim a part of the Indian Union. Thus, Sikkim became a State of the Indian Union with a popularly elected Chief Minister on April 26, 1975. Monarchy was abolished.

This fairy-tale State of India nestles in eastern Himalayas amidst orchids and oranges fanned by colourful butterflies, and overlooks the magnificent Himalayan peak KANCHENJUNGA (8,534 metres) the third highest in the world. Kanchenjunga is revered by the Sikkimese as their protective deity. It shares its borders with Tibet in the north, Bhutan in the east, Nepal in the west and the State of West Bengal in the south.

With an area of 7,300 sq. km. and measuring approximately 100 km. from north to south and 60 km. from east to west, the elevation ranges from 244 metres to 8,534 metres above sea level. Population is a little over 400,000.

Till the 18th century, the inhabitants of Sikkim were Lepchas, cultivators of Mongol origin, who came here in the 8th century. Then came the Bhutias from Tibet, who were sheep and yak breeders and traders. In the 18th and 19th centuries, a large number of immigrants of Nepalese origin came to Sikkim and they now constitute over 50 per cent of the total population. It is, therefore, an interesting mix of ethnic population — a friendly, colourful and simple people.

Amidst the grandeur of the mountain peaks, lush valleys, fast flowing rivers, terraced hills, Sikkim offers to visitors a rare and singular experience. Within a matter of hours, you can move from the subtropical heat of the lower valleys to the cold of rugged mountain slopes that reach up to regions of perpetual snows.

Sikkim can be reached both by air and by land routes. The nearest airport is Bagdogra from where you hire a jeep or taxi to reach Sikkim. From nearby Siliguri, there is a regular bus service operated by the Government of Sikkim to GANGTOK, the capital. The other convenient route is to go from Darjeeling to Teesta Bazar on the way to Kalimpong by bus and then take another bus from Kalimpong to Gangtok. The journey from Siliguri or Kalimpong to Gangtok is breathtaking. The Teesta Valley and the Teesta River dominate the scene for quite a long distance. A British naturalist, Dr. Joseph Hooker, wrote about Sikkim as early as 1849: "The view of the snowy range is one of the finest in Sikkim, the eye surveying at one glance the vegetation of the tropics and the Poles." Nothing has changed since then.

Desmand Doig, a journalist-artist, wrote not too long ago. "It is a moving experience to see a lama dressed in an impressive mask and brocades of God Kanchendzonga, prance and whirl against the backdrop of the mountain itself. So might have the Gods of classic Greece danced on Olympus."

Sikkim is Nature's own museum. Imagine a lake in the midst of a luxuriant forest and not a single leaf floating on it. And, even if a little leaf falls, a bird picks it up instantly. So the legend goes. This is the *Wishing Lake* or Tsho - she-Tsho as the Sikkimese call it.

You can also lose yourself in the romantic solitude of mountain meadows, cascading rivers or densely forested ridges. There are opportunities to float on the rivers by raft or seek out rare wildlife. During your wanderings, it may be interesting to look out for an electric blue butterfly. Hear a cuckoo gayly singing for you. Sikkim is also home to such exotic birds as woodpeckers, kingfishers and a hundred other varieties. The lingering fragrance of flowers is not something you can forget on your return. The State offers 4,000 varieties of plant species — magnolias, rhododendron, drons, janiers, blue poppies, primulas — and orchids in stunning sizes and colours.

Sikkim is home to the rare Red Panda, peering from a tree top. There are musk deer, the Himalayan black bear and yaks in the Alpine zone.

Religion Dominates Life
Religion forms the main thread in the fabric of life of the Sikkimese. With close to 194 monasteries, the influence of Buddhism is all-pervasive. Even in the remote mountain regions, near wind-swept summits, fringing monasteries or private houses, flutter the ubiquitous prayer flags.

The main monasteries are PEMAYANGTSE and TASHIDING in west Sikkim, ENCHEY in Gangtok and RUMTEK near Gangtok, RALONG in south and PHODONG and TOLUNG in north Sikkim. Influencing the lifestyle and cultural heritage of the people, each monastery is host to a number of festivals which are a singular experience in pomp and pageantry. The lama dances complete with fierce masks, gorgeous brocade costumes, music and chants are at once evocative and out of this world.

The Sikkimese Nepali is the inheritor of the legacy of Hindu traditions. The visitor to Sikkim is spellbound by the colourful festivals of Dasain/Tower celebrated by the Hindu Nepali population. Invocations are made to Goddess Durga and barley seeds are planted in prayer rooms. Their other important festival is Dipavali in October-November.

Exploring Sikkim

A perfect symbol of the confluence of the past and the present is Gangtok, the capital of Sikkim. Built on the flank of a ridge, Gangtok is 1600 mts. above sea level. The town's unique ambience derives from its happy blend of tradition and modernity. Alongside the deeply felt presence of stupas and monasteries, Gangtok also bustles like other small towns. Outside Gangtok, peace and solitude prevail everywhere.

AROUND GANGTOK

The HANDICRAFTS & HANDLOOM EMPORIUM is Centre for promoting and keeping alive the traditional arts and crafts, a veritable storehouse of exquisite carpets, blankets and shawls in 'Lepcha' weaves. (Closed on second Saturdays and Government holidays.) It is run by the Government and prices are fixed.

The DEER PARK is a haven for nature lovers, where the Red Panda and fleet-footed deer can be observed in their natural habitat. An imposing statue of the Buddha is situated here. (Open from 8.00 a.m. - 11a.m. on working days and 8.00 a.m. to 5.00 p.m. on holidays.)

DO-DRUL CHORTEN (Stupa) is one of the most important Stupas of Sikkim, built by Trulsi Rimpoche, head of the Nyingma Order. Valuable relies and two statues of Rimpoche are to be seen here.

The RESEARCH INSTITUTE OF TIBETOLOGY is a world renowned centre for study of Buddhist philosophy and religion, a treasure house of rare thankas, statues, over 200 Buddhist icons and prized objects of art (closed on second Saturdays and Government holidays).

The ORCHID SANCTUARY is an exotic sight of over 200 species of orchids set amidst a beautiful landscape. Situated just below the Institute of Tibetology. Sikkim is one of the few places in the world with such a diverse (600) variety of orchids.

The ENCHEY MONASTERY, 3 km. from Gangtok, is 200 years old built on the site blessed by the great Tantrik master, Lama Druptab Karpa, known for his flying powers. Religious masked dance is performed on the 18 and 19th of the 12th Tibetan month.

The ORCHIDARIUM is maintained by the Department of Forests. Here one can see a spectrum of colourful orchids and other rare tropical and temperate plants.

The PUMTER MONASTERY is a must for every visitor. Situated 24 km. away, the seat of the Kagyu Order, this is a close replica of the original Kagyu in Tibet. Here one can find some of the most unique art objects of the world.

TASHI VIEWPOINT is situated 8 km. from Gangtok. This site offers a breathtaking view of the majestic MOUNT KANCHENZONGA and MOUNT SINIOLCHU.

PHODONG MONASTERY, 38 km. from Gangtok, is one of the six major monasteries of Sikkim. About 4 km. from Phodong is the uniquely architectured LABRANG MONASTERY.

A Mountain Adventure

If you visit Sikkim and you are young at heart, you are bound to undertake some trekking — that is the best way to see this beautiful State. The unspoiled natural splendour and tranquillity of the countryside has made some regions of Sikkim ideal for adventure tourism. Listen to the sound of the winds among the trees, feel the way of the rocks, watch the snowclad peaks as you trek up a mountain side dwarfed by the ramparts of the echoing cliffs.

Trekking at a leisurely pace takes one from YUKSAM situated 5800 feet above sea level to DZONGRI (13,800 ft.) in almost two days. All along the route one wonders at the spectacular mountain scenes. And for those who would like to rough it up a little more, the trek from Dzongri to GOCHALA through spectacular majestic mountain ranges is equally rewarding.

If you feel inclined you can even go on a yak safari — another experience unique to Sikkim.

And those who want to see some white water action there is plenty in store for them. The rivers of Sikkim sparkle and beckon. River rafting tours and kayaking are organised on the Teesta and Rangeet rivers.

Among its wildlife sanctuaries, the Kanchenjunga National Park with an area of 850 sq kms is the largest. Ecologically untouched, it provides natural protection to flora and fauna.

GANGTOK

GENERAL INFORMATION

Population: 50,000 (1991 census)
Altitude: 1547 metres (5152 ft)
Climate

	Temperature	
	Max.	Min.
Winter	13^0 c	0^0 c
Summer	23^0 c	21^0 c

Season: Mid-February to late May and October to mid-December.
Clothing:
Summer: light woollens.
Winter: heavy woollens.

HOW TO GET THERE

By Air: Bagdogra (124 km) is the nearest airport. Indian Airlines services connect Bagdogra with Calcutta, Delhi, Patna, Guwahati and Imphal.

By Rail: The nearest railway stations are Siliguri (114 km) and New Jalpaiguri (125 km). They are connected by rail to Calcutta, Guwahati, Patna, Delhi, Bhubaneshwar, Madras and Trivandrum.

By Road: Gangtok is connected by road to all the important places in the east. It is
67km. from Kalimpong,
124km. from Bagdogra,
88km. from Darjeeling (direct route),
119km. from Darjeeling via Kalimpong,
584km. from Patna and
725km. from Calcutta.

There are regular bus services from Gangtok to Rumtek, Siliguri, Bagdogra, Kalimpong and Darjeeling.

LOCAL TRANSPORT
Tourist cars, luxury coaches, jeeps, landrovers and wagonnettes are available.

CONDUCTED TOURS
Half-day tour of the city. Half-day tour to RUMTEK MONASTERY.
Information: Sikkim Tourist Office, Mahatma Gandhi Marg, Gangtok. *Phone*: 22064.

Note: Foreign nationals require permits to visit Sikkim. Intending visitors should apply to the Ministry of Home Affairs, Government of India, New Delhi, through Indian Missions abroad at least six weeks in advance. Permits are issued liberally for visits up to 7 days for Gangtok, Rumtek and Phodang. Tourist groups are given special permits of 10 days for trekking in the Dzongri area, if accompanied by guides assigned by the Govt. of Sikkim.

WHERE TO STAY (STD CODE: 03592)
STANDARD
1. Tashi Delek
   Phone: 22991, 22038
   Fax: 03592-22362
   Cable: NORKHILL
2. Nor Khill
   Phone: 23186-7
3. Netuk House
   Phone: 22374
4. Martam Village Resort
   Phone: 23314

BUDGET
5. Hotel Mayur
   Phone: 22752, 22825
6. Tibet
   Phone: 22523
   Fax: 03592-22707
7. Central Hotel
   Phone: 22553
8. Orchid
   Phone: 22381
9. Denzong Inn
   Phone: 22692

WHAT TO SEE
1. CHORTEN, a stupa built in 1945, is a great religious centre with valuable relics and two huge statues of Guru Rimpoche (Padmasambhava).
2. DEER PARK with a statue of the preaching Buddha.
3. ORCHID SANCTUARY with over 200 species of orchids.
4. TSUKLA-KHANG, the royal monastery of the former Chogyals or rulers of Sikkim. It has priceless Buddhist treasures.
5. ENCHEY MONASTERY with its exhibits of images and religious objects.
6. RESEARCH INSTITUTE OF TIBETOLOGY has a large collection of icons, tankhas (tapestries) and rare books.

EXCURSIONS
1. ORCHIDARIUM (14 km), of the Forest Department maintains this with a wide variety of orchids and exotic plants.

2. RUMTEK MONASTERY (24 km), noted for its carved and painted woodwork, magnificent murals, icons and rare manuscripts.
3. PHODANG (28 km), site of one of the most beautiful monasteries.
4. PEMAYANGTSE MONASTERY (137 km), at a height of 2085 metres. It is the starting point for visits to the holy Tashiding Monastery, pine-forested Yaksam, Dhubdi (Sikkim's oldest monastery), and treks to Bakkhim and Dzongri (3962 metres). There is a Tourist Lodge at Pemayangtse.
Food: Chinese and Tibetan is more popular. Indian and continental food is available in major hotels.

SHOPPING
Hand-woven woollen carpets, blankets and shawls, Lepcha woven bags, *choksies* (tables) exquisitely carved and painted handmade dolls, painted masks, bamboo artifacts and handmade paper. Sikkim also makes its local liquor out of paan (betel leaf).

FESTIVALS OF SPECIAL LOCAL INTEREST
1. Religious MASKED DANCES performed by Lamas for two days at Enchey (January), Rumtek (February to June), Phodang (November and December) and Pemayangtse (February).
2. LOSOONG is Sikkim's New Year's day (November-December) when the Dance of the Black Hat (denoting the triumph of good over evil) is performed.
3. PONG LHABSOL (August-September) celebrated in worship of the mountain, Kanchenjunga. Colourful masked dances are performed by Lamas in the courtyard of monasteries.
4. HARVEST FESTIVAL celebrated in December.
5. DANCES BY THE LEPCHAS, the original inhabitants of Sikkim (December).

TREKKING
Sikkim, with its flora, is a paradise for trekkers.
1. The most popular trek is from Gangtok to Pemayangtse via Rumtek. Then on to Yaksum, Bakkhim and Dzongri.
2. A popular low-altitude trek is from Namchi to Pemayangtse back.
3. There are many other treks such as:
   (a) Pemayangtse to Gangtok — 9 days.
   (b) Naya Bazaar to Gangtok — 8 days.

You can hire equipment from Sikkim Tourist Dapartment or bring it with you.

Sikkim Tourist Office makes arrangement for trekking in the state and yak safaris. Arrangements can also be made through the Himalayan Mountaineering Institute, Darjeeling. (See under Darjeeling).

Entertainment Office
Gangtok shuts down early unless there is a festival or *chaam* (dance)

under way. Hotels and most good restaurants have bars. Try the local brandies or *chang*—just remember these are strong.

Within the Tashicho Dzong Monastery, Gangtok.

Chapter 28

ISLAND RESORTS OF INDIA
Andaman & Nicobar Islands and Lakshadweep

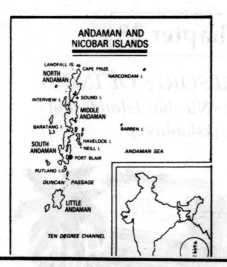
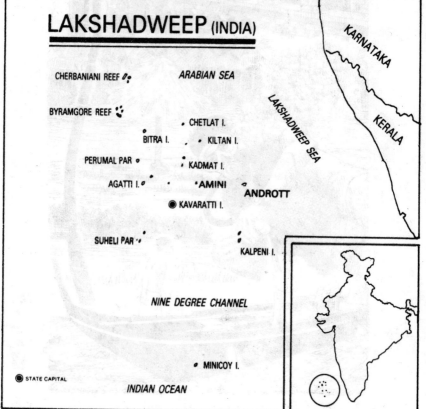

ANDAMAN AND NICOBAR

Opened recently for international tourism by the Government of India, Andaman and Nicobar Islands are located in the heart of Bay of Bengal in an idyllic and tranquil setting away from the mainland of India. Of the 321 islands of this archipelago which stretch from the tips of Burma, the Philippines, Malaysia and Indonesia, only 328 are inhabited. The islands are tropical with rain forest, beautiful, crescent-shaped beaches and clean lagoons edged by coral reefs. The rich flora and fauna makes these islands an ideal holiday resort.

PORT BLAIR, its capital is 1200 kilometres south-east of the coast of West Bengal and 1190 kilometres east of Madras, almost equi-distance from both Calcutta and Madras. There are regular air services of Indian Airlines from Calcutta and Madras. The flight takes about two hours.

One can also travel to Port Blair by sea. Regular shipping services ply from Calcutta, Madras and Vishakhapatnam to Port Blair. The voyage takes about three days and the ship stays for two days in the Port.

The islands are a Union Territory of India which means that the territory is centrally administered and the local Governor who runs the administration is responsible to the Central Government. The area is 8,247 square kilometres and population about 280,000.

The islands are home to some of the ancient aboriginal tribes speaking different languages of their own. The tribes fall in three main groups. The Ongas, concentrated on the little Andaman are small, dark-complexioned tribe of hunters who wear no clothes other than tassled genital decorations and they love colourful make-up. The Nicobarese whose home is in CAR NICOBAR are fair-complexioned people. They have started adjusting to contemporary way of life. They live in organised villages and survive on fish, coconut and pigs. The last group — the Shompens — are found on GREAT NICOBAR. They shy away from contacts with the immigrants and have not yet integrated.

When the British took over the islands in 1869, they used them as a penal settlement for freedom fighters of India. They imprisoned them in the dreaded CELLULAR JAIL — now a national monument. Most of them perished during their imprisonment due to torture or diseases. Prisoners who survived till independence were freed. Many prisoners settled in the islands after their release and they now make a major part of the population of these islands.

These are evergreen islands of tropical forests with exotic flora, birds, coral reefs, lagoons and abundant marine life. Some of the trees reach the enormous height of 43 metres with branches spread out to form large canopies. Among animals, there is vast variety of deer, wild cats, iguana and pigs. Wild goats roam about in volcanic islands of BARREN and NARCODAM. Islands are also home to the green lizard, found nowhere else in the world except in Madagascar. Besides, there are many varieties of reptiles. The sea around supports a fantastic variety of fish— tuna, sardine, anchovy, barracuda, mullet, mackerel, pomfret, hilsa, crab and oyster. The rivers of Andamans hold crocodiles. There are exotic trees with pale, pink, scarlet and orange flowers — some very fragrant. There are shrubs bursting with flowers like the yellow hibiscus and white lily and a myriad of orchids.

Agriculture is the primary occupation of the people. They grow rice, coconut and arecanut. Attempts are also being made to grow spices and rubber on a large scale. Timber is the primary export of the islands.

PORT BLAIR

Port Blair has some fine hotels including one run by the Welcomgroup chain. Visitors have to stay in Port Blair. They are not allowed to stay on other islands. However, your hotel can easily arrange visits to neighbouring islands.

The capital was named after Reginald Blair who conducted surveys of the area in 1789. Until World War II, it was essentially a penal settlement. It was only after independence that Andaman became a good town with modern facilities of transportation and communications. The town has excellent roads and plenty of taxis.

Built in 1906, the CELLULAR JAIL — now a national monument — held over 400 political prisoners during the struggle for independence. It is a massive whitewashed building facing the sea. It had 698 cells. The Museum within shows the instruments of torture used by the jailors.

The ZOO ON HADDO PROMONTORY has some interesting animals like the salt-water crocodiles, hornbills and crab-eating monkeys.

The ANTHROPOLOGICAL MUSEUM exhibits mini models of villages of local tribes. There is a BURMESE TEMPLE at PHOENIX BAY and a well-equipped COTTAGE INDUSTRIES EMPORIUM. Port Blair also has the largest air-conditioned HERBARIUM in India.

From MARINE JETTY, you can take a ferry to ABERDECON MARKET on. VIPER ISLAND, where executions used to take place, or go past the CHATHAM SAW MILL - one of the oldest and the biggest saw mills in Asia.

Scuba diving

The majority of the inhabited islands are reserves where tribes are protected from contact with the outside world. Only a few are open to the visitors. Most hotels and tour operators in Port Blair organise picnics, scuba diving and snorkelling trips. An overnight trip to CINQUE ISLAND is also offered which includes small trek through the forests giving opportunities for bird-watching.

The closest beach is CORBYN'S COVE — 6 kilometres from the town. The hotel here offers various facilities including wind-surfing and they have equipment for all kinds of water sports. There are beaches also at WANDOOR BEACH, 25 kilometres and SHIRYA TEPU at the southern tip of the island. Other places worth a visit are the BOTANICAL GARDENS, 14 kilometres, BURMAH NALLA and WIMBERLYGANJ LUMBERING CENTRE, in the jungle.

Other interesting places are BARREN ISLAND, known for boiling water which flows out of an extinct valcano. CHIRYA TAPU is the Birds' island in Hindi. MADHUBAN (14 kilometres) is the place where wild elephants are tamed and trained for timber work. MOUNT HARRIET on top of a hill was once the summer resort under the British. It is now a good place to have a bird's-eye view of Port Blair. ROSS ISLAND has the ruins of the British Chief Commissioner's residence, a church, a temple as well as other offices of the government.

Car Nicobar is a flat island compared to the Andaman group which is hilly. Interesting sights here are huts built on stilts. The people enter into the floor of the hut by a ladder. Landing at Car Nicobar can be exciting. At low tide, one may have to wade in water to the shore from a motor boat or canoe.

There are inter-island ships which can take you to different islands. Harbour cruises are arranged by the local administration in fibre-glass boats.

LAKSHADWEEP - The Resplendent Island

Yet another island resort opened very recently for tourism are the Lakshadweep group of islands, scattered some 200 to 400 kilometres west of the Kerala coast. It is an archipelago of 27 coral islands — only ten of these are inhabited by some 50,000 people. People here are like those in Kerala and they speak Malayalam. The majority of the population consists of Muslims converted to Islam in the seventh century A.D. by an Arab missionary, Hazarat Ubaidulla.

The people here are highly civilised and cultured, although they are somewhat shy because of their isolated existence for centuries. Crime is totally unknown. People live on fishing and coconut cultivation. Land is very fertile. Coir industry, based on abundant supply of coconut fibres, also provides employment to people.

Fishing in a lagoon

The climate is tropical, ranging throughout the year from 20⁰C to 32⁰C. From May 15 to September 15, the islands are closed to tourists because of turbulent sea and heavy monsoons.

Only five islands have been opened to tourists to make sure that environments are not affected. Of these four are open to domestic tourists and only one — BANGARAM ISLAND — is open for foreign tourists. The four other islands are KAVARATTI, KALPANI, KADMAT and MINICOY. Accommodation consists of tourist huts on the beach. At Bangaram, the Bangaram Beach Resort is a 30-room hotel of international standards. On other islands facilities are minimal. Lakshadweep is for those who want to get away from the hustle and bustle of crowded cities and want to enjoy peace and quiet on the sea. The late Prime Minister Rajiv Gandhi made Bangaram popular by spending his holidays here with his family. Day tourism is being promoted by administration by allowing passenger liners to anchor off the permitted islands so that the tourists can go ashore and return to the ship the same day. Three passenger liners ply between Cochin and Lakshadweep islands.

Vayudoot operates regular flights from Cochin to Agate island — the closest inhabited island to Bangaram. From Agate passengers are brought to Bangaram by fast boats and brought back to let them catch the departing flights.

Although the total area of all the islands is mere 32 square kilometres, the islands are so spread out that this Union Territory of India has 20, 000 square kilometres of territorial waters and 700, 000 square kilometres of economic zone. The smallest inhabited island is BITRA (0.1 square kilometres) with a population of 181. Kavaratti is the administrative capital of Lakshadweep islands. It is also the most developed island and can boast of 52 mosques. The biggest, the UJRA MOSQUE - is said to have been built of driftwood. Other attractions of the island are an aquarium with a vast variety of fish and beautiful coral formations. Marine life on the lagoon along the island are out of this world.

Lakshadweep islands lie one beyond the other, threaded by almost a continuous line of silver sand beaches and fringed by dense rows of coconut palms. The calm, clear stretches of blue water are ideal for swimming, water skiing, scuba-diving or snorkelling. Of the five islands open to tourists, Kalpani is one which is surrounded by three uninhabited islands sharing the same large lagoon . Tourist facilities include glass-bottomed boats that reveal the fascinating world of underwater fish and beautiful coral formations.

Minicoy, another permitted island, has a hundred-year-old lighthouse built by the British. The island has one of the largest lagoons in the archipelago. The inhabitants of Minicoy are somewhat different from other islanders in dress, food and language. Their language is Mahl, written from right to left in Diveji script. They have an endearing folk dance called Lava performed by men.

Tuna fishing, wooden handicrafts and boat building are their principal occupations.

Bangaram is a beautiful island, uninhabited, for use of the international tourists. Huts have been put up with modern facilities to

The uninhabited Pitti island

house and look after the international tourists. It has three more similarly uninhabited islands close by which can be visited by tourists. All the four islands share the same lagoon. It is great fun to watch the changing colours and shades of water in the lagoon at different hours of the day and moods of sky from time to time.

Facilities for communication with the mainland and between the islands have been improved in recent years. Tourist facilities in the shape of luxury cruise ships to go round the islands are being developed. Potentially, the archipelago could offer an interesting holiday for cruising in the crystal-clear waters of the lagoons. It provides opportunities for deep-sea fishing and for bathing on lonely beaches in the way you want.

This archipelago in the Arabian sea was called Laccadives during the British Raj, an anglicised name given to original Lakshadweep. The new name was given to these islands in 1973.

ANDAMAN & NICOBAR ISLANDS

GENERAL INFORMATION

Population: 277,989 (1991 census)
Altitude: 79 metres (263 ft)
Climate

	Temperature	
	Max.	Min.
Winter	31^0 c	22^0 c
Summer	31^0 c	24^0 c
Rainfall	999 mm	58 mm

Season: September to April for those who wish to swim, dive and take part in under-water sports.
Clothing: Cottons throughout the year. (Carry an umbrella or raincoat with you.)

HOW TO GET THERE

By Air: Indian Airlines services connect Port Blair with Calcutta and Madras.
Recently, private airlines too have started operations.
By Rail: Nil
By Road: Nil.
By Sea: Passenger ships ply between Port Blair and Calcutta/Madras/Vishakhapatnam. Travel time three days one way.

LOCAL TRANSPORT

Tourist taxis, unmetered taxis and buses available. The Marine Department operates regular inter-island ferry services from Port Blair to other points. Helicopter services now operate from Port Blair to the northern and southern islands.

CONDUCTED TOURS
1. Half day sightseeing tour of PORT BLAIR.
2. WANDOOR tour: Full day.
3. CHIRYA TAPU tour: Full day.
4. CORBYN'S COVE tour (on Sundays only): Half day.
5. HARBOUR CRUISES:
   (a) A two-hour harbour cruise thrice a week.
   (b) Regular harbour cruise from Phoenix Bay Jetty.

Information: Directorate of Tourism *Tel*: 20642

WHERE TO STAY (STD Code: 03192)
DELUXE
1. Welcomgroup Bay Island
   Phone: 20881
   Fax: 21389
   Cable: WELCOTEL
STANDARD
2. Andaman Beach Resort
   Phone: 21462, 21465
   Fax: 21463
   Cable: TRAVELAIDS
3. Shompen
   Phone: 20360, 20425
4. Suiclair's Bay View
   Phone: 20973, 20425
   Telex: 0695216SLRAIN
BUDGET
5. Teal House
   Phone: 20642
6. Hornbill Nest
   Phone: 20018
7. Dolphin Yatri Niwas
8. Hotel Shalimar
   Phone: 21963
9. Nicobar Cottage
   Phone: 20207
10. Negapode Nest
    Phone: 20207

Reservations: Directorate of Tourism, Port Blair *Tel*: 30933 *Fax*: 20656

ENTRY FORMALITIES
Foreign nationals travelling individually are given permission by the Immigration authorities to visit Port Blair Municipal Area, Jolly Buoy and Cinque Islands for a period of 30 days, on arrival at Port Blair.

Permits can also be obtained from Indian Missions abroad and the Regional Immigration authorities at Bombay, Delhi, Calcutta and Madras.

Foreign nationals in groups of 6 to 20 are allowed to visit GRUB, RED SKIN, SNOB and BOAT ISLANDS with prior permission from the Chief Secretary, Andaman and Nicobar Administration, Port Blair.

Indians do not need permit. Permits are, however, required to visit Nicobar island - available from Deputy Commissioner, Port Blair.

WHAT TO SEE
1. THE CELLULAR JAIL, the Bastille of India, now a national memorial, where India's freedom fighters were incarcerated by the British in single room cells from where they could not

see or communicate with anyone. Also Museum attached to the Jail.
2. The CHATTAM SAW MILL where rare species of timber can be seen.
3. MARINE MUSEUM with 350 species of sea-life.
4. ANTHROPOLOGICAL MUSEUM.
5. CORBYN'S COVE, a picturesque beach.

EXCURSIONS
1. BURMAH NALLA (17 km.) where lumber operations are carried out by trained elephants.
2. MADHUBAN (14 km) where elephants are trained.
3. SIPPIGHAT FARM (14 km). Agricultural demonstration farm where tropical cash crops and spices are grown.
4. WANDOOR BEACH (28 km) offers a picturesque landscape and is ideal for swimming. This area has been declared a Marina National Park.
5. CHIRYA TAPU (30 km). This southern tip of South Andamans is also known as the Bird Island.

CRUISES AROUND THE HARBOUR
1. HOPE TOWN, Panighat. Lord Mayo was assassinated by an Afghan convict here.
2. NORTH BAY, a long and sandy beach.
3. VIPER ISLAND, which used to be the penal settlement before the construction of the Cellular Jail.
4. ROSS ISLAND, administrative headquarters during the Raj days. There are many monuments here.
5. GRUB, RED SKIN, JOLLY BUOY, BOAT SNOB and CINQUE ISLANDS. These are picturesque Islands offering exotic coral and marine life. Sandy, virgin beaches and crystal-clear waters are ideal for snorkelling, diving and under-water photography.

SHOPPING
Shell craft, shell jewellery, wood carvings and tribal crafts are available in the markets and in the emporia.

SPORTS
Diving, windsurfing, fishing angling, water-skiing, sailing, snorkelling, collecting rare shells on the beaches and studying under-water marine life. Equipment for the above is available on hire from the Andaman Beach Resort, Corbyn's Cove.

INDIA'S NEIGHBOURING COUNTRIES

Chapter 29

NEPAL
A DESTINATION FOR ALL SEASONS

Scaling the misty heights

The world is no longer a mystery. There are no new countries to discover and no new regions to explore. Yet, Nepal is one destination which is still unique and not known to most people of the world. It is shrouded in mystery.

A visit to Nepal is like a trip through the time-machine. There are many areas in Nepal which have yet to emerge from the Middle Age, areas which are still not connected by roads and where people have seen neither a rail nor an automobile. The hardy people of this only Hindu kingdom in the world are brave though somewhat shy, yet warm and hospitable.

Nepal is also the land of great contrasts. Its unconquerable mountain peaks provide a vivid contrast with hand-sculpted landscape of farms in mountain valleys. The tiny compact houses of the people provide another interesting contrast with the vast, icy glaciers and mighty highland vistas. The lowlands of the Terai are a mere one hundred metres above sea level, yet the country's highest mountain EVEREST soars over 8800 metres. The distance between the two extremities, as the crow flies, is not more than 150 km. This, together with monsoon rains along the slopes facing south has resulted in compacting virtually all climate zones on the planet earth. The country, therefore, provides a safe home to a variety of birds, animals and plants.

The Himalayas are the youngest and the highest mountain chains in the world. About a third of its 1000 km. long Himalayan range lies within Nepal. It has a convergence of 1310 magnificent pinnacles and peaks over 6000 metres including the world's eight of the 14 giant peaks over 8000 metres high. The world's highest peak Mount Everest (Sagarmatha) and the third highest KANCHANJUNGA (8848 and 8586 metres respectively), are in Nepal. The other six peaks in Nepal are LOHTSE (8816 metres), MAKALU (8463 metres), CHO OYU (8201 metres), DHAULAGIRI (8167 metres), MANALSU (8163 metres) and ANNAPURNA I (8090 metres).

Nepal, with an area of 144, 577 sq. km., is landlocked. Roughly, it is of the size of England or Florida in the United States with a population of

Mt. Everest   Mt. Ama-Dablam

20 million. About half a million people now live in the capital, KATHMANDU.

Geographically, the country lies between 80.4' and 88.12' east longitude and 26.22' and 30.4' north latitude. It is bounded on the north by Tibet — the autonomous region of China; on the east by Sikkim and West Bengal; on the south by Bihar and Uttar Pradesh and on the west by Uttar Pradesh. Climatically, it lies in the temperate zone with the added advantage of altitude. Except for the Terai region in the extreme south, even the mid-valleys are seldom higher than 1220 metres above sea-level.

Till 1951, Nepal was a closed book for foreign visitors. Up to 1964, it was the mystic land reserved only for hardy climbers and explorers. In recent years the country has opened its doors wide to foreign travellers and about 400,000 of them are able to make it to the wonderland every year. Major airlines like Lufthansa, Thai, Indian Airlines, and of course, the national carrier Royal Nepal Airlines link it to the rest of the world. Experienced tour operators of Nepal provide excellent service.

The country can be broadly divided into three regions:

HIMALAYAN REGION: The altitude of this region ranges between 4877 metres and 8848 metres with the snow-line running around 4877 metres. It includes all the major peaks of the Himalayas mentioned above.

MOUNTAIN REGION: This region accounts for about 64 per cent of the total land area of the country. It is formed by the MAHABHARATA RANGE which soars up to 4877 metres. To its south lies the lower CHURIA RANGE whose altitude varies from 6210 metres to 1524 metres.

A breathtaking view of the Himalayas

TERAI REGION: The lowland Terai region which has a width of 26 to 32 km. and a maximum altitude of 305 metres occupies about 17 per cent of land area. KACHANAKAWAL, the lowest point in the country, has an altitude of only 70 metres. It is located in Jhapa district of eastern Terai. This goes to prove that the country is a destination for all seasons. It welcomes visitors both in winter and summer. One often wonders why Western visitors prefer Nepal only during winter months. The only reason appears to be that they combine their Nepal trip with the visit to India, where winter months are generally preferred. About 60 per cent of foreigners come to Nepal from Delhi. The off-season of Western visitors is a boon to Indian visitors who make use of good Nepalese hotels during summer months at highly discounted prices. If you opt to visit Nepal in summer, surely you will find the trip very economical. And enjoy the pleasant climate too. Indians constitute over one-third of foreign visitors. Indians do not require visa to enter Nepal.

HISTORY

One knows very little about the early history of Nepal. It is believed that the first inhabitants of Nepal were of Mongoloid or Tibetan stock who migrated to the fertile valleys in the south. They were mainly Buddhists, following the Tantric rituals of Tibetan Buddhism. In the early centuries of the Christian era, they were joined by Indo-Aryans from northern India who were Hindus. Gradually, the Hindus took charge of the country. They were followed by a tribal group called the Lichhivis who were also Buddhists converted by Lord Buddha himself. But, very little is known of their history. Nepal in those days was divided into small principalities which were fighting against each other. It was not till the arrival of the Mallas from north India that Nepal was launched into in its first flowering of social and artistic creativity. The Mallas also took control of a major part of present day Nepal and Tibet. But, pattern of small, independent kingdoms continued and Nepal could not be unified. The Mallas love for art and architecture was at its peak. They had three separate kingdoms in the Kathmandu Valley itself, with their capitals at Kathmandu — then known as Kantipur; PATAN, called Lalitpur, and BHADGAON, then called Bhaktpur. From then onwards, the history of Nepal is better documented. They have left their stone inscriptions in temples and carved them on the bases of statues.

As the Mallas grew weaker due to family feuds, they were replaced by another dynasty — the Shahs. It was during the rule of King Prithvi Narayan Shah (1730-75) that Nepal became more unified. He came from the Gurkha region. He was the first to use these tough fighters to strengthen his rule. The Gurkhas are still valued as great fighters and a large number of them are serving in the Indian and British armies. Their pensions and salaries remitted to Nepal are still the largest source of foreign exchange earnings of the country. Now, income from tourism is higher. The present King Birendra Bir Bikram Shah Dev, is the 10th in the dynasty. The King Prithvi Narayan Shah was responsible for the exclusion of European traders from the country whom he did not trust. As the Shah dynasty became weak another clan — the Ranas—took over in 1846. The monarch only became a figurehead while the Ranas ruled the country. The British were able to pressurise Nepal when Nepal lost a war to the British in 1817. Nepal accepted nominal allegiance to the British. As a result, the Gurkhas fought several wars for Great Britain. They sided with them during the first War of Indian Independence in 1857. The British were so pleased with their loyalty that they returned some of the territories they had occupied after the defeat of the Nepalese. Subsequently, the Gurkhas fought other battles for Britain, including World Wars I & II. They fought in all parts of the world.

After a popular revolution masterminded by the ninth King Tribhuvan of Shah dynasty in 1950-51, the Rana regime was wiped out with the assistance of India. King Tribhuvan died in 1955 and was succeeded by his son Mahendra, father of the reigning king. Nepal became a member of the United Nations in 1955.

King Birendra, the present King, abolished party system. Only a person acceptable to the king could be appointed Prime Minister.

A popular democratic revolt in 1990 led to the re-establishment of a multi-party democratic system based on adult franchise. The new democratic Constitution of the kingdom was promulgated on November 9, 1990. The king remains the titular head of the government. In 1994, Nepal elected communist party to form the government which has since been replaced by coalition government.

THE PEOPLE

The 20 million people of Nepal consist of an assortment of races and tribes living in different regions. They follow varied customs, traditions, wear different costumes and speak different languages and dialects. The Gurangs and Magars live mainly in the west and on the southern slopes of ANNAPURNA HIMACHULTI and GANESH HAMAL. The Rais, Limbus and Sunwars inhabit the eastern mountains. The Sherpas popularly known as "tigers of snow" live up to a height of 4000 metres. The Newars mostly inhabit the valley of Kathmandu. The Tharu and Dhimals live in the Terai region. The population of Nepal is concentrated around Kathmandu, Patan, Bhadgaon, BIRATNAGAR, BIRGUNJ, NEPALGUNJ, BHAIRAHAWA and other new towns in the Terai region. The Gurkhas inhabit mountainous areas. Brahmins, Chhetris and Thakuris are spread all over the country. Nepali written in Devanagri script is the official language and is spoken by most people. English is taught in High Schools. Literacy in Nepal is only 29 per cent and per capita annual income US $ 180. 90 per cent of the population are Hindus, 5.3 per cent Buddhists and the rest others.

RELIGION, CULTURE AND FESTIVALS

There is a complex blending of Hinduism and Buddhism in Nepal. Although a Hindu kingdom, all deities are worshipped by Hindus and Buddhists alike. A remarkable feature of the land is the mutual bond of friendship between the people of the two religions. The exquisite Nepalese pagodas enshrine colossal bronze and stone images. The traditional Hindu temples and Buddhist stupas preserve fascinating wood carvings and stone sculptures. The rich cultural heritage of Nepal is manifested by the diverse social customs and hundreds of festivals. Some of these include Babarsha, the Nepalese New Year's day (2nd week of April), a national holiday celebrated with great pomp and show at Bhadgaon, Linga Jatra or Bisket is celebrated on this day and Baisakh Purnima (May), the birthday of Lord Buddha is celebrated with great veneration. Homage is paid to the 'Light of Asia' at SWAYAMBHU, LUMBINI and other places. The Red Machhendranath Rath Jatra is a spectacular chariot festival in Patan (begins in April and lasts for months). A similar festival in Kathmandu, known as White Machhendranath Rath Jatra is lasts four days (March-April). Dhumji is celebrated by Sherpas during July. Loshar Festival is observed by all Tibetan-speaking people.

Gai Jatra — the new festival—is an 8-day carnival of dance and music. On the first day of the festival, families who have witnessed death during the year send persons dressed up as cows to parade through the main thoroughfares of the city. DESAIN, Durga Puja, is the principal festival of all Nepalese, celebrated with great fanfare and rejoicing (October). A fortnight's holiday is declared for the nation. INDRA JATRA (August-September) is the occasion for worship of Lord Indra, the king of the gods in heaven. Kumari worship is the main attraction of this festival. DIWALI, the festival of lights is celebrated for five days in October-November. SHIVARATRI, the night of Lord Shiva, is famous for the fair held at PASHUPATINATH TEMPLE (February-March).

GHORE JATRA, literally the festival of horses, horse-chariot races as well as other sporting events are the main attractions.

EXPLORING NEPAL

For tourists not in a hurry, Nepal offers a holiday for at least 10 to 15 days. But, those pressed for time are advised to confine their discovery to the Kathmandu Valley.

The Kathmandu Valley houses not only the capital city but also several other ancient towns, monuments and architectural wonders. The valley is not high — about 1500 metres — giving it an excellent climate most of the year. It is seldom very cold, there is no snowfall in the valley. It is ringed by high mountains which can be viewed clearly from vantage points at the foothills around Kathmandu. It also provides an

A family of elephants at chitwan National park.

opportunity to undertake more difficult treks up in the mountains and excursions to nearby places.

An half-an-hour flight out of Kathmandu towards the west brings you to the valley of Pokhra. To the southwest near the Indian border is the ROYAL CHITWAN NATIONAL PARK GAME RESERVE. The Park has TIGER TOPS and similar other game-watching towers and lodges. Other attractions of Nepal are trekking and river rafting in SAGARMATHA (EVEREST) NATIONAL PARK from where the ascent to Everest starts. A trip to LUMBINI, the birthplace of Lord Buddha in the Terai region, is a must for Buddhists and those interested in Buddhism.

The lowlands of Terai are semi-tropical and physically and ethnically closer to India. In fact, Lumbini is more easily accessible from India—if your mission is to visit all places of interest connected with the life of Lord Buddha.

KATHMANDU

Kathmandu, the commercial, administrative and social capital of Nepal, is one of the most picturesque capitals in the world. The name is derived from Kasthamandap, an imposing wooden pagoda near the HANUMAN DHOKA PALACE. This city of half a million inhabitants was built in its present form by King Gunakama Dev in A.D. 723. The original name of the city was Kantipur, the glamorous city. The city claims to have some 2,000 temples and shrines.

The most interesting things to see in the capital are clustered around the old towns between the old marketplace and the shopping centre along the New Road. Around central DURBAR SQUARE are the ROYAL PALACE, a number of interesting pagodas and temples and the KUMARI HOUSE, the residence of the Living Goddess.

Black Bhairab

The massive stone image of the terrifying Black Bhairab god was once used as a kind of lie-detector. Criminals were brought here to confess. If a person spoke a lie on oath, it was believed, he would die immediately. Fear and faith made them confess.

Hidden behind the temple wall of the Black Bhairab is an even more terrifying aspect of Bhairab, the WHITE BHAIRAB. The image was built in

1794 by the third king of Shah dynasty — Rana Bahadur Shah. Today, it is used as the symbol of Royal Nepal Airlines. It is opened only during Indrajal Festival in September. But, you can have a look at the temple through the lattice.

Hanuman Dhoka is the historic palace and temple complex. In its large compound, there are many different courtyards and buildings. One of them, the TELAJU TEMPLE, is a fine three-tiered temple built in the 16th century. Being the Royal chapel, it is closed to foreigners and is opened only once a year to the Nepalese. Along the outside wall of the palace, you discover an inscription written in 18 languages. It was ordered by King Pratap Malla who himself was a poet and a scholar. Among the 18 languages are English and French also. Close by is the King's statue, seated with folded hands and surrounded by his four sons. There is a popular belief that milk will flow from the spot in the middle of the inscription if someone can read all the 18 languages. By the main entrance to the palace complex is the statue of the monkey god Hanuman who played a great role in the service of Lord Rama in the epic *Ramayana*. The statue is shielded by a golden umbrella and the face is covered by red paste. The gilded carvings on the doorway are very well done.

The Royal Palace in the complex is called the HANUMAN DHOKA PALACE. It was built by King Pratap Malla in the 17th century but has since been renovated by the successive kings who lived there till the end of the 19th century. There are several courtyards inside the palace. You can enter a famous one — the NASAL CHOWK — which can hold up to 10,000 people for ceremonial occasions. In the centre of this courtyard is a platform used for royal coronations. On one side is the seven-tiered temple devoted to Hanuman. Here, one can climb on the top of the nine-storey BASANTPUR TOWER overlooking the courtyards and the Kathmandu city.

Looking out on Durbar Square is the residence of the living Goddess, Kumari Devi, a little girl who is selected from a caste of Newar goldsmiths after extensive rituals at the age of 5 or 6.

During the Desain festival, she is installed on a throne in a room she lives in. The spirit of the goddess is believed to enter her body after the ceremony. For three days in September during the Festival of Lord Indra, she is taken out in Kathmandu on a chariot followed by a procession. She gives her blessings to the king and receives a gold coin in return. Kumari remains at her residence till her puberty, when another living goddess is chosen.

The little girl is not supposed to go to school, a teacher comes to teach her. Her expenses are borne by a temple trust. After losing her goddess status, she is free to do whatever she wishes and even get married. But, there is a prevalent superstition that the man who marries her could die in six months. However, this is not true as some men who married the former goddess have outlived her.

The central courtyard of Kumari's house is superbly crafted with extensive carvings on windows and balconies. One can often see the child goddess in the upstairs window, but photographing her is not permitted.

There are some more temples in the Square with erotic carvings on the struts but the best ones are in the JAGANNATH TEMPLE, near the Hanuman Temple. Explanations have been offered for the existence of erotic carvings on temples but the amusing one is that the Goddess of Lightning would not strike on such a temple—the goddess being a chaste virgin.

The KASTHMANDAP from which the capital derives its name is an intricate wooden temple carved from the timber of a single tree. It was built near Hanuman Dhoka by King Lakshmi Narasingh Malla in 1596. The adjacent three-tiered TRILOKYA MOHAN is a Vishnu temple with a statue of the kneeling Garuda facing it. Close by is the MANJU DEVI TEMPLE, again with some erotic carvings and the SIVA PARVATI TEMPLE where images of the God and the Goddess look out from the window on what is happening on the streets below. The white neo-classical building looking out of place is the GADDI BAITHAK which was built as a palace during the Rana period.

Across the Kasthmandap temple is the small MARU GANESH TEMPLE, a popular temple always humming with activity. As you walk down the Durbar Square, there are more interesting sights to discover. Lining the street are open-fronted shops, sacred Hindu shrines with superb silver-worked images of gods and goddesses. Street vendors display exotic goods coming from all parts of Nepal and the hill folk come down in their traditional costumes to buy them. Through these narrow streets, a traffic consisting of cycle-rickshaws, hawkers and flute-sellers flows constantly. Tibetan monks and Hindu priests mix with the crowds, along with a few foreign tourists and an occasional wandering cow. The scene appears to be from a medieval story book.

In the bazar area, there are more temples. The white MACHHENDRANATH TEMPLE has a three-tiered pagoda-style roof and is set in a courtyard of secondary stupas and shrines around it. Traditional Nepalese music is played in the evenings. In the main INDRA CHOWK, there is another major three-tiered temple — AKASH BAIRAVA. The temple image is taken out and paraded through the streets of Kathmandu during the Indra Festival in September. The Indra Chowk is also a busy shopping centre for Nepalese goods. If you are interested in buying Nepalese caps, you will find them in plenty.

The next square is called ASAN. It is the busiest square of the country with six roads radiating from it. The three-storey high pagoda is dedicated to Goddess Annapurna — the goddess of prosperity. A major Himalayan peak is also named after the Goddess.

Also look for the SINGH DURBAR, an impressive stucco palace of huge dimensions close to the PARADE GROUND. At one time, the palace housed several offices of the Nepal Government. An earthquake damaged the building in 1934. The impressive main facade and the reception hall area have survived.

Close by is the MARTYR'S MEMORIAL, an archway containing statues of major participants in the 1950-51 revolution against the ruling oligarchy of the Ranas. The present Royal Palace is located at the end of the Durbar Marg. It is a modern building built not too long ago.

The NATIONAL MUSEUM OF NEPAL is 2.5 km. west of Kathmandu and one can walk to it in less than half an hour starting from Hanuman Dhoka. It has a rich collection of weapons and artefacts from ancient and medieval times. The museum is open every day except on Tuesdays.

Kathmandu also has its NATURAL HISTORY MUSEUM, located 3 km. west and run by TRIBHUVAN UNIVERSITY. It has a unique collection of 14,000 samples of butterflies, fish, reptiles, birds, mammals, plants and fossils collected from within Nepal.

Close to the National Museum is SWAYAMBHUNATH, a magnificent stupa set on a hill 77 metres above the Valley. The approach from the east is through steep stairs, but if you climb from the west, the ascent is gradual. The spire rises from the base, capped by a gilded pinnacle. Painted on the four sides of the spire bases are the all-seeing eyes of Lord Buddha. On the hill top, there is a mosaic of small Buddhist Chaityas and Pagodas.

If you are fortunate to be in Kathmandu during full moon, spend some time at night at Swayambhunath. Be sure to wander around the rear of the main stupa. There are many white stupas here that glow under the full moon.

Geologists now accept that the Kathmandu Valley was once a lake and according to a popular legend the hill on which the pagoda stands, was then an island.

KIRTIPUR

The medieval town of Kirtipur is situated on a ridge to the southwest of Kathmandu. To get there, it is better to take a bus or taxi to the University and then stroll up to the Ridge where the town is located. Kirtipur is a centre of cloth weaving and dyed yarn. The Ridge offers a panoramic view of Kathmandu with Himalayan peaks rising behind it.

When Prithvi Narayan Shah conquered the Valley in the eighteenth century, Kirtipur put up a stiff resistance, causing heavy losses to the invading army. In order to avenge the death of his soldiers, the King cut off the noses of all able-bodied men in town. It is said that people in this town have their noses shorter than those of most other Nepalese.

The TRIBHUVAN UNIVERSITY CAMPUS is located at the foot of the hill.

Just past Kirtipur is CHOBHAR GORGE, a very scenic spot. It is believed that gods cut this gorge to drain the water from the Kathmandu Valley when it was still a lake. On the hill-top is the Buddhist temple of ADINATH.

BODHNATH

Some 8 km. north-east of Kathmandu is Bodhnath, a colossal stupa — one of the world's largest. It is said to contain the bones of one of the Buddhas who preceded Gautama Buddha. Painted above are the all-seeing eyes of Lord Buddha.

Built by Lichchavi king Mana Dev in the fifth century A.D., Bodhnath is constructed on an octagonal base inset with prayer wheels. This is also the centre of Nepal's Tibetan Buddhists. In the surrounding houses, you can see many Tibetan monks who have come here to study.

Pashupatinath temple at the extreme left

On a trip to Bodhnath, you can also visit one of the holiest Hindu Temples in Nepal, PASHUPATINATH, a temple dedicated to Shiva on the banks of the Bhagmati River. Hindus from all over the Indian subcontinent come here for pilgrimage. Local Hindus are brought here for cremation in the river. In February-March, the great Shivaratri festival attracts hundreds and thousands of pilgrims.

Foreigners may not enter the temple compound, but they can have a good view of the whole complex from a higher vantage point.

Just beyond the Pashupatinath Temple and on the banks of Bhagmati river is another temple, GUHESHWARI, dedicated to Goddess Parvati — consort of Lord Shiva. The structure is built on the principle of Tantric Yantra, a geometric triangle. It signifies the spirit of female procreation.

Not far is the ROYAL WILDLIFE SANCTUARY OF GOKARNA. It is situated on the banks of the river Bhagmati, some 12 km. east of Kathmandu. The sanctuary has herds of elephants and deer.

DAKSHINKALI TEMPLE — the temple dedicated to Goddess Kali—is located the southern edge of the Valley. Here goats are sacrificed to please the goddess. The temple is about half an hour's drive from Kathmandu.

Many Nepalese families take a vow before the goddess that if their wish is fulfilled, they would offer the sacrifice. After the sacrifice, part of the meat is brought home for a feast.

Between Chobhar Gorge and Dakshinkali, a small lake is all that remains of the big lake which once engulfed the Valley. Another interesting stop in the area is SHESH NARAYAN PAGODA, built in the shadow of a limestone cliff.

The world's largest "Sleeping Vishnu" is the greatest attraction of the BUDHANIKANTHA TEMPLE, some 10 km. north of Kathmandu. It is attributed to 8th century A.D. No one knows who built the statue. Legend has it that it was accidentally unearthed by a farmer. Each November, a festival is held here when the god is believed to wake up. Prayers take place here every morning around 9 a.m. A school started by the British is located nearby.

PATAN

Five km. south-west of the Kathmandu valley is Patan, also known as Lalitpur (the city beautiful). It is the second largest city of the kingdom and the most Buddhist also. It is famous for its artistic temples and sculpture. To understand the religion and culture of the Himalayan kingdom, it is necessary to visit this ancient town. The access is easy — buses and auto-rickshaws ply to this little town, or you can make a trip by a hired bicycle.

Patan was once an independent kingdom under Malla rulers and a centre of craftsmanship, which it still is. Visitors today can find superb souvenirs in paintings, bronze, brass, stone and wood. Many small shops cater to the needs of discerning tourists.

DURBAR SQUARE is located in the centre of the city. It has ancient palaces, Hindu temples, Buddhist shrines and many fascinating sculptures.

Close to the Durbar Square is HIRANYA VARNA MAHAVIHAR, an outstanding Buddhist monastery built in the 12th century. It takes its name from the gold-plated roof which was dedicated by a rich merchant. Patan once had many families of affluent merchants who had become rich from trade with Tibet. Inside the monastery there are many prayer wheels and scenes from the life of Lord Buddha on the walls. The courtyard has a richly decorated three-storey temple with a golden image of Lord Buddha. This monastery is quite unlike anything else in Nepal.

Nearby is the 5-storeyed temple dedicated to Shiva, known as KUMBHESHWAR. The water in the courtyard spring is said to be coming directly from the holy lake in the GOSAINKUNDA. In Durbar Square itself is the ancient palace of Patan. Most of the buildings were built during the 13th century by the Malla king Siddhi Narsingh. The ROYAL PALACE and TEMPLE stand on the right side. Towards tho west are KRISHNA TEMPLE and a host of other temples. Patan's biggest marketplace, the MANGAL BAZAR, is part of the scene.

The first temple to the right of the square is the three-storey BHIMSEN TEMPLE. You notice it by a pillar in front with a lion on top. Bhimsen was one of the five Pandava brothers in the *Ramayana*. The SHIVA TEMPLE is the second one with five stone elephants guarding the door.

The third temple is dedicated to Krishna. Built by King Siddhi Narsingh Malla in the 17th century, it bears the influence of Indian architecture — unlike the usual Pagoda style. It is regarded as one of the finest examples of Nepalese craftsmanship. The mythical Garuda kneels atop a pillar facing the temple. The carvings on its four pillars tell us the story of *Mahabharata*. The second floor depicts scenes from the *Ramayana*.

The temple has been built entirely of stone and as has been the practice Nepal, no nails have been used. Also set on a high pillar is the statue of King Yoganarendra Malla who ruled Patan in the 18th century. A bird stands on top of the statue and legend has it that it will fly away one day. Next to the king is another white Indian style temple followed by a 3-storey Shiva temple with erotic sculptures. The big bell in the Shiva temple was rung by people to draw the attention of the king to their complaints.

The Royal Palace is marked by its golden gate and bronze windows. It is believed that the spirits of the Malla kings still reside there.

TALEJU TEMPLE is another landmark. Built in the 13th century and dedicated to goddess Taleju (Parvati), it has excellent wood carvings. In its courtyard stands a four-storey Pagoda with white statues of goddesses Ganga and Yamuna guarding it. The main palace is at the end of the courtyard and outside the palace are statues of the Ganesh, Narsimha and Hanuman.

MAHABUDDHA TEMPLE — the temple of one thousand Buddhas—is located at the south of Durbar Hall. Built in the 14th century, the temple was severely damaged by an earthquake in 1934. Each brick used in the temple contains an image of the Buddha. You can climb on the top and have a good look of the Patan town.

Nearby is RUDRA VARNA MAHAVIHAR, another Buddhist monastery similar to one with the gold-plated roof.

The TEMPLE OF RATO (Red) MACHANDRANATH is a little away from the centre of Patan. It has a fine image of AVALOKETESWARA which is taken out in a procession during a festival in June each year.

During his visit to Kathmandu Valley 2300 years ago, Buddhist emperor Ashoka is supposed to have created four stupas indicating the boundary of Patan. You can still see the grassy humps where they once stood.

JAWALAKHEL is the area where a Tibetan refugees camp is located. Set with the Swiss assistance, it has a handicrafts centre selling carpets made by the refugees which are very reasonably priced. The area now has also some of the upmarket hotels — Narayan and Himalayas.

Patan also has a zoo housing many specimens of Himalayan and Terai wildlife including deer and the Bengal tiger.

BHAKTAPUR (BHADGAON)

Founded in A.D. 889, Bhaktapur — or the city of the devotees—is some 20 km. to the east of Kathmandu. Its popular name today is Bhadgaon. It was the earliest of the three major cities of Kathmandu Valley to attain a high level of artistic achievements. The town has remained relatively unchanged over the centuries. Although its streets and lanes are untidy, there is no question about the artistic quality of the creations of the people of this town. DURBAR SQUARE is the area where most activity is concentrated.

Some experts believe that the artistic excellence of Bhaktapur is far superior to that of other towns of the Valley. It contains some of the finest architectural showpieces. Its golden effigies of kings and mythical figures, perched on pillars and roofs and deities looking out from their shrines are fantastic.

The ROYAL PALACE OF BHAKTAPUR was first constructed in the 15th century. Later it was renovated in the 17th century. Within the compound is one building with 55 windows. Part of the palace has been converted into an ART GALLERY which has many rare paintings and manuscripts. Adjoining the Gallery is the GOLDEN GATE OF BHAKTAPUR built by the last Malla king in the middle of the 18th century. According to historian Percy Brown who visited Nepal in 1912, this was the liveliest work of art in the whole of Nepal. A Garuda — the vehicle of Lord Vishnu—tops the gate and is shown eating serpents. The multi-figure siding the Garuda is goddess Durga. A statue of King Bhupatindra sits with folded hands on top of a pillar facing the gate. This Malla King was responsible for most of the building activity in Bhaktapur.

Another gate dating from 1696 is guarded by two huge lion statues. Alongside are two other superb statues of Shiva in his incarnation as Bhairva and his consort Parvati as Ugrachandi.

Moving to SQUARE TAUMADHI, you can see Nepal's

Nyatapola Temple

largest Pagoda, the NYATAPOLA TEMPLE. The 55-storey temple is the highest temple in the valley and a fine specimen of Nepalese architecture and crafsmanship.

The foundation stone of this temple was laid by King Bhupatindra Malla himself who ordered its construction. The stairway leading to the temple is flanked by two wrestlers, then two elephants, two lions, then two giraffes and finally two goddesses. Wood carvings in this temple are some of the best in Nepal. A fine view of the temple can be had from the road leading out of the valley towards the Tibetan border.

The two-storeyed BHAIRAVNATH TEMPLE stands on the right of Nyatapola Temple. It was built in the 17th century but was reconstructed after severe damage was done to it in the earthquake of 1934. Only four minutes walk from Bhairavnath Temple is the square where DATTATRAY TEMPLE and PUJAHARI MATH monastery stand. Built in the 15th century, the Dattatray Temple is the oldest in the area and is dedicated to Lord Vishnu. There is a pillar on top of which Garuda sits with his traditional weapons. It is believed to have been built from the wood of a single tree. The Pujahari Math monastery is equally ancient and is extraordinarily rich in wood carvings. A head priest still lives here. The area is of special interest since it was one of the most extensively restored sections with West German aid. The work has been done with aesthetic care. It also incorporates water and sewage systems for the benefit of the community living here.

Returning to the old road, it may be worthwhile to visit the village SANO THIMI, famous for its pottery and folk dances.

MOUNTAIN FLIGHTS

If you happen to be in Nepal between June and September, you can have an experience of your lifetime. There are regular mountain flights operated by the Royal Nepal Airlines giving you a breathtaking view of the Himalayan peaks. The flight takes off early morning each day and it flies for an hour over the Himalayas. The plane, a Boeing 727, can fly at a height of 6000 metres. During the flight, you can view eight out of the ten highest peaks in the world, from a distance of only 20 km.

The plane flies along the length of the mountain ranges in both directions giving opportunity to passengers on both sides of the aircraft to view all the peaks. A mountain profile is handed over to you before you take off so that you can identify each peak. At the end of the journey, the passengers are given a certificate by the Airline to certify that they have been greeted by Mount Everest.

This is a unique flight. India too has followed Nepal's lead and the Indian Airlines offers once weekly flights over the Himalayas during season.

This is, however, not the only way to view Himalayan peaks. Since mountains are not clearly visible from the Kathmandu valley, there are excursions out of Kathmandu to get you a good view. Near Kathmandu, the most popular dawn-excursion to view the Himalayas is from the village of NAGARKOT. Situated on the ridge to the north-east, it offers a view stretching from DHAULAGIRI in the west to KANCHANJUNGA in the east. Several travel agencies operate these dawn excursions costing US dollars 5 to 6. A better option would be to stay overnight at NAGARKOT and view the mountains at dawn. This course is recommended for the young who can trek to the ridge after they get down at the Nagarkot bus stop. In recent years, Nagarkot has developed into a kind of a resort where there are a few budget hotels for an overnight stay.

After mountain viewing at Nagarkot, you can walk along the ridge to the famous temple of CHANGUNARAYAN — a pagoda-style temple dedicated to Narayan (Lord Vishnu). Garuda the mythical man-bird, which is the mount of Vishnu stands, with folded hands in front of the temple. This is a very popular temple visited by thousands of pilgrims.

Another place for mountain viewing is DHULIKHEL, just outside Kathmandu Valley. Buses leave every hour and travel on a good road towards the Chinese border. Dhulikhel is at an altitude of 1500 metres and viewing from here is considered better than Nagarkot. Access to this place which is district headquarters is easy. Basic accommodation facilities are available. It offers a superb view of the CHO OYU in the east to HIMALCHULI in the west.

Another mountain viewing site is the 8,000 feet pass of SIMBHANJYANG or DAMAN along the main road leading to the Indian border. It is 120 km from Kathmandu. Although at lower altitude, some people believe that this is the best place for mountain watching. On a clear day, you can see from here DHAULAGIRI, ANNAPURNA and EVEREST — all the three peaks.

There is a view tower fitted with long-range telescopes. Overnight accommodation is available.

RAPTI VALLEY - CHITWAN GAME RESERVE

Apart from mountains, Nepal has several wildlife sanctuaries or as they call it here, Game Reserves. Touristically, the most popular area lies in the lowlands of the Terai - the semi-tropical Valley of Rapti. It has thick forests, elephant grass and rivers. Here some of Asia's rare animals live and they are protected. They include the one-horned rhinoceros, tiger, leopard, gaur, deer, wild boar, crocodile — and even the fresh water dolphins. A large part of the Valley has been earmarked as a national park — and is now called the Royal National Chitwan Park. Strict conservation policies are followed. The Park is open to tourists. A popular attraction of the Park is the Tiger Tops, a vast lodge in the forest built at tree-top level. A half-hour flight from Kathmandu brings the visitors to an airport called MEGHANTIA. From here you travel to Tree Tops Hotel by elephant or by landrovers.

It is an interesting place to experience the fun of seeing wildlife. The owners of Tiger Tops also run some tented camps away from the main hotel which are relatively inexpensive.

Following the lead given by Tiger Tops, other operators have also set up similar and even better camps. One of these is Temple Tiger, also in the same area. Visitors can undertake river Safaris which include shooting the rapids and camping by the riverside.

Air journey is not the only way to reach the Royal Chitwan Park. By road it is about 5 hours drive from Kathmandu over a 200-km. mountain highway that ends at the edge of the Narayani River. The drive passes through terraced rice fields and beautiful villages along the banks of the Trisuli and Narayani rivers - a unique experience. The Temple Tiger people offer to take you to their camps by rafting through their rivers.

Other National Parks

Other major National Parks are ROYAL BARDIA NATIONAL PARK, SUKLA PHANTA WILDLIFE RESERVE, SAGARMATHA(EVEREST) NATIONAL PARK, LANGTANG NATIONAL PARK, SHEY PHOKSUNDO NATIONAL PARK, RARA NATIONAL PARK and the ANNAPURNA CONSERVATION AREA.

The Royal Bardia National Park is about 400 kms west of Kathmandu on the banks of the Karnali river and has an area of 968 sq. km. The higher grounds of the Park have deciduous forests of sal. The porous slopes support large open grasslands locally known as "phantas".

The Bardia National Park is home to a vast variety of animals who live in and around these phantas. Some of these animals are spotted deer, hog deer, sambar, wild boar, barasingha or swamp deer. Two species of monkeys—the langur and the rhesus macaque—are also seen in large numbers. Small herds of elephants too are visible. A few one-horned rhinos from the neighbouring Chitwan Park have been relocated in this Park which should multiply over the years.

Access to the Park is five hours' drive. The best time to visit is April to November.

The Sukla Phanta Wildlife Reserve, a 155 sq. km. area, lies along the Indian border. It was once a reserve for the Ranas of Nepal for their hunting pleasure. The park provides a safe sanctuary to such endangered animals as the barasingha or the swamp deer and the pygmy hog. Among other animals found here are herds of deer, nilgai, wil jackal and elephants. The best time to visit is April to

among the natural heritage sites of the world is the erest) National Park. It includes MOUNT EVEREST, LHOTSE, DOBLAM, KANGTEGA, GYACHUNG KANG, etc. The nal Park is the rugged areas of 1148 sq km. It is the dy Sherpas who have over the years helped mountaineers to conquer major peaks including Everest. The first men on Everest were a Nepalese Sherpa Tenzing Norgay and a New Zealander Sir Edmund Hillary.

In 1979, the Sagarmatha National Park was declared a World Heritage Site. The wildlife found in the park includes the Himalayan Tehr, goral, musk deer, pikka (mouse hare) and weasel. Other occasionally seen animals are the Himalayan black bear, wolf, lynx, and the snow-leopard.

To visit the park, it is recommended that the services of government-approved outfitters should be used.

Nepal's largest national park is called the SHEY PHOKSUNDO NATIONAL PARK. It has an area of 3555 sq. km. in western Nepal. The park was established to preserve the trans-Himalayan ecosystem found only in a few areas of Nepal. The park includes many mountains over 6, 000 metres and also the Shey Monastery, the PHOKSUNDO LAKE and the LANGU GORGE. The wildlife includes a good population of blue sheep and goral, musk deer, leopard, wild dog, wolf, marmot and the langur monkeys. The higher reaches are the haunt of the elusive snow-leopard. The adjoining Tibetan region is home to such animals as the great Tibetan sheep, wild yak, Tibetan gazelle and the antelope. The area is generally inhabited by the people of Tibetan stock.

The RARA NATIONAL PARK is the country's smallest national park - 370 km. north-west of Kathmandu. It is also the most scenic park of the country and protects some of the most beautiful Alpine and sub-alpine ecosystem of the Himalayas. The centrepiece is the pristine lake of Rara also known as MAHENDRA TAL — the biggest lake in Nepal. It is surrounded by rich forests. CHURCHEMARA DANDA at 4, 087 metres is the best vantage point to get a stunning view of the lake; forests and the surrounding mountain ranges. The Rara National Park comes within the catchment area of the Karnali river — one of the three principal rivers of Nepal. The habitat supports animal life like red panda, black bear, yellow-throated martin, goral, serow and musk deer.

Access is not easy — a brief flight followed by a three-day trek.

The KHAPTA NATIONAL PARK is the newest protected area, a plateau of grass and forests. It is located at an elevation of 3000 metres in the far west. The habitat provides good cover for bear, leopard, barking and musk deer, and a vast variety of birds including impeyan, koklas and kalij pheasants. The park represents one of the few remaining mid-mountain ecosystems. To reach it, travellers will have to combine hiking with a brief flight.

The ANNAPURNA CONSERVATION AREA encompasses 2, 500 sq. km. of mountainous terrain, containing some of the world's highest peaks and deepest river valleys. For thousands of years, hill people have scratched their living out of the steep hillsides in the region. The advent of tourism and the phenomenal rise in population has triggered a process of environmental deterioration. To take care of the new problems, King Mahendra Trust for Nature Conservation launched in 1986 the Annapurna Area Conservation Project with international help. Its objective is to integrate environmental conservation with development which can sustain the people. As part of the project, courses in conservation are taught in the local schools.

POKHRA

Few places in the world have such splendid variety of natural beauty crammed into one small area as the Pokhra Valley in western Nepal. Linked with Kathmandu by Prithvi Highway and the Indian border-town of BUNAULI by Sidharatha Highway, Pokhra has daily bus services to and fro from these towns. All major cities including GORKHA within the kingdom are linked to Pokhra.

Royal Nepal Airlines operates daily services between Kathmandu and Pokhra.

The valley of Pokhra abounds in lakes, PHEWA, RUPA and BEGNAS being the most famous one and KHASTE, DIPANG and MARDI being the smaller ones located out of town. Sporting activities like canoeing and swimming are conducted on Phewa together with angling of 'mahser' fish found in the lake.

There are two Tibetan settlements near Pokhra and one can see women weaving exquisite carpets using traditional designs. Both these settlements are famous for traditional Tibetan handicrafts and souvenirs crafted mostly by the deft hands of the refugees.

Pokhra is full of exotic places of interests. The SETI RIVER GORGE (the river flows some 300 feet below the earth's surface), DEVIN'S FALL where the cascading water vanishes underground, the MAHENDRA CAVE full of stalactite and stalagmite formations.

Although a base for all treks to the Annapurna region, several mini treks can be organised from Pokhra, notably to SARANGKOT. The four hours' hike to the top of this hill offers the hiker a spectacular view of Phewa Lake, the entire Annapurna Range, the Seti river and the village of HYANGZA.

A one night trek to NAUDANDA and GHACHOWK, KHASTE and OPPANG TAL from Pokhra can also be made. From Naudanda, the twin peaks of the MACHHAPU-CHHARE or the FISH TAIL MOUNTAIN can be seen.

Of the longer treks the most often tried is the trip from Pokhra to JOMSON. The journey along an ancient trade route between Nepal and Tibet takes about seven days and often one comes face to face with mule caravans transporting goods between the Tibetan border and the Pokhra town.

A walk through the Pokhra bazar, starting from RAMESWAR TOLE till BIND BASINI TEMPLE will bring the visitor across the diverse tribes and unhurried life of the people. The stone altar under trees locally known as 'chautaras' are also a peculiarity of this place.

A visit to RAM GHAT, the widest section of Seti river, is an exhilarating experience. Ram Ghat is also the cremation ground of Pokhra.

TREKKING AND ADVENTURE

Over half the 300, 000 foreign visitors who visit Nepal every year come with the idea of an adventure holiday — it may be a short trek or a major expedition into the mountains, a peep into the wildlife parks of Nepal or a walking tour. The prime motivation is an open air holiday under the blue Himalayan sky. Never mind if you are not a trained mountaineer. Nepal is known as a trekkers' paradise. Trekking in Nepal is free from seasonal or age limitations and the possibilities are unlimited. To suit special interests like bird-watching, plant-hunting, butterfly collection or just to be close to Nature, there is no better way than to trek in Nepal. And see the plus point—whether you are an adolescent of 15 or in the age group of 60, it makes no difference.

White-water rafting

If you are not a trained mountaineer or cannot withstand rigours of a long trek, try white-water rafting. River-rafting is not as demanding as trekking but the excitement is greater. For the less adventurous, there are opportunities in the Pokhra Valley for fishing, swimming and canoeing or just boating. Then, there are wildlife national parks — some like the famous Tiger Tops Parks provide excellent accommodation and food amidst the wild jungles. To experience wildlife viewing, seated on a trained elephant can be something to remember for lifetime.

No special experience is required for rafting trip although kayaking, a new sport introduced in Nepal, requires some expertise. As long as you do not mind doing some paddling and have no objection to getting wet, you are a good candidate for a white-water trip on the stormy rivers. You are perfectly safe as the helmsman provided by Your Tour Operator will help keep your raft on course — and you too.

The tours last from three to nine days and prices depend on the types of services you need. All-inclusive trips costing US$ 40 to 75 per day include the services of cooks who cook for you and take care of your creative comforts. Tenting equipment moves with you.

There are three main rivers where rafting is currently done: Sun Kosi, Trisuli and Narayani River in Kali Gandaki. The first two are the most popular ones. Recently, some tour operators have started rafting in Central Nepal and the Tamor river in the east.

A permit is required for rafting too. But, these formalities are taken care of by your tour operator.

TREKKING TO EVEREST

Can you trek to Everest? Not really. But, you can do the second best thing—be very near Everest and its lower ranges. Royal Nepal Airlines operates a daily STOL flight to an airstrip called LUKLA. It is close to NAMCHA BAZAR, the last human settlement before ascent to Everest starts. This is the flight most Everest expeditions take to save fifteen days of trekking to reach Namcha Bazaar by the surface route.

If you take this Everest flight, be prepared to be stuck up there for a couple of days if weather gets bad and the flight cannot take off. Visibility suddenly becomes poor. There are some hotels there with basic facilities to provide you accommodation.

PILGRIMAGE TO BUDDHA'S BIRTHPLACE

For the followers of Lord Budha and those interested in Buddhism, Lumbini (original name Rummindei) — a small town in the Terai region—is the most important site. It was the place where Lord Buddha was born around 544 B.C. His father was the ruler of a small State in this area. His mother was on her way to her father's house when he was born at a small place where she had halted.

Tvangboche Monastery

All travellers who enter the country overland from India through Nepal's Terai region pass by Lumbini. Apart from being the holy region where the Buddha was born, Terai is the granary of Nepal and is home to Royal Chitwan Park which we have described earlier. Lumbini is only a few kilometres across the Indian border in Nepal.

From Kathmandu, you can fly to Bhairava. Lumbini is only 22 km. from the airport. It may be advisable to stay overnight in Bhairava which is a district headquarters town and head for Lumbini in the morning. There are hourly buses to Lumbini which are very inexpensive. Lumbini too has basic accommodation for visitors.

Emperor Ashoka, one of India's greatest kings who did the most to spread Buddhism in the world, visited Lumbini in 259 B.C. to worship at the place where the Buddha was born. In order to identify the place with Lord Buddha, he erected a giant pillar. The pillar is the only proof that Lord Buddha was born here. The place is of prime inportance. Other attractions are the temple of his mother Maya Devi and a tank where she took bath before giving birth to the Buddha.

Excavation work undertaken recently has unearthed two Chaityas dating back to the 3rd century B.C. The Chinese traveller Huien Tsang who later visited the place had seen these buildings and described them. The Chaityas disappeared during the course of centuries in the absence of patronage. A Tibetan monastery built in 1975 has interesting paintings on its walls and also a massive bronze image of Buddha. Another monastery has a white Buddha image donated by the Burmese.

Lumbini is being developed as a major place of pilgrimage with the assistance of United Nations thanks to the vision of its former Secretary General U Thant, who was a devout Buddhist. Around the pilgrimage sites now there are green lawns and gardens.

It is interesting to note that Muslims constitute almost half the population of Lumbini though their population in the whole of Nepal is negligible.

NEPAL

TRAVEL INFORMATION

Area: 141, 577 sq. km.
Population: 20 million
Capital: Kathmandu (Population 300, 000)
Entry: Biratnagar (100,000) Pokhra (50,000)

By Air: Nepal is adequately served by major international airlines besides its own national carrier - Royal Nepal Airlines (RNAC). Among the international airlines operating to Kathmandu are China (CAAC), Lufthansa German Airlines, Pakistan International Airlines, Indian Airlines and Thai International.

Within Nepal, the national carrier, RNAC, has an extensive network using small planes to meet the requirements of tourists.
By Land: Nepal is a landlocked country. By land the most convenient entry point from India is through the Terai region by a picturesque highway built by India. There are other land entry points from where foreign travellers can enter into Nepal. These are:
1. Kakarbhitta
2. Birgunj
3. Kodari
4. Sunauli

5. Nepalgunj
6. Dhangadi
7. Mahendranagar

Facilities for changing foreign exchange are available at all entry points.

Within Nepal, public buses ply on most roads and it is not difficult to reach any part of the country through public transport.

There is no passenger railway network within Nepal.

Those entering Nepal by their own cars must be in possession of valid international carnet.

PASSPORTS AND VISAS

All visitors to Nepal (except Indian nationals) must hold a valid passport and visa. Tourist visas can be obtained for a fee of US $ 10 from any Royal Nepalese Embassy or Consulate valid for a period of 30 days.

Visas can also be obtained for 15 days on arrival at the Tribhuvan International Airport, and at the other above-listed entry points. Visas can, if necessary, be extended on arrival in Nepal at the
Department of Immigration,
Tridevi Marg,
Kathmandu.
Tel. 412337

On arrival at the TRIBHUVAN INTERNATIONAL AIRPORT, Kathmandu, you are required to produce your disembarkation card and on departure an embarkation card is required to be filled in. Departing passengers have to pay an Airport Tax of Nepalese Rs. 450 levied on all passengers leaving by international airlines. There is a domestic airport tax of Rs. 20 to 30.

FOREIGN EXCHANGE REGULATIONS

Payments in Nepal are made in Nepalese currency. Facilities for converting foreign currency into Nepalese currency are available at the international airport, banks and hotels. At your hotel you must settle the bill in foreign currency.

Tourists are advised to obtain receipts for the exchange of foreign currency. It will enable them to re-convert their leftover Nepalese currency into dollars at the time of exit.

Tourists other than Indians are not allowed to bring in Indian rupees. Indian rupees are freely accepted in shops and bazars.

BANKS

Kathmandu banks are open from 10 a.m. to 2.30 p.m. from Sunday to Thursday and between 10 a.m. and 12.30 p.m. on Fridays. They are closed on Saturdays and other holidays.

CUSTOMS

All baggage must be declared and cleared through the customs at the port of entry. Personal effects are permitted free entry. Duty on articles brought in by the visitors varies according to the volume and value of the goods. A tourist may bring in dutiable goods, such as tobacco and liquors, free of duty and other taxes subject to the following limits:

Cigarettes 200 sticks
Cigars 50 sticks

Alcoholic liquor 1 bottle (not exceeding 1.15 litre in all) or 12 beer cans

Visitors are also permitted to import the following articles for their personal use:

One pair of binoculars, one ordinary camera with 15 rolls of film, one radiogram, one record-player with 10 records, one radio, one tape recorder with 15 tape reels or cassettes, one perambulator.

Import of these articles is subject to re-export. Antiques and precious or semi-precious stones bought by tourists must be cleared and a certificate obtained from.

His Majesty's Government of Nepal,
Department of Archaeology,
Ram Shah Path,
Phone 215358.

Other prohibited goods for export are gold, silver, precious stones, wild animals and their skins, horns, etc., all drugs, processed or in natural state. Carrying narcotics, arms and ammunition is strictly prohibited.

RESTAURANTS AND FOOD

Almost every kind of food representing the culinary arts of many parts of the world can be found in Kathmandu. Leading hotels may have several restaurants under one roof serving a wide variety of dishes. Imported and domestic liquors and wines are available in hotels and bars. It is usually safe to drink boiled and filtered water.

TIME

Nepal time is 5 hours 45 minutes ahead of Greenwich Mean Time and 15 minutes ahead of Indian Standard Time.

OFFICIAL HOLIDAY

Government and most other offices work six days a week. Saturday not Sunday is the weekly holiday in Nepal. Other holidays are listed in the Nepal Gazette.

WORKING HOURS

Government offices open from 1000 hrs to 1700 hrs in summer and till 1600 hrs. in winter. On Fridays, offices are open till 1500 hrs only.

ELECTRIC CURRENT

220 volts/50 cycles. Most important cities of the kingdom have electric supply.

BROADCASTING

Nepal Radio broadcasts English news and other programmes regularly during the day. Broadcasts start at 6 a.m. and last till 10 p.m.

TV broadcasts started in Nepal only in 1985. Timings are: Mornings 7.30 a.m. to 8.30 a.m. Evenings : 6.30 p.m. to 10 p.m.

ENTERTAINMENT

Entertainments cover a wide range. One can enjoy theatrical shows including cultural and classical performances. Cinema halls screen Nepali, Indian and Western movies.

Major hotels have well-stocked bars and nightly dance and music.

TOURIST INFORMATION

His Majesty's Government of Nepal, Department of Tourism, runs an information counter at its office in TRIPURESHWAR to provide tourist information and guidance to visitors. It distributes booklets, folders, posters and stickers to tourists free of cost. Besides, there are Tourist Information Centres run by the Department of Tourism in other cities and towns.

TREKKING PERMITS

Any foreigner intending to trek in any part of the kingdom of Nepal shall have to obtain a trekking permit from the Department of Immigration. Permits are issued for trekking in any part of the country except in areas restricted to foreigners by government regulations. Trekking guide lists are available.

Travel Agencies and Tour Operators

Nepal has a long list of Government approved travel agencies and tour operators. The list can be had from the Tourist Office. The largest and the most experienced agency of Nepal with its own vast transport fleet and guide services is:
Yet Travels,
Darbar Marg,
Kathmandu
Tel.: 221234
Fax: 977-1-226153

ROYAL NEPALESE EMBASSIES ABROAD

His Majesty's Government of Nepal maintains enbassies and consulates in the following cities:
Bangladesh - Dhaka;
China - Beijing;
Consulate in Lhasa;
Egypt - Cairo;
France - Paris;
Germany - Bonn;
India - New Delhi;
  Consulate in Calcutta;
Japan - Tokyo;
Myanmar - Yangoon;
Pakistan - Islamabad;
Saudi Arabia - Riyadh;
Thailand - Bangkok;
United Kingdom - London;
Russia - Moscow;
USA - Washington.
And a Consulate in Hong Kong.

All these countries have also their diplomatic missions in Nepal.

WHERE TO STAY (STD Code: 977-1)
Kathmandu
DELUXE
1. Hotel Annapurna
   Phone: 221711
2. Hotel Everest International
   Phone: 220567
3. Hotel Soaltee
   Phone: 272550
4. Hotel Yak & Yeti
   Phone: 413999
STANDARD
5. Hotel Malla
   Phone: 222683
6. Hotel Narayani
   Phone: 521442
7. Hotel woodland
   Phone: 222686

Budget
8. Hotel Bule Star
   Phone: 211470
9. Hotel Crystal
   Phone: 223611
10. Hotel Yellow Pagoda
    Phone: 220338
11. Hotel Aloha Inn
    Phone: 522797
12. Hotel Ambassdor
    Phone: 414432
13. Hotel Bajra Guest House
    Phone: 271824
14. Hotel Blue Diamond
    Phone: 226392
15. Hotel Gautam
    Phone: 215016
16. Hotel Manaslu
    Phone: 410071
17. Hotel Mt. Makalu
    Phone: 223965
18. Hotel M.H. International
    Phone: 411847
19. Hotel Panorama
    Phone: 221502
20. Kathmandu Guest House
    Phone: 413532

Chitwan
Standard
1. Tiger Tops Hotel
   Phone: 57
Budget
2. Hotel Wildlife Camp
   Phone: 24
3. Adventure Jungle Camp
   Phone: 40
4. Chitwan Jungle Lodge
   Phone: 30
5. Elephant Camp Hotel
   Phone: 24
6. Gaida Wildlife Camp
   Phone: 41
7. Jungle Safari Camp
   Phone: 41
8. Mechan Wildlife Camp
   Phone: 32

Pokhra
Standard
1. New Hotel Crystal
   Phone: 20035
Budget
2. Hotel Fish Tail Lodge
   Phone: 20071
3. Hotel Mount Annapurna
   Phone: 20037
4. Hotel Mandar
   Phone: 20268
5. Rajbhandari Guest House
   Phone: 20203

Nepalgunj
Budget
1. Hotel Sneha
   Phone: 30
2. New Hotel Bheri
   Phone: 40

Dhulikhel
Budget
1. Dhulekhel Mountain Resort
   Phone: 32
2. Hotel Sun-M-Snow
   Phone: 24

Janakpur
Budget
1. Hotel Welcome
   Phone: 60
2. Hotel Rainbow
   Phone: 28

Birgunj
Budget
1. Hotel Suraj
   Phone: 54
2. Hotel Diyalo
   Phone: 42

3. Hotel Samjhana
   Phone: 50
4. Hotel Kailash
   Phone: 62

Bhairahawa
BUDGET
1. Hotel Himalaya Inn
   Phone: 55

Lumbini
BUDGET
1. Lumbini Carden Guest House
   Phone: 30

Coloured garlands for sale at **Durbar Square**

Chapter 30

BHUTAN
THE LAND OF THE DRAGON

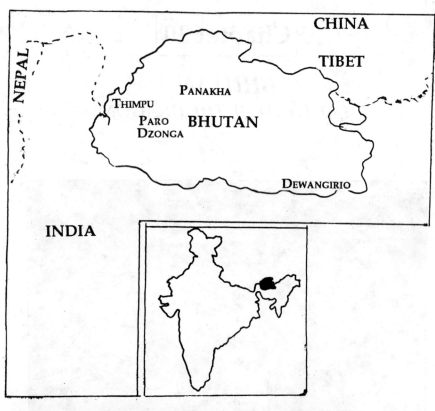

A view from Dochu La Pass

The author James Hilton who created fictional Shangri-la in his classic *Lost Horizon* could not have imagined that something like that existed on this earth. Bhutan, the mystic Himalayan kingdom, answers to his description. Only a few thousand foreigners have been fortunate enough to visit this Shangri-la during the two decades that it has been opened to international travellers. The entry to this land is restricted to retain the ancient charm of this kingdom and save the citizens from outside influences. The country was first opened to foreigners on June 2,1974 when some 150 dignitaries from different countries of the world were invited to attend the Coronation—a three-day spectacular ceremony — of the present King of Bhutan, Jigme Singye Wangchuk, who was crowned at the young age of 17. After the Coronation, the Government decided to open the kingdom for foreign tourists utilising the accommodation built for the guests who came to Bhutan.

The entry is restricted by keeping the prices of package tours offered by the Bhutan Tourism Corporation Ltd. and limiting visas to those who want to visit Bhutan on their own. Bhutan Government has fixed 4,000 foreign visitors per year as the outer limit for inbound foreign tourists to their country to preserve their culture. No wonder, therefore, in Bhutan you do not meet a single picture postcard vendor or someone trying to force you to buy local souvenirs.

Bhutan was totally closed to foreign visitors till 1974 except some Indian visitors. The country has treaty arrangements with India under which India guides the kingdom in respect of foreign relations. Bhutan Tourism Corporation or simply Bhutan Tourism is responsible for pioneering tourism. Privatised since October 1991, it has competent staff and offers totally integrated services. The organisation does not have any overseas office at present.

Druk Air, the country's national carrier, has recently opened offices in some of the neighbouring countries like India, Nepal and Thailand. These offices are a good source of information. Otherwise, address your enquiries to:

Bhutan Tourism
PO Box 159,
GPO, Thimphu,
Bhutan.
Tele: 975-24025.
Fax: (975)22479/23392.

Till Druk Air started flying in 1983, the only access to Bhutan for tourism was through India's Darjeeling and Sikkim areas. The air services connect Delhi with PARO via Kathmandu. Paro is the only airport in the country — not very far from the capital THIMPHU. It takes only two hours to reach Bhutan from Delhi by air. Accommodation in its hotels, motels and camps is comfortable though not luxurious. Continental,

Indian and Bhutanese food is served at its hotels. People are warm, hospitable and always smiling. They love to meet and entertain foreign visitors.

If you opt to fly to Paro from Calcutta or Delhi by Druk Air, take a seat on the west side of the Bhutan-bound jet. Your effort will be rewarded with an unobstructed view of the Mount Everest on a clear day.

HISTORY

Written history finds Bhutan first mentioned in the seventh century, when Buddhism reached the land. Temples built at this time still stand, revered by all the Bhutanese.

A century later, the saint, Padmasambhava, spread the Buddhism faith throughout Bhutan. After a long period of internal strife, the country was united by Shabdrung Ngawang Namgyal who consolidated his spiritual and temporal authority over Bhutan amid frequent battles with Tibetan and Mongolian armies.

The Shabdrung established the Drukpa Kagyupa tradition of Mahayana Buddhism, from which Bhutan derives its native name of Druk Yul — Land of the Dragon. The sect has continued to this day without interruption as the state religion.

The small country of Bhutan has remained isolated and independent for centuries. For 300 years, following the arrival of westerners, only 13 European expeditions are known to have passed through Bhutan's borders.

GEOGRAPHY

Situated in the heart of the great Himalayas, the world's mightiest mountain ranges, Bhutan is flanked on the north and north-east by Tibet. To the west and east, the rugged mountain ranges separate Bhutan from the hill districts of India. In the far north is the most forbidden barrier of all — the savage and eternally snowclad peaks of the Himalayas — some of them soaring over 7500 metres high. In the far south of the country, the foot-hills of the kingdom merge into the forests of Sikkim and north-eastern plains of India's West Bengal and Assam.

The kingdom is spread over an area of 75,000 sq kms, about the size of Switzerland, and a population of only 1.4 million. No formal census, however, has ever been taken. Buddhism is the State religion of the country - a school of Mahayana or Tantrik Buddhism. Buddhism has shaped the country's destiny since it was introduced 1100 years ago. It has played vital role in the life of the people.

An unspoiled country with unique cultural heritage for a thousand years, Bhutan is different from anything in the neighbouring countries of the Indian subcontinent. The country was never colonised, and it remained unaffected by outside influences and Western culture.

Climate and Seasons

The climate of Bhutan varies from the subtropical to the arctic and within one hour you can move from one climate to the other. Most towns that host cultural tours have warm and autumn days with cool nights in spring, cold with sunny skies in winter, and warm, generally sunny summer with light monsoon rainfall.

Temperatures vary greatly between day and night at different altitudes. Layered clothing for changing conditions is recommended.

The People

The people of Bhutan fall into three broad ethnic categories: the Sharchops, who live mostly in the eastern region, the Ngalops, living in the western part of Bhutan, and the people of Nepalese origin who generally live in the southern part of the kingdom.

The national language of Bhutan is Dzongkha, with each region having its own dialect. English is understood, as it has been the medium of instruction in most public schools since 1960.

People seem to wear a constant smile. Perhaps it is due to a feeling of contentment because of their Buddhist faith or because of security felt by the people due to the lofty Himalayas protecting them from the outside world. Whatever may be the reason, the people project a sense of happiness which is visible on their faces

With the opening of roads in recent years, small towns have sprung up near the roads. Occasionally, you see a twentieth century automobile parked outside a thousand-year-old monastery. But, most people of Bhutan live the life as they lived several hundred years ago. They live in rustic rural homes surrounded by fields of rice, maize, buckwheat and wheat. At higher altitudes, they live in nomadic tents woven with yak hair. The tough life has moulded their character.

Western dress is still an exception in Bhutan. Men wear traditional *Gho* — a knee-length robe usually made from hand-woven fabric in interesting patterns. Women wear the ankle-length *Mira* — woven in patterns distinct to each valley.

The Bhutanese love festivals, and many of them last several days. Dancing, singing, feasting and sports are an integral part of each festival.

Visitors are welcome to join them and partake the hospitality of the people.

The most important sport or pastime of the Bhutanese people is archery. Archers throughout Bhutan take great pride in hitting any part of a plate of the size of a dinner plate from a distance of 450 feet. Every village has its own archery range, and high-spirited competitions take place as part of every festival

Flora and Fauna

Like the climate, the flora and fauna of the country offers tremendous contrast. The rivers of Bhutan cascade down from the frozen glaciers to feed the fertile valleys below. If you follow the rivers upstream, fern and forests of oak and other deciduous trees give way to evergreens — such as pine, spruce, hemlock, cypress and juniper. Mountains of rhododendrons blaze with colours in the spring. Even on the high mountain passes above the tree line, tiny alpine flowers can be seen dotting the wind-swept ground.

At higher altitudes, herds of yaks graze as do the wild, goat-like blue sheep. At times, you can spot the *Takin* or once in a while even the elusive snow-leopard. At lower altitude, you can see in Bhutan's forests small game—wild boar and Himalayan bear. In the Manas Wildlife Sanctuary which extends into Assam, elephants, tiger, rhinoceros, buffalo, deer and Bhutan's own golden langur monkeys abound.

Important places of tourist interest are now accessible by road. Much of the rugged beauty of the country can be seen along these roads. Visits to *Dzoinga* and temples enables visitors experience Bhutan of the past and present. Spectacular masked dances are part of the tourist itinerary and visitors can see a local festival unexpectedly during their trip. The festivals are so frequent.

PARO VALLEY

For a first time visitor to Bhutan, the best introduction to the Dragon Kingdom could be an ancient circular watch-tower perched on a steep ridge and overlooking the patch-work rice paddies of the Paro Valley. Built around 1657, the white and brown ringed fortress was made the NATIONAL MUSEUM in 1967 — the country's only archive. The Museum has old coins and the costumes of the people of this country at various times of its history. There are the ancient weapons including also bows used in archery. The brass and copper housewares are good examples of Bhutanese craftsmanship. The PHILATELIC GALLERY near the top of the Museum may be of great interest to western visitors. Stamps are a big business in Bhutan and are an important source of foreign exchange. Their postage stamps are sought by collectors as they cover a wide range of subjects and are beautifully printed. On October 30, 1967, Bhutan issued the world's first three-dimensional stamps in commemoration of

National Museum

man's conquest of space. The world's first steel stamps, printed on hair-thin steel foil, reflects the importance of steel industry in the economic development of Bhutan. They have printed silk stamps with religious motifs of Bhutan. The King of Bhutan has been featured on a series of gold embossed coin stamps. Bhutan was the first country to introduce "Talking Stamps" in 1973 — these were, in fact, gummed miniature phonograph records playing Bhutan's national anthem. However, it may be interesting to note that despite some of the finest postage stamps, Bhutan has no strong postal system. Even today, runners carry messages across the country where no road links exist. Perhaps, to provide a contrast, the Museum displays a fragment of the moon's surface brought by Neil Armstrong in July 1969.

If ever there were a place where nature and man conjured to create their clearest image, it must be the Valley of Paro in the kingdom of Bhutan. Paro, the town with the only airport in the country, is unique in beauty and in history. To the north, MOUNT CHAMOLHARI (Mountain of the Goddess), reigns in white glory and the glacier waters from its "five sisters" peaks plunge torrentially through deep gorges, finally converging to form the Paro Chu river that nourishes the rice fields and apple and peach orchards.

The TAKTSANG MONASTERY, literally meaning 'Tiger's Nest', has been built around the cave where Guru Rimpoche — and later his follower Dubthak Singye — meditated. It clings, seemingly impossible, to a cliff of rock 800 metres above the valley floor. A visit to this monastery is a challenge, exhausting, thrilling and profoundly mystical. According to a legend, Padmasambhava flew on the back of a tiger from Tibet to this place. But now you do not have to use tiger transport as you can either trek to the temple or use a horse as your transport.

Across the river, on the knoll that rises from the river, stands the elegantly symmetrical RIMPUNG DZONG (Rimpung meaning literally heap of jewels) commanding a view of the Paro Valley stretched out below. Today, it houses the Paro monastic body and the office of the Dzongda (district commissioner) and Thrimpon (district judge). But, until some centuries ago, it was an impregnable fortress that repulsed invasions from Tibet.

The THONGDROEL, the most sacred giant painted and appliqued scroll depicting the eight manifestations of Guru Padmasambhava with the two attendants, Khendu Yeshey Tsogyel and Khandu Minona Rawa, is displayed for a few hours on the concluding days of the Paro Tesechu festival held from the 10th to the 14th day of the Bhutanese lunar calendar's second month. It is unfurled before dawn for only a few hours before the direct rays of the sun strike it. Approximately 400 years old, it is easily susceptible to damage from sun rays.

KYICHU LHAKHANG, one of the kingdom's oldest and most sacred temples, and DUNGTSE LHAKHANG are other centres of attraction

Built on a hillside overlooking the beautiful Paro valley, Hotel Olathang offers accommodation in the main building as well as in 14 cottages sprawled over 43 acres.

THIMPHU

THIMPHU, the capital of Bhutan since 1960, lies at an elevation of over 7600 feet in a fertile valley transversed by the Thimphu Chhu River.

TASHICHO DZONG, the main secretariat building, houses all the Ministries, the National Assembly Hall, the office of the King and the

Tashicho Dzong

Throne Room. It is also the summer residence of the monk body and the religious chief, the Je Khempo.

In the NATIONAL ASSEMBLY HALL, the two-storey high statue of Lord Buddha, wall paintings depicting the twelve stages of Buddhahood and columns of Kanju and Tenju exemplify the supremacy of religion over politics.

The yearly Thimphu Festival is held in the courtyard directly in front of the National Assembly Hall. Housed in the UCHI, the tall citadel-type temple in the middle of two courtyards, is one of the two largest thankas (religious scrolls). Unlike the one in Paro which is displayed once a year during the Paro Festival, this one is displayed to the public only once in 25 years. During the renovation of TASHICHO DZONG, the Uchi was left undisturbed.

Prominently standing out in Thimphu is a stupa-styled monument dedicated to the late King, His Majesty Jigme Dorji Wangchuck, the father of modern Bhutan. The paintings and statues inside the stupa provide a rare insight into Buddhist philosophy. The town of Thimphu is nothing like what a capital city is imagined to be. Nevertheless, for Bhutan, it is a fitting and lively place. The shops sell wares from tea to horseshoes and cooking oil to cloth fabrics. And wooden houses stand side by side with concrete buildings, all painted and constructed in traditional Bhutanese styles. The HANDICRAFT EMPORIUM displays a wide assortment of handwoven and crafted products.

Eight kilometres from Thimphu stands the SIMTOKHA DZONG on a lofty ridge. It still enjoys the strategic importance today that it did in 1627 when it was first built by Shabdrung Nawang Namgyel — the first King of Bhutan.

Hotel Motithang at Thimphu played host to numerous Heads of State and Government on the occasion of the coronation of His Majesty, King Jigme Singye Wangchuck. Built in classical Bhutanese style, this palatial hotel is located at a height of 2560 metres above sea-level on 20 acres of land.

PUNAKHA

Drained by the Phochu and Mochu rivers, the fertile valley of Punakha produces rich crops of rice and fruits, including mangoes, bananas and oranges. It has a temperate climate. Until 1955, Punakha served as the capital of Bhutan and even today, it is the winter seat of the Central Monk Body. In 1637, Shabdrung Ngawang Namgyel built the FORTRESS OF PUNAKHA at the junction of the Phochu and Mochu (Male and Female) rivers (which actually converged right in front of the Dzong) to serve as both the religious and administrative centre for Bhutan.

Punakha Dzong houses many sacred temples, including the MACHHIN LHAKHANG, where the embalmed body of Shabdrung Ngawang Namgyel lies in state in keeping with tradition. Everyday rituals, including the serving of meals, is carried out as it was during the Shabdrung's life.

Damaged four times by fire in the late 18th and early 19th centuries and by earthquakes in 1897, the Punakha Dzong has also suffered devastation by floods which sweep down the valley as the snows melt in the great northern glaciers. The Dzong (named Punthang Dechen Phodrang) was completely restored under the direction of the present King.

Punakha Dzong

The road from Thimphu to Punakha is crossed through a 10,218-foot high DOCHU LA PASS. It offers an enchanting views of alpine snows and a magnificent canvas of colour — a profusion of red, pink, white, yellow and purple rhododendron blossoms.

The Valley is also home to the sacred Jampe Lhakhang and Kurje monastery. The body marks of Guru Padmasambhava are to this day imprinted on a solid rock. Both temples are believed to have been built in the eighth century by Sindhu Raja whom Padmasambhava cured of his ailment.

WANGDIPHODRANG

On the east-west traverse and road beyond Thimphu lies the valley of WANGDIPHODRANG, at the junction of the Mo Chu and Tang Chu rivers. At the confluence of the rivers stands the WANGDIPHODRANG DZONG. For many centuries, it was the seat of one of Bhutan's most powerful dzongpons. The higher reaches of the valley provide rich cattle pastures. Yak dairy research station has been set up at GOPGONA.

TONGSA

Midway between HA in the far west and TASHIGANG in the far east stands the striking TONGSA DZONG, ancestral home of Bhutan's royal family. Both Ugyen Wangchuck, the Penlop of Tongsa who was elected the nation's first hereditary monarch, and his successor King Jigme Wangchuck, ruled the country from this ancient seat. All four kings have held the post of Tongsa Penlop prior to being officially crowned. The present king was appointed Penlop in 1972, shortly before his succession to the throne. The dzong was built by Ngawang Namgyel in 1648 and later enlarged and decorated. Because of its once strategic position, the only connecting route between the eastern and western sectors of the central region, the Tongsa Penlop could effectively control the court. Among the Dzong's treasures is a magnificent collection of rhino-horn sculptures. Tourists stay at a comfortable Motel Sherubling.

BUMTHANG is also the home of the great Buddhist teacher Pemalingpa, to whose descendants the present dynasty traces its ancestry. Pemalingpa was a blacksmith who was led by mystic forces to discover spiritual treasures at the bottom of a burning lake. Not knowing how to spread the word contained in the treasures, he hid them away until one night the Daklinis, or female heavenly spirits revealed to him the power to preach. Legend also tells us that as he spoke, flowers dropped from the sky and vanished into rays of light. Hotel Wangdichhaling plays host to visitors during their stay at Bumthang.

TASHIGANG

In the far eastern part of Bhutan, on the banks of the Dangme Chhu lies Tashigang, the hub of the region's largest and most important district. Once the centre of a busy trade-route with Tibet, Tashigang is today the junction of the east-west highway with a road which runs north from the foothill town of SAMDRUPJONGKHAR. Vividly coloured handloomed cloth and silk, spun from cocoons bred on castor oil plants, are local specialities. Tropical crops and fruits thrive. The TASHIGANG DZONG, from which the whole of the eastern region was governed from the late 17th century until the unification of the country at the beginning of this century, stands on a steep ridge above the Manas River. The dzong was built in 1667 by Chogyal Minjur Tempa, Bhutan's third Deb.

A comfortable Motel, the Kelling, can be used as a base for visiting this area.

MONGAR

To the southwest is Mongar, next to Tashigang, the second largest settlement in the east. Mongar is the site of one of Bhutan's newest dzongs, built in 1930 following the traditional architectural pattern. The Motel Shongar provides pleasant accommodation for visitors.

Adventure
Bhutan is just not for culture alone. It is also a place for experiencing a little bit of adventure in the mountains or to enjoy an outdoor holiday. The best adventure treks are available, depending upon the

physical conditions of each guest. Treks start from semi-tropical forests right up to the snowclad mountains. For the more adventurous, some of the highest peaks of the country and swift rivers have been opened. The rivers in Bhutan are for rafting experience. The challenge is one of the most exciting in the Himalayas. Visitors are provided well-trained guides who have good knowledge of history and traditions of the country and are well versed in English language.

In India, Bhutan tours are packaged and marketed by Indo-Japan Tours. Chandralok Building, Janpath, New Delhi-110001. They offer tours ranging from 5 days and four nights to 8 days and 7 nights in association with Bhutan Tourism Corporation.

<u>Information</u>: Royal Bhutanese Embassy, Chandragupta Marg, Chanakypuri, New Delhi-110021. *Tel*: 604070.

INDEX

Abbe Faria Statue, 408
Aberdecon Market, 595
Abi Gamine, 158
Achabal, 208
Achalgarh, 277
Adalaj Vav, 361
Adhar Devi (Arbudha Devi) Temple, 276
Adinath Temple, 264, 318, 335
Afghan Church, 371
Aga Khan Palace, 377, 378
Agartala, 572, 573, 578
Agartala Raj Bhavan, 572
Agate Island, 597
Agra, 13, 52, 53, 54, 55, 57, 59, 71, 111, 113, 149, 151, 176, 177, 180, 231, 245, 255, 260, 271, 281, 286-291, 299-301, 313, 319, 491
Agra Fort, 111, 289, 300
Aguada Beach, 408
Aguada Fort, 404
Ahar, 264
Ahar Museum, 271
Ahmedabad, 107, 118, 137, 181, 343, 348-350
Ahmedabad Zoo, 350
Ahmednagar Fort, 378
Ahmedpur Mandvi Beach, 357, 364
Aihole, 424, 431-434
Aiyappan-Kurukku, 446
Aizawl, 571-572, 577
Ajanta Caves (Cave Temples), 7, 55, 56, 57, 60, 114, 367, 375, 379-380, 392-394
Ajmer, 120, 153, 262

Ajmer Tomb, 269
Akash Bairava, 612
Akbar's Fort, 294-295
Akbar's Mausoleum, 300
Akbar's Tomb, 53, 54, 55, 57
Alagar Kovil, 483
Alappuzha (Alleppey), 443, 447, 452
Albuquerque Mansion, 405
Alchi Gompa, 211
Alibaug Beach, 374
Alibaug Fort, 379
Alibaug Temple, 384
Aligarh, 291
Allahabad (Prayag) (Vatsa), 116, 281, 294-295
Alleppey (see Alappuzha)
Almora, 283-284, 310
Altinho, 408
Alwar, 260-262
Alwar Palace, 261
Alwaye, 452
Ama Doblam, 620
Amanat Khan Serai, 232
Amar Mahal Museum, 205
Amar Sagar, 275
Amarnath, 154, 199
Amarnath Cave, 199
Amaravati, 108, 496, 498
Amba Mata Temple, 354
Amber, 112
Amber Fort, 53, 54, 55, 57, 59, 60, 112, 256, 268
Amber Palace, 112, 268
Amboli, 383-384
Amer, 257-258
Amritsar, 96, 121, 229-233

Anamalai Wildlife Sanctuary, 171, 476
Anamudi Peak, 437
Anand Bhavan, 294
Ananda Bazar, 519
Anandpur Sahib, 230
Anantnag, 200
Anantpur, 495
Andaman and Nicobar Islands, 593-596
Andhra Pradesh, 120, 124, 166, 180, 245, 489-504
Andrews Memorial Hall, 536
Animeshlochan Chaitya, 547, 557
Anjengo, 438
Anjuna Beach, 405
Anjuvannam, 438
Ankh Macholi, 291
Ankleshwar, 347
Anna Samadhi, 480
Annapurna Peak, 605, 608, 609
Annapurna Area Conservation Project, 622
Annapurna Conservation Area, 620, 621-622
Anthropological Museum, 595, 600
Anugul, 514
Anukil Thakur's Ashram, 554
Apollo Bunder, 371
Aquarium, 442
Araku Valley, 504
Archaeological Museum, Goa, 404
Archaeological Museum, Tanjore, 469
Archaeological Site Museum, Konark, 520
Archaeological Site Museum, Sarnath, 305
Archaeological Survey of India, Khajuraho, 317
Arjuna's Penance, 464
Armenian Church, 529
Art Gallery, Baroda, 347

Art Gallery, Bhaktapur, 617
Art School, 527
Arunachal Pradesh, 561, 567-568, 580
Arunachal Pradesh Museum, 577
Arunachala Temple, 467
Asan Square, 612
Ashoka Pillar, 295, 334, 557
Ashokan Column, 551
Ashrafi Mahal, 337
Assam, 5, 24, 31, 117, 124, 137, 165, 166, 245, 561-566
Astamudi Lake, 443
Auli, 155
Aundh Nagnath, 384
Aurangabad, 7, 52, 55, 56, 57, 58, 60, 71, 176, 180, 367, 379, 380, 391, 393
Auroville, 477
Avaloketeswara, 616
Avantipur, 208
Ayodhya, 293-294, 466

Baba Atal Rai Tower, 232
Baba Bakala, 232
Babri Masjid, 293-294
Bada Bagh, 275
Bada Ganapati, 337
Badal Mahal, 264
Badami, 424, 425-426, 413-434
Badami Cave Temples, 108, 425, 432
Badami Fort, 426, 432
Badrinath, 252, 282, 283, 284
Baga Beach, 405, 408
Bagdogra, 59, 62, 533
Bagh Caves, 337
Bagmola Beach, 405
Bahu Fort, 205
Baidyanath Dham, 554
Baijnath Temple, 224
Bakkim, 589
Balak Tirth Temple, 357
Balighat, 513

Balsamand Lake, 273
Bamyan, 114
Banbasa, 31
Bandhavgarh National Park, 168, 335
Bandipur National Park (Tiger Reserve) 167-168, 421, 429, 430-431, 476
Bangalore, 56, 57, 58, 59, 61, 71, 133, 145, 162, 176, 177, 180, 181, 415-416, 427-430
Bangalore Museum, 416
Bangalore Vidhan Sabha (Vidhana Saudha), 415, 429
Bangaram Beach Resort, 597
Bangaram Island, 597
Banjara Darwaza, 493
Banqueting Hall, 460
Bara Bazaar, 577
Bara Imambara, 292-293
Bara Khamba, 427
Bara Shigri, 157
Barabati Fort, 512
Baradari Palace, 493
Baramula, 196
Barari Caves, 554
Bareth, 328
Barmer, 275
Baroda, 180, 347-348, 361
Baroda Museum, 347
Baroda School of Indian Art, 347
Barpeta, 575
Barrackpore, 527
Barren Island, 594, 595
Basholi, 205
Basilica of Bom Jesus, 403
Bassein Sea Fort, 378
Bastar, 330
Batasia Loop, 542
Bathing Ghats, 338
Batote, 206
Battis Shirale, 388, 391
Batul, 329
Baz Bahadur's Palace, 337
Bedsa, 381

Begnas Lake, 622
Belur, 57, 111, 429
Belur Math, 62, 539
Belur Temples, 58, 414, 419, 420, 529
Benares Hindu University, 297, 305
Bengal, 14, 15, 114, 118, 122, 123, 124, 130, 137
Bengal Club, 528
Benisagar Dam, 335
Bennarghatta National Park, 168, 429
Benog Hill, 309
Benoy Badal Dinesh Bagh (BBD Bagh), 524, 525, 526
Beraghat, 329
Betla National Park, 550
Betul Beach, 408
Bhadgaon, 54, 607, 608
Bhagalpur, 554
Bhairavnath Temple, 618
Bhairahawa, 608, 630
Bhaja Caves, 381, 391
Bhakra Dam, 23, 27
Bhaktapur (Bhadgaon) 617-619
Bhandarkar Oriental Research Institute, 391
Bharat Bhawan, 325, 332
Bharat Kala Bhavan Museum, 305
Bharat Mata Temple 297, 305
Bharatiya Lok Kala Mandal Museum, 264, 271
Bharatpur, 149, 151, 165, 260, 261, 277
Bharatpur Bird Sanctuary (Keolodeo Ghana) 269, 278
Bharatpur Fort, 262
Bharatpur Palace, 278
Bhartrihari Caves, 338
Bhatta Falls, 309
Bhattiprola, 496
Bhavnagar, 180, 184, 358
Bheemunipatnam, 504

Bherugarh, 323
Bhim Baithak, 325
Bhimashankara, 384
Bhimbetka, 332
Bhimsen Temple, 616
Bhimtal, 308, 310
Bhitar Kanika Sanctuary, 170
Bhodnath, 54
Bhojpur, 332
Bhopal, 152, 313, 325-326, 331-333
Bhopal Museum, 332
Bhubaneswar, 52, 62, 71, 105, 109, 133, 176, 179, 507, 508-510, 513, 515, 516-519
Bhubaneswar Museum, 517
Bhutan, 5, 31, 131, 633-642
Bibi Ka Maqbara, 112, 380, 393
Bidar, 502
Bidon Falls, 567
Bihar, 15, 31, 95, 141, 167, 245, 281, 545-558
Bihar Institute of Handicraft and Design, 556
Bihar-Sharif, 552, 558
Bijapur, 414, 426-427, 434
Bijli Mahadev Shrine, 219, 222
Bijnor, 155
Bijolia, 262
Bikaner, 66, 266
Bikaner Fort, 266
Billing, 162
Bind Basini Temple, 623
Bindu Sagar Lake, 508
Biratnagar, 608
Birds' Island, 595
Birgunj, 608, 629
Birla Academy of Art and Culture, 529
Birla Mandir (see Lakshmi Narayan Temple, Delhi)
Birla Planetarium, 494, 529
Bishop Falls, 567
Boat Snob Island, 600
Bodh Gaya, 62, 93, 294, 298, 545, 546-547, 556, 557-558

Bodhi Tree, 557
Bodhnath, 614-615
Bogmalo Beach, 408
Bolar, 413
Bolghatty Island, 445
Bolghatty Place, 445
Bombay (*See* also Mumbai), 7, 12, 19, 22, 54, 56, 57, 58, 59, 60, 61, 62, 63, 71, 72-73, 97, 113, 122, 132, 133, 144, 145, 147, 151, 153, 162, 177, 179, 180, 181, 367
Bombay Gymkhana, 376
Bombay-Pune Highway, 162
Bomdila, 568
Bondla Forest, 405, 409
Borra Caves, 504
Botanical Gardens, 62, 475, 539, 567, 595
Brahma Temple, 318, 335
Brahmakunda, 568
Brahmeshwar Temple, 517
Brammahi, 158
Brihadeesvara Temple, 56, 58, 109
Brindavan Gardens, 418, 429
British Residency, 493
Budhani Kantha Temple, 615
Buddhist Stupas, 106
Buland Darwaza, 15, 290
Bull Temple, 416, 429
Bumbetka, 113
Bumthang, 641
Bunauli, 622
Bundi, 262
Burj Museum, 287
Burma, 11
Burmah Nalla, 595, 600
Burmese Temple, 595
Bushy Dam, 383
Butterball, 464
Butterfly Museum, 577

Calangute Beach, 404, 405, 408
Calcutta, 6, 8, 9, 14, 16, 19, 31, 51, 54, 59, 62, 71, 74-75, 113, 127,

130, 132, 133, 144, 145, 147, 176, 177, 179, 523-532, 537-540
Calcutta High Court, 526-527
Calcutta Raj Bhavan, 526
Calcutta Town Hall, 524
Calico Textile Museum, 361
Calicut (Kozhikode), 446
Cambay, 347, 350
Camel Breeding Farm, 266
Candolin Beach, 404
Cannoor (Cannanore), 446, 447
Car Nicobar Island, 594, 595
Caranzol, 405
Cardamom Hills, 437
Catholic Church, 473
Cellular Jail, 594, 599
Central Cottage Industries Emporium, 245
Central Museum, 259, 268
Chadwick Falls, 217
Chail, 220
Chalukyan Badami Caves, 114
Chamba, 157, 223
Chamba Bridge, 325
Chamundi Hill, 162, 417
Chanchal Forest, 534
Chandarnagore, 532
Chanderi, 328
Chandigarh, 23, 151, 162, 190, 215, 228-229, 233-234
Chandipur, 513
Chandragiri Fort, 498
Chandragiri Mahal, 498
Chandraprabha Forest, 305
Chandrodaya Mandir, 537
Changabang, 158
Changunarayan, 619
Chankama, 298
Chankramana (Jewel Walk), 547, 557
Channakesava, 420
Channapatna, 416
Chapel of St. Catherine, 403
Chapora Fort, 405
Char Minor, 419-493, 502

Charaideo, 565
Chashma Shahi, 196, 208
Chatham Saw Mill, 595, 600
Chaturbhuja Tample, 319, 335
Chaukhamba Peak, 282-283
Chaumukha Temple, 264, 353
Chausath Yogini Temple, 317, 335
Chepauk Palace, 460
Cheria Palli Church, 445
Cherrapunji, 6, 567, 575, 577
Chhatri Bagh, 337
Chhindwara, 329
Chhota Nagpur, 554
Chhoti Dargah, 552
Chidambaram 457, 467
Children's Park, 350
Chilka Lake, 7, 513, 514, 515, 517
Chimmi Ghat Masjid, 550
China Bhavan, 536
China Hills, 284
Chingleput, 462-463
Chinhat Picnic Pavilion, 303
Chini-Ka-Roze, 289
Chirya Tapu, 595, 600
Chisti's Tomb, 290
Chitrachal Hill, 564
Chitragupta Temple, 316, 335
Chitrakoot Falls, 330
Chitralayan Art Gallery, 442
Chitpore, 524
Chittoor, 495
Chittorgarh, 262, 263, 271
Chittorgarh Fort, 149
Chitwan, 629
Chitwan Park, 620
Cho Oyu Peak, 605, 619, 620
Chobhar Gorge, 614, 615
Chola Tanjore, 114
Chola Temple, 56, 58
Cholamandal, 481
Chor Bazar, 376
Chorten, 588
Chorwad Beach Resort, 61, 364
Chow Mahal, 493
Chowpatty Beach, 372, 374

Chowringhee, 524
Chowringhee Gate, 527
Chrisneshwar, 384
Chunar Fort, 305
Church Gate, 372
Church of St. Cajetan, 404
Church of St. Francis, 444, 452
Church of St. Francis of Assissi, 403
Church of Our Lady of Expectations, 461
Church of Our Lady of Immaculate Conception, 408
Church of the Most Holy Rosary, 413
Church of the Sacred Heart of Jesus, 529
Churchemara Danda, 621
Churia Range of Himalayan Mountains, 606
Cinque Island, 595, 600
Circular Road, 524
Citadel, 275
City Palace, 259, 268
City Palace Museum, 271
Climere Wildlife Sanctuary, 476
Cochin (see also Kochi), 56, 57, 58, 59, 61, 62, 97, 178, 437, 444-445, 597
Coimbatore, 476
Colaba, 375, 376
Colgang Temple, 554
Columbia Hills, 373
Colva Beach, 408, 505
Connaught Place, 239, 245, 246
Convent of Church Assissi, 403-404
Convent of Our Lady of the Rosary, 404
Cooch Behar, 523, 535
Coondapur Beach, 429
Coorgh, 413
Corbett National Park (Tiger Reserve), 161, 165, 171, 283-284, 309-310

Corbyn's Cove, 595, 600
Cottage Industries Emporium, 595
Cotton Exchange, 376
Courtalam, 474
Covelong Beach, 462, 481
Crafts Museum, 113
Craganore, 438, 447
Crawford Market, 376
Crinoline Falls, 567
Crocodile Farm, 363, 429, 463, 481
Crusoe Island, 454
Cubbon Park, 415, 428
Cuddappah, 495
Cuttack, 512

Dabhoi, 348
Dachigam Wildlife Sanctuary, 167, 208
Dada Hari Vav, 361
Dadra and Nagar Haveli, 358-359
Daksum, 208
Dakshineswar Kali Temple, 529, 530, 539
Dakshinkali Temple, 614, 615
Dal Lake, 8, 191, 192, 195, 196, 208, 209
Dalhousie, 205, 219, 233
Dalhousie Square, 525
Dalma Wildlife Sanctuary, 167
Daman, 619, and Diu, 357-358
Damodar Valley Project, 554
Dampa Wildlife Sanctuary, 169
Dariba Kalan, Chandni Chowk, 245
Darjeeling, 5, 6, 7, 59, 62, 147, 179, 523, 533-535, 540-542
Darjeeling-Rangeet Valley Ropeway, 542
Darranga, 575
Darya Daulat, 416
Dasavatara Temple, 108
Dasawamedh Ghat, 296-297
Dattatray Temple, 618
Dattia, 321-322

Daulagiri Peak, 283
Daulatabad, 379, 380-381
Daulatabad Fort, 60, 393
Dauli, 517
Daw Hill, 535
Deeg, 287
Deeg Fort, 278
Deer Park, 585, 588
Dehotsarga, 364
Dehradun, 155, 161, 215, 283, 285
Delhi (Old Delhi; New Delhi), 6, 9, 13, 14, 15, 19, 22, 31, 52, 53, 54, 55, 57, 58, 59, 60, 62, 63, 66, 68, 71, 73, 74, 111, 113, 116, 122, 127, 129, 133, 140, 144, 145, 147, 149, 151, 152, 157, 161, 162, 165, 176, 177, 179, 180, 190, 215, 236-252, 255, 281, 286, 313, 319
Deo Tibba Peak, 157, 158, 218
Deodari Waterfalls, 305
Deogarh, 108, 554
Depot Hill, 309
Desert National Park, 275
Desert Sanctuary, 171
Deshnoke, 266
Devi Chinnamasta Temple, 554
Devi Jagdamba Temple, 315, 316
Devil's Fall, 622
Devlali, 162
Dewas, 322
Dhakna - Kolkaz Sanctuary (Tiger Reserve), 169
Dhanbad, 552, 554
Dhami Sagar, 573
Dhanushkodi, 473
Dhar, 338
Dharamsala, 161, 162, 215, 219, 233
Dharmajika Stupa, 298
Dharmasura, 157
Dhanladhar, 218
Dhaulagiri Peak, 605, 619
Dhawa Wildlife Sanctuary, 273
Dhenkanal, 514

Dhirdham Temple, 541
Dhobi Ghat, 373
Dhoongri Temple, 222
Dhuandhar Falls, 329
Dhubdi, 589
Dhubela Palace, 335
Dhulikhel, 619, 629
Dhumekh-Stupa, 298
Dibrugarh, 563
Digha, 537, 540
Dilli Haat, 246
Dilwara, 109
Dilwara Jain Temples, 264, 276
Dimapur, 569
Dimna Lady, 554
Dipang Lake, 622
Diu, 364
Diwan-e-Aam, Agra, 287; Delhi, 242, 251; Fatehpur Sikri, 291; Jaipur, 259
Diwan-e-Khas, Agra, 287-288; Delhi, 242, 251; Fatehpur Sikri, 291; Jaipur, 259
Do-Doul Chorten, 585
Dobolim, 62, 404
Dochu La Pass, 632, 640
Doll Museum, 113, 268
Dolphin's Nose, 504
Dona Caterina Tomb, 404
Dona Paula Beach, 408
Doars, 542
Dr. Graham's Home, 535
Dras Valley, 201
Dudhsagar Waterfalls, 405, 409
Dudhwa National Park, 171
Duladeo Temple, 319, 335
Duliagan, 565
Dumbur Falls, 573
Dunagiri, 158
Dungtse Lhakhang, 638
Durbar Square, 63, 610, 611, 615, 619
Durga Temple, 297, 305, 424, 432
Durgapur, 531, 536
Durgiana Mandir, 229, 232

Durrang, 566
Durung Glacier, 156
Dutch Fort, 473
Dutch Palace, 444, 451
Dwarka, 343, 364, 466
Dzoinga, 636
Dzongri, 587, 589

Eagle's Crag, 535
East India, 5, 127
Eastern Ghats, 7
Edapalayam, 446
Ekambareswara Temple, 466
Eklingji Temple, 264, 271
Elephant Waterfalls, 567, 577
Elephanta Caves (Temples), 55, 58, 60, 108, 374-375, 387
Ellora Caves (Cave Temples), 6, 7, 12, 55, 56, 57, 60, 108, 124, 367, 375, 379-380, 391, 392-394
Enchey Monastery, 585, 586, 588
Ernakulam, 441

Fagu, 220
Faizabad, 293-294
Faluknama Palace, 502
Fashion Street, 376
Fateh Burj, 262
Fatehsagar Lake, 55, 263, 271
Fatehpur Sikri, 13, 15, 53, 54, 55, 57, 59, 60, 111, 149, 289-291, 300
Fatula, 201
Ferozeshah Katla, 237-238, 251
Fiang Gompa, 211
Fire Temple, 529
Fish Tail Mountain, 622
Five Raths, 465
Flora Fountain, 372
Fort of Jaisalmer, 118
Fort of Janjira, 379
Fort Saint George Museum, 113, 459, 460, 480
Fort William, 524, 527
Fortress of Punakha, 639

French Rocks, 416

Gaddi Baithak, 612
Gagan Mahal, 427
Gahirmatha, 514
Gaitor, 268
Gallery of Modern Art, 259
Ganapatipule Beach, 384
Gandarbal, 199, 208
Gandhi Ashram (Sabarmati Ashram), 360
Gandhi Bhavan, 332
Gandhi Ghat, 539
Gandhi Maidan, 550
Gandhi Memorial, 486
Gandhi Memorial (Mani Bhavan), 387
Gandhi Memorial Centre, Library, 360
Gandhi Museum, 472, 483
Gandhigram, 483
Ganesh Hamal, 608
Ganga (Ganges), 5, 53, 54, 60, 62, 118, 155, 160, 281, 284, 464, 549
Gangaikondacholapuram, 111, 468
Gangetic Valley, 285-286
Gangotri, 154, 155, 282-283
Gangtok, 59, 120, 542, 584, 587-590
Garampani, 577, 580
Garhmukteswar, 161
Garhwal, 155, 281-282
Garhwal Himalayas, 5, 155, 281-285
Gateway of India, 371, 374, 387
Gateway of Victory, 290
Gaumukh Temple, 277
Gaur, 537
Gauriphants, 31
Gaya, 550-551, 558
Geological Survey of India, 527-528
Ghachowk, 622
Ghana Bird Sanctuary, 170

Ghantai Temple, 318
Ghantal Temple, 375
Ghantasala, 496
Gharial, 579
Ghat Shila, 554-555
Ghats of Varanasi, 112
Gheem Rock, 534
Ghoom Monastery, 62, 534, 542
Ghoom Sanchal Ridge, 533
Gir National Park, 60, 167, 354-355, 358, 362-364
Girmar, 353, 354-355
Glen, 220
Goa (See also Daman, Diu), 52, 60, 62, 97, 119, 131, 167, 177, 181, 357, 397-410
Gobind Palace, 321
Gobind Sagar Lake, 23
Gobindwal Saheb, 232
Gochala, 587
Godwin-Austin, 5, 6
Gol Gumbaz, 13, 112, 414, 426, 434
Golconda, 493, 495, 502
Golconda Fort, 58
Golden Gate, 617
Golden Temple (Hari Mandir, Harminder Sahib), 96, 121, 229, 232
Golden Temple of Vishwanath, 297, 305
Golghar, 549
Goli, 496
Gomateshwara Statue, 10
Gompa of Kaushik, 204
Gomukh Glacier, 284
Gopal Bhavan, 278
Gopal Mandir, 338
Gopalpur-on-Sea, 179, 513, 517
Gopgona, 640
Gorai Beach, 374
Gorakhpur, 295
Gorkha, 622
Gorsain, 155
Gosainkunda, 615
Govind Devji Temple, 268

Govindapur, 524
Govindjee Temple, 573
Grand Ancient, 485
Grand Trunk Road, 15
Graves of Nizam Ali Khan, 492
Great Nicobar, 594
Great Stupa, 333
Greater Kailash Market, 245
Griddhakuta, 552, 558
Grove of Perfect Being, 509
Grub Island, 600
Gufa Mahadev, 307
Guheshwari Temple, 614
Guindy Deer Park, 462, 476
Gujarat, 9, 12, 97, 122, 167, 245, 343-364
Gulbarga Fort, 414
Gulmarg, 60, 156, 162, 192, 195, 198-199, 208, 209, 210
Gun Hill, 309
Gundu Island, 452
Gunner Falls, 567
Gupta Hindu Temple, 334
Guru Shikhar, 277
Gurgaon, Upper Assam, 565
Guruvayoor, 447
Guwahati, 71, 563-564, 574, 575, 577, 580
Gwalior, 112, 151, 180, 184, 300, 313, 319-321
Gwalior Fort, 151, 319
Gyachung Kang, 620
Gyan Bhandar (Library), 275

Ha, 640
Haflong, 580
Haji Ali, 384
Haji Matang, 384
Hajo, 564
Halebid, 57, 111, 429
Halebid Temples, 58, 414, 420
Hampi, 111, 422-423, 433
Hananakonda Hill, 497
Handicraft Emporium, Thimphu, 639

Handicrafts and Handloom Emporium, Gangtok, 585
Handloom House, Calcutta, 532
Handola Mahal, 324
Hanging Gardens, 372, 373, 387
Hanuman Dhoka Place, 610, 611
Hanuman Statue, 616
Hanuman Temple, 612
Hanuman Tibba, 218
Happy Valley Tea Estate, 542
Har-ki-doon, 283
Haramuk Mountain, 199
Hari Parbat, 197, 208
Hari Parbat Fort, 194
Haridwar, 116, 161, 252, 283, 466
Harike Head Works Sanctuary, 170
Harmandir Sahib Temple, Patna, 549, 556
Haryana, 118, 227-234, 245, 281
Hasimara, 535, 536
Hassan, 176, 420
Hathi Gumpha, 513
Hathu, 157
Hauz Khas Village, 252
Hawa Mahal, 255, 259, 268
Hayagriba Madhav Temple, 564
Hazara Pama Temple, 423, 433
Hazarat Bal Mosque, 490
Hazarduari, 537
Hazaribagh, 553
Hazaribagh Wildlife Sanctuary, 167, 554
Hazratbal, 197
Hebrew Synagogues, 529
Hemis Gompa, 121, 211, 202, 203
Hemkund, 280, 282
Hill-Top Fort, 320
Hills of Karbi Anlong, 580
Himachal Pradesh, 4, 81, 158, 161, 162, 167, 201, 205 215-224, 227, 245, 281
Himachal State Museum, 220
Himalayan Monasteries, 159

Himalayan Mountaineering Institute (HMI), 534, 541
Himalayas, 5, 8, 22, 131, 147, 153-159, 200, 215, 218-282, 283-284, 533, 605, 642; important peaks of, 157-158
Himalchuli, 619
Himayat Sagar, 502
Hind Old Mahal, 337
Hiranya Varna Mahavihar, 615
Hiuen Tsang Memorial Hall, 558
Holy Cross Church, 462
Homes for the Dying, 530
Hope Town, 600
Horiyuji, 114
Hoshang Shah's Tomb, 337
Hoshangabad, 113, 329
Hot Springs, 222
Howrah Bridge, 16
Hoysaleswara Temple, 420, 421
Humayun's Tomb, 241, 251
Hundru Falls, 553
Hussain Sagar Lake, 494
Hussainabad (Chhota) Imambara, 293, 302-303
Huthising Jain Temple, 361
Hyangza, 622
Hyderabad, 19, 58, 59, 61, 62, 71, 122, 131, 133, 139, 140, 145, 179, 181, 245, 489-496
Hyderabad High Court, 493

Ibrahim Rauza Mosque and Tomb, 112, 427
Ice House, 461
Idgah Hills, 326, 332
Imambara, 302
Imphal, 71, 176, 570, 571, 577, 580
India Gate, 117, 239, 243, 251
Indian Museum, 113 527, 539
Indira Chowk, 612
Indo - Saracenic Palace, 417
Indore, 61, 162, 313, 322, 336-338
Indra Kila Hill, 499
Indrasan, 158

Institute of Oriental Studies, 347
Intanki Wildlife Sanctuary, 169
Islamnagar, 332
Itanagar, 71
Itmad-ud-Daula's Tomb, 289, 300

Jabalpur, 313, 329-330, 340
Jadavpur University, 529
Jag Mandir Palace, 263, 271
Jagannath Temple, Kathmandu, 612; Puri, 121, 510-511, 519; Ranchi, 553
Jagannathpur Village, 553
Jagat Ambika Mata Temple, 264
Jagatsukh, 222
Jagdish Temple, 55, 271
Jagmohan Palace, 418
Jahangir Mahal, 288, 322
Jahangir Nicholson Museum of Modern Art, 113
Jahaz Mahal, 324, 337
Jai Mandir, 258
Jai Vilas Palace, 320
Jaigarh Fort, 257, 258
Jaikwadi Project, 393
Jain Stupas, 108
Jain Temple, Calcutta, 539; Dilwara, 109, 264; Jaisalmer, 275; Malabar Hills, 373; Ranakpur, 56
Jaipur, 52, 53, 54, 55, 57, 58, 59, 60, 112, 145, 149, 151, 176, 178, 180, 182, 231, 255, 256, 257-260, 266-270, 286
Jaipur Zoo, 259
Jaisalmer, 55, 56, 149, 151, 260, 265-266, 274-276
Jaisalmer Fort, 118, 254, 265
Jaisalmer Lake, 264
Jakhu Hill, 220
Jakhu Temple, 216
Jakrem, 567
Jakrem Hot Springs, 577
Jalan Museum, 556

Jaldapara Wildlife Sanctuary, 172, 535-536, 542
Jallianwala Bagh, 232
Jalmandir, 552
Jalpaiguri, 523
Jama Masjid, Agra, 289; Ahmedabad, 348, 350; Bijapur, 414, 427; Bhopal, 332; Delhi, 13, 14, 111, 238, 243, 251; Fatehpur Sikri, 290; Mumbai, 374; Mandu, 325, 337; Srinagar, 196
Jambukeshwara Temple, 485
Jammu and Kashmir (*See also* Kashmir, Srinagar), 5, 6, 13, 15, 121, 155, 158, 162, 167, 176, 189-212
Jamnagar, 346, 352
Jampe Lhakhang, 640
Jamshedpur, 6, 554
Janakpur, 629
Janardhan Temple, 443
Janjira Sea Fort, 385
Jantar Mantar, Delhi, 241, 250-251; Jaipur, 259, 268; Ujjain, 338
Japanese Buddhist Temple, 529
Jasidih, 554
Jaswant Thada Cenotaph, 55, 273
Jaunpur, 305
Javeri Temple, 318, 335
Jawahar Bal Bhavan, 494
Jawahar Burj, 262
Jawahar Tunnel, 13, 206
Jawalakhel, 616-617
Jehangir Art Gallery, 372
Jetpur, 354
Jewish Synagogue, 452
Jhansi, 53, 54, 320, 321
Jhansi Fort, 321
Jharipani Falls, 309
Jhaveri Bazar, 376
Jhelum, 195, 212
Jodhabai Palace, 290
Jodhpur, 55, 56, 57, 58, 149, 151, 180, 182, 260, 265, 272-274

Jodhpur Museum, 273
Jog Falls, 413
Joginder Hagar, 215
Johari Bazar, 259
Jolly Buoy Island, 600
Jomson, 622
Jorhat, 580
Jorasanke, 529
Joshimath, 155
Jowai, 577
Jubilee Hall, 494
Juhu Beach, 374, 387
Jullundar, 230
Juma Masjid, 417
Junagarh, 343, 354-355, 358

Kachana Kawal, 607
Kadmat Island, 597
Kailasa Temple, Daulatabad, 380, 381; Ellora, 108, 380, 413
Kailasanatha Temple, 381
Kailash, 154
Kaiser Bagh, 293
Kakarhwa, 295
Kala Bhavan, 536
Kala Pahad, 494
Kaladi 447
Kalahasti, 498
Kalahati, 162
Kalakad Sanctuary, 171
Kalakshetra, 461
Kali Temple, 527
Kalibangan, 9
Kalijal Island, 515
Kalikata, 524
Kalimpong, 535, 542, 584
Kalka, 215
Kalpani Island, 597
Kamakhya Temple, 563, 575
Kamakshiamman Temple, 466
Kameng, 568
Kamet Peak, 155, 158, 282
Kamla Nehru Park, 387
Kamshet, 162
Kanakdurga Temple, 499

Kanauj, 291
Kanch Mandir, 61, 337
Kanchenjunga, 533, 534, 583, 605, 619
Kanchenjunga National Park, 587
Kanchipuram, 61, 109, 137, 457, 462, 466-467, 480
Kanchipuram Temples, 56, 58, 105
Kanda, 310
Kandriya Mahadeva Temple, 315-316, 317, 318, 335
Kangra, 162, 223, 227, 233
Kangra Fort, 219
Kangra Valley, 219, 330
Kangtega, 620
Kanha National Park, 165, 168, 328-329, 338-340
Kanheri Caves, 375, 387
Kanjitu Peak, 156
Kankaria Lake, 350
Kanniyakumari (Cape Comorin), 473-474
Kanpur, 152, 292
Kapaleeswara Temple, 461, 480
Karakoram, 189
Karamibag, 554
Karang, 570
Karapur, 419
Karbi Anlong Hills, 580
Karbi Villages, 580
Kargil, 201
Karla Caves, 108, 381, 382, 383, 388, 391
Karnal, 230
Karnala Bird Sanctuary, 169, 385
Karnataka, 10, 13, 111, 120, 124, 162, 167-168, 245, 413-434
Karnataka High Court, 415
Karol Bagh, 245
Karwar Beach, 429
Kasauli, 162, 220
Kashi, 296
Kashmir (See also Jammu and Kashmir; Srinagar), 7, 8, 18,

20, 60, 95, 129, 136-137, 139, 162, 163, 231, 245
Kasthmandap Temple, 612
Kasturba Samadhi, 391
Kathgodam Tibba, 309
Kathgola, 537
Kathmandu, 52, 53, 54, 131, 606, 607, 608, 610-613, 614, 615, 619, 620, 621, 622, 628-629
Katra, 205
Katra Mosque, 537
Katrain, 222
Kausani, 310
Kavaiyar Palaces 442
Kavaratti Island, 597
Kaveri Arts, 417
Kaziranga Wildlife Sanctuary, 165, 166, 564-565, 575, 578-580
Keahreswar, 510
Kedarnath, 154, 252, 282-283, 284
Kedarnath Sanctuary, 172
Keibul Lamjao National Park, 169
Kempty Falls, 309
Keoladeo Ghana National Park, 261
Kerala, 11, 22, 96, 97, 114, 118, 123, 124, 168, 195, 245, 437-454
Keshod, 60
Keylong, 223
Khadakvasla, 377
Khadi Gramodhyog Bhawan, 532
Khajuraho (Temples) 53, 54, 60, 71, 105, 109, 119, 124, 176, 178, 295, 313-319, 334-336
Khajuraho Museum, 315, 317
Khalse, 202
Khandagiri, 513
Khandala, 382-383
Khangchandzonga National Park, 171
Khanvel, 358
Khapta National Park, 621
Kharagpur, 10
Khas Mahal, 251, 288
Khaste Lake, 622

Khilanmarg, 162
Khimsar, 180
Khopoli, 382
Khuda Baksh Oriental Library, 549
Khusrau Garden, 295
Kihim Beach, 385
King Kothi, 493
Kirti Stambh, 271
Kirtipur, 613-614
Kishtwar, 156, 206
Kochi (Cochin) (*See also* Cochin) 447, 450-453
Kodaikanal, 7, 474-475, 483
Kodarma, 554
Kohima, 568, 569, 577, 580
Koina, 570
Kokthang, 158, 159
Kolahoi Glacier, 200, 209
Kolar Gold Mines, 416
Kolhapur, 184, 367, 378
Kollam (Quilon), 447
Kolleru Pelicanry, 166
Konar Dam, 554
Konark, 52, 62, 105, 506, 507, 508, 511-512, 516, 517, 520
Konark Temple (Sun Temple), 111, 351, 506, 507, 511-512, 517, 520
Kondapalli, 499
Kota, 262
Kotagiri, 476
Kothandaraswamy Temple, 473
Kottakal, 452
Kottayam, 445, 452
Kovalam Beach, 61, 176, 442-443, 449
Kozhikoda (Calicut) 446, 447
Krishna Temple, 445, 447, 615
Krishna Vilas, 263
Krishnagar, 537
Krishnagiri Upavan National Park, 381
Krishnarajasagar Dam, 418, 419

Kuari Pass, 155, 284
Kud, 205-206
Kufri, 157, 217, 220
Kukarail Reserve Forest, 303
Kulu and Manali, 7, 123, 156, 157, 201, 217-218, 219, 220, 221-224
Kullu Pumori, 158
Kumakarom, 152
Kumaon, 155, 310
Kumaon Hills, 282, 283
Kumaon Himalayas, 281-282
Kumarhar, 549
Kumari House, 610
Kumbakonam, 468
Kumbhalgarh, 264
Kumbeshwar Temple, 615
Kumhrar, 556
Kun Peak, 156, 158
Kundale, 446
Kunzam, 218
Kurge Monastery, 640
Kurukshetra, 230
Kurnool, 495, 497
Kurseong, 535, 542
Kurusadai Island, 473
Kushinagar, 295, 305, 548, 556
Kushinagar Temple, 294
Kutch (see Rann of Kutch)
Kyichu Lhakhang, 638

La Martiniere, 529
Labrang Monastery, 586
Ladakh, 6, 124, 131, 189, 190, 197, 199, 200-204, 209, 212
Ladh Khan Temple, 424, 432
Lady Hydari Park, 577
Lahaul and Spiti Valley, 156, 157, 217, 218-219, 223
Lake of Ho Return, 568
Lakshadweep (Laccadive), 452, 596-598
Lakshman Tilla, 293
Lakshmana Temple, 316-317
Lakshmi Narayan Mandir, Patna, 550

Lakshmi Narayan Temple (Birla Mandir), 244, 251
Lakshmi Temple, 316
Lakshmi Vilas Palace, 348
Lal Tibba, 309
Lalbagh (Botanical Gardens), 415, 428
Lalitgiri, 512, 513
Lamaguru, 201-202, 211
Land's End, 307
Langtang National Park, 620
Langu Gorge, 621
Lawson Bay, 504
Le bong Race Course, 534, 542
Ledo, 568
Legislative Assembly, Calcutta, 527
Leh, 121, 131, 156, 190, 200, 201, 202-204, 208, 210-212
Leh Khar Palace, 210
Leh Monastery, 210
Leh Mosque, 210
Lenin Sarani, 529
Leo Pargial, 158
Lepakshi Temple, 429
Lhotse, 620
Lidder Valley, 199
Lidderwat, 200
Lihir Gompa, 211
Lingaraj Temple, 508, 509, 517
Linking Road, 376
Lion Capital, 107
Lion Safari Park, 387, 429
Lloyd Botanical Gardens, 541
Lodurva, 275
Lohagarh Fort, 278
Lohtse Peak, 605
Loktak Lake, 570
Lonavala, 382-383, 391
Lonavala Caves, 388
Longtalai, 572
Lothal, 9, 107, 343, 350-351, 361
Lotus Mahal, 423, 433
Lotus Tank, 557

Lucknow, 122, 292-294, 295, 301-303
Lucknow Residency, 303
Ludhiana, 230
Lukla, 624
Lumbini, 294, 295, 547, 609, 624-625, 630
Lungleh, 572

Machhapu-Chhare, 622
Machhendranath Temple, 612
Macchin Lhakhang, 639
Madarihat, 536
Madh Beach, 374, 387
Madhava Temple, 512
Madhuban, 141, 359, 552, 595, 600
Madhya Pradesh, 8, 105, 109, 119, 162, 168-169, 245, 281, 295, 313-340
Madras, 12, 14, 19, 56, 57, 58, 59, 61, 62, 71, 75, 113, 127, 133, 144, 145, 147, 178, 180, 181, 245, 459-462
Madras Aquarium, 261
Madras Government House, 460
Madras High Court, 460
Madras Snake Park, 461-462
Madras University, 460
Madurai, 56, 58, 61, 120, 176, 457, 470-472, 482-483
Madurai Museum, 483
Madurai Temples, 105
Mahabaleshwar, 7, 383, 391
Mahabaleshwar Temple, 233
Mahabalipuram (Mamallapuram), 61, 457, 462, 463-465, 480
Mahabalipuram Temples, 56, 58, 109
Mahabharata Range of Himalayan Mountains, 606
Mahabodhi Society Library, 298
Mahabodhi Temple, 298, 546, 547, 557
Mahabodhi Tree, 557

Mahadeo Hills, 313
Mahadev Temple, 316
Mahakal Cave Temple, 534
Mahakaleshwar Temple, 337
Mahalakshmi Temple, 374
Mahamakham Tank, 468
Mahamandir Temple, 273
Mahabarinirvana, 552
Maharaja Scindia's Palace, 323
Maharashtra, 6, 110, 114, 122, 141, 162, 169, 245, 367-394
Mahatma Gandhi Bridge, 550
Mahendra Cave, 622
Mahendra Tal, 621
Maheshwar, 337
Mahesmurti of Elephanta, 108
Mahishasura Mardhini Cave, 465
Maithon, 554
Majorda Beach, 408
Makalu Peak, 605
Makhdum Kund Hot Springs, 552
Malabar Hills, 373, 387
Malabar Point, 372
Malana Valley, 218
Malda, 537
Malda Museum, 537
Mallegitti Shivalaya Temple, 426, 432
Malik-i-Maidan, 427
Mall Hill, 309
Mall Road (Street), 215, 216
Mallikarjuna Temple, 425, 432, 497
Malpe Beach, 429
Mammallapuram, 107, 176
Man Mahal (Palace of Honour), 265
Mana Peak, 158, 282
Manak Chowk, 349
Manakavala, 454
Manali (*see also* Kulu), 159, 162, 224
Manali Sanctuary, 167
Manalsu Peak, 605
Manapadu, 462

Manas Wildlife Sanctuary, 166, 565, 575, 577, 580, 636
Manasbal, 199
Mandalong, 568
Mandar Hill, 554
Mandhata, 322
Mandi, 161, 218
Mandore Gardens, 273
Mandren Beach, 408
Mander, 61, 313, 322, 323-325, 336-338
Mandu Monuments, 61
Maner, 552, 556
Mangal Bazar, 616
Mangaldas Market, 376
Mangalgiri Temple, 499
Mangalore, 180, 429
Mani Bhavan (Gandhi Memorial), 387
Maniharon Ka Rasta, 259-260
Manikaran Hot Springs, 222
Manipur, 169, 245, 561, 570-571, 577
Manori Beach, 374, 387
Masar Lake, 205
Mantralaya State Secretariat, Mumbai, 372
Mapusa Market, 408
Marble Palace, 529, 539
Mardi Lake, 622
Margoa, 62, 404
Mariamman Teppakulam Tank, 472, 483
Marina Beach, 460-461, 480
Marina National Park, 600
Marine Drive, 372, 374
Marine Jetty, 595
Marine Museum, 600
Martand, 208
Martyr's Memorial, 550, 613
Maru Ganesh Temple, 612
Marul, 201
Marve Beach, 387
Mashobra, 220
Mashro West Peak, 156
Matangeshwara, 335
Matheran, 7, 147, 381-382, 391
Matheran Hill Resort, 388
Mathura, 108, 122, 251-252, 286-287, 300, 466
Mathura Museum, 252, 286-287, 300
Matri Mandir, 477
Mattancheri, 438
Mausoleum of Sher Shah, 553
Mawphlang, 577
Mawsynram, 567
Mayadevi Temple, 547
Mayapur, 537
Mayem Lake, 409
Mecca Masjid, 492, 502
Meena Bazar, 287
Meenakshi Sundareshwara Temple, 120, 468, 470, 472, 482
Meerut, 286
Meghalaya, 96, 97, 162, 561, 566
Meghalaya State Museum, 577
Meghantia, 619
Meguti Tample, 424
Meharangarh Fort, 55, 272
Mehrauli, 122
Mehsana, 351
Melkote, 416
Memorial Church, 292
Memorial Pillar to George V, 236
Memorial to Swami Vivekananda, 474
Menal, 262
Menthosa, 157, 158
Meru Peak, 156
Metcalfe Hall, 527
Mettupalayam, 148
Mhow, 162
Milam Glacier, 310
Milang River Basin, 157
Minicoy Island, 597
Miramar Beach, 408
Mirik, 542
Mirzapur, 113, 137, 305

Mizoram, 97, 561, 571-572, 577
Modhera, 351, 361
Modhera Temple, 110
Moirang, 570
Mollem Wildlife Sanctuary, 167
Mongar, 641-642
Monghyr, 550
Monte Sante, 404
Monument of Polius, 477
Moradabad, 245
Morgim Beach, 408
Mormugao Harbour, 404
Moti Mahal (Pearl Palace), 265
Moti Masjid, Bhopal, 332; Delhi, 242, 251
Mount Abu, 7, 55, 56, 264, 265,276-277
Mount Ama-Dablam, 605
Mount Chamolhari, 637
Mount Everest, 6, 62, 533, 605, 618, 619, 620
Mount Harriet, 595
Mount Kailas, 504
Mount Kanchenzonga, 586
Mount Siniol Chu, 586
Mudumalai Wildlife Sanctuary, 171, 429, 476
Mughal Fort, 550
Mughal Garden, New Delhi, 239
Mughal Gardens, Srinagar, 60, 194, 196, 208
Muktanand Ashram, 388
Mukteshwar, 308
Mukteshwar Tample, 509-510, 517
Mukut Parbat, 282
Mulbekh, 201
Mulbelkh Monastery, 211
Mulkila, 158
Mullakkudi, 454
Mumbai (See also Bombay), 367-377, 385-389, 391
Mumbai High Court, 372
Mumbai Old Secretariat, 372
Mumbai Race Course, 373
Mumbai Raj Bhavan, 372

Mumbai Town Hall, 372
Mumbai University Buildings, 372
Mundanthurai Tiger Sanctuary, 171
Munnar, 446, 452
Murshidabad, 537
Murud Janjira, 162, 374, 384
Murud Janjira Beach, 387
Mussoorie, 7, 161, 283, 308-309
Mysore, 56, 57, 58, 61, 123, 162, 176, 181, 184, 416-421, 429
Mysore Maharaja Palace, 57, 58, 417

Naargarh Fort, 151
Nabadwip, 537, 539
Nag Devata Temple, 309
Nagaland, 169, 245, 561, 568-569, 577, 580
Nagaon Beach, 385
Hagarhole Wildlife Sanctuary, 419, 429
Nagarjunakonda, 108, 496, 498
Nagarjunakonda Island Museum, 496
Nagarjunasagar Dam, 496, 502
Nagarjunasagar Srisailam Sanctuary, 166
Nagarkot, 619
Nagaur, 273
Nagerhole National Park, 168
Naggar, 222
Nagin Lake, 192, 195, 196, 197, 208
Nagpur, 367
Nahargarh Fort, 258, 268
Naik Temple, 468
Naini Lake, 307, 308
Nainital, 7, 161, 283-284, 306-308, 310
Nakhoda Mosque, 529
Nakkil Lake, 277
Nalanda, 62, 548, 551-552, 556, 558
Nalanda Institute, 551
Nalanda Museum, 558
Nalanda University, 551-552 558

Nambor Reserve Forest, 580
Namcha Bazar, 624
Namika - La, 201
Nanda Devi, 155, 158, 282, 310
Nandan Hills, 554
Nandankanan, 514, 517
Nandavan, 155
Nanded, 384
Nandi Hills, 416, 429
Nandi Statue, 417-418
Nanga Parbat, 198
Napier Museum, 449
Narasimha Statue, 423
Nareodam Island, 594
Nariman Point, 372
Narkanda, 157, 161, 220
Narmada, 325
Narsimha Statue, 616
Nartiang, 577
Narwar, 320-321
Naseem Lake, 196
Nashik, 367, 384, 388, 391
Nataraja Temple, 467
Nathdwara, 264
Nathmalji Ki Haveli, 275
National Art Gallery, 461
National Assembly Hall, Thimphu, 639
National Defence Academy, 377
National History Museum, 613
National Institute of Design, 361
National Library, 527
National Museum, 113; Nepal, 613; Paro Valley, 636, 637
National Museum of Natural History, 113
Naubhat Pahad, 494
Naudanda, 622
Navratna Kali Temple, 529
Nava Nalamda Mahavihira, 558
Nawabganj Bird Sanctuary, 303
Nawangar, 352
Nayyar Dam, 450
N.C. Mehta Collection, 361
N.C. Mehta Museum, 350

Neer Mahal (Palace of water), 573
Nehru Bazar, 260
Nehru Planetarium, 387
Nehru Science Centre, 387
Nehru Science Museum, 113
Nehru Zoological Park, 494
Naminath Temple, 264, 354
Nepal, 5, 6, 8, 30, 53-54, 62, 114, 295, 605-630
Nepalganj Road (Rubaidiha), 31
Nepal Gunj, 608, 629
Neral, 381
Netrahat, 553
New Churachundpur, 570
New Jalpaiguri, 533
New Vishwanath Temple, 305
Nilachala Hill, 563
Nilgiri Tahir (I bex), 476
Nilgiri Hills, 722, 147, 162, 476
Nilgiri Parvat, 18
Nilkanta, 158
Nilkanta Temple, 325
Nine Planets Temple, 564
Nishat Bagh, 208
Nishat Gardens, 194, 197
Niwas Garden, 268
Nizam Palace, 490
Nizamat Killa, 537
North Bay, 600
Nun Peak, 156, 158
Nyatapola Temple, 617, 618

Observatory Hill, 541
Old Bazar, Hyderabad, 492
Omkarreshwar, 322, 337
Ootacamund (Udhagamandalam) (Ooty) (*See* Ooty)
Ooty, 7, 147, 148, 178, 181, 429, 475, 476
Oppang Tal, 622
Orcha, 321-322
Orcha Fort, 321
Orcha Temples, 321
Orchid House, 541
Orchid Sanctuary, 586, 588

Orchidarium, 586, 588
Orissa, 7, 15, 105, 109, 121, 138, 141, 169-170, 245, 507-520
Osean, 273
Osman Sagar, 494, 502
Osmania University, 491, 493
Oudh (Kosala), 281, 293

Pachad, 378
Padam, 159
Padmaja Naidu Zoo, 534
Padmanabhapuram Palace, 443, 449
Padmanabhaswamy Temple, 442
Padri-Ki-Haveli, 549
Pahalgam, 195, 196, 199-200, 208, 209
Pakhal, 502
Palace of Water, 573
Palace of Winds, 291
Palakkad (Palghat), 447
Palamau, 554
Palamau Wildlife Sanctuary, 167
Palampet, 497
Palghat (Palakkad), 447
Palika Bazar, 246
Palitana, 352-353, 364
Pallava Panamalai, 114
Pallava Temples, 109
Palolem Beach, 408
Panch Mahal, 291, 493
Panchakki, 380, 393
Panchchuli, 158
Panchet Dam, 554
Panchgani, 383
Panchisi, 291
Panchmari, 7, 329, 332
Pandav Falls, 335
Pandavleni, 381
Pandua, 537
Pangso Pass, 568
Panhala Hill Fort, 378
Panna Diamond Mines, 335
Panna National Park, 335
Panvel, 379

Pao Mecca, 564
Papanatha Temple, 425
Papsura, 158
Parade Ground, 613
Parambikulam Wildlife Sanctuary, 168
Parasurameshwar Temple, 510, 517
Parbati Valley, 218
Pari Mahal, 196, 208
Parihaspur, 196
Park Street, 529
Parli Vaijnath, 384
Paro Valley, 636-638
Parshnath Hill, 552
Parshuram Kund, 568
Parsi Tower of Silence, 373
Parsvanath Jain Temple, 318, 335
Parthasarthi Temple, 480
Parvati Hill, 391
Parvati Temple, 317
Paschim Daroja, 550
Pashupathinath, 54
Pashupatinath Temple, 614
Patan, 54, 352, 361, 608, 609, 615-617
Pathankot, 190, 215,
Pathar-Ki-Masjid, 550
Pahar Masjid, 196
Patiala, 220, 232
Patna (Pataliputra), 6, 13, 62, 72, 176, 180, 545-546, 555-557
Patna Museum, 549, 556
Patnitop, 206
Patrola Fort, 233
Pattadakal, 434-425, 431-434
Patwan Ki Haveli, 275
Pavel, 437
Pawapuri, 552, 556, 558
Peacock Island, 564
Peermade, 445, 450
Pemayangtse, 59
Pemayangtse Monastery, 585, 589
Pen Temple, 384
Periyar Dam, 454

Periyar Game Sanctuary, 483
Periyar Lake, 56, 58, 445, 446
Periyar Wildlife Sanctuary (Tiger
    Reserve), 164, 168, 445-446,
    450, 452
Phewa Lake, 622
Philatelic Gallery, 636
Phodong, 585
Phodong Monastery, 586, 589
Phoemix Bay, 595
Phoksundo Lake, 621
Pichola Lake, 56, 57, 60, 263
Picture Gallery, 293, 303
Pindari Glacier, 310
Pinnacle Peaks, 156
Pipli, 517
Pir Panjal, 189, 218
Pirotan Marine Sanctuary, 167
Pitalkhora, 381
Pitti Island, 598
Point Calimere Sanctuary, 171
Pokhra Valley, 622-625, 629
Ponda, 60, 408-409
Pondicherry, 176, 476-477, 485-486
Porbandar, 358, 364
Port Blair, 72, 593, 549-596
Powai Lake, 385
Pratap Memorial, 271 (Pratap
    Smarak), 264, 271
Pratapgad Fort, 378, 391
Prayag (See also Allahabad), 116
Prince of Wale's Museum, 113,
    372, 387
Project Tiger Sanctuary, 165
Prospect Hill, 220
Public Gardens, 494
Pujahari Math, 618
Pullamangis Temple, 468
Pumter Monestery, 586
Punakha, 639-640
Punakha Dzong, 640
Pune, 151, 153, 162, 367, 377-379,
    389-392
Punjab, 23, 156, 170, 190, 215, 227-
    234, 245

Punmudi, 450
Purana Mahal, 278
Purana Qila, 238, 239, 240-241, 251
Purandar Hill Fort, 378
Puri, 52, 62, 121, 507, 508, 510-511,
    516, 517, 519-520
Puri Beach, 520
Pushkar, 262, 269
Pushkar Lake, 124, 269

Quila House, 550
Queen's Bath, 423, 433
Queen's Necklace, 387
Quila-i-Kholina Mosque, 240
Quilon (See also Kollam), 437, 443
Qutb Shahi Tombs, 112, 493, 494,
    502
Qutub Minar, 14, 111, 237, 238,
    239-240, 251

Rabinder Bharti Museum, 113
Rabindra Bharati University, 529
Rabindra Sarobar, 529, 539
Radhakishorepur, 573
Radhaswami Samadhi, 300
Raghunath Temple, 205
Raghunathji Temple, 272
Raigad, 378
Rail Museum, 113, 152-153
Railway Coach Factory, 459
Raison, 222
Raj Bibi Mosque, 348
Rajghat, 243-244, 251
Raja Kelkar Museum, 378, 391
Raja Mann Singh Tomar Palace,
    112
Raja Rani Temple, 509, 517
Raja Vishal Ka Ghar, 551
Raja's Palace, 571
Rajabai Clock Tower, 372
Rajaji Hall, 460, 461
Rajaji National Park, 284
Rajarappa, 554-555
Rajarappa Waterfalls, 554

Rajasthan, 22, 118, 119, 121, 124, 137, 150, 153, 170-171, 245, 255-278, 281
Rajdari, 305
Rajgarh Palace, 335
Rajgir, 62, 547-548, 556, 558
Rajkot, 352, 354
Rajneesh Ashram, 378
Ralong, 585
Ram Ghat, 623
Ram Niwas Gardens, 259
Ramachandra Temple, 433
Ramakrishna Mission Beach, 504
Ramakrishna Mission Institute of Culture, 529, 539
Ramappa Temple, 497
Rameswar Tole, 623
Rameswaram, 145, 457, 472-473, 483
Rameshwaram Temple, 26, 105
Ramgarh, 308
Ramgarh Fort, 297
Ramnagar Fort, 305
Rampur, 416
Rampur Bhushair, 160
Rana Kumbha's Palace, 271
Rana Pratab Sagar Dam, 262
Ranakpur, 55, 56, 264, 277, 278
Ranakpur Temple, 271
Ranchi, 553
Ranchi Hill, 553
Raneh Falls, 335
Rang Ghar, 565
Rang Mahal, 242, 251
Ranganatha Temple, 469
Ranganathittoo Bird Sanctuary, 168, 418, 419
Ranganathswamy Temple, 473
Rangaun Lake, 335
Rangeet Valley Ropeway, 534
Rani Gumpa (Queen's Cave) 513
Rani Padmini's Palace, 271
Rani Rupmati's Mosque, 361
Raniganj, 30, 531
Ranikhet, 161, 283-284, 310

Ranjit Vilas Palace, 362
Rann of Kutch, 5, 167, 344
Ranthambor Game Sanctuary, 165, 269
Rabti Valley, 619-622
Rara National Park, 620, 621
Rashtrapati Bhawan, 117, 118, 239, 243, 251
Rathong, 158, 159
Ratnagar, 557
Ratnagiri, 512-513
Ravanaphadi Cave, 432
Razdi, 343
Red Fort, 13, 113, 117, 238, 242, 251, 252
Red Fort Museum, 113
Red Skin Island, 600
Research Institute of Tibetology, 585, 586, 588
Residency Building, 293
Rexual, 31
Rewa Kund Lake, 325
Riasi, 205
Rimpung Dzong, 637
Rishabdeoji Temple, 265
Rishikesh, 118, 160, 283
River Front, 305
Rock-cut-temple, 107
Rock Fort, 61, 484
Rock Fort Temple, 469
Rock Garden, 228, 234
Roerich Art Gallery, 222
Rohru, 220
Rohtang Pass, 159, 217, 218, 223, 224
Roopmati's Pavilion, 337
Roopnagar, 332
Ropar, 107
Rose Garden, 229, 234
Ross Island, 595, 600
Royal Bordia National Park, 620
Royal Chitwan National Park Game Reserve, 610, 619, 620, 624

Royal Palace, Bhaktapur, 617; Kathmandu, 610; Patan, 615, 616
Royal Polo Grounds, 571
Royal Wildlife Sanctuary, 614
Rudra Varna Mahavihar, 616
Rumi Darwaza, 292-293, 302
Rumtok Monastery, 59, 585, 589
Rundranagar Lake, 573
Rupa Lake, 622
Rupnarainpur, 531

Sabarmati Ashram (*See also* Gandhi Ashram), 349
Sach Khand Shri Huzur Sahib Gurudwara, 384
Sadaquat Ashram, 550
Sadopanth Peak, 283
Safdarjung's Tomb, 243, 251
Sagarmatha (Everest) National Park, 610, 620, 621
Saharanpur, 121
Saheed Minar, 528
Saheliyon-Ki-Bari, 55, 263, 271
Sahet-Maheth, 295
Saif Khan's Mosque, 550
Saila, 273
Saint John's Church, 525
Saint Thomas Mount, 461
Sajjangad Fort, 378
Sakerbagh Garden Zoo, 354
Salapar Bridge, 160
Salar Jung Museum, 58, 490, 502
Salem, 476
Salim Mahal, 260
Salim Mosque, 260
Salim Singh Ki Haveli, 275
Salt Lake, 524
Sam Sand Dunes, 275
Sambalpur, 514
Samdrupjongkar, 641
Samudra Beach Resort, 357
San Thome Cathedral, 461, 480
Sanasar, 206
Sanchal Lake, 534

Sanchi, 107, 313, 326-328, 333-334
Sanchi Temple, 312
Sandakphu, 534, 442
Sandipam Ashram, 338
Sanganer, 268
Sanghameswara Temple, 425, 432
Sangeet Bhavan, 536
Sangrama, 198
Sanjay Gandhi National Park, 373
Sanjay Park, 307
Sankasya, 303
Sankat Mochan, 220
Sanskar Kendra Municipal Museum, 350
Santinath Temple, 318
Santiniketan, 536, 539
Saptadhara, 552
Saptaparni Cave, 552, 558
Saptasaya, 514
Sarabhai Calico Museum, 350
Sarangkot, 622
Sardar Samand Lake, 273
Sariska, 261
Sariska Game Sanctuary, 170, 269
Sarkhej Monuments, 350
Sarkhej Roza Tomb, 361
Sarnath, 6, 53, 54, 62, 296, 297-298, 305, 548
Sarnath Museum, 19, 107, 298
Sas Bahu (Mother-in-law-Daughter-in-law) Temple, 320
Sasan Gir, 355
Sasan Gir National Park, 355
Sasaram, 552-553, 556
Sasir Kangri, 156
Sat Tal, 307
Satara, 162
Satkosia Gorge Sanctuary, 169, 514
Satpura National Park, 169
Saurashtra, 122, 352
Scindia's Palace, 323
Sculpture Gallery of Archaeological Survey, 432

Sculpture School, 61
Sea View Point, 383
Secretariat Building, Goa, 402
Secunderabad, 494
Semdia Fort, 291
Senate House, 460
Seti River Gorge, 622
Shafat Glacier, 156
Shah Hamdan Mosque, 196
Shah Majaf Tomb, 293
Shahi Masjid, 550
Shaking Minarets (Jhulta Minar), 360
Shalimar Gardens, 196, 197, 208-209
Shamla Hill, 326, 332
Shankar Gompa, 211
Shankaracharya Hills, 196
Shankaracharya Temple, 195, 197, 208
Shanwarwada, 391
Shatrunjaya Temple, 352
Sheesh Mahal, 258, 263, 288, 322
Shekhawati, 124
Sher Mandal, 240, 241
Sher Shah Masjid, 556
Shesh Marayan Pagoda, 615
Shey Monastery, 202, 211, 621
Shey Palace, 211
Shey Phoksundo National Park, 620, 621
Shillong, 72, 162, 176, 566-567, 575, 576-578
Shillong Golf Course, 577
Shillong Peak, 567, 577
Shillong Raj Bhavan, 567
Shimla, 7, 147, 157, 161, 162, 179, 215, 217, 218, 219-220, 227, 233
Shinde's Chhatri, 391
Shirdi, 384, 388, 391, 393
Shirya Tapu, 595
Shishu Bhavans, 530
Shiva Temple, 467, 553, 616
Shivling, 158

Shivneri Fort, 391
Shivpuri, 300, 320
Shivpuri National Park, 300-301
Shore Temple, 463-464
Shreyas Folk Art Museum, 350, 361
Shri Gopal Ganapati Temple, 409
Shri Govindji Temple, 570
Shri Madhavdeva Shrine, 575
Shri Mahalakshmi Temple, 409
Shri Mahalsa Temple, 409
Shri Mangeshi Temple, 409
Shri Nagesh Temple, 409
Shri Raghunathji Temple, 277
Shri Ramnath Temple, 409
Shri Saptakoteshwara Temple, 409
Shri Shanta Durga Temple, 409
Shrine of Srisailam, 497
Sibsagar, 565, 575
Sickle Moon, 158
Sidheswar Temple, 510
Sidi Bashir Mosque, 348
Sidi Sayyid's Mosque, 350, 361
Sigao, 404
Sijan, 346
Sikandarabagh, 303
Sikandra, 53, 54, 55, 57, 59, 111, 287
Sikkim, 120, 131, 158, 171, 583-590
Sileh Khana, 259, 265
Siliguri, 533, 535, 584
Siliserh Lake, 260
Silk Weaving Factory, 418
Silver Street (Old Delhi), 245
Simbhanjyang, 619
Simhachalam Temple, 488, 504
Simhanath Temple, 512
Similipal National Park, 514, 518
Similipal Wildlife Sanctuary (Tiger Reserve), 170
Simtokha Dzong, 639
Simultala, 554
Sindh Valley, 199, 201, 203
Sindhudurg, 379

Sindri, 554
Single Bazar, 534
Singh Durbar, 613
Singhgarh, 162
Sinhagad Fort, 391
Sippighat Farm, 600
Sirgirya Caves, 114
Siridao Beach, 408
Sirvan Village, 363
Sisodia Gardens, 268
Sisodia Palace, 268
Sisupal Garh, 510
Site Museum, 334
Sittannavasai, 485
Sleeping Vishnu, 615
Snake Park, 429, 480
Sofa Shahouri Masjid, 404
Solang, 162, 224
Solang Nala, 159
Solang Valley, 218, 222
Somnath Temple, 61, 344, 356-357, 358, 363
Somnathpur, 61, 111, 418
Somnathpur Temple, 414, 418, 420
Son-et-lumiere, 61
Sonamarg, 199
Sonauli, 30
Sone Bridge, 25
Sonepur, 550
South Extension Market, 245
South India, 5, 7, 22, 105, 111, 122, 123, 127, 130-131, 134
Space Research Centre, 416
Spiti Valley, 156
Spituk Monastery, 204, 211
Square Taumadhi, 617
Sravanabelagola, 61, 419, 420, 429
Sravasti, 303, 548
Sri Chamarajendra Art Gallery, 418
Sri Chitra Art Gallery, 449
Sri Jambukeswar Temple, 469
Sri Lanka, 11, 114
Sri Ranganatha Temple, 416
Sri Venkateshwara Konda, 504

Srinagar (*See also* Jammu; Kashmir), 5, 18, 28, 60, 162, 179, 180, 184, 190, 191-197, 198, 201, 205-208
Sriniketan, 536
Srirangam Island, 469, 485
Srirangam Temple, 61, 105, 469
Srirangapatnam, 57, 58, 61, 416, 418,
St. Andrew's Church, 526
St. Augustine Tower, 404
St. Francis' Church, 444, 452
St. Francis Xavier 403
St. Mary's Church, 460
St. Paul's Cathedral, 528-529
St. Thomas' Cathedral, 372
State Archaeological Museum, 494
State Astronomical Observatory, 307
State Government Emporias, 245
State Legislature, Hyderabad, 494
State Library, Bangalore, 415
Statue of Duplex, 477
Statue of Joan of Arch, 477
Statue of Lord Buddha, 494
Statue of Netaji Subhas Chandra Bose, 527
Stok Kangri Peak, 156
Stone Monolith, 465
Stupas, 333
Suchindram, 449
Sukh Niwas, 258
Sukhna Lake, 234
Sukla Phanta Wildlife Reserve, 620
Sulakshi, 564
Sultan's Battery, 446
Summer Hills, 216, 220
Summer Palace of Tipu Sultan, 57, 58
Sun Temple, 111, 351, 506, 507, 511-512, 517, 520
Sunder Nagar Market, 246
Sunder-Dhunga, 155

Sunderbans, 17, 524, 539
Sunset Point, 382
Suraj Bhavan, 278
Suraj Kund, 118, 319
Surat, 137, 344, 346, 347
Surinsar Lake, 205
Suru Valley, 201
Sutanati, 524
Swayambhu, 609
Swayambhunath, 613

TV Tower, 9
Tadoba National Park, 169, 385
Taj Bawdi, 427
Taj Garden Retreat, 178
Taj Mahal, 13, 53, 54, 55, 57, 111, 112, 113, 149, 260, 263, 271, 281, 285, 287, 288-289, 300, 367, 491, 528
Taj-ul-Masjid, 325, 332
Takdah, 542
Taktsang Monastery (Tiger's Nest), 637
Talegaon, 162
Taleju Palace, 616
Tambdi Surla Temple, 409
Tamil Nadu, 117, 138, 139, 162, 171, 245, 457-476
Tanjore (Thanjavur) 467-469
Tank Square, 524
Tanqueber, 467
Tamsa Lake, 388
Tapobana, 554
Tapovan, 155
Tara Devi, 220
Taran Taran, 232
Tarangiri, 158
Taraporevala Aquarium, 373, 387
Tarnetar, 122
Tashicho Dzong Monastery, 590, 638-639
Tashi Viewpoint, 586
Tashiding, 585
Tashiding Monastery, 585, 589
Tashigang, 640, 641

Tashigang Dzong, 641
Tata Theatre, 372
Tattapani, 160, 220
Tawang Monastery, 568
Tea Gardens, 575
Tea Plantations, 580
Teen Murti, 236
Teen Murti House, 252
Teerathgarh, 330
Tehri, 155
Telaju Temple, 611
Telangana, 495
Telika Mandir, 340
Telugu Lalithakala Thoranam, 494
Temple Museum, 483
Temple of Lord Venkateswara, 494
Temple of Mirabai, 263
Temple of Rato (Red) Machandranath, 616
Tengnoupal, 570
Tezpur, 566, 575
Thadlaskein Lake, 577
Thangu, 570
Thangasseri, 443
Thanikkudi, 454
Thanjavur (Tanjore) 56, 58, 109, 137, 485
Thar Desert 22, 149, 161-162, 275
Thekkady, 56, 58
Thekkady (Periyar) Wildlife Sanctuary, 441 (*See also* Periyar Wildlife Sanctuary)
Theosophical Society, 461, 480
Thevali Palace, 443
Thiksey Monastery, 202, 211
Thimphu, 633, 638-639
Thiruchirapalli, 457
Thirukkalikikundram, 463, 480
Thirumalai Naik Palace, 472
Thiruvananthapuram (Trivandrum), 62, 72, 437, 441-442, 447
Thiruvananthapuram Museum, 442

Thongdrod, 638
Thousand-Pillared Temple, 497, 498
Thrissur (Trichur), 447
Tibet, 155, 156, 157, 281
Tibetan Monastery, 222
Tibetan Refugee Self-Help Centre, 535
Tiffin Top, 307
Tiger Hill, 59, 62, 534, 542
Tiger Project Ranthambore (Tiger Reserve), 170
Tiger Reserve, Sunderbans, 172
Tiger Tops Park, 619, 620, 623
Tilaiya Dam, 554
Tipu's Foot, 416, 429
Tipu's Palace, 416, 429
Tirthamukh, 573
Tiruchirapalli (Trichy), 468, 469-470
Tirumalai Nayak Palace, 483
Tirupati Temple, 497-498
Tiruttani, 498
Tiruvannamalai, 467
Tolung, 585
Tomb of Itmad-ud-Daula, 53, 54, 55, 57
Tomb of Nawab Ali Khan, 293
Tomb of Queen Khurshed Begum, 293
Tomb of Sufi Saint Moinuddin Chisti, 262
Tongsa, 640-641
Tongsa Dzong, 640
Tonnur, 416
Topchanchi Lake, 554
Toranas (Four Gateways), 333
Torna Hill Fort, 378
Tower of Fame, 263
Tower of Victory, 263
Tribal Museum, 359
Tribhuvan University Campus, 614
Trichur (*See also* Thrissur), 118, 447

Trichy, 56, 57, 58, 59, 61, 484-485
Tricuta Hill, 265
Trikut, 554
Trilokya Mohan Temple, 612
Trimbakeshwar, 383-384
Trineteshwar Temple, 123
Tribolia Bazar, 260
Tripura, 56, 245, 572-573, 578
Tripureswari Temple, 573
Trisul Peak, 158, 283, 310
Trivandrum (*See also* Thiruvananthapuram), 145
Tsemo Gompa, 211
Tsukla-Khang, 588
Tulsi Lake, 388
Tulsi Manas Temple, 305
Tulsishyam Hot Springs, 356, 364
Tungabhadra Dam, 423
Tvangbocha Monastery, 624

Udai Sagar Lake, 263
Udaipur, 55, 57, 58, 60, 149, 151, 176, 178, 182, 260, 263-264, 270-271, 277, 328
Udaipur Fort, 271
Udaipur-Khandagiri Caves, 517
Udayagiri, 512, 513
Udaypur, 328
Udaypur Caves, 334
Udayeshvara Temple, 328
Ujjain, 313, 322-323, 336-338, 466
Ujjayanta Palace, 573
Ullal Beach, 429
Umaid Bhavan Palace, 273
Umananda Temple, 564
Unjha, 351-352
Unkoti Tirtha, 572
Uparkot Fort (Upper Fort), 354
Upper Lakes, 332
Uran Beach, 387
Ushakothi, 514
Uttar Pradesh, 5, 15, 31, 95, 119, 121, 137, 158, 161, 165, 171-172, 215, 245, 281-310, 321
Uttara Khand, 282, 283

Uttarayan Complex, 536

Vadakkunathan Temple, 447
Vadodara (Baroda), 347-348, 361
Vagator Beach, 405, 408
Vahahe Temple, 335
Vaigai Dam, 483
Vaishali, 548, 550-551, 556
Vaishali Museum, 551
Vaishnava Monastery, 575
Vaishno Devi Shrine, 205, 222
Vaital Temple, 510
Vaitarna Lake, 388
Vajrasana, 557
Vajreshwari Hot Springs, 388
Valley of Flowers, 282, 284
Valia Palli, 438, 445
Valluvar Kottam, 480
Valvan Dam, 383
Vamana Temple, 317, 335
Vanganga Project, 359
Vamvihar, 358
Varadarajaswamy Temple, 466
Varaha Temple, 316-317
Varanasi (Kashi), 6, 31, 53, 60, 62, 72, 105, 137, 176, 178, 245, 281, 285, 286, 294, 295-297, 303-306, 322, 466
Varanasi Ghats, 296-297
Varkala, 443
Vasco Da Gama City, 404
Vashisht, 218
Vashistha Ashram, 564
Vasisht Baths, 222
Vedanthangal Bird Sanctuary, 171, 467, 481
Veechar Utensil Museum, 361
Venbanad, 443
Veraval, 355, 357
Versova Beach, 387
Viceregal Arch, 402
Viceregal Lodge, 220
Vichitra, 536
Victoria and Albert Museum, 113
Victoria Memorial, 525, 528, 539

Victoria Memorial Hall Museum, 113
Victoria Terminus Station, 373
Victory Tower, 271
Vidisha, 328, 334
Vihar Lake, 388
Vihara Temple, 298
Vijayawada, 498-500, 503-504
Vikram Kirti Mandir, 338
Viper Island, 595, 600
Virupaksha Temple, 422, 433
Vishakhapatnam (Vizag), 500
Vishala, 350
Vishalgad Hill Fort, 378
Vishnu Temple, 554
Vishnupad Temple, 550
Vishnupur, 536
Vishvanath Temple, 317
Vishwa Shanti Stupa, 558
Vishwabharati International University, 536, 540
Vishwanath Temple, 297, 335
Visveswarayya Industrial Art Gallery, 416
Vittala Temple, 422, 433
Vrindaban, 286, 300

W. Ibbi Gamin Peak, 282
Walkeshwar Temple, 373
Wandoor Beach, 595, 600
Wangdiphodrang Dzong, 640
Wangdiphodrang Valley, 640
Wankaner, 362
War Memorial, 477
Ward Lake, 567, 577
Warrangal, 496-497, 502
Weaver's Service Centre, 387
Wellington Island, 441
West Bengal, 17, 30, 31, 123, 172, 245, 523-542
West India, 124, 127, 129, 134
Western Ghats, 7
Whispering Gallery, 426
White Bhairab, 610
White Field, 429

White Needle Peak, 156
White Sail, 158
Wild Ass Sanctuary, 167
Wild Flower Hall, 217, 220
Willingdon Island, 444
Wimberlyganj Lumbering Centre, 595
Wishing Lake, 584
Worli, 141
Wood Fossil Park, 275
Writers Building, 526
Wular, 198, 199
Wular Lake, 21
Wynad Wildlife Sanctuary, 476

Yadavindra Gardens, 234
Yak Dairy Research Station, 640
Yamnotri, 154, 282-283
Yercaud, 476
Yuksam, 587, 589

Z-1 Peaks, 156
Zanskar, 206
Zanskar Mountain Range, 155-156, 189, 190, 200
Zanskar River, 159
Zanskar Valley, 159
Zoji La Pass, 199, 201
Zoo on Haddo Promontory, 595
Zoological Gardens, 9
Zoological Park, 542
Zorawar Fort, 202